IRVING LAYTON

A PORTRAIT

ELSPETH CAMERON

IRVING LAYTON

A PORTRAIT

Copyright © 1985 Elspeth Cameron

All rights reserved. No part of this book may be reproduced or transmitted in any form or by any means, electronic or mechanical, including photography, recording, or any information storage or retrieval system, without permission in writing from the publisher.

First published in 1985 by Stoddart Publishing Co. Limited
34 Lesmill Road
Toronto, Canada
M3B 2T6

CANADIAN CATALOGUING IN PUBLICATION DATA
Cameron, Elspeth, 1943-
Irving Layton, a portrait

Bibliography: p.
ISBN 0-7737-2051-0

1. Layton, Irving, 1912- Biography.
2. Poets, Canadian (English) — Biography.*
I. Title.

PS8523.A98Z6 1985   C811'.54   C85-099021-1
PR9199.3.L39Z6 1985

Front cover photograph by Arnaud Maggs
Back flap photograph by John Goddard

COVER DESIGN
Brant Cowie/Artplus

Printed and bound in Canada

For my father,
whose insistence on public school education I finally appreciate

and my mother,
who gave me *The Amazing Pranks of Till Eulenspiegel*

Contents

Preface
Acknowledgements
Flamplatz   1
Romania   4
Montreal   16
Death   31
Transitions   37
Revenge   43
Suzanne   47
Adrift   50
Revolution   57
The Politics of Love   60
Russia   67
Seeing Red   74
Feeling Blue   87
The Sultan of Sixth Avenue   92
The Farmer Thinks   95
Lynched   101
A Fuller Brush Man   105
The Farmer Leaves a Wife   110
Many Worlds   114
Icons   120
Modernism   124
War   131
The Hat-Check Girl   136
Here and Now   139
Yes, Sir!   154
Bohemia   166
The "Proletarian Poets"   171
Poet by Default   187

Target Practice	196
Vexed Questions	204
Superman	224
An Attractive Bulldozer	239
Dear Desmond	250
At Odds	256
Anti-Romantic	259
Portrait of the Artist	272
Backflips	274
The Sorcerer's Apprentice	278
The Day Aviva Came to Paris	305
A Very Rich, Rich Year	308
A Tall Man Executes a Jig	312
Mirror Reflections	336
A Greek Tragedy	343
A Question of Value	348
Armchair Traveller	361
Où Sont Les Jeunes?	363
Over-Exposed	371
Marion	376
Sceneshifter	382
Gypsy Jo	408
The Meshugas	415
Two Bar Mitzvahs	427
All That I Prize	432
Anna	447
Reunions	451
Endnotes	462
Bibliography	505
Index	508

Preface

There used to be a psychological personality test that was based on preferences for shapes. There were four to choose from: circle, square, triangle and zig-zag. If you chose the circle, sexuality was supposed to be uppermost in your temperament. The square indicated a longing for security; the triangle, intellectual strength. The zig-zag was understood to reveal a creative personality.

Although it is years since I thought about this simplistic method of character analysis — which I regarded as an amusing game — it came back to me after finishing this book. It seemed to me that the "shape" of a zig-zag perfectly represented the character of Irving Layton, and even the pattern of his life and the movement of his poems.

The experience of feeling my way into his frame of mind and following the events of his life has been like riding an emotional roller coaster, itself a sort of zig-zag of sudden twists and about-faces. The zig-zag is an image of power. As lightning — its natural manifestation — it is the epitome of destructive power. But it is also the instinctive movement of animals in fear. In a desperate effort not to be any one place too long, never to be a steady target, the panic-stricken rush from one randomly selected spot to another along the path of retreat. Even in popular folklore, the zig-zag has been known to convey such principles. The revolutionary bandit Zorro, for example, "the fox, so cunning and free," struck blows for justice apparently coming out of nowhere, and "signed" his victims with his sword with the letter "Z."

Layton, who like Zorro usually has been firmly convinced that his destructive acts have been carried out to set right an unjust world, also hated to be unmasked. When literary critic George Woodcock analysed his poetry in 1970 as the work of a modern Proteus — that god of infinite disguises and changeability — Layton wrote to him, "I hate being defined: even as Proteus."

This hatred of being pinned down, of being made to be one defineable entity, frequently led Layton to alter or invent facts. I have come across three different dates (March 5, 9 and 12) for his birth, offered each time with apparent sincerity. Summaries of his past life given in spontaneous newspaper interviews were often highly distorted. In one of these he described his marriage to his first wife as having lasted only a few months when in fact he lived with her for five years and was technically married to her for almost a decade. Such distortions were characteristic of his family generally. Coming from a peasant background of limited education, unaccustomed to keeping written records and much given to story and song, the moral point of anecdote assumed much greater significance for them than literal accuracy. Yet even within this context, Layton seems to have been first among equals. His older brother observed shrewdly that even as a boy Layton created the world to suit himself in order to avoid suffering. Others — friends like American poet Cid Corman and Layton's third wife (to whom he was never actually married) Aviva — have described him as someone who makes the world up as he goes along so that no one can enter. Canadian literary critic Desmond Pacey, the man who was probably his best friend, once wrote him in exasperation that he was the "greatest phoney ever."

Listening to Layton speak, or studying his letters and expository prose, the movement of his mind often can be seen to take the characteristic shape of the zig-zag. When a student at Queen's University who was preparing a paper on his work in 1960 wrote to ask him whether he was an existentialist, Layton offered this fascinating description of his own work:

> [A great number of] my...poems...are...concerned with [the] darker side of man's nature. My concern with it came to me first of all from my own temperament, and then from Dostoevsky and Freud. I knew all about "dread", "anguish", etc., etc., the special vocabulary of the German existentialists, Jasper, Heidigger and French ones too — Sartre, Camus. Nevertheless if I must be called an Existentialist, it should be understood that I

am one only in the sense that Neitzsche can be called one. Like him my thought is exploratory and plunging; like him despite the poet's and thinker's necessary alienation, I love laughter and celebrate joy. Most emphatically, I do not repudiate Reason, though I am with Neitzsche in exalting the Dionysian state of ecstasy as the highest good obtainable by man. In the face of terrible dilemmas and unavoidable pain, men, I think, will do better in trusting to courage, laughter, and joy than in relishing the darker emotions for their own sake as some of the existentialists seem to me to be doing. And certainly *Reason*, rather than *Faith*!

I am a Romantic with a sense of irony. It's the latter which differentiates me from those rather humourless Romantic poets, Wordsworth, Shelley, Keats. Even granting they did have a sense of humour and fun, they were certainly devoid of a sense of irony, or self-consciousness that might have preserved them from a solemnity they often mistook for sublimity.

I dislike "vagueness", "fog". I abhor sentiment and sentimentality — this, with my love of clarity, hardness, precision, would almost make me a classicist, except that I wholeheartedly believe that all good and great poetry is "revelation" and that the poet leaves this stale, empirical world only to return to it laden with epiphanies. Please do not make the mistake of thinking that when I call this world "stale" and "empirical", I mean to dispraise it absolutely. Personally, I find the world a most exciting and colourful place to live in. It's only in comparison with the riches and more vivid world of poetry, that I find the existent world wanting and defective. Anyhow, it's the tension between the two that makes for poetry, as it makes for thought, and probably also for the highest ecstasies of love.

This passage does not bear logical analysis. Though it reveals that Layton was well-read, it shows equally that he sometimes did not grasp in any penetrating way what he had read. His clichés about the Romantics, for instance, are useless as criticism and his grouping of the existentialists diminishes insight rather than enlarges it. There is, too, plenty of "vagueness" and "fog" to be found in many classicists, T.S. Eliot for example. As some of his correspondents were to note on other occasions, Layton uses terms like "Romantic," "classicist" and "existentialist" without precise or consistent definitions of their meaning.

What Layton's self-description does demonstrate is his ability to dart quickly from one major figure or concept to another so that an *image* is conveyed of his own importance and power. He tells his student that on the one hand he doesn't repudiate Reason, but on the other hand he exalts Dionysian ecstasy. He is a Romantic, but he is also an ironist. He likes clarity, but is not an empiricist. He is worldly, but not at the expense of otherworldliness. In short, he is everything to everyone. He cannot be categorized. Having aligned himself with every major thinker, artist and "school" he can muster for the moment, he conveys an impression that he partakes of all their many virtues and strengths. So rapidly does he reel off names and terms that the many inconsistencies in what he actually says all but escape notice. The risk in such a tactic, of course, is that some readers will associate him not with all the noble qualities of the company he says he keeps, but with their several weaknesses.

The zig-zag shape of Layton's thought and actions has not been well-suited to logical or analytical thought. His prose, though notable for its striking imagery and muscular manipulation of language, is not otherwise impressive. But in his poetry, the impulsive and erratic nature of his mind and heart emerged as strengths. Darting, as he did, from one style of language (classical, intellectual, sensual, colloquial) to another, anxious not to be tagged finally as "romantic," "classical," "American," "Canadian," "European," "ethnic," "mythological," or anything else, Layton kept in suspension so many modes that in the best of his poems he spoke in an absolutely unique and ingenious voice. One of his favourite techniques was to pluck a line from a first draft and set it down elsewhere in the poem. He thus disrupted even the hint of linear development in his own poetic free-association. The result, when he was at his best, is some of the freshest, most lively and startling poetry this country has ever produced.

Acknowledgements

The person who has helped me most with this book is Irving Layton. From that autumn day in 1981 when he suddenly asked me over lunch in the University of Toronto Faculty Club whether I would be interested in writing his biography, he has been co-operative and helpful. Despite a date book that contained so many appointments that it looked like a chess board, he was readily available for interviews and patiently told me without complaint about his life and the circumstances in which many of his poems were written. He helped me track down several of his acquaintances, introduced me to family and friends and even gave me special permission to examine those of his papers in the Concordia Library that he had sealed in envelopes to be opened only after his death. He provided me with photographs, showed me the many paintings and drawings done by various artists that relate to his life and kept me posted about his latest projects. He kindly took the trouble to arrange, with useful results, for notarized requests to go on my behalf to the F.B.I. and the R.C.M.P. He promptly and clearly replied to letters containing lists of questions. Above and beyond these many practical details, he has approached the whole endeavor in a spirit of lively interest and encouragement which helped me feel enthusiastic about the hard work involved.

The arduous task of assembling a truly formidable array of Layton materials was financed by the generosity of the Social Sciences and Research Council of Canada. With these funds, I was able to hire Ruth Panofsky full-time for two years. Ruth proved to be an untiring, meticulous research assistant, whose positive attitude to the project was a constant source of support for me. I am grateful also to Geri Sarits-Fine, my unflappable checker and to Stephanie Gould, Elaine Nascimento and Sophia Tsiliggiri, who typed the manuscript.

It would be impossible to name each of the many, many

people who agreed to be interviewed. Meeting each of them was for me an education and a pleasure. So varied and widespread were Layton's acquaintances that I could not hope to see them all. I am, however, convinced that I have heard from a fully representative sample of the kinds of people he knew. Some interviews from among those I conducted over a four-year period were exceptional. I am especially grateful to Layton's second wife, Boschka, who spoke so candidly about her years with Layton, showed me her drawings and paintings of him and gave me copies of the poems she had written about their time together. I am profoundly sorry that she has not lived long enough to see this book. I am equally grateful to Aviva Layton who was so generous with her time and who allowed me to sift through the boxes of photographs she has kept, many of them containing pictures of Irving's life at times when she herself was not part of it. I admire the courage of both these women, and of the many other women who spoke freely with me of their relationships with Layton. It was brave and generous, too, of Louis Dudek, who had suffered considerably from Layton's personal attacks, to agree to give his account of their past dealings. I was touched also by my interview with Henry Moscovitch, whose doctor assured me that he would not be disturbed by recalling the past, but whose mental anguish was nonetheless palpable. I would also like to thank all the members of the Lazarovitch family who assisted so readily in reconstructing their lives in Romania and Layton's early childhood in Montreal. It is a stroke of luck to have a subject like Layton who is the youngest in a large family. It is ideal to have friendly co-operation from no fewer than four older siblings: Gazella Goldberg, Dora Pleet and Harry and Hyman Latch. A unique family member whose recollections were especially useful has been Layton's nephew, Bill Goodwin, who has been close to the uncle only four years his senior and who has remained a friend and frequent companion.

A number of people assisted me by lending me access to their diaries or private correspondence with Layton. Such materials are often the most difficult to track down, but sometimes prove to be highly significant. Of paramount importance were the letters of the late Desmond Pacey. I am deeply grateful to Mary Pacey, his wife, for access in her home to these letters, for the hospitality I enjoyed with her family and for her permission to quote without restraint from the letters. I appreciate especially having been given Suzanne Rosenberg's "Memoirs" and Dean Baker's "A Fool's Long Journey" — both unpublished personal recollections involving Layton. I owe a special thank-you to Steven Osterlund DaGama whose letters were lost by the mail system between Ohio and Canada, but who, despite this upsetting mishap, continued to give his support to my project. Although copies had been taken, the originals may never be recovered. Others whose letters from Layton proved important were Barry Callaghan and John Brebner. I am grateful to Earle Birney who accompanied me personally to his special file concerning the aborted attempt to hire Layton at the University of British Columbia, a file that is kept closed in the University of Toronto Library. Layton's publisher, Jack McClelland, also co-operated fully by giving me access to and allowing me to quote freely from the Layton files at McClelland and Stewart and the collection of Layton papers at McMaster University. Excerpts from previously unpublished letters of William Carlos Williams, Copyright © 1985 by William Eric Williams and Paul H. Williams; used by permission of New Directions Publishing Corp. agents.

Important information resulted from discussions with Annette Pottier, Frank and Marian Scott, Miriam Waddington, Amos Saunders, Musia Schwartz, Karen Pietkiewitz, Veneranda McGrath, Leonard Cohen, Fred Cogswell, Robert Creeley, Rochel Eisen, Gertrude Katz, Milton Lackman, Irwin Miller, Joyce Dawe Freedman, Saul Muhlstock, Louis Muhlstock, Alvia Neiss, Shirley Ross, Lucinda Vardey, Marion Wagshall, Andy Wainwright, Audrey Sutherland, Scott Symons, Samuel Margolian, and Ann Madras, among others.

A number of people gave me unique assistance. Dorothy Rath, whose hobby for over a decade has been to gather everything she can about Irving Layton, might well have refused to share her extensive collections of materials. Instead, she gave me complete access to it and assisted with the compilation of the bibliography I needed to prepare before writing the book. I appreciate Stanley Ryerson's assessment of Layton's M.A. thesis from the perspective of someone who was a Marxist in Montreal at the time it was written. Brenda Panofsky and Lilly Yampolsky translated some Yiddish materials for me; Professor Jacques Kornberg and Isaac Shoichet, both of the University of Toronto, helped me with details of Hebrew and Yiddish and with Jewish customs generally; Professor Ruth Wisse, of McGill University, helped me understand something of the history of the Jewish community in Montreal. A number of scholars in Israel — especially Daniel Ben-Natan and Arie Schachar — generously helped me understand the background of Layton's family and directed me to materials in libraries and museums there that proved to be important. I am grateful also to Francesca Valente for photographs and information about Layton's trips to Italy and for her translations of Italian materials. I was pleased to be given photos by Hyman Latch, Aviva Layton, Audrey Sutherland, Irma Zack and Mary Pacey. Gerald Hallowell offered me editorial guidance and encouragement at an early stage of writing.

I am indebted to a large number of librarians and archivists who have assisted me in locating and using Layton materials from Canada and the United States: Joy Bennett, Librarian, Concordia University Library, Montreal; George F. Butterick, Curator, Literary Archives, The University of Connecticut Library, Storrs, Connecticut; Mary Flagg, Manager and Research Officer, Archives and Special Collections, Harriet Irving Library, University of New Brunswick, Fredericton, N.B.; Anne Goddard, Arts Archives Co-ordinator, Manuscript Division, Public Archives, Ottawa; Rachel Grover, Thomas Fisher Rare Book Library, University of Toronto, Toronto; Sheila Latham, Canadian Literature Librarian, Toronto Public Library, Toronto; Katherine Laundy, Librarian, National Library, Ottawa; Pat Norman, Librarian, John P. Robarts Research Library, University of Toronto, Toronto; Brian M. Owens, Archivist, McGill University Archives, Montreal, P.Q.; Glen Makahonuk, Librarian, Special Collections, University of Saskatchewan Library, Saskatoon, Saskatchewan; Apollonia Steele, Special Collections Librarian, University of Calgary, Calgary; Charlotte

Stewart, Director of Research Collections, McMaster University Library, Hamilton; David Walden, Archivist, British Archives, Manuscript Division, Public Archives, Ottawa; Robert Weaver, CBC, Toronto and Bruce Whiteman, Research Collections Librarian, McMaster University Library, Hamilton.

I have enjoyed working with my editor, Ed Carson. His steady appraisals have helped me to reconsider and revise my manuscript in an atmosphere of calm encouragement and optimism.

Above all, I appreciate the loving support and practical help my husband, Paul Lovejoy, has given me. He and our three children — Beatrix, Hugo and Henry — have kept the whirlwind experience of writing about Layton firmly anchored in the comfortable round of domestic events.

Flamplatz

Flamplatz! she thundered.

Where was that miserable child of hers? He was living up to her name for him too well: *Flamplatz,* exploding flame. She simply couldn't control him.

Where was that nuisance? That last-straw insult to her life! "I wish that he would break a bone and never make his way back home!" she expostulated in crackling Yiddish rhyme.

His brother Harry had tried once again to cheat at prayers today, skipping the pages. And stupid enough to get caught by his father, too. He'd learn his lesson or be turfed out of the house once and for all. He was almost as stupid as Larry, her *Megele.* Good-looking enough *he* was, but dull as a donkey.

Keine Lazarovitch stopped just long enough to look up as the bell in the grocery rang once again. That made five customers already. How God had cursed her with this tiresome existence! Perhaps if she turned the grocery over to Dora, the only reliable child she had, she could take a rest later. She — Keine Lazarovitch! Up at five to bake; all day long tending her parlour grocery on Ste. Elizabeth Street; then sewing late into the dark Montreal nights. As if eight children in three rooms weren't enough, she had to take in orphaned cousin Fanny, too! Well, they weren't so low as Karpal, the rag-picker from Galicia next door with his yard full of junk. Or those young French-Canadian sluts upstairs with their late-night sailors. She grabbed her broom and thumped it up on the ceiling. The sounds of laughter and bottles subsided a little.

Where was he, her *Flamplatz,* now that she needed him to drag his long-handled cart through the snow and down those dreary dozen blocks to Bonsecours Market; needed him to wait in the long shadow of that big monument to some English somebody-or-other, needed him to haul back to the parlour grocery the beefy red tomatoes, juicy pears and sleek black eggplants she would bargain for there. "Would that his bowels should twist him up double, then that the wind should give his gut trouble! If only *Flamplatz's* father's seed had melted when it came to breed!"

"*Flamplatz!*"

In bounced Issie, her *Flamplatz,* a squat, dark, round-headed child of six with the intense blue startle of her own father's eyes.

"May a fire strike thy soul and burn it till it's black as coal!" She let go yet another rhyming curse. But, before she could unleash more of the same on her youngest offspring, he darted to her side and began to rub her belly in an intimate, calming way, crooning, "*Mama bakele. Mama bakele.*" Immune to the barrage of insults that had terrified two of his older sisters into early marriages; turned one older brother out of Montreal and into a loveless marriage and the small business of a Jewish family in Trois Rivières; and daily sent another brother, Hymie, out onto the streets to brawl and fight with French Canadians who shouted *"Maudits juifs!"* with infuriating regularity, Issie loudly announced his readiness to go to Bonsecours Market, a hunk of chocolate from his mother's shop shoved deep in his worn jacket pocket.

"Well, my *strulick,* my little man, we're off then." But not before she turned a critical eye towards the back room, and added, "Look at your father in there with his holy books! What good is Hebrew here? Would that worms his flesh might eat, he brings us neither drink nor meat! We're not in Tirgul Neamt any more, and never will be. What's needed now is strength."

That night, almost all her Yiddish rhyming curses spent,

she cast a quick look into the dingy front room where Fanny and Dora shared a bed and Larry and Harry sprawled in their usual disarray. She crossed the kitchen, with its black wood stove and corner-cupboard toilet, to the bedroom and glanced over to the cot where her husband, Moishe, slept with his favourite, Hymie — the brawling brute *Guzlin*. Imagine it! she thought. And Moishe, so mild himself, like the pale milk he scarcely could hoist onto the stove for curdling. He was saving the few pennies he made from his *brindsa* cheese to send Hymie to Yeshiva. That bully would never go to Yeshiva!

If only each from my womb had slid as early as my first child did. Even *Flamplatz*. I almost lost him, too, because of my great sickness. Didn't the doctor in Romania, because of that same sickness, shake his head and say, "If she ever delivers this child, that'll be the day I grow hair on my palms!"? And didn't my mother draw that sickness from me by stretching her hands out over my belly and saying, "No one knows what that child may become. You are a fruitful tree and I a barren woman. May the disease that is meant for you, befall me!" And wasn't the child born circumcised — miraculous! — needing only a ritual cut at his *bris*? Our "Messiah"! May he be destined for greatness, that one!

Had anyone suggested that he might become a poet, she would have loosed lightning bolts of scorn and a thundering belly-laugh. She shook her head and chuckled bitterly as she removed the *sheitl* that *Flamplatz* called her "dead hair" and dropped her teeth into the glass beside the bed.

With only the faintest hint of tenderness, she shifted *Flamplatz,* her little *srulickel,* from the centre of her narrow bed and climbed in. In the few seconds before sleep, she felt him turn and reach for her.

Romania

The Lazarovitch family had come from Tirgul Neamt, a small, humble village in northern Romania. It lay at the foot of the heavily wooded Carpathian mountains that separated the district of Moldavia from Bucovina to the north-west, and Austro-Hungary to the south-west. In the late nineteenth century, Romania resembled a crescent moon, the melancholy Carpathians outlining its western concave edge; the Black Sea, with its Danubian Estuary, embracing its convex exterior. For centuries, visitors to Moldavia, where Tirgul Neamt was located, had been struck by the sudden openness of rich, loamy farmland that stretched out from the base of the jagged, pine-capped Carpathian pinnacles. Everywhere, nature flourished without much cultivation: fruit trees, red raspberry bushes, green artichoke and the homely cabbage multiplied in profusion. Crops of maize for *mămăliga* (pudding), the staple fare of the area, rippled golden in the fields where peasants in coarse, loosely belted white tunics and trousers applied old-fashioned tools to the tasks of sowing and reaping for the boyars. Damson plum trees offered clusters of purple fruit to the local manufacturers of *ţuica,* the ever-popular plum brandy. Above, on the mountain slopes, woodsmen felled the trees for buildings and implements, sending the logs by local tributary toward the Siret River, where they would zig-zag down to the Danube, then to the Black Sea for export. Vendors with carts heaped with bright, scissored petals offered their wares for homemade rose jam. In the yard of each peasant cottage stood a couple of farm animals: chickens, a pig and cow, perhaps; or a horse to pull cart and sleigh for the more fortunate.[1]

In a land traversed by nomadic gypsies whose dark powers and talents were discredited but nonetheless feared, superstition was rife. "Any phenomenon, or effect of unknown causes," observed an English doctor who studied Romanian customs "scientifically" in the middle of the nineteenth century, "is regarded by them as a miracle. They look upon a solar eclipse as a fray between the infernal dragon and the sun.... They believe in fairies, monsters, both horrid and picturesque, strolling vampires, sorceries, and the blighting charms of the evil eye. [They] hardly [dare] go out after sundown on Tuesday or Friday for fear of being whisked away by witches."[2] In some areas of the country, they safely kept all their clipped fingernails lest in the after-life they be sent to gather them from earth with their own eyelashes.[3] Four centuries earlier, when Romania included what is now Transylvania, the dreaded Vlad III, "The Impaler" — better known as Dracula — terrorized his subjects from a mountain castle on the Arges River, roughly two hundred fifty kilometres south-south-west of Tirgul Neamt. Dracula's fondness for extreme sadism (one of his favourite pastimes was eating meals in a room surrounded by his victims, who were slowly dying by various types of impalement, and he frequently ordered the genitals cut off those who offended him however slightly) gave rise to the ghoulish legends and tales associated with the region today.[4] Such superstitions were inextricably bound up in religious beliefs; peasant women, for example, were reputed to avoid sewing on Tuesday (the most unlucky day, because it was thought to be the day creation occurred) "for fear that the Saviour would feel every stitch and thus be crucified anew."[5] Animal legends often accounted for the creation of the world, the Romanian mind seeing little distinction between man and the creatures among whom he lived. It was widely regarded as a sin to kill a frog or a tortoise or a hedgehog, for these three especially were thought to have been God's helpers in making the world. To Romanians, "a sort of brotherhood existed between God and the devil, both having had a vital role to play in man's creation, according to legend, a situation accounting for such proverbs as 'God is great, but the devil is clever also'."[6] Strolling theatrical performers recalled and re-enacted these fears and beliefs on feast days. The *călusari*, for example, travelled through the villages each spring. An initiated group of male dancers, wearing over their coarse peasant shirts straps of embroidered cloth representing different mythological figures of animal origin believed to be connected to fairies and to the intricate movements of the sun, moon and stars, danced themselves into a frenzy in the attempt to ensure "that darkness will be followed by light."[7] An important figure was the "fool" or "dumb man," who represented the sun-god: either he was killed and revived, or he carried a phallus and killed a stag to acquire its powers.

The music and poetry of Romania characteristically ran the gamut of sentiment. Village fiddlers, called *lăutari*, travelled from village to village, accompanying themselves on stringed instruments while reciting the *doina*, or lyric poetry of the Romanian peasantry. The *doina* usually began with the words "green leaf," followed by a plant's name chosen to rhyme with what followed. Typically, these lyric poems expressed life's emotional quandaries: grief, exile, death, worship of creation, fear of oppression, celebration of carousal and wine and, most often, the trials of love. The *doina* were recited or sung as suited the occasion; when sung, the melody was a melancholy succession of prolonged, often throbbing sounds.[8]

This mediaeval, serf-like existence was not an aspect of life only in remote northern villages like Tirgul Neamt, where peasants who had been "crushed to the earth for centuries"[9] supported the land-owning boyars. One observant British traveller, who crossed the country in 1865, experienced the sensation of "having quitted the modern world" on his entry to Romania; he felt as if he were

> under some strange spell that had turned the hand of Time's clock several centuries backwards...into a land of

the Middle Ages. There were a few large fortunes amongst the boyars — but very little education, and less probity. Official corruption was a prevalent malady.... Social immorality had attained its apogee.... Divorce was as common as the open disregard of the marriage tie. Nine-tenths of the population did not know how to read or write. The army was officered in a manner which defies description, and is much better forgotten than recalled. Like the Ireland of fifty years ago, Romania suffered from the curse of absenteeism. The money wrung from the soil by the peasant's labour was chiefly spent out of the country. Paris, Vienna, Milan, Rome, and all the European hells during the gambling season, were the favourite residences and resorts of the Romanian boyars, whose agents squeezed the tiller of the soil to within an inch of his life, enriching themselves by that process.[10]

A year after these observations, in 1866, a Jew, Moses (Moishe) Lazarovitch, was born in Tirgul Neamt. The time and place could not have been less auspicious. That year, after the brief but chaotic interregnum that had followed Prince Cuzo's abdication from the throne, Carol Hohenzollern Sigmaringen was nominated to rule Romania, and a new constitution was established.[11] Luckily for Romania, Prince Carol was an "austere" man[12] and "a born soldier"[13] who, according to one observer, "made a considerable impression on the shifty, impulsive, Oriental-minded boyars by his strict Prussian uprightness, quiet, unemotional bearing and steady adherence to the principles of order and discipline."[14] But, unluckily for the Jews, many of whose families had inhabited Romania for centuries, his spectacular *tour de force* to make his country governable was accomplished, in part, at their expense: "Jews found little mercy or justice beneath the sceptre of Prince Carol,"[15] observed historian Edmund Ollier in 1890.

By the time Prince Carol took power, the Jews in Romania posed a dilemma that was largely economic. Those emigrating from Russia and Galicia during the first half of the nineteenth century had joined their Romanian counterparts to establish small towns, centres for the exchange of merchandise. In doing this, they pioneered as commercial "intermediaries" between the boyars and their peasants.[16]

In the semi-feudal society of Romania, the gradual emergence of a Jewish commercial middle class was unwelcome, to say the least. Anti-Semitic writings in the country can be traced back as far as the seventeenth century.[17] Romania, like other Eastern European countries, deplored, with a fear born of ignorance and superstition, the existence in their midst of a people so different from themselves in custom, dress and religion. According to historian Carol Iancu, "the special dress of the Jews caused an unfortunate *quid-pro-quo* among the peasants, who thought of them as the same Jews who...had crucified their Saviour."[18] Though most Jews wore the standard woollen clothes of the period[19] (not as heavy as the coarse ones the peasants wore),[20] the beards of the men and the *sheitl* (wigs) donned by the women as part of the marriage ceremony set them apart. The few Hassidic Jews, who maintained the black robes and *shtramel* (three-cornered fur hats) of Polish origin, excited special attention.[21] Ironically, Jews were detested largely because their disciplined observance of religious law highlighted the degeneracy of the peasants with whom they shared the northern towns.[22] Because they lent money for indulgences they did not share, owned the hostels frequented by Christian orthodox peasants and sold liquor they did not themselves drink, they were blamed for "exploiting the weaknesses and lack of foresight of those around them."[23] But the initiation of Prince Carol's forty-eight-year-long reign commenced a new era, during which Jews became subject to greater restrictions in almost every aspect of their lives.

These restrictions began to accelerate noticeably after the Congress of Berlin, attended by Germany, Austro-Hungary, England, France, Italy, Russia and Turkey at the conclusion of the Russo-Turkish War (1877–1878). At about the same time as young Moishe Lazarovitch celebrated his *bar mitzvah*, the recognition of Romania's independence by these more powerful nations helped inflate the Romanian nationalism that would swell during the next half century.

Although the Congress of Berlin proclaimed the equality

of all people without regard to religious belief, one article of the Treaty of Berlin that resulted afforded the Romanian government an opportunity to persecute the steadily growing population of Jews who had appropriated such occupations as tax-collectors, book-keepers, salesmen of liquor (over which one boyar held a monopoly), money-lenders and a host of small trades and crafts such as tailors, weavers, shoe-makers, tinsmiths, cabinet-makers, rug-weavers and blacksmiths. Though the treaty did not specifically mention the Jews at all, it contained harsh regulations for the treatment of "non-naturalized foreigners."[24] By subsuming all Jews into this category, although most of them had been born to families who for generations had lived in Romania, Prince Carol's government gradually and relentlessly denied Jews their rights as citizens.

In 1881, when Romania was transformed from a principality into a kingdom, with Carol its king, "official" anti-Semitism began to gain force. Though new laws in the 1880s attempted to appease land-hungry peasants by making land purchases possible, the absence of available property frustrated those who could own land in theory but not in practice. To stem discontent against the state, the government pointed to those few Jews who, by gradually earning money in trade, had joined the boyars as land-owners. The government successfully redirected the peasants' anger away from themselves towards the Jews.[25] "The Jews are the cause of our troubles,"[26] ran one popular slogan that attempted to keep more than a million peasants content with the same amount of land that was shared elsewhere in Romania by a mere four thousand boyars. The problem was bad in the southern district of Wallachia, where the Jewish population had grown from nine per cent to almost eleven per cent of the total; but in northern Moldavia, where most of the Romanian Jews lived, the problem was acute. In some places such as Jassy, Moldavia's capital city, Jews made up half the population; in Tirgul Neamt, to the west, the proportion of Jews expanded from twenty-seven per cent in 1859 to forty per cent near the end of the century.[27]

Life for Jews in Romania was far more precarious in 1890, when Moishe Lazarovitch (whose family came from Budapest) married Klara (known as Keine) Wolfsohn, than it had been a quarter-century before. The growth of the Jewish population in proportion to the Christian orthodox majority led to fears about "the Jewish infiltration"[28] of Romania. For Moishe Lazarovitch, a book-keeper in a small timber company that cut wood from the Carpathian slopes,[29] as for other Jewish merchants and artisans in Moldavia, this meant a number of quite specific constraints. At any moment, for example, Moishe could have been expelled from his homeland. Since 1879, Jews had been stopped in a number of Moldavian cities and forced to leave the country as "vagabonds" because they did not possess the correct documents. With little or no access to passports or citizenship papers, and with the government's abuse of the legal process by which they might have become "naturalized" (only eighty-five Jews were naturalized between 1879 and 1900), Jews were vulnerable at any time and place. Raids on outlying villages were not uncommon; Jewish men were rounded up, escorted to the border and warned not to return to Romania. Such expulsions were legally organized after 1881 and, although they were supposedly aimed at Russian nihilists who had taken refuge in Romania, the government took this opportunity to get rid of Jewish intellectuals, artisans, rabbis and women.[30] This situation was particularly grave for the Lazarovitches because Moishe's young wife was the daughter of a cotton manufacturer of Russian origin.[31]

Moishe and Keine, like most Jewish merchant families at the time, lived in a tiny community of Jews; theirs was twenty or thirty miles outside Tirgul Neamt. Their first child, a son, died soon after birth, but it was not long before a second son, Abraham, was born in 1893. Over the next fifteen years, at intervals dictated by nature, their family grew to seven: four sons and three daughters. Though Abraham, like his father, was a thin, physically feeble boy, he soon began to drive their one lame horse into the fields to help pull stumps from the land. The other children had chores as well. To them, the austere Carpathian backdrop was nothing more than a reminder that life in Romania was hard, doubly so for a Jew.

"We did not have a good home," Gazella, the Lazarovitches' second child, commented about her first fourteen years in

Romania. "We were very poor; my mother didn't seem to want any of us; we all wanted to run away from home. I liked living with my grandmother in Tirgul Neamt, where Avram and I stayed so we could go to Hebrew school. She was a much better mother than our mother." Frustrated with her impoverished existence, to which each of her children added further to demands she could not meet, Keine turned her considerable wrath against those dependent on her for their lives. To each in turn she gave a Yiddish nickname that conveyed the particular flavour of her contempt: the elegant Gazella who, like her father, was fussy about food and cleanliness, became *Printzesen* (the one who thinks she's a princess); Esther, who inherited her mother's dark vitality and large, beaked nose, was alternately *Chora,* (the black crow) and *Cruminas* (the crooked nose); Larry (inexplicably called Oscar), who couldn't keep pace with his mother's quick wits, was *Megele* (a cretin, moron or donkey); Harry was the *Shegetz* (because he wouldn't follow Jewish traditions); Hyman, who soon demonstrated the same tough belligerence as Keine, became *Guzlin* (the strangler). Only Dora, strong and stocky like her mother but mild and sweet-tempered like her father, escaped a fixed insult, though she too felt the almost continuous force of her mother's raging tongue.[32]

Moishe, despite his poverty and "limited experience" in business, was determined that his children would perpetuate the orthodox tradition in which he had been raised. Drinking, dancing and cards were strictly forbidden (he and Keine had never indulged in such pleasures); Friday nights would find him hurrying home to light the *minora* before sundown and say the *kaddish* over the wine. Each Sabbath, and whenever he could on weekdays, he attended one of the town's three nondescript, wooden, unheated synagogues. Keine had cut her luxuriant black hair when they married, and now wore the *sheitl* that traditionally concealed beauty from all and ensured that she should not tempt even her husband. As soon as Avram and Gertie reached the age of six or seven, off they went to Keine's parents in town, glad to exchange their burdensome, cramped life in a tiny rural hut for schoolwork in German and Hebrew at a small *cheder*. With the money Keine earned from the feathers she plucked from her chickens and turkeys, she paid her parents for the children's board. Gazella remembers Tirgul Neamt as a small city, with public gardens. "In the evenings we would go there and listen to military music, sitting at small tables, drinking black coffee and eating cookies, or we would go to a hall and watch a Yiddish play." The "military music" was one of the many expressions of growing Romanian nationalism. The "plays" were the main cultural backlash of Jewish nationalism, for it was in northern Romania, at about the time Moishe was ten, that Avram Goldfaden, father of Yiddish theatre, directed the first professional Yiddish play in a cabaret garden in Jassy.[33] Goldfaden explicitly aimed to merge the poems of Yiddish troubadours with the folk-lore of the Moldavian peasantry to stir the Jews to take pride in themselves and resist oppression. His satirical, didactic plays, some of which the Lazarovitch family saw, soon became popular throughout Moldavia and beyond. To later historians, "their creation [was] a significant cultural crossroads, since it marked the point at which Yiddish 'jargon' passed into the language of the country."[34]

Throughout Romania, the zenith of dramatic art was *Hamlet*, which had been translated into Romanian from French and first performed at the National Theatre in Bucharest in 1884. Wherever it played, it was hailed as a major cultural event; Hamlet's crisis, and the emotional speeches that flowed from it, struck a sympathetic chord among Romanian people. To this day, a statue of Manolescu, the original translator (who also acted the role of Hamlet), stands costumed as Hamlet in the Athenaeum in Bucharest.[35]

Impoverished as the family was (the four-room house of Keine's parents in Tirgul Neamt appeared relatively luxurious to Avram and Gertie), their food was wonderful. "The fruit and vegetables had much more flavour there than any I've eaten in North America," Gazella recalls. "We had ripe tomatoes and pears, plums and other berries. We often ate the local porridge [mămăliga], but my mother made good *challah*, *knishes* and cookies which we washed down with strong black coffee."

The family accepted the miraculous as a central aspect

of life. They were all raised on Old Testament Bible tales that emphasized mysterious transformations, dreams and wonders — stories taught in school as part of their religious heritage and retold at home in Yiddish by the garrulous Keine in an even more colourful fashion — and they absorbed a good deal of the peasant superstition with which they were surrounded. Both Gazella and Harry recall powerful magical sayings about the hated Christian church in Tirgul Neamt, sayings that they believed. "If you dared to look at the steeple, you'd go blind," Harry recalls. "And it was said that if you could throw a penny over the point of the cross, the church would fall down."

"If you passed a church," Gazella remembers, "you must never look at the cross. I had a special power," she goes on, recollecting the nights she secretly stayed up with her brother Abraham, telling fortunes behind curtained windows with a kind of Ouija board. "I got 'the power' from one of my auntie's husbands who was a rabbi's grandson. One night, I remember, we were up until five in the morning, and people would come to ask us about the future; each of us put a finger on the board and the answers would just come."

In the next two decades, the acceleration of anti-Semitic legislation impinged directly on the simple lives of the Lazarovitch family. Sporadic expulsions of Jews from the countryside and towns,[36] the gradual exclusion of Jewish students, first from public and secondary schools, then from universities,[37] the initiation of laws that prevented Jews — often for "sanitary" reasons — from many of the occupations they had formerly taken up, restricted Jewish freedoms until, by 1910, only naturalized Romanians were allowed to be doctors, midwives, veterinarians, druggists, liquor salesmen, grocers and workers on state projects such as railways and public works.[38] Above all, stricter application of military duties[39] led to increasingly larger waves in the emigration of Romanian Jews which had begun just before the turn of the century.

It was a confrontation between Abraham Lazarovitch and the Romanian militia that spurred the family's emigration to Montreal.[40] In Moishe's youth, Jews had not been expected to serve in the Romanian army. (On the contrary, they were required to sign a declaration of renunciation, which stated that "as sons of non-naturalized foreigners they expected neither to be recruited nor to be protected by Romania"). But, since 1882, they had been required to enlist after age eighteen simply because they were born in Romania. To compensate for what was seen as "the unfair exemption of Jews" from military service in previous years, the new regulations were applied with as much severity as possible. Since Jews could not become officers in the army nor enrol in military schools or rural regiments, they became a distinct and frequently abused minority group within an institution that had not often been noted for compassion.[41] Under the guise of military discipline, and fired up with a nationalism that was becoming more ardent, Romanian officers easily could unleash brutality against the religious group that had been disliked, envied or misunderstood for centuries, and whose numbers were growing. Gazella recalls: "When Avram reached an age where he would have to spend three years in the army, and we knew he would be hurt there because we didn't have enough money to bribe the officers, he decided to go to Montreal where my mother's sister had started living a few years before. One day, two officers passing him with one of his friends in the street had slapped him across the face. We all knew what would happen to him if he stayed in Tirgul Neamt. I went with him, though I was only fourteen, because I was the closest to him, and that way my mother got rid of two of us instead of just one. I was very sorry to leave all my friends. We knew we were going somewhere where we wouldn't even know the language."[42]

Abraham and Gazella went first to Chernovitz in Bucovina, where their father's sister, Frieda, arranged for their transport from Antwerp. There they waited four weeks for the ship that took them by steerage on the three-week trip to Quebec. Then they journeyed by train to Montreal.

The emigration of East European Jews, organized in part by the Jewish Colonisation Association, was stupendous; Abraham and Gazella were only two in a much larger panorama. From the date of the first recorded entry of eleven Romanian Jews to North America in 1881[43] (into New York), until the eve of the Great War in 1914, approximately ninety thousand Jews (roughly one-third of the Romanian Jewish population) transplanted themselves to Paris, London, Argentina, the United States and Canada.[44] Their overwhelming sense of loss is simply expressed in one of the many "emigration" songs that originated near Tirgul Neamt, where Jews had once made up half the population:[45]

> What pain we feel
> On leaving home
> When forced to abandon
> Our beautiful homeland
>
> Our thoughts will turn back
> For eternity
> All our lives we'll recall
> Dear Romania!

In the Second World War, Tirgul Neamt would be emptied of its Jews when they were expelled to the district capital, Piatra Neamt. There, by 1950, only about five thousand Jews were left. By 1970, there would remain only three hundred families.[46]

Montreal

"When the rest of the family finally came to Montreal in 1913," Gazella recalls, "it was the first time I saw the baby. Israel Pincas, they had called him. He was so cheerful and beautiful. One of the first things we did was get him a cradle. After all, our little 'Messiah' was special!"[1] Issie — or *Flamplatz* as his mother called him — would try out several names before settling on Irving Layton.[2]

In 1913, Montreal was a bustling commercial city spread out between the regal mountain backdrop and its protected island harbour. The immediate impact of the completion of the transcontinental railway had been to accelerate Montreal's transformation from a provincial outport to the "City of Merchant Princes." Since the end of the 1880s, the port had become the major centre for exports of cattle and wheat, which were shipped by rail from the interior. In the seven months of each year when Montreal's docks were not ice-bound, steamers from across the Atlantic jostled for space and the wharves were crowded with imports from European countries. Montreal was the largest city in Canada, boasted the second-largest port on the continent (after New York's) and claimed to handle a third of the nation's commerce. Its citizens fully believed that it was becoming another New York; St. Lawrence Boulevard, its main north-south commercial artery, was thought of as Canada's Fifth Avenue.[3]

But St. Lawrence Boulevard (or "the Main," as it was familiarly called) played an important role in Montreal that had no counterpart in its American antecedent. This was the street that sliced the city into two distinct and private halves: French to the east and English to the west. The French comprised roughly two-thirds of the city's population of more than half a million. The English — who at the turn of the century had made up the other third — were declining in proportion. By 1920 they would make up only a quarter of the city's inhabitants. In 1913, however, as boatloads and trainloads of immigrants flooded into the city, a new strain — neither French nor English, but mainly Jewish or Italian — was rapidly coming into its own, upsetting the old bi-cultural pattern.

Despite this potentially disruptive intrusion — of which the Lazarovitch family formed a tiny part — and despite the fact that the French, not the English, prevailed in Montreal, the city viewed itself, through the filter of its influential English-language newspapers, as a typical Anglo-Saxon, Victorian-Edwardian community with a French-speaking population large enough to warrant bragging that it was "a microcosm of the composit [sic] Dominion of Canada."[4]

In fact, the city was dominated by Scottish merchants and bankers and English press lords and professional men who had secured their fortunes amidst the uncontrolled economy of a burgeoning commercial empire. A new arrival to the city in 1913 could hardly overlook the solid, ornate buildings that spoke of wealth and power in the commercial districts that rose northwards from the placid St. Lawrence River, nor the huge, ostentatious architectural vagaries, with their towers and turrets, that lined the fair, broad streets of the residential "Square Mile" and graced the southern slopes of the royal mountain itself. Indifferent to the city's poor (six thousand of whom protested on May Day beneath the red flag), Montreal's rich drove their spirited horses along fashionable Sherbrooke Street, past McGill University with its fine trees and winding drives, where within the past decade Professor Ernest Rutherford had won the Nobel Prize for chemistry and was now engaged in theories about the structure of the atom; tobogganed in quaint outfits down the mountain's public slides in winter; took the "Mountain Lift" from Fletcher's Field to the Look-Out in summer, where they could stroll in the 460-acre park or gaze with pride onto the river, across St. Helen's Island park and over the eastern townships towards the American hills, which could be glimpsed on a clear day; or attended the St. Andrew's Ball in the ballroom of the palatial Windsor Arms Hotel. To them it was of little concern that prices had been rising at an alarming rate in the past few years or that unemployment was increasing dramatically.

Yet to anyone walking through its streets, Montreal had a Continental flair that was unmistakeable and singularly un-Protestant. Though a tram system had been built in 1907 and automobiles were appearing in increasing numbers since the turn of the century, horse-drawn vehicles still predominated. The French were Roman Catholic, as were significant numbers of the English: three-quarters of the populace all told. Ecclesiastical buildings were everywhere: the landmark harbour churches of Notre Dame Cathedral and the seventeenth-century Bonsecours Church, and convents, monasteries and numberless neighbourhood churches. The city's several public squares — among them Dominion Square, Victoria Square and Place d'Armes — were elegant, tree-lined parks that contained gravel walks and well-groomed gardens with public monuments that lent an old-world European grace. To many of its citizens, Montreal was the "Paris of North America."

In the two years since the two eldest Lazarovitch children had left Tirgul Neamt, they had done their best to adapt to this new and — to them — overwhelming city. It had not been easy. Abraham wore himself out lugging his two valises full of tablecloths, shirts and sheets up and down the cobbled, refuse-filled streets of downtown Montreal, eking out only enough as a "customer pedlar" (pedlars who established a regular clientele) to pay his board to his Auntie Sigler, a widow with a family to support. Gertie put in long hours at a factory "adorning ladies' hats" for five dollars a week. Though they could not afford street-car tickets, they did keep aside a little change to go weekly to the movies or to an ice-cream parlour, their only diversions.[5]

Their father, Moishe, could not speak or write English, so

he had no hope of finding work as a book-keeper, as he had in Romania, especially in a city feeling the pinch of unemployment. Deeply depressed, he assuaged his longing to return to Tirgul Neamt by staying in the bedroom behind closed doors, fastidiously groomed and dressed, poring over the *Tanach* (Old Testament), the *Talmud* (commentaries on the Bible) and other inspirational rabbinical tracts and books he had brought with him. For hours at a time he would disappear to pray in the local synagogue on Cadieux (later De Bullion) Street — one of the many synagogues improvised in vacant stores or community halls to serve the small groups of fifty to two hundred of the three *landsleutes* (groups who emigrated from the same town or country in Europe).[6] His rabbi was Abraham Schecter, whom the family had known in Romania.

It was Keine who proved most resourceful in these strange circumstances. By word of mouth, she tracked down Mrs. Wiser, a woman she had known in Romania who ran a store on St. Lawrence Boulevard that supplied Jewish customer pedlars with goods to sell. From Mrs. Wiser, Keine and Moishe rented the four-room downstairs flat of a little unpainted shack crammed into a small alley on the east side of St. Elizabeth Street, just above de Montigny. Drawing on her experience as a girl helping her mother to run a tiny grocery business from their home in Tirgul Neamt, she appropriated the narrow front parlour for a shop.[7]

The Lazarovitch family was completely typical of the enormous demographic shift in which they had taken part. Their shack at 183 Ste. Elizabeth Street was situated almost exactly in the centre of "the area of first settlement" of Eastern European Jews in Montreal.[8] This area, bracketed by St. Lawrence on the west and St. Denis on the east, boxed in by Craig to the south and Duluth on the north, stretched like an elongated rectangle directly north from Champs de Mars in Old Montreal. Formerly a French-Catholic district that constituted the St. Louis ward of the city, it was rapidly becoming Montreal's *shtetl* of immigrant Jews.

Though individual Jewish settlers had been trickling into Montreal since 1760 — the first synagogue was established in 1777 on Notre Dame near the courthouse — immigration had not become significant until the very end of the nineteenth century, when a wave of Jews from central and eastern Europe took flight for survival. The Lazarovitch family arrived at the height of this immigration.[9]

According to sociologist Judith Seidel, the number of Jews in Montreal more than quadrupled from 16,401 (0.3% of Montreal's citizens) in 1901, to 74,564 (1% of Montreal's citizens) in 1911, an increase of 355%, compared to an increase of 34% in the population generally. Romanian Jews like the Lazarovitches were especially numerous in Montreal. (Russian Jews tended to settle on the prairies; Polish Jews, who arrived mainly after 1920, preferred Ontario.) Compared to immigration in the United States, Canadian Jewish immigration included far fewer German Jews,[10] a factor that led historian Arthur Ruppin to speculate in 1934 that a different sort of North-American immigrant was emerging: "Canada, which in the 19th century received no German-Jewish immigrants, lacks a Jewish upper class. Most of the East European Jews are still petty traders, commission agents, or are in the fur or clothing trades, and in a few handicrafts."[11]

Ruppin's statement certainly applied to the Jewish community in Montreal. In the year of the Lazarovitches' arrival, approximately forty per cent of Jewish men and twenty per cent of Jewish women older than ten (Abraham and Gertie among them) were employed in commerce or manufacturing, as opposed to eight per cent of the general population.[12] In other words, immigrants from Romania and elsewhere began to ply the very trades that had made them an envied emergent class in Europe. In Montreal, too, they would play a major role in transforming economic life. As L. Rosenberg has theorized, "It is the Jewish population of Canada which has converted Canada from a country which was a producer of raw furs to export to other countries, into a country which dresses, dyes, and makes up all the furs it required for its own use." And, in Montreal (and elsewhere in North America), as in Europe, Jews would be envied. Discrimination persisted against them: they were excluded from heavy industries, and from positions in many large firms and elsewhere; they were ineligible for clubs and hotels and other recreational facilities where business contacts are often made and maintained; some companies refused to employ them or did so only on a very limited basis.[13]

Moishe, like other Jewish men, thought he would continue the orthodox customs of his Romanian days, but history dictated otherwise. Assailed by unfamiliar expectations in a city much larger than any he had known, unable to read or write either of the two major languages, confined to a community that was dramatically usurping a vocal, displeased French-Canadian *quartier,* Moishe Lazarovitch lost, almost overnight, his authority in the family. That authority had previously radiated through him to the family from the religious rituals he had conscientiously observed in Romania. But, in the North-American setting, even the authority of the synagogue was undermined: "As a house of assembly its function... atrophied; as a house of study [it became] weakened and [gave] place to independent institutions; [only] as a house of prayer it remains.... Here may be seen the Jews with their long beards, their long coats, *yarmulkah* (little silk caps); and the women with their *sheitl* (wigs) and head-shawls. However, those who still observe these customs in dress are not always in the majority...but the *talith* (praying shawl) is used in every orthodox synagogue."[14]

Seidel speculates that the single most "inexorable factor" that eroded Jewish tradition in Montreal was economic necessity. This was undoubtedly true for Romanian Jews between 1899 and 1910; they had, on average, $16.82[15] on entering North America, and for them the abrupt dislocation from an agricultural to an urban setting[16] meant that skills in subsistence farming were no longer useful. In Montreal, as elsewhere in North America, "the exigencies of competing for a living have made it impossible for the vast majority of Jews to honour Saturday as their Sabbath.... Daily synagogue has been restricted to the very pious, most of whom are retired or otherwise free to spend the necessary time." This assault on Jewish observance, Seidel concludes, "constituted a very powerful assimilative force.... A whole set of attitudes towards the preservation of religious ritual [was] weakened."[17]

Moishe fiercely resisted any dilution of orthodoxy. Though Keine's sister had abandoned the *sheitl* shortly after arriving in Montreal some years earlier (an act that so embarrassed her that she would not send a photograph of herself back to Romania),[18] Moishe forbade Keine to do the same. "Superstition prevailed," Hyman observes. "Our father was uneducated. He had never heard of physics and chemistry or science. He only knew what Moses had said on Mount Zion. It was ludicrous. On Saturday we couldn't light a match to start the stove — even if it was thirty degrees below. One of us would be sent out to find a *shegetz* (gentile boy) who, for ten cents, would light a paper to get it going. The ragged kids we approached on the street were usually too scared to come and do it."[19]

In the absence of a wage-earning occupation, Moishe had the leisure to attend synagogue frequently. He made cheese in the tiny kitchen and sent Hyman, his favourite, with baskets packed full to deliver to his eight or ten customers. Hyman recalls: "His cheese-selling, which he eventually gave up because he was too frail to lift the huge tin cans on and off the wood stove in the kitchen, only paid for his own few needs, with a little left over to save for me. He was determined I would become a rabbi. For a long time I went along with this idea of his. I used to go to synagogue and sit on hard chairs in a bare room in a neighbourhood house with him. I was well ensconced in religion. I had a retentive memory and knew the whole book of prayers by heart. He concluded I was religious; actually, I was just too lazy to learn to read Hebrew."[20] "I used to go with him once in a while on Fridays to the *mikvah* (ritual bath house) on La Gauchetière," Layton would recall, "but I didn't like the hot steam which he believed purified him before the Friday night prayers. I still can't reconcile my feelings of confusion at his reverent lighting of the *minora* candles on the stove right next to the putrid little cupboard-like toilet that was jammed up against it in one corner of the kitchen. The divine and the earthly were inseparable to me."[21] Hyman comments: "When our *kvetching* (complaining) mother berated him for being useless and not supporting us, he would simply say 'God so willed it.' He believed that everything was ordained. It seemed to us that he mortgaged the present for a heavenly future."[22]

The dislocation of roles Keine and Moishe experienced was

not unusual in North America. Jewish patriarchs typically found their contemplative authority undermined by the practical skills their wives possessed. The tensions between Moishe and Keine were not unlike those that can be glimpsed in A.M. Klein's 1933 portrait of the Gellers in his short story "The Seventh Scroll":

> Reb Yekuthiel Geller was utterly miserable in his new environment, among the barrels of briny herring, the boxes of dried pears, the pyramids of sardine-cans. He longed for the cool repose of his study, with its fragrance of phylactery-leather, its aroma of citron in cotton wool. Here in the narrow grocery of his new wife, where he could not take a step but he bumped into a crate of cubed sugar, or tripped over a clattering pail, or awkwardly elbowed down from the shelf a ketchup bottle, he was veritably in exile. The sounds, the smells, the very taste of the atmosphere in the grocery nauseated him. Those days when he had fingered the tassels of a prayer-shawl, or crooned over a holy book, or written his scrolls of divine dictation now belonged to a remote and enviable past.
>
> For the marriage had not prospered as well as the ebullient Kalimeyer had prophesied. The grocerylady — that was what the neighbours called her — had, he soon discovered, an indomitable will beneath that pious perruque of hers. She did faithfully observe the Sabbath, it is true, but that, Yekuthiel maintained, was religion well directed. A shrew of her kind needed some liturgy to mellow her. She was finicky, indeed, in her fulfilment of the dietary injunctions, but that was no difficult matter for a wife who fed her mate on a diet of ill-prepared meals, and of menus of monotonous identity. Even the consolation prize of her merits had been delicately exaggerated; she did not have, Yekuthiel soon found out, a handsome savings account hidden in her stocking, or in her bosom, or in any other of the concealments which womanhood has invented.
>
> At first she had treated him with respect. A scholar and a man of saintly ancestry was no common catch for

a widow. She had even boasted of her recent acquisition to her neighbours. She had allowed him, moreover, to continue his work while she wrapped her parcels, and hopped about the store like a live broomstick. But when she discovered that he was dedicating his Torah scroll to his late wife, jealousy made her sharp bones glow like embers. The gall of the man! Her husband, and offering a Torah in the name of his first wife. It was like adultery, she swore. She began to complain about the arduousness of her duties in the grocery; it was a shame that a man should sit at home, waste his time in writing scrolls which nobody would buy, because they were not even offered for sale, while she sweated and worked herself to the bone to provide his bread. At length he consented to help her out in the store. When Mrs. Geller considered the aid and succour which he gave her, it turned out, in her depreciating phrase, that he was no more than a message-boy. It was a ludicrous sight, indeed, to behold him, his little beard pointed forward like a goat's, his fragile body bent, and his eyes, dreamy and nostalgic,— drawing by a long handle a little cart, laden with wrapped kippers, wax-papered loaves, jars of preserves, and bags of fruit. When he was not running errands — leading his cart and tramping through the street, on the road and not on the sidewalk, like a pony, his plight was even worse. He had to stay in the store, serving Mrs. Itkovitch with a half-pound of sugar, or Mrs. Cohen with two pickles, of those that are three for five, please. His slightest error was visited with condign punishment by the vigilant and fastidious Mrs. Geller. She would let loose her vixen tongue upon him, and flog him with insults, in the sight of no matter how many customers. And all day long it was: Wrap those loaves! What, are you standing there like a *golem*? Weigh those onions! Are you going? for today or for tomorrow? Come, trundle yourself! She no longer called him Yekuthiel, only plain, imperious Yukel.

 At home in the double-parlour she would pounce upon his slightest gaucherie, his most innocent comment as an excuse for prolonged harangues, characterized mainly by the fact that they consisted of her own refutations of her own objections, and subsiding only when she realized that she was carrying on a marathon monologue. A scold among the scolds in Israel, her full-mouthed, spicy maledictions, had they any potency, would have thrown blight and bane upon an entire seraglio of husbands, let alone the poor, hunched, humble, self-effacing Yukel. For to her the process of cursing was a ritual, a sort of witch's incantation. Her ingenious oaths, moreover, tripped featly from her tongue in rhyme: did he gently suggest that the tea was cold, quick came the answering echo: May you soon grow old. Did he faintly remonstrate that the meat lacked pepper, out of her mouth it leaped — May you become a leper. These, however, were merely conversational couplets, extemporaneously uttered to express mild displeasure; it was when she observed him in the dining-room at his seventh scroll, that an avalanche of maladies, a torrent of afflictions, a tornado of calamities, rushed, streamed, and whirled from her termagant lips. But Yekuthiel, long-suffering and adept at volitional deafness, persisted in his labours, and was now completing the Book of Numbers.[23]

The Lazarovitches' move to Montreal called for radical adaptation, for changes that were much more easily made by European women than by their men. In the Lazarovitch family, as in many other North-American Jewish immigrant families, the attitudes and skills of a patriarch soon seemed irrelevant. Wives, whose complaining once would have been contained within the larger and stronger framework of their husbands' acknowledged superiority of learning and faith, became dominant in the family. Their complaints were no longer minor episodes in a life lent dignity by a reverent patriarch. They became the major theme in lives governed by new realities.

Layton would remember his father as a "dark, brooding, silent man" with "a strong sense of the unimportance of this world" who "spoke not more than ten words to me. I remember only one conversation with him. We were walking down the street. It was winter, and he stopped and looked up at the sun and said some profound, mystical thing about Nature being 'God's garment' as if it were some enveloping presence. The Hebrew patriarchs (whom he with his full black beard resembled) were more real to him than his own family." Moishe Lazarovitch was stirred to action only when his boys refused their holy observances. Then he would spank them or tie them to the bed-post until they relented. Though reports of Moishe's indifference to all but his offspring's souls may be somewhat exaggerated, they convey an alienation from the father felt by all the Lazarovitch children, even by the favoured Hyman, to whom his father made special small concessions, like hand-feeding him soup at the table on Fridays. Shut away behind a green door from the bustling activities of the kitchen, where Keine sliced fresh, raw potatoes directly onto the black Quebec wood stove as a fried snack while directing her miniature empire of grocerydom — a child noisily dispatched here to deliver fruit, another sent there with a sack of flour or a package of candles — Moishe "converted the bedroom to a sanctuary and communicated with the angels."[24] His excessive spirituality, directly underneath the mysterious comings and goings that often took place upstairs — drunken sailors in the passageway, occasional police raids with speedy, shameful exits — struck Hyman, who had a talent not only for memorization but for story-telling, as ludicrous. "What was going on upstairs was what the landlord was doing to us downstairs," he comments wryly. "While my father was downstairs praying with his candles and trying to reach the gates of heaven, upstairs they were making it into paradise momentarily."[25]

The brothel scraps above were part of the dominant French-Canadian context in the St. Louis ward, which Hyman remembers as "rampantly anti-Semitic." Moishe and Keine must have found the prejudice mild by comparison to what they had known in Romania, but its degrading ferocity struck all their children. To venture into the street was to encounter comments such as *"font à yell"* (go to hell!), *"maudit juif"* and "Jesus-killer," as well as the rhyme to slur the poverty of all foreigners, "Greenhorn, popcorn, Five cents a piece." "The police were French-Canadian, need I say more?" Hyman comments. To his younger brother Issie, the peal of church bells on Sundays and other Roman-Catholic holidays was a reproof not unlike the volleys of horse droppings heaved regularly down the alley towards their shack. At Easter, especially, gangs of French or Italian boys would descend upon their enemies — descendants of the Jews who had, in their opinion, crucified Christ — to exact revenge with broken bottles and knives. "I remember taking terrible beatings," Hyman says. "I had to organize a group of half a dozen guys who would retaliate if one of us was waylaid. Issie wasn't a great fighter, but he didn't back off either. We used to run across the rooftops to avoid them."[26]

The Lazarovitch children responded in different ways and degrees to the hostile climate.[27] The girls (except for Dora, who helped her mother with the smaller children and the grocery) worked in clothing factories until Keine deemed them ready for marriage in their mid-teens. To her, daughters were pawns to be traded for whatever financial security some suitable Jewish husband could offer. Gertie, "the Princess," was sent, protesting, into a loveless bond with a coarse, aggressive Romanian called Strul Goldberg, who cynically made an excellent living as a pedlar of religious items to Roman-Catholic monasteries and convents. He boasted openly of his sexual prowess with nuns and other women customers, and asserted frequently, "I'm better known in the province of Quebec than Jesus Christ!" Gertie's tears of protest (which prefaced a lifetime of suffering, numerous breakdowns, three marital separations and a son who comitted suicide) were met with Keine's scathing remark: "So you're hiding something under your apron, are you?" Esther, "the Crooked Nose" or "the Crow," was bartered a couple of years later to Benny Cohen, another customer pedlar. Within three months, she arrived home with a black eye. As an old woman she would become senile and would be put in the Maemonides Home. Of the three Lazarovitch girls, only the kindly Dora, who mothered the younger children and Keine herself on those occasions when her formidable energy gave way, was spared. But the inoffensive Dora sacrificed the education she wanted and earned. When she won a scholarship to teachers' college after public school, Moishe was adamant. There were no women teachers in Romania, and no daughter of his would become one. Such freedom for women was scandalous. She stayed unmarried — helping her mother — until she was in her late twenties. Then she married a heavy-built pedlar, a quiet, reverent man, who took her to Brockville, where they ran a store together.

As for the five Lazarovitch sons, Abraham, still boarding with his Auntie Sigler, strenuously peddled his wares and grew more and more sickly. Tuberculosis had begun to take hold. Harry, "the *Shegetz*," a thin, pale, sensitive boy, would maintain later that he was "more affected by the misery around than his brothers." As soon as he arrived in Montreal, at the age of eleven, he began to work evenings and Sundays for Mrs. Wiser, running errands or descending into her damp, foetid basement to stock goods for the five dollars a month he dutifully turned over to his mother. "I didn't see eye to eye with my father about religion," he admits sadly. Harry was kicked out when he was fourteen or fifteen because he wanted to shorten morning prayers. Feeling responsible for his mother, he visited her only when he had money to take. Oozing eczema on his hands lost him a job milking cows in the Eastern Townships, and he went to Sherbrooke to try to find work in a munitions factory. "I was a strange kid in a strange town," he recalls. "The Jewish woman where I was boarding had ten kids and thought my eczema might be contagious, so she threw me out. I looked up the most prominent Jewish businessman in the place, but he wouldn't help me. In the end, it was the poorest family in town who took me in. Even so, they weren't as badly off as my family. They were Roman Catholic. I couldn't understand their kindness to a Jew." Despite his bitter rebellion against his father, Harry preserved what he calls "old-world notions." "I've slept only with one woman [whom he met and married in Sherbrooke]; I think honesty is the best policy; self-praise is no recommendation; a man should be as good as his word. I never learned to have fun. I was satisfied just to get by, just to work and pay my bills." Larry, considered by the family to be the most handsome Lazarovitch son (he bears a striking resemblance to the actor Clark Gable), put in his stint at Mrs. Wiser's, and also was turfed out in his mid-teens.

He lived on the streets of New York for half a decade; then, after an incident in which a man came after him with a knife because he was having an affair with the man's wife, Larry turned to Keine, who "arranged" a marriage for him through a *shotgun* (marriage-broker) in Montreal. "He couldn't battle life," Hyman observes of the handsome, likeable brother Keine called *Megele*. "He was an introvert like our father. He bought a farm in Ste. Sophia, outside Ste. Agathe, where he lived away from other people. He became manic-depressive. He died in middle-age because he just gave up. He just wouldn't *try*. He's the tragedy in our family."

The two youngest Lazarovitches — Hyman and Israel — undoubtedly got the best deal in the family, though that wasn't much. Each of them was "taken up" by one of the parents: Hyman by his father, Issie by his mother. Neither had the delicate, sensitive nature of Gertie, Harry or Larry: "they were more robust and aggressive, they had more fun," Harry recalls. Hyman was a tough bully, who dominated his peers with his fists and with the ghost or adventure stories he would spin so convincingly at dusk on the porch stairs. When he was twelve, Hyman reminisces, he rejected the Jewish tradition his father planned for him by telling Rabbi Schecter, "You take a flying fuck!" He continues. "We weren't allowed to be sick. My mother was too busy to be a mother. She was a barracuda. Once, when I had a toothache, she said, 'You must have sinned. Just pray and it will go away.' I was turning somersaults from the pain. Finally, she gave me a dime for some toothache drops. It didn't take Einstein to see that those drops were more potent than God." It wasn't long before he, too, was "tumbled out" to join Larry on the streets of New York in the swelling ranks of those poor who were gravitating towards the Communist party in protest against the oppression of a capitalist sytem. His later life (which encompassed a plethora of professions, from leather goods to carpets) speaks of revised political views.

It is Hyman who most clearly remembers the odd way in which their mother's favourite, *Flamplatz,* responded to their home life. "He didn't suffer as he should have. He was the only one who escaped all that. His special pastime for a while was skating to bed on the water that had dripped down the walls during the day and froze at night." Faced with stark physical conditions and emotional turmoil, the youngest Lazarovitch, favoured by the surly, clamorous mother with whom he continued to sleep throughout his childhood, imagined into existence a world as sunny and cheerful as his own ebullient nature. Physically robust and somehow able to penetrate through his mother's façade of hostile curses to her earthy humour and gruff tenderness, he found the strength to have fun. When reality was painful or ugly, he habitually re-invented it. Competing with Hyman as a storyteller, in imitation of their mother's homespun fables of biblical miracles and proverbial superstitions, he made up life as it went along. "He was lost once, and no one bothered to look for him. A couple of French-Canadian kids brought him in and asked for some candy as a reward," Hyman recalls. "Even *that* didn't seem to bother him." To him, the springtime strip-down of wallpaper and the handing along the line of buckets of scalding water Keine heaved, cursing, onto the cockroaches was not work but high adventure. Savouring the physical, making of each sensuous detail an intensity of the moment, Issie transformed potential pain into intense beauty and, sometimes, unspeakable pleasure.

Death

Flamplatz was on fire.

He was in his sixth year. It was Friday night, and he could hear his mother talking loudly to some of her Romanian friends in the dining room. The glasses from which they were drinking coffee clinked softly. He had gone into the toilet with his candle and set it down on the floor. Suddenly, he looked down to see long flumes of flame licking upwards from the hem of his white nightshirt. They were exquisitely beautiful. He exploded with pain.[1]

"He was in bed for several weeks afterwards," recalls Dora, who nursed him, though she was only thirteen. "Those burns were terrible. But he was so good, so uncomplaining. He just stayed in bed under the comforter drawing with a paper and pencil and kept himself happy."

Keine railed her Yiddish rhymes against fate. "Whether we're rich or whether we're humble, we end up in dust or ashes that crumble," she expostulated with a deep, bitter laugh. "When we get older, our blood just runs colder; as for our ears, they no longer hear." Wasn't it enough that her youngest child lay in bed, refusing to help her, taking valuable time from Dora, who should have been weighing sugar or making up barrels of pickled tomatoes or *schmaltz* herring? No. God had also arranged for her eldest son, Abraham, to be ill, so ill he'd gone up to the Mount Sinai Sanatorium at Ste. Agathe in the Laurentians to rest and breathe the fresh air. He wanted her there. It sounded serious. Hadn't she told him that if he broke off his engagement to that Jewish girl, God would punish him? Stupid boy! Just think of the bills the two of them would bring upon her head!

Tomorrow, she thought, was one Sabbath she would not be visiting her grandchildren to make them cookies or *kugel* and cook them *knaidle* (chicken soup with dumplings). She would miss the snug comfort of Gertie and Strul's big brass bed, where she liked to climb in with the children after dinner and tell them stories and fairy-tales.[2]

Two or three weeks after the doctor had come running to treat the screaming Issie, Keine abandoned him to nurse Avram up north. When she returned, what seemed like a lifetime later, though it was only a month, it was to announce that Avram had died. The doctor said it was tuberculosis. She knew better. God had punished him.

Because of his long recuperation, Issie entered grade one at Alexandra Public School on Sanguinet Street in the middle of the year. His arrival did not go unnoticed. Saul Muhlstock, a Galician Jew whose family had brought him to Canada when he was a small child, remembers being a student supervisor of the school playground when he was eleven. "Mr. F.H. Spinney, the teacher in charge, called me over and pointed at a short, stocky boy with a shock of black hair who resembled a Shetland pony. 'Keep your eye on that one, he's a live one,' he told me. Invariably at recess, when the boys and girls would pelt down the stairs to the basement or outside, Issie was on the floor with some guy. Though he was very small, he would not be pushed around. He meant what he said, or else. Even much bigger kids took notice of him. One day I went up and pulled him out of some melée or other and said, 'Who do you think you are? You're acting like a little Napoleon around here.' The name caught on. 'Nappy,' we all called him. I still do."

With hindsight, Muhlstock speculates, "I was struck by his leadership qualities, though, to my thinking, he did not contrive nor control [them]; he could only *be*, because he could no other.... Much of his pugnacious, pushy attitude was also a determination to impress the girls; it was a way of saying 'I may be small, but oh, my!' He may have had the natural will to define, express and vaunt his gift of a richly encarved sexuality."[3]

Issie was interested in women. One day in a restaurant, he had seen one of the Miss Cooks. The thin, short one. She and the tall, stout Miss Cook had lived upstairs from Issie, before the noisy young French-Canadian girls moved in. The thin, short Miss Cook asked him to visit her for tea. Over sugared tea and jam tarts, she explained how lonely she was. Her husband had died. She held up a photograph that showed Issie all the bullet marks he had worn as proudly as a row of medals. They played dominoes. Issie told her fortune. She thought he had "powers" and told him so. Or had he told her? Anyway, he foretold her marriage to Mr. Palmer. Issie knew Mr. Palmer was interested in the lonely Miss Cook. He felt the same way. The two Miss Cooks were from Sussex. He liked the English.[4]

And women were interested in Issie. The first was Minnie (they called her "Minnie-Ha-Ha"). "For a penny she would let the boys kiss her hand," Hyman recalls. "She was nine and had bad pimples. Issie said her pimples were like cheerful cherubs dancing in the moonlight. It was about the same time he coined a word for money: 'snook.' I had a snook, he'd say. It meant both money and where it came from."[5]

"Then there was cousin Fanny who let us boys gaze at her adolescent nakedness, and sometimes even let us touch her 'there' and 'there'. I was consumed with feeling," Issie would recall later. "It increased my pleasure to know that it was forbidden. That I shouldn't be doing it. The tension between denial and desire evoked the keenest delight."[6]

As soon as Issie learned to read, his interest turned to the erotic. Whenever he had a "snook" — even five cents — he'd buy or trade second-hand boys' magazines like *Fame and Fortune* or *Pluck*. "I read a great deal," he recalls. "It was junk, if you wish, but it gave me delicious moments. I would get some candy, take one of these magazines and climb up on the roof to sit leaning against the chimney. At first it was cool, but as the sun started to climb it began to warm up. Some of them were very sleazy: war comics or horror comics stapled in the middle between lurid covers. I got my first notions about England from *The Magnet,* an adventure series about English school boys. I read all of G.A. Henty's books. From episodes I read about the Tong Wars, I fostered an exotic image of Orientals. I remember walking down La Gauchetière, through the Chinese district, imagining romantic adventures. It gave me tremors."[7] It also gave him tremors to see Miss Benjamin, his sixth-grade teacher, flush when she got confused. He would ask her to help him so she would stand beside his desk. He watched that bold, mottled blush sweep down from her cheeks to her neck and into the mysterious folds of her open blouse. He'd known what to do when she gave him a detention. He slipped a poem about her beautiful blush onto her desk. It had worked. Indeed, it had more than worked; convinced that he was "a young man of unusual gifted talents," she had moved him to the back of the class, given him a dictionary, and left him alone to "do his thing."[8] It gave him tremors, too, to watch one of the girls at school say "prunes." How her mouth would form the most delicious pout, as if her lips invited kisses. "Prunes," he asked her to say over and over again. "Prunes. Prunes. Prunes."[9]

In contrast to the sensual thrill of boys' adventure stories, Issie disliked the religious instruction in Hebrew texts his father severely forced him to attend at a local *cheder* (religious school) every day after school until he was thirteen. "It was a waste of my glorious boyhood," he protests now. "I spent hours in the company of my *lerner,* a pathetic, sadistic little man, who made me laboriously translate certain sections of Genesis or memorize long Hebrew passages. It was boring, stupid and ill-taught. I can only read a little Hebrew today, but without much understanding."[10]

Issie was in his twelfth year. He had eluded a bar mitzvah. His father was sick. At first Moishe grew quiet, though, given his usual withdrawal, it went largely unnoticed. Then, limb by limb, he gradually became paralysed. At the end, in the winter of 1925, he lay cold with fever; the family crammed into his "sanctuary" and gathered around his bed. Keine supported his neck and urged him to eat, but he was too feeble to do anything but cough dryly, covering his bearded chin with his one good hand, the one he didn't write with. He could not speak.

Keine had written for a *refue* (remedy) to the chief rabbi of Israel. Couldn't he send something to save her husband? He was only fifty-four. Two years ago he had felt well enough to open a tiny shop for Larry and Harry (then thirteen and ten), but it had failed a month later.

Moishe had been dead for two weeks when the container of earth arrived from Israel with the instructions. "Put the *tfillin* [phylacteries for the head] on his head, and spread this holy earth upon his legs."[11] Years later, in a story called "A Death in the Family," Layton would recreate his reaction to his father's death and to the friends and relations who clustered in the dingy little dining room to moan and weep as Issie was held up, terrified, to look into the coffin at the limp, lifeless corpse:

> He did not stop, but ran into the bedroom, closing the door behind him. There was no one in the room. He was glad to be in here all by himself. He was glad to find the room bright with sunshine. He thought: "My father was here a week ago," and he instinctively glanced at his bed in the corner. It was made up, the white coverlet snug and unwrinkled, as if it had never been slept in.
>
> At that moment the bells from the nearby church began to ring loudly and cheerfully; the peals came over the narrow back street and across the yard and straight into the room, filling it with a deafening tumult. When the bells stopped and the echoes retreated, it seemed to the boy that someone outside was still flinging grains of music against the windows shivering in their wooden frames. He was so absorbed that he completely forgot the dark faces on the other side of the closed door. He knew, but how he did not know, that the men were washing his father's body. Quickly, he dismissed the image from his mind.
>
> He ran from one corner of the room to the other, in dizzying circles, leaping over the jagged spears of sunlight as if they were real and could trip him up, and only when he was out of breath did he stop. He put his hand into his pocket and came up with an elastic band and a green button that had come off his jacket. He carefully pulled the elastic through the holes of the

> button and twisted it round and round with a mad kind of happiness. He put the ends over his thumbs and moved his hands backwards and forwards as though he were playing an accordion and listened to the whizzing sound it made, like the wings of a giant fly. When he tired of that, he wound the ends up on the iron knobs of the bed and pulled the button towards the floor as far as it could go and releasing it gave a loud squeal each time it flew upwards.[12]

Issie had learned how to deal with any reality he did not like. Just as his father had closed the door on the physical, hurly-burly of their kitchen to enter more spiritual realms, Issie easily imagined another, better world into being and threw himself into it. But that world could not have been less like the fastidious, religious world his father had treasured. Issie's world was more like Keine's — full of physical sensations and emotional power.

"A Death in the Family" reveals Issie's skills in evasion, and also shows how strongly the adolescent boy associated death with sexual guilt. Something about his brother's death — Avram was punished because he had betrayed a woman — his father's useless pale corpse and Issie's comprehension of the sexual humiliation his older sister was suffering at the hands of her crude husband coalesced into an almost metaphysical repulsion. But an exhilarating sense of freedom triumphed. His father's disappearance forever from the bedroom left Issie sole possessor of his mother, his *maidele* (sweetheart). He was her *strulick*,[13] her *Flamplatz*, her favourite. For the time being, he would continue to share her bed, reaching for her, past the unsavoury memory of his father, looking away from her "dead hair" and the teeth in the bedside glass as she joined him, burying his nose in her sweet-smelling flesh.

Transitions

The death of Moses Lazarovitch in 1925[1] was a marked turning point for his family. Gone were the enforced *kiddish* (morning) prayers, the pressures to attend synagogue and the feared visits to *mikvah* and *cheder*. No more would the younger, recalcitrant Lazarovitch boys be punished at home or dragged by the ear past their jeering French-Canadian peers, those *schkotzin* (gentile riff-raff), by a father distracted and appalled by their dilatory behaviour. With the disappearance of that meek, contemplative presence behind the green door, a presence that had set holy visions apart from the daily wheel of ordinary life, the restraints of old-world longings disintegrated, and the family — now solely under the wing of their practical, adaptable barracuda[2] of a mother — took a quantum leap forward towards assimilation.

Once she got her hands on Moishe's few savings, along with those of her son Abraham, Keine moved her family about ten blocks north, out of their rented Ste. Elizabeth Street rooms to 4158 Avenue de l'Hôtel de Ville. Her purchase of a tiny, unpainted, run-down shack with clothes-lines out back and a store out front, though it raised their standard of living hardly at all, made the family independent.

The Lazarovitches' move typefied the demographic realignment of the European Jewish community in Montreal in the first quarter of the century. The family had first taken up lodging in the centre of the first area of Jewish immigrant settlement; their second house was almost exactly in the middle of the next main area of settlement that sprang up as many Jewish families moved away from the seedy Montreal downtown into a slightly better environment. In 1911, the St. Louis ward, in which their Ste. Elizabeth Street house had been located, contained the largest representation of the city's Jews. But by 1921, the St. Jean Baptiste ward, which included Avenue de l'Hôtel de Ville, had surged to the fore as Montreal's unofficial Jewish "ghetto."[3] As the Jewish community was rapidly radiating outwards — north and west into Laurier, Notre Dame de Grace, Westmount, Outremont and other areas of the city — the most dramatic increase of Jewish population took place in the St. Jean Baptiste ward, where the 2,911 Jewish citizens enumerated in the census of 1911 had swelled by 303% to 11,712 by 1921. During the same decade, the Jewish population in the St. Louis ward increased only slightly, by 6%. The total Jewish population in Montreal in 1921 was 45,014; the ward to which the Lazarovitches moved in 1925 harboured more than a quarter of the city's Jews. That ward of St. Jean Baptiste was bounded by Park Avenue on the west and St. Denis on the east, and stretched north from Sherbrooke Street to Mount Royal Avenue. Especially north of Pine and south of Rachel, Jewish immigrant families crowded together to form the "ghetto." The north-south artery that neatly bisected this ghetto through the middle was still St. Lawrence Boulevard.

Then as now, St. Lawrence Boulevard — "the Main" — formed the business and amusement centre of the community. At all hours of the day and night, people of unmistakeably middle-European stock darted in and out of the shops, banks and factories that announced in Yiddish as well as English the nature of their contents. Here were the food shops: butchers whose windows displayed the *kosher* meat symbol and announced their affiliation with the *Vaad Hair* (the Jewish Community Council), which guaranteed that the ritual slaughter by a qualified *shochet* had taken place; fish markets; delicatessens where the prized *schmaltz* herring, sauerkraut and lox (smoked salmon) could be obtained;

bakeries selling the ritual Sabbath *challah* (white egg bread), earthy caraway-seed and pumpernickel, beside which the *goyisheh* (non-Jewish) bread seemed unbaked and tasteless; grocery stores that sold Sabbath candles, vegetable-oil soap for dishes, Passover products, *halvah* (a cream-cheese-like confection made of nuts) and other special products; dairies where cream cheese, sour cream and milk products were freshly made; and sweat-shops, many of them Jewish-owned, in which clothes, hats and furs were manufactured in the vast needle-trade of Montreal. At the hub of this bustling mercantile community was the "Rachel" market, at the corner of Rachel and St. Lawrence streets, where French-Canadian farmers brought fresh produce to be bargained for and sold. In the midst of this market, Keine was often to be seen, her *Flamplatz* at her side with his makeshift cart, haggling over the fruit and vegetables she would take four blocks away to her new grocery parlour to sell to local customers. She was one of the many older women who still dressed in the European way, a shawl over her head and shoulders and a dark heavy sweater to keep her warm. Her type was beginning to stand out among the younger women who often were attired in clothes from the nearby factories that, though cheap, represented the height of fashion. Everywhere, inside the cramped, shabby stores and outside in the open market, Yiddish was the language of trade.

Among the many small grocers' shops that had sprung up in the area, one in particular irked Keine: the Steinbergs'. Mrs. Steinberg's business on St. Lawrence seemed to be prospering in a way that Keine's wasn't. She blamed her sons. "Why can't you be like Mrs. Steinberg's boys?" she would angrily remonstrate. "Their hands aren't always filthy so that the customers complain after deliveries! They aren't always disappearing just when they're needed to help! Why did God give me the useless sons and her the good boys? Why don't you follow their example so that we can put some decent clothes on our backs and better food on our own table? That I should live to see this morn! Would that you had not been born!" But her *kvetching* did nothing to instil responsibility in her sons, and she looked on in helpless rage as Mrs. Steinberg gradually built her family business into a grocery empire.⁴ When his mother began to curse like this, Issie sought refuge in graveyards. He liked the solemn, quiet stones and the tremors he felt thinking of the mystery of death. Somehow he felt close to his father there.

The streets that fed into the Main and those that paralleled it were frequently reminiscent of the streets in Europe from which their inhabitants had originally come. The close-set houses, which gave directly onto the sidewalks, were two- or three-storey buildings, usually in need of repair. "Although low rentals and deteriorated buildings are the rule here," one observer in the early thirties recalled, "the anonymity, disorganization, and degradation of a slum, while not entirely absent, are not characteristic."⁵ Religious values, still largely undiluted, and the extension of these values into communal rituals and cultural traditions, unified the members of ghetto life and gave them a sense of purpose that provided a formidable resistance to ethical erosion. Knowing the intolerable situations they left behind, possessing a common language to bond them — despite their various countries of origin — and hopeful of successes in the New World that would have been impossible in the old, these Jews, like others elsewhere, bore their deprivations without becoming utterly desperate. Mindful of the needs of their new community, they used their new freedom to institute the organizations that could best fulfil them — not only the synagogues, but also the Hebrew Old People's Home on Esplanade Avenue (1910); the Montreal Hebrew Orphans' Home (1912); the Young Men's Hebrew Association (which by 1912 had more than twelve hundred members); the Jewish Immigrant Aid Society (1920); and the Canadian Jewish Congress; as well as a wide network of parochial schools: the first Talmud Torah in 1903; the United Talmud Torahs of Montreal, which included five schools (1917); the Peretz Schule, with its emphasis on Yiddish (1912); the "Folk Schule" or Jewish People's School, which emphasized Hebrew (1914); and the Workers School (1927). Though they lived in a situation that in many ways pressed them centrifugally into a North-American community via the many tramways and bus lines that led outwards from the "ghetto" to greater Montreal, the centripetal strength of their traditions and customs, and the skill with which they set up an appropriate infrastructure, ensured that their assimilation would not be sudden. The unique character of Montreal, divided as it was between French and English with two languages, religions and traditions, did not encourage assimilation as powerfully as a monolithic society might have done.

It was certainly heedless of this intensely transitional phase of his family's existence that Issie Lazarovitch walked the long ten blocks from their new home in the St. Jean Baptiste ward back to the Alexandra Public School in the St. Louis ward for the months of May and June in 1925 to complete his public-school education. Yet in that back-and-forth journey lay a timely paradigm. Issie's walk to the old ward, where he had experienced his father's drive to maintain rigidly orthodox patterns of life, then forward to the new ward, in which his mother sought release from the hardships that had resulted from orthodoxy, suggested the wavering between self-limiting conservatism and individualistic experimentation, which the Montreal Jewish community, in its rapid adaptation to new circumstances, was experiencing on a much larger scale.

During the summer of 1925, having left the name "Nappy" behind at Alexandra Public School, Issie was sent, like his brothers before him, to Mrs. Wiser. There, dressed in soiled overalls, he would help stock the shelves in her damp and musty basement. "It was taken for granted that I would become a customer pedlar, now that I was finished school," Layton recalls. His family could imagine no career other than this, except perhaps that of a shipper or cutter. Abraham had been a pedlar, as had his other brothers and his two brothers-in-law, Strul Goldberg and Benny Cohen. It was Strul and Keine who conspired to urge Issie to take up his bags and walk. So it was over to Jeanne Mance Street that the thirteen-year-old Issie would go, striding down from Mrs. Wiser's on Pine Avenue, his two valises loaded down with buttons, linens, brushes, jewellery and sewing notions — all the familiar staple wares of customer pedlars. "At first, I felt anxious," he later recalled, "but I turned out to be good at it. I proved to be a born salesman."[6] Like his mother, Issie was quick with words and shrewd at bargaining. He was also handsome; his intense blue eyes contrasted dramatically with his thick shock of black hair, and his voice was magnetic and compelling. He was possessed of unusual charm.

The end of that summer brought into the open a conflict that was to become crucial. Issie wanted more education. The prospect of a dreary life of peddling, hauling heavy valises around the streets, did not appeal to him. Compared to that, school didn't seem like work at all. He also longed to return to an environment where his keen appetites for a fantasy life of romantic adventure, fostered by literature and history, might be satisfied, even partially. At the end of public school, he was still an avid reader, devouring boys' magazines and adventure stories with keen interest. Had he not been the youngest Lazarovitch, he would not have had a chance to fulfil his wishes. Baron Byng High School, a Protestant-English institution and the only high school in the "ghetto," charged a small fee for attendance each month. This meant that Keine, instead of receiving four dollars a week direct from Mrs. Wiser for Issie's peddling, as she had all summer, would have to spend a few dollars a month on his schooling. None of her other children had gone past public school, not even Dora with her scholarship. Perhaps it was because he was her favourite; perhaps it was because her ambitious nature saw and seized an opportunity for her *srulickel* to make more money in the long run; perhaps it was her conviction that her "Messiah" was special — born circumcised, though that was most probably the result of a common birth defect[7] — or perhaps simply because of her obstinate nature, she ignored her son-in-law Strul's advice and the urgings of her daughters and agreed to pay for the schooling. In the fall of 1925, Israel Lazarovitch entered high school.

Revenge

> At Flores in the Azores, Sir Richard Grenville lay,
> And a pinnace, like a fluttered bird, came flying from
>   far away:
> 'Spanish ships of war at sea! We have sighted fifty-three!'[1]

Tennyson's memorable opening to "The 'Revenge': A Ballad of the Fleet," thundered out — perfectly enunciated with an English accent — from the lips of Amos Saunders. "Sandy," as he was known to the students of Baron Byng High School, had graduated in political economy from University College of Wales in Aberystwyth, taught in Northumberland, England, then emigrated with his wife to Montreal, where he had taken a position at the High School of Montreal until 1925. That was the year of major expansion in Baron Byng High School. Saunders, like several other British schoolmasters, had transferred there to help deal with the many new enrollments.

To the boys of Room Twenty-four — mainly Jewish, like the rest of the students — Sandy was "a grand fellow." He had a reputation for being tough, and consequently was given the most difficult boys. "They were the best ones," he recalls. "A month after I got them, even though there were fifty-five or so in a class, they felt as if they belonged to a family. I'd sit on them for the first little while until they knew I was boss. I got the good ones to help the poor ones. You could leave school at fourteen in those days, but I was usually able to keep them in high school longer than they intended to stay. I guess I had something in common with them: I believed in fair play; I loved justice."[2] Saunders also loved books, especially poetry, or "poi-try," as he pronounced it in the British way. He quoted lines and phrases extensively to illustrate whatever he said. He bought *Chums,* the *Boys' Own Paper* and *Chatterbox* in the after-Christmas sales and circulated them in an attempt to instil the love of reading in his boys.

Believing that "the purpose of life is to *serve*," he considered his teaching job a vocation of almost Messianic proportions. If the boys would read, or listen to the great thoughts, sublimely expressed, of the major "poits," they might make a qualitative leap in life from the physical to the moral and aesthetic.

So the burly, well-groomed Sandy, his brown eyes flashing, read to his boys in Form 8(2) from Tennyson's rousing ballad. The poem was based, they learned, on Sir Walter Raleigh's 1591 report of the *Revenge*, a tiny English ship that single-handedly engaged the Spanish fleet of fifty-three men-of-war off the coast of Africa:

> The little *Revenge* ran on sheer into the heart of the foe,
> With her hundred fighters on deck, and her ninety sick below;
> For half of their fleet to the right and half to the left were seen,
> And the little *Revenge* ran on thro' the long sea-lane between.
>
> Thousands of their soldiers look'd down from their decks and laugh'd,
> Thousands of their seamen made mock at the mad little craft....

Sitting near the back of the class, "insolence on his face,"[3] sat Issie Lazarovitch, transfixed, "astonished that anyone would take words that seriously."⁴ Mocked for his mad belligerence and his small, stubby body, he, too, had flung himself through the lines of bigger, stronger boys. Goaded by wounded pride, he knew what it was like to make those blind, doomed rushes at those who mocked him. He boxed and wrestled. And he knew the sweet taste of revenge. As the impassioned British voice of the kindly, idealistic Sandy pounded out the lines that caught the very rhythms of pummelling fists, something clicked into place in Issie's small experience. Here were *Boys' Own* adventures raised to a more intense level than any he'd known. Here was a drama he recognized well: the beleaguered underdog against the heathen Roman Catholic, upholding "duty," "Queen and Faith" "like a valiant man and true." Here was history brought alive in words he recognized from his readings of Henty — "power and glory," "perilous plight," "musketeers," "devildoms" — all cast in the dramatic rhyme his mother used and interspersed with the curses that had issued from her lips for as long as he could remember. And all this was coming at him through the one teacher in the school with the dark visionary eyes of his father, the only one who commanded his respect. "Poi-try," he saw, was power.

By the end of Form 9(2) in 1927, Sandy had managed to convince Issie Lazarovitch that the pen was sometimes mightier than the fist. Every Saturday, Issie would walk all the way from City Hall Avenue to the second-hand bookstores on Vitre and Bleury streets to pick up a collection of Tennyson or a copy of the *Nation* or *New Republic* or a dictionary. He had become a bibliophile. Issie's tribute to Sandy — couched in the highly literary nineteenth-century English he was rapidly absorbing from Saunders and from his readings in English poetry and classics such as *The Count of Monte Cristo* (his favourite book at age fourteen), *The Three Musketeers* and several of Sir Walter Scott's and Bulwer-Lytton's novels⁵ — emerged in a character sketch he penned as his second year of high school drew to a close:

28th June 1927

Sandy

Sandy, as I affectionately call him, is a stocky well-built

Englishman. He (stands) is medium sized and wears an habitual good-humoured smile which inspires all who meet with him with confidence. Looking into his face I could not help noticing his aquiline nose and brown eager eyes peering at me with as serious a look as ever I beheld. And his form, ah, such an athletic figure, his broad Herculean shoulders and well-proportioned limbs; a chest which betokens good lungs and a strong heart.

About his mouth are those lines which give to a person strength of character and personal force — will power, yes, perfect strength of will. But it is not that thin dry, hard mouth of Ropespierre [sic]. No! a thousand times, no! it is an open, a frank a genial expression, an expression that fills you with delight and wonder. And then, people say if you can control yourself, you can controll [sic] others. And sure enough it is true. Ever-smiling, ever laughing, not from a sense of duty but from pure open-heartedness and geniality. Altogether he presents a figure that call [sic] for admiration and respect, a person to love and honour and defend (if need be) unto the last.

I. Lazarovitch[6]

Suzanne

It was a cold night. With violent ferocity the wind swirled down from the mountain through the streets of the St. Jean Baptiste ward, throwing gigantic white pinwheels of snow in its relentless course towards the river. There were only a few wagons and carts out tonight, the horses shrunk into their traces, their heads turned to shield them from the barrage of icy flakes. Drifts higher than the tallest man had begun to form along the roadside. Tomorrow it would be shovels and curses until a path was cleared. In the meantime, no one who could avoid it went out.

Inside the lower flat of a run-down house on City Hall Avenue, a light burned late. Issie was reading, his face flushed with the thrill of adventure. The cracked wooden door opened and slammed shut. It was Keine, back from a neighbour's. They had come that afternoon to ask her to listen to some dispute or other, to offer her advice. She had thrown down the pants she was sewing for him, wrapped her head and shoulders in her black shawl and left, muttering to herself.

While she was gone, Dora had flown into a fury. Why wasn't he helping her? He was so lazy. Reading? Who had time to read with so much work to be done? She had threatened once again to destroy his books. She had pulled some of them from the shelf onto the floor. Two were ripped.

"A trouble that comes regularly is no trouble at all," Keine, shaking snow from her shawl, announced in exasperation. The curses began to build. It was as if she herself were the winter wind freezing each shabby stick of furniture in the cramped suite of rooms with a blizzard of blasphemy.

Issie inhaled the odour of rotting vegetables from the parlour grocery. He'd forgotten to deliver that order to — who was it? — the Rosenbergs. They lived in a flat over on Drolet Street, three blocks east. Issie closed his book and slipped it quietly behind the chair. He strode purposefully to the small window, drew back the worn curtain and peered through the cold, frost-caked window-pane. Outside, the trees were frozen with ice, their spiny fronds encased in crystal that reflected haloes of light from the street lamps above. It was beautiful, magical, terrible. Before his mother could build to a final crescendo of insults, he grabbed her shawl, hung it on its hook and began to rub her stomach with his small, knowledgeable hands. "*Mama bakele,* I'm just leaving now." Before she could answer, he darted into the grocery, thrust his short arms into a ragged coat, seized the two or three bags, and was off.[1]

The wind was against him. His flat platform sled with its long awkward handle kept sticking in the snow and tipping over, scattering the groceries into the fine white powder that lay luminous on the deserted streets.

He reached the Rosenbergs' and rang the bell. A nine-year-old girl answered, a two-year-old boy clinging to her knees.

"Shurri, let go! Let go!" she commanded, but her brother clung to her, whining and gazing up at the snowy, black-haired apparition that had appeared in front of him. It was one of the sons of that woman she feared, the woman who wore those long, wide unfashionable skirts. The one whose dark, thick hair refused to submit to pins and combs and sprang — almost alive — in wavy, snake-like curls out of the bun at the nape of her neck. She always scowled like a witch. Perhaps she *was* a witch. It was best to cross the street when you saw her coming.

"Shurri! Come on!" she continued in a heavily accented voice. "Mother will soon be home from work. Ah," she said to Issie. "I've had to mind him all year. I've missed school and everything. Who are you?"

Issie could not reply. He had never seen a girl quite like this. She was not at all like cousin Fanny or Minnie-Ha-Ha with her pimples. This girl had gleaming, fair hair and dark eyes like the heroines in his books. Her skin was like peaches. Peaches with lights inside. Her cheeks were as red as the apples that had just spilled into the snow. He drew himself up as tall as he could and handed her the groceries.

"There was a haughty and independent air about him which told me that he hated his dull job of grocery boy no less than I resented being turned into a nanny and spending all day with my brother, rather than learning at school and playing games with my peers," she would later write. "My gaze caught the intensity in his deep blue eyes. The strength in them communicated itself to me. Often, after that brief encounter, I mused upon that boy with the intense look, hoping to meet him again."[2]

The name of the nine-year-old girl was Suzanne.

Adrift

Issie's childhood ended in the spring of 1929. That was when Keine — his *mama bakele* and *maidele* — set up house with Kalman Hershorn,[1] a lusty man who was reputed to have cut off a finger to escape military service in Russia. Now that her *Flamplatz* was fifteen and, in her opinion, a man, Keine decided arbitrarily that her long stint of rearing children was finally over. She greedily seized what remained of her own life. At last, her cumbersome *sheitl* could be abandoned for a new husband who was not as orthodox as Moishe had been. Like herself, Hershorn was vigorous, and he loved life. Even in his eighties, though he and Keine had long been separated, he would declare how he used to "love to lie on top of her."[2] Hershorn had money, enough to move Keine up and out of the Jewish getto of the St. Jean Baptiste ward to the western section of Notre Dame de Grâce, where they lived (though she kept and rented the shack on City Hall Street) in what, for her, was relative splendour in an apartment at 4136 Decarie, near Broadview. Though Issie visited once or twice a week, he never felt comfortable there. Disliked by her new husband, he had not been invited to the celebration of their new home and was distinctly unwelcome.

How could she reject him? Her little *strulick*, her own *Flamplatz*. He felt almost sick with grief. He wasn't ready to leave.

She had more money now. Why wouldn't she give him some? Why wouldn't she look after him? Where could he turn?

Almost simultaneously, Issie was undergoing rejection on another front. A job with the Hebrew Orphans' Home, which he had begun the previous summer, had ended abruptly. It seemed as if he had brought the disaster upon himself. Inflamed with idealism and a pity that more accurately might have been turned on himself, Layton saw only corruption and the abuse of power in the orphans' home. Feeling orphaned himself, he took it upon himself as a personal crusade to alert the board by assembling a delegation of former supervisors and resident nurses. The meeting had no effect. He then resorted to the desperate tactic of getting the boys and girls to stage a protest on the games field with placards that read WE WANT JUSTICE and DOWN WITH THE BYES (the couple superintending the home). He was fired from a job he could ill-afford to lose. (Within a couple of years, his predictions were realized: the Jewish Community Social Services closed down the institution and placed the children in foster homes.[3])

He began, unhappily, to drift. First he went to the home of his sister Esther. There, under the unsympathetic eye of her husband, Benny Cohen, who thought of himself as something of a Russian gentleman, Issie was not allowed to sleep on the living-room couch, but was relegated to the floor with a couple of old blankets. Keine would visit him at Esther's from time to time, bringing him food — chicken soup and other dishes (a kindness she never paid any of her other children). But when she left, Esther would take whatever she wanted — even the meat from the soup — for her own three hungry children.[4] When he was really starving, Issie would go to Gertie's relatively wealthy home on the Esplanade and, after 1929, to her even more luxurious home on Ducharme, in Outremont. There he would steal food shamelessly, stuffing his pockets with bread and vegetables. Her husband, Strul, was quickly rising in business as a self-sufficient (and, to Issie, unbearably pompous) importer, accountant and packager of goods from abroad. When he caught his good-for-nothing brother-in-law stealing, Strul cuffed Issie's ears and sent him flying with a string of abuses. Gertie, whose fear of Strul overcame any compassionate feelings she may have had for her youngest brother, stood by and gave Issie nothing.

In an article he wrote much later for the *Maclean's* column "My Most Memorable Meal," Layton captured the humiliation he felt at about this time. "Every time I reached out for anything or to anyone, I felt as if my hands were cut off at the wrist," he would later remember.

> The meal I remember best wasn't a meal at all. It was a descent into the valley of humiliation, a discovery of the abysses of human snobbishness, a sore trial — but a meal it definitely was not, unless eating humble pie constitutes one. In a hurry, you see, I had stumbled into a restaurant that catered only to the well-heeled. There was nothing on the ordinary plate-glass window, the unostentatious door, to let a fellow know he was standing on the outskirts of a domain where stomachs were coddled with pâtés, lobster salads, and choicest wines.
>
> I entered and took my seat at an empty table and began drumming on the innocent-looking tablecloth. Presently the waitress came and handed me a menu. The prices for a meal ranged from two seventy-five to fifteen dollars, and all I had in my pocket, grown suddenly clammy and ill-ventilated, was eighty-five cents. Then my distressed eye noticed the chopped liver, which could be ordered *à la carte*.
>
> "I'll take that," I said, pointing casually. She inclined her head statuesquely. "Yes," and waited, pencil on pad. "That's all, just the chopped liver."
>
> She stared at me and as the horrible truth broke in upon her, waves of boredom, pity and contempt washed across her face. She removed the menu from my faltering hand as if she feared contagion. While she was gone, I had the chance to observe the other diners at the tables next to mine. Their teeth and lips were closing happily over their morsels of thick plutocratic steak, the succulent gravy on the plates making brown pools of composure....
>
> I swallowed the liver in two swift bites, but the waitress kept her back toward me. I could not ask for my check without raising my voice, and this I could not do. When

she finally came, she handed me the bill as coolly as before and cleared away the offensive dish so that no tip of mine would sully it. This was the most crushing blow of all.

I staggered to my feet. How they carried me past the hilarious diners — I was sure they had remarked the whole thing from beginning to end — and past the supercilious cashier, I shall never find out.[5]

It was books that lay behind Issie's conflicts with his family. Certainly, it was books they blamed for his lazy waywardness. Lined up like a battalion against him were Keine, Strul, Benny, and his sisters Gertie, Esther and Dora. Were it not for his books and his silly notions of education, he would be out on the street earning a decent living as a *handler*. And were it not for his books, he would be making money, instead of spending it in second-hand book-stores. Were it not for those books, full as they were of scandalous and unorthodox ideas, he would be more reverent, less curious, more respectful, less audacious.

Keine had heard of nothing more ridiculous than the ideas of this *schmegegee* (fool), Darwin. How she roared out her loud belly-laugh to hear her youngest — her *srulickel* — lecture her seriously about how man had descended from apes, not God. Did he think she was crazy to believe such garbage? And a trial in a real court in the United States about it? Such nonsense! This education of Issie's was addling his brain. He was worse than his father — poring over useless books, instead of putting bread on the table. For this she was paying her hard-earned money to Baron Byng School? Then she must stop sending it.

As for Dora, she'd tried. Again and again, when she was frustrated beyond measure at her *bratchik*'s (little brat's) laziness — lying around reading, instead of helping — she'd attacked him, pulled his shaggy, ungroomed hair and headed for those shelves, intent on ripping to shreds his precious books. Inexplicably, it was Keine who had interceded.

To Gertie and Esther, busy raising their young families, Issie was a curse, filling the heads of their young children with inflammatory, irreligious thoughts, not to mention talking them out of their spending money and their treats. The further away he was kept, the better. Gertie, especially, was vigilant, for Issie practically had adopted her eldest son, Vehlvel (so-named for her mother's father, Vehlvel Moscovitch), "Bill," as he came to be called. On Saturday mornings the two would be off — Issie a mere four years older than his younger, look-alike nephew Bill — to Diamond's Book Store on La Gauchetière, where the clean-shaven Jewish owner regularly offered advice to Issie, who regularly persuaded his nephew to "share" his weekly allowance to buy the *Nation* or the *New Republic.* Once he stole a rare book, Plato's *Laws,* from the McGill library, felt guilty and replaced it. As if to justify himself, he slipped out of Diamond's with *How to Improve Your Character.* Amos Saunders remembers being presented with one of these books, an edition of Coleridge and Wordsworth, in which Issie had written on the frontispiece, "Remember me." On the fly-leaf of a used collection of John Keat's poetry, which Issie bought in 1928 when he was about to turn fifteen, he typically inscribed in his beautiful flowery script:

> I. Lazarre
> 4158 City Hall
> Montreal
> Can.
> Student of Literature

He signed it "Isadore."[6] "I. Lazarre, Student of Literature" posed a profound threat to the real and increasingly powerful social order to which his family belonged. Worse than studying poetry with a passion incomprehensible to everyone (except Amos Saunders), he was actually writing it. In third-rate, highly imitative romantic verse, he was flinging his heart to a stony world. Typical of these verses are eight lines he wrote at about age fourteen, which he included in his short story "The Philistine" (1944):

> Come, my love, since life is short
> And stormy as the ocean's breast,
> We'll anchor safely at love's port
> And loudly laugh at fortune's jest.

> Soon will our toiling lines be spent
> And dust and ashes be our clay;
> So, dearest, to our heart's content
> We'll live and love this very day.[7]

Keine's response to his poetic pretensions was a shrug of her bulky shoulders and the comment: "He'll grow out of it when he gets married."[8]

Some time during grade ten, in 1928, Issie dropped out of school. He had taken a delivery job at Macy's drug store, which kept him up until midnight; so days at the beginning of the term had been spent dozing in school[9] and it wasn't long before the attractions of independence outweighed the lure of learning. Unwelcome at his mother's new home with Kalman Hershorn, shunned by his sisters, who were doing their best to raise their own families, Issie rented a "cupboard-like room"[10] for himself on De Bullion Street.

Though his mother and sisters continued to urge him scornfully to make something of himself, he stubbornly resisted their efforts to press him into an ignominious life of working hard to make money. He had quit school and continued to work just enough to keep him in food and second-hand books.

When he could find students, he taught English to Jewish immigrants at the rate of a dollar or seventy-five cents for an hour's private class in his room. Most of his students were women whose personal lives were desperately unhappy. "Many were unmarried and really needed male company," Layton recalls. "I was sometimes aware of their sexual hunger."[11] Others were married, sometimes unhappily. In his short story "The English Lesson" (1945), he explores the nature of such encounters, casting himself in the role of victim, unfairly mistaken for a gigolo and attacked by jealous husbands. His portrayal reveals his boredom with situations he knew were hopeless educationally but upon which he depended for money:

> he stole another glance at his wrist watch. The lesson was nearly half over. He now knew for a certainty that her English was a twisted, unsalvageable wreck. A prophet's lifetime would be needed to weed even a corner of the

luxuriantly over-run garden of her speech. Were he honest — or even moderately well-off — he would tell her so.[12]

Though Layton maintains that "[his] code, [his] timorousness, and [his] sense of gallantry" kept him from taking advantage of such women who "with animal eagerness" sought to master English and unburdened their troubles under the guise of practising "conversational English," the story is suffused with an atmosphere of guilt and self-loathing. At the very least, Layton recalls these early encounters as crassly exploitive emotionally and financially, and rationalizes his character's "dishonesty" as a temporary stop-gap measure in a life destined for greater things:

> Anyway, it was a livelihood. Far better than working for some insensitive exploiter, punching a clock.... And his textbook was coming along fine. It was almost done, all except for the final chapter on the adverbs. His "English Made Easy" would sell at least ten thousand copies. The Government was bound to encourage immigration after the war. Ten thousand? Why not twenty thousand?[13]

Though the fifteen- or sixteen-year-old Lazarovitch could not hope to follow the career of his model Amos Saunders, he could do the next-best thing: he peddled his skills in English and earned enough to give him time to write. He convinced himself that he was helping unfortunate immigrants like his own family and he obtained a little emotional gratification by spending his time with older, often motherly, women who naïvely admired his learning. Like his father, he rejected a miserable utilitarian life and retreated to a room full of books where he could study and imagine into existence a world better than the real one.

Revolution

The Montreal of the late twenties, into which the beleaguered young Lazarovitch drifted without purpose from Baron Byng High School, was one of increasing political ferment. The Wall Street stock-market crash in 1929, and the rapid increase in unemployment that followed it, exemplified dramatically the theories of those who had become critical of a capitalist system in which the bourgeoisie luxuriated in power at the expense of the working class. Such theories gained wider credence as that economic vortex drew more of the bourgeoisie into the ranks of the workers and the unemployed.

To the Jewish community in Montreal (and in Canada generally), such ideas were hardly novel. Socialist theories already had been widely disseminated in the Eastern European countries from which most of the Jews had come. In Romania, for example, at the time the Lazarovitch family emigrated, Constantin Dobogreanu Gherea had popularized the ideas of Karl Marx in a series of books written between 1884 and 1894,[1] and a number of socialist journals had begun to appear in the large cities.[2] Jews in Jassy, the major city near Tirgul Neamt, looked to the Russian Jewish Socialist party, the *Bund,* which sought to unify and make self-sufficient the Yiddish-speaking Jewish workers of Lithuania, Poland and Russia.[3] Though Moishe Lazarovitch seems to have been ignorant of or uninterested in these developments, his oldest son, Abraham, was not. Members of the family recall that Abraham read the Yiddish newspapers in Montreal, which continued to spread left-wing ideals across the Atlantic.

Sixteen-year-old Issie was exposed to these socialist ideas and soon fell under the spell of the Communist cry for revolution. The excitement of the Russian Revolution and the Winnipeg General Strike of 1919 and the establishment of the Worker's Party of Canada at Guelph in February 1922, which became the Canadian Communist Party in 1924, provided the backdrop for Issie's indoctrination.[4] As Tim Buck, Communist party leader from 1929 to 1962 (after the Canadian Communist Party was outlawed in 1941, the Labor Progressive Party replaced it in 1943), remembers it, the twenties were "a period of great militant working-class struggles and, simultaneously, of cunningly engineered anti-working-class schemes"[5] set against the larger backdrop of "the rise of American imperialism to world primacy."[6] Canadian Communists endeavoured to demonstrate that the gathering economic crisis was not "an unavoidable natural disaster," and Tim Buck, in his *Steps to Power* (1925), a widely circulated revolutionary pamphlet, outlined how the workers could take their unhappy fates into their own hands. But Buck later came to realize that capitalist interests in Canada were too deeply entrenched to be dislodged.

> [The] Canadian bourgeoisie was exercising sovereign authority in all distinctly Canadian affairs. With the merging of bank and industrial capital, the rise to power of the finance-capitalist oligarchy and the increasing participation of the Canadian monopolists in the imperialist struggle for division and re-division of the world market, Canada had become an imperialist state. The monopolists maintained vestigial forms of colonial relationships to Britain as barriers between their monopolistic privileges and the advancing forces of the workers and farmers. But, while preserving these obsolete forms of colonial subordination, the Canadian monopolists were already looking towards a junior partnership in United States imperialism for themselves....the Canadian

monopolists deliberately betrayed the century-old dream of Canadian independence for their personal profit and class privileges.[7]

This concept of Canadian society was one Issie Lazarovitch found heady and appealing. His family had experienced the exploitation of the worker by capitalist factory owners, merchandisers and importers. But it was less as a representative of his people than as an individual that Lazarovitch was attracted to left-wing meetings in 1928. The struggle of the working class for freedom and power paralleled his own personal struggle.

His mother, her new husband and his two brothers-in-law, especially the belligerent and obnoxious Strul Goldberg, were infused with the capitalist spirit, determined to acquire power and wealth through economic advancement. They thought Issie's education at Baron Byng High School provided him with a great advantage in the quest for the same objectives. But education had steadily built up in Issie a different set of objectives, life-aims that ran counter to those of his family elders. Clinging tenuously to that persistent, contradicting refrain of his mother's that he was their "Messiah," destined to be great, and her saying that *chochma* (wisdom) was the virtue most worth pursuing,[8] an image reinforced by his father's disdain for and withdrawal from the material and economic realm of life, Issie had become convinced not that he might rise to higher economic status, but that he could supersede it. What looked like shiftlessness and lack of ambition to his family was really an ambition much greater than anything any of them were capable of imagining, an ambition entirely and angrily at odds with their own mercantile aspirations. Thus, the rhetoric of socialism that young Lazarovitch first espoused, and the more extreme rhetoric of Communism he soon adopted, coincided with a surging tide of energy from within, a personally enacted "revolution" in which he was the "oppressed" and "exploited" in an unfair "capitalist" world. He whole-heartedly joined the struggle to throw off the chains of bondage.

The Politics of Love

Quietly, Issie opened the unlocked door of the dingy, two-room apartment on Drolet Street, spat on his left hand, ran it over his "unmanageable black straight hair"[1] and crept in. Good. Excellent. Mrs. Rosenberg, that unorthodox, chain-smoking woman who fascinated, shocked and exhilarated him with her fiery political diatribes, was out early this morning with her son, Shurri. And Suzanne, his "Russian princess,"[2] was alone, waiting for him. He carefully passed the "cheap, haphazardly arranged furniture"[3] and went into the well-scrubbed, unheated bedroom where he knew she would be lying warm beneath the tattered covers her mother was so proud of. The Rosenbergs were not filthy bourgeois, like the stinking capitalists they saw entering the factories wearing expensive clothes and brandishing polished canes. They were workers, wearing their poverty and the great cultural tradition of Russia, which they considered their most important baggage when they emigrated to Montreal in 1922, like a badge of honour. Only a revolution could make Canada, or the world for that matter, what it ought to be: a place where books and ethics mattered more than money.

He tripped over a volume of Lermentov, regained his balance, bent over and kissed her on the neck.

Zaftig,[4] he thought. "*Zaftig*," he said. "You are voluptuous like a luscious plum. Your skin is ripe with the fullness of a summer's day," he murmured into her soft fair hair. They kissed. Automatically, he reached down to rub her stomach. She pushed his hand away and quickly got up, laughing. He'd have to leave the room until she dressed for school.

Issie was disappointed. He thought Communists would do anything. Why did Suzanne have such strict morals? He stepped into the front room, sneaking a quick glance at her before closing the door.

Soon Suzanne appeared. She was wearing the ridiculous clothes her mother made: long skirts and old-fashioned blouses. She put on her green silk hat with the turned-up rim. She looked like nothing he had ever seen before, but that didn't matter. What mattered was their conversation. They talked excitedly all the way to Baron Byng, where Suzanne's mother had sent her as preparation for a university education. Why was her mother so strange, Issie asked. She wasn't strange, Suzanne replied. She was a graduate of the Sorbonne. She had been a railway engineer. She was a fervent Communist dedicated to the Party and the revolution that must soon take place. And Suzanne was, too. She was one of the most active members of the Young Communist League.

Since she had been about fourteen, Suzanne had been sent to address large groups of workers on behalf of the Party. Mainly, she spoke to the middle-aged Anglo-Saxon workers during their meal breaks at the big Northern Electric Plant. With her good looks, resonant voice and recently acquired command of English, Suzanne made an inspiring speaker. "With their lunch baskets and...milk bottles in their laps,... they welcomed the diversion of a young girl getting up to speak to them, telling them to unite against their bosses.... Knowing nothing of these workers' conditions, three topics were open to me: the international situation, the doom of capitalist society...and China. I would get on top of a crate. And from all sides came the greeting: 'Hello, Rosie, how is China getting on?' 'Rosie' because of my pink cheeks."[5]

Suzanne quickly interested Issie Lazarovitch in her ideas. She took him with her to Horn's Cafeteria, on the Main, a popular hang-out of the Young Communist League members. "We would buy a cup of coffee for five cents, and argue all evening about politics," she recalled. "There were times when I did not want to be seen with Irving, because he was, being a socialist, so to say, on the other side of the fence, and my comrades, particularly the leaders, regarded the relationship with disapproval. But Irving and I were in love."[6]

As luck would have it, there was a sudden change of directive from Suzanne's "leaders." She and her comrades were told to penetrate the socialist ranks and try to win over members to the Communist cause. She was sent to meetings of the Young People's Socialist League, which were often chaired by David Lewis, to accomplish this mission.

Her friend Issie could not have been more pleased to be "infiltrated." For hours, he and Suzanne would walk together through the streets of Montreal talking and arguing about politics.

"Here," she said one night at Horn's, "read this!" She handed him a copy of Nickolai Bukharin's *ABC of Communism*.[7] When she next saw him, he was quoting from it.

Suzanne Rosenberg was on a collision course with the law. Her pro-Communist speeches (composed, she later admitted, by interweaving statements lifted from several of the major party publications),[8] were exceedingly high-profile. Partly because she was so pretty, she drew crowds, not always serious ones. "I was a plump, well-fed, rosy-complexioned high school kid and I talked to these mature and seasoned workers about the exploited, downtrodden and starving masses of China with the cocky assurance of ignorant youth," she recalled. "They listened amusedly, grinning and joking.... I imagined I already heard the death rattle of capitalism and [that] revolution was just around the corner."[9]

She was barely fifteen when she found herself in the detention room of the local police station, then shoved into "the gloomy cell with its grimy cement floor" along with several girls and young women from "Montreal's notorious red-light district, close to the harbour."[10] Although she was released almost immediately on bail and the arrest was "a trivial affair,"[11] it had serious repercussions. She was expelled from Baron Byng High School. Mrs. Rosenberg successfully interceded with Mr. Astbury, the principal, even though she knew that "in the eyes of the Party leadership," her promise that

Suzanne would remove herself from the Young Communist League was "a breach of discipline."[12] The event increased Suzanne's significance to Issie Lazarovitch, who saw her more than ever as a heroine: a beautiful, passionate, articulate political martyr.

As for Suzanne, she had fallen in love with Issie because he was so different from the other teen-agers she met. "My Canadian peers," she recalls, "were too flighty and mindless for my taste. They had not the slightest interest in the problems that fascinated me. None of them had heard of Spartacus, my great hero. The name of Lenin meant nothing to them. And when I held forth on the Russian Revolution, of which, after all, I had first-hand knowledge, they ran off to play baseball or to peruse the comics."[13]

In her youthful and bookish lover, Issie Lazarovitch, she found a soul-mate, someone with whom to argue and debate. "We would talk our heads off about literature, politics and philosophy. But when it came to Communism, we quarrelled bitterly. Invariably, he carried a bundle of books under his arm and also a notebook in which he jotted down words and expressions, their meanings and examples of their usage."[14] Anne Madras, the daughter of a Jewish immigrant grocer, a member of the Young Communist League and Suzanne's only girlfriend at Baron Byng, remembers her culture-loving parents "standing in the street listening at a crack in the wall to hear the opera." She also recalls Issie Lazarovitch's passion for the English language. "He would come into my place and throw a dictionary into my lap, saying 'Ask me any word! I know them all!' I'd try to catch him, but I never could. He *did* know the meaning of any word I picked."[15]

With Suzanne, Issie would go out walking and talking, sometimes until midnight or three in the morning. "I was especially attracted to his beautiful voice," she recalls. "Though his skin was pimply then and he had an arrogant bearing, his eyes were such an intense blue against his thick black hair that even the whites seemed blue."[16] Together they read and discussed Shaw, whom he liked and she didn't; and Wilde, whom she liked and he didn't. "He'd sell his children for a paradox,"[17] Issie would exclaim, apparently ignorant of Wilde's sexual proclivities. In retrospect, Suzanne concludes that, while she was unoriginal, Issie seemed a highly original person[18] with a much larger view of life than her own. As they talked in the park atop Mount Royal looking out over the twinkling lights of the city or at Horn's Cafeteria, he would consider her statements carefully, "knitting his brows and frowning before he leaned forward to speak."[19] "Shakespeare embodied the pessimism and collapse of the feudal system," Suzanne would declare, parroting the current Communist view. "What about the exuberance and optimism of Shakespeare's comedies?" he would parry.

Issie's courtship of his first sweetheart suggests that he not only had read but sought to imitate the romantic poets. One warm night, after an evening of argument at Horn's, they walked up the streets of the rich "heady with the fragrance of lilacs."[20] Issie climbed up one of the fences, helped himself to the lilacs, jumped down and handed the bouquet to Suzanne. But when they were back downtown, reality intruded on the romantic evening in a way that must have been humiliating. "I noticed by the street light that he had a big tear in the seat of his trousers," Suzanne recalls. "Possibly they were the only pair he owned. On my doorstep he blurted out that he was famished: he had not eaten anything that day and had no money.... If I gave him food, I knew I would have to face my stern mother in the morning and listen to a cascade of severe reproaches.... I turned away and quickly vanished into the house." For the last birthday he would spend with her, her sixteenth, in 1929, he rounded up the money to buy two second-hand books for her: H.G. Wells' *The Outline of History* and a volume of Shaw's plays. "These two writers were among our mentors," Suzanne remembers. "We were romantics, hoping for a better world. We were enchanted by the humanitarian views and faith in science H.G. Wells proclaimed. We believed with this writer that national and racial feelings would gradually vanish and that the world was headed for harmony, understanding and peace."[21] That evening, to celebrate, they went to see an English company's production of Shaw's *The Apple Cart,* for which Issie had managed to buy tickets. When everyone rose before the performance to the familiar chords of "God Save the King," Suzanne alone remained seated. "The idea of paying homage to a king or a political leader has always been repugnant to me....I sat through the entire anthem without the least fear of consequences, [though] I knew that it would not gain sympathizers for my cause."[22]

Suzanne remembers the room her sweetheart took at 3848 De Bullion Street when he was in grade ten. "I was really impressed with that tiny little place. It was littered with books. It was not at all clean and was furnished with only a desk or table and a cot with an old gray blanket. But it was his place. He gave lessons there to immigrants who needed to learn English. When I went there, he would read to me. He always gave me a book inscribed with a poem he had written."[23]

One of these poems, "The Vigil," was to be the first Lazarovitch published. At A.M. Klein's suggestion, he sent it to the *McGilliad,* a short-lived university publication. It appeared with the signature "Irving Lazarre" in April 1931. The romantic, free-form musing gives an accurate impression of his notion of a writer at the time: sensitive, anguished and sensual:

>Evening....Feathery grass....Boughs
>That coldly lift a silent offering....
>The shadowy swaying of trees,
>Like graceful forms in a moveless dance....
>The yearning stillness of an ended night,
>And clouds, the colour of oyster shells,
>
>Clustered about a comfortless moon....
>Dawn....A crayon held in a master's fingers
>Pencilling in soft outlines the earth....
>The hills: Humps that tell laconically
>The labouring age of earth....
>And suns that turn the wayside streams
>To moving panes of light....[24]

In the spring of 1931, not long after her sixteenth birthday and not long after "Irving Lazarre" had passionately defended freedom of speech at a meeting of the Young People's Labour League on 19 February, Suzanne's mother announced they were going back to Russia within days. Disillusioned with the Canadian Communist Party and convinced, finally, that collectivization in the Soviet Union had resulted in the death, arrest and deportation of thousands of hard-working peasants, she had decided that the first priority for all devoted Communists was to build socialism in the Soviet Union. Despite warnings from the Canadian Communist Party that such efforts would be futile, she organized a group of thirty or forty immigrant Canadian families, mostly Ukrainians and Russians, pursuaded them to pool their personal savings to buy farm machinery as a gift to the Soviet Union and left Montreal for the farmland near Odessa.[25] Suzanne was distraught. "I opposed [my mother's decision] vehemently, but to no avail.... I did not share her view about the need for Communists to go and build socialism in the Soviet Union rather than fight for a better life in their own land.... I had come to regard Canada as my homeland, and hated to leave it, [but] her decision was irrevocable.... I even wrote a letter to Tim Buck...to which he did not deign to reply."[26]

Wearing a light-green spring coat with a squirrel collar (her mother abandoned her own Persian lamb coat, bought long before in Europe, because "It would look too 'bourgeois' in a country where all were 'equally rich or poor'")[27] that was to serve her through many a severe Russian frost to come, Suzanne said goodbye to Issie and, "with a strange premonition of calamity," lay awake all night, weeping hysterically into her pillow. The young lovers "vowed that [they] would soon meet in a land with better prospects than [those they] faced in Canada during the troubled time of depression."[28] As soon as he could manage it, Issie promised to join her in Moscow.

Russia

Suzanne's abrupt departure for the Soviet Union posed a serious dilemma for Issie. Should he try to obtain the necessary documents and join her? In the spring of 1930, a year before Suzanne left, his formal education had come to a halt in one final turbulent episode at Baron Byng High School. Though he had persuaded Mr. Watson, one of the teachers there, to take him back into grade eleven, his independent reading, aggressive nature and political involvements made him a feisty trouble-maker in classes noted for their rigid conformity.[1] A staff composed almost entirely of British Protestant school-teachers, with their ideals of gentlemanly behaviour and fair play, was unlikely to deal wisely with class after class of underprivileged Jewish children, especially one student in particular who read widely and thought himself more adept in the literary classics than they were and who was also highly skilled in the rhetoric of left-wing politics. Against a prickly background of unpaid fees, he had a run-in with Mr. Steeves, a teacher who especially disliked him. When Mr. Astbury, the principal, demanded that he apologize to Steeves, Lazarovitch angrily strode to the school library and ostentatiously sat reading a book.[2] Though it was a scant two months before junior matriculation from high school, Lazarovitch was expelled.

The young Lazarovitch wanted to become a teacher, a position that, for Jews, was impossible to attain without undergoing years of anti-Semitic comments and risking unemployment in the end. The Roman-Catholic schools in Quebec were staffed by Catholics; the Protestant School Board was set on hiring British-born masters; and the parochial Jewish schools, of which there were now several, preferred orthodox Jews as teachers. In the absence of any of these general qualifications, the pursuit of a teacher's certificate was inadvisable.

As best he could, Lazarovitch continued to drum up private students to tutor in his cockroach-infested room during the winter. During the summer he picked up odd jobs. If he were to leave for the Soviet Union, where undoubtedly he could find a job teaching English, he would need at least a certificate of junior matriculation and a passport. He had neither.

It was David Lewis and A.M. Klein who intervened to ensure that young Lazarovitch would matriculate. Klein, with whom Lazarovitch met frequently to discuss poetry, politics and life in general, tutored him in Latin, his weakest subject. Though Klein was already established as a poet, Lazarovitch did not wish to imitate either his poetry or his Zionist politics. Nonetheless, Klein's presence as a Jew and a poet who had achieved distinction made it clear that writing was an avenue open to him. As he put it much later, Klein's very existence "pursuaded me that the poet need not be completely a leper, an outcast."[3] Lewis donated the ten dollars Lazarovitch needed to take the McGill high-school leaving examinations.

While he and Suzanne sent anguished letters back and forth between Montreal and the Soviet Union (her first telegram had said simply "Love"), he contemplated the possibility of joining her. It was the extremity of her political views that dissuaded him. Though there was much that they shared, and although he "loved her spirit," he thought her "superficial"[4] and he was sceptical of her passionate dedication to the Marxist-Leninist cause. He preferred to use Communist ideas as a kind of intellectual punching-bag against which to test the strength of his own views, and he indulged in the rhetoric of socialist and Communist meetings as a testing-ground for his increasingly explosive language. In fact, he was most drawn to Trotsky because of his internationalism and humanism and was deeply critical of Trotsky's expulsion and subsequent assassination by Stalin. He was even more critical of the purges, rumours of which had begun to circulate through North America in the late twenties. "Once, I insulted Lenin and [Suzanne] cried all day," he recalls. "She used to denounce me as a social democrat."[5] One thought undoubtedly plagued him: that, even if he were to find work in the Soviet Union, his life might be endangered. Furthermore, what about his poetry? What good would it be to carry around his dictionary and notebook in a country where virtually no one else spoke English?

Suzanne's letters tugged at his heart and he found her idealistic purposefulness appealing at a time when his own life lacked direction. She wrote to him on 1 June 1932, almost a year after her arrival in Odessa, after reading a letter from him that had "driven her crazy" and set her hands trembling so she could scarcely reply:

> My dearest Irving,
> Irving if you still love me, we must see each other — surely that is not impossible. It must be arranged. All these months I have been planning, planning. You see I shall probably soon be in Paris or in Berlin. You can surely get to Hamburg or Sherbourg some how. I shall write all particulars to-morrow. If I'll be in Europe I will have a little money. Write how you stand financially? Why are you not studying? Where were you born? Are you a Canadian citizen. Write all these particulars. Write the truth — do you seriously want to go to Russia. Write immediately what you have taken. I have already spoken about you in Moscow.
>
> I shall do everything in my power if you want to come here to help you get into the Soviet Union and help you to settle here.
>
> Irving I love you and O how I want to see you and

give all that my love can offer — I love you — what else can I say — I cannot write any more.
>With love
>Always yours —
>desperate Suzanne.

>P.S. My health is now down at the present time for I have lived through a lot of suffering, disappointment and critical mental unrest. How is your health, are you working?
>Send your poetry and write in details your plans concerning the Soviet Union, what documents you have, etc. I am dying to see you — *Economics is the bottom of everything, of all our suffering — if our economic circumstances were different no doubt by now we would have been to-gether.*
>Don't forget ever your
>Suzanne.

>P.S. If only every word of this letter could be an embrace and a kiss of our love. O if only this letter could convey to you my real sentiments! But I trust that you who have always understood will understand now too.
>O how I would love to embrace a thousand times that head of yours......
>Love,
>Suzanne.[6]

A year and a half later, Lazarovitch had not forgotten Suzanne. Nor, judging from their correspondence, had he entirely abandoned the thought of joining her in Moscow, where she had found a good job proofreading foreign dictionaries for a Soviet encyclopaedia. He had begun teaching English to immigrants in evening classes at the Jewish People's Library. And his politics were moving further left. In the opening speech of the Canadian Labour Defence League, on 18 March, "Irvine Lazare" praised the "free and Socialist State known as the USSR" to "tremendous applause" and critized Canadian socialist leaders Woodsworth and Heaps as "fakers in the worst sense" for their failure to defend the working class.[7]

Though he was upbraiding Suzanne unjustly for getting involved in "affaires d'amour," as he delicately called them, he was by no means chaste himself. He had enjoyed a brief fling with Nina Caiserman, an ardent member of the Young Communist League whose sister, Ghitta, became a noted painter.[8] Miriam Waddington, then a seventeen-year-old student and budding poet, remembers him calling and inviting himself and his nephew, Bill, over to her friend Marjorie Firestone's. "They came over and talked," she remembers. "Marge had a school-girl crush on Irving, who to her seemed like a glamorous 'older man.' I didn't find him attractive. I went for a walk with Bill until 3:00 AM. (I got hell from my mother). When we left, Marge and Irving were necking on the sofa. A few days later, Marge, who thought she was smart, gave him a book inscribed, 'To Irving, for services rendered!' Irving's response to this was, 'If I had gone to bed with her, she would have given me the complete library of Harvard Classics!'"[9]

Despite such escapades, Irving expected Suzanne to remain faithful and kept alive the hope that he might join her. She adamantly denied his accusations that she had other suitors. She loved the poems he sent her and was waiting for him, hoping that he would come to her despite the overwhelming disadvantages he would face if he moved to Russia. A long letter from her on 10 January 1934[10] reflected her awareness that Soviet officials might censor her mail. Though she worded her message delicately, she risked describing Russia's deplorable conditions. That way her lover would know the truth. When he joined her, he would not be able to say she hadn't warned him. In her letter, Suzanne enumerated carefully the drawbacks of Russian life. The best accommodation she and her mother had been able to find was a two-room apartment without running water several kilometres outside Moscow. They both worked hard from early morning until late at night at jobs in the city; between them, they earned six hundred rubles a month. (Shoes, by comparison, cost one hundred twenty to two hundred twenty rubles.) There was no question of buying clothes or furniture; they ate, she reported, "meagrely." But so great was her commitment to the arts that she went weekly to a theatre or opera performance. Though Suzanne had located an Anglo-American school where Issie might teach, he would need a certificate of high-school graduation. The libraries, he ought to know, had no modern English literature at all. Subjects for books — if he were to write any — would be chosen by the publishing houses. If he came as planned, he would need to bring enough money to live on for at least a month.

Despite the hardships, Suzanne remained loyal to her political cause. "To build socialism is not as easy a task as some people imagine," she reported. "The people have been deprived of the very necessaries, for a more or less comfortable existence, so that heavy industry, the very essential for Socialism, may be developed.... Dearest, I think that the struggle that is going on here is the most interesting and... worthwhile. What I mostly fear is that perhaps you will not share my views." Suzanne had joined the Romsomol nucleus, hoping to become a member of the Russian league eventually. Her political activities (which involved courses every other day) included learning to shoot with a rifle. "Our nucleus," she wrote, "is a shock brigade that serves as an initiator."

It is clear from Suzanne's letter that she expected her "beloved" to accept the limitations she described:

> Write heaps and heaps about yourself. O what joy your letter shall bring to me. Write immediately. To-day I shall drink a toast to your health and our love. I believe that our love shall compensate all economic routine matters. We must rise above these, you and I. Together we must learn to live. I love life and so do you.... I think the best time for you to come will be in August when I shall have a month's vacation. Then we could spend our honeymoon to-gether, and in September you will start work.... I think you will find teaching very interesting here since the Soviet system of education runs on different principles than the capitalist.

Suzanne offered practical advice for Issie's journey: that he must bring as many books — especially books of poetry — as possible, that he must have his educational certificates (papers

Lazarovitch had not yet earned) and a visa, that he must bring all his clothes plus anything he could collect from his brothers, especially woollen underwear and sweaters (which were unavailable in Moscow) for the severe winters and any other personal trifles. But first he must write to the principal of the Anglo-American school and apply for a job teaching English and literature. Suzanne pledged that she would go in person to support his application.

"Well good-bye my love," she concluded, after inquiring about his mother, Anne Madras, David Lewis and some of their "Yipsel" friends.

> Remember I love you now not a bit less than I loved you when I last kissed you good-bye. A curse on that day!
> Please, dearest, answer immediately.
> Ever and always
> With Love
> Your
> Suzanne

Seeing Red

Genus: Lazarrovitch [sic]
Species: Irving Peter
The above was first found in Roumania some years ago.

On account of his massive brain, it took seven storks to carry him when he was born. Four of them dropped dead immediately after; two acquired varicose veins, and the other ruptured himself.

After a precocious and stormy youth in which he became actively and militantly interested in politics, he boosted the prestige of Mac[donald College] by entering as a freshman.

For the last three years he has cut a swath across the life of the college that will be sung about by the bards in years to come.

Our Peter is Mac's all time outstanding orator, and has given many well attended public lectures in various parts of Canada.

He is always at his best when he "sees red."

Good old Pete![1]

This excerpt from the student newspaper at Macdonald College, the *Failt-Ye Times,* appeared on 25 October 1935 under the column POISONALITIES. It offers a capsule insight into the way Lazarovitch was perceived by his fellow students. Though not tall (a little more than five and a half feet), he was stunningly dark, slim (125 pounds) and handsome. There was a resemblance in the Lazarovitch boys to the swarthy, swashbuckling Hollywood stars who were then beguiling the popular market. In contrast to his brother Larry, who resembled Clark Gable, Peter, as Layton now called himself, preferred to think of himself as a second Benny Leonard, the Jewish-American boxer who had retired as undefeated lightweight champion in 1924 after 29 bouts in the ring. Not only did Lazarovitch resemble Leonard physically; he also identified with the cocksure determination of the small, pugnacious man who was famed for his ability to snatch victory out of the fire when the odds seemed against him. Lazarovitch had been doing his best to excel at boxing since he was twelve or thirteen, when he had worked out intermittently at the University Settlement. Upon arriving at Macdonald College in the fall of 1933, he joined the boxing and wrestling clubs. His experiences as "Nappy," the notorious street-wise scrapper, gave him an advantage. And, at twenty-one, he enjoyed at least three years' edge over the other freshmen. But he could not rise to the dizzying heights he dreamed of as a champion. Often he was second, even in the 440-yard dash of 1935, but second was not good enough. He had to dominate. He wanted glory and power. Though he turned out for the first trials on 6 December 1935, from which boxers would be selected to compete on the McGill Collegiate team for the 1936 Assault-at-Arms,[2] his name does not appear among the eleven who showed up for final competition two months later.[3]

That Pete Lazarovitch was attending Macdonald College at all was a bizarre phenomenon. The institution had begun in 1907 at the whim of its eccentric founder, Sir William Macdonald, a Montreal tobacco millionaire who abstained religiously from smoking.[4] Macdonald, a "shy and unassuming man" who lived "as simply as a street-car conductor" and conducted his business from cramped, dingy offices on Notre Dame near Place d'Armes, had built up a reputation as "the greatest philanthropist in the British Empire."[5] Though he was profoundly ignorant of the realities of agricultural life (on one occasion he watched, fascinated, for several hours as chicks hatched in the Macdonald College incubator in the poultry department; he emerged, exclaiming, "I never knew that that is how chickens came!"),[6] he entertained extravagant notions of the sound moral fibre of rural life and earnestly set about establishing a college for farmers. In tandem with Mrs. Hoodless of Hamilton, Ontario, who sought to interest the public in the better training of women for housekeeping and home-making, Macdonald donated the funds necessary to purchase a vast tract of farmlands and town lots in the parish of Ste. Anne du Bout de l'Isle and the town of Ste. Anne de Bellevue, which bordered on the Ottawa River to the south and stretched almost up to the Lake of Two Mountains on the north, at the west end of Montreal Island. On this lovely, treed estate were the main building (which included a library and an assembly hall), the chemistry building, the biology building, agriculture, poultry, horticulture, parasitology and high-school-teaching training buildings and separate student residences, each with its own gymnasium, for men and women. The principal's residence, named "Glenaladale" after the estate of Sir William Macdonald's ancestors in Scotland and his own farmhouse in Prince Edward Island, and the loftless stone row cottages for employees combined to give the place something of the air of a Scottish feudal estate. The livestock was imported: in 1908, the college bought a herd of Ayrshire cattle; soon after, milking Shorthorns; in 1912, four Clydesdale mares; in 1913, a flock of south-country Cheviot sheep; and numerous breeds of swine. This was a deliberate ploy on Macdonald's part, and one he believed would enhance the nature of his educational enterprise: "The conditions of residence life and the accessibility of senior staff, all living together on the same campus, would...make it possible to achieve something like the medieval ideal of a community of scholars rather than a series of autocratic departments."[7]

In its fledgling year, the college attracted 215 students: 38 in agriculture, 62 in household science and 115 in teaching. By 1933, when Lazarovitch enrolled in agriculture, numbers had doubled to a total enrollment of 528: 173 in agriculture, 111 in household science and 244 in teaching. Since 1924, the college had been involved in recruitment programmes in

British public schools. In co-operation with the Canadian Pacific Railway, representatives from the college enticed British boys, who for one reason or another had poor prospects at home, to answer the challenge of a burgeoning pioneer society, and to avail themselves of free transportation on the CPR to work on Canadian farms as part of their training at Macdonald. As a result of the recruitment programme, a substantial proportion of agricultural students were British boys. As for the Quebec students, some had marks too low to warrant university education at McGill; some were from rural Quebec and had a vocation in one of the three college spheres; and some came from families whose incomes during the Depression years made the payment of university fees impossible.

Lazarovitch fell, somewhat uncomfortably, into the latter category. It was not students like Lazarovitch whom Doctor W.H. Brittain (who became dean of agriculture in 1934 and vice-president of the college in 1935) had in mind when, in 1955, he praised the "wide cultural contacts" available to students in residence at the college. Lazarovitch must have seemed to have more affinities with the Poles, Italians, Romanians and other racial groups whose "sturdy arms," along with those of the Cockney English and burred Scots, heaved the original buildings into place in a scene reminiscent, to Brittain's nostalgic eye, "of that distant time when the race of men gathered on the Plain of Shinar to erect a tower that would reach to heaven."[8] Heaven, in Macdonald College's view, was attainable through one of two routes, both Protestant: St. George's Anglican Church and the United Church of Ste. Anne de Bellevue. A sung grace preceded every meal in the dining hall on the main floor of the women's residence. Lazarovitch was one of the school's few Jews.

It was a former classmate from Baron Byng High School, Alec Alvarine[9] (with whom Lazarovitch had set up a mutual cheating system: Alvarine sneaked math answers to him in exchange for assistance on English exams), who had tipped off Lazarovitch to the means to a higher education and a temporary escape from the exigencies of tutoring and odd jobs that bored him and were becoming more difficult to scrounge as the Great Depression inexorably took hold. The first two years of agricultural courses at Macdonald College were free. The last two years would cost a mere fifty dollars each. The Quebec government, anxious to develop farming in the province, offered subsidies of nine dollars a month to "Quebec students from farming communities." It didn't take even Baron Byng mathematics to figure out that this subsidy would help pay living costs. Lazarovitch appealed to his sister Gertie for a monthly "loan" of five dollars to augment this. She agreed in the hope that at last her no-good *schmegegee* of a brother had decided to apply himself to practical matters. "She made me sweat each time she parted with the paltry sum," he recalls.[10]

With a confidence born of his experience as a tutor, his age, his physical vigour, his training in the urban arena of Montreal's left-wing politics, his association with public figures like David Lewis and A.M. Klein (who had managed to get Lazarovitch to sit still long enough to absorb the information necessary to obtain his senior matriculation) and with all the excitement of a young man embarking on a new phase of life, anxious to establish his niche in an entirely fresh pecking order, Peter Lazarovitch burst through the door of his residence common room to engage in what he had every reason to expect would be an intellectual fray. It was a spectacle that might stand as a symbol of the delicate pivot on which Canadian social evolution teetered in those few years before the outbreak of war. Canada had been drifting further away from the colonialism Macdonald College still encouraged; the influx of European immigrants had risen steadily to significant proportions; left-wing politics had unmistakeably gained a wider following among the thoughtful, the oppressed and the well-informed. The entrance of an energetic, dark Romanian Jew into that common room, filled with effete, fair-haired Englishmen and country bumpkins from the small villages of Quebec, signified a crossroads of social history. As Layton remembers it,

> There they all were, all healthy-looking English philistines, red-cheeked, blue-eyed, with not a thought in their heads and here was myself, eager, enthusiastic, concerned about the affairs of the world, the rise of Naziism,

> the unemployment situation and in no time I got myself involved in an argument, thinking that the people in front of me were characters in Horn's Cafeteria. I was met with incomprehensible stares. After a while I could see that they regarded me as some sort of queer animal who had somehow or other been let in by some grotesque mistake.[11]

Lazarovitch was not put off by his reception. Quite the contrary: he sensed the opportunity to seize and hold sway over minds less astute, temperaments less assertive and backgrounds less experienced than his own. Where most people would have felt rejected and unaccepted, Lazarovitch felt superior. He perceived the situation as one in which he could exercise his powers to their limit. No one would dare try to stop him.

He regarded his subjects (agriculture, botany, chemistry, English, mathematics and physics) as mere inconveniences to the development of his mind. One fellow-student who did not want her name disclosed vividly remembers Lazarovitch. The girl who, according to him, was his "only comfort" at Macdonald was enrolled in household science and was graduating that year from courses different from his. Even so, she explains, it was impossible not to notice him. Though Lazarovitch never showed up for the Sunday-afternoon singsongs, teas or formals that provided opportunities for students to meet each other, he was always at student assemblies and public debates. "After a speaker was finished," she recalls, "[Peter] would stand up and challenge him. Sometimes he would leap onto the stage, grab the microphone and proceed with his views on the speaker's subject. At a time when we women students wore uniforms and the nondescript staff generally held the attitude, 'We know best, and we know everything,' no one knew how to cope with him. It simply wasn't done. The things he said were certainly challenging to the speaker, and it made for some outstanding occasions. I don't think anyone at the College had his ability with words. He had a golden gift."[12]

Layton applied his "golden gift" on behalf of any of his fellow students who responded. Falling easily into the role of tutor, a role he had brought to perfection over the preceding three years, a role he had played since adolescence in relation to his cousin, Bill, who had dutifully followed him to the second-hand book-stores on Notre Dame and had read whatever his friend-uncle-mentor recommended, Lazarovitch occupied a position somewhat parallel to and, at least in his own imagination, superior to his teachers at college. He must have been an odd sight on campus, striding athletically and purposefully along, clutching a disarray of the latest political journals and literary classics in his arms, none of them related in the least to his studies. "He gave me books to read," recalls the girl to whom he felt closest, a girl who grew up in an artistic and musical Westmount household surrounded by literary classics, "many books on philosophy, social and literary criticism and politics. One, a critique of Hegel, was particularly difficult. Over a period of time, I became aware that he had extraordinary patience and a unique quality of questioning. Through careful discussion, he could elicit some of the meanings of what he had given me to read. Parallel with that was the extraordinary impact modern poetry had on me through him. He gave me anthologies of American poets like Whitman, Frost and cummings. He *glowed* when we talked about it. When I think of the cups of coffee we consumed in a student place in the village a short walk from the campus! He was probably one of the very best teachers I've ever had."[13]

It was inevitable that there would be a confrontation between Macdonald College and Pete Lazarovitch. His activities at the college suggest the swift, aggressive tactics of a persistent mongoose in a den of sleek, somewhat lazy cobras. He tried boxing, wrestling and track and field. When those failed to produce the euphoric state of indisputable success, he tried debating (he and Robert Flood defeated the Oxford-Cambridge team by negating the statement "It were better to have written Gray's 'Elegy' than to have conquered Quebec"),[14] poetry and drama. His name pops up everywhere in the *Failt-Ye Times* and the Macdonald Annual in whatever aspect of college life he could compete with some chance of glory.

It was as a member of the Social Research Club, where he became president in his second year (after indifferent first-year grades: two failures; two marks in the sixties; and seventies in English),[15] that Lazarovitch finally fixed on the means by which he could exercise his powers to their fullest. The result was a series of confrontations that destroyed the student council, split the college asunder and finally provoked enquiries from the departments of Agriculture, Justice and Immigration of Quebec, not to mention invoking ridicule from the *London Times*.

Lazarovitch's summary of the aims of the club, newly under his leadership, smouldered with the passionate political rhetoric with which, through Suzanne (with whom he was still corresponding) and left-wing leaders like David Lewis, he was enkindled, a fire kept alive by indefatigable reading in current political journals like the *New Republic*.

Using the pseudonym "Pero" — the nickname (meaning "pen") that Gleb Krzhizhanovsky, a friend of Lenin's, had given to Trotsky in tribute to his success as a writer — Lazarovitch undertook a series of political commentaries in the *Failt-Ye Times*. (Layton later claimed that his use of Trotsky's nickname was a coincidence.)[16]

The 18 October issue of the student newspaper launched a broadside attack on the recent federal election, in which Mackenzie King had replaced R.B. Bennett. "Never in the history of this country," Pero adamantly maintained with an authority culled from numerous journals and newspapers of the time, "have the issues before the electors been so confused and shadowy or more unrealistic. For neither of the two traditional parties faced up squarely to the problem of unemployment or to the equally pressing problem of progressive social legislation.... Mr. Bennett as well as Mr. King hastened to save the country from Communism; the former with perhaps a trifle more poise and skill owing to the experience gained by his 'narrow escape' from Moscow's paid agents." Entries that followed, with pressing regularity and urgency, included the disaster of Mussolini's rise to power in Italy; the threat to world peace posed by Japanese aggression in northern China (in an issue of the paper that was almost sabotaged by students when it was delivered at the train station); Europe's inevitable move towards war; and a comparative statistical analysis of staple crops for the years 1929 and

1933-1934 to illustrate "the plight of the French-Canadian farmer." By 29 November 1935, a month and a half after "Pero" (soon afterwards I.P. Lazarovitch) took up the pen, the storm broke. Warnings in the *Failt-Ye Times* had been oblique and ineffective: "Have you heard of the third-year 'Freshman' who was seen out with the young Jewish girls? signed PEEP" went unnoticed in a late October issue; the POISONALITIES profile appeared in the same issue. By the end of November, a letter to the editor signed "COLLEGE SENTIMENT" appeared, accusing the *Failt-Ye Times* of publishing "the personal views of political events from one extremely Communistic view point. Such utter drivel" was no more than "one man's extremely odd views of world affairs." It was "high time" something was done.

> War and the suppression of civil liberties are the burning issues today. A two-fold purpose motivates the activities of the Macdonald Research Club; first to consider impartially the main trends of the present economic system and the basic changes that should be affected [sic], second, to arouse and organize campus sentiment against the twin menace of War and Facism.[17]

The Social Research Club began opposing these evils with a vengeance during the 1934 school year. In addition to the regular presentation of papers by members, it set up a library, disseminated anti-Fascist handouts and issued a questionnaire to evaluate Macdonald College students' views on war. Guest speakers included Stanley Ryerson, who attacked Fascism; I. Wallace, of the Canadian Defence League, who spoke on "Civilization at the Cross Roads;" the Reverend Lovell Smith, who extolled pacifism; and Doctor Norman Bethune, whose talk was called "What I Saw in Russia." But when Lazarovitch invited Canadian Communist Party leader Tim Buck to address the group, other students let him know he had gone too far. The principal of McGill, when asked, had no particular objection. According to Doctor W.H. Brittain, then dean of agriculture, the student council resigned on principle, a new council replaced them, passed a unanimous motion denouncing the Social Research Club's choice of speaker, then stepped down to let the original council back into office.[18]

By the 1935 school year, having barely made the grades to enter third year (five failures; a seventy-six in economics; an eighty-nine in English literature), Lazarovitch used his position as president of the Social Research Club to wangle a weekly column called CURRENT HISTORY in the *Failt-Ye Times* under his pseudonym "Pero."

Week by week, letters to the editor flooded in. Some attacked "College Sentiment;" some attacked Lazarovitch anew; some tried to take a more objective middle ground. The student council met and passed a resolution of "complete confidence" in Lazarovitch; one of the paper's editors resigned. Though other students had dumped garbage on his bed and "hazed" him in swimming, Lazarovitch had a heyday. In a self-parody headed "CURRENT HYSTERICS (as seen by Students)," he let fly a heavy-handed satire in the form of a fairy-tale about a terrible Red Ogre who was mean to little boys, did not believe in Santa Claus and had decided to hate "a nice, nice man called 'Mucilage', or something."[19] Nor did this piece entirely vent his spleen. In one of several poems that appeared in the *Failt-Ye Times* under the pseudonym "Blissless Carmine,"[20] he addressed the muse of music and fixed on "the mournful dirge that some call tune" that preceded each college meal. In attacking the Anglican sung grace, he was lashing out at the whole charade Macdonald College presented to him: it seemed unrealistic, materialistic (though in no Marxist sense), hypocritically religious and, possibly worst of all, unaesthetic.

> The fate whereof I speak is simply this,
> A grace that's sung, and elsewhere in the land
> Is always spoken in simplicity.
> And not in prostitution of thy name.
>
> In daily fear of hearing holy grace
> Sung in the mournful dirge that some call tune,
> Do I this more than bestial torture face,
> Must I miss all my meals to have some peace,
> Must I be starved to death because of thee
> Dear Muse? No, No! There is indeed a way.

> Go ope' the eyes of them that cannot see
> Let light shine where a Stygian darkness dwells,
> And grace that's *quietly spoken* shall precede
> A Symphony of music, wondrous sweet,
> That masticating jaws make as they feed.[21]

The elements of this undergraduate satire are uniquely Layton. Such a poem could only have been written by someone steeped in Shakespeare, Milton and Pope. Yet these lines also betray the old rhyming curses of Keine Lazarovitch, returning always to the simple physical truths of a peasant culture and to the enduring insight that man, beneath all his pretensions, is an animal. Beyond both these influences, literary and familial, is the fresh and jarring sound of someone whose native language is not English, but to whom the sensual and intellectual twists and turns of the language give inordinate delight. Neither Shakespeare nor Pope nor Keine Lazarovitch would have used words like "prostitution," "bestial" and "masticating" in such a context. And, as in the poems he would later write with considerably more skill, Lazarovitch wields his final line as if it is a knockout blow towards which all the preceding feints and dodges have been leading. It must have been with savage pleasure that Lazarovitch read, in the issue that followed one containing his poem "...And Sendeth Milk" (about the tiny, inadequate jugs, which needed constant refilling, on the residence table) that a Macdonald cow had attained a national record production of milk and butter-fat.

By the end of January 1936, the vice-president, secretary and treasurer of the *Failt-Ye Times* had resigned. Professor S.R.N. Hodgins (editor of the *Journal of Agriculture* for the province of Quebec and advisor to the student paper) had written a letter to the editor of the *Failt-Ye Times* to complain about Lazarovitch's haphazard and misleading use of statistics on Quebec farmers, and the department of immigration requested samples of his work. Upon receiving copies of everything he had publically printed, they opened a file on him in Ottawa. One letter to the editor claimed in alarm that excerpts from "CURRENT HISTORY" had been held up to ridicule in the *London Times* as samples of what colleges in the colonies were up to. Questionnaires were passed among the students regarding the advisability of continuing the column. Students became anxious about how the college's reputation might affect their futures. By Valentine's Day 1936, though I.P. Lazarovitch was still listed against "CURRENT HISTORY" on the *Times* masthead, the column, now subtitled "An Open Forum of Opinion," was written by John Osborne. One after another, fellow students attempted, without success, to replace the incisive (though derivative) political and economic commentary Lazarovitch had established. In one final dynamic column,[22] Lazarovitch attacked the British Cabinet for being sympathetic to Naziism and praised Soviet Russia and France for upholding world peace, a movement to which he was actively committed through the National Committee for World Peace, where Lazarovitch was one of seven elected members. "Only confirmed blockheads, cretins and intellectually crippled epigones," he frothed, "can dream of a 'New Deal' for Europe."[23] Keine should have been proud of him.

But Keine was not proud of him. How she must have cursed when he failed his third year, at the end of 1936. Like the mother in his story "A Game of Chess" (1944), she sarcastically blasted him: "[He] reads so much, he hasn't time for studies."[24] Despite the cram sessions for which he had become legendary (one of these, on English, in his first year, resulted in passes for everyone and several unheard of "firsts") and his ability, reported by Bevan Monks, a fellow student, to memorize "complete sets of lecture notes borrowed from conscientious students,"[25] he still had not passed second-year calculus or third-year biochemistry and had not shown up to write third-year biophysics on the unsubstantiated grounds that he was "feeling unwell."[26]

Lazarovitch turned for solace to Rochel Eisen, a kindly woman six years older than himself. Rochel was a librarian at the Jewish People's Library. She recalls that he used to storm into the library in search of socialist books and periodicals. Full of admiration for his intellectual vigour, solicitous about his well-being and interested in his writing, Rochel became a handy source for his insatiable political and economic interests and a close friend as well. She read him Yiddish poetry and attempted to interest him in Hebrew, but found that "he would make no effort at it."²⁷ When the library closed, he waited on the steps for her and they would walk, perhaps to the park or up on the mountain, talking of social change, of the beauty of the world around them, of the literature they loved and the loneliness and insecurity they each knew.²⁸

On 22 September 1936, Oscar (a nickname Larry had acquired) went in person to ascertain his brother's status in what ought to have been his last year at Macdonald College. Three days later, a letter arrived on Decarie Boulevard, care of their stepfather, Kalman Hershorn.²⁹ Re-admission was impossible.

What was *Flamplatz* up to now?

Feeling Blue

The summer of 1936 had been hot. Lazarovitch fled Montreal "with its dirt and its sadness and its terrible enervating heat," leaving the "dismal room of his [St. Dominique Street] boarding house with its noisy, vulgar children and their screaming mothers." He turned for solace to the Cusinières, who lived in a tiny derelict cottage, one of "a handful of tumbledown, wooden shacks confronting the river"[1] in Val Cartier near Ste. Anne de Bellevue.

Mme. Cusinière was a plump, life-loving Parisienne whose husband had left her. Mimi and Calin, her two daughters, also plump and life-loving, were Lazarovitch's contemporaries. It had been through the delightful Mimi (who had been one of the few students at Macdonald to defend his left-wing journalism in the *Failt-Ye Times*) that they had met.

Lazarovitch latched onto this rollicking household partly to exchange "the stink of garbage and children's pee"[2] that permeated his room in town for "the vital sunlight" that streamed through the clear, fresh air of Val Cartier. Together they would walk, admiring in detail nature's beauties, even Lazarovitch's "beloved crows."[3] More important, he found in this all-female household the comfort and attention he craved. He was their "chou chou," their "Waou Waou" or "dear little Laz."[4] With the solicitous cluckings and fussings of a trio of mother hens, they filled his empty stomach with wholesome country food (including rashers of bacon and pork, about which they joked endlessly with their "little Jew"), stroked and groomed him and listened sympathetically to sorry tales of his family's coldness. Even though their English stumbled awkwardly, they took down his words in dictation as if he were a king. (His first short story, "The Philistine,"[5] was recorded by Mimi that summer). He became the centre of their lives.

To the Cusinières, "cher La-Laz" was not only a fitting object for almost endless maternal ministrations, but he also provided an assertive male presence in the house; he filled the void left by M. Cusinière. He tutored the girls in English and lectured them on the evils of the social and political scene. Numerous letters from the three women to him during that summer and on into the fall are extravagantly affectionate and playfully critical by turns. They offered what Keine Lazarovitch might have offered had life treated her better. "We all miss you here," Mimi wrote after only a few days' absence. "Mother misses her abstraction, Calin her Tou-Tou, and I the lecture in political economy — we will always be gratefull [sic] to you for the many things you taught us —. But on the other hand, what peace we enjoy! No more glass of water impatiently called for in the morning, Mother and I eat the bacon and eggs, we don't need to set the table at mid-day ect. [sic]"[6]

Unemployed, coldly rejected by his family (especially his sisters and mother), who thought he should be earning his keep at twenty-four, Lazarovitch was close to a physical and emotional breakdown. His health was poor (the Cusinières treated him as an emaciated semi-invalid, frequently kept him in bed, cheerfully tolerated his resting and reading on the grass and administered to his ear-aches and viral infections). He knew he would not gain re-admission at Macdonald College. He had become disillusioned with the "freaks and chatterers" at Horn's Cafeteria who, he now thought, met "to exchange their sense of failure for moral indignation [and] palmed off on each other their bonelessness for idealism."[7] What was he to do next?

One option was marriage, a subject he discussed frequently

with the Cusinières. Comforted, well-fed, buoyed up with renewed self-confidence, he would strike out for Montreal where — he told Mimi, Calin and his "petite mère Mouchkette" (as she called herself) — there were "real girls,"[8] preferably with "Latin temperaments,"[9] "Nina [Caiserman] foremost among them."[10] Despite the showers of kisses and other demonstrations of affection "Laz" enjoyed at the Cusinières, his relationship with his two jovial, well-endowed contemporaries was not sexual. Instead, he seemed to have looked past their "red cheeks" and "simple hearts" towards the secret of congenial family life. The Cusinières advised him to get married, in particular to the cousin of his brother-in-law, Faye Lynch. "Laz" was thinking seriously about this. Playfully, he had broached the subject by proposing to all three Cusinières, who as playfully refused. Mimi wrote: "As mother and Calin tell you, the three of us sacrifice ourselves and refuse your demande [sic] in marriage! But really, if that girl is as nice as is said and has a good education why should you not marry her? You must take someone not too young, who could take care of you, and understand your writing — and your hand writing! — Beside [sic] if her father is so kind, she probably has a good characteer [sic].... About that, you can be sure that we will tell your future wife what your pet volutés are: washing your nose and ears; she will certainly be delighted to here [sic] that!"[11] Calin, taking into account the girl's "rich father," advised him, "if you can find happiness and material security in that union, don't hesitate. You will always be able to follow your litterary [sic] vocation. You eat enough of misery bread: that food is no longer necessary to your genius."[12]

The Cusinières' letters reveal their awkward struggle with the inappropriate readings suggested by their dear "chou chou." With genuine mystification, they offer naïve comments on Gorki, Tolstoi, Chekhov, Poe, Marx and Lenin. Mimi once inquired innocently what the British North America Act was.[13] To them Laz, who was consuming endless books about diverse subjects and writing short stories, must have seemed a remarkable genius. Their practical efforts to find him a job (they acquired a letter of introduction from their friend Mr. Harvey to Abel Vineberg, staff correspondent at the

Gazette, for example) seem pathetic in their eagerness to please. More to the point was their common-sense advice about daily life: not to apply so much hair oil, to tell his sisters that he wouldn't bother them further if they provided him with a new suit, to take as much milk and fresh fruit as possible and "very very important" to "see men about dogs regularly."[14]

But the Cusinières' shack was, in the end, a mere stopping-off place. The thing that really compelled — then, as strongly, repelled — Lazarovitch was the disturbing presence of Mme. Cusinière. As his short story "Vacation in La Voiselle," based on his stay with her, makes clear, her warm maternal treatment more than bordered on the seductive. "At certain moments," he wrote of Mme. Tipue in his story based on "actual fact,"[15] "even an ugly woman, if she has lived for some time with the wind and the sun, can be sexually attractive. Even if she is old enough to be your mother. And perhaps just because she is that old...there still clings about her an animal smell."[16] Mme. Cusinière, who admitted she preferred the sensual novels of Zola to the more political works of Tolstoi,[17] exercised this kind of attraction for her "little Laz." In a letter dictated to Mimi (since she could not write English), she wrote, "At night, when I go to sleep, I wish to hear you say again: 'I can't sleep, I would like you to come with me!' Polisson! Talk like that to a woman of my age!" On another occasion, she closed a letter, "And now, good night, my little Laz. I won't say that I cover you with kisses; the saying is common-place; further more, given the [small] surface you offer, my heart would no [sic] be satisfied. Let us say that we send you as many kisses as the holy King David and his august son, Solomon, had legitimate wives and concubines together! Ah! Ah! that is better isn't it? Little polisson! My dear little Laz, those jokes are unworthy of my age. Those women of fourty! [sic]"[18]

Fictionalizing the one occasion on which he actually came close to filling the most compelling void M. Cusinière had left behind him, Layton, in "Vacation in La Voiselle," dramatizes a conversation in which Mme. Tipue calls softly to the young man, Hugo, from her bed. She proposes sex on the grounds that the crucifix, which normally protects her from sin, has fallen down. Hugo, both attracted and repelled by "the fold of stomach that lipped over the shiny black belt" Mme. Tipue wore by day, is torn and intensely uncomfortable. Before long he must leave their home. Lazarovitch's self-disgust with his exploitation of the Cusinières' hospitality and generous hand-outs,[19] and his horrified awkwardness when confronted with the sexual advances of his "mere Mouchkette," propelled him onward.

The Sultan of Sixth Avenue

In the autumn of 1936, twenty-four-year-old Irving Lazarovitch strolled down Sixth Avenue in New York City, one arm thrown nonchalantly over the shoulder of his brother Hyman as if he had not a care in the world. The Great Depression was ravaging the city. The streets were filthy, bums slept on benches under newspapers or in bus-stops and the unemployed lined up daily at the soup kitchens for their meagre rations. Issie was staying with Hymie in the latest in a series of unpaid-for rooms in the Bronx. They were broke again. No money for rent. No money for food. Between the two of them, they could only scrounge seventy-five cents, which jingled loosely in their pockets. "I was sick with worry," Hyman recalls. "But not Irving. 'Hey,' he said cheerfully as we passed a barbershop, 'we need a haircut.' That meant spending twenty-five cents apiece. In he goes and settles into the chair. I can see him there still, leaning back with a steaming white turban of towel on his head, a manicurist working over his fingernails, someone else shining his shoes. 'But Irving,' I was protesting, 'all we've got is seventy-five cents, and you get a haircut, a shoeshine and a manicure?'" Irving tossed the barber seventy-five cents (twenty-five cents less than the total bill) and the two of them sauntered back to spend their last night in Hyman's unpaid-for room. "After that, I called him 'The Sultan of Sixth Avenue.' He looked great; I looked terrible. As we walked, he got deep into a lecture on Harold Laski — how he was a fraud and a fake. I just felt terrified. I couldn't concentrate on what he said. All I could think was what would become of us?"[1]

Hyman and his brother Larry had been eking out a hand-to-mouth existence in New York since 1925 or so, when the resourceful Keine had paid a Jewish agent twenty dollars apiece to smuggle her teen-age sons, under the name of "Leizer," across the United States border. She hoped they would have more chance of work there than they had around Montreal. Mostly, according to Hyman, she wanted to make sure that they were far enough away not to ask her for money or food.

"They were horrible times," Hyman recalls. "I remember one occasion when a group of people organized to remove my furniture when I was evicted from one of my rooms in the Bronx near Third Avenue. I was hit on the head by a marshall. My ear was bleeding all over the place. Some people may think that Jews stick together when there's trouble. Well, they don't. Gentiles were no better. As for the French-Canadians, they were starving too. In those days, you worked twelve hours a day in factories for seven dollars a week."

It was Irving who brought the gospel of Marxism to his brothers. The three of them joined the bread-lines, where a handful of cracked wheat cost two cents; a ration of milk, one cent; a spoon of honey, one cent and a cup of coffee, two cents. "Irving and I sold newspapers for a while. We'd go barefoot into bars that were covered with spit, dust and filth. I wore a shirt people thought was painted on me. It didn't take Irving long to convince me that there was something wrong with the world, and that that 'something' was capitalism. I wanted to change things, so I became a radical. In fact, I was a sort-of leader in one of the groups in New York under an assumed name. The three of us used to go to the Communist meetings. We heard Earl and Bill Browder, American leaders of the Communist Party. They were amazingly powerful. 'Capitalism is tottering!' they would declaim. 'The brotherhood of man will triumph.' I never participated, but Irving sure did. I remember one meeting of the Socialist Labor Party which convinced us we could vote our way into the system, form unions and take over all the industries.

Irving leapt up and spoke so eloquently. He challenged the Party founder, Daniel DeLeon, and annihilated the meeting."

Hyman recalls that his brother complained one day that he had never had sex, a complaint that reflected his needs rather than his personal history. "I took him over to Harlem where you could get a black prostitute for a dollar. Up the stairs he went, and I waited around outside in the street for an hour or so. When he came back down, I eagerly asked him, 'Well? How was it?' He looked elated. 'Nothing happened,' he said. 'She was interested in poetry, so I read her some. She liked it!'

"Irving dealt with the horror of that mid-Depression year in New York with an air of indifference," Hyman reports, amazed that his brother could so easily withdraw from the harsh realities that pressed in relentlessly upon them. "He never cared about money. His head was in the clouds, in political theories and economic analysis. I was the only one that protested about our mother and sisters — especially Gertie. While we were starving in New York, she and Strul (who was earning a thousand dollars a week) were taking vacations in Europe in the 30s, 'business trips' she called them, on which Strul would establish contacts for his thriving import trade. And Dora and her husband were getting by all right in Ottawa. But there was no kindness for us. They could have done something to help us, but they didn't. Like our mother, they were indifferent to our suffering. They just thought we should work. If we couldn't get jobs, they said, then it must be our fault. I even married to eat, a girl I met who had a job. I had to steal the food for our engagement party. When I took flight from Detroit to Montreal soon afterwards, when I heard her ex-boyfriend was after me with a knife, Gertie (who acted as an arbitrator with the immigration authorities sent by the girl's parents) didn't take my side. She and my mother took the girl's side. That was one time Gertie did give me money: ten dollars for the train fare back to Detroit. Eventually, I quit the job I got through my wife, then quit a second job and left her by fleeing to Toledo.

"I guess Marx didn't harm me after all. I've bought and sold properties, worked a number of businesses and trades. Instead of changing the world, I've made a few dollars."

The Farmer Thinks

In a letter written by Eugene Forsey to David Lewis on stationery embossed CO-OPERATIVE COMMONWEALTH FEDERATION, Boîte Postale 265, MONTREAL and dated 2 September 1937, the following matter was raised:

> I had a visit from Irving Layton (sometime Lazarovitch), one of your old YPSL members. He has had three-and-a-half years at Macdonald College, where he has won golden opinions from his professors, and where he organized and carried on with great success a Social Research Club. He now has the offer of a job with the YMHA, but doesn't want it if he can get — a job as CCF organizer! His idea is to get a job with a farmer, for which he'd get enough or almost enough to keep him alive, and in his spare time, with such money as the CCF could pay him, to organize the rural voters. Stan [Allen] and I were on the whole favourably impressed with him. He is not, I think, a Trotskyist, nor a disguised Communist; and he obviously has brains. He says he wants to make this job of CCF organizer his life work.[1]

Forsey went on to inquire about the possibilities for Layton. He seemed willing to consider sending him out to the Eastern

Townships of Quebec or to find him a position in Ontario.

That month, Layton (as he had called himself since his return from New York) re-entered Macdonald College in a manner that reflected his current political passions and his considerable life experience. He could transfer credits from the two economics courses he had passed in his stab at third year, and he re-enrolled in the physics course for which he had never written the exam and in the chemistry course he had failed. That was routine, as was the addition of a new course on vegetable crops that enabled him to list "horticulture" as one of his major subjects. What constituted a radical departure from the norm was the means by which he had set out to acquire his second major subject: economics. Of the eleven subjects he undertook that year, his one sociology course ("The Family") and all five of his economics courses were located at McGill. They were "Canada: Geographic, Industrial & Economic Problems;" "Labour Problems;" "Money & Banking;" "Canadian Social & Economic Statistics & Statistical Method" (taught by a left-wing contributor to the League for Social Reconstruction, Leonard C. Marsh); and "The Government of Canada" (taught by Eugene Forsey, who thus almost immediately would get to know in person the man about whom he had enquired just before the fall term began).

"My chief impression of him as a student in the Government of Canada course," Forsey recalls, "is that he was not really much interested. He was too engrossed in Marxism and in working-class political activity to acquit himself academically as he was capable of doing."[2] Although the curriculum at Macdonald College had been undergoing revision steadily over the years to bring it in line with courses for degrees in other faculties of McGill University, it would not be until 1945, eight years later, that students majoring in economics would be directed to McGill for some of their courses. Simply by following his personal interests, and through understanding because of his age (he was now at least four years older than his classmates) that courses at McGill from some of the leading political luminaries of the Canadian CCF would provide a grander stage for his oratorical talents and political ambitions, Layton engineered a unique education for himself. It could be said that from 1937 until his graduation in

1939 he was more a McGill undergraduate than a Macdonald College student, though with his grades as they stood he never would have been admitted to McGill as a full-time third-year student.

By coincidence, a new policy worked out between the *Failt-Ye Times* and the *McGill Daily* played into his hands. The *Times* was about to be incorporated into a weekly section of the *Daily*. Under the utterly misleading heading, "The Farmer Thinks," Layton began, on 3 November 1937, a new column, which, along with the poems he also contributed, would reach a wider, more intellectual audience, whose interests covered a much broader scope, than CURRENT HISTORY had done. Layton's first subject was the St. Francois-Xavier co-operative movement in Nova Scotia, which he praised. As in the *Failt-Ye Times*, he also tried his hand at satiric verse, this time under the heading "Poetic Socialism." In heavy-handed doggerel couplets, in a poem called "Portrait Of A Pseudo-Socialist," he blasted Professor H.D. Brunt, a man whose comfortable position at the college seemed to Layton to have taken the bite out of his political sympathy with the left. (Brunt had, by some divine intervention, become a lecturer in economics, although his training and department appointment were in English.) A second poem, an attack on the British "appeasement" proposal to outlaw the bombing of cities, rudely exposed hypocrisy: "we'll humanize this war, for fear/Of awkward revolution in the rear."[3] On 10 November, Layton condemned the farmers for re-electing Mitchell Hepburn as premier of Ontario. His prose was so lavish and convoluted it reads today like that of a Renaissance historian. Although he seems to have regarded his poems as "off-the-cuff" barbs, mere embellishments to the weighty matter of his prose diatribes, "Thaumaturge," which appeared in the same issue, carried its message more effectively than his column:

> I've reached the gutter, true
> And like a mud-veined jut of ice
> That throws itself against the gutter's bars
> I wait until I thaw completely out.

self-pitying? Yes. Extravagant? Yes. But in his ability to

compress thought, feeling and intense sensual experience into images (an ability that made his prose sound archaic and cloying), Layton demonstrated a talent for poetry he did not yet realize he had. For the most part, his poems were silly, imitative (especially of Shakespeare and the Romantics), clumsy and sentimental.

On 19 November 1937, Layton's denunciation of capitalism described the farmer as "the prize porker about to be slaughtered." On 31 January 1938, he exposed "gluts and surpluses of wheat" as endemic to the capitalist system; on 2 February, in his last contribution to "The Farmer Thinks," he condemned the profit system. In an article called "Culture and Capitalism," he rhapsodized in a most un-farmerly fashion:

> Of what use, then, are the lyrics of Shelley or Heine to a fascist aviator blasting the dark-skinned natives of Ethiopia?...tiny coteries and select literary cliques suddenly spring up and begin to flourish like cobwebs in a deserted room. Preaching a farrago of nonsense, they have lost touch with the vital forces of the day....The enemy is not only in Germany and Italy. The enemy is within the gates.

Layton addressed his questions to the world at large, but also to himself. What *was* the relationship of culture to economic realities? This was a drama he had witnessed from birth. His father, after all, like a "cobweb in a deserted room," had pursued his culture with not the slightest regard for "the vital forces of the day." His mother, with all the skills of a professional orator, had commandeered those forces into sustenance for a battalion of children. Were impulses such as hers "Fascist"? Or "capitalist"? Certainly it was she and her legion of daughters who were now bringing all the power at their command to bear on him to work, to earn a living, to join the ranks of capitalists. The enemy *was* "within the gates." Layton saw the same tug-of-war in A.M. Klein. Was he a man of culture, a poet? Or was he a perpetrator of the profit motive, a lawyer? Klein was of the last generation not to be torn into choice, though the inherent tensions of this conflict would eventually fracture his sanity. Layton's circumstances were such that he would have to confront the issue.

How could he keep in touch with "the vital forces of the day" and "preach a farrago" without becoming a capitalist like his mother? How could he be a custodian of culture like his father without shutting himself away in a "deserted room"? How could he retain the best of both worlds when they seemed, like his parents, diametrically opposed?

After an appeal to J.S. Woodsworth (whom he had publicly denounced as a "faker") in mid-November, in which he continued his campaign to find a place for himself in the CCF (as well as requesting some free maps of Canada),[4] Layton's potential political career was crushed by the party's national secretary, David Lewis: "Regarding the student Irving Layton," he wrote to Lucy Woodsworth who, in her husband's absence, had forwarded Layton's request to Lewis,

> It so happens that I know the young man. I have had many years of experience with him and his work and I am afraid that it has always been disappointing, inasmuch as he used to be inclined to unreliability both as to his promises and his facts. I am making enquiries from friends in McGill as to exactly what his column in the "McGill Daily" is. I shall write to Mr. Woodsworth just as soon as I have any information. In the meantime I would suggest that Mr. Woodsworth delay any definite or lengthy reply until he hears from me. I want to assure you that the above is not written lightly nor on second hand information. Layton, whose real name is Lazarobitch [sic], was well-known to me over a period of years before I left for England in 32. In fact, he was one of the large group of young people whom I trained in Socialism through the Young People's Socialist League.... I also know that he has been with the Young Communists League, with Trotskyist elements, and has, in general, been wandering all over the plot. At the moment he is making every effort to get on the inside of the CCF, for his appeal to Mr. Woodsworth is not the first one. Knowing him and knowing his past, I have been advising great caution until we can be more certain of his bona fides.[5]

This letter must have crossed one of 6 December from Eugene Forsey to David Lewis, reporting his impressions of

Layton's *McGill Daily* column, "The Farmer Thinks." Forsey appears to be unaware that Layton is one of his students. He also either overlooks Layton's poems in the *McGill Daily* or dismisses them as unimportant:

> As far as I could judge on a hasty reading, they say pretty much what we should say on all three subjects, though they are not very profound (like my own journalistic efforts, alas!), and their style is rather lush. The chief thing that strikes me about them is that no Quebec, and probably no Ontario, farmer would have written them. But they are none the worse for that! He does not, as far as I could see, mention the CCF, or any other party, at all. I should not call them Communist articles, or Trotskyist, or United Front, or anything specific in that way. His general line on foreign policy is that the democratic nations should stand together and adopt a strong policy, and that if they do there is no danger of war. On the other subjects he is even less specific.[6]

Lynched

On 19 December, the *McGill Daily* printed a short story by "Irvine" Layton, "Silhouette of a Man." It was a maudlin, overwrought tale of an embittered, starving and unemployed man who waits in vain on a park bench for a rich young woman who has promised to help him. It prefigured Layton's imminent marriage.

Layton met Faye Lynch through his sister Esther, whose second husband was related to her uncle, a man named Margolian, from Yarmouth. That winter, Faye had moved to Montreal.[1] Though she was not beautiful — short and dark and, for her age (a year older than Layton), decidedly overweight — she was good-natured, responsible and affectionate, and her face showed the sweet openness of those who bear their lot with equanimity. Had it not been for one small coincidence, Layton probably never would have married her.

In the summer of 1938, he could not afford to attend the first World Conference on Agriculture, which was being held at Macdonald College. Despite the sporadic cheques sent his way by his brother Hyman (who was taking full advantage of his new position in a government job as a supervisor of cheque payments to help out members of his family),[2] Layton had no choice but to work as he had done every summer. He was back as a waiter at M. Greenberg's Hotel, Presqu'Isle, the

Jewish resort in Ste. Agathe, later to be immortalized (as Rubin's Hotel Lac des Sables in Ste. Agathe) by Mordecai Richler in *The Apprenticeship of Duddy Kravitz*.[3] As a result of his incendiary involvement in a strike of Greenberg employees,[4] Layton was fired in mid-summer. He returned to Montreal, embittered, hungry and unemployed. He somewhat desperately called the people he knew, but they were all gone. Finally, he thought of Faye who, he vaguely recalled, worked as a book-keeper and stenographer for Salig, a junk-dealer. Had his other friends been home, he never would have bothered.

"She showed me genuine affection in every way," Layton recalls. Unlike the disappointed wretch in his story "Silhouette of a Man," Layton found he could rely on Faye for food, for money and for sex. "Although I never loved her," he admits, "I enjoyed her sense of humour and admired her practicality. She had pride in herself, despite her obesity. If I had looked like that, I would have been embarrassed, but she was plucky." Layton basked in her solicitous attention, as indeed he might under the circumstances. And Faye had another suitor, Hyman Jacobson, who was pressing for an engagement, a situation that piqued Layton's intensely competitive nature. Once Faye rejected Jacobson for him, Layton felt responsible. "I loathed myself for allowing this to happen," he recalls, "but I felt guilty about stopping her engagement to Jacobson." This thought bore out a highly moral inscription he had jotted down sometime that year on the back cover of Communist Party Leader Earl Browder's *The Democratic Front for Jobs, Security, Democracy and Peace:* "Nothing so weakens character as an unperformed promise."[5] In the back of his mind also lingered a superstitious thought that helped keep him on the path to marriage. His brother Abraham's fatal tuberculosis had been dramatized many times by Keine as divine vengeance. By now, the story was woven into the warp and woof of Lazarovitch legend. Abraham had broken his engagement; the woman's parents had asked their rabbi to pronounce a curse on him; shortly afterwards, his tuberculosis had gripped him until he had wasted away at Ste. Adèle, near the very place Layton had just left in considerable confusion. Was it possible that to betray a woman was to invite such disaster? The appeal of comforts, responsibility born of irresistible competitiveness, superstition and the lure of steady financial support combined to render a facsimile of love. On 13 September 1938, only a couple of months after that first phone call, just as his final year at Macdonald College got underway, the two were married. According to Hyman, his brother had married for the same reason he had: to keep an empty stomach full. "We married to eat!"[6]

On Faye's salary, the couple rented a tiny apartment on Crescent Street. Despite their shared sense of humour (a robust "Keine Lazarovitch" outlook on life), Layton almost immediately felt trapped. Faye's plucky self-esteem soon seemed to him a little ridiculous, even overbearing. He began calling her "the General." He objected to her lack of interest in his avid intellectual pursuits. She had "a completely unliterary and anti-literary mind," he would later reflect.[7] Certainly she must not have appreciated the gang of enraged cadets from the McGill contingent of the Canadian Officers' Training Corps who tried to force their way into her apartment in response to a poem her husband (who was out) published in the 28 November issue of the *McGill Daily*. In "Medley for Our Times," Layton had sneeringly alluded to the widely honoured Remembrance Day rite of poppy sales and had referred to the army veterans who sold them as "be-medalled bums." It was, he claimed in a subsequent letter of self-defense to the *McGill Daily*, an attack on a system of government that had led to widespread unemployment, not a slight against the dignity and courage of soldiers.[8]

Probably in large part due to the nourishment, stability and comfort Faye provided, Layton passed his final year at Macdonald College in May 1939 with the highest grades of his four years there: his average was 71.3%. His economics and English marks were outstanding; again, he had managed to include two courses from McGill. He never did pass physics. Against the grindstone of Eugene Forsey's course on the history of political theory (in which he received his top mark, ninety),[9] Layton had honed his skills of political discussion to more than undergraduate perfection. In an impressive essay on Machiavelli for that course, he wrestled with the complexities of dictatorship from a Marxist stance, drawing parallels with the contemporary world and suggesting analogies with his own life. He perceived Machiavelli as an astute thinker who had stripped the hypocritical mask from stark animal realities that lay beneath man's pious religiosities. Changed modes of production, he observed, had ushered in a new era represented especially by the "rising burgher class" who stood to profit most from change. The power of the state had replaced church rule and ethical considerations had been "brushed aside." "[Machiavelli] failed to reconcile his power politics with a clear ethical principle," he concluded. But he added, "Perhaps...the dialectical approach is warranted which regards good and evil as the necessary component parts of the evolving whole."[10]

Somewhere along the way he had begun to groom himself carefully. His wardrobe included three-piece suits or tweed jackets with leather patches. He smoked a pipe. Beside his *Clan Macdonald* graduation photo, in which he looks dapper and prosperous, though swarthy and less dignified than the Scots and English lads who surround him, is a cheeky sum-up of his years at the college that must have been written by himself:

> LAYTON, IRVING PETER
> "As full of wisdom as a cheese of mites."
> *Biography:* Born Neamtz, Mar. '12. Came to Canada in 1913 to avoid conscription. Educated Montreal. Nocturnally devoured Ibsen at Horn's Cafeteria. Phrucology decreed entering Mac '33.
> *Activities:* Intercollegiate wrestling '33-'34; Pres. Social Research Club '34-'36; Intercollegiate Debating '34-'37; Interfaculty Boxing '34-'35; *Failt-Ye Times* '35-'36; College play '35-'36; McGill Daily '37-'39.
> *Hobby:* Soap-box oratory.

A Fuller Brush Man

With good cause, Layton's fellow-students at Macdonald College had been anxious to control his flamboyant and provocative political columns. Graduates with a B.Sc. (Agr.) commonly turned to the provincial government for jobs. It was not in their best interests to come from a college branded "Red." That summer of 1939, as the world trembled, poised on the cliff-edge of Hitler's war, Layton must have seemed one of the least desirable of employees, though both Doctor J.E. Lattimer, who had taught him economics, and his chairman, vice-principal W.H. Brittain, filed strong letters of support as reference at his request.[1]

At first he tried the Canadian Jewish Congress. On 18 May 1939, he wrote, with his best manners (and someone else's handwriting), from his apartment with Faye at 1175 Bishop Street to H.M. Caiserman, then general secretary of the congress in Montreal. He did not mention that he was married or that he had been involved with Caiserman's daughter when they had both been in the YCL in the early thirties. Layton outlined his accomplishments at Macdonald College and asked to be made educational director:

> Throughout my College years I have been interested in

> Youth work and my experience in that regard has been a wide and fruitful one....
>
> My interest in Jewish Congress work is a profound and urgent one: my aim is to contribute something to that work. I share your fear of and detestation for fascism in all its forms and desire strongly to translate both into effective action. In all this I see the urgency of enlisting the support of young people, of opening their eyes, of showing them clearly this menace which Fascism and Nazism [sic] represent against our democratic institutions and democratic way of life. More immediately, Jewish Youth must be awakened to the ghastly danger which those doctrines embody against their faith, their rights and their dignity as human beings. No greater satisfaction in life can come to me than to help bring about such an awakening.[2]

When Layton's willingness "to work hard and to go wherever you might send me" failed to move Caiserman, he tried something else. Wishing to establish his identity as a farmer in order to seem more palatable to the CCF, and also wishing to escape from Faye, who had begun impatiently pressing for a family, Layton visited his brother, Oscar (Larry) Latch (the surname Larry, Hyman and Harry adopted), who had bought a farm in Colchester, New York, where he could eke out a living. Pictures show Layton, amiable in his unkempt clothes, feeding chickens or standing in sunny fields wrestling a bull calf.

It was Faye's parents who rescued the couple, inviting them to come to Yarmouth, near Halifax, Nova Scotia, where Faye's father had a clothing store. Suitably outfitted and financed by his father-in-law, Layton renewed his efforts to obtain a job with the CCF, this time by applying in person to H.I.S. ("Ingi") Borgford, the provincial secretary of the party, who worked for the Halifax YMCA. Borgford checked Layton's credentials with Stan Allen and reported back to David Lewis, unaware that Lewis already knew Layton. "Layton called on me," he wrote on 27 November 1939, and

> has good appearance though quite aggressive. Assured

me he was not or never had been a C. party member, though a YCL'er at Macdonald U. This of course would not mean anything if he were really a party member. They are such awful liars and proud of it as a tactic even in face-to-face relations.

The CCF here needs the stimulus of new blood, but with this word from Stan I felt I must exclude Layton. What can you tell me of him?[3]

The "word from Stan" Borgford quoted as follows: "Layton is really Lazarovitch, a Communist and a bad one. He's tried innumerable ways to enter the CCF before & we wouldn't trust him an inch. Any really CCF man has his membership card. Avoid him."

Unaware of his now entrenched and somewhat exaggerated reputation within the CCF, Layton requested a reference from Dean W.H. Brittain after meeting Borgford. "I do not need to tell you how important this position is to me and how desirous I am of procuring it," he wrote to Brittain on 11 October 1939. "I would put my whole heart into my work and try hard to bring credit to the University that gave me my education."[4] As he waited, optimistic by disposition, Layton took a job as a Fuller Brush man. "He was a Fuller Brush man only in theory," says Faye's cousin, Sam Margolian, a merchant who had graduated in law from Dalhousie in 1935. (Later he taught at Osgoode Hall and practised with Brown, Master in Toronto.) "I remember him stretched out comfortably under a tree smoking his pipe on the Dalhousie campus reading books he took out of the Dalhousie Library. That's how he sold Fuller brushes! He had taken an apartment with Faye near the campus. I was living in a room at the Lord Nelson Hotel, a treat I'd promised myself if I ever became rich. Irving considered my room a haven where he could escape from his wife. We used to have heated political discussions. He was a devout Communist in those days, and tried to persuade me that they had the solution to all the world's ills. Really it was poverty that made him resent society and put him into the Communist revolutionary view. He subscribed to the *Bulletin* of the Brookings Institute. I remember particularly discussions we had about whether or not Russia would invade Finland. Layton vowed that Russia would never invade Finland. 'If they do,' he claimed, 'I'll leave the party.' He completely accepted Russian propaganda."[5]

After six months as a Fuller Brush man, Layton began selling insurance for Confederation Life. Finally, he heard that his application to the Department of Agriculture had been turned down. Reluctantly, he agreed to carry through on his father-in-law's proposal to set him up in a haberdashery shop in Halifax.

The prospect was laughable. With political views such as his, views he did not hide under a barrel (in fact he attended local "cell" meetings of the Communists in Halifax),[6] Layton never could have settled in to conduct a small business. He had eluded his mother's crafty machinations and those of his sisters to make him a capitalist money-earner. He had fought and finagled for his education, an education that had confirmed his notion of himself as a man of large ideas about political and economic change, as one above or outside the fates in which lesser men had unwittingly been entrapped. He was not about to throw in the towel now, especially for a woman he did not love. As the summer of 1940 drew to an end, disillusioned by Russia's treaty with Germany and her invasion of Finland in November 1939, he hitch-hiked alone to Montreal. In a letter he wrote to a friend much later, Layton recalled, "I broke no Olympic records in either enterprise [Fuller Brushes and Confederation Life]. But society said I had a wife to support and those were the only jobs open to a burgeoning madman with a BA. When one of the local merchants, a prominent charity-minded Jew, told me my radical activities were menacing the welfare of the right little tight little community of Jews, I decided it was time for me to leave behind my wife and whatever ambitions I had of becoming the president of Confederation Life."[7]

The year spent in Montreal was an endless limbo of melancholy. Layton seemed destined to an inglorious career teaching English to immigrants at the Jewish People's Library, where he began employment in September. He felt trapped in a marriage to a woman he increasingly loathed, for Faye had pursued him to Montreal, insisting he honour his vows, settle down to a job and support her while she bore his children.

Layton would look back on that winter with Faye in a spirit of exaggeration so strong it betrays the depths of his disgust with her. "I never loved her," he reminisced. "She was obese — probably 350 pounds. And she had so much black hair on her face she had to shave daily. I used to watch the bristles gradually push through her white face powder with horrified fascination. One night, when she reached out for me, I ordered her not to touch me. I jumped out of bed, ran to the gallery three stories up, leapt onto the balustrade and threatened to throw myself onto Dorchester Street below. Luckily she didn't come near me."[8] One of Layton's brothers recalls that, during that year, Irving forced Faye to sign a contract promising to lose a certain amount of weight if she wanted him to remain with her.[9] Judging from the tone and imagery of his poem "English For Immigrants," Layton turned to his students for comfort and a feeling of self-esteem:

> And I am Caesar I cry I am Saint Francis,
> I am this misty slate and a lump of chalk:
> They only climb from their steep silence and stare.
> So I call for the raven in their throats
> And their cleft tongues toss on a bed of fever
>
> Yet from me, a hawk, they take whatever feather
> Can start their heavy wishes under a stone.[10]

The Farmer Leaves a Wife

The summer of 1941 found Layton on a farm next to his brother's in Colchester, New York. There he could work the fields (one of the few kinds of labour he enjoyed, probably because of the chance to be outside), relish the jolly camaraderie of the male trio formed by himself, Oscar and his nephew, Bill (whom he had persuaded to join him), and, most important, escape from Faye. Faye was proving to be a loyal and stubborn woman, not content to be rid of an uncaring and exploitative husband, but determined to make him change his ways by any means she could. Without a shred of pride, she approached Rochel Eisen at the Jewish Library, asking where Irving was to be found, pleading for help getting him back.[1]

Rochel knew well enough where Irving was. On his frequent trips into Montreal, he took advantage of their earlier brief intimacy and of her usefulness to him as a provider of books and journals, by staying overnight at her apartment. These sojourns created much tension, as a series of letters[2] reveal, written by Rochel during the week-days when Irving had returned to the farm.

Rochel was a diminutive woman, pale and delicately beautiful, completely devoid of the earthiness and humour Layton usually found attractive in women. She had come to

Montreal in 1923 at age seventeen from Volyn, in the Ukraine, emotionally scarred by a war that had left her sensitive and fearful of other people to an extreme. Along with a polite thoughtfulness of others and a febrile imagination nurtured by extensive reading, it was her inclination to lean on strong individuals that drew her to Layton. "When I read your letter," she wrote to him on 1 August 1941, "I had a vision of a narrow but forceful river breaking its way through stony walls. You are talking with so much love and enthusiasm of your new experience [on the farm]! It is really wonderful to feel that one does something! You always do, because you always see so much in everything and learn from all. 'An open mind' as they say in yiddish."[3] Layton's forcefulness both attracted and frightened Rochel. His moods were very unpredictable. Whereas she was meticulously reliable, giving him precise information about where she would be, with whom and when, he turned up, or didn't, according to his own whims. He asked her to do favours for him involving other women he knew: she reported "regards for you from Martha — Gaspé Coast;"[4] and sent a message for "the young lady who is reading Strachey's book."[5] She was surprised to learn that he was still having his mail received and forwarded by Faye, and wondered if he was still seeing her. Wistfully uncomprehending of Irving's relationship with his wife, she described Faye's visit to the library: "She returned her book & went down to the musicale. She looked very nice, even pretty. Her eyes were particularly lovely. We only exchanged a few words."[6]

Rochel's discontent over the question of love arose, and increased, during the summer. What is love? She must have wondered. To her it was steady and patient faithfulness. But to Irving, it seemed to mean something different. At the beginning of the summer when she admitted, "My heart is trembling right now, and I am sure it is because I love you,"[7] she was responding to what she felt were similar feelings in Irving. He had written "we are both patient people," urged that "we be honest with each other" and expressed confidence that "time will bring happiness to us."[8] By the end of the summer, confused, lonely and bitter about his "unpossessiveness," she had become less trusting. "You certainly have a peculiar understanding about my friendship, thinking that mine was simply a passing mood because we had such happy hours," she wrote. "I see the two of us like two huge rocks, strong and pointy and very closely situated near each other, enjoying mutually the warmth of the sun and transferring the heat to each other like most devoted loving friends. I can also see and feel how the rocks are swirling with happiness and, it seems to me, they are even moving in their eternal firmness when a cooling rain comes down their cheeks, and in their jolly dance the streams of water forget their straight course and jump from one rock to another creating a net that knots them."[9] In this far-fetched image (a richly imaginative one that helps explain Layton's fondness for her), Rochel seems to recognize their essential separateness. The kind of man she needed was one with whom she could feel secure about sharing her refined interests. That man she had actually met just before the summer began, and there are occasional references to him in her letters.

Melech Ravitch was forty-eight, eighteen years older than Rochel. A well-established poet and essayist who had emigrated to Montreal that year from Varsovie, he became an important figure in the Canadian Jewish scene.[10] Because of his commitment to the preservation of Yiddish culture, he was asked to organize a programme for immigrants that would offer courses in English, French and Yiddish literature. Ravitch, in fact, had much in common with Irving, but while he was mature and purposeful, Irving, twenty-four years his junior, was struggling still to discover what his purpose might be. At first, Rochel regarded Ravitch as an interesting (and refreshingly "punctual") acquaintance, someone with whom it was a privilege to read and discuss essays and poems. But it was Layton, she believed, who was "the only one that knows me best."[11] She wrote to Layton: "Mr. Ravitch and I were reading an essay: 'Perpetual Peace' by Kraus, in which there are many interesting and contemporary thoughts. Still I would like some day to read it with you. I am sure you will make many things clear for me, and we may develop interesting thoughts."[12]

Although she would remain true to her vow that "Some day I'll say with pride, '...and mind you, I have had the honor to be a personal friend of this great poet!'",¹³ "Perpetual Peace" was something she never was to share with Layton. When Melech declared himself, she accepted and they set up house together.

Many Worlds

Every person lives in many worlds. But
there is one world among others that includes
all the others. He is, indeed, fortunate who
discovering, dwells in it. And it sometimes
happens!
Wishing you, with all my heart, a new year filled
with happiness —
          Your devoted friend,
          Irving Layton

This dedication, neatly and floridly inscribed inside the 18 December 1941 issue of Rochel Eisen's copy of the *Forge*,[1] hinted at depths of meaning Layton may not have realized. On the surface, it referred to the subject of his first major essay: Harold Laski.[2] The *Forge* was a McGill student journal that featured poetry and prose on cultural and economic subjects. Though Layton was not officially enrolled at McGill, he had managed to have his essay on Laski published in the journal. Harold Laski was a timely but unusual subject for the *Forge*, whose contributors were mainly upper-middle-class undergraduates interested in sports and student politics. Among their wholesome, naïve offerings, Layton's article seems an odd duck. The tone he adopted (no doubt in imitation of the many economic tracts and periodicals he had been reading) was that of a man much older than himself. He sounds like an earnest professor emeritus or an ambassador of long experience haranguing colleagues of middle age who have not kept up with their jobs.

Harold Laski was a man Layton could easily idealize. Laski had taught at McGill during the Great War before returning to England to take a position at the London School of Economics and help found the British Labour Party. Since Layton's early admiration of British boys' annuals and his profound response to Amos Saunders, who had taught British literature so passionately, he had been an Anglophile. The literary universe of English romantic poets and Victorian essayists had been for years a haven into which he could retreat from unpleasant reality. His tweeds and pipe, even many of his spoken phrases, were affectations, evidence of the extent to which he was attempting to act out the role of an English gentleman. Layton admired Laski's Marxism. "Acute, and wielding a vigorous prose," he wrote, "he has consistently preached the by no means popular gospel that liberty is an illusion."[3] Laski's quest for a better world, one free of poverty, class privilege and complacency, was probably the "one world among others that includes all the others" to which Layton alluded in his inscription for Rochel. But the fact that Laski preached an unpopular gospel was probably more compelling to Layton. Certainly, in his article about Laski he attempted to do the same himself.

Because of his passionate involvement with his material, Layton could not treat his subject objectively. There is an interplay between the intellectual position he argues, the broader context of the Jewish community he reflects and even the personal experience he has known.

The conflict between two distinct strands of the Jewish tradition, ethical idealism and entrepreneurialism, had been exacerbated by North-American conditions. These tended to open vistas of much greater scope for capitalist ventures than had been possible in Europe, a fact that undermined the orthodox, religious and disciplined-intellectualism side of Judaism. To Layton, who had observed and disapproved of this tendency in the Jewish community of Montreal, Laski seemed to present a political life-view that restored the moral, ethical side of life to a position more nearly equal to that of the more banal but necessary provision of life comforts. Laski represented a valid intellectual position that reflected the aims of the international socialist movement to which so many Jews had been attracted. Layton's fascination with Laski was a logical extension of his eclectic political career; it also was disturbingly personalized as a struggle in himself between the forces represented by his father and mother.

In the essay, the ghosts of Keine and Moishe Lazarovitch hover very near. Layton observes that critics have attacked Laski's works, as Keine once had assaulted or "dismissed" Moishe's studies, as "the erudite vagaries of a pedant." Like Moishe, and indeed like all Jewish orthodox men, Laski seems to Layton a man of ideas and ethics; at other times, Laski seems to resemble Keine: in his "impassioned pleas," his "powerful" portrayal of a "grievous" economic dilemma and his "perception of a disadvantaged group." Laski's description of capitalism — "ruthlessly crushing" opposition — also seems akin to her, whereas his endorsement of the pure ideals of democracy echoes Moishe. Layton's observation that "capitalism no longer found the marriage connection tolerable; it simply kicked its sleeping partner [democracy] into a concentration camp and turned the key," may have arisen from the image of his weak, idealistic father shut in his room communing with his Maker while Keine stridently denounced him.

Layton could easily respond to the struggle he depicted because it triggered memories of that unresolved struggle between ethics and greed within his family and within the immigrant Jewish community at large. He responded to Laski because Laski, like Moishe, was a custodian of conscience and, like Keine, expressed himself often and vigorously. Laski's exhortation, "Ideas arm themselves for battle," may have seemed to resolve the two opposite and unresolved worlds that co-existed in the Lazarovitch household into a satisfying, if temporary, unity. Layton would not have to dispense with Moishe's ideals in order to retain Keine's vigour. Neither would he have to endorse her crass material motives in his own entrepreneurial drive. He could, like Laski, be "shrewd" and "alive" without being "ruthless." He could enlist his energies on the side of the oppressed without becoming a "pedant." Harold Laski, Layton concluded, "is one of those rare persons whose thought grows with the times. Unlike the doctrinaire intellectual, he does not attempt to force the facts to fit his theories, but builds his theories out of the living substance and reality around him." The essay is a celebration of process and dynamic growth through the interplay of opposites. That Layton's prose style was too stilted and affected to embody such a theory effectively is not surprising.

As 1941 slid into 1942, the year Layton would turn thirty, he had not resolved his life into any satisfactory unity. He did not like having to choose. As his inscription suggested, he "lived in many worlds." As a result, he seemed to have no centre. The "Notes on Contributors" in the *Forge*[4] present him as a "Graduate Student," the only one among a number of undergraduates. If this was so, it was unofficial. Though Layton sat in on classes he wished to hear at McGill, and continued to read economics and political science (in which the "Notes" said he was pursing an MA with a thesis on Harold Laski), he did not officially enrol in McGill's graduate faculty until 1945, when he took two half-courses ("Contemporary Economic Theory" and "World Economic Survey Since the Great War"), in both of which he received sixty-five per cent.[5] Layton's student-self was an odd one: it tended to become its opposite — that of teacher — with surprising ease. Layton still was a teacher; he tutored privately and gave official classes in the evening at the People's University at the Jewish People's Library where Rochel worked. There, he was considered excellent: patient, sympathetic, dramatic, inspiring. Before his classes (full of people whose immigrant status he well understood and whose painfully limited knowledge of English made them humble and appreciative), he was transformed into a god-like idol.

Another of his "many worlds" was his life with Faye. "Married four years now," the "Notes" describe him, quoting Layton's acerbic comment: "My best ideas come to me at 3 or 4 in the morning, to the great annoyance of my wife." Faye, who continued to work as a book-keeper, had taken an apartment on Prince Arthur Street, conveniently near McGill. When it suited Layton (which seems to have been quite often), he went "home." He had left Faye without really leaving. Relying on her when he needed her, but feeling no commitment to her, he was both "married" and "free." The world that would come later — not to resolve these many worlds into the "one world" he longed for but to "include all the others" — was the world of poetry. But at that moment, it was the least important of his "many worlds." The "Notes" include an interesting sleight-of-hand, for in stating simply that Layton had been a contributor to *Canadian Forum* and *Saturday Night,* the two most prestigious Canadian periodicals of the time, they imply that his contributions were essays like the one in the *Forge.* In fact, they had been poems: "Debacle,"[6] "Beneath The Bridge"[7] and "Providence."[8] All three were unremarkable. Their conventional rhyming four-line stanzas betrayed the fact that Layton had more or less given up reading poetry in favour of his "studies." He had begun attending the evening meetings of McGill's English Literary Society, which offered lectures, but he was not thinking of himself mainly as a poet. But poetry seems to have offered a number of attractions. It was a commendable pursuit for an educated man; it enhanced his status and immediately placed him above the ordinary; it was another vehicle through which to preach political and economic gospels; it satisfied a direct physical pleasure in the manipulation of words whose meanings he loved acquiring and whose sounds thrilled him more; and it was a proven method of courting, attracting and impressing women. Layton's comparison of summer raspberries to nipples and his forthright query about how contemporary world affairs could ever be written about with the same appreciation as the natural beauty described by the romantic poets prefigured things to come. But his most urgent concern was voiced in "Providence":

> With careful fragments do we build our lives
> Unknowing, when the wind moves nearer,
> How a certain governance contrives
> The show before a comic mirror....[9]

Layton was trying to outwit providence. By not choosing

from among his "many worlds," he kept open a dazzling number of options. With an adroitness he had not yet turned to his writing, he eluded every possible category — student, teacher, husband, lover, intellectual, poet — by switching on instinct from one to the other. He could not be "fated" to anything. When he stopped long enough to examine what these "careful fragments" he was building into a life might actually reflect, he feared, or perhaps hoped, that it was all nothing more than "The show before a comic mirror."

The most painful reality of all was the truth, which hardly had a chance to intrude itself as he flipped from one role to another: he was hurting people. So fool-proof was his strategy that he could not see what effect a poem like the one he wrote about Rochel ("To R.E.")[10] might have on her. The poem pictures her as a sort of vampire-nun who exudes an atmosphere of mourning and urges some man to hurry up and sacrifice his freedom for her womanhood by marrying her. To Layton, there was no discrepancy between such sentiments and his affectionate inscription on the *Forge* a few months earlier.

Icons

It was a crisp evening in late fall of 1941 at a lecture of McGill's English Literary Society that Louis Dudek and Irving Layton met. That they were to be chemical elements that precipitated a cultural transformation could not have occurred to them. They simply liked each other.

Dudek was a tall, gangly, bright-faced man, six years younger than Layton. His open expression, alight with enthusiasm for poetry, suggested the vitality of his origins. These were not distinguished: his mother was a Protestant Liverpudlian who had met and married his Catholic Polish father in the working-class district of east-end Montreal. His paternal grandfather had smelted iron in the Ukraine. His father had fled from the poverty of a small store in Warsaw to Montreal, where he had earned enough as a fireman and as a beer delivery-man for Frontenac Breweries Ltd. to put Louis through McGill. Dudek — tall, fair, gentile, rough-mannered — and Layton — burly, dark, Jewish, shrewd — might well have been icons of two vigorous European strands that were now having an impact on Canadian society. Had their families stayed in Europe, they never could have entered a university; it had taken the hard work of only one generation under the favourable skies of Canada's social and political milieu for them to obtain university degrees. More than that, they had acquired sufficient skill in English to attain literary sophistication the equal of any native-born Canadian. Beyond that, they had aspirations to become writers themselves.[1]

Since graduating in 1940, Dudek had succeeded in earning his living as an advertising copy-writer and free-lance journalist. He had much in common with Layton. "We got on like a house afire," Dudek recalls. "We shared so many attitudes, saw exactly the same point of view. It was a matter of class origin." Dudek remembers walking up the hill, talking in an animated way with his new friend, to his apartment with Faye on Prince Arthur Street. "We looked over Layton's copy of what was then the only little collection of modern poetry in Canada, *New Provinces*. We laughed at some of the dinky, avant-guardism poems in there. We said, 'Man, we are going to do something far more radical, more realistic, more relevant than this stuff.' To us, those poems were far too picayune. I always called those poets 'the meticulous modern.'"[2]

Dudek found Layton's marriage to Faye "rather puzzling," but he did not question it. "Faye was in full flower; she was as beautiful as a rose," he observed. "But they were oddly matched as a couple. He was young, bouncy, handsome and a poet. She was dumpy, soft and sentimental. I gathered she was putting him through college."

New Provinces had been edited by A.J.M. Smith and F.R. Scott in 1936.[3] Both poets thought of themselves as decidedly modern, international and daring. Their idea of modern poetry was manifest in their selection: poems by A.M. Klein, Leo Kennedy, Robert Finch, E.J. Pratt and, of course, themselves. The poems ranged from short imagist works in the manner of the American Ezra Pound to satires aimed at the silliness of previous romantic poetry (such as that of Bliss Carman) to social and politically conscious poems in the style of Auden and Spender. Their aims were ambitious. In the preface,[4] Scott outlined the need for more vitality in Canadian poetry. Satisfied that new techniques had been readily available through developments in British and American poetry since the twenties, he argued for more substance in poetry. "The economic depression has released human energies by giving them a positive direction," Scott pointed out. "The poet today shares in this release."

Smith's more controversial theory (not printed until much later) scathingly described Canadian poets of the time as "half-baked, hyper-sensitive" souls out of touch with the realities around them:

> Capitalism can hardly be expected to survive the cataclysm its most interested adherents are blindly steering towards, and the artist who is concerned with the most intense of experiences must be concerned with the world situation in which, whether he likes it or not, he finds himself. For the moment at least he has something more important to do than to record his private emotions. He must try to perfect a technique that will combine power with simplicity and sympathy with intelligence so that he may play his part in developing mental and emotional attitudes that will facilitate the creation of a more practical social system.
>
> Of poetry such as this, there is only the faintest foreshadowing — a fact that is not unconnected with the backwardness politically and economically of Canada — but that Canadian poetry in the future must become increasingly aware of its duty to take cognizance of what is going on in the world of affairs we are sure.[5]

What struck Dudek and Layton as funny was the discrepancy between this philosophy (with which they mainly agreed) and the poems that were meant to illustrate it. The poems definitely showed an awareness of some of the more recent currents of English-language poetry, and were not nearly as effete and parochial as most poetry of the time, but the notion that they embodied "vitality" and were "alive" or did much to further "a more practical social system" seemed absurd. They tittered over the poems in *New Provinces* like adolescents reacting to the earnest efforts of their parents to keep abreast of things.

The contributors to this "first anthology of modern poetry in Canada" were, in some ways, another generation. It was not so much a question of age, though E.J. Pratt at fifty-four really was old enough to have fathered the twenty-four-year-old Layton and his eighteen-year-old friend. The ages of the other contributors ranged from twenty-seven to thirty-seven.

It was more, as Dudek observed, a question of class, and of the attitudes that spring from deeply imbedded experience. Robert Finch, for example, was an American from Long Island who had been educated at the Sorbonne and was teaching seventeenth- and eighteenth-century French poetry at the University of Toronto, where Pratt had been teaching English in Victoria College for years. Leo Kennedy, a protégé of Pratt's, had spent his early childhood in England, graduated in business from the University of Montreal and earned a reputation for being "the sprightly leader of Canada's 'graveyard school' of metaphysical poetry."[6] His models were T.S. Eliot and Sir James Frazer. A.J.M. Smith was the son of English immigrants wealthy enough to provide him with a home in Montreal's prosperous suburb of Westmount, and an education at Cambridge, in England. He was immersed in his MA on Yeats and the symbolist movement at McGill. F.R. Scott, the son of an Anglican clergyman, had been a Rhodes Scholar at Oxford and was teaching law at McGill. Even A.M. Klein, the only Jew and the youngest of the group, seemed a much more elevated figure than either Layton or Dudek. Though he, too, had been brought from the Ukraine as an infant, he was solidly ensconced in the orthodox traditions of his family and earned a good living practising law in downtown Montreal. His temperament was far more like Layton's father's than like Layton's.

These men had all grown up on the wrong side of the class fence to convince men like Dudek and Layton. Their radicalism was intellectual and aesthetic; it had not been forged in the fiery furnace of poverty and strife. Dudek and Layton must have wondered how three university professors, a graduate student, a lawyer and a businessman could understand a thing about the evils of capitalism or the role of the poet in "the creation of a more practical social system" such as Scott had outlined. Their poetry was pitched too high, like their status in society. Art had been for too long the preserve of an aristocratic class. Canada, from the beginning, had come from the peasants of England and Europe, and finally, in Dudek's opinion, the time had come for a voice of a deeper tone, one that was lower down on the social scale, to be heard. But how?

Modernism

Modernism in Canadian poetry had not sprung crisp-imaged into the literary scene of 1936 with *New Provinces*. As early as the first year of the Great War, there had been distinct stirrings: moves to liberate methods and substance. Arthur Stringer, a free-lance journalist, poet and novelist from Chatham, Ontario prefaced his 1914 volume of undistinguished poems with a mandate "to free Canadian poetry from the trammels of end-rhyme."[1] Stringer's mandate was (possibly accidentally) timely, for Ezra Pound's theories of *imagisme* and free verse had been published less than a year before,[2] and free verse still floated in the limbo of experimentation.

By the end of the Great War, altercations between old and new proliferated until they became commonplace in literary journals. In Toronto's *Canadian Bookman*, J.M. Gibbon (who later became president of the Canadian Authors' Association) astutely analysed the strengths and weaknesses of new poets like Pound, Eliot and Sandburg. By comparing the writing of these Americans to an older, characteristically British type of poetry, Gibbon accepted what was becoming increasingly obvious: the Great War had transformed man's perception of the world, and a new kind of artist was expressing the new perception. A year later, F.O. Call prefaced his mediocre volume of poems with a plea for "the rejection of the hackneyed limitations imposed by end-rhyme."[3] Call's rather precious title, *Acanthus and Wild Grape*, and his odd mix of free-verse poems with more traditional forms, do not now seem particularly modern, but for his time they were experimental.

In practice as well as theory, the influence of a unique vision and language had begun to appear. The poems of W.W.E. Ross, Dorothy Livesay and Raymond Knister (all of whom, except Livesay, would remain relatively minor figures on the literary scene) showed traces of what was elsewhere being called "modern." Their work was published in American literary magazines and in the *Canadian Forum* and *Saturday Night*, both of which (but especially the radical *Forum*) were more sophisticated and less conservative than the *Canadian Bookman*.

But modernism crept slowly into the Canadian literary scene. The vast majority of poems written and published during the first quarter of the twentieth century were flowery, insipid romantic lyrics or narrative sagas. These were often competent imitations of the English nineteenth-century tradition from which they derived, but they adopted the mannerisms of their originals without much vigour. Poets usually attempted descriptions of the Canadian landscape and climate in a poetic language and in the controlled forms that had organically risen from the softer climes of the poets they took for models: Wordsworth, Keats, Shelley and Blake. Typical of such poems is "Vestigia" by Bliss Carman, a fey, "aery-faery" rendition of pantheistic yearning:

> I took a day to search for God,
> And found Him not. But as I trod
> By rocky ledge, through woods untamed,
> Just where one scarlet lily flamed,
> I saw his footprint in the sod.[4]

The poem, one of his best-known, was written in 1921 near the end of his career. It illustrates what, for most Canadians, was then the essence of poetry: rhyming lines, a deep response to the beauty of nature, religious belief and a "literary" vocabulary ("trod," "untamed," "flamed"). Archibald

Lampman's poem "Reality," written four years later, in 1925, provides a useful example of how the persistent imitation of nineteenth-century romanticism obscured changes that were taking place in twentieth-century Canada:

> I stand at noon upon the heated flags
> At the bleached crossing of two streets, and dream
> With brain scarce conscious now the hurrying stream
> Of noonday passengers is done. Two hags
> Stand at an open doorway piled with bags
> And jabber hideously. Just at their feet
> A small, half-naked child screams in the street,
> A blind man yonder, a mere hunch of rags,
> Keeps the scant shadow of the eaves, and scowls,
> Counting his coppers. Through the open glare
> Thunders an empty wagon, from whose trail
> A lean dog shoots into the startled square,
> Wildly resolves and soothes his hapless tail,
> Piercing the noon with intermittent howls.[5]

Though Lampman records how the "reality" of poverty, starvation and suffering intrudes itself on his romantic stance as a detached dreamer, he presents it without comment in traditional sonnet form. To him, it is merely a colourful spectacle. He does not betray any sympathy for the sufferers, nor does he acknowledge that there may be something amiss in a political and social system in which such a scene can occur. It is tempting to see Layton (who was still very young at the time Lampman wrote the poem) in that "small, half-naked child." As long as poetry remained the preserve of a privileged, educated class, squalour would remain picturesque, part of a literary convention of ugly, sometimes comical rustics, buffoons and riff-raff. What would happen when the poor acquired a voice?

It was with the Newfoundlander E.J. Pratt that a new voice began to be heard in Canada. His first book of poems appeared in 1923, between the publication of Carman's "Vestigia" and Lampman's "Reality." Temperamentally, Pratt was not a romantic. He grew up on the coast, so he knew how destructive nature could be. He responded to it with firm admiration and respect rather than with soft dreaminess. But despite his experimentation with free verse, Pratt was not really a modern. His long, muscular sagas (*The Titanic, The Witches' Brew, Brébeuf and his Brethren*) and his shorter ballads and lyrics followed the pattern of epic poems or the more intellectual works of the nineteenth century. He sought to reconcile deeply held religious beliefs (he was trained and had practised briefly as a Methodist minister) with the advances of science and technology he encountered as a student of behavioural psychology.

But modernism would arise in an urban setting, not in a Newfoundland outport. It would take account of and express social realities that were a tangible part of every-day life. Though poverty no doubt stalked the paths of coastal villages in Canada, only a few people were poor, or the entire community was poor. In the cities, people were poor by class. Only in urban centres were there sufficient numbers of people for the effects of post-war industrialization to slice society into visible compartments.

Though they were not the first to notice, the intellectuals were the first to speak. On 8 October 1924, as twelve-year-old Layton was entering his last year at Alexandra Street School, A.J.M. Smith began editing a special "Literary Supplement" to the *McGill Daily*. Smith, an undergraduate in his last year, had to fight for his literary interests. He had let down his parents by failing most of the Cambridge local examinations (he passed English and history) and "wasting" his time haunting English book-stores and reading the new war poets and imagists. After graduating from Westmount High School, he was on his way to a university degree. But it was a science degree; their choice, not his. His "Literary Supplement" for the *McGill Daily* was an outlet for what really interested him: the creation of a literary sophistication such as the one he had directly experienced when he was in England. The supplement, which featured some of Smith's poems and called for a new kind of poetry that would incorporate symbolism and myth, folded in March at the end of the school year. Smith graduated in science and turned full-time to his poetic interests, enrolling in the MA programme in English.

Before his classes started in the fall, he met Frank Scott,

who had just returned from Oxford to study law, and asked him to co-edit the "Supplement" for the next school year. Leon Edel, later famous for his massive and perceptive biography of Henry James, was entering his junior year in arts at McGill. He remembers Scott in the fall of 1925 as a "tall, angular young man, who with uncommon use of words and a brilliant and often searching gleam in his eye, confronted, and...no doubt affronted, Montreal."[6] Scott, Edel recalled, had a crucial part to play as the literary group's "pipeline to respectability."[7] When McGill, under the principalship of the former head of Canada's wartime army, General Sir Arthur Currie (who "thought of McGill as a kind of military backwater after Vimy Ridge and Mons"[8]), was a Victorian "semi-soldiery," Scott negotiated the supplement through the waters of imminent censorship. Though Smith intended to continue the *McGill Daily* "Literary Supplement" in the fall of 1925, an uneasy student council refused to vote the publication funds. Out of these ashes rose the *McGill Fortnightly Review*, a financially solvent outlet for Marxist observations and modern poetry. Scott's prestigious family, his recent education at Oxford, his legal aspirations and his tendency to express his deeply felt socialism in a light, tongue-in-cheek manner made him an effective ambassador. He struck a tone that convinced Currie that the *McGill Fortnightly Review* was mere undergraduate exuberance and not serious political activism.

In fact, Scott's defense of the freedom of undergraduate speech in the red-carpeted, mahogany-furnished chamber of Currie's office ushered in a new era of Canadian poetry. In the *McGill Fortnightly Review*, Scott published his satiric attack on the trivial Victorianism of the Canadian Authors' Association, using T.S. Eliot's "The Hollow Men" as a model. "What academic literary review on the entire North American continent," Edel asks, "could boast in the mid-twenties of an article on *The Waste Land* (by Smith), or a brilliant parody of Gertrude Stein (by Scott), or a piece on Joyce (by himself)? We were modern in the *Fortnightly* long before Edmund Wilson put the moderns together in *Axel's Castle* and the avant-garde became a subject of respectable study in academe. We also had articles on Canadian politics by

Eugene Forsey, the future senator, on trade unionism by Allan Latham, and a wide variety of reviews and discussions of politics and the arts."[9] The *Fortnightly* folded on 27 April 1927 with the graduation of its contributors, who believed that it was up to the next wave of students to forge their own magazine according to their own political and aesthetic lights.

After teaching briefly in a Montreal high school, Smith was off to Edinburgh on a fellowship towards the Ph.D. he would receive in 1931 on the metaphysical poets of the Anglican Church in the seventeenth century. Scott, who became a member of the Montreal law firm Lafleur, McDougall, Macfarlane and Barclay, started up a new magazine, the *Canadian Mercury*, with Louis Schwartz, who later founded the American Abelard Press, and Leo Kennedy. The magazine's colophon pictured a plump, naked Mercury thumbing his nose at — to judge from the magazine's contents during the few months of its existence — Victorianism and Canadian parochialism, the old guard of that insufferable garrison mentality Northrop Frye would later describe. In December 1928, in an essay called "The Future of Canadian Literature," Kennedy pled fervently for the rescue of Canadian letters from "its present affliction of infantile paralysis." He attacked the CAA as "a pillar of flim-flam." He agreed with S.I. Hayakawa that "The bulk of poems written in Canada, may be briefly classified under four heads. They are, Victorian, Neo-Victorian, Quasi-Victorian, and Pseudo-Victorian."[10]

The stock-market crash of 1929 ushered in an era in which Smith's, Scott's and Kennedy's views converged with the ideas of society at large. Because Montreal was the centre of Canada's economic life, it was inevitable that the crash and the Depression that followed it would have a profound effect on the city. Observations, like Scott's from the mid-twenties, that the rich were exploiting the poor and, in all the splendour of their Christianity, stood indifferent to the suffering they could have helped, seemed prophetic. What had sounded like mere book-learning, abstract intellectual debate, had become the grim reality of mass unemployment, starvation and revolt. Layton had glimpsed Scott at meetings of the Young People's Socialist League in the thirties: "He didn't strike me as true or sincere," he recalls of the man whose attention had turned quite dramatically from poetry to constitutional law. "He seemed aristocratic." No matter how dedicated Scott may have been to the emancipation of the oppressed, he never could have appealed to a man like Layton, who was a valid spokesman for revolution because he had been born into the class that was being exploited. As Leonard C. Marsh's *Canadians In and Out of Work* (1940) reveals, the Depression hit Montreal Jews especially hard, because the kinds of employment (mainly skilled, clerical and managerial) they had typically undertaken were among those soonest lost.[11] While Scott enjoyed credibility as a socialist (as his career illustrated), Layton and some of the members of his family were among those who had lost jobs and starved. By the early forties, partly because of the steady self-improvement of the new waves of immigrants who had arrived a generation before and partly because the Depression had acted as a great leveller in society, bringing the classes in Canadian society much closer to each other, the modern movement in poetry had reached the point of what Louis Dudek was to call "cell-division."[12] One set of aesthetic theories could not contain a Frank Scott and an Irving Layton.

In the spring of 1942, six months after he had befriended Layton, Dudek had boldly taken some of his own poems to show Doctor Harold Files, professor (later chairman) of the department of English at McGill. Files referred Dudek to one of the undergraduates from his creative-writing class who showed exceptional promise, John Sutherland. Excited at finding another "modernist," Dudek sent Layton along to meet John, too. Sutherland was the catalyst who would transform the separate elements represented by Dudek and Layton into a new, potent "cell" of modernism, one that was international by birth, leftist as the result of direct experience, rebellious and vital of necessity.

War

On 15 July 1942, Irving Peter Layton enlisted in the Royal Canadian Artillery in Montreal. Two weeks later he officially was given the rank of provisional second lieutenant and sent immediately to Brockville. On his Officer's Declaration Paper, he lists himself as "Married" to Mrs. Faye Layton (LYNCH) and living at her address, 538 Prince Arthur Street West, Montreal. He describes his profession as "Physical Instructor & Lecturer, Literature & Science, Jewish University, Montreal 1 Year" and "Private Tutor." He entered his religious denomination: "Unitarian."[1]

Why Layton should suddenly decide to join the Canadian active service is puzzling. He had frequently stated in his writings that he was a pacifist. He had showed no interest in serving the Allied cause by enlisting when war broke out in 1939, nor did his knowledge that European Jews were being persecuted previously elicit this response (though it did elicit much moral outrage in print). As a public supporter of left-wing politics, he must have thought the army represented everything he most despised.

In his short story "A Game of Chess" (1944), based on his experience in the army where his brother Hyman soon joined him (though not as an officer), Layton reports a conversation between two brothers:

"You enlisted because Russia was attacked. Isn't that the reason?" David stared for a moment at his brother as if he were trying to recollect something and then said vehemently:

"Yes, of course! Before the Soviets got into it, this war was just another filthy imperialist swindle. Same as the last one. A bloody scramble for markets, for cheap labour and big profits."

"And what about the unemployed? The war was sprung to kill them off. You forgot to add that one, David."

"Very, very clever... it's still a good explanation. Do you know a better one? What about the Depression? There was no money then. But there's lots now, eh. Everyone is working. Why? Just answer me that one!"

"I'm a soldier," Ben smiled, "not a speech-maker. That's your department."

"To hell with you! It's morons like you that have gotten us into this mess. Sure, you'll do your duty all right. But ask you to think — that's too hard. It's much easier to die nobly, isn't it brother?"

Ben filled his pipe carefully and lit it....

Then, more softly and as if he were explaining to an invisible audience, [David] said: "Big words don't fool anyone. You're found out eventually... Hell, Ben, can't you guess?"

Startled, Ben looked up.

"Guess what?"

It was as though one of the chessmen had spoken.

"I couldn't make her suffer anymore. When I told her I wanted to break the engagement she cried. I tried to explain myself to her, but it was too late. Anyhow she wouldn't listen. She just kept crying hysterically and her eyes became swollen and I hated her because I pitied her and because she made me make her suffer...

"But maybe I did love her. Maybe I loved her without knowing it.... Hell, I'm all mixed up."

...David went on as if in a trance:

"There was nothing left between us except her suffering. She'd begin to cry after I had humiliated her and her tears would make me pity her. Then I'd take her in my arms and feel happy such a warm bond existed between us." David pulled his lips into an ugly ironic grimace. "Real love and sympathy. Yah....

"Do you see now why I enlisted?"

"I even thought myself a superior person because I had those feelings. What was the truth? I was a sentimental weakling in the grip of a ruthless bitch bent on having me fertilize her ovaries. What a farce! Did I say I loved her? Listen carefully.... I loathed her for being too ugly and insensitive to permit me to go on playing my role to the end."

"What role? I don't understand," Ben said.

David looked at his brother incredulously. "Didn't I explain? I guess I didn't. I imagined myself some kind of glorious saviour to the unmarriageable, the crippled.... You know how hideous she was."[2]

Though Layton renames his characters and reverses the usual family chess winner and loser (making himself, instead of Hyman, the habitual winner), he admits that David's reasoning about his fiancé, Bella, is "very close to what was going on in my mind about my wife Faye at the time I joined the army."[3] Layton's brother Hyman confirms this theory: "My brother joined the army to escape from Faye."[4]

It is difficult to imagine anyone less suited to military discipline than Irving Layton. As a letter to A.J.M. Smith, asking to have some of his poems included in Smith's forthcoming anthology *The Book of Canadian Poetry*, reveals, he thought his training in the physics and mathematics of radio and television was so much nonsense. "When I Kill a Nazi," he wrote to Smith from the officers' mess in Kingston, "it will be by a close application of the Sine Curve multiplied by $\tan \frac{0\sqrt{(1-x)^2}}{cr^2 (a-b)}$ or some such intricate formula like that... I hope the censor doesn't become suspicious and think I'm giving away valuable military information."[5] George Edelstein, who arrived in February at Camp Petawawa where Layton had been transferred after six months in Brockville and a few days in Kingston, thought him "strange."[6]

He suffered from a peculiar type of military absentmindedness. After the first rifle practice he was shunned on the firing range for he had fired into other targets on either side of his — which was untouched. We were also in constant danger for he would drag his loaded rifle unconcernedly on the ground.

On "Shoots", when he was troop commander in charge of the firing orders for the 25 pounders, a deathly silence would descend on the area. Everyone had taken cover while grim-faced senior officers glared and N.C.O.'s cursed. When the last round had been fired, and the Observation Party recalled — they displayed an understandable reluctance to leave their bunker during Layton's command — we would celebrate our "baptism by fire". Despite his military failings, he was quite popular for he was always cheerful and willing to assume extra duties.

Then the new buildings were ready and we moved in, two officers to a room. Irving Layton, our "reader", and I were assigned to the same cubicle. Immediately we found that we had certain things in common. My pipe tobacco, for instance — I bought it and he smoked most of it in large-bowled pipes; Montreal was our home town and both of us had attended McGill University.

He was an interesting companion, after I made certain allowances for some of his peculiarities. Time meant nothing to him. After a night out I would literally stagger in and collapse on the bed; then he was ready to start a discussion about his current reading. My entreaties to turn out the light were useless. He would murmur "Soon, soon," and continue talking — smoking constantly. I solved this problem by learning to sleep in a fog-like atmosphere, in a lighted room. The worst period was during his bout with Marcel Proust. It took him about two weeks and to this day I refuse to read *Remembrance of Things Past*.

That summer I went overseas. I remember him walking with me to the final assembly. Gunners, with their heavy kit bags on their shoulders, marched across the earthen parade ground, their boots swirling the sand and distorting their shapes in the sunlight. He looked at them and said: "They don't even look like men any more."[7]

"I was the only officer that was interested in talking about the source of the war — the national socialists, Hitler, why we were fighting," Layton recalls. "I made myself an eccentric. My brother officers, who spent most of their time drinking rum and Coke in the mess, used to taunt and bait me. But I took their measure quickly. They were stupid. All they wanted was to stay comfortable, ignorant and untroubled."[8]

The Hat-Check Girl

In late November 1942, Irving Layton was in Montreal on leave from Camp Petawawa when he heard that "someone as cuckoo as you"[1] was the cashier at the Venus Restaurant on St. Catherine Street.[2] "You should just see her," his sister-in-law, a waitress at the Venus Restaurant, told Layton. "She sits there reading Trotsky's *The History of the Russian Revolution* and sketching the people who come in and out. Her name is Betty Sutherland."

The name registered. It didn't take Irving long to discover that Betty was the sister of John Sutherland, the poet at McGill. John, stung with bitterness when some of his poems had been rejected by *Preview*, a literary magazine begun by F.R. Scott and Patrick Anderson[3] in March 1942, had just begun a mimeographed rival publication, *First Statement*, and predicted that "almost everyone is a potential critic of this magazine."[4] The publication sounded like a likely outlet for Layton's controversial writings. He telephoned Betty and made an appointment to meet her and show her some of his poems.

He tilted his military cap to a jaunty angle and marched briskly through the cold over to her room in a large boarding house on Stanley Street. Finding the door unlocked, he strode in. Her room was empty. He waited impatiently, pacing back and forth in front of the large window, anticipating with pleasure the impact he felt sure he and his poetry would make.

It was not long before Betty arrived, wearing an old racoon coat from the Salvation Army. No one had told him she was the most beautiful woman alive! And working at the Venus Restaurant! He chuckled. She looked like Barbara Stanwyck — no — Ingrid Bergman...that was it![5] Blonde and serene, she disarmed him. He rose to his feet, stretched out his hands and embraced her.

Later, in the coffee shop of the Ford Hotel on Dorchester Street, he sat opposite her and read his poetry, glancing up as often as possible to fix his eyes on hers. "The poetry he read that first day was awful," Betty recalls. "It absolutely stank. It was too conscious of politics. It had terrible rhymes. There was no heart to it. I had read Louis Dudek's stuff by then and loved it. When I told Irving what I thought, he was taken aback. He saw I was going to be a hard nut to crack."[6]

Betty and John Sutherland had drifted to Montreal from Lockeport, Nova Scotia by separate routes. Their father, Fred, was a prosperous travelling salesman, a man with wonderful appetites and a jolly nature occasionally disrupted by jowl-shaking tempers. Their mother was artistic, a contralto who loved playing their grand piano, telling stories and drawing. Tuberculosis had claimed her too soon in 1926 when John was seven and Betty six. Immediately after her mother's death, Betty began to paint. The two children became close through loss, then drew even closer when their father remarried in 1930. They perceived Dorothy McNicol, their new stepmother, as "neurotic, strict and hating children."[7] Before long there were three more children, one of whom was Donald Sutherland, later to become a prominent actor and film-star, but by then, Betty and John had turned elsewhere for fulfilment: John to literature and philosophy, Betty to art. From 1932 to 1940, she studied painting in St. John, New Brunswick under Millar Brittain and others. John had gone to Queen's University in 1936. At the end of that academic year, he was sent back to Lockeport to recuperate from tuberculosis of the kidney, which had developed after an athletic injury.[8] He never recovered fully, and his slow convalescence in a household where he did not feel loved brought Betty to his side. As much as she could, Betty nursed him for four years in Lockeport during holidays and between art-school terms. "We became very, very close," she recalls. In 1941, against the doctor's express orders, John left Lockeport to enrol in English at McGill, supporting himself by working as a night clerk in the Simcoe Hotel at the bottom of Peel Street. Betty went to New York to study painting at the Art Students League. Lonely and unable to find a job, she joined John in Montreal in July 1942, at almost the same time Irving was enlisting in the army.

"I was ripe for the picking," Betty observes. "I had come to Montreal instead of going home because I was twenty-two and it was about time to begin to live. I had had a few escapades — most recently, a boyfriend who had told me that he was separated and living with his mother. I had just realized he was married and not separated." Despite her opinion of Irving's poetry, she fell in love with him. "We had common interests. We were equal: he wrote and I drew. Although I thought his poetry was shit, I believed I could help him improve it. I was drawn to him because he was fascinating. He has a fascinating face to draw."

From December 1942, Layton took as many weekend leaves as possible. In the train station at Montreal, two women were always waiting for him: Betty — blonde, lithe and gentile — and Faye — dark, heavy and Jewish. "She was huge, probably 350 pounds, but she had a beautiful face, a madonna face with rosy lips," Betty recalls of the woman who spurred black jealousy in her heart. "She would stand there, waiting for Irving to get off the train, looking daggers at me. I can still picture him stepping off the train, so handsome and slim in his uniform. He would start towards me, then veer towards her, then back towards me, back and forth until he had to choose."[9]

Here and Now

At some point during the first two months of 1943, the colourful kaleidoscope of Irving Layton's life took a sudden twist. For the first time, poetry took precedence over all his other "many worlds." Partly, he could not bear to hear Betty Sutherland praise Dudek's poetry and damn his. With intense competitiveness, he set about reversing her views. Louis had begun writing tough, clenched little imagist poems in the manner of Pound. Irving studied these carefully. What did Dudek have that he didn't? It had been one thing to sneer over *New Provinces* with him almost a year before; it was quite another to replace the poetry of what Louis had called those "meticulous moderns" with something more punchy, more down-to-earth. Mainly, Layton struggled to impress Betty. He must write something she would admire. She was angelically beautiful. She was *zaftig*. He must have her.

"Some of the poems he sent me from Camp Petawawa were really good, quite unlike the stuff he first showed me,"[1] Betty recalls. She was particularly impressed with "Drill Shed," a free-verse imagist poem that incorporated scientific images, like Eliot's in *The Love Song of J. Alfred Prufrock*, to undercut its romanticism:

> The passive motion of sand

> Is fluid geometry. Fir needles
> Are the cool, select thoughts
> Of madmen; and
> Like a beggar the wind wheedles
> Pine cones from the pines.
> Inside there's no violence,
> Only the silence
> Of an empty church;
> Drilled zygotes shift
> From foot to foot or lurch
> With half-closed eyes against the guns
> While the ackeye shows
> With delphic joy
> The deeper things a dial sight knows;
> Curious now,
> I marvel how
> Lord Euclid's dream
> Can stiffen a boy.[2]

Instead of complaining directly as he had in "Debacle" about the impossibility of tackling romantic subjects like beauty and truth in a modern era gone mad with mechanical megalomania, Layton deftly incorporated modern cynicism into his poem. His allusions to "delphic joy" and "an empty church" were not watered-down romanticism; they were bitterly ironic. The modern marvel he describes tongue-in-cheek is the "romance" of technology: the perverse power of science and technology to "stiffen a boy." The poem's sexual overtness and unusual vocabulary ("zygotes" and "ackeye") are characteristically "modern," but they are also characteristically Layton. Coming from a background where the most basic facts of life were omnipresent and savouring, as he had for years, the sound, taste and texture of odd English words, he was perfectly situated to express some of the new freedoms modernists had fought for. It had taken only Betty's scorn for his traditionally romantic and philosophical rhymed poems to prod him into a more contemporary ironic stance. Though he did not comprehend it then, the tenets of modern poetry proffered the ideal way to resolve the domestic conflict he had experienced as a child. In poems like

"Drill Shed," he could hold in ironic suspension the dreamy otherworldliness of his reverent father and the scathing satire that poured from his mother.

Betty's praise for the poems he was writing was a heady aphrodisiac. It gave him an image of himself he could esteem, that of a powerful and persuasive poet who could elbow his way into the Anglo-Saxon establishment he had first admired in the English boys' magazines of his adolescence. The blue-eyed, fair-haired Sutherlands must have seemed like denizens of an artistic heaven from which he had felt excluded for years. They presented him with concrete criteria for a success he had vaguely sensed for some time. If he had to write ironic poetry to gain romantic bliss with Betty, and publication in *First Statement* with John, he would do so. He could assume, he thought, any persona at all.

Layton's passionate and determined pursuit of Betty forced him to make a choice. He would have to abandon Faye and his role as husband. Though he was ambivalent about her for a time after meeting Betty, his thoughts eventually became clear. She represented one of his many worlds that must, indeed should, be discarded. He saw her as the representative of everything from which he longed to escape: middle-class values of financial stability; the unenlightened ignorance of his own Jewish lower-class family; the smothering comfort of a food-centred woman; and, most of all, in her demand that he father a family, the hated Life Force that Shaw so insightfully had revealed in women. Life with Betty would be of a higher order altogether. They would embark on a bohemian adventure spiced with sex and oblivious to worldly values. As an artist, she, too, valued freedom; she would not pressure him into marriage or demand that he make money. Certainly, she would not want a child.

It was not long before he took Betty to the poetry readings at Frank and Marian Scott's home in lower Westmount. Now he, like Frank, would have a woman who was a painter. He could belong to the very group that wanted to snub him. Marian Scott, who was becoming an artist of note, remembers Irving and Betty arriving at 451 Clarke Street to join the group of poets who gathered from time to time to read poems to each other. "Irving was in uniform. He struck me as quiet and deferential, though a bit surly. Betty was very beautiful, an earth-mother kind of woman. I remember her settling down on the floor like a mushroom. Irving would drop his satchel in the hall when he came in, but eventually someone would ask if he had brought any poems and he would go and get some and read. He was really on the fringe of the group. Once, Faye rang up about 4 AM asking where Irving was long after he'd left."[3]

Faye was determined not to lose Irving. He had left her before and come back. Surely he would tire of this new *shiksa* who was, after all, a gentile. But, as long as he was in the army, she could not keep track of his whereabouts. She would do what she could to get him discharged. According to Betty, with whom Irving was spending most of his leaves, Faye contacted army officials and informed them that Irving was a Communist, telling them to check the files Irving said had been assembled during his outspoken years at Macdonald College.[4] The RCMP paid a call to Eugene Forsey, asking if he knew where Layton was. "I didn't, and I said so," recalls Forsey, "adding that I'd be grateful if the officer, if he found him, would tell him (ask him, rather) to come and see me, as he was behind his work, and I had not laid eyes on him for some considerable time." Forsey was surprised to find the RCMP looking for Layton. "My impression of him, politically, was that he was a Marxist Socialist, but not a Communist: too much of an individualist to conform to party discipline.... He gave me a book by some Marxist thinker, probably Sidney Hook."[5] It is likely that Layton was already on the point of being asked to leave the army because of his conspicuous incompetence, as he maintains.[6] Indeed, he deliberately may have exacerbated army officials at Petawawa so that he could be released to live with Betty and begin an exhilarating new life as a modern poet. On 12 June 1943, after only eleven months in the army, he received an honourable discharge.

Betty was not entirely pleased. "I was worried when Irving dumped himself in my lap," she recalls. "I had liked the idea of a lover who would disappear from time to time. He had an oppressive ego and it had always been a relief when he left. Whenever he wrote a poem, he had to read it out loud to me at once. Having him around every day was too much. I was pretty independent and wanted to be left alone most of the time to paint."

Betty's father was irate when he heard that she had taken up with a Jew. He made a special visit to Montreal in the summer of 1943 to talk her out of it. As if to create a confrontation, Layton made sure his army suitcase — with his name on it — was visible under her bed. In the dispute that followed, Betty stood up to her father. Indeed, as is often the case in such matters, his reprisals drove her closer to her lover. As for Layton's family, they were equally distressed. How could he leave Faye? She was such a nice, long-suffering (and wage-earning) Jewish girl. He must get over his madness and go back to her, start a family. He was thirty-one and behaving as if he were three. Faye would never allow a divorce, and they didn't blame her. Keine swore that Betty would never be admitted to her apartment. But Betty was just as pleased about Layton's Jewishness as he was about her being gentile. "Because of Hitler and the war generally, I had strong feelings about the Jews," she observes. "I wanted to show that I was not prejudiced. Loving Irving, I felt as if I were making up for the awful things that had happened. I still feel constant to their race."[7]

Before Layton was discharged from the army, he published a few poems in John Sutherland's *First Statement*. From the outset, he demonstrated a shrewd sense of salesmanship, for a number of these poems had already been published in the *McGill Daily* and elsewhere.[8] Sutherland, who seems not to have realized he was recycling Layton's poems, lavished praise on his friend, whose left-wing politics he had begun to admire and absorb. "Here is a stanza from an unpublished[9] poem by Irving Layton, called 'Restaurant De Luxe,'" he wrote in an article called "Three New Poets," about Kay Smith, Louis Dudek and Irving Layton:

> For this one moved her silver knife
> To cut each bramble from her life,
> And this one had a wondrous spoon
> With which she ladled out the moon.

> The use of the moon for fantasy and the clear-cut images are reminiscent of Miss [Kay] Smith. Both poets have a moral interest and this urge to find the symbol. Layton, perhaps, speaks with more directness and masculine vigor as in "Day." He may write a pure description of nature, such as "Vigil," but his personality is not so deeply involved in the web. He writes a poem, still complex and mysterious, in which nature symbols are largely absent. "Providence" seems to contain the seeds of a personal mysticism, and, if one remembers his Hebraic inheritance, it appears possible that this strain in his poetry will develop with time.
>
> Layton bears some resemblance to Abraham Klein. Both have a love of romantic beauty, coloured by the poetry of the Old Testament; both have a satirist's pleasure in the affairs of human beings. But whereas Klein was engaged in unearthing relics of forgotten personalities, Layton only mentions the rabbi in passing....
>
> Layton's interest is in politics, and this frequently shows itself in his poetry. "Say it Again, Brother," soon to be published in *ALERT*, is reminiscent of Sandburg, but has more vigor and a more consistent poetry than other poems of this kind. "Obstacle Course" is a fusion of the two interests: fantasy is coupled with vigorous criticism....
>
> Here are three poets, not lacking in imagination or intellectual power, who are producing work that is much more honest and wholesome than that of our modernist school. What they write is essentially readable, and it is valid and real as poetry.[10]

The diversity of Sutherland's praise of Layton's work indicates the extent to which Layton was experimenting at the time. Sutherland drew attention to the mutually contradictory elements of "masculine vigor" and "fantastic invention;" "realistic political satire" and "Hebraic mysticism;" "clear-cut imagism" and "love of romantic beauty." Layton was a man for all critics. Despite Betty's criticisms, he had not yet found his voice. Indeed, since he had no qualms about re-publishing poems he had written as much as five years before, he didn't seem to have taken seriously her criticisms of his earlier work. It is probable that he had no clear idea what he wanted to write, what stance he wished to adopt or how he wanted to express himself. It wasn't clear that he thought of himself as a poet. His most coherent and original efforts in those early issues of *First Statement* were the short stories he had started writing during his years at Macdonald College. The first to appear, "The Parasite"[11] (about his stay at the Cusinières') drew an intense stream of abuse from poet Patrick Waddington, the husband of Miriam Waddington, in April 1943, when Layton joined the editorial board of *First Statement*. Waddington was the first critic to sound a note that would be repeated throughout Layton's career: the "critical" condemnation that is really a virulent personal attack:

> This [story] was so vulgar as to demand condemnation. The very title is in the worst vein of self-exhibitionism and poor taste. If you wish, you may boast of a vice, but you cannot expect a reader to be unduly interested.
> But for the rest of the picture — one smiles at the double debasing-and-flattering portrait of the dreamer, the poet, the much-loved, the burdened by art speaker who is made welcome for his beaux yeux and charm at the house of the two sisters.
> '"There now, eat, you good-for-nothing," she clucked noisily.'
> Oh, that picture — culled from how many forgotten stories and adolescent images of the poor but beloved poet! Made to eat by his luckier but intellectually inferior admirers. I cannot believe in him. I cannot believe in the tale of poverty, of hunger and despair, nor that he believed himself a parasite; that he would not indignantly deny the charge made by another. Not, certainly, because such a thing is not extremely likely. Not because I cannot believe that the matter is true. But we are not speaking of material truth, we are speaking of artistic, of literary validity. In literature the experience is nothing if the meaning and the expression are not there. A man may have all kinds of unusual experiences, but if they mean little to him they mean nothing to us; if they mean a

distortion to him they mean an irritation to us. But if he interprets life anew for us, it is everything and everything may be forgiven.

Truth may be found anywhere and lies anywhere. In Mr. Layton's story the facts are undoubtedly true. But who cares? — for the thought, the feeling, the conclusion are all false. To get a meaning from this incident he stretches out his feelings painfully, exaggerates, perverts, exhibits and deceives himself and attempts to deceive the reader. The result is not sympathy of [sic] surprise or pity — but shame. Shame for the speaker.

Why? Partly because Mr. Layton is speaking of himself. The extension of emotion which is permissable in the third person is not in the first; it is too close to us. It is like a man pushing his face into yours when he talks to you. Involuntarily you turn your face aside. But Mr. Layton gives us no relief. Alas, like an old farceur, an unnatural exposer of himself, he has not learned the dignity of privacy, the strength of restraint. He neither laughs nor condemns himself, nor is impartial, but loves, pities, caresses and admires that person whom he shows us.

Bad art is a departure from truth; truth in art is not material but moral. We do not have to believe in Don Quixote charging the windmills to know what Cervantes intends. It is here Mr. Layton has lost himself.[12]

Waddington's vehemence may have sprung from jealousy of John Sutherland, for Waddington's wife, Miriam, had become close to Sutherland. Betty remembers once when her brother bicycled all the way from Montreal to Toronto and back just to see her. ("It was the summer of 1943, I think, when he borrowed that bicycle. I can picture him still as he looked when he returned: tanned, lovely-looking, cigar in hand.")[13] Layton may have seemed to Waddington too closely associated with the Sutherlands. More likely, Waddington was simply repelled by the characteristics that made Layton such a prime candidate for a place in the literary scene of the time: his outspoken vulgarity. The irrationality of some of Waddington's arguments, the vagueness of his aesthetic theories and the angry tone of his remarks suggest that he could not tolerate that boisterous, calling-a-spade-a-spade voice from lower down on the social scale. Boors like Layton, he concluded, could not and should not attempt literary endeavours. They should cultivate "restraint."

For Betty, Layton wholeheartedly did what he had done only sporadically for Faye. Undertaking a series of menial jobs — as "bus-boy, waiter, salesman, clerk, boxing instructor, proof-reader, and lecturer,"[14] by his own account — he did his best to earn some money. Betty, meanwhile, continued to work as a cashier in restaurants like the Oxford Hotel & Grill, Diana Grill and Schnapp's which, by her description, were "mostly deserted." "I never worked in a classy place," she recalls. Their real work was Art. Betty painted and sketched in their threadbare apartment over the Junior League of Montreal Superfluity Shop on University Street. Irving continued to write. His closest associates were Louis Dudek and John Sutherland, who continued to publish his poems and stories in *First Statement*, convinced that Layton had the makings of a great literary figure: "He and Louis sparked each other in those days,"[15] Betty recalls. Dudek remembers a famous meeting between the two of them that expressed the excitement and visionary sense of future greatness they shared: "We walked along Jacques Cartier Bridge one cool summer's evening to a spot out over the river where we could look back to the lights of St. Catherine Street. We spoke of poetry and our future so positively. We believed we each had a great career ahead."[16]

In 1945, *First Statement* began its New Writers chapbook series on the printing press Sutherland had bought in 1943. Layton's book was first in the series. Its title, *Here and Now*,[17] threw down the gauntlet to the "meticulous moderns," to critics like Waddington and to the world at large. These poems, the book's title implied, were not weak imitations of previous poetry, nor were they effete and aristocratic. In a society levelled by the Depression, a new voice announced itself. It could not have been heard even a decade earlier. It was, in Layton's opinion (and Dudek's and Sutherland's), the voice of "here" and "now."

Layton comically undermined the usual pretentiousness of

authors introducing themselves to the public. The volume's fly-leaf said he had begun to write poetry "at an early age to defend himself from bored, underpaid and incompetent teachers," and alludes to the "Marxist outlook" he gained from his experiences. Oddly, considering his refusal to father a family (backed by Shaw's theories of women as naturally predatory), he describes himself as having "a great love for children and a frustrated desire to like their parents." Perhaps the child he most had in mind was himself; the parents, his own.

Judging from all this scaffolding, *Here and Now* ought to have been a landmark in Canadian poetry. With an ambivalence that was prophetic, it was and it wasn't. The thirty-two poems are a puzzling mixture of old and new, skilled and unskilled, imaginative and pedestrian. An anthropologist reading the volume in a vacuum would have difficulty classifying the author. Was he middle or upper class, as the sedate, free-verse poem "Mortuary"[18] might suggest? Or was he lower class, as "Mother, This Is Spring,"[19] in which the poor decry the rich, would indicate? Was he an intellectual, as in "Spinoza,"[20] or a street-wise realist, as in "Waterfront"?[21] Was he a traditionalist, expressing his originality by reworking archaic poetic forms, as the eighteenth-century "Epitaph For A Wit"[22] implied? Or was he an extremely up-to-date modernist, as his awkward, rhyming parody of Auden, "The Modern Poet,"[23] claimed? He might be Jewish, yet some poems took an agnostic or even anarchic stance. A literary critic would find traces of A.M. Klein, T.S. Eliot, Walt Whitman, John Donne, the Bible, Keats, Shelley, Blake, Byron, Shakespeare and Pope as well as Auden. Some poems were as spare and angular as a skeleton; others were as florid and expansive as a rug from Bessarabia. Saccharine sentimentality stalked these pages, but so, too, did an authentic depth of feeling. Some were forced and tortured; others quite surprisingly felicitous. Reading these poems is like looking at those children's books that invite you to mix and match the heads, limbs and bodies of a series of figures: the clown's head with the devil's tail on a dragon's midriff. Their effect is bizarre, sometimes absurd, almost surrealistic. Best among them are ironic poems like "Drill Shed," which Betty had so liked, poems that yoked sentimentality neck-and-neck to bitter anger, and a couple of poems written in the summer of 1944 in which Layton drew on the unique milieu of his childhood with a mixture of shrewd, tough observation and bittersweet nostalgia. The best of these is "De Bullion Street," notorious as Montreal's red-light district when Layton was a child. The poem appeared in *First Statement* in March 1944:

> Below this broad street inverted bell-jars
> Hanging from wooden crucifixes drop
> Tiny moons upon the shaven asphalt;
> Rouged whores lean lips to narrow slits: they stop
> The young soldier with his bag of salt.
>
> Under the night's carapace, the soft lanes
> Are listening ears where sudden footfall
> Starts a choir of echoes. A red light winks
> Viciously; and the wind's occasional
> Sigh lifts from the garbage pails their stinks.
>
> Here private lust is public gain and shame;
> Here the Oriental and the skipjack go;
> Where those bleak outposts of the virtuous
> The corner mission and the walled church grow
> Like hemorrhoids on the city's anus.
>
> O reptilian street whose scaly limbs
> Are crooked stairways and the grocery store,
> Isolate, is your dreaming half-shut eye:
> Each virgin at the barricaded door
> Feels your tongue-kiss like a butterfly.[24]

This poems flaunts images that shock, in much the same way as Eliot's "patient etherised upon a table." Layton's comparison of the corner mission and the walled church to "hemorrhoids on the city's anus" is especially repulsive — more repulsive, probably, to English-speakers than to one who had acquired English as a third language and thought of "hemorrhoids" as an interesting-sounding word. "Isolate, is your dreaming half-shut eye" is clumsy and pretentious. "Private lust is public gain" seems too directly didactic. Yet these flaws do not destroy the overall effect of the poem. Partly because the poem's excesses are restrained by formal rhyming stanzas and partly because the mix of dreamy romance and pungent realism is nearly balanced, the poem works. Layton's extraordinary flair for language — "carapace," "bell-jars," "scaly" — conveys the vigourous earthiness of a mysterious and sinister sub-culture.

In part, the startling unevenness of individual poems and of the collection overall was the result of publishing so many poems that had been written over a fairly long span of time. Only about a fifth of the poems were new. The rest already had been published elsewhere, many of them twice. More than half of them had been published two or more years before; one ("A Jewish Rabbi/My Father") had appeared in the *McGill Daily* in 1938. These were hardly "here and now." Though poets commonly collected poems already published singly into books, Layton seems to have had, from the outset, a commercial attitude to his work — not surprising, given that on more than one occasion he had been a pedlar, numbered several pedlars and businessmen as his immediate relations and had undergone relentless pressure from his mother and his brother-in-law, Strul Goldberg, to get busy and get rich. Not that publishing poetry was likely to make Layton rich; but the marketing notion of quantity sales seems to have been instilled in him, despite his denunciations of the get-rich philosophy. The more poems you published, he seemed to think, and the more often you re-published them, the better poet you must be.

This had been brought home to him with the publication of *Unit of Five* the previous year.[25] The collection of poems that purported to present the five most important modern poets had not included Layton; it featured Louis Dudek, Raymond Souster, James Wreford, Ronald Hambleton and P.K. Page. Layton had taken his exclusion hard. It had seemed like a deliberate snub, and it had made him determined to include as many poems as possible in his first book.

John Sutherland, as his editor and publisher, ought to have curbed Layton's expansiveness and culled from the manuscript of *Here and Now* the handful of poems that deserved publication. But Sutherland's notions of his own criteria seem vague. They were defined largely against the standards the *Preview* group of "meticulous moderns." And his friendship with Layton, whose emotional left-wing politics exerted considerable influence over him, may have blurred his judgement temporarily. Layton seems not to have been able to tell the difference between his poems. His omnivorous, unsupervised reading had packed his mind with ideas and his imagination with models, but he really had no criteria for subject matter, taste or style — and where could he have acquired them? He tried everything, discovered what drew praise or insult from whom, assessed the situation, dropped what didn't work and tried again. The trial-and-error process had its pitfalls. Having learned to be immune to the outrageous and incessant cursings of his mother, seeing them not so much denigrations as awesome, comical explosions behind which lay a tenderness and favouritism reserved for him alone, Layton looked upon criticism, especially the more virulent sort, as perverse manifestations of affection. He had enjoyed the outrageous attacks of his fellow-students at Macdonald College, received their sarcasm as his self-important due and banged into the fray with all the gusto of Keine herself. (One of the reasons he had identified with Harold Laski, and continued to do so, was the fact that Laski had been savagely scape-goated by his critics.) With this attitude towards criticism — he was virtually immune to it — Layton was unlikely to feel criticism as criticism, or to take it seriously. Praise was praise, of course, and that reinforced his talents. But blame for his flaws was also praise, praise concealed behind a tempestuous, confrontational attack that would soon blow over. Fighting was inventive and fun, but to Layton it simply wasn't real.

Not that the criticism Layton received for *Here and Now* provided much praise or blame into which he could sink his teeth. There were only a few notices. One, by poet Margaret Avison in *Canadian Forum* in May 1945, admired "Mother, This Is Spring," but damned the collection as generally being "not really poetry," but rather the "fitting [of] an impersonal 'guise' over...naked conviction, emotion, vision."[26] Layton responded to Avison's accusation that "the fusion necessary to poetry" might occur once his techniques or his conviction developed with a scathing (and arrogantly "British") response in June 1945: "Mr. Layton's statements are not really poetry. Really? Since I do a fair amount of reviewing myself I know how damnably easy it is to dress up a purely personal reaction.... It consists of laying down some principle or canon purporting to have universal aesthetic validity and then proceeding to show how, in this line or that, the writer has contravened it. Theorem, QED, bring in the undertakers!"[27] Layton quoted lines from "The Swimmer," "Newsboy" and "Proof Reader," inviting Miss Avison "to roll her tongue around them and tell me once again that they're not [poetry]." Avison apologized for singling out Layton for faults found in many poets, but stuck to her guns: "The statement presupposes an exalted standard. But we need such a standard. For that reason, I cannot apologize for my comments."[28] F.W. Dupee, in the *Nation*, singled out "De Bullion Street" to categorize Layton as a stark, plebian realist and satirist: "anger is always leaping right out of Layton's poems and at your throat, often busting up the poems in the process. Yet for all their snarling, bottom-dog attitudes they often succeed in convincing us of their reality."[29] *Canadian Author and Bookman* seemed puzzled by Layton's unusual reactions to nature, and summarized the book as a collection of occasional poems reflecting life today.[30] Alfred C. Ames, in *Poetry*, also singled out "De Bullion Street" and portrayed Layton as "Left," contrasting him to B.H. Reece ("Right") and R.B. Campbell (as the infinitely preferred "Centre"): "the rebel is so thoroughly dominant that one feels the author is little interested in anything but protest...in the absence of disciplined expression and some elevation of feeling beyond disgust and anger, [these poems] do not guarantee the achievement of poetry of a high order."[31] The important summary of the year's poetry by E.K. Brown in "Letters to Canada" of the *University of Toronto Quarterly*, which had begun in 1936, dismissed Layton with condescension: "the belief that drugs or drabs are the catalysts for poetry is outmoded — and in Mr. Layton's poems [about the political and social problems of the immediate present] there is very little passion, except in the trivialized form of resentment. No one will ever call him tame, however, and his rich chunks of experience are unfailingly interesting."[32]

Yes, Sir!

"The autumn sun spilled like a light sauterne over the yellow desks and collected into irregular patches on the floor. There was a friendly, industrious atmosphere in the room."[1] The year was 1946. The school, in the basement and first floor of a converted old mansion facing the broad expanse of Fletcher's Field, which lay at the foot of Mount Royal on Esplanade at the corner of Rachel,[2] was a new Talmud Torah enterprise called Herzliah Junior High School. The British history and English teacher for the first year of Herzliah's operation was Irving Layton. The school had been set up by a group of orthodox Jewish parents — pedlars, clothing manufacturers and real-estate men — who wanted to preserve Jewish tradition and provide a secular education strong enough to ensure their children access to Canadian advanced schooling and universities. Though there were socialist undercurrents at the school, and some notably left-wing teachers, like Victor Byers and Alma Prince, Herzliah lay somewhere right of centre in the extraordinary political spectrum that characterized Jewish educational institutions in Montreal.[3] Furthest left was Morris Winchevsky School, an anti-Zionist, Communist institution eventually padlocked by Duplessis. Furthest right was Adath Israel Academy, a modern, orthodox Zionist school in Outremont, the residential area of

Montreal into which successful Jews from the downtown areas of first and second settlement had moved.[4]

Layton was not involved in the complex internal politics of the Jewish community. It is doubtful that he was aware that the first ultra-orthodox Hassidic community had sprung up in 1941, and he probably couldn't have named many of the Jewish organizations that flourished in the city, except the *Folks Universitet* (or Jewish People's University), an open university in the tradition of European countries, whose classes were held at the Jewish People's Library, where he taught. He simply needed a job, and loved to teach.

He aspired to be a university professor of economics or political science, a voice that would be heard throughout the country urging social revolution and achieving it. To steal a phrase he once applied to Harold Laski, he had ambitions to be "the one-man brain trust" of Canada. In the past year he had successfully completed two half-courses ("Contemporary Economic Theory" and "World Economic Survey Since the Great War") at McGill University and had written an MA thesis on Laski.[5] But Layton's performance in McGill's MA programme had been disappointing. He had been steeping himself in contemporary political writings for more than a decade, and at age thirty-six he was a good ten years older than the average MA student (though a number of older veterans, roughly five years older than the average, also had enrolled at the war's close); he had already published his article on Laski in *The Forge* in 1941. He ought to have produced brilliant results. This simply was not the case. His mark on both half-courses was sixty-five per cent,[6] the lowest mark a graduate student could receive and still pass. His earlier near-worship of Laski had abruptly switched to complete condemnation. In his thesis,[7] he set out to determine "to what extent, if any, Laski is justified in thinking of himself and in getting others to think of him as a Marxist." His conclusion was that "Laski's claim [to Marxism] is utterly lacking in foundation and must be disregarded by any alert and well informed student of the subject." Layton levelled an extravagant accusation at his former hero: "by employing Marxian terminology for his own purpose, [he] has robbed Marxism of its revolutionary content, thereby completely emasculating and distorting it. That purpose, I believe, was to graft his earlier political doctrines, his individualistic pluralism, upon the vigorous tree of Marxism; and the result...is the rather spongy fruit — social Democracy."[8]

Layton's feisty thesis used Marx, Engels and Lenin — especially Lenin — to demonstrate that the essence of Marxism lay in revolution. From this Marxist-Leninist perspective, he deplored Laski's distaste for violent radical action, saying it resulted in "idealistic social democracy and eclectic hodge-podge." Layton thus took sides with Laski's critics, whom he had lambasted five years before. He boldly described Marxism, and betrayed his fierce identification with it, as "a blazing furnace which rapidly consumes as so much rubbish all teleologies, all perfectionisms; it is the declared and uncompromising enemy of absolutisms in any form, of all ethical and idealistic hankering." There is no doubt Layton aimed to set the world afire with his inflammatory words. So caught up was he in his own powerful rhetoric that he read aloud section after section of his thesis to his phlegmatic mate. Friends remember Betty lolling back comfortably on their tatty furniture, almost asleep, rousing herself from time to time to comment softly, "The bastard!" Even this token approval spurred Layton to new rhetorical heights.

As Layton's views on Laski suggested, he now wholeheartedly backed the Communists, with whom he had before merely flirted. With more certain ardour, he became a member of the Labor Progressive Party of Canada, though one week later, apprehensive that he might be jeopardizing his career, he destroyed his card and withdrew his membership.[9] It is possible that he was alarmed by the Gouzenko scandal, which broke in mid-February that year. Like most Canadians, he was shocked to learn that the Russians were using Canadian Communists as spies.

Not surprisingly, even his friends were unsure of Layton's political views. A Labor Progressive Party member had offered her house for the launching of Patrick Anderson's collection of poems *A Tent in April*; when she discovered that Layton was to be one of the guests, she told Anderson she would have to cancel the party. Anderson's recollections of the situation give a good impression of the way Layton was seen at the time:

> She never realised the book was being published by First Statement and that she cannot possibly be connected in any way with an organization which contains, so she says, a real live Trotskyite. This terrible person is Irving Layton whose enormous fluent assurance and air of tousled sturdy candour I have always rather mistrusted. Irving is undoubtedly a renegade Marxist and a Koestler fan and I never feel comfortable when he begins a sentence with "Passionately as I admire the Soviet Union..."
> Was she quite certain about Irving? Did she know he had a photo of Stalin in his room? Didn't our Victory Bookstore sell the magazine of which he was, after all, only a member of the editorial board? She promised to consider the matter....
> But later last night...she phoned again. It was quite impossible.... Already one of the guests had complained. I quite saw her point. If Layton was as bad as all that...if he was thought to be.... But was he? I seemed to remember a very pro-Soviet article of his, and another one about the L[abor] P[rogressive] P[arty] which also appeared in the magazine. I knew too that he has enemies and that there are many besides myself who suspect his mixture of the slick and rugged. Anyway, I told her I would say that one of her children was sick and that the party would have to be held somewhere else....
> I am not absolutely convinced that the stories about Layton are true enough or important enough to justify the bother.[10]

Layton's insistence that Communist revolution was the only route to a classless society, and his view that Laski's theories of change through due parliamentary process amounted to a cowardly evasion that was bound to reinforce a capitalist-run democracy, were not unusual stances to take in 1946. Stanley Ryerson, who was then national educational director of the

Labor Progressive Party and editor of the party journal, *National Affairs*, observes that Layton took "what for the period was a fairly orthodox Marxist viewpoint in developing an interesting political theoretical critique of Laski's political position."[11] Ryerson's views were similar to Layton's, but Ryerson, a trained scholar with a committment to the Communist cause, already had begun the series of high-profile publications that would examine French-Canadian history from a Marxist perspective. He knew what he was talking about. Layton's thesis advisor was Raphael Tuck, an Englishman, who had been educated at the London School of Economics, Canterbury and Harvard. Tuck was a visiting member of McGill's department of economic and political science for only two years (1945 to 1947), where he taught sections of the department's core courses. Layton's thesis was the only one he supervised at McGill, and it is likely that Layton chose him rather than one of the senior members of the department (Forsey recalls that Layton was assigned to him but did "very little work")[12] because he could thereby start fresh instead of encountering the prejudice of his former teachers, and also because he could discuss Laski with an Englishman who had direct experience of British politics.

Layton's outside examiner was Frank Scott, who by this time had become nationally renowned for his role in founding the League for Social Reconstruction and the Cooperative Commonwealth Federation. Scott must have read Layton's thesis in something of the same state of mind as a knight plucking a gauntlet from the floor. There was no love lost between the two men: one born to power, the other aspiring to it. They were temperamentally different: Scott (tall, slim and fair) was all air (some of it hot) and cool water; Layton (short, dark and burly) was fire and earth. To some extent, the stage was set by their differing attitudes to poetry. There, too, they were on opposite sides. It was not just that Scott was spear-heading the *Preview* poets while Layton belonged to the *First Statement* group. Scott's clever and witty poems made some of Layton's look like the work of a clumsy buffoon. Yet there was something about Layton's poems that made Scott's work seem thin and effete, disconnected somehow from the realities of flesh and blood. Scott slipped easily into Oxonian snobbery and aristocratic wit, occasionally at Layton's expense; to Scott, Layton sometimes seemed the worst sort of vulgar little upstart. To Layton, Scott seemed like Laski: a weak, hypocritical man unfairly invested with political prestige. Scott hardly could have overlooked the double meaning of some of Layton's more personal blows in the thesis. Though addressed to Laski, they applied also to Scott, who was repulsed by any hint of violent revolution and who believed that social democracy could gradually emancipate the working class in Canada. Scott's connection with the CCF, and Laski's role in the British Labour Party, revealed similar ideological stances. Their ideas and their actions were comparable, and Layton knew it and attacked them both. Layton's hard-punching accusations that Laski was an "eclectic" or "idealist" given to "fits of high academic scorn;" that he was "drunk with a sense of hypothetical power;" that Labour governments were doomed to "failure, impotence and humiliation" and represented, as Lenin said, "a paradise for the rich and a trap and a snare and deception for the exploited;" that to social democrats (always in danger of becoming Fascists) "Parliamentarianism and democracy are sacrosanct idols," had more than overtones of his personal opinion of Scott.

Scott reacted as any man might when confronted with overwhelming insults to the beliefs he held dear. He let it be known that he did not think Layton's thesis was sound. According to Layton, he even attempted to fail it, but could not do so because Tuck thought quite highly of it. The thesis was accepted, though its fuzzy political thinking (Layton, for example, argued that Nietzsche and Marx were similar) prevented it from being on the cutting edge of contemporary political thinking. Probably Layton's diatribe had as much to do with his father as with F.R. Scott: Moishe had been the ineffectual idealist locked in with his sacrosanct idols, a father who had reneged on his role of interacting in the here-and-now to take leadership of an oppressed family under the none-too-comforting wing of a rampaging mother. Though Laski's theories at first had suggested to Layton a plausible integration of the two worlds of the Lazarovitch household, further consideration had shunted Laski off into that back room with his useless books and irrelevant visions, leaving Layton the full and equally vehement protégé of that blazing furnace, his mother. What began as ironically balanced appreciation of Laski became diatribe as Layton moved further left. Nonetheless, the fact that someone like Layton should have been in such a position, completing an MA and confronting F.R. Scott, one of the top political and legal minds of the country, with theories that by accident, not conveyed tradition, bore a striking resemblance to the theories that intellectuals had begun to articulate in the country of his birth, was nothing less than a cultural phenomenon.

In Romania, Layton never could have aspired to education beyond the basics, in all likelihood would have become a merchant or farm-hand, and certainly would have remained mute. Layton's position in May 1946, upon graduating from McGill, was a nexus of ironies. Since his discharge from the Canadian Army in 1943, he had been disallowed entry to the United States. Twice, en route to visiting his brother in New York, he had been turned back at the border. This meant that he was listed by United States immigration officials (via the RCMP) as an undesirable alien: the reason, his brief membership in the Labor Progressive Party and his public Communist activities. Although Layton had dropped any notion of Russian Communist allegiance when Russia invaded Finland in November 1939, his political perspective had shifted further and further left. The most dramatic shift had coincided with his discharge from the army, a fact that may have had much to do with his disillusionment in what he saw going on (or not going on) in army life.

Although he assiduously had pursued his political studies ever since, as his thesis on Laski demonstrates, he had done so in a vacuum. He had not associated closely with other Marxists or Communists of the time, men like Stanley Ryerson or Tim Buck, for example. He stood, a peculiar figure, isolated from the other far-left-wing intellectuals of the time on whose views he might have sharpened his own. He was passionate in his political beliefs, and those beliefs had been developed not in the way a careful, disciplined political thinker might have constructed a belief-system, but erratically, sporadically (for he was also drawn to the others of his "many worlds") and instinctively. Though he clearly understood bits and pieces of what he had read, he often confused the positions of others, preferring dynamic rhetoric to measured thought. He thus drew upon himself all the deprivations an inflammatory left-wing extremist could expect without reaping any of the benefits of an intellectual in the forefront. His thesis demonstrated less that he could think than that he could feel, especially about the sound and persuasive potential of rhetorical language. Though his degree did not succeed in preparing him to be a politician or a professor (he entertained fantasies of power in both areas), it did develop his skills in forging images and rhythms that might compel. On several counts, he could not hope for the moment to join the staff at McGill or any other Canadian university, but he could and did continue to teach evening classes for immigrants at the Jewish People's Library (later the Jewish Public Library) and day classes at Herzliah. At the library, which he liked to refer to grandly as the Jewish University though it was actually the People's University, his students had a lamentable knowledge of English. At Herzliah, his students were children. In his classes he found a theatre for the forceful rhetoric he had tried to develop in his MA thesis and wished he were demonstrating elsewhere.

"It was a gray, dim, serious time [at Herzliah]," recalls Ethel Roskies, a student in Layton's first class there. "Many of the teachers were Europeans who had lost their families during the war that had just ended. There was a sort-of hot-house atmosphere at Herzliah then: we understood that we were the cream of the crop; we had to be bright enough to have been chosen competitively; we were the ones who were going to replace the six million that had died."[13]

Among the sober, dedicated staff at Herzliah, Layton was unique. Most of the teachers were quiet and restrained, polite and docile. Layton, in his crumpled shirt and trousers that didn't match, was an explosive volcano who erupted with enthusiasm and sarcasm by turns. In the first class, Roskies says, Layton asked his students to name the great living poets they knew: "In the list we drew up, Irving Layton's name was there. False modesty was not one of his problems. He was not a good teacher in any conventional sense. He was not patient or kind. He fired chalkboard erasers at you if he didn't like your answers. He broke all the rules. We'd never seen anything like him. Most of our parents were immigrants who had sacrificed long hours of work on our behalf. Most of the adults we knew were very, very cramped. Their mentality was that the world was flat: one step and we'd fall off. They thought there were dangers everywhere, especially the danger of assimilation. He was completely different from this. He was an adult who seemed to be having fun, and that was a contradiction in terms. He boxed, which the men we knew didn't (physical activity was done by *goyim*, not Jews). He had a body he was proud of, while we had been raised to think that if you could use your head you didn't use your body. He smoked, which just wasn't done. With his full head of dark hair in a world bereft of young men by the war, he stood out amongst the grey and the bald. He was full of energy, larger than life." Only much later, with the hindsight of womanhood and a Ph.D. in psychology, would Ethel recognize the strong sexual dimension of Layton's appeal.[14]

Alvin Neiss, now a druggist, who stood near the bottom of the same class, agrees that Layton was an exceptional teacher: "His methods and means were not run-of-the-mill. He was a fanatic. Everything had to be letter perfect. I still remember all about 'epithet' and 'rhyme.' Not only did he throw chalk at me, but he hurled insults if I disturbed the class. He'd shout, 'You haven't a brain in your head!' or 'You're nothing but a clod!' Things like that. I think he did it to get a rise out of the class, or to impress them and show how serious he was in what he was doing. He used to read his own poetry to us. He mentioned Louis Dudek and gave credit to others in the literary field, too. At least we were never bored. He'd mix religion and politics with literature; he was quite the radical. He tried to convey the importance of both the physical and the spiritual side of life. He was full of pep; I could never keep up with him. The thing he most impressed on me was that you had to stand up in life, no one would carry your banner."[15]

The dark-haired, vivacious Ethel, now a university professor, was profoundly influenced. "I was his teacher's pet," she recalls: "In my family, I was brighter than my sister, but not as nice. The two characteristics were thought to be antithetical. I was the rebel. Layton sanctioned this. He instilled an ideal that is with me today, that it's okay for a woman to be bright. After all, it was revolutionary at Herzliah, girls getting a boy's education. It was because of his political enthusiams that I went on to get an MA in political science at McGill. He introduced me to the idea of theatres, a love I still have, and he shared his passion for second-hand book-stores. I can't pass one even today without going in to see what they have. Perhaps most of all, he showed me that life can be fun, that *work* can be fun."

In his short tale "A Plausible Story" (1954),[16] Layton fictionalized his first two years at Herzliah. He based the plot on the contrast between Ethel Goldstein and her "nice" sister, Edith, whom he taught in 1948.[17] Judging by the sharp, satiric sketches of teachers in his story, Layton loathed his colleagues. The narrator, based closely on himself, thinks they are ridiculous and contemptible. To tolerate working with them, the narrator sustains an elaborate fantasy life in which he plays Creator: "I don't remember exactly when I first began to copy the Omnipotent; probably at the beginning of my career as a pedagogue.... In the courtyard, in the classrooms, in the Headmaster's office, my writ ran everywhere; and my rule, like that of the Creator Himself, was as sweeping as it was not-to-be-seen. No one ever arose to challenge it and no one, as far as I can recall, ever complained. My colleagues innocently did my bidding; they accepted without a murmur their prescriptive existence."[18]

This megalomaniac instructor, who has developed a number of dramatic tactics, such as thrusting out his jaw and fixing a single inoffensive child with a stare to control his class, is perplexed by the hatred of the character Ava Rickstein, based on Ethel's sister. He bitterly thinks of Ava as his "masterwork, a figure I'd raised from the depths to tease my brain with hints of man's illimitable perversity." Why, he wonders, does she not respond as her sister, Evelyn, did to his "best roles": Shelley, Lincoln, Debs, Papineau? When he finally perceives the depths of Ava's jealousy for her more brilliant sister, the irony of his "creation" of a "sensitive, perverse and intractable" human being that could not more resemble himself strikes home. Like God, he has created an offspring in his own image who must be sacrificed.

Though it is presented in a self-mocking way, much can be understood from this story about Layton and his sense of limitless power as a teacher. Here, in capsulated form, are some of the attractions teaching held for Layton: his enjoyment of domination; his ingenuity as a rhetorical tactician and actor; his pleasure in a captive audience; his success as a popular teacher among dull colleagues. Here, too, are its drawbacks: the oppressive boredom of a regulated institutional life; his flippant rebellion against some of the subject matter he was expected to teach; the hours spent with stupid students; the unending vigilance teachers must maintain over children; the sense of his own abilities wasted and life by-passed. Though Layton's impetuous actions may have scorched more than a few dullards, they sometimes sparked a lasting brilliance. When he acknowledged Ethel Roskies' abilities with the gift of a second-hand copy of George Bernard Shaw's *The Intelligent Woman's Guide to Socialism and Capitalism,* inscribing it "For Ethel, whose fine mind and questioning spirit fill me with admiration and wonder,"[19] he set unimaginable goals and a future career.

Year after year, he inspired scores of students who never forgot him. On his copies of each session's yearbook, he collected signatures that showed what the students had experienced in his class.

> To a poet, novelist, teacher and 'human'. Herzliah will never forget you,
>
> Irwin Gotler[20]

> Your name shall be enlocked in my book of memories forever. You have whetted my poetical appetite and for that I can never repay you.
>
> A lonely poet, Charles Spector[21]

> The two years spent with you have been great and the knowledge gained immense. Let's make it two more (if you don't mind),
>
> Abraham Engel[22]

Some periods were good,
Some periods were bad.
Sometimes you were happy.
Sometimes you were mad.
Composition, Literature, History and such
I can never repay you,
I owe you too much!

Martin Nathanson[23]

Mr. Layton, your chief aim has been to get us out of hell. I think you have succeeded with me and I am very very grateful.

Your friend, Golda Malus[24]

Dear Sir, in all my life I have never come upon a person quite like you, as fascinating, interesting and well-meaning as you have been. To me you have been a friend and a father as well as a teacher. I could never express in words how I feel so I'll do it by trying to be the kind of person you would like me to be. Your friend, pupil and admirer,

Fruma Gewurz[25]

Layton profoundly affected most of his youthful students. He impressed on them a philosophy of life that valued the arts, loved learning for learning's sake and bridged the abyss, which usually characterizes schoolwork, between play and intellectual achievement.

Bohemia

To those who knew them, Irving and Betty seemed idyllically happy. Working their motley jobs — Betty as a cashier, Irving as a teacher at Herzliah Junior High School and the Jewish People's Library — they earned enough for their few needs. Their unmarried, chaotic co-existence looked like everything bohemia ought to be: a life dedicated to sex, politics, the arts and learning. In their stark and cluttered studio on the east side of City Hall Avenue between Rachel and Duluth, near the Rachel Market at the heart of Montreal's second area of Jewish settlement, they lived in happy deprivation. "The bathtub was in the kitchen. I washed our clothes in it by hand. There was ice on the bedroom floor in winter. Rats occasionally ran across our chests at night, but I loved it there," Betty comments. "It was good for me as an artist. I had to know all that to create." To Irving's swarthy and swashbuckling energy, Betty played the quiet, flaxen-haired introvert. "I was speechless at the parties and poetry-reading gatherings we went to," Betty recalls. "I never was a great talker. It was only when we were alone that we talked and talked together."[1]

Audrey Aikman, who had come from England to McGill in 1940 and, after serving on the editorial board of *First Statement* for a year, had married John Sutherland, thought Betty and Irving were extremely well-suited: "I thought of them as being a very happy couple, always."[2] Aikman recalls being puzzled at the effect Irving seemed to have on other people: "I accepted him as a friend, but I never experienced his fascination, as everyone else seemed to do. I was at ease with him and couldn't understand the importance or strength of his personality. I observed, from the outside, that he liked to dominate anyone with whom he was in contact. I thought at the time that this must be part of his gift as a teacher. This trait had an unfortunate aspect: he had to lead, he could not follow."

From the inside, Irving and Betty's relationship was mostly fun: painting, writing, reading, sharing scorn for bourgeois, materialistic conventionality, sensing that rebellion was the consort of creativity. But there was a darker side. "It was a love-hate relationship from the start,"[3] Betty recalls. "He made excuses to go out, and he would stay out. I was sometimes in tears. There was a student he spoke of for a while. There was never anything definite, but I was tortured." Layton insists he was "completely faithful to Betty during the fifteen years we were together."[4] "If that is true," Betty comments, "he was pretending for some reason that things were happening. He frequently behaved as if he was carrying on."[5]

By July 1945, their relationship had come to the point where it had to alter. "Irving got this idea that we should have children. 'We'll have beautiful babies!' he'd exclaim." For the three years he had been living with Betty, he had been pestering Faye to grant him a divorce. She adamantly refused. Though marriage was impossible, Layton became obsessed with having children, as if it would bond him and Betty in a "natural" marriage. "He got me pregnant, really, to convince me that he loved me," Betty observes. "I remember that July day our child was conceived. We went to bed at 10 AM and talked all day. 'I'll give you a baby — a wonderful little kid!' he kept saying. He thought it would solve everything. We began to make love, knowing I was fertile. At the last possible moment, he withdrew and said, 'I changed my mind.' By then, I'd been swept into the fantasy he'd created, and it was too late to stop. He didn't consider what I might think at all."[6]

It would be difficult to imagine a more scandalous situation than the one Layton had created for himself. Pregnancy outside marriage would have been enough to spark indignation, but pregnancy with a real wife only blocks away added to the flames. It was only two years since Gwethalyn Graham's novel *Earth and High Heaven*[7] had rocked Montreal to its foundations. By describing a love-affair between an upwardly mobile Jewish man and an enlightened, well-bred Westmount girl, Graham had attacked prejudice and the compartmentalization of ethnic groups in Montreal. Partly because of its explosive subject matter, the book struck instant notoriety, was a best-seller in the United States and Canada and won the Governor-General's Award. But Irving and Betty's relationship went much further than the one Graham had depicted. Graham's young Jew was a respectable lawyer and a captain in the Canadian army, her Westmount girl an intelligent newspaper-woman, still living at home, with the ability to negotiate past her parents into marriage with her lover. The novel's scandals were mild compared to the one Layton created. He had managed open adultery, political notoriety as a Communist and a taboo-breaking Jewish-Gentile relationship. Now he would add to his credentials the stigma of an illegitimate child.

Betty's pregnancy understandably set several people astir. Her brother, John, took Layton aside. "He was worried about Irving's intentions," Audrey Sutherland recalls. "He had a private talk with him, not an angry conversation, but to express his anxiety."[8] A.M. Klein strongly advised Layton not to marry a Gentile.[9] Faye, in desperation, sent off a letter to Betty's father, Fred Sutherland, accusing Betty of enticement and pregnancy. Sutherland, who was vice-president and general manager of the New Brunswick Electric Power Commission, was alarmed. "The first ambassador from the Sutherland family was my mother," Louise Scott, Betty's cousin and a noted Montreal painter, recalls. "She was sent to Montreal to report on this exotic creature, Irving Layton. Although I was only six when this happened, I know there was a great commotion in the family about whether he was Jewish or Communist or both. My mother was quite charmed by him and came back to say that she saw nothing wrong. It was all a great disappointment to Uncle Fred, who was an irascible individual anyway."[10] Keine was shocked. What was her *Flamplatz* up to now? Getting his *shiksa* pregnant with a wife just around the corner? At Keine's thundering insistence, Betty agreed to convert to Judaism. Although "Sarah" was the standard name for women converts, Betty recalls, she wanted to take the Russian-Jewish name for her real name, Elizabeth. In a small ceremony presided over by a rabbi, "Betty" became "Boschka." Although she continued to be called "Betty," she formally legalized her Jewish name in the early 1970s, and began using it then.

Betty's conversion had the dubious benefit of opening the corridors of communication with Keine, who had abandoned Kalman Hershorn as suddenly as she had moved in with him and taken a room on Mount Royal Avenue. Keine never really was satisfied with Betty. "The first day she visited us, she made us some chopped eggplant and salt for breakfast. It looked awful to me, but it was very good. She was a marvellous cook. I liked her. She was a magnificent looking woman with white hair, olive skin, black shining eyebrows over bright black eyes. I did many drawings of her. She reminded me of my grandmother Sutherland who was food-centred and very physical. Keine was very funny, loved cracking jokes, wrote a little poetry herself. She was smarter than all Hell. But she was a holy terror. She resented me for being a *goy* and found fault with everything." Betty, who did little housework and seemed oblivious to the dirt and chaos around her, refused to keep kosher. " 'Bubba,' as we called her, would get after me: 'That's the wrong fork! You forgot the prayers! Where are the candles?' It was no picnic. When she got mad at me, Irving would just laugh. He never defended me."[11]

On the evening of 7 April 1946, Maxwell Rubin Layton was born. Betty and Irving were having dinner with John and Audrey Sutherland when Betty went into labour. "She must have kept it to herself for quite awhile," Audrey recalls: "All of a sudden she announced quietly, 'This child is about to be born.' We phoned a taxi. Then we talked nervously for half an hour. When the taxi still hadn't appeared, someone went out and flagged one. Irving and Betty bundled into it and sped off to the hospital. We were all so childish and inexperienced. It didn't occur to me to go with her to help or even just talk to her. She didn't have so much as a toothbrush with her. I remember thinking afterwards 'Surely they're not going to take a baby back to that awful studio of theirs?'"[12]

That summer, Betty and Layton rented an old, run-down summer place in the Eastern Townships. There Betty spent the summer with Irving's nephew, Bill Goldberg, "in Platonic bliss." Layton, who appeared only on the weekends, had a job in Montreal. Keine began to invade the household. Now that she was ageing, she turned to her favourite *Flamplatz* to look after her. While Betty tended Max, Keine would *kvetch* and complain. Asthma had become her latest affliction, and *Flamplatz*, her *srulickel*, was the only one she believed capable of giving her the emergency injections she needed during the attacks, which usually took place in the middle of the night. Irving, who assumed this responsibility completely (and, Betty thought, idiotically), would be up to tend her or off across Montreal, when she wasn't staying with them, to give her the injection. "Once when Bubba was staying with us for a month or so — I forget why — she would bring people in and show them the room with me and Maxie in it and offer it to them for rent! I would go into a rage and shout, 'It isn't *for* rent. It's my home!'"[13]

Max's birth finally convinced Faye to give Irving the divorce he had wanted since 1941. In February 1948, shortly after the divorce became legal, Irving and Betty married. In a magnanimous gesture of forgiveness that ensured his grandson would not be raised in utter squalour, Fred Sutherland gave the couple the down-payment on a charming little house in Côte St. Luc, set among farm lands in the rural north-west outskirts of Montreal.[14]

The "Proleterian Poets"

Robert Finch won the Governor-General's Award for his collection, *Poems*, in 1946. This seemingly innocuous event, one that ought to have provoked celebration and the usual flurry of congratulations, became a *cause célèbre* and triggered momentous events in Canada's fragile bid for poetic modernism. Finch was an academic in the French department at the University of Toronto. A protégé of E.J. Pratt's, he was an American who had come to Toronto for his undergraduate degree, then gone to the Sorbonne, where he laid the groundwork for a distinguished scholarly career in seventeenth- and eighteenth-century French poetry.[1] Finch had been one of the six poets whose work provoked Layton and Dudek to incredulous hilarity when they read *New Provinces*. His poems were mainly lyric. They had some modernist elements: Finch resembled Scott in his deft satire and Smith in his cool-toned, metaphysical wit. His poetry reflected the fact that he was a refined and highly trained aesthete (he painted and played the harpsichord) who reacted against the emotional excesses of the Romantic movement by being reticent and allusive. Though Finch, like Layton, often chose subjects from ordinary life, his treatment of them was more detached and less political. Layton indelicately celebrated the vitality of the ugly; Finch delicately raised the commonplace into the sphere of aesthetic perfection. He described a truck viewed from a train window, for example:

> The dark green truck on the cement platform
> is explicit as a paradigm.
> Its wheels are four black cast-iron starfish.
> Its body, a massive tray of planking,
> ends in two close-set dark green uprights
> crossed with three straight cross-pieces, one
> looped with a white spiral of hose.[2]

When John Sutherland heard the award announcement, he was indignant. How could the award go to Robert Finch? Raymond Souster and Louis Dudek, P.K. Page and Patrick Anderson had published books of poems with his First Statement Press. In a scathing attack[3] on the criteria for poetry that had misled a committee of judges to make their decision, Sutherland let fly resentments that had been percolating for almost a decade. Singling out the worst of Finch's lines ("Your treason is my reason,/Your poison is my raisin"), and analysing in devastating detail one of Finch's sonnets, Sutherland highlighted the absurdity, pretension and self-consciousness of Finch's poems. He waxed most indignant at Finch's detachment, accusing him of playing "with rhyme and metre like a kitten with a ball of wool" and indulging in nothing more than "mental gymnastics" or "verbal chess." Sutherland wrote: "His method is one of compilation rather than of composition. It merely suggests that a knack for making word pictures has been gradually transformed into a hobby.... How did *Poems* receive the national award for poetry in a year which saw the publication of some unusually good books?" In a list that concisely summarized Layton's, Dudek's and his own objections to the poetry scene in Canada, he offered some possible reasons:

> 1. Respectability. Finch is professor of French at the University of Toronto.
> 2. Precedent. The award has a habit of going to the sturdy Western farmer type or the etherialized academician. It has recently been granted to the following writers:

1942 — Anne Marriott   1943 — A.J.M. Smith
1944 — Dorothy Livesay 1945 — Earle Birney
        1946 — Robert Finch

3. Naïve wonder. Mr. Finch kept his first book up his sleeve for twenty years.

4. Fairness. Ryerson Press had won many times and Oxford never had.

5. Respect for age. Mr. Finch was old enough: the other candidates were not.

6. Sanctimoniousness. Mr. Finch was morally correct and sounded religious.

7. Hypocrisy. The politics of the younger writers was "out of place" in poetry.

8. Snobbery. Finch was billed as a talented musician and painter.

9. Credulity. The judges accepted Finch's verdict on his own work:

> His lines run wherever his pen goes,
> Mine grope the miles from heart to head;
> His will tire before he does;
> Mine will move when I am dead.
> ("Poet on Poet")

10. Ignorance. The judges knew of, but had not read, Louis Dudek, P.K. Page or Patrick Anderson.

11. Ignorance. The judges had not read Finch.

None of these reasons entirely satisfy me, but the thing is hard to explain.

Sutherland's blast, which was printed in August 1947, shattered the tenuous and uneasy consolidation of modern poets that had begun less than two years before in Montreal. Ironically, he had been the one who had initiated the consolidation. In a letter dated 27 March 1945 from First Statement Press, at 635 St. Paul Street West, to the editors of *Preview* magazine, he had asked for an amalgamation of the two magazines, outlining a number of practical steps for doing so. It is clear from the letter that F.R. Scott was perceived as the leader of the *Preview* group and that Sutherland and Layton were the most influential of the *First Statement* editors. "We believe that we can work with you to our mutual benefit,"

Sutherland wrote, "but if you feel that an amalgamation would be against the interests of *Preview*, you are, of course, under no obligation to consider our offer."[4] *Preview* and *First Statement* were amalgamated, and the new magazine was called *Northern Review*. The first issue was published in 1945. But after Sutherland's criticism of Finch's award, Scott and Smith, as well as A.M. Klein, Patrick Anderson, P.K. Page, Ralph Gustafson and Neufville Shaw resigned. In a brief announcement in the October/November 1947 issue of *Northern Review*, the truncated board of editors outlined the situation:

> The reason for these changes was a difference of opinion about editorial policy, particularly concerning criticism and reviews. The immediate occasion for disagreement was a review of Robert Finch's poems by John Sutherland, which appeared in the last issue. The editors who resigned maintained that this review, and similar pieces of criticism, were too harsh and unjust for publication, while the present editorial board held that criticism of this kind was badly needed in Canada. Our readers can form their own opinions in the matter.
>
> Elsewhere in this issue we have printed a short letter from P.K. Page, at her request, stating that she was ignorant of the review on Finch. Perhaps we should mention that our regional editors never saw contributions to the magazine before they were printed and were not entitled to vote on them.
>
> The present editors are John Sutherland, R.G. Simpson, Mary Margaret Miller, John Harrison, Irving Layton and Audrey Aikman. We intend to carry on *Northern Review* in its present form. We hope that the concentration of responsibility in the hands of a smaller editorial board will result in greater efficiency and a more interesting magazine.[5]

In his 1928 article "Wanted: Canadian Criticism," A.J.M. Smith had called for "the critic-militant." Now that he was faced with one, it was another story.[6]

The inability of the *Preview* poets, whose literary sympathies lay with Finch, to tolerate outspoken criticism of Finch's poetry or an attack on the committee that awarded him the prize set a pattern for Canadian poetry. Instead of developing a modern tradition based on some common denominators within which individual voices might follow unique paths, the bridge Sutherland had precariously built crashed into an uncrossable chasm. The two modernist groups had much to offer each other. First, there was strength in numbers in any arts undertaking in Canada, where publishers were few, distribution was unreliable and the public generally was predisposed to ignore creativity. The *Preview* group had respectability — even prestige — education, business contacts, organizational and administrative abilities and money. The *First Statement* group had a different class experience and the bold determination to cut a swath through the pretensions of respectable middle-class gentility; they wanted vigorous realism and fresh language. The *Preview* group professed left-wing politics, modern poetry and vitality for the arts, and the poets of the *First Statement* group were ready to catch them out when they failed to live up (or rather down) to their own principles. Through the *Preview* poets, the *First Statement* group could gain access to Canadian institutional life and to arenas where their voices would be heard. After 1947 the two groups stood on opposite sides, enemies instead of colleagues who agreed to differ, each group convinced that the other had missed the point about poetry, each determined to prove it.

    Almost immediately, Sutherland wrote a brilliant, polemical introduction to a collection, *Other Canadians*, which he was editing for his press. As its title suggests, the anthology was a cheeky answer to *New Provinces*. Smith's *Book of Canadian Poetry* (1943) was the first major overview of Canadian poetry presented with the kind of knowledgeable enthusiasm of one at last certain that his country has a literary tradition and that he himself is a major figure in its most recent and best "school." But Smith's elitist introduction had antagonized Sutherland, and the *First Statement* group generally, because Smith had described modernism in a way that would accommodate the poetic theories and poetry of the *Preview* poets but exclude the poems of Layton, Souster and Dudek. He divided Canadian poetry into chronological sections such as

"The New Nationalism;" "The Golden Age" — Romantic nature poetry, Carman, Roberts or Lampman — and "Modern Poetry: the Cosmopolitan Tradition." He dismissed many earlier poets, as all the moderns had, for what Scott in 1927 had wittily called "their zeal for God and King, their earnest thought" and for their rhapsodic-idiotic nature worship. When he contrasted them to a "cosmopolitan" modernism, he betrayed his own bias:

> The poets of today, inheritors of what I.A. Richards has called the "neutralisation of nature," have turned away from all this. They have sought in man's own mental and social world for a subject matter they can no longer find in the beauty of nature — a beauty that seems either deceptive or irrelevant. Their early simplicity, assumed in reaction to the overloaded diction of much Victorian verse, has been replaced by a variety of individual and subtle rhetorics derived in part from Pound or Eliot, the later Yeats, or the seventeenth-century metaphysicals. Generally speaking, it is the poetry of ideas, of social criticism, of wit and satire, that has replaced the descriptive or contemplative poetry of the nineteenth century.[7]

When Smith used the term "cosmopolitan," he meant those who had a breadth of education and sufficient taste and international experience to lay claim to being cultured and sophisticated. He meant people like himself — he had lived in England and taught at Michigan State College, in East Lancing — or Robert Finch, who had been to the Sorbonne, or Scott, who had been a Rhodes scholar at Oxford. He did not mean "cosmopolitan" in any sense that might have included a Romanian-born Jew with an MA from McGill who read Marx, Engels and Lenin. Though Smith claimed that "The new poetry is rich and various," his "new poetry" was not various enough to include Irving Layton.

Northrop Frye, who reviewed Smith's anthology for *Canadian Forum*,[8] mentioned that there were omissions but offered no examples. He thought the collection's striking "unity of tone" came not from "limited sympathies" on Smith's part, but from the material itself, which he treated as fully representative. (Frye, an ordained minister who was exactly Layton's age, lectured in English at Victoria College, University of Toronto, and became Canada's foremost literary critic.) He devoted most of his review to exploring the nature of the Canadian identity as expressed by the poems Smith had chosen. The cool tone of the anthology suggested to Frye "a frostbite at the roots of the Canadian imagination," which produced "a disease for which I think the best name is prudery...." Frye was struck, as Louis Dudek had been in *First Statement* in 1944,[9] "by the predominance of university and professional people" who were Canadian poets. He was not put off by this; indeed, he offered words of benediction. He deplored poets who insisted that direct experience must be their education, and observed: "There has on the whole been little Tarzanism in Canadian poetry." He approved of poets who were "curious universal scholars." For poets who were scholars, however, Canada posed special difficulties. It would be difficult, perhaps impossible, to extend a cumulative literary tradition when their own tradition had been inevitably fractured because they existed in a colony that was disrupted by co-existence with another tradition, that of French Canada. In this cultural disturbance, "the traditions of Europe [he seems to have meant Britain, as well] appear as a kaleidoscopic whirl with no definite shape or meaning, but with a profound irony lurking in its varied and conflicting patterns." That "irony" gave rise to "a poetry of incubus and *cauchemar*" in Canada. By not exploring Smith's omissions in his review, and by treating the collection as representative, Frye did much to reinforce and disseminate Smith's biases about poetry, biases that had informed Smith's selection for *The Book of Canadian Poetry*. (Later anthologies attest to this. One of them, for example, does not even mention Robert Finch.)[10]

Smith's anthology was an ideal target for Sutherland, and Sutherland took aim with so many arrows that his introduction to *Other Canadians*[11] is jarring and confusing. But, all told, his attack was powerful and justified. His introduction, as Louis Dudek stated,[12] endures as "a standard reference in Canadian criticism." Essentially, Sutherland thought Smith's theories sounded like the high-pitched death-rattle of literary colonialism. Though Smith claimed to be *au-courant*, Sutherland thought he was out of date. This situation was ironic, for Smith had taken pains to outline the "progress" of Canadian poetry since the Romantic nature poets to show how "modern" he and his contemporaries were. To Sutherland, Smith was guilty of the same shortcomings as the earlier poets. Smith had accused them of using art as a means of expressing religious or transcendental beliefs. Now Sutherland pilloried Smith and his associates for disguising similar beliefs under the pseudo-religious terms "metaphysical" and "aesthetic." "Many changes are rung upon the same old theme," Sutherland wrote, "sometimes in the name of history and tradition, and sometimes in the name of that pure aestheticism which...is nothing less than the history and tradition of the human spirit wrapped in a papal bunnyhug." Sutherland accounted for "the close air and literary smell" of the work he criticised by drawing attention to the personal backgrounds and temperaments of the poets in Smith's anthology:

> The poets of the forties are English by origin and birth, and the new poetry is predominantly English in tone. James Wreford, Ronald Hambleton, P.K. Page, Patrick Anderson, were all born in England or educated there: what they produce must seem strange and alien to those who, in a way still undefined, feel themselves Canadians.... It is this division between the poet and his audience which is of crucial importance today. Our poetry is colonial because it is the product of a cultured English group who are out of touch with people who long ago began adjusting themselves to life on this continent. The lack of all rapport between the poetry and the environment is one of the factors accounting for the incredibly unreal and ethereal quality of some of the new poetry.

Sutherland thought the burning question for contemporary poets was: Were poets to come from the class of society that traditionally had the leisure and education to read, write and contemplate literature, or were they to come from a class excluded until recently from having a voice? It was not enough for middle-class writers to believe, in principle, that the poor should get a better deal, and to write about them from the safety of their economic bastions of power, Sutherland thought. The poor must speak for themselves in their own words. Sutherland attacked "Bishop Smith" as "a traditionalist and classicist" whose "spiritual father" was T.S. Eliot. "Regarding with trepidation the example of America, he flies to European fields and to those sheltered haunts where the 'classical' tradition still maintains itself." Smith was trying to remind Canadians that their poetry was "more truly Roman than we could ever have imagined in our wildest dreams." What was wrong with this group of English-born, English-educated or English-admiring poets was clear to Sutherland: "We can state the whole problem of [literary] colonialism in terms of the poet's relation to his audience." He theorized that the advent of socialism in Canada was in the process of altering Canadian society and that poetry must express this alteration and address those who were taking part in it.

> The poet retains *human* attributes in spite of being a poet...his materials are *tangible* [italics added]...and... he has something to say which frequently has meaning for the ordinary man.... If God still talks to these poets in private, he carries less weight than Karl Marx or Sigmund Freud. The seven-day fireworks of the world's creation matter less than the creation of the socialist state; the cure of earthly ills is to be achieved by economics or psychology rather than by divine intervention. These poets are interested in events and ideas whose importance is neither ephemeral nor imaginary to the living and thinking individual; they *intend* at least to speak to the average man of everyday realities and of the principles which operate in them.

To Sutherland, this approach to poetry, radically different from Smith's, meant evolving away from English models and English aesthetics: "Canadian poetry struggles to follow the American example even while its dominant bias remains

English." He identified the struggle as "the inevitable halfway house from which Canadian poetry will pass towards an identity of its own."

Sutherland thought that contemporary English poets W.H. Auden, Stephen Spender, Dylan Thomas and George Barker directed poetry towards socialism; thus the English bias. He thought the American influence, which he believed would temporarily supercede English influences until Canadian poetry acquired its own identity, stemmed from Carl Sandburg, e.e. cummings, Marianne Moore, Karl Shapiro and Kenneth Fearing.

But Sutherland's main point was that the times called for a Canadian poetic voice from lower down on the social scale. Predictably, Dudek and Layton were two of the three poets Sutherland singled out as most significant. The other was Raymond Souster, a young bank clerk in Toronto who, according to Sutherland, "has a freedom of form, and an ability to handle colloquial language...a way of calling a spade a spade...[that is] the embodiment of the common man." These three poets, Sutherland maintained, "are not middle-class but proletarian in origin.... They have followed American literary models rather than English ones, and they are the first poets of more than passing interest of whom this is true. In their work one finds a more Canadian point of view, a greater interest in themes and problems of a Canadian kind, and a social realism which distinguishes it from the political make-believe of other poets." In Layton's poems, Sutherland found "a hard-fisted proletarianism which makes it potential dynamite in the closed chamber of Canadian letters." He singled out three poems: "De Bullion Street," "Newsboy" and "Words Without Music."[13]

Of Sutherland's three poets, Layton was probably most representative. He had endured the poorest background, worked the most menial jobs, stood furthest left politically and was a secularized Jew. Unlike Dudek and Souster, Layton represented the literary evolutionary process Sutherland described. It was true that Layton admired his American models for their colloquialism, their free verse and their North Americanism. But, because he had entertained a rich fantasy life about the English *literati* since he was a boy, and because he had, until recently, worshipped British Fabianism, he also represented the English bias Sutherland disdained. Layton's second book, *Now is the Place*, published at his own expense in 1948 (one of only thirty-five books of poetry published in Canada that year), contained a brief, humorous foreword (signed "I.P.L.") that treated Sutherland's theories about modern poetry as truth and assumed that Layton was the best representative of them. Layton's foreword does not bear close scrutiny as to logic. It sets out to shock, harass and revolutionize in his best Keine Lazarovitch style.

> NOW IS THE PLACE to say that the existing economic system, by forcibly subjecting millions of human beings to wage-slavery, is immoral and wicked; but marvellously designed to keep alive at the top a handful of parasites....
>
> NOW IS THE PLACE to say that the multi-national and potentially colorful spirit of Canada can be rescued from the dominant anglo-saxon pattern of hypocrisy, prudery, and complacent dullness only by the free and abundant use of four-letter words....[14]

Tongue-in-cheek, the dust-jacket blurb presents Layton as all things to all people. For intellectuals, he is the MA in economics from McGill; for patriots, his army service is mentioned; for Communists, he appears as the teacher (where he teaches is not mentioned) who believes that "the nation's schools are a deliberate and well-organized conspiracy... designed to produce slaves rather than free men;" for the literary, he is one of the "active spirits" behind *First Statement* and *Northern Review*; for the conventional, he is (untruthfully in spirit, if not in fact) married with one child; for the non-literary, his favourite sport is boxing. For Jews, his foreword referred to "the warnings of the great Hebrew prophets from Isaiah to Jesus." It was a masterpiece of marketing. How could he lose?

For all its huffing and puffing about its urgent relevance, *Now is the Place* consisted mainly of material Layton had already published. Two short stories were reprinted from a 1946 issue of *Northern Review*. About half the twenty-seven poems had appeared previously; fourteen were from the

1945 *Here and Now*. Only five poems were printed for the first time, though six were reasonably recent: they first had appeared within the past two years in *Canadian Forum, Contemporary Verse* and *Northern Review*. Oddly, the dramatic events that recently had altered Layton's life did not much affect his poetry. Of the five new poems and the six recent ones, only one dealt with his personal life. "To the Lawyer Handling My Divorce Case"[15] is an undistinguished free-verse poem that explores the sense of anonymity, insignificance and absurdity felt by a client discussing his divorce with a lawyer. (The poet pictures himself as "undersized;" in another poem, "The Eagle,"[16] he is met by princes "taller than I.") Layton's most recent poems included a range of forms (some had rhyming couplets), but were most frequently free verse. Though he relied on vivid images, the poems cannot be termed imagist. In a style that had become uniquely his own, Layton expanded on or embellished images within a form that originally was designed to shrink them. He was at his best in "Karl Marx":

> Now the winds are lashed howling to the poles
> And these bones charged with lightning
> While his secular horse,
> The shadow removed like a halter,
> Moves magisterially into the sun,
> And O you black ugly beast O my beauty
> Churn up these white fields of leprosy![17]

He was at his worst in "A Poor Poet Is Grateful For A Sudden Thaw":

> The snow shows darkly under your heels,
> In places it looks like oyster shells,
> The wakes of autos are like fat eels,
> The sidestreets blossom with lovely smells;
> Men are raising a shout in the town,
> It might even bring the System down —[18]

The elements in his poems — good, bad and indifferent — were the same: every-day occurrences recounted with the immediacy of a first-person point of view; left-wing political pronouncements or subjects; images, often of animals, noteable for an earthiness possible only to one who had grown up among almost constant evidence of bodily functions; an English notion, drawn largely from Romantic poetry, of what poetry is and ought to be; an American grasp of compact, hard-punching colloquial forms; an unabashed admiration of and sensual engagement in the English language, especially erudite, coarse and tactile words. The result was an all-options-open poetry. Each poem could be read as all things to all people; or, to put it another way, no poem could be criticised for not doing something poetry was supposed to do. Layton resembled a cook faced with a shelf of international cook-books. Without adopting the assumptions and ingredients of any one authority, he found it impossible to tell what to mix with what, and when. The elements sometimes fell into place all wrong. At other times, they comprised units of astonishing felicity. No single poem was consistently good, though some were almost completely dreadful.

Now is the Place, the sixth book in the New Writers series from First Statement Press, was reviewed — evidence of the effervescence of the Canadian poetry scene, and of the keen interest in poetry in the post-war period. Sales for all books in the series, which cost $1.25 each, were small — none exceeding five hundred copies. Robert Weaver, who was at the hub of the Canadian literary wheel, reviewed *Now is the Place* for "Focus on '48" on CKEY radio in Toronto on 18 July,[19] before John Sutherland's review appeared in *Northern Review*. Weaver praised the artistic nature of the book (the cover, a sketch by Betty, depicted slum children playing in the street and a mother leaning in a doorway) and contrasted it to other recent books of poetry (probably Ryerson's chapbooks), which seemed "to depend on school texts for models and a paste pot and discarded newspapers for materials." Weaver focussed on Layton's proletarian side and highlighted the influence of "the American realists."

> He is a political leftist and...this fact is of literary as much as political significance. It means, most obviously, that Layton is in revolt against many aspects of our

society, but it also means that his revolt is not sterile and irresponsibly individualistic.... It is difficult...to write of the poor, especially of the alien poor, without being destroyed by pity or sentimentality. Layton usually manages a dry, clear compassion; he has much humour and a lusty and probably basically non-Canadian appreciation of all aspects of life.

At his best, Weaver said, Layton's irony was "beautifully sustained." But what did Weaver mean by "non-Canadian?" Perhaps Layton's angle of vision was not typically Canadian because it was not reticent, cautious or polite. Weaver described the New Writers series as "our legitimate literary underworld" and praised it (somewhat inconsistently) for its "long overdue attempt...to smuggle into Canada literary techniques and intellectual attitudes in keeping with our time." Weaver noted that the work of "this energetic Montreal group has been greeted with indifference or active hostility by most of our established literary figures," and he predicted that Layton would not find "the mass-audience that proletarian poetry must theoretically demand." In a note to Layton, Weaver admitted that his review had been "pretty hasty work and I'm afraid superficial."[20] Certainly the review failed to note the enormous debt Layton owed to the English Romantics and eighteenth-century poets, like Pope. If Layton was the proletarian, realistic writer Weaver described, he was different from other such writers. He was florid while they "pared down;" he was disorderly while they were fastidious; though his language was at times colloquial, like theirs, it was at other times archaic, even flowery.

In the August *Northern Review*,[21] Sutherland predictably praised the book he had edited, especially the fiction, where he believed Layton's talent lay: "the two short stories are the best yet written by a Canadian." His comment that only "about four" of the poems in the collection could be called poetry is enigmatic. It raises questions about Sutherland's editorial policies. He stated that "three-quarters of the poems are of small value except as restoratives from our puritanical drought." Why, then, did he publish them? Would Layton not revise? Sutherland included four of the poems from *Now Is*

The Place in *Other Canadians*[22] and accepted at least seven other Layton poems for *Northern Review* in the past two years. Had he not already accepted that they were poems? He seems to have wanted to use Layton's work to attack the elitism of other Canadian poets. He claimed that *Now Is The Place* was "unusual among books by the younger Canadian writers in appealing directly to ourselves rather than to our lurking snobbishness." Almost defensively, Sutherland humorously highlighted the connection between Layton and Wordsworth, which was "their joint capacity for emotion recollected in tranquility. The difference is that, while Wordsworth recollected daffodils, abbeys, etc., this poet recollects selling newspapers, buying bad fish, walking innumerable times under the obscene cross squatting on Montreal Mountain, and similar emotions. Moreover, his tranquility takes the form of anger." In Layton's defense, Sutherland asserted that Layton was a "rebel" with "guts." "This has irked conventional people, and irked still more those who can only pose as rebels. He will never turn these disadvantages to account until the day of the transvaluing."

A more thoughtful review than Weaver's or Sutherland's was Harry Roskolenko's in the June 1949 issue of a journal coincidentally called *Here and Now*. Roskolenko reviewed *Here and Now* and *Now Is The Place* in an article called "Post War Poetry in Canada." He called Layton "the Marxist who sees the over-all condition of man and society and intends to tell you just what is to be done — and he does it, openly, big, sarcastic and sweating at it. The symbols of our day are pulled taut and all that is recognizable comes into focus, the poem of disintegration, the neon-blasted cities." Roskolenko noted that Layton's satire was neither "neat" nor "refined" (he contrasted Layton with the academic poet Roy Daniells), and that Layton preferred "the obvious explosion, the gag instead of sly wit, the broadside instead of the pin-prick." To Roskolenko, Layton was "sophisticated" in literature and politics. In a few incisive sentences, Roskolenko conveyed Layton's real gift and appeal as a writer:

> From this sophistication [he] has extracted the core, entered into the centre, broken through the centre and

come back to the surface again. It is as athletic as it is intellectual and emotional.... The total process is visible in the bold, strong, often too-persuasive indictments of social-minded poems. The language is often a cannon rather than a sword; the splash too great; but the purpose...is good. The imagery is active; like all things that make a parade and the watcher at one and the same time. For it is the Marxist parade walking through the war, the world that makes men war — all neatly companioned by a marginalia of fact resolving so many fictions that only the obvious fiction of the poet remains at the end.

Unlike other reviewers, Roskolenko saw Layton's "many worlds" and grasped that the only common denominator was Layton himself.

By 1948, Layton was conspicuous in the world of Canadian poetry. He had published two volumes of poems (excluding reprints, a total of about forty-six poems) and had made numerous contributions to several of the most prominent literary journals. Sutherland's attack on Smith's literary elitism in his introduction to *Other Canadians* in 1947, and his singling out of Layton as one of the three major proletarian voices in recent poetry, was well and widely understood. Given these facts, one would expect some of Layton's poems to appear in the revised second edition of A.J.M. Smith's *The Book of Canadian Poetry*, which was published in 1948. There were thirty poets represented in Smith's section called "Modern Poetry": Scott, Smith, Finch, Anderson, Page and E.J. Pratt (who was sixty-five) were included. So were Louis Dudek and Raymond Souster, two of the "proletarian" poets Sutherland had mentioned. The anthology did not include Irving Layton.

Vehlvel Wolfsohn, Keine Lazarovitch's father, a cotton manufacturer in Tirgul Neamt, Romania.
CREDIT: BRIAN MERRETT
DONATED BY GAZELLA GOLDBERG

Gazella Lazarovitch, nick-named Printzesen *(the Princess), in her mid-teens at about the time of her marriage to Strul Goldberg.*
CREDIT: BRIAN MERRETT
DONATED BY GAZELLA GOLDBERG

Keine Lazarovitch and her girls in Montreal about 1920: Sarah Latch (Harry's wife) standing left; Gazella (Printzesen) standing right; Ester (Chora or Criminas) seated left; and the aimiable Dora.
CREDIT: BRIAN MURRETT
DONATED BY HYMAN LATCH

Keine Lazarovitch with her son, Hyman (Guzlin) about 1924.
CREDIT: BRIAN MERRETT
DONATED BY HYMAN LATCH

"Nappy" Lazarovitch (upper left) and the boys in his graduating class at Alexandra Street School, June 1925.
DONATED BY IRVING LAYTON

Miss Benjamin, the Grade Six teacher whose extraordinary blush inspired Issie Lazarovitch to write one of his first poems, seen here in her graduation photograph a year or two before she taught him.
DONATED BY IRMA ZACK

Sixteen-year-old Lazarovitch at the Hebrew Orphans' Home in Montreal where he was fired for initiating a protest against the administrators.
CREDIT: BRIAN MERRETT
DONATED BY IRVING LAYTON

Vehlvel (Bill) Goldberg at eighteen with the twenty-two year old "uncle" Lazarovitch who would be his friend for life.
CREDIT: BRIAN MERRETT
DONATED BY HYMAN LATCH

Israel Lazarovitch's student card photo for 1929-30, the year he was a member of the Young People's Socialist League in Montreal.
DONATED BY IRVING LAYTON

Isadore Lazarre's first love, Suzanne Rosenberg, his "Russian Princess" and an outspoken member of the Young Communist League in the late 1920's.
CREDIT: BRIAN MERRETT
DONATED BY IRVING LAYTON

ABOVE: *"Too young for all that pride"*: wrestling a bull calf on the farm.
CREDIT: BRIAN MERRETT
DONATED BY HYMAN LATCH

TOP LEFT: *The Cuisinières' "dear little La-Laz' relaxing on St. Helen's Island near Montreal.*
CREDIT: BRIAN MERRETT
DONATED BY HYMAN LATCH

MIDDLE LEFT: *"As full of wisdom as a cheese of mites"*: Irving Peter Layton (with pipe) and some of his colleagues at Macdonald College in 1937.
CREDIT: BRIAN MERRETT
DONATED BY HYMAN LATCH

The Lazarovitch boys at Larry's (Oscar's) farm: left to right Harry (the *Shegetz*), Hyman (*Guzlin*), Issie (*Flamplatz*) and Larry (*Megele*).
CREDIT: BRIAN MERRETT
DONATED BY HYMAN LATCH

TOP LEFT: Lieutenant Layton and his wife Faye Lynch ("The General") in 1942.
CREDIT: BRIAN MERRETT
DONATED BY IRVING LAYTON

TOP RIGHT: A 1940s sketch of Layton asleep by Betty Sutherland: "he had a fascinating face to draw".
CREDIT: BRIAN MERRETT
DONATED BY BOSCHKA LAYTON

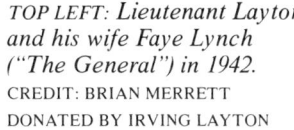

MIDDLE LEFT: "Hubby-cat" and "Wabby-puss" (Irving and Betty) enjoying the bohemian splendour of their home in Côte St. Luc.
CREDIT: BRIAN MERRETT
DONATED BY AVIVA LAYTON

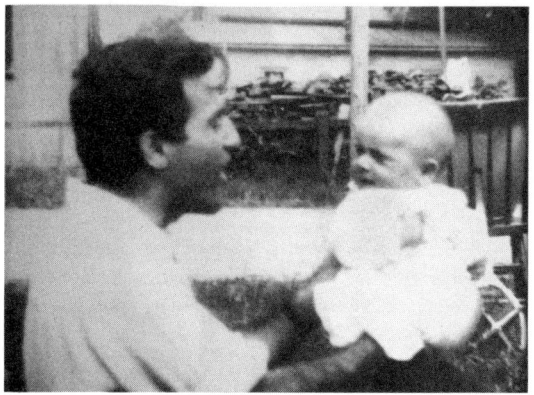

Irving plays with Max during a weekend visit to the run-down cottage where Betty and Bill Goodwin were spending the summer of 1946 "in Platonic bliss".
DONATED BY AUDREY AKMAN

Games on Fletcher's Field near Herzliah in the 50s.
CREDIT: BRIAN MERRETT
DONATED BY AVIVA LAYTON

"They sleep without dreams or nightmares": Layton, full of life, in the mid-50s.
CREDIT: BRIAN MERRETT
DONATED BY AVIVA LAYTON

Betty, Max and Sissyboo (Naomi) about 1955.
CREDIT: BRIAN MERRETT
DONATED BY AVIVA LAYTON

Poet by Default

Between August 1948 and August 1949, Betty and her brother, John, drove Irving Layton to poetry, but not in ways one would expect. Though Betty soothed, admired and stabilized her husband, it was not these qualities but her unexpected pregnancy that forced his hand. And though John Sutherland edited, published and encouraged his brother-in-law, it was, paradoxically, his criticism, not his praise, that most affected Layton.

At the beginning of 1948, even though he had just published *Now Is The Place*, poetry was not foremost among Layton's "many worlds." As a writer, he was torn between poems and short stories. But neither literary activity seemed as important to him as his aspiration to become a university professor. Despite his frequent diatribes against academics, especially those who wrote poetry like Finch, Pratt, Smith and Scott, he clearly entertained ambitions for a university post. He had passed McGill's Ph.D. preliminary oral examination in political science and the French requirement in December 1947; he enrolled in the Ph.D. programme in 1948 and would re-enroll in 1949.[1] Frank Scott had agreed to supervise his thesis on Laski in political science. As some of his poems and short stories strongly suggested,[2] Layton did not enjoy the long hours, tedium and lack of intellectual challenge he experienced teaching immigrants and Jewish children. What he did like about teaching — being centre-stage, exercising power, arousing curiosity in others, scrapping in debates — could have been enjoyed much more in a university setting. There he could triumph over equals, debate with more agile opponents and work shorter classroom hours. Teaching at Herzliah and the Jewish People's Library was better than most other ways to make a living, but he had his eye fixed higher, on the very occupation he frequently professed to despise. Had he successfully proceeded to a Ph.D. in political science, he readily would have obtained a university job. He would have devoted more of his time and energy to writing political theory and giving lectures in the academic circuit, where he would have been in demand as an entertaining, vigorous speaker. It is difficult to speculate what role creative writing might have played in his life; probably, it would have been a minor one, though he almost certainly would not have abandoned it outright. In all likelihood, Layton would have become an authority in political science who wrote poetry on the side; like Frank Scott, a professor who wrote poems after his other responsibilities were discharged.

As far as the less pressing matter of poetry versus short stories, John Sutherland ought to have known his brother-in-law better. It was clear from his observations in *Northern Review*'s July/August 1948 issue that he wanted to encourage Layton to write short stories instead of poetry. ("It...seems obvious that Mr. Layton's talents lie in fiction rather than poetry.") Surely he realized that Layton was too rebellious to follow meekly anyone's advice. What spurred Layton was rejection, not praise. It was to Sutherland's insults that he responded, not to his commendations. Sutherland had written that "about three-quarters of the poems are of small value except as restoratives from our puritanical drought," claiming that only a few "probably indicate that Mr. Layton is a poet of some sort." The best way to get Layton to do something was to tell him, preferably in an insulting way, that he could not or should not do it. His family had told him he should get a job in business; he had slipped through their fingers. Everyone had said he never could get a university degree; he had managed a B.Sc. and an MA and was bent on getting a Ph.D. People had urged him not to marry a gentile; he had gone ahead and done so. Jews, he had been told, could not hope to become teachers; he would show them. So only four poems deserved to be called poems? So he was good at short stories, but not good as a poet? He'd be a poet!

Almost immediately after Sutherland's review of *Now Is The Place*, Layton resigned from the editorial board of *Northern Review*, which overnight became a less controversial journal. He disclaimed any input into the introduction to *Other Canadians*, although he had actually contributed a great deal. (Betty recalls that he dictated whole sections to John.[3]) Their friendship began to disintegrate.

John Sutherland had played a crucial role in directing Layton away from short stories and towards poetry, but Betty played a more decisive role in shaping her husband's future life. Sometime in August 1949, proving truth in the old proverb "new house, new baby," Betty became pregnant. Though she had a weak heart, from rheumatic fever in childhood, and had been advised, after Max was born, that she should not have any more children, she was pleased. Their rural cottage at 8035 Kildare Avenue, in Côte St. Luc, with its large, sunny garden, seemed idyllic. There "hubby-cat," as Betty called Layton, and "wabby-puss," as Layton called his wife, from the German *wiebe* (woman), could live close to nature in middle-class domestic bliss.

Though a number of factors conspired to end Layton's academic career, the birth of Naomi Parker (Betty's mother's maiden name) on 1 May 1950 was most significant. "Dear Frank," Layton wrote to Scott on 23 January 1950:

> Since the Ch[ristmas] break, I've thrown out the notion I entertained in October that I could get any work done on my thesis. As I wrote Dr. Thomson — I had made the mistake of confusing ambition with ability. My teaching duties have been much heavier than I thought they would be, leaving me almost no time for any outside reading and study. The school [Herzliah] asked me to take over Latin, Geometry, and Algebra, subjects that I'm very rusty in, it has meant hrs. of real effort to get

myself to *a pt.* where I could *make* any sense trying to explain them to a very sophisticated group of young persons. I had to take on more hrs. of teaching because Bet's expecting in May, I have a blasted mortgage to pay off, and a highly capricious Chev. Model 1938 that I've got to keep in good humour. At present, I'm toiling for these different institutions and it seems that the harder I work the more deeply I crawl or rather plunge into debt.

That's the situation Frank. There's no sense in pretending to myself that I'm working on a Ph.D. Thesis when I'm not. And it's no good for my morale. So I've decided to call it a day, but before I write the thing off, I want to thank you and to tell you how much I appreciated the intelligent and sympathetic ear and tongue you gave to my brief effort. You were wunderbar. The longer I live, the more I learn to value your many rare and excellent qualities.[4]

A week later, Scott replied:

I am very sorry to learn that you cannot continue with your work.... I was personally enjoying working with you, and I should have liked to have seen the thesis you would eventually have written. I think you perhaps are particularly qualified to write on the subject you chose. However, I can appreciate the difficulties you face, and I must say that I think your decision is a wise one. Maybe someday you can write on this same subject even though you are not a graduate student.[5]

Layton observed that the early fifties were, for him, a period of frenetic activity: "I was working three or four teaching jobs at a time: Herzliah steadily, Jewish immigrants some evenings, part time classes in literature at Sir George Williams University [which he used to call "the happy hunting ground for easy diplomas"][6] other evenings, assisting in political science classes at McGill. For each of these jobs I was being paid as a part time lecturer at only $3.00–$4.00 an hour. One year I taught all of Shaw's plays at the Jewish People's Library. The next year it was all of Shakespeare's plays. I was teaching political and social philosophy, modern British and American poetry, Canadian literature, plus all the subjects Herzliah now expected me to do. And Betty was becoming more and more ambitious as a painter. After the children began going to a Jewish parochial school, she took a studio on Duluth Avenue. Our lives got to be very hyper. I seemed to have excess energy. I thought at the time that I had to do it for financial reasons, but maybe I was crazy without knowing it."[7] For relaxation, they went to the homes of their literary friends for informal evenings, reading poetry, drinking coffee or tea (liquor, because of the expense, was a rarity) and talking about the arts, politics and life generally. In the summers, they took cottages where they could be inexpensively obtained: north to the Laurentians or south to the Eastern Townships. Once, they agreed to be gardeners in exchange for free room and board. Even on holidays, Betty recalls, Irving kept frantically busy, walking, swimming, when in town boxing or playing handball and reading "three or four books a day."[8]

Out of this ferment of excessive activity came poems instead of a political thesis, poems piqued into existence partly by John Sutherland's remarks. Layton's third collection, *The Black Huntsmen*, dedicated to "Elizabeth the Good" (Betty) and published by Layton, appeared in 1951. It contained no short stories. Again, Layton depended heavily on published material. More than half of the thirty-nine poems already had been published: fifteen had appeared in one or the other of his first two volumes; seven had appeared in both. In a prefatory note, Layton claimed that the poems reprinted from earlier collections, "with the exception of De Bullion Street and The Swimmer...have all been revised in some detail." This statement was misleading. Most of his revisions were minor. In "Church Parade,"[9] for example, he simply moved every other line a few spaces to the right; in "Stolen Watch,"[10] he split one line into two and substituted the more general "a hammer" for "his Meccano." Two poems, "Newsboy" and "The Modern Poet,"[11] were not revised at all. To five poems he gave new titles; for example, "To the Lawyer Handling My Divorce Case" became "Existentialist." Though there were nineteen new poems (of which four shortly afterwards would be published in literary journals), they were mainly undistinguished. Several of the nineteen were reprinted rarely or not at all. Layton's best poems were still "Newsboy," Stolen Watch," "Proof Reader," "De Bullion Street" and "Gents Furnishings."[12] "The Swimmer," which had appeared in *Here and Now* and *Now Is The Place*, was his strongest and most typical poem, and one that struck universal appeal:

> The afternoon foreclosing, see
> The swimmer plunges from his raft,
> Opening the spray corollas by his act of war —
> The snake heads strike
> Quickly and are silent.
>
> Emerging see how for a moment,
> A brown weed with marvellous bulbs,
> He lies imminent upon the water
> While light and sound come with a sharp passion
> From the gonad sea around the Poles
> And break in bright cockle-shells about his ears.
>
> He dives, floats, goes under like a thief
> Where his blood sings to the tiger shadows
> In the scentless greenery that leads him home,
> A male salmon down fretted stairways
> Through underwater slums....
>
> Stunned by the memory of lost gills
> He frames gestures of self-absorption
> Upon the skull-like beach;
> Observes with instigated eyes
> The sun that empties itself upon the water,
> And the last wave romping in
> To throw its boyhood on the marble sand.

This athletic, free-verse poem, written after a day at Caughnawaga,[13] threads Layton's boyhood memories of "fretted stairways" and "slums" into the web and woof of man's universal memory of an idealized, pre-evolved state. With resonant images drawn from nature and the world of animals, Layton celebrates the aliveness of life and hints at the deathly "self-absorption" that maturity involves. The swimmer is in his element, revelling in purposeless, sensual play. He is Layton as a wayward boy, all men with their illogical, instinctive drives and, ultimately, mankind. The poem resembles Wordsworth's "Intimations on Immortality" and Walt Whitman's *Song of Myself*, but its language is tougher and more savoury, its concept bolder and more sexual.

Reviews of *The Black Huntsmen* were not ecstatic. Poet Anne Marriott, in the *Canadian Forum*, found Layton's newer work "disappointingly strained and weak,"[14] and speculated that anger might have made him inarticulate. Northrop Frye (whom Layton had attacked for being unable to distinguish between poetic "flame" and critical "wax" in a poem called "Butchevo, The Critic") observed in "Letters in Canada: 1951"[15] that the book's "successes are quiet and the faults raucous." Frye objected to Layton's "militant," overly moral imagination; accused him of being "a noisy hot-gospeller" in most of the poems; and complained that "One can get as tired of buttocks in Mr. Layton as of buttercups in the *Canadian Poetry Magazine*." But Frye accurately sensed that beneath the strident tone lay another Layton: "There is a real poet buried in Mr. Layton, a gentle, wistful, lonely and rather frightened poet who tells us how his childhood love for Tennyson grew into a defiant fear of a hostile and pursuing world." It was Earle Birney's radio review on CBC's "Critically Speaking," on 15 July 1951, that most upset Layton. "He's rough and tough with language," Birney said, "spits audibly in the sink, slaps buttocks with a sombre zest, and retires early to the delights of the bedroom. He can unfortunately be bad-tempered, egotistic, childishly crude, and sentimental." Birney also noted that Layton's collection was "made up largely of selections from two previous volumes."

Birney's criticism drew from Layton his first written diatribe against a critic, on 22 July 1951:

Dear Mr. Birney:
    Honesty, if not critical acumen or sensibility, is asked from a reviewer. I'll not waste good typewriter ink in telling a lanky hayseed from the provinces what I think

of him: you can, if you try, muster sufficient intelligence to guess. But — you uncoiled tapeworm of asininity — where did you ever get the notion that I never wrote any prose? Were you, by any chance, trying to give yourself a cheap continental hug at the taxpayer's expense as the only Canadian poet who could manage other forms of writing? True, I have no novel to my credit, one blown out of the arsehole of a broken-down humorist in the last stages of the ST. VITUS DANCE — the jerky movement of the dance assisting the said propulsion — but surely even an ignorant worm like yourself must know that I have a creditable half-dozen published short stories to my name.

Moreover, you asserted with the glibness of a practiced liar that the Black Huntsmen was very largely made up of poems from my two previous volumes. In any language, Mr. Birney, that's a real stinkeroo. You probably picked that one up from Johnnie Sutherland, but even that doesn't excuse it's [sic] repetition on a national hook-up. The new poems constitute about half of the book.

Again, were you something more than a mediocre poet turned huckster, you would have mentioned the fact that most of the old poems had been revised in some detail. Indeed, to take care of superranuated [sic] dodos like yourself, I mentioned the fact twice; once, at the beginning of the book, and again at the end. What excuse, Mr. Birney, did you have, beside dishonesty, for not referring to this knowledge; unless it was the rage to compound the lie that the new volume was nothing else but the old volumes between different covers?

It concerns you to know that I am currently engaged in writing a poem called 'The Ballad of the Clotted Arsehair'. I have allotted several memorable verses to yourself.

      Irving Layton[16]

It was his best Keine Lazarovitch style. Six days later, he sent Birney a telegram, which arrived soon after the letter: I THOUGHT YOUR REVIEW OF THE BLACK HUNTSMEN SILLY AND RATHER PREJUDICED BUT MY LETTER WAS SILLIER PLEASE

EXCUSE MY BAD TEMPER A THOUSAND SINCERE APOLOGIES. On 2 August, Birney replied: "The letter made me feel you were in an abnormal state, and I had not proposed answering it, but your telegram assured me the state was temporary." Birney, who claimed he never bothered answering reviewers, calmly analysed his remarks and apologized for not referring to Layton's short stories: "I read your book with an open mind; I said what I thought; and I gave final emphasis to what I liked. Also, I gave you as much time as the others whose work I liked better."[17] But Layton could not let the matter alone. Almost immediately, he wrote back to Birney. Though the voice of Keine Lazarovitch does not thunder so loudly in the second letter, there are low rumblings; Birney is "pig-headed;" he's "a half-ass poet;" his discussion is "idiotic." "The volume contained such splendid poems as 'Auspex,'[18] 'Mrs. Fornheim, Refugee,'[19] 'Mont Rolland,'[20] 'The World's a Tavern,'[21] 'The Poet and the Statue,'[22] 'Elan,'[23] 'Gothic Landscape,'[24] 'The Swimmer,' 'De Bullion Street,' 'Drill Shed,'" Layton concluded, "any one of which would have made your fame and fortune."[25] At the bottom of the letter Birney added a note: "And then he met me and made it up!"

Target Practice

In August 1951, Louis Dudek returned to Montreal from New York. He invited Layton and Souster to meet him for lunch at his grandmother's farm on the banks of the Little Jesus River in Charlemagne, Quebec. The gathering was an important one for all of them. Souster commented: "I'll always remember the day...with Louis Dudek throwing the first two issues of Cid Corman's *Origin* down on the picnic table and saying, 'This is typical of what the nuts in New York are doing these days.' I remember casually flipping through both copies and then giving them back to him; I was not yet ready for Charles Olson and Robert Creeley. But the next year something led me back to those two issues, and then Louis came to Toronto in May and left me as a gift *The Collected Later Poems of William Carlos Williams*. From that time on my world of poetry assumed largely its present shape."[1]

Even at an ostensibly friendly picnic, Layton and Dudek had reason to regard each other with caution. When Dudek left for New York in 1943, they had seen eye-to-eye on politics and literature. But Dudek had been developing rapidly in directions Layton could not follow. Dudek had attempted a graduate degree in journalism and history at Columbia University, but he had soon transferred out of journalism (about which he would remain sceptical) into literature. His

MA thesis examined Thackeray as a writer and editor. His doctoral thesis, a defense of private presses and little magazines (later published as *Literature and the Press*), was directed by Lionel Trilling, who was associated with *Partisan Review*. Under Trilling's influence, Dudek began to alter his political views. The radicalism he had first heard from Frank Scott's lips in a speech at Montreal's Musée de Beaux Arts was refined into a gentler liberalism. "Trilling had once been Marxist, but he had become critical of Marxism. He pushed me out of simple radicalism into a more analytical point of view on society's relationship to literature."[2] With the excitement such intellectual discoveries can engender, Dudek wrote to Layton in 1947 to share some of these views. "He wrote back to me all right," Dudek recalls: "He was so insulting — it was one of his maniacal letters — that I never wrote back. He accused me of selling out. Selling out! In those years I was doing odd jobs like door-to-door surveys for the *New York Times* and wrapping parcels in the mail room at Columbia University — $10.00 a week jobs! I found his rigid Marxism intolerable. So for several years we were incommunicado. I didn't love him that much. I didn't miss him. I put him down for a loss. Anyone who writes like that isn't a friend."[3]

When Dudek began teaching at McGill University, he drove home a point that Layton rather would not have faced. The two men had started out from more-or-less equal lower-class backgrounds, with about the same talent, intellectual and literary aspirations and no money. Both had wanted a doctorate. Layton had had to back off, but Dudek was well on his way to completing his degree and had a job at McGill. Dudek had something Layton wanted, a career he had had to give up. The lanky, fair-haired gentile was to be the professor. Then Layton must oppose intellectuals and be the poet.

When he slapped down those first two issues of *Origin* on his grandmother's picnic table, Dudek unknowingly presented Layton with an intensely personal challenge. Dudek made no secret of his new American contacts. Through Cid Corman, editor of *Origin*, he had become acquainted with a number of writers, including Ezra Pound. Dudek had written admiringly in 1949 to Pound, who was confined for treason in Washington's St. Elizabeth's Hospital. Pound had responded and set in motion a correspondence. Dudek was soon running errands for Pound, sending him books and materials. Dudek was on the inside, right up to date on American writing. His prestige provoked Layton in the extreme.

Souster had written to Dudek in New York, suggesting they start a small magazine. At first, Dudek refused. As Frank Davey has shown,[4] Dudek wished to avoid a confrontation, especially with John Sutherland, and on his return attempted to fit into the literary gatherings at Frank Scott's, which included Phyllis Webb, Hugh MacLennan, A.M. Klein and Neufville Shaw. In December 1951, in imitation of an idea of his called "Poetry Grapevine," which had worked briefly in the United States, he began what he called (with oddly Arthurian overtones) a "postal round table," which included Layton on its mailing list as well as poets across Canada, among them James Reaney, Anne Wilkinson, James Wreford, P.K. Page, Roy Daniells, Alan Crawley, E.J. Pratt, Neufville Shaw, A.J.M. Smith, A.G. Bailey, Miriam Waddington, Dorothy Livesay, Kay Smith, Ralph Gustafson, Robert Finch, A.M. Klein, Phyllis Webb, Margaret Avison, Anne Marriott, John Sutherland, F.R. Scott, Raymond Souster, Earle Birney and W.W.E. Ross. Modernism was no longer a Montreal movement; it had become a national phenomenon with regional distinctions. Dudek's fresh-faced enthusiasm, in tandem with genuine international authority, held out the possibility of a wide-flung support-system for a broad range of Canadian poets. The one chink in his apparently flawless armour was his marriage, which had broken down at the end of his New York years. Betty telephoned him not long after the fall term at McGill began, and persuaded him to reunite with Stephanie, whom he had married in 1943.

Souster was not content to leave the publishing of poetry mainly in the hands of *Northern Review*. He thought Sutherland's editorial policies somewhat old-fashioned and conservative. In October 1951, he told Dudek he planned to publish *Contact*, a little magazine to be based in Toronto that would be more innovative and experimental than *Northern Review*. Though Dudek did not think Souster's scheme a threat to Sutherland, Sutherland refused to co-operate. In November, Dudek wrote in frustration to Souster:

"J. Sutherland is dead as a doorknob. He's waiting for something to drop into his lap." When the first issue of *Contact* arrived from Toronto, Dudek was clearly elated.[5]

Contact was the logical culmination of the new forces Dudek unleashed on the Canadian poetry scene. Through his contacts, especially Cid Corman, he drew on a wide network of North American poets. While Sutherland remained nationalistic in his attempt to build and define a Canadian school of letters, Souster devoted more than half of each issue of *Contact* to writers outside Canada. As Frank Davey concludes: "The message which they projected through *Contact* was clear: Canadian poetry magazines were conventional and parochial; Canadian writers were isolated and technically naïve; international writing was rapidly leaving a static Canadian literature behind."[6] Among *Contact*'s contributors were well-known non-Canadian poets: Denise Levertov, Guillaume Apollinaire and Wallace Stevens and the poets associated with the experimental North Carolina school Black Mountain College, Charles Olson and Robert Creeley.

Souster sat firm at the helm of *Contact*. Cid Corman proposed an amalgamation of *Origin*, *Contact* and the English magazine *The Window*; Dudek suggested that Souster share the editorship of *Contact* with himself and Layton. Souster refused both offers. This crucible of literary pressures resulted in a book that featured poems by Layton, Souster and Dudek, printed on Souster's printing equipment in Toronto at the poets' own expense. In January 1952, Souster approved Dudek's first idea for a name: "TRIO? Or some name of a 3 headed beast." But they needed a publisher. Souster and Dudek shrank from approaching McClelland and Stewart, whose Indian File series on Canadian literature provided a possible outlet for their book, or Ryerson Press, whose chapbooks offered another. They thought the Indian File series hopelessly out of date; and each had published with Ryerson and felt that they had been edited out of existence. Thus, *Cerberus*, named after the three-headed dog who guards the gates of Hell, was published with Contact Press in April 1952.

Layton's brief introduction to the twenty-one poems that made up his third of the book betrays an angry sense of injustice. The introductions of Souster and Dudek assume common denominators between the three poets; Layton's announces their differences. "Dudek, Souster and I hold different opinions on a number of subjects, ranging from the war in Korea to the optimum size of women's bathing suits." He was prepared to concede only that the three poets were brought together to say "a loud nix to the forces high-pressuring us into conformity or atomic dispersion."[7] In other words, even in a revolutionary publication that shunned conventional publishing outlets for poetry and took a deliberately nose-thumbing attitude to the literary community, Layton took the stance of a "bright rebellious talent" and refused to be part of a group of three. He attacked his usual targets: Canada's philistinism, business and technology-oriented education, middle-class morality, the genteel tradition — all "the gilded and gelded." But there were some new objects of attack, which smacked of more personal grievances: "right-thinking social workers" (could he have had Miriam Waddington in mind?) and university graduates (could he have been taking furtive aim at Dudek?). While Souster praised Olson in his introduction, Layton praised Walt Whitman, with whose "barbaric yawp" he felt comfortable.

Most of Layton's poems in *Cerberus* were highly personalized attacks that correspond to the tone of his introduction. For the first time, all the poems in the collection were recent and appeared for the first time in 1952, either in the book or in *Contact*. Though they are some of his worst poems, they convey much about his state of mind at the time. He seems to have been knocked off balance and to have lost some of his self-confidence as a poet in the flurry of activity precipitated by the return of Dudek. The most painful poem is an attack on his brother-in-law, the man who launched his poetic career, John Sutherland. It is called "Good-bye Bahai." ("Baha'ism" is a belief in the unity of all religions; the Baha'i faith was founded in 1863 by a Persian, Mussein Ali.)

>he sniffs trends like a butcher
>meat;
>he's a punctilious critic and
>what he does not comprend
>he has his wife read

and explain to him. She does that well.
on hot summer nights her green fingertips
budding innumerable little wineglasses
she has the appearance of a fallen dryad.

a monk with a novel refectory joke
he looks at you
out of the corner of his mouth;
he has trouble with molars.

good-bye Bahai.
I know an austerer religion,
having seen their etiolated faces
bent over
arcana canadiana.[8]

He also attacked Earle Birney ("Little David")[9] as a drunk in a privy; Northrop Frye ("The Excessively Quiet Groves")[10] as a useless archaeologist; A.J.M. Smith ("News of the Phoenix")[11] as a drunk who fancies himself Yeats; Miriam Waddington ("Poetess")[12] as cute and pimpled; and Raymond Souster ("Letter to Raymond Souster")[13] as too much influenced by American colloquialism. (Souster admired the poem.) Layton also criticised the *Report* of the Massey Royal Commission on National Development in the Arts, Letters, and Sciences in Canada.[14] The *Report* had stated that 423 books of poetry and drama were published in Great Britain in 1948, 504 books of poetry in the United States and only 35 books of poetry in Canada.[15] His few love poems and more general poems suggest a bleak, distorted view: love turned to ashes, young women turned to crones, lost joys. Only rarely are there lines or groups of lines as good as those in "The Swimmer." The collection reads like the bitter, somewhat uncontrolled cries of a man in pain.

Critical response to *Cerberus* probably confused the tiny audience the book addressed. The Toronto *Globe and Mail* gave it a "medium-voiced" affirmation on the grounds that it was "a good thing" for the Canadian public to encounter a little vigour.[16] James Reaney, in what Raymond Souster thought was a "mixed-up hodge-podge,"[17] found a "unity of tone" amongst the three poets and described the book as "canine... funny, obscene [and] unusual." He thought the three contributors had previously been "gray poets" (had he read Layton's earlier volumes?) and thought their new "energy" was commendable.[18] B.K. Sandwell didn't much like the element of social protest in the book.[19] Northrop Frye "blushingly" recognized the satire on himself (he thought it was Layton's best), and praised the wistful and unique poem "To a Very Old Woman." Generally, Frye found two problems in Layton's militant writing: first, his "conception of effective language as deriving from vocabulary rather than rhythm," and "the tendency to talk about writing poetry instead of presenting it." But probably none of these observations leapt out at Layton when he read Frye's review. What probably piqued him most was Frye's statement: "Mr. Dudek's ideas are more advanced than those of his two collaborators, and so it is not surprising that he writes with more authority than they do."[20]

Layton was being ranked lower than Dudek, and the enterprises he had hoped Dudek and Souster (those two fellow "proleterian poets" singled out in Sutherland's *Other Canadians*) would launch successfully were not succeeding as they had hoped. Though they tried every marketing gambit they could devise (Layton sent a copy to the governor-general and received a formal thank-you letter from his secretary),[21] they had to admit, with Souster, that "we're a few isolated guys in a nation of 12,000,000 trying to put something we think is important over."[22] *Contact* magazine did not launch Canadian poetry into a larger sphere; *Cerberus* proved neither high-quality nor revolutionary; the publication of *Canadian Poems: 1850–1952*, edited by Layton and Dudek and printed by Souster's Contact Press (Jack McClelland turned it down as a publishing venture because of reprint fees), failed to replace A.J.M. Smith's *Book of Canadian Poetry* as the standard Canadian poetry anthology and textbook.

Sometime in the winter of 1952, Layton met Dudek for a game of handball. Somehow the game ceased to be merely a game. "I stopped for a rest during one of the matches," Dudek recalls, "and Layton started sounding off at me that he was Jonathan Swift and Shakespeare rolled into one.

"'Irving, this is crazy talk,' I told him. 'Talk about what you've written, not these meaningless generalities.'

"'Whoever wins the next game is the better poet!' Layton boasted."

They returned to their play like two madmen. The score went from 20-19 for Dudek to 20-20; then it was 22-23 for Layton, then 24-24. They leapt to make fantastic saves. Not stopping to rest or talk, they sweated it out with intense competition until, finally, in exhilaration, Irving won 31-29. "After we showered, both of us exhausted," Layton recalls, "Louis asked me if I thought he was a major poet. I told him I thought I was a major poet, but he was only a minor one. I still think so. He has a modest lyric talent, but his spark was doused by intellectuality."[23]

Vexed Questions

"Life's funny," Layton wrote in January 1953 to the American poet Robert Creeley, who was spending the year in Mallorca, Spain. "Last night we celebrated *CIV/n* [their new poetry magazine] with an orgy and to give the issue the proper send-off we all undressed and sat about holding each other's privates (sounds gruesome now). And I thought to myself, 'This is our [eighth] wedding anniversary and the first time my wife has ever touched another guy's penis.' Life's funny, ain't it? The surprises and coincidences that happen in it! But let's save all that for my poems."[1]

Layton had never met Creeley, but Raymond Souster sent Creeley Layton's third volume of poems, *The Black Huntsmen* (1951), and Layton followed up by writing to Creeley. Creeley wrote back to him in February 1953 admiring the poems Layton had published in Cid Corman's *Origin* and soliciting more of them to publish on his Divers Press in Mallorca. Thus began an intense three-year correspondence.

CIV/n had begun when a few younger Montreal poets, newly graduated from university, approached Louis Dudek for advice.[2] Dudek had suggested the title, which came from Pound's statement: "CIV/n — not a one-man job." ("CIV/n" was Pound's shorthand for "civilization.") The first mimeographed issue, edited by Aileen Collins and designed by young Montreal sculptor Buddy Rozynski, received editorial advice from Louis Dudek and Irving Layton. By the end of its seven issues, which spanned two years, poems and essays from such up-and-coming young writers as Leonard Norman Cohen (who accompanied his poems by strumming on a guitar), Phyllis Webb, Gael Turnbull, Doug Jones, Eli Mandel and Avi Boxer had been printed alongside work by older writers such as Souster, Patrick Anderson and F.R. Scott and three American writers with whom Layton and Dudek were quickly becoming more familiar, Cid Corman, Robert Creeley and Charles Olson. *CIV/n* was a vehicle for presenting a new evolutionary development in modern Canadian poetry.

John Sutherland's *Northern Review* concentrated on more dignified Canadian poems (his "golden boy" was South African Roy Campbell). But the three "proletarian" poets he had hailed in 1947 — Dudek, Souster and Layton — had bridged the generation gap, identified with the free-wheeling and often satirical energy of younger poets and joined them in their new magazine. *CIV/n* recorded the literary discussions (including, for example, thoughts on Marshall McLuhan's new theories and outrage at Ezra Pound's incarceration) and the newest poems being read at the homes of several Montreal poets. The fourth issue contained a sketch of Dylan Thomas by Betty Layton and the poem "Elegy on the Death of Dylan Thomas" by Phyllis Webb. (The Welsh poet visited McGill in the fall of 1952, and went to Layton's house afterwards. Layton commented, "I could never see what all the fuss about Dylan Thomas was about. He's written about half-a-dozen admirable poems, but surely no more. Louis and I brought him...home, but I think he was too spiffilated to know where he was.... He was a short, balding man with the face of an amiable broker.... I couldn't help thinking that he looked like a blurred copy of...an unheroic Winston Churchill."[3]) According to Ken Norris,[4] *CIV/n* "bolstered" the advance towards modernism begun by *Contact* (which continued to be published until late 1954) and succeeded in "pushing poetry forward to a condition of Modernism resting on the most solid of foundations. Although the socialist verse of the forties had suffered a defeat, social force and consciousness were still necessary in verse, as well as a moral integrity and commitment to language."

The old *Preview* group had dispersed. Though they were

pursuing individual careers as poets, they had left behind any sense of group identity after their resignation from the editorial board of *Northern Review*. Patrick Anderson separated from his wife and left for England. He returned to teach at McGill for two years (1948 to 1950) with his English lover, Orlando Gearing. ("We all called him 'Orlando Furioso,'" Betty recalls.[5]) In 1950, P.K. Page married W.H. Irwin, commissioner of the National Film Board; he became an ambassador in 1953 and they travelled to Australia, Brazil and Mexico. A.M. Klein assisted Layton with the revision of some of his poems for *The Black Huntsmen* in 1951. But he was already showing signs of the psychological stress that would lead to two suicide attempts in 1954, after which he became a recluse. (In 1953, Layton described him as "Too smug, too petit-bourgeois. A considerable talent hamstrung by a worldly wisdom: poetry doesn't long survive here. I don't think he'll ever write another poem."[6]) F.R. Scott continued to hold literary evenings at his home on Clarke Street and joined the *CIV/n* group at theirs. He was a brilliant constitutional lawyer and was concentrating his energies on his career in politics and law. In 1952, he spent a year in Burma as Canada's representative to the United Nations. (After meeting Scott, Cid Corman observed, "[He] is good to want to be part of the whole boost [of Canadian poetry], but I suspect there is too much disinterest...insufficient direct involvement in what goes; I mean; his own work."[7])

As the forties came to a close, Sutherland lost touch with the new poets. Although he was attracted to Layton's left-wing theories in the late forties, he turned away from thoughts of social purpose and towards the conventional teachings of the Roman Catholic church, which he had previously denounced. He and Layton always had temperamental differences, and Sutherland complained that Layton had not pitched in with the menial jobs of setting type, printing, distribution and correspondence as much as other members of the *First Statement* group.[8] In fact, John Sutherland was slowly dying. As his energy drained away, he needed a philosophy that would lend meaning to his suffering. Nothing could have been more alien and incomprehensible to Layton than Sutherland's new "morose religiosity."[9] Robust with life, Layton sought to divest himself of all pre-packaged philosophies and to find a language to celebrate the powerful throbbing in his own veins. As Sutherland became more religious and contemplative, Layton stood back and laughed satirically at his sickly brother-in-law, the man who had said *he* was no poet.

Life, energy and meaty discussions of poetry were found in the trio Sutherland had singled out in *Other Canadians* in 1947. Dudek was back in Montreal, armed with his copies of Cid Corman's *Origin* and his contacts with Pound, Creeley and Olson, and the two rivals sparred frequently. They both wrote to Souster in Toronto. Dudek held up "the nuts in New York" (the new poets who had been influenced by Pound) as the latest word in modern poetry. He might just as well have held up a target in front of Layton's broad beaked nose. Layton was disarmed by Dudek's academic success and dismayed by his intimacy with American writing. Dudek overshadowed him at present, and Souster, with his Toronto press, sat nicely at the hub of Canadian modern poetry. But it would not last. Layton must find out all he could about these Americans.

Layton's *Love the Conqueror Worm*, printed at his own expense (two hundred dollars for four hundred copies, which would sell for a dollar each) by Souster at Contact Press, appeared at the end of the first week of February 1953. With the exception of the long rhyming satire "Ah Rats!!! (A Political Extravaganza of the 30's)," reprinted from a 1938 issue of the *McGill Daily*, it was his first solo collection of entirely recent work. The poems in the collection differed significantly from the poems in *Cerberus*. These were less personal, more universal; less Marxist, more idiosyncratic. As Souster wrote, "you have done some of your best work in the last year or so."[10] In many of the poems, Layton had a more detached outlook on life. He deepened his defense of the force of life with mythological rather than political underpinnings. "How different, how less generous our political climate is today than say, two decades ago," he now claimed.[11]

The timing of the book could not have been better. Without it, he probably would not have been treated as an emerging poet by the Americans he courted. And it was his third book. He looked like a poet who spoke with authority.

One of the poems from *Love the Conqueror Worm* provoked an on-going discussion with Creeley, Olson and Corman, writers with whom Layton kept up a voluminous correspondence during the next few years.

Robert Creeley thought the best poem in the book was "Vexata Quaestio."

>I fixing my eyes upon a tree
>Maccabean among the dwarfed
>>Stalks of summer
>Listened for ships' sound and birdsong
>And felt the bites of insects
>>Expiring in my arms' hairs.
>
>And there among the green prayerful birds
>Among the corn I heard
>>The chaffering blades:
>"You are no flydung on cherry blossoms,
>Among two-legged lice
>>You have the gift of praise.
>
>"Give your stripped body to the sun
>Your sex to any skilled
>>And pretty damsel;
>From the bonfire
>Of your guilts make
>>A blazing Greek sun."
>
>Then the wind which all day
>Had run regattas through the fields
>>Grew chill, became
>A tree-dismantling wind;
>
>The sun went down
>>And called my brown skin in.[12]

In his inimitable style, peppered with swear words, Creeley wrote on 17 February to praise the poem. He also asked for poems for a book he wanted to publish: "16 pages, say, or 24 or 32."[13] "You can use these forms [those of writers like Auden, Spender and Eliot]," Creeley wrote in April:

> with a tenseness, and thus a "rightness," utterly the issue of your own emotions.... I like, for example, the title poem of *Love The Conqueror Worm*, for this fact — the kind of quite literal verbal quickness in that fourth stanza, that it does go, right there, into a *sound* altogether the fix of what is being said. A lot of poetry doesn't, or buzzes on, irregardless. Death, Love, Hate, all the christly blah — all the same. Again I like your poems for the same quickness...like the Vexata Quaestio. Damn fine verse.... I like your poems, anyhow, because you do damn well invest formal or traditional metrics...with your own immediate presence. And you also experiment, within this area, to such an extent that you make a lot of so-called "avant-garde" types look that much the sicker.... Anyhow, you are the one. You have a very damn *melodic* line, I haven't heard poems making this literal music for god knows how long.... Your wit is likewise very great indeed — and damn well do tell me, since it came up via a man writing me, if Vexata Quaestio is "self-satiric" — if it isn't of course here I am with my pants down.... Anyhow tell me, I like it very, very much. (...anyhow would you do me the tolerance of damn well saying it, on a small single piece of paper, "I, Irving Layton, declare sd poem to be 'self-satiric'").

Creeley's response to Layton's work was amazing. Creeley's poetry was not at all like Layton's. His poem to the American poet he most admired, William Carlos Williams, was called "W.C.W.":

> The pleasure of the wit sustains
> a vague aroma

> The fox-glove (unseen) the
> wild flower
>
> To the hands come
> many things. In time of trouble
>
> a wild exultation.[14]

The poem might speak of exultation, but its cool, sparse, condensed form did not seem exultant. It displayed what Layton called "a gnomic quality." And Olson also wrote tough, short, tight little poems, like "These Days":

> whatever you have to say
> leave the roots on, let them
> dangle
>
> And the dirt
>
> just to make clear
> where they came from[15]

Though Layton would have agreed with the thought in both poems, he never would have expressed it in such a flat, understated or technically experimental manner. Oddly, Creeley liked Layton's work for Layton's use of the English tradition as his point of departure.[16] What Layton saw, or said he saw, was "a common outlook, a common philosophy, a kind of angry secularism, a poetic down-to-earthiness...which has 'come out of the war'."[17]

Creeley's observations drew a quick response from Layton: "Vexata Quaestio: subject or theme, Hebraism vs. Hellenism; modern man torn between the Hebraic/Christian impulse toward good and the Greek impulse toward beauty and self-expression, ends up by having neither the one nor the other. The soul of the modern is a battlefield where the two dominant cultural strains of Western Europe have been fighting it out for supremacy. The poem is self-ironical, of course; springing as it does, from an ambiguous experience and an awareness of its implications, but it's self-ironical in the sense that it speaks, at least I hope it does, for Everyman."[18]

To Creeley, Layton's theory (which was reminiscent of Matthew Arnold's essay "Culture and Anarchy") sounded like a lot of "very damn" or "christly" nonsense. "I don't finally read the poem with those implications," he wrote back,[19]

> or if I do they are anyhow so submerged in the content I feel them call it, but don't actually come to this form of identification. After all, the poem has a sharpness, and a kind of pulled-in humor which is very much the surface incident — and "surface" in no way to intend a diminution of same. I mean, it is primarily you & the goings-on, here, that pulls me up short, and makes for my own respect and admiration. There are damn beautiful ironies, in the poem, and these I think exercised most clearly on the man writing, — say, the last line. Or the wind which becomes the "tree-dismantling" wind, etc. Or the bites of insects, etc. God knows the "disillusion" is there, like you have it here, in the notes but whether one, or the reader, more precisely, would be willing to extend all this immediacy to the abstraction: "Hebraism vs. Hellenism..." I can't quite now grant you.... You don't ever want to speak for "Everyman", when you can speak so damn finely for yourself. Or tell me if it isn't the precision of the emptiness, in just yourself, that makes any of it possible. Or that any emotion, clearly, is first found in one's own body, etc.... For myself, there is an *active* line or movement all through Vexata Quaestio...that makes the tension.

Creeley's comments triggered a response from Layton that gives a clear description of his method of writing poems. (He included a full-dress theorizing in the preface to *The Laughing Rooster* in 1964.) "Of course, no poem is really paraphrasable," he wrote on 26 May 1953, while Betty was at a sketch class and three-year-old Naomi was asleep at his side, sucking her thumb.

> There's always the residue, the POETRY, that escapes through the web of words. Saying that VEXATA QUAESTIO

is about the conflict engendered in the modern's mind by Hellenism and Hebraism, I did not think to suggest that I started out with any two such abstractions in my mind, and constructed the poem with any blueprint in front of me. No poem is ever made that way, as you know. The origins of poems are obscure; only when the poet is uncommonly self-analytical can he trace the beginnings, the obscure urges or irritations, behind the finished work. For myself, I find when I'm really "hot" that the commencement of a poem takes place with a rush of images to my head which I put down on paper as swiftly as they occur. When the stream stops coming, I look at what I've written and try to decipher as best I can what it is that my "unconscious" is trying to tell me, and only when I detect some pattern trying to realize itself to my mind do I sit down to the actual composition of the poem. The quality of irony which you rightly detect in the poem is the self-ironic smile of a man who sees the drift of the joke — and sees that the joke is on him. But all irony in poetry, I believe, is the consequence of the two antithetical roles the poet embraces, that of passionate participant and detached observer. It springs from his ability to keep a number — the more the better — of contradictory thoughts and emotions in suspension. A really good poet is capable of going off vigorously in several directions at once. I do not say he does, only that he's capable of doing so. The distinction is important.[20]

Layton's remarks reveal that poetry offered him the opportunity to express the many worlds of his personality without having to integrate them. In the creative process, he could "keep a number — the more the better — of contradictory thoughts and emotions in suspension;" he could go off "vigorously in several directions at once." Nothing bothered Layton more than giving up some side of his many-faceted self — as, for instance, he had been forced to do when he could no longer entertain hopes of obtaining a Ph.D. He points to the two main "roles" he experienced and describes them as "antithetical": the role of "passionate participant" and the role of "detached observer." These roles can be traced back to his parents, to Keine, an extreme version of the passionate participant, and Moishe, an equally extreme version of the detached observer. These were roles well-suited to Layton's poetic needs, and John Sutherland had observed how closely they approximated Wordsworth's notion of the dynamic of poetic creation: "emotion recollected in tranquillity." But Layton amplified these two primary and, as he had experienced them, antithetical roles. Under the general rubric of "passionate participant" might be included his roles as political agitator, student radical, illicit lover, athlete, literary revolutionary, husband, father and teacher. Under the heading "detached observer" might fall such roles as meditative reader, political theorist, social critic, essay-writer and student. In some areas of his life, roles overlapped and "antithetical" roles collided. As a teacher, for example, he would confront his class as a superb rhetorician and sustain the role of passionate participant. But as many poems attest, he was also, perhaps simultaneously, a "detached observer" of the students, of the nature of education, of the frustrations of attempting to impart knowledge to those who had little wish to acquire it. The key word is "roles." To Layton, no one aspect of his complex existence was "it." Those who saw only an upstart immigrant huckster missed the extent to which he could adopt the role of the tweedy, pipe-smoking British gent. Even Betty, who lived closely with him for years, could not mirror a satisfying image. When she did a portrait of him that year, he rated it only fair. "Like all people who sit for their portrait, I have the feeling that all the complexity that goes into the making of my personality doesn't get included in the arrangement of paint. I've often observed the sitter's dissatisfaction with the portrait of himself even though it appears so excellently real to others. I suppose that is because each person knows himself for being the multitudes he really is behind the skin of his face, and smiles to himself to think that any artist can hope to portray them in any single canvas."[21] Did Layton have a "core" of identity, or did he flip, with ingenious dexterity, in and out of a number of possible roles, many of them inconsistent with one another? Did he will the changes? Or were they uncontrolled responses to immediate situations?

One thing was certain: the satirical poems, such as those in *Cerberus*, spun from the sequence of social or political observation (the detached observer) and the railing or ranting against what he saw (passionate participant). Like Keine, Layton quickly grasped either the broad outlines or the revealing details of man's foibles, and brazened out his complaints. Like Keine, too, he generally gave vent to such exposés in rhyming couplets. This "pea-shooter" side of his nature would culminate in *The Long Pea-Shooter* (published in 1954), "about forty poems, say verses rather, of no great value as poetry, but valuable in the sense that this is what this country needs." Layton saw such poetry as "folk verse" or "doggerel," a form he thought was much neglected in the twentieth century.[22] Betty decorated the cover of *The Long Pea-Shooter* with an insolent, Puckish sketch of her husband. Layton dedicated the book to Robert Creeley.

Poems like "Vexata Quaestio" were different from these satiric "verses," as his description of the process by which he wrote such poems reveals. "It's odd how I'll write a serious poem about SADISM, DEATH, etc. and then bubble up to the surface with something like O.B.E. or SENSIBILITY."[23] In his "surface" satires, his feet were firmly planted on the earth; he knew his point of view. But in "Vexata Quaestio," he floated, like a swimmer, in a vaguely remembered medium. He held inconsistent points of view suspended in ironic balance. He became "really 'hot,'" a "passionate participant" in that undefined world of the imagination to which he had so frequently retreated from the tensions around him as a child. After the "stream" of images emerged, he became the "detached observer": he deciphered and granted order and form to what had occurred. The act of writing did not resolve "contradictory thoughts and emotions." It expressed them, usually ironically, and always sensually, with the kind of immediacy felt by children.

To take the measure of the American poets in 1953, Layton had to read Charles Olson's theory of "open verse." The theory was articulated in "Projective Verse,"[24] an essay central to modernist American literature. Layton first caught wind of it from Cid Corman, who hitch-hiked first from Dorchester, Massachusetts to Toronto, where he stayed with

Souster for a week, then to Montreal, where he visited the Laytons. Layton was not impressed with Corman. Instinctively, he felt he had encountered a lesser man. "He's a difficult man to please," Layton wrote to Ann Creeley the day Corman left. "He talks about literature as if he had a stuffed nose. I wish he had more joie de vivre in him, he's a man of such excellent parts, but a bad poem — or one he considers so — seems to cut into his flesh like a cut sardine tin. Truly he suffers too much."[25] Corman me a number of the *CIV/n* group in Montreal, canvassed subscriptions for *Origin* and took back with him the latest magazines and books on Canadian poetry. He also left Layton a copy of Olson's "Projective Verse." Layton was puzzled. "What do you mean by 'open,'?" he wrote to Bob Creeley. "I find [Olson's] prose abominably affected and opaque. So unless you, or someone else, explain to me what is being meant I'm afraid I shall never know."[26] He could not understand Olson's theory.

Creeley explained by return mail:

> Thinking of Olson's open verse. Perhaps that is a hard introduction although he doesn't at all mean it to be such. I don't have a copy here, but it's been such a bible for me in many ways that I can almost quote it by heart. The concept of "open" verse (granting the obvious perhaps antithesis of "closed") bases itself on the assumed necessity...of making each poem autonomous — which is nothing very new. But the further assumption is that forms accepted from another time or usage carry with them a predetermined character which may or may not prove inimicable to the given poem under hand.
>
> All of which is goddam vague I know.... How the hell best to effect a structure, i.e., in the attempt to find an alternative to such accepted and partially at least predetermined forms such as sonnet, villanelle, & so forth. Taking it further, there is the like problem of a predetermined metric, of iambs, & so on & so on which already have too much the character of an a priori observation, rather than a present base for actual rhythms in any possible poem.
>
> So what can serve as alternative. The answer clearest

to hand is, or lies in, the breath — the way a man says a thing, or anything, and how his own breathing affects the disposition of his language in any given instance.... In other words, the poem starts with the first word — and not with an assumptive "metrical" pattern....well, I hate the fucking dogma, either way. It seems to me that the given breath component, in any group of words (having sequence, etc., etc.), can well be used as a partial or even total means for their scoring in "lines". That has given me, if I make it to begin with, a clear means of dealing with that part of structure in a poem.... But what Olson wants to emphasize, insofar as I understand him, is that a poem suffers too much if it is considered as anything but the given poem, under hand. That, further, a poem is an actual high energy construct, and that said energy can declare a multiplicity of forms, all depending on the circumstances involved. One job is to allow for that complex of possibility, and to work more accurately and closely in our own apprehension of what "form" can literally be. As well, Williams' sense comes in here too: "Therefore each speech having its own character the poetry it engenders will be peculiar to that speech also in its own intrinisic forms." All of which to put weight on the one apparent fact, that, writing, we have our surest materials in the particulars of our own speech, and that the acceptance of generalized or abstracted systems of "form" lessen that edge to a sometimes disasterous extent. (Your own victory, put it, consists in a hell of a great part, in not having ever dulled the edge of your own speech for any purpose — and still it is the dismal tragedy of almost all the flops in both the US and Canada. They never learn.)... "Open" verse may very well be a disposition of the mind, rather than a formal methodology for dealing with the problems of poetry. But I think one can amount, very nearly, to the other. Williams again useful. The poet thinks with his poem, in that lies his thought, and that is the profundity.[27]

Because he still could not understand, Layton resisted the theory of "St. Olson the Baptist," as Layton called him.

Creeley tactfully speculated that Layton was already writing "open verse." Layton wrote to Creeley on 22 July 1953:

> I seemed to see a dogma taking shape before me, a new coterie of mystifiers complete with banners and slogans, pressing their thumbs to the eyeballs of other poets. What a relief to find myself completely mistaken! The nightmare ended. More, to find like that famous character in one of Molière's plays, that I had always been writing "open verse" without knowing it. I like your statement, "It's a disposition of the mind, rather than a methodology."...certainly in my own practice I've never imposed dead form upon what I happened to feel and want to say at the moment.... each poem was a many-sided invasion of the unknown with the final product, the poem, as much of a surprise to me as to anyone.... Successful poems are the happy union of form and content...but the partners...must be anarchistically free.[28]

With a quizzical sense of bewilderment at Corman's interference and Layton's thick-headedness over "open verse," Creeley wrote to Olson at the end of July: "it sounded to me as though Cid had made the whole thing a good deal more of a mess than it was before. I.e., your article couldn't have stimulated all that confusion by itself."[29] Or could it?

After carefully examining Layton's poetry, Olson concluded "that the syntax is of the man's own making, not something accepted as a canon of the language in its history."[30] Layton's unique syntax created what he called "the crisis of the third foot," by which he meant that Layton showed a peculiar use of English poetic metre in which the third and fourth sections of a four-section line resulted in a verse that was not based on the syntax of the completed thought. Taking a line like "I dance my shanks, here, in the field, reply," Olson concluded: "Layton pushes past [the third foot], falls from the cliff of that foot and then remounts the line, makes it have a second life."[31] In using English as no native English-speaker would use it, Layton gave his poetry a liveliness and flexibility English seldom had. It was for this that Olson and Creeley admired him most.

As 1953 drew to a close, Layton, at Creeley's request, called in a professional photographer for the first time.

> Yesterday we had the photographer in to take some pictures of myself and the family.... Great fun, except that Max had to be coaxed into dropping his scowl and smiling at the birdie. The photographer turned out to be a woman I had known many years ago — member of a study group which I had organized all of twenty years ago. She said I hadn't changed a bit — except for more fat around my neck and belly. It's outrageous how I've put on weight in the past few years; this despite vigorous games of handball once and sometimes twice a week, as well as swimming and lots of hard work. I guess I'll never work those glycerol lumps off unless I cut out the bread and potatoes of which I am inordinately fond.[32]

It is tempting to see, in that December photograph, the portrait of a happy man. Almost everything Layton had aimed for, and more, had come to pass in the previous year. He had worked with Dudek on *TRIO*, a three-sided collection of *CIV/n* poets — Gael Turnbull, Phyllis Webb and Eli Mandel. (He thought it was "a much stronger book than *Cerberus*.")[33]

Layton had become the darling of the American poets. Creeley was finishing work on *In the Midst of My Fever*, a collection that would be a knockout. Layton was negotiating about an American-Canadian anthology for the spring that would include six American and six Canadian modern poets. As well, the Americans preferred Layton's work to Dudek's. Creeley had written in July to tell Layton he didn't like Dudek's recent collection: "I can't make the damn tone, the 'I assume he died...' Goddamn arch, etc. of the book, [I] like 'An Air by Sammartini' — also sense of last poem, tho drags, but honest. There is pretty much emptiness, for me anyhow, otherwise."[34] Layton championed Dudek, but at the end of the year Creeley wrote a long critical letter about Dudek's work. Creeley concluded: "Jesus, God, Irving, I do *not* see why you think this poem a good one. I hope to christ I don't seem here utterly unreasonable, i.e., I started off I think ok, but I know at this point I'm screaming again — it has that fucking *effect* on me. I cannot damn well stand what he is doing. It grates on my nerves like a file."[35] Creeley wanted Layton to write a "core" of three or four poems for *Black Mountain Review*. (Creeley had been asked to begin the magazine after he returned from Spain to teach, with Olson, at Black Mountain College, the avant-garde school in North Carolina where John Cage, Buckminster Fuller, Josef Albers, Paul Goodman, Merce Cuningham and Robert Rauschenberg had gathered.) Creeley also wanted Layton as a guest lecturer at the college for the summer. Creeley wrote to Olson:

> I think Layton would almost damn well weep, with gratitude, to get a chance there. He's about forty now, or one or two years over, and seems to have come up very damn much the hard way, and much against everyone around him. Anyhow he's faced the provincialism there too long, without a vacation — and to get to BMC at least would also put him clear of the Canadian business for long enough to rest. I like him very, very much — what I know of him through the letters and poems. He's got wit, i.e., a humor that almost none of the others there have. He also has a wild ear, and a damn fine sense of rhythms. In that particular backwash I think he's forced to "formalize" his thinking much too much, or at least in a priori comment, etc., etc. — but give him any kind of oats, etc., and think he would breeze in ahead of almost anyone else I could think of. I think he would make, and is, a wild "teacher". His very care for people would make him that.[36]

To his chagrin, Layton could not accept Olson's exciting long-distance telephone invitation to come to "Candy Mountain," as he called Black Mountain College.

> It would be splendiferous to see you and work with you, but alas the stars are not disposed for that at the moment. I've got three teaching commitments, not one of which I can wash my hands of without making a considerable stink. Had Olson written to me earlier I might have been able to swing a sabbatical leave from the High

School where I am teaching, though the matter of money may have thrown me in any case since my future is heavily mortgaged in the way a teacher's usually is. Payments on the house, on the car, etc. You know the routine. Still, I'm crazy enough to have given the plan a whirl.

But hold on a moment. I'm forgetting the McCarran act. Years ago I was a hot left-winger (what bright boy wasn't?) and the American immigration has me down for a dangerous subversive. Two years ago I wanted to visit my brother who lives in Ellenville, N.Y. and I was stopped at the border with the pound of salami and smokemeat which my brother ordered and which he never got. The border officials made me turn back and for the following week the family had salami and smokemeat served up in a variety of fancy dishes. I filed a protest which was sent to Washington, but the only consequence of that was to make the temporary exclusion permanent. So the big boys of Washington wrote me. However, one is able to make an appeal after a year's passage and this I have since done. So far I haven't heard from them. Quite frankly, I'm not too optimistic, considering the moral and political climate that now prevails in the U.S. Things will change, of that I'm quite confident, but until it does, every independent-minded person, both at home and abroad, will be regarded by the present American government as a reckless bomb-thrower.[37]

In his personal life, everything seemed "splendiferous." Though he and Betty had financial worries, they were getting some breaks. In 1950, Layton bought the farm lots that bordered on their property, an investment that sponsored a studio for Betty and a bedroom in their house for Max.[38] That fall, Betty earned a hundred dollars from sales during her first two shows: one in Saint John, New Brunswick, the other at Macdonald College. Layton and Betty enjoyed "a four-day picnic," driving from Quebec to Murray Bay in August, "sleeping under the broad smile of heaven."[39] ("Give me a mattress any time," Layton commented.) His letters reveal an energetic, cheerful man at ease with his body, his marriage and, seated in his summer holidays at the white table with his thesaurus and dictionary under the Bo tree in his rural back garden, his life's work. Even his teaching, which at times dragged him down, seemed halcyon: "If I didn't enjoy teaching as much as I do," he confessed to Cid Corman,

> I would cut my throat.... One of the courses I give is Political Theory — the thing I majored in at McGill. Because I don't want to forget the subject I spent so much time learning about, I try to arrange a course in it each year at the Institute for Jewish Studies. This year I have a group of fourteen, very keen. I've been going through Plato with them, right through the *Republic, The Statesman,* and that work of his dour old age, *The Laws.* What I like about these courses is that they make me go back to the sources again, and from year to year I find my views becoming acuter and more comprehensive. Then again, it provides me with something else besides poetry to think about, gives me an additional perspective on the world. I think if my poetry has any breadth at all, I can put it down to "double vision."[40]

But Layton more often criticised than praised teaching. "Now I can settle down to the more civilized and welcome business of writing my own poetry instead of discussing someone else's which has always struck me like using another chap's prick for screwing."[41]

Gradually, all the hard work — the money donated to help publish younger poets and sponsor little magazines, the hawking of books (in March 1953, at a Jewish Library meeting, Layton sold fourteen copies of *Love the Conqueror Worm* and was not above peddling them to his classes and sending his pyjamaed children around at parties to sell copies to guests[42]) — was beginning to pay off. In 1954, the CBC began a poetry-reading radio series of three half-hours, paying poets fifty cents a line. Within a year, Robert Weaver arranged for Layton to read a few poems.[43] Through the efforts of a few dedicated volunteers, markets for poetry were beginning to open up in regional centres like Winnipeg.

A number of poets and sympathetic critics were strategically placed at Canadian universities (Layton saw students as his main potential audience and market):

> There's Desmond [Cole] at Sir G[eorge Williams]; L[ouis] D[udek] at McGill; Eli Mandel, a fine poet, teaching at — of all places — St. John's Military College, and he's got for three colleagues very wide awake chaps who don't equate poetry with either Trees or Daffodils. There's Doug Jones teaching at another military college at Kingston (beginning to sound pretty subversive); [Desmond] Pacey's at Dalhousie; [Earle] Birney at Victoria, and so on.... Really, the sky is beginning to clear. Those chaps I named, and I could add another half-dozen, are A-1 [and] are giving a new and modern twist to the teaching of poetry, bringing the poet as the "Informer" (MacNeice's word) getting a whole new generation to look at poetry with different eyes.... Maybe I'm kidding myself, but...I sometimes think the situation is a lot better than some poets realize; that the world is changing, that the rule of the middle-class with all...that has meant for culture...is now coming to an end.[44]

On Saturday 14 November, Layton and Dudek were off to Toronto; Layton bragged it was "the first time Montreal poets [had] been asked to read their verse in another city, and it may well set a shining precedent."[45] He reported, "Our trip to Toronto [which he concluded was a "hateful place"] was a brilliant success. There was a good turnout, made me and Louis realize that there were lots of people still interested in poetry, if only the poet could find means of breaking down the wall between them and him. We think we have the answer...a series of six poetry readings [here] starting in February... [with]...Frank Scott [to] lead off."[46] Layton thought Canada was enjoying a "poetic flourish." So did the Americans. ("I sense a quickening in Canadian verse. A likelihood of fine, perhaps its finest, work," Corman had written in September to F.R. Scott).[47] Within a year, in response to the publication of *The Long Pea-Shooter*, Ezra Pound sent him a "history-making" post-card that said simply "CHEERS." Layton wrote to Creeley:

One word, ONE WORD, but the approval of a man whose excellence you...venerate, and it's enough to make a chap feel that he hasn't altogether wasted more than fifteen years of his life learning the niceties of his craft. It fills me with the delight of a bird at dawn because it was the publication and after-effects of [*The Long Pea-Shooter*] which led to a serious quarrel between me and Louis the Dudek; me holding forth that writing pea-shooters required O so much craft and cunning, cunning running along the blood & into the fingers that held the pen. Ah well, let me not spoil the grandeur and innocence of the birds' dawnsong by anything so foolish as a human gloat.[48]

A.J.M. Smith could no longer exclude Layton from his anthology of Canadian poetry. For the forthcoming revised edition, he requested six poems: "The Cold Green Element," "Keewaydin Poetry Festival," "Birds at Daybreak," "For Louise, Age 17," "The Poetic Process" and "The Epitaph for an Ugly Servitor."[49] The Canadian poetry scene was coming into its own, and it seemed to Layton that he stood, strong arms akimbo, at its centre.

Superman

"My wife is the most understanding woman a writer could have," Layton wrote in a letter to Robert Creeley in the summer of 1953. He was responding to Creeley's request for more poems, which Creeley hoped to place in *Atlantic Monthly*, the *New Mexico Quarterly* or the *Kenyon Review*. Layton replied, "All this is predicated upon the hypothesis that my wife doesn't clout me on the head for being such an unsociable beast who spends his vacations staring into space and muttering insanely to himself instead of taking the family to the beaches." He had been quick to add, "But I do her an injustice."[1]

Betty was understanding. She continued to cushion Layton's sometimes irascible temperament in a soothing, non-judgemental, serene manner. She was as unlike his railing mother as any woman could be. But tensions were building. Like all couples, they had acquired a backlog of minor grievances that called for adaptation. One sore point was Betty's housekeeping, or the lack of it. "I remember Irving cleaning up with a broom," Louise Scott comments. "He was always correcting Betty on her housekeeping. He was shocked at her casualness. He likes his comforts. He has moderate habits; he's a very middle-class guy in lots of ways. She would just roar with laughter at his domesticity."[2] Miriam Waddington remembers him pumping her and her husband (who were considered the most "square" of the artistic community) about whether they had a cleaning woman and whether Pat's shirts were sent out to a laundry. "'See?' he'd expostulate to Betty. 'She irons his shirts!'"[3] Betty had proved more than a match for his bohemian side.

And she resented the on-going intrusions of her mother-in-law. "Once Bubba and Irving destroyed my living-room. They threw everything out and bought a new settee, curtains and chairs. He was like that. He liked to disrupt things periodically. I suppose it was funny, but sometimes he'd get mixed up and introduce me to people as her, as Keine."[4] Much worse were his intense and vindictive hatreds. "He could be so full of fun and we shared many nice, blooming kinds of moments. Usually he was cheerful and affirmative, joking and relaxed. But his hates I couldn't take. Louis was fairly tolerant of him, but Irving would go into such a rage over him. And he said such awful things about my brother. I remember going to Frank Scott's one quiet Sunday evening when everyone had books or new poems to read from. Irving had brought a poem he'd just written, 'When It Came to Santayana's Turn.' He asked me to read it out loud for him. When I realized as I read that it was an awful attack on John, whom I loved and who was very sick, it was too late for apologies."[5]

The children were also a source of friction. Though both Betty and Irving were loving (Marian Scott thought them excellent parents), attention for the children sometimes seemed like attention subtracted from each other. They were extremely permissive: friends recall that they boasted of how they allowed the children to ride on Layton's back when he was making love to Betty, a situation he drew on for the poem "Eros Where the Rents Aren't High."[6] Miriam Waddington remembers taking her son, who was about Max's age, over to play: "Max kept hitting Johnnie, but Betty just laughed. I never took him there again." But the growing children were nudging their the parents into middle age and imposing living limits on their free-form existence. "Irving blew hot and cold with the children," Betty recalls. "He was not good at their birth times (he tended to disappear with his nephew Bill). I think it was because, for once, he was not centre-stage. Sometimes, though, he'd come in and be 'father'. Then he was so wonderful, so good at it and so charming that I'd feel jealous."[7]

In 1953, as Irving was hitting his stride as a poet, Betty was coming into her own as a painter. Though both needed outlets for their talents, Layton's needs took precedence. It was not that he did not encourage his wife. He had faith in her talents and was extremely proud of her. "News of Bet's exhibition. Terrific," he wrote to Cid Corman after her first exhibition in Saint John, which he had cheerfully sponsored with the three hundred dollars she needed for framing and transportation. "The curator of the Art Gallery or Museum or whatever they call it over there phoned long distance in ONE afternoon to tell her that she was a genius and that he was going to devote the rest of his life to make that fact known."[8] Louise Scott recalls that he was always supportive of Betty's artistic ventures, sometimes more than Betty: "She was lazy and he pushed her. She never applied herself fully to her drawings, though there was no question of her talent. Painting is a hard job. You can't just pop in occasionally at the plant."[9] But Layton sometimes saw Betty's talent as an extension of his own and her work as taking second-place to his. "Her cooking may leave much to the imagination," he commented to Creeley, "but with brush or pencil she's a genius. Well, this summer she turned out some excellent things, strong and sensitive. In many ways, I think you'll find that her work has many of what I imagine are my own qualities."[10] But when Corman came to visit the Laytons in June 1953, though Irving complained that she fried better eggs for Cid than for him,[11] he never mentioned that she was a painter or showed Corman any of her work. "I take the blame for your not seeing any of Bet's paintings,"[12] he wrote to Corman after Corman apologized for overlooking Betty. Layton attributed the oversight to his enthusiasm for discussing "open verse" with Corman.

Things had already begun to come to a head between Layton and Betty in the spring of 1953. Sculptor Buddy Rozynski had finished some pieces that were to be used as illustrations in the second issue of *CIV/n*, and there was a party to show the pieces at the Laytons'. Most of the Laytons' social evenings had centred on poetry; for the first time the evening's subject was closer to Betty's expertise than to Irving's. It was the first time she stood up to him in public. "Irving went into a big spiel that Buddy should make duplicates of his sculptures and sell them for $2.95. I knew some technical things about sculpture and I told him he was stupid to say such a thing about a work of art. In a way, I did it just to see how it would sound. Things became very stormy after that. He never treated me the same again."[13]

As Betty remembers it, each of them needed more than the other could provide. Somehow, the magic had gone out of their relationship. "There was a discussion we had up on the mountain one day about this," Betty comments. "It was a calm discussion in which we both admitted that we needed the outlet of affairs. I told him who I thought my first lover would be and named a Jewish friend of ours. "'Please don't make it anyone I know!' was Irving's response."[14]

Irving Layton, in his "idyllic" bohemian life in rural Côte St. Luc, was in crisis. On 17 April he sent off a new poem, "In the Midst of My Fever." (It was the title poem of the 1954 collection published by Creeley in Spain.) Layton commented, "By means of ambiguous imagery (suggesting elation and disgust), I've tried to communicate what it must feel like to be a middle-aged man having a late spring."[15] He claimed that the poem had a "kinship" with "Vexata Quaestio." He wrote in the first person:

> In the depth of my gay fever, I saw my limbs
>   like Hebrew letters
> Twisted with too much learning. I was
> Seer, sensualist, or fake ambassador; the tyrant
>   who never lied
> And cried like an infant after he'd had to
>   to succour his people.
> Then I disengaging my arms to bless,
> In an eyeblink became the benediction
>   dropped from the Roman's fingers;
> Nudes, nodes, nodules, became all one,
>   existence seamless....

In his letter, Layton wrote as if he were only imagining the late spring of a middle-aged man in his poem. But the tone and subject of many of his poems at the time, and a noticeable shift in his poetic theory, suggest he also was living it. At about this time, he and Louis Dudek tried their hand at writing radio plays. The plays were rejected by Nathan Cohen for television presentation because there was "too much exposition, and not enough interplay of character or conflict,"[16] but they reveal much about the men who wrote them. Dudek had devised most of the farcical plot for "The Ambassador,"[17] a political satire in which the Russians decide to buy up cheaply all the remaindered Canadian books. It was a humorous comment on the huge amount of Canadiana selling for cut-rate prices in the book-stores across the country. Layton provided the idea for the other play, and it reflected his determination not to grow old. "The Old and Quiet Ones"[18] featured the Lovejoys, an old couple who rent a room from a suspicious, Keine-like landlady who assumes they will be quiet tenants, only to find that they kick up their heels as much as any young couple would.[19] When Layton sent off "Bacchanal" (an eat-drink-and-be-merry poem) and "Portrait of Aileen" (a poem about Aileen Collins of *CIV/n* who had begun a relationship with Louis Dudek),[20] he put forward a theory that sounded impersonal, but that was intensely specific:

> I think I prefer Bacchanal of the two, but the latter is the more ambitious poem. What I wanted to say in that poem is that the capacity to destroy without scruple is one of the constituent elements of perfection, the line you picked out, THOUGH AN INCREDIBLE WOUND IN THE AIR ETC. But this person is tortured by her awareness of the Fly, symbol of corruption, and that that is omnipresent: the flowers choke the weeds. The problem is one that is faced by every sensitive, moral personality of our time and one that threatens to split human consciousness apart. The sudden realization that there are no easy answers to this moral dilemma, that the quicksands of awareness threaten to drag us down into the bogs of weakness and futility, if not of desperation, is what "has taught me severity, strictness of speech." The

other poems, as you say, are slight things in a dry season. Finger exercises, if you will; though the Priscilla poem is interesting psychologically, and intended to be moving, in the last line, anyway.

Layton's "moral dilemma" did threaten to split his consciousness apart, as the poem suggested. "Seer," "sensualist," "fake ambassador," "tyrant," "infant," these were but a few of the mutually contradictory worlds Layton felt free to inhabit. Like a reckless juggler of disparate objects, he wished to keep switching roles so fast that only "benediction" remained — surely a mock benediction — that would be his gift to the world. Only when the moral dilemma itself was depicted through art (sculpture, painting, poetry or whatever) could these human inconsistencies be contemplated in all their irony. His marriage to Betty, like any single role or human enterprise, was merely a role. To make it "the" role, he must sacrifice some sides of himself that he was not willing to part with. Was the poet not engaged in a drunken Bacchanal of words? Wouldn't he become sterile and dull if he did not continuously feed off life itself? Hadn't he for years been showing how deadly middle-class conventions were? How stupid he would be to allow himself, of all people, to get trapped. Wasn't the poet a kind of Nietzschean Superman, above the laws that governed more ordinary men? Didn't he believe, like Blake, that "the sources of poetry were enthusiasm & inspiration"?[21] How could he write unless he allowed himself to live?

As his marriage to Betty ripened into the calm plateau of middle age, Layton thought his crisis was a moral dilemma; he did not consider that it might be an aesthetic one. Since his poetry was so often autobiographical, he had depended on intensity of feeling in his personal life to fuel his poems. The subsiding of passion in his marriage threatened the very quality of his poetry, and the lack of passion seemed permanent to him. If he were to detach his poems from experience, he would have to change as a poet. This might have meant development into new forms — the epic, narrative or dramatic verse, for example. But Layton did not wish to rely on his imagination to fuel his creativity. He chose instead to shatter the calm so that he could deepen and heighten his emotional landscape. The challenge he might have sought in new poetic spheres he began to create for himself in his own life. He voyaged to extremes of emotion that ordinary men could only guess at.

Layton claims that his hunger for life took a vicarious form. Certainly, he was fascinated to hear from one of his Jewish immigrant students, Helen Achtman, that she had saved her husband's life in Maidanek, Poland by trading sexual favours with Nazi officers.[22] He wrote a story about this episode called "Mrs. Polinov," and offered it to Creeley in August 1954 with the apology, "Prose isn't my medium."[23] His "coffee romances" (meetings at coffee shops after class with students), as he called them, exposed him to many men and women who told him their stories and troubles. Out of the more intense and fruitful of these encounters came poems like "Mildred," about a woman Layton consoled after a man she loved had left her, and "For Priscilla," about a woman to whom he felt powerfully attracted but who seemed to him "a female hyena," voraciously eager to prey on his "rotting psyche."[24]

The poems Layton wrote in the midst of his fever, most of which are collected in *The Long Pea-Shooter* (1954)[25] and *The Blue Propeller* (1955),[26] give the general impression of a man contemplating a series of bizarre reflections of himself (and passers-by) in a multitude of carnival-distorting mirrors. Poems like "On First Looking into Stalin's Coffin,"[27] "May Day Orators"[28] (which reduced his former idols David Lewis and A.M. Klein to sheer buffoonery) and "My Favourite Colour's Green"[29] indicated that he had put his Communist beliefs behind him. "Prologue to the Long Pea-Shooter" begins:

> A friend tells me I must not write
> About the workers and their sad plight,
> ...For it's the season now to cavil
> At Original Sin and Evil.[30]

Though Layton wrote the lines facetiously, and was still capable of writing a strongly revolutionary proleterian poem like "Address to the Undernourished,"[31] he had set aside the more doctrinaire aspects of Communism to unleash a spate of bitter and cynical poems on the human condition — as represented by himself.

As always, Layton declared himself most often on the side of life and energy. Using the teachings of D.H. Lawrence and Friedrich Nietzsche, two of his favourite writers at the time, he called attention to the joy and exuberance of natural existence. Power, he often seemed to be saying, is in things as they are. "Alas, my whales are *only* whales!" he noted in "No Moby Dick,"[32] a short diatribe against interpretive literary critics.

Frequently, he located life and energy in his marriage with Betty through poems written directly or obliquely about her.[33] For example, "Look, the Lambs Are all Around Us!":

> What luck, what luck to be loved
> by the one girl
> in this Presbyterian
> country
> who knows how to give
> a man pleasure.[34]

But even a tender, intimate poem like "How Poems Get Written" hinted at trouble:

> Like
> a memory
> torn
> at the shoulders,
> my darling
> wears
> the chemise
> I gave her —
> a wedding gift.
>
> At night
> I tap out
> my poems
> on her hip bone.

> When
> she can't
> sleep
> either
> we write
> the poem
> together.[35]

As Layton said in "Love's Diffidence,"[36] familiarity and comfortable co-existence were apt to make love elusive. Layton's pro-life, pro-energy stance contained the seeds of destruction, for it was a young man's philosophy and he was advancing anxiously into his mid-forties. His emotional inclination to locate vitality and growth in youth (to his own distress) is best seen in a poem called "Maxie," about his school-aged son:

> I suppose, spouse, what I wanted
> was to hold the enduring folds
> of your dress. Now there's this.
>
> This energetic skin-and-bones. You'll see,
> he'll pummel the two of us to death,
> laughing at our wrinkled amazement.
>
> Yes, though his upthrust into air
> is more certain
> than delight or unreason,
>
> and his active pellmell feet
> scatter promises, elations
> of breast and womb;
>
> yet his growing up so neighbourly
> to grass, us, and qualifying cobwebs
> has given me a turn for sculptured stone.[37]

It is as if Layton saw his son usurping the role that was one of his "many worlds," a playful, energetic lover soon capable of giving "elations" to "breast and womb." Though Layton temporarily could accommodate this incursion by seeing his son as an extension of his own phallic self, the days of accommodation were numbered. His last thought is of "sculptured stone," perhaps a statue (the monument capturing Max's cocky youth that is the poem itself) or a gravestone marking the end of youthful — and especially sexual — vitality for the father. One facet of himself Layton kept glimpsing in life's mirror was the grotesque reflection of old age: "For an Older Poet in Despair with the Times,"[38] "Now That I'm Older,"[39] and "Against This Death"[40] suggest the development of a new role for Layton, that of an aging, death-anxious man. It was a role he associated with his father, whose paralysis and death had made him a terrifying and pitiful object of anger to his youngest son. In poem after poem, Layton suggested he was not ready to give up the sexual role of active participant in favour of detached observer.

With almost phobic intensity, Layton wrestled with the concept of impotence, not simply in its sexual aspect (though that preoccupied him in a number of poems), but in the most general way. Did growing old necessarily involve loss of vigour? Did one have to give up some aspects of active involvement in the world and settle (this word sounded to Layton like "die") into a more contemplative, less physical mode? He identified the many forms of impotence from which he wished so fervently to disassociate himself. He attacked ministers for their mildness, critics for their lifelessness, Canadians generally for their bland, snow-like "innocence" and lack of philosophical concepts. He attacked the more refined poets for their aesthetic sterility, colonials for their syncophantic deference, society women for their lacquered, doll-like artificiality, students for their emotional superficiality, professors for their bland mediocrity, T.S. Eliot for his "poetry without zest" and Norman Levine for being a "third-rate" writer. He even turned on his own hero, Lawrence, calling him "an inverted Puritan and a passive male."[41] In a devastating poem called "Impotence" that recalled impressions of his sick and dying father, he lashed out at John Sutherland:

Health to him is an offence.
He can make nothing of sense

> But wraps it in altar-cloth
> And calls on Angels of faith,
> Who're strengthless when he's in bed
> To give him the needed aid;
> Thereupon over his male loss
> He makes a sign of the Cross
> And endows God with a son,
> Himself having none.[42]

In another violently crude poem, "Mr. Ther-apis,"[43] Layton attempted to equate the modern sterility of middle-class married males with primitive Greek rites, and he depicted a wife castrating her husband.

Against these thoughts of ageing, impotence and death, Layton set a series of *carpe diem* poems like "Bacchanal" ("Come, pleasure's my god and yours") that have a biting edge of self-mockery. Layton was aware that one of the most grotesque buffooneries was the St. Vitus dance of those determined to retain their youth. "Composition in Late Spring"[44] (a title that recalls his comment to Creeley that he wished to imagine a middle-aged man experiencing a late spring) begins, "When Love ensnares my mind unbidden/I am lost in the usual way" and continues in a surrealistic, free association of images to the conclusion, "I'm a Doge, a dog" — which is to say, both kingly and animalistic as a poet-trickster. Several poems Layton does not associate with Betty philosophize that men and women alike are made for each other's pleasure. "What Ulysses Said to Circe On The Beach of Aeaea"[45] explores an adulterous episode; "The Greeks had a Word for It"[46] (the word is "phallus") light-heartedly raises uncontrollable sexuality to a mythological level; the companion poems "Marius" and "Marie"[47] explicitly explore male and female sexual lust. The poem "Misunderstanding"[48] (a pun on "Miss, understanding") showed a student of English rejecting a pass from her teacher. In a poem called "Enigma," Layton explores the enigma of a poet who is married:

> The friend supplicated: Take my wife;
> we are free, we free ones,
>   of vernacular prejudice. Joy only
> is the reasonable man's philosophy.

And when after the cocktails I did
he was affable and
ashamed, but not of himself, magnanimous
and more than ever in his own eyes splendid.[49]

As always, the problem was who to be. Poets, by definition, were not monogamous. They celebrated life, love and joy spontaneously, turning down no opportunity to savour life to the full. On the other hand, the myth of monogamy was attractive. To be faithful to one beautiful woman, grow with her, father her children, know depth instead of breadth of experience: that, too, was appealing. By glancing now in this mirror, now in that, wryly enjoying the ironies of juxtaposing one reflection with another, Layton tried out different guises, none of which seemed just right for his multi-faceted self. He especially liked to imagine himself dead, as in a poem called "Lines on Myself":

Here rots Irving Layton
Claimed by no kith or kin;
Friends I had none, for who
Could love an ironic Jew?

Being a misanthrope
I gave mankind rope,
But women I loved well
And still want them in hell.

Next I loved poetry,
Though knew the poets lie;
I sometimes loved the sun,
Clouds and thoughtless children

All mercurial things:
Streams, air, bright-coloured wings.
I hated cruelty.
The world's well rid of me.[50]

As the poem suggests, Layton's "mercurial" multiplicity of selves sometimes led to self-disgust. He had begun satirizing what he called "manunkind's" faults and vices not from the point of view of a detached observer, but as a fellow-traveller. Poems like "Human Being"[51] (about an aggressive housekeeper the Laytons hired to help out while Betty was in hospital suffering from Bell's Palsy, a viral infection of the nerves which left her face partially paralyzed), did more than expose the ironic malice of a specific person: they illustrated what Layton had come to see was endemic in human beings generally. He knew. He was living it.

With traditional black images or allusions to darkness, Layton revealed the blot that lay in every human soul: the fly or the "charred fingers" that lay behind perfection in "Portrait of Aileen,"[52] or, in a lighter moment, the energetic, indestructible ants that emerge as onto a moonscape out of the dust of Betty's emptied vacuum cleaner in "The Ants."[53] In "Author, With a Pipe in His Mouth," he pictures a writer staring out across the darkness towards his neighbour's:

> My mind, at night, facile
> > as the moon,
> but the heart dark
> > as the vegetation
> at my feet.[54]

What he needed was freedom, freedom to be whatever he was required to be at any given moment. In one of his most eloquent poems, "Metzinger: Girl with a Bird,"[55] he "interpreted" a painting he had seen in one of Betty's art books. By projecting his own feelings onto the details of the painting, he represented several aspects of his own situation, this time without humour. The girl dreams of flight (symbolized by the bird), Layton imagines, from a "monster" or "tyrant" with whom she lives. Though she "wills" and has an "appetite" for flight, she is not yet sufficiently "indignant" to take action against her own unhappiness. Layton sees her as "impotent."

In the first week of July 1954, Betty took action. For several months there had been plans for a poetry weekend on Doug Jones's island, Keewaydin, near the Royal Military College in Kingston where Jones taught. "All the poets of Canada have been invited," Layton wrote excitedly to Creeley, "though we don't really expect them all to show up. We'll be happy if about fifteen can make it, this country is so damned sprawling and big. But we expect to have fun, with an island all to ourselves, a large rambling house, and the feeling of importance we'll all have in being the initiators of the first Poets' Festival in the history of this dominion. Ain't that something?"[56]

"That's where I had my first love affair since our marriage," Betty recalls: "We took the kids, there were lots of good friends there. Some did the cooking. There wasn't much work to do; we just had fun. The last evening we were sitting around the living room. I sat on Frank Scott's knees facing him. A young poet called John Paul Harvey was sitting on the floor beside Frank's chair. He took my hand. Irving was sitting across the room facing Frank and me. He could see it all. He said, 'I think I'll go to bed. Come on, Bet.' 'No,' I said. 'I think I'll stay.' He went off upstairs alone. I got off Frank's lap and lay down across John's knees. I wasn't drunk, I was just having fun. Suddenly, Irving sped down the stairs and gave John a judo chop to the nose. He pulled me upstairs by the arm, threw me into bed and fucked me. I gritted my teeth and bore it. Soon afterwards, I got up and went back downstairs. I tripped over John in the dark and more or less fell onto him. It was the most glorious thing. He made love to me. I went back upstairs afterwards with love bites on my neck. Irving had heard it all. The next morning he and John went for a boat ride and talked things over. They shook hands on the dock and then we went back to Côte St. Luc."[57]

It is impossible to tell whether Layton mainly perceived life as serving his poetry or poetry as serving his life. But one poem stood out from the torrent of poems that flowed from him in the mid-fifties. In "The Birth of Tragedy," Layton described the way in which writing poetry could make an ageing middle-aged man into a Neitzschean Superman, resolving his "many worlds" into "that one world that contains them all."

> And me happiest when I compose poems.
> Love, power, the huzza of battle
> are something, are much;

yet a poem includes them like a pool
    water and reflection.
In me, nature's divided things —
    tree, mould on tree —
    have their fruition;
I am their core. Let them swap,
bandy, like a flame swerve
I am their mouth; as a mouth I serve.

And I observe how the sensual moths
    big with odour and sunshine
    dart into the perilous shrubbery;
or drop their visiting shadows
    upon the garden I one year made
of flowering stone to be a footstool
    for the perfect gods
    who, friends to the ascending orders,
   sustain all passionate meditations
and call down pardons
for the insurgent blood.

A quiet madman, never far from tears,
    I lie like a slain thing
    under the green air the trees
inhabit, or rest upon a chair
    towards which the inflammable air
tumbles on many robins' wings;

    noting how seasonably
    leaf and blossom uncurl
and living things arrange their death,
while someone from afar off
blows birthday candles for the world[58]

An Attractive Bulldozer

It was 1955, the year after Dylan Thomas drank himself to death; the year the *Times Literary Supplement* declared Mazo de la Roche (whom Layton called "Mazola Roche") the greatest Canadian author; the year before Elvis Presley swept the North-American popular-music scene with songs so raw, so sexual, so subversive that his gyrations would soon be censored from the waist down on Ed Sullivan's popular Sunday television show. Layton had much in common with Presley. They were both, as Layton described himself, "un-genteel" and "un-academic." Uninhibited in their expression of a vulgar sexuality that rebelliously shattered the veneer of post-war middle-class complacency, both spoke with the voice of the poor and downtrodden, hostile to a civilization accustomed to ingrained snobbery and prejudice. Each displayed the colour and vitality of ethnic groups the WASP majority would just as soon have forgotten, Elvis drawing on black southern music, Layton on middle-European Jewish peasant inventiveness. And they looked alike: dark, wild, sensual, insolent.

Layton was conscious of the ripeness for social revolution that swept Elvis into the lime-light in the mid-fifties; he was conscious, too, of the role he might play. As Pound had speculated, civilization was "not a one-man job," but smashing that civilization might be. "The hard rock metaphor that you used some time ago in reference to *The Long Pea-Shooter* comes to mind here," Layton wrote to Bob Creeley:

> For this country the shits and pisses etc., the sex and scatology are a necessary antidote to the prevalent gentility and false idealism.... I am convinced that the only protest, the only effective protest that a man can make today to the pressures seeking to annihilate him either physically or spiritually is the biological one. It is for our time that the paradox is reserved that the soul must be saved by the body, the highest by the lowest; and men's equal claim to life, liberty, and the pursuit of happiness [is] justified by their common possession of an anus. The teachings of a vaporous Christian idealism for almost two thousand years has falsified our position; to remind ourselves that men in addition to being God-seekers and truth-seekers are also farting and excreting animals is a piece of wisdom that might save us from the follies of pride and overweening ambition.[1]

Or, as he wrote to Desmond Pacey, a professor of English at the University of New Brunswick whose field was Canadian literature, "Art is ecstasy...it's a crazy dance on a heap of burning coals and it's not reason but intuition in Bergson's use of the term that keeps [the artist] from toppling into the flames or scorching his heels too badly, keeps him aware of the flow."[2] All this from a man who frequently claimed to hate theories.

Layton's success with *In the Midst of My Fever, The Long Pea-Shooter* and *The Cold Green Element* had fanned his ambitions. Modern Canadian poetry was more or less established, and he longed to try his mettle in a larger arena. "[Bet and I] are thinking quite openly of making a break," he wrote to Creeley, who was in Mallorca, early in 1955. "How much would it take for a family of four to live in Mallorca. I mean the minimum. Would an income of $1200 do it? Would there be any way of supplementing that income by work as a teacher? It might well be Mallorca or Israel or Italy for us.... After all I have gone skiing and have made my obeisances to this country and its national sport by writing a poem about it."³ Layton hated winter. His first and last attempt at skiing, in contrast to the rhapsodic loveliness of the poem, "Canadian Skiers," which arose from it, had been anguished. "With my first fall I broke my bamboo ski pole, so I had only one pole to engineer the difficult feat of climbing the hills which loomed now high and monstrous before me. A few hours later and many falls to mark the passing time I thundered down an insignificant gradient, fell, and sprained my ankle. That put an end to all further skiing for the day. On my way to the car I discovered that my keys were gone.... Now I hobble around the house and listen to Bet's encouraging compliments and the poorly concealed derision of my children."⁴ Layton saw photos of sun-swept Mallorca, and thought Creeley was "in heaven." He also envied Gael Turnbull, a Canadian poet living in London, England, and Cid Corman, who was travelling around Europe on a Fulbright Scholarship, and Norman Levine, who was in St. Ives, Cornwall.

Layton and Betty applied for Canadian Government Overseas awards, offered by the Royal Society of Canada to sponsor artists abroad. Olson, Creeley and Corman had convinced Layton that as long as he stayed in Canada, he was trapped in a provincial backwater. "The most important reason to get you out of Montreal," Corman wrote him, "is to free you of an abiding provincialism, which I think you can sense yourself. It doesn't mean that you must become slick or urbane or sophisticated or that you must thereby improve, but I think you have it in you to be a much better poet than you even are now — but I feel that you need such a distance for a year or two."⁵

Layton had not been encountering unmitigated praise like Corman's from all quarters. Some students at Sir George Williams University had staged a protest after he read from and tried to flog *The Long Pea-Shooter*. They were outraged at his revolutionary views and insulting opinions. But Neil Compton, a friend of Layton's who had attended some of his literary gatherings and who was strategically placed as chairman of the English department, intervened and ensured that Layton was not fired.⁶ Layton also had nettled a number of writers in Toronto. "Took along a group of [your] poems... to our last poetry group meeting at Louella Booth's, and the inevitable reaction — much shaking of heads and mutterings about your fondness for 'dirty' words. In other words they don't see past the exteriors of the poem into the heart, the meat."[7] Nor were American poets without reservations about Layton. Paul Blackburn, Robert Hellman, Mason Jordan Mason, Larry Eigner, Thomas White and William Bronk were critical. "Don't know why the kids in New York are quite so eager to blast your work," Corman had written Layton. "Their commentaries, as far as they go, are vague and not convincing. Perhaps they have some minor points, but they press them damn hard and seem reluctant to see your qualities."[8] It was a blow, especially to Layton's precarious finances, when McGill dropped from its reading list the anthology of Canadian poems he and Dudek had edited. "We have reason to believe," he wrote to Creeley, "the higher-ups took a good hard look into its contents and yelped blue murder."[9]

The Royal Society grants did not come through. Neither this nor the criticism discouraged Layton. Nor did the customs stamp OBSCENE on a package of copies of *In the Midst of My Fever* in 1957 upset him. On the contrary, he was convinced that his detractors were either jealous or puritanical, and that his scatological verse was necessary. In fact, out of 117 poems published in book form (not counting repeats), Layton had used "dirty" words only 18 times.[10] This was excessive only in terms of Canada's puritanical literary taste, not in terms of English literature at large, which by then included Lawrence, Joyce and Miller. It was true that *Canadian Poems: 1850-1952* "frankly preferred poems which show a dark grain of fact running through them, which are challenging and experimental," but that hardly constituted obscenity. The closest any Layton poem in the anthology came to being risqué was the line from "Vexatia Quaestio": "[Give] your sex to any skilled And pretty damsel," a line as notable for the archaic word "damsel" as for the controversial word "sex."

Inclined by temperament to see criticism as sour-grapes praise, and observing that it arose from widespread repression throughout society rather than from any neurosis in himself, Layton readily shrugged off such barbs. In fact, he thrived on them as a boxer delights in his punching bag.

More believable and more plentiful were the kudos that had begun to shower him as thick and fast as after-concert flowers. The American poet revered by Creeley, Olson and Corman — William Carlos Williams — had responded with a glowing letter from New Jersey to Layton's canny gift of a copy of his *The Long Pea-Shooter* (dedicated to "a great poet"): "You have opened up the whole northern sky for us!... You have let in the air among the objects and people of our lives which was very necessary at the present time.... I will never be able to look north without thinking of you from this time forth.... Your abandon, without restraint, to printed page amounts to genius!"[11] A small trickle of fan letters had begun. One, from Austin, Texas asked to review *In the Midst of My Fever*. Canadian critic Hugh Kenner, who was in California, commented on the dust-jacket copy on Layton's books:

> ANTICLIMAX OF THE YEAR: "Irving Layton, of Montreal, teaches at Sir George Williams College." One could envisage him rolling his ironic eye at *any*thing but an asst. prof's duty schedule.... Wonderful discovery that something has begun happening up there in the attic since I slipped out of it ('48). Norry Frye, he was a prof. of mine, and in 1947 he said, "What a pity Joyce and Yeats couldn't have had my Blake book. All the time it would have saved them." Jamie Reaney I chiefly remember as spilling ink all down the front of his ulster and being hysterically annoyed with the janitor who confiscated the empty bottle on the museum floor; Birney as wearing blue spectacles. And there was the prof. who said on CBC ('46) that Canadian poetry suffered too much from "too much Eliot," by which he meant not enough Tennyson. Anyway, you boys have made the break, and I can only congratulate you; not that I want to go back."[12]

A.J.M. Smith included Layton in his forthcoming revised version of *The Book of Canadian Poems*. (The anthology held its own in the face of the demise of *Canadian Poems 1850–1952*.) Smith also solicited some of Layton's satirical verses for an anthology he was planning, with F.R. Scott, of irreverent

Canadian satires. The volume, *The Blasted Pine*, included Layton's "From Colony to Nation" as one of its three keynote poems. Smith reviewed *The Long Pea-Shooter* and *In the Midst of My Fever* for CBC radio on 17 April 1955; he gave both ecstatic reviews. Souster told Layton that he thought *In the Midst of My Fever* should win the Governor-General's Award, but that P.K. Page's book, *The Metal and the Flower*, in the respectable McClelland and Stewart "Indian File" series, would probably win instead. (It did.) Even Northrop Frye had changed his tune. In his "Letters in Canada" summarizing Canadian poetry for 1954, he singled out Layton for some remarkable praise. He did not like the satires in *The Long Pea-Shooter*, claiming they conveyed "a depressingly unreal world" in which "a conscience-driven and resentful mind...sees modern society as a rock pile and the poet as under sentence of hard labour." But he hailed *In the Midst of My Fever* as the work of "an erudite elegiac poet, whose technique turns on an aligning of the romantic and the ironic." Frye found "something of value on nearly every page... [from] a poetic mind of genuine dignity and power.... An imaginative revolution is proclaimed all through this book... we see a new excitement and intensity in the process of writing."[13] Layton's "straight, solid tones" (as Olson described his voice) proved excellent for radio, and offers from the CBC increased. Layton also began what would become a long and intimate friendship with Desmond Pacey. The two men were temperamentally congenial, as a first meeting proved, and the tall, amiable, good-hearted Pacey took over where Dudek, after increasing differences of opinion, had left off as the man with whom Layton could spar with ideas. Pacey had approached Layton in preparing an article on Canadian literature for an encyclopaedia. Before long, Pacey was giving Layton the kind of approval he needed: serious recognition from someone whose views he respected, who would stand up to him, whose down-to-earth attitudes he shared and who, in turn, held the craft of writing in high esteem. Pacey, ambitious to become a writer himself, had written some poems and short stories and published some children's books. After watching a television programme on Beethoven, Pacey wrote to his new friend: "Beethoven reminded me of you — the same downrightness & force & faith in the creative spirit."¹⁴

Layton began to act the role of the distracted poet in earnest. Steve Cumas, a friend of his and Betty's, recalls a visit from the Laytons to his cottage at Lac Marois. "We'd all be enjoying the gay, effervescent warmth of each other's company," Cumas observed. "But Irving would always be careful about drinking. Suddenly, he'd get up and disappear, his lips going up and down mouthing words the way a child sometimes does. It was almost like watching a regression. He'd go outside and fumble around with bits of paper. He gave the impression that writing was his main drive at the time."¹⁵

As Layton looked into the world's mirror and saw reflected back no less than genius, the first of his followers began to emerge. Already Norman Levine had "established contact" with Layton; he had visited Layton in Montreal and written occasionally from Cornwall. The relationship was that of younger Jewish writer to older Jewish writer (not unlike Layton's earlier relationship to A.M. Klein); Levine wanted assistance and was eager to belong to a community of writers, yet he essentially considered himself Layton's equal. George Johnston, another young writer, sent a letter¹⁶ to which he had attached "a light verse" about Layton (an abysmal piece called "The Gentle Poet"), and asked for copies of Layton's *In the Midst of My Fever* after reading Toronto professor Milton Wilson's review of it.¹⁷ Johnston had disliked *The Long Pea-Shooter*, but wrote out of curiosity and the desire to be informed about Canadian poetry. His was the first of hundreds of letters Layton would receive, with poems attached, from people who responded to Layton's poetic voice as to something familiar and inspiring. Henry Moscovitch, a grade-eight student at Herzliah when he first met Layton, was mesmerized. The son of a Romanian Jew, Moscovitch looked enough like Layton to make a passable job of imitating him. Soon he was spending his spare cash at second-hand bookstores, spouting Marx and Neitzsche and writing poems. He dressed like Layton, sounded like Layton and, whenever possible, was with Layton. In October 1955, a thirty-five-year-old factory worker from Vancouver who dabbled in modern literature and had decided to go to Europe to become a writer landed on Layton's doorstep. He had read

Layton's work with "amazed delight." In a state of "identity-crisis...like a ghost in transit from life to death," he stayed overnight with the man who had a personality like "an attractive bulldozer." He soaked up energy and inspiration from "the quality that makes Layton so attractive to the young... The 'Live, live, for tomorrow we die!' bit, and the thought behind it is absolutely damn well authentic," he would later maintain.[18] The middle-aged visitor was Al Purdy.

Layton's voluminous correspondence throughout 1955 reveals his prodigious energy (he was still teaching at several institutions, albeit with occasional planned "truancies") and the irresistible self-image of "genius." It also reveals his astute flair for business dealings. Generous with his time and money for friends, he had negotiated and funded the editing and printing of a collection of Corman's poems, and was acting as a one-man distributing centre for American poetry magazines and books, which he often manoeuvred through customs himself. He arranged for Souster's books of poetry to be in the National Library in Ottawa (his own were already well-stocked). His poetic output was becoming so prolific, to the wonderment of all his correspondents and fellow poets, that he was faced with a log-jam of his own books. He had published *The Cold Green Element* and *The Blue Propeller*. He was preparing his first "selected poems," which would include his best work from all his books, several of which were already out of print. And he had two new volumes almost ready. One he originally titled "the bloody i," a title Pacey, among others, persuaded him to change to *Music on a Kazoo*; the other was called *The Bull Calf and Other Poems*. Because the fate of the selected poems, eventually titled *The Improved Binoculars*, rested in the uncertain financial hands of Jonathan Williams, a young American publisher at Black Mountain College who had taken over Layton's work from Creeley when Creeley found duty regulations between Mallorca and Canada impossibly complex and expensive, it was taking much longer to print than the two projected volumes at Souster's Contact Press in Toronto. Layton's top priority was the prestigious *Improved Binoculars* (which he referred to as "Tibby") because a book of selected poems signalled the established major writer. With astounding efficiency, he sent installments of money to Williams, got editor Lorne Pierce (who regarded him with cautious awe) at Ryerson Press to order and pay for two hundred of the five hundred copies printed, lined up the possibility of an "Indian File" series publication as backup in case Ryerson failed (though he refused to be contained in the "Indian File" format), persuaded Gael Turnbull in England to find a British distributor (Frederick Woods, who took a hundred copies), encouraged Jonathan Williams to request an introduction from William Carlos Williams (which the poet wrote) and entered an advertisement for the book in *Queen's Quarterly* at his own expense. When Lorne Pierce drew back from committment to Tibby, implying he would order *The Bull Calf* instead, Layton astutely delayed publication of the two proposed volumes until Pierce reneged.

But Pierce, or rather the editorial committee of his publishing house, which was affiliated with the United Church, did one final about-face that left Layton without a Canadian publisher for his book. Two of the poems proposed for Tibby were offensive to Ryerson's committee. "De Bullion Street," which described a "mission" and a "Church" as "haemorrhoids upon the city's anus," and "The Poetic Process," which alluded to "the blood and balls of Christ," seemed too strong to be included, and the committee decided not to act as Layton's Canadian publisher. Pierce (who recommended Layton for a Guggenheim, which he did not get) explained to Layton:

> Certainly this collection will consolidate your position. You already know what I think of the best of your work, all of which is here. Some erotic things I dislike. The "blood and balls of Christ" is so violently offensive to all Christians that it makes the book unpleasant, to say the least, to a large part of your potential audience. Erotic poetry forms an important part of the great tradition, but I dislike this focus on the genitals, say, moist with dancing, and such. You achieve the artistic expression of such experience quite splendidly very often by implication and suggestion and veiled metaphor, and are best

when you avoid this latrine cartoon business. Your best friends, I think, would not want you less passionate, but less heavy-handed.[19]

Pierce also said, "My difficulty is that I did not see the proofs [because Williams did not send them] and so had no chance of objecting to a few poems that would cause a tense time in our publishing committee."[20] Though Layton offered to withdraw "De Bullion Street" and agreed to replace the word "balls" with the word "bones" (a "trifling" change, he said), it was too late.[21] Pierce turned over Ryerson's two hundred copies to Layton and offered to pay the customs duty. Ryerson's name would be removed from the copyright page.

Layton's angry letter to the Toronto *Telegram* and his interview with the *Globe and Mail*[22] did nothing to change the situation, but they did stimulate sales (the first printing of five hundred copies was sold out by November 1956). They also caught the notice of the man who would become his Canadian publisher: Jack McClelland of McClelland and Stewart.

This fracas with Ryerson Press over the language of his poems marked a major milestone in Layton's ongoing — and largely justified — battle for more freedom of speech in literature. It focussed his attention on sexual expression, and he began to define quite clearly his own philosophy on the subject. "Yes, sex," he wrote Desmond Pacey:

> as much as one's system needs & can take, and not only of the legalized love-making variety, but anywhere and with anyone who can kindle the sacred flame. *Even with one's own wife*, and solely. The thing is much too important to trifle with. Most men and women go about like corpses or zombies, because they're badly repressed by conventional fears. He'd be mankind's greatest benefactor who could persuade it (mankind) that the ecstasy of sex is a wholesome good that's entirely independent of the foolish moralities which have been erected by the fear-ridden and the unadventurous. I believe that a great change is on the way, one that Freud started, but which will go beyond anything even he dreamed of. Yes,

sex — but have you never heard of...unorthodox ways of love-making which the puritanical leave with a horrified shudder to the gaily uninitiated![23]

After *The Improved Binoculars* appeared in late December, Layton sent Williams a list of people to whom copies should be sent at Layton's expense. The list included: Northrop Frye in Toronto; Malcolm Ross at Queen's University; Cyril James, principal of McGill; Eli Mandel; Robert Weaver at the CBC; Desmond Pacey at the University of New Brunswick; Pacey's colleague Fred Cogswell, editor of *Fiddlehead*, a well-established literary magazine; Layton's brothers Hyman and Larry; Governor-General Vincent Massey; and the honorable Louis St. Laurent.[24] The publisher's blurb for Tibby advertised Layton as "the First Great Canadian Poet...one of the most popular poets of his time." With a characteristic demand for last-minute changes, Layton wrote to Williams in early December, "I think Tibby is going to be a huge success."[25]

Dear Desmond

8035 Kildare Ave.,
Côte St. Luc, Que.,
June 28, 1955.

Dear Desmond:[1]
Thanks for your altogether good and wise letter. Read today N[orthrop] F[rye]'s review of *In the Midst of My Fever* and your description of it is certainly accurate.[2] After all the knocks I've given him, what he wrote was great-hearted and magnanimous. It distressed me sufficiently to make me write him to tell him that I thought so. My beef — if I still had enough wind left in me to make one — is that he's characteristically blind to the virtues ("a depressingly unreal world")[3] of *The Long Pea-Shooter*. But he does quote from it, and admits the lines stick.

A conspiracy? I don't know, but what would you call it? Consider the following facts objectively. I've been writing poems and stories for about a decade and a half and during that time I've appeared more often than any of my contemporaries in American magazines and books and received reviews and notices from them which few of these same contemporaries could match, beginning with a review of my first book, *Here and Now*, by F. Dupee in the Nation. He was writing about [Ralph] Gustafson, F.R. Scott and [Patrick] Anderson as well as myself and for each of us, I believe, it was our first appearance in print. I think I can truthfully say that I came off best. I was published in *Voice* and *Commentary*, and was the only other Canadian poet besides Klein to appear in a New Directions Annual. Observe. I am not mentioning my recent forays into Am. publications such as the *Black Mountain Review & Origin*, but confining myself strictly to the past. Now, although reasonably good grounds existed for considering me a writer of some seriousness and talent I have been kept out of the following Anthologies:

1. Smith's Book of Canadian Poetry (original and revised)[4]
2. Gustafson's[5]
3. Birney's Twentieth Century Canadian Poetry[6]
   and to be released soon —
4. Klinck and Wells [sic] (I don't know its title).[7]

When Smith was planning to bring out the first edition of his *Book of Can[adian] Poetry* he asked me for some poems, said he was going to use them. He never did. Bringing out his revised edition, he put in Miriam Waddington, Louis Dudek, [James] Reaney and [Douglas] Le Pan, the last two recent arrivals but again gave me the back of his hand though by then I had something like five volumes of verse to my credit and had appeared consistently in about a dozen mags both here and abroad. Perhaps more to the point I had also written, among others, the following poems:

1. Newsboy (Poetry, Chicago)
2. Jewish Main Street
3. Drill Shed (Poetry, Chicago)
4. The Swimmer (Poetry, Chicago)
5. Gothic Landscape (Commentary)
6. Mrs. Fornheim, Refugee
7. Mont Rolland
8. De Bullion Street
9. Week-end Journey
10. Proof Reader
11. To A Very Old Lady
12. Poet and Statue [sic]

Now any one of these poems is as good a poem as I ever hope to write and certainly, without wishing to force insidious comparisons, as good as some of the things which he included by others. Smith's sudden espousal, therefore, of my "new-found" talent cannot but put a wry smile on my lips, remembering as I do his studied neglect of that same talent in the past. Perhaps the unpleasantest duty I ever had to perform in my life was to point this out to him by letters after his laudatory review of my books on *Critically Speaking*.[8] I'm no asslicker and I do not "butter the reviewers" even after they have shown themselves to be disposed favourably. The truth is the truth, and I'm beginning to suspect that the reason I'm disliked is that I refuse to convert literature to a parlour-game, albeit an engaging one. "You weigh me down" Johnson reminded Lord Chesterfield on an occasion memorably analogous to my own. I am unkind? I cannot help it; like Shaw I have perfect eyesight.

Furthermore, Des, if you compare the reviews which my book received in this country with the reception of those books elsewhere you will again note an astonishing discrepancy. It began with my first book and has continued right up *until the present*. I'm thinking of Woodcock's review in the *Queen's Quarterly*;[9] also neither Smith nor Frye are reconciled to the *L.P.S.* Well, to convince you that the pattern has not altered, both William Carlos Williams and Pound wrote to congratulate me on *The Pea-Shooter*, the former going so far as to say that he had something to learn from me. I could list a half-a-dozen other Am[erican] & English poets who find *The Pea-Shooter* tops — among Canadians, you're the only one who's been really enthusiastic.

To continue this melancholy and, I fear, rather boring tale. Two years ago or it may have been last year, Frye had great praise for Elizabeth Brewster and even Anthony Frisch (both of which he currently dismisses with a curt nod) but could find very little to praise in so fine a volume of poems as *Love The Conqueror Worm* though it contained two genuine masterpieces "Cemetery in August" and "Death of Moishe Lazarovitch," neither of which he mentioned though both contain ample evidence of the "pity and terror" he today belatedly discovers in "Westmount Doll"[10] (not half so good a poem as either one above).

What about my short stories? The story is the same — and short. Along with poems I've written about a dozen of them. When my *Vacation in La Voiselle* first appeared in *Northern Review*, Knopf wrote to ask me whether I would care to submit a longer work or a book of stories for their consideration so impressed, they wrote, were they with its excellence. *Death In The Family* evoked the same enthusiasm and the same request for manuscripts from the Dial Publishing House in New York. In recent years a spate of anthologies of Canadian short stories were published. Is either *Vacation in La Voiselle* or *Death In The Family* to be found in any of them? "A Game of Chess"? Do you think "A Plausible Story" will ever find its way into an Anthology, though it was featured in *Origin*? Or "Mrs. Polinov"?[11]

Had I been one who discouraged easily, I should have given up writing a long time ago, certainly after Birney's snide & patronizing review of *The Black Huntsmen* which held me up to ridicule across the country (it was on "Critically Speaking") and to which there was no chance of reply. That book contained some of the best things I had done up until then, including *The Swimmer, Mrs. Fornheim, Refugee, Mont Rolland, Auspex, Drill Shed, Afternoon of a Coupon Clipper*, etc! You'd think, however, from his remarks that I sat composing (or is it "de-") in a brothel and didn't know my left hand from my right. Or read Marriott's snippy review of *Love The Conqueror Worm* in *The Canadian Forum*. Fortunately, I was born on the wrong side of the tracks: before I encountered critics and reviewers, I had fistfights every day of my public school life with the toughs that flourished in the slum neighbourhood, and sometimes, in fact frequently, it was bottles and jack knives. I learned to give as good as I got — and never to whimper. I also learned that if you had it in you, come hell or highwater, you'd earn their respect. But you had to stay in there, and keep on pounding. It's a lesson I never forget, and today I'm grateful to the anonymous Italians, Poles, Hungarians, and French-Canadian delinquents who taught it to me. After a broken nose and a slit cheek, what's a Frye or a Smith?

I tell you all this not to bore you or to give you the colour and dimensions of the chip on my shoulder, but because you're a literary historian. Figuratively speaking, these matters are your bread-and-butter. The facts are, I believe, largely as I state them. You will note I've deliberately avoided the part which John Sutherland and his subsequent defection played in all this, which was not inconsiderable. But that deserves a separate treatment, and in any case I gave you some inkling of its scope and nature when you were here. Since I have no reason to believe that the response which my poems evoked in this country was due to my odious personality — most of the reviewers and critics had never met me — I could only conclude that both the matter and style of what I write were what gave offence. And since I never doubted either my talent or my dedication and saw myself passed over in favour of the mediocre but adaptable, I further concluded that the nub of the matter was that my view of the world and what poetry is differed strikingly from theirs. It's still the brittle and the desiccated in what I would hardly call poetry at all, but a species of verse — that are most admired by our academic critics. Only in this last review by Frye do I notice a slight shift of value with passion and spontaneity being preferred to labour and intellect. Could be I've educated him? Though his remarks on Smith and Scott are opposite and discerning, he still over-values them, as he most certainly does Miss Page, whose last book sounds like nothing so much as a parody on her earlier one. I've yet to see him or any other Canadian critic give both Dudek and Souster their just deserts [sic]: but there are all kinds of kudos for Anderson whose phoney English accent was apparent to the reviewer in *The Nation* more than a decade ago. Frye's review both of *The Colour as Naked* and the second book by Le Pan will one day give him nightmares — that is, if he continues to mature. No, Des, the kind of poetry that's valued here though I admit changes are being made and the plaster is beginning to crack is still the "clever", the "involuted", the "commentless". For my money, Frye gives himself completely away and reveals his limitations when he speaks of *The Long Pea-Shooter* as a "depressingly unreal world." To a professor in a library or a comfortable armchair, or engrossed in symbolic-psychological-blah blah analysis no doubt it is; but to me who lived it, it isn't. *The Long Pea-Shooter* is a genuine touchstone: as long as the Smiths, Fryes and "who-nots" are against it, I'll go on believing that criticism in Canada has not emancipated itself from the "genteel tradition" and that the profs, the older ones anyway, have refused to acknowledge the changing Zeitgeist. One revealing item that should speak volumes to you. Smith told me in conversation that "Marie" in the *L.P.S.* and "De Bullion Street" in *The Black Huntsmen* were both masterpieces of their kind — but of course would never use them in his projected *The Blasted Pine*:[12] too raw, you know. The Blasted Pine indeed!

Well, I won't apologize for this rather lengthy letter. If it has bored you or irritated you, in all fairness you'll have to admit you brought it on yourself. One shouldn't go around poking a hornet's nest with a stick.... I'll enquire about [outlets for] your bks [of children's stories][13] this week. The poems were for your own pleasure. I'm glad they gave you some. Bet and the kids say hello to you.

All the best.
Irv

At Odds

It is March 1955. Irving Layton sits in the McGill University library. In front of him on the table are periodicals, the *New Republic, Yale Review* and *Philosophy*. He has just finished reading Frieda Lawrence's revelation about her talented and erratic husband. He stops reading to write a letter to Bob Creeley. He is sleepy, he tells Bob: "My eyelids come down like weights of lead or iron, and to the amused surprise of my studious neighbours I make off into a world which is much simpler than the one I know when my eyes are open. My pleasant after-reading nap sometimes lasts for two hours; by now, I've learned how to slide into forgetfulness without the least discomfort or loss of dignity. I can even fool strangers or the librarian seated at the table some distance away from where I am into thinking I am absorbed profoundly by some esoteric thought. Very truthfully, they may think to themselves that they've never seen anyone with so much concentration written upon his face!"[1]

It is August 1955. Irving reclines at Lac Minerve, County Labelle, in the Laurentians, with Betty, "Maxie" and "Sissyboo." He has left behind his Côte St. Luc living room with the painting of a nude over the fireplace. (He has often said of the painting, "That's Betty. It pays to advertise."[2]) It is their second summer holiday at the lake. Irving is happy. "In the past ten days we've...slowly straightened out our reflexes. The sounds we hear are all pleasant ones: voices across flowing water, the loon's call, etc. Sissyboo has learned to swim very well and she can also row.... Betty is looking magnificently beautiful, and I've written five moderately successful poems. Max and I have started reading the Bible together — *there's* poetry for you — and intend to go right through it. After that we'll go through the Odyssey and the Illiad [sic]. Max is an appreciative listener, it's a pleasure to read to him. He takes everything in and the comments he makes are amusing and intelligent. He's a very great joy to me."[3]

One of the "five moderately successful poems" Irving has written is for Betty. It is called "Letter From A Straw Man."

> I loved you, Bobbo, even when you knuckled me
> And pulled the straw out of my breast,
> Pretending to weep yet secretly glad to note
> How yellow and summer-dry the stuff was.
>
> You will surely recall how amazed
> We both were the straw was endless;
> At the time I did not know it was your fingers
> Made the straw grow there and blaze
>
> Yellow in the fierce sunlight...How when
> I once caught your cold blue eye
> It first burned like sulphur, but affected
> Let down a tear like a drop of dirty sea-water
>
> Into my prized open chest; though after that
> Encounter of our eyes your own —
> The pitiful one — grew into a porcelain
> Saucer white and blind. That I could understand.
>
> But why did you give great handfuls
> To the visiting firemen? And when the mayor
> Asked for some to decorate his fireplace,
> Why did you not refuse? No, rather,

Plunging your delicate green fingers
Into my gaping breast you drew
Out for him the longest stalk
Which he snatched with a cough and a compelling eye.

I have left you for another,
Who wears black panties and is as crazy as the birds;
But when the straw comes away in her hands
She is careful to burn it immediately afterwards.[4]

Anti-Romantic

Aviva Cantor waited on the icy steps outside the apartment she shared with two French-Canadian girls on the east side of Montreal. She hadn't known there would be French people in Canada. Now she was stuck with two of them, and it was lonely, not being able to talk. Jesus, it was cold! Where was he anyway? In Australia, she'd have known where to go, how to find the kind of people she liked: bohemian, off-beat, literary. But here.... Well, it was worth a try. The one person she knew in Montreal, Harry Hooten, was from Sydney, too. He wrote poetry. That man in New Brunswick he'd told her to write to, Fred something-or-other at *Fiddlesticks* magazine, had written back telling her to try Frank Scott or Louis Dudek or Irving Layton. Irving! What a name! It was a joke, really. She'd never heard anything like it. He had said, "Layton really is a lively chap." That gave her some hope. Frank Scott had been out when she called. Saying "Irving" over the phone had almost done her in, but she was desperate. She couldn't stand this stuffy, confusing Montreal much longer unless *something* happened. His rich voice had boomed out over the phone. "Come on over to our next gathering. I'll pick you up Sunday evening." It wouldn't be as good as Australia, though. There was no one here like that — mad as hatters, they'd all been, flaunting sex like a revolutionary flag flying in the face of society. There was a battered-up Volkswagen swerving down the street. Was that him? It was amazing that he'd bother. Jesus, it was cold![1]

He couldn't have missed her, even though she was tiny. Her hair was dyed bright brass. "Aviva — that's a laugh — on a day like this. Means 'springtime' doesn't it? Jump in." "As he drove me to his little Hansel and Gretel cottage in the woods," Aviva recalls, "he told me he was thinking of buying a yacht. I couldn't figure him out, but he was terribly attractive. I loved his voice. I asked him if he was married. 'Very much so,' he replied. 'And I have two kids.'" Aviva was disappointed.

"Betty was very, very beautiful," Aviva said, recalling that first party at the Laytons'. "And she was a good painter. Her paintings were all around the room. Louis Dudek was there with Aileen Collins. And Louise Scott, Betty's cousin, who was starting her career as a painter too. It was just like Sydney, not my oppressive middle-class business family, but the part of it I'd loved — drinking and talking on and on about books." At age twenty-one, Aviva could not have been more different from Betty. Betty was quiet; Aviva talked non-stop. Betty was slow-moving, comfortable, serene; Aviva was pert, vivacious, restless. In her semi-autobiographical novel, *Nobody's Daughter*,[2] she compared the character Eve, partly based on Betty, to Ingrid Bergman; and the narrator, partly based on herself, to the cute dancer Jane Powell. Aviva's Australian accent, which to Irving's Canadian ear sounded something like the cultivated British accent he had so admired in Amos Saunders and others, lent a curious "double effect" to the colourful vulgarity of her expressions: vodka and gin were "leg-openers" and couples necking were "knee-tremblers." (Layton quickly incorporated these expressions into his poem "The Newer Critics.")[3] Aviva strutted around the Laytons' living room like a bantam cock. She soon became a regular at the Layton's Sunday-evening get-togethers.

"On one of those evenings Louis had brought a Greek-Canadian sculptor along. He said something about Nietzsche — all of whose works I had read — and I went berserk," Aviva recalls. "The sculptor was pissed off and said, 'I wish I didn't know you.' That made me even more brash. I began screaming about Nietzsche, reeling off examples like crazy. I made a mess of the party. Actually I was dying to make an impression on this group so that I wouldn't be treated as a nonentity. I was very young and I was pretty ignorant. I only knew about Nietzsche because Harry Hooten was mad keen about him. Louis never did change his impression that I was an aggressive fool. Irving had not been much attracted to me before that evening, but after that he took an interest."

Irving called Aviva at the Jewish General Hospital, where she was disconsolately working as an x-ray technician. He came to see her and took her out for a cup of coffee. After that, he was a regular visitor at the hospital. He didn't come in quietly: he let everyone in the place know that The Poet had arrived. Layton wrote a poem called "If You Can't Scream," in which he saw himself as a little "all-odds-against-me" David taking aim at his Goliath-like fate: "my stoned eyeballs tighten/in the neat slingshot/of your posterior."[4]

One afternoon, he took Aviva for a drive: "He was nervous. I couldn't understand why he felt it necessary to give a long speech, a sort of preamble to making a pass. It went something like this: 'When Gabriel came to Michael he told him he couldn't get into heaven. When Gabriel asked why, Michael told him he'd only done good deeds. "You've had opportunities for joy and you didn't take them," Michael said. "So you're damned for the greatest sin of all: not living!"' Irving was very shy and very awkward. He took so long getting around to it that I nearly froze to death. He kissed me with his lips closed. Eventually, I needed to pee. He looked away. While I was gone, he wrote that poem 'You went behind a bush to piss./Imagine Wordsworth writing this' ("Anti-Romantic").'[5] After that day, I could see that we were going to have an affair. Though I went to his literary gatherings a couple more times, I knew that they would be closed to me from now on. I moved out of my shared apartment and took another one nearer Irving in the Snowdon area. He was inhibited sexually, puritanical, not at home in his own body. For weeks he would only touch me, fumbling foreplay stuff. He was more comfortable doing that. I guess he felt guilty. He was unable to penetrate me for a long time."

To Fred Cogswell, editor of *Fiddlehead* in New Brunswick,

who had sent Aviva to Layton, Layton wrote a note: "I've met a nurse from the Jewish General Hospital in Montreal. She has a beautiful set of teeth and nothing behind them."[6]

In fact, Layton was drawn to the voluptuous, grey-eyed Aviva as if to his own image suddenly become female. In her novel, "Anna" — based partly on Aviva — and "Alex" — based partly on Layton — bear an uncanny resemblance to each other. She describes the peculiarly "androgynous" nature of their relationship, based on her own experience with Irving:

> Our bodies were so much alike — legs that looked as if they should be rooted into the earth, strong, stocky bodies, peasant faces — that making love to each other was like making love to oneself. But the fucking was only the foreplay. The *real* fucking was the talking. That's what we really came together for. We displayed our lives in front of each other like shrewd Jewish merchants in a richly stocked bazaar. We loved each other's wares; fondled and pinched and caressed the objects of each other's past lives. "I can't talk with Eve," said Alex. "She won't listen anymore. She closes herself against me." I couldn't open the lid of my life wide enough. Its jumble of rubbish spilt around us. Under Alex's gaze, it turned into an avalanche of brightly coloured jewels.
>
> I knew then that Alex was mine. Apart, we were mortal. Together, we possessed an androgynous power.[7]

During the affair, Betty faced a different crisis: she had become pregnant by her lover, a black construction worker name Basil. Layton knew that she was having an affair: he waited up one night for her return. She climbed quietly in through her studio window to find him propped up in bed reading, a bitter smile on his face. "Come here!" he commanded. As she stood beside the bed, he slid his hand under her skirt to see if her pants were sticky. They were. Like a man demented, he beat his head against the wall. Betty decided to have an abortion.

She went into the hospital where, because of her heart problems, she had to be x-rayed before any surgical procedure.

The technician who performed the x-ray, which revealed "gross cardiac enlargement," was Aviva Cantor.

About this time, Betty dramatically lost her fabled beauty. Stress exaggerated the Bell's Palsy she had contracted after Naomi's birth and the disease further afflicted her face. As the paralysis got worse, one side of her face stayed slack and twisted forever, and one eye rolled up as if blind. The smile that had reminded so many people of Ingrid Bergman had become a startling grimace. To her friends, Betty's physical transformation seemed an important factor in the deterioration of the marriage.[8] But Layton, whose version of events differs from Betty's, thinks the disease struck later, after the couple had separated.[9]

Aviva spent only a few months in her spartan apartment in Snowdon. Layton visited her there frequently during the spring of 1957. Suddenly, a real "love-nest" was available to them. A friend of Aviva's, a "kept" woman who had a flat at the Croyden Apartments at 3445 Côte des Neiges in downtown Montreal, had to leave in a hurry for New York. "She left everything in the apartment," Aviva recalls. "It was mad. It was a real courtesan's place like something out of Berlin in the 1930s: pink satin sheets, the lot!" Aviva split the cost of the apartment with an intern from the Jewish General Hospital, who used it twice a week for his affairs; for two nights a week, Aviva slept surreptitiously in the intern's room at the hospital. ("I had to use a bedpan so that I wasn't spotted in the toilet!") "Irving used to come swaggering in and drink all the intern's Drambuie," Aviva remembered. When the Croydon almost went up in smoke that summer, Irving wrote his poem "Esthetique." "Out of the rubbish burning and burning comes/ Mozartian ecstasy leaping with the flames." It wasn't long before Aviva was also making love to the intern. "I almost married him," says Aviva. "At the end of the summer I went with him to Boston where he worked in a down-town hospital. We took a little garret apartment on Beacon Hill. I got a good legal job. I had no responsibilities. Life was wonderful. I loved Boston. We used to go to Cape Cod which was a bit like Sydney. Later we lived in New York. I enjoy life in suspension."[10]

Though Aviva was happy in Boston and New York with her "adoring and loving" intern, she kept up a correspondence with Layton. "He used to write almost every day from his class at Herzliah: wonderful, beautiful, funny, tender, passionate love letters. I treasured them. They must have been the most beautiful letters in his life. He made up fairy-tales for me — all about butterflies, princes and princesses. I wrote back at least once a day. But eventually he wrote a terrible, hurtful letter, asking me to destroy the letters, to burn them at once. I would have done anything he asked. I burned hundreds of letters and even sent a telegram to report that I had done what he wanted."[11]

Because he frequently had the impulse to join Aviva, Layton made a concerted effort to have his name cleared for entrance to the United States. In February 1957, he asked Olson, Creeley, Jonathan Williams and Paul Metcalfe to send letters to Customs and Immigration testifying that his presence in the United States would be "beneficial." His friends sent the letters, and Layton received notification from the department of immigration that he must show proof that he had been actively anti-Communist for at least the past five years. By the end of 1957, he had still not received clearance, though he had a lawyer helping him.[12]

In the fall of 1957, about a year after Aviva left for Boston, Layton demanded that she return to Him: "When I got back to Montreal, it was to total nothingness," Aviva recalls. "When I appeared, he retreated. My life was like a mediaeval monk's. Finally, I took a basement apartment at 3360 Ridgewood Avenue where he would come to see me. He was very uneasy. He thought Secret Service men might be watching us to collect evidence, and that if they were he might lose his job. Later, I moved out to a depressing place on Stanley Street behind one of the first vegetarian restaurants in Montreal. Where my window looked out was all the rubbish from the restaurant and lots of huge plump grey rats who fed on mouldy vegetables. At midnight, Irving used to rush out with a spade to kill the rats. I furnished the place from the Salvation Army with a mattress on the floor and lots of Indian covers."[13]

While she was living on Ridgewood Avenue, Aviva met

John Mills, another writer, who got her a job at a Classics bookstore, where he worked. Mills hated Layton and thought he was absurd. He did his best to convince Aviva that the man she called "a God" was not even a reasonably good poet. In a later, fictional representation partly based on Layton and Aviva, Mills created the characters Isaac Stein and his young "wife," Susan:

> Unlike most of Canada's poets, Isaac Stein was no gentleman. He was short, stocky, pugnacious, huge-headed, bushy-maned with violent, half-crazed eyes which impaled you like Klieg lights. Other than this the chief thing about him was his solipsism — fundamentally he could not accept your separate existence. All the same you had to admire the tremendous efforts he made to recall the names of those shadows residing in a world which ceased to exist the moment he closed his eyes. He forced himself to act as though there *were* an external reality. His usual technique was to address you firmly by what he thought was your name, emphasizing it as though he wished to prove to you, triumphantly, that you possessed a Being and that he had remembered you. Thus I have been poked in the ribs, glared at, argued against in that deep rapid voice whilst being addressed as "Fred", "Graham", "Archie" and once, even, "Jean-Claude".
> Isaac swung open the door and ancient-marinered me straight away.
> "Yes, my friend? What can I do for you?"
> I slipped past him into the living room while, frantically, he rushed down the corridors of his mental waxworks to select the appropriate dummy.
> "Haven't seen you for a long while," he said, playing for time. "Take a seat. My wife'll make some coffee. What've you been doing with yourself?"
> "I've been away, Isaac."
> "Did you go to North Beach, David? To Sausalito? Did you see my friend Lawrence Ferlinghetti?"
> But with a cry of "Marcus!" his wife rushed in and threw her arms around my neck. I caught his eye.

> Finally he was in control of the situation. I was the man he'd invented called Marcus Smith whom he'd turned into a criminal, then sent to the bug-house. Now, by some stroke of unconscious genius, he had brought me back — almost flesh and blood, one of his most successful achievements. He gave me a relieved smile.[14]

Layton seemed to thrive on the chaos in which he lived. Though he still wrote a few poems on subjects unrelated to his intense and wildly fluctuating situation, most of those he wrote after meeting Aviva expressed various points of view on his personal crisis, though they were not necessarily views held by himself. For some time — definitely from 1953, when he first became aware that he was in the midst of a "late spring" fever — he yearned for more freedom than his marriage to Betty allowed. In a sense, they "announced" to each other that affairs were probable, if not imminent. Although Betty fell first, Irving had long appropriated freedoms that were easy enough to rationalize as "coffee romances," some of which had gotten well past the chit-chat stage. And after all, hadn't Bob Creeley just left his wife and family, euphoric with the freedom it gave him to write poetry? Earlier Layton poems like "Metzinger: Girl with a Bird" had expressed the longing for freedom, but not the actuality. Now several poems picked up that theme, treating it more strongly: "A Roman Jew To Ovid" (a pun on "a roamin' Jew" and originally titled "An Errant Husband"), "Individualist," "Whatever Else Poetry is Freedom" (it took him six months to find a concluding stanza)[15] and the stately and complex "On Seeing the Statuettes of Ezekiel and Jeremiah in the Church of Notre Dame." In the last poem, the best of the four, Layton expressed his "aching confraternity" with the statues of two great Old Testament figures "captive," "bored" and "incensed" amongst "saints" in the church of "Notre Dame" (the "holy" mother).[16]

As some of his poems suggested, Layton had come to see his marriage to Betty as a captive state and himself a kind of immobilized captive statue. Earlier, he had praised marriage, despite its imperfections, in "The Longest Journey": "Yet the good life holds:/ Like great art, is unsensational; and there time/ Does not rush upon us but unfolds."[17] Now, even though his thrilling experiences with Aviva rushed in upon him, he could still see Betty and his marriage to her as true, their love as a "sacrament," as in the work called "Poem."

> I would for your sake be gentle
> Be, believe me, other than I am:
> What, what madness is it that hurls me
> Sundays against your Sunday calm?
>
> True, there's enough gall in my ducts
> To cover an area, and more:
> But why you — free from evil, poor bird?
> Why you — my heart and saviour?
>
> I swear I'm damned to so hate and rage.
> But your fair innocence is my guilt;
> And the stream that you make clear
> I must, to fog my image, fill with silt.
>
> Bear with me, bear with me —
> Your goodness, gift so little understood
> Even by the angels I suppose
> And by us here somewhat undervalued
>
> Is what I hold to when madness comes.
> It is the soft night against which I flare
> Rocketwise, and when I fall
> See my way back by my own embers.[18]

Nothing could have been more tender than some of the poems he wrote at this stage. "Song for Naomi," his lovely tribute to his six-year-old daughter, for example, or "Berry Picking," the reverential description of Betty at home in nature at the cottage at Petit Lac Long, Terrebonne County, in the Laurentians, where they spent the summer of 1957. These two poems are among his most widely anthologized.[19]

But a fiercer, darker side of his feelings about his wife erupted as often. In "Autumn Lines for My Son,"[20] he wrote, "turn from the women yearning/ To become wives, and their encircling arms:/ Monstrous circle where Love's garrotted." For Tibby, he revived "Enigma," the poem about a man offering his wife to a friend (first published in *The Blue Propeller*). In subsequent volumes are poems like "Letter from a Straw Man," which revealed the anguish a man can feel at his wife's betrayals. When a second Keewaydin poetry weekend was proposed, he wrote to A.J.M. Smith: "I think we can organize something better this time than a prolonged petting party."[21]

Many of the poems that spun from his deepening involvement with Aviva were not the celebrations of ecstasy he frequently said poetry ought to be. Most of them were critical of woman's lechery and deceit, and suffused with guilt at man's self-indulgence. Though he trotted out allusions from classical myth to disguise and dignify his affair, he could not conceal his own sense of its sordidness. Sometimes he perceived himself as "Odysseus in Limbo" (a pun on "in limbs, Oh!") with his "Nausicäa" (Betty was, by implication, a patient Penelope). The name "Nausicäa" suggested Aviva's youth (she was exactly half his age when they began their affair, twenty-two to his forty-four), and also the gut-churning "nausea" Layton sometimes felt when he thought about what he was doing. At other times, he recorded the deliberate entry into a "perverse" lust ("Lesbia") as if he knew what it was like to enjoy striding wide-eyed into Hell itself.[22]

Though Layton wrote a moving tribute to Marilyn Monroe, "Earth Goddess,"[23] and seemed eager to embrace a philosophy of sexual freedom, his guilt proved a formidable obstacle. It was impossible to know whether the burning he experienced was pleasure or pain

> By Ecstasies Perplexed
>
> By that, by this, by sharp ecstasies perplexed,
> illumined, a saint streaked with foibles,
>   I wore at the heart a hairshirt of fire,
> wrapped my thighs in a loincloth of bees.
>
> Honour foreswore and talent, and with these
> burnished those bluedyed baubles which hang

> amorously from sad and arid bantam trees
> in one-room apartments cheaply furnished.
>
> Yet now with lust and indignation spent
> and even remorse and other troubles
>   I ask whether by deliberate will I went
> or frenzy at a woman's beauty.
>
> And cannot answer. But recall
> a flaxen-haired boy five years old
>   who one bad night put fire to his gown
> and watched the flames about him rise blue and gold.[24]

Of this poem, Layton's friend Al Purdy, who knew nothing of Layton's personal dilemma, commented, "I have the feeling that you are feeling your way into something else, that you are changing like the Phoenix before my eyes.... [that this] is an interim period."[25] When Layton was with Aviva, it seemed, he could not get his role as a husband and father out of his mind; when he was with Betty, as in the sardonic poem "How Domestic Happiness is Achieved" (by not spending much time together), he could only "curl up in my most/ lascivious thought of you/ and try to sleep" ("From a Lawnchair").[26]

Many of his most moving poems described situations in which an animal or person is suddenly struck down in punishment. The most famous is the tenderly eloquent "The Bull Calf,"[27] in which a young calf, full of life and promise, is methodically disposed of because he is male. In "The Mosquito," Layton pictures himself as a cruel and indifferent fate dealing out death to the insect who has demonstrated his "stupid extravagance" by showing himself, "letting the sun/ betray him." In "Cain,"[28] the poet sadistically shoots a "self-infatuate" frog to show the absurdity of aspirations in the face of death. (The poem was based on a real incident in the summer of 1957 when, to Betty's horror, Layton gave Max an air-rifle and went "frog shooting" with him at Petit Lac Long.) In "Firecrackers,"[29] Layton drew on the stories of the Tong wars he had read as a boy; he pictures an innocent Chinese child unaware that, because of his explosive fun, he is about to become the victim of a large, predatory osprey. Some of the poems that treat the theme of imminent punishment relate that punishment to a Jewish father; for example, "Fiat Lux."

> Do not, son,
> the Sabbath dishonouring,
> switch on the lights, the black beard said,
> for with a quiver from His bag of cloud
> God kills in a revenging wrath.
>
> Alone in the dark shall the boy sing?
> Shall he pray? No, let his father pray.
> His father's lips are red, red and full,
> and the beard black. Bald and skinny the boy
> stared at the switch, a nipple marooned in the wall,
> and could not keep his trembling hand from it,
> no more than Achan from an emerald.
>
> The dull metallic click he heard
> was like a small bone that had snapped
> perhaps in his skull
> or somewhere below his perspiring neck;
> and though the room,
> reeling with vertigo, filled
> with a salt light that all but blinded him,
> God has yet not struck or killed.[30]

Partly as a contrast to himself, to his daring the fates and choosing life over respectability no matter what the cost, and partly as a salve to his pricking conscience, Layton continued his attacks on poetry that was effete, academic, not rooted in flesh-and-blood experience. His new target was Jay Macpherson, whose graceful, pristine mythological poems were being heralded in Toronto. Layton also used Freud (whose biography by Ernest Jones he had just read and disliked) to attack T.S. Eliot in "The Love Dream of W.P. Turner,"[31] a poem about the dangers of emotional repression.

William Carlos Williams, to whom the manuscript for *The Improved Binoculars* had been sent, responded in superlatives: "You have one of the major talents of the age, I only wish I were half as good." He singled out "Rose Lemay" (a poem about the old housekeeper Layton had hired when Betty was hospitalized)[32] and called it "as near a perfect poem as I hope ever to see." Williams offered Layton advice:

> You spoil many of your poems, more than half of them, by your perfectly horrible inversions of the normal phrase... nothing more than a bad habit that you have acquired from your studies of past verse... Get over it. Stick to the contours of the modern idiom. You must go over all your poems with the keenest eye you can muster, with a view to eliminating every one of [them] that you cannot alter to read more normally. It goes without saying that in some of them you will fail. Cut them from your mind and forget them.... I have given you a cruel job to do on your own work. You'll have to be ruthless. Out of the holocast [sic] will emerge some of the greatest poems ever written in the language, but only if you do your work well.[33]

Layton had created a living hell for himself and was enjoying to the full all its emotional extremes. Suspended between two women, each of whom seemed alternately sinister and marvellous, filled with anxiety about the consequences of what he called his "madness," fearing the imagined retribution of his father for playing with fire and breaking time-honoured laws, aware that, as each year went by, his son nudged him closer to old age, Layton immersed himself in frenzies of sexuality with Aviva and, in an ironic, new-awakened passion, with his wife. And just as he juggled the old and the new, the past and the future, the mistress and the wife, he sported with poetic techniques and angles of vision in an endless permutation of juxtapositions. The effect was intense and bizarre. "He knows the colours of the spectrum, and how all the colours are split off from it," William Carlos Williams wrote in his introduction to *The Improved Binoculars* with more insight than his description of Layton as a "backwoodsman" might imply. "If you want him to be true to yellow, he will be true to red; and if to green, he will be true to purple or brown or black or the most heavenly blue.... As far as deftness in the craft of a poet, I think he can do anything he wants to."[34]

Portrait of the Artist

As he frequently remarked later, Layton paid a high price for the freedom he believed was a necessity for his art. He jeopardized the friendship and respect of many of those who had forgiven, even enjoyed, his idiosyncracies. According to Louis Dudek,[1] Layton changed dramatically when he gained the attention of the American poets Williams, Creeley, Olson and Corman. Dudek remembers a literary gathering at the Laytons' in late 1953 or early 1954, which was held to organize an issue of *CIV/n*. The young poet Bob Currie, who had recently emerged in the Montreal scene, was, at the outset, dazzled by Layton's exuberance. He was soon disillusioned. Dudek recalls:

"I drove over to Irving's with Currie that evening, and Currie said, 'I can't stand Layton's egotism. It's unbearable. If there's any more dogmatic egomania tonight, let's come down on him hard.' At the party, people sat around as usual and sang or read something. Others would offer their comments afterwards. Irving got up and read some squibs he'd written and Currie lashed out at him. I backed Bob. The next day Irving phoned me and was very hurt. What had upset him the most was that some of his best friends had been there. So I told him that in my opinion there was a real problem with his attitude and that he should do something about it. There was hardly a poem he wrote in which he was not the central figure. As for Bob, he more or less dropped Layton after that evening.

"[Layton] didn't do anything about it, though. In fact, it got worse. I'm certain that his mania was connected with the recognition the American poets were giving him. I didn't wholeheartedly go along with the American poets — either with their poetry or with their criticism — and neither did Irving. But he managed to be published by them and keep his views secretive. As I see it, there were two periods in Irving's life: one before the early 50s when he was cool, had good views of life, politics and family; and now this one in which his ego was unbearable. He was like Mohammed Ali, the boxer, going around boasting, 'I am the greatest!' Before that, there was no one I'd rather discuss things with. After that, it wasn't a discussion any more. Losing the friend I cared about, seeing him turn into someone I didn't like with no possibility of reconciliation was terrible. It was like those lines of Coleridge's in *Christabel:*

> Alas! they had been friends in youth;
> But whispering tongues can poison truth;
> And constancy lives in realms above;
> And life is thorny; and youth is vain;
> And to be wroth with one we love
> Doth work like madness in the brain.

You can't replace a friend of your literary youth.

"The final break — after several minor rifts — came when I found out he was moving in with Aviva. It was the same secretiveness he'd shown with the American poets. He'd been seeing Aviva for some time before any of us knew. When he moved out, I stopped seeing him. He didn't come to my house. I wouldn't visit him at his new apartment. Other things drew both of us out and carried us in different directions."

Dudek was one of Layton's many literary and artistic associates to whom Betty showed the painting she had done in anger after Irving openly took up with Aviva. It showed Aviva laid out on a kitchen table, Irving's huge, black-maned head between her legs.[2]

Backflips

Keine Lazarovitch scowled like a black thundercloud. Her gold ear-rings quivered with the force of her idignation. No. Definitely not. She would never move in with her *Flamplatz* and his new woman. Betty was his wife. She was the mother of his two children. Even if she wasn't Jewish. It had been one thing to stay with them for awhile; but this was quite another.

Now that she'd left her second husband and moved, she wanted to buy another house. Her *strulick* had found her an ideal building. That's what he said: "Ideal." The front was a doctor's office; that seemed safe enough. It was on Mont Royal near Esplanade, only a couple of blocks from his Herzliah school. Her *srulickel* had promised to drop in every day. That would be nice. With asthsma you could never tell. Layton recalls:[1]

"When my mother learned that the previous occupant had died in the place, she would have none of it. She had sold her other place to an old man, but she had put in a special clause that if she changed her mind within a certain period of time she could reclaim it. Once she learned a death had occurred where she was moving, she wanted to move back to the old place. I met with the son of the buyer on Fletcher's Field to try to sort it out. He had gone to see her already, but all she did was cry. He agreed to give her back the building. After a couple of days, I called him because nothing had happened and my mother was worried. The son brought me the contract. His father had scissored out the clause she had added. So I went to see the old man. We both went to my mother, but all she would do was shrug her shoulders. Eventually I found another place for her above a grocery run by a French-Canadian woman who did nothing but complain about the roof leaking and the cellar smelling of refuse. A little while later, the old man came back to me to ask if I would give him a character reference in court. I actually went down and did it. Soon afterwards, I ran into his son who told me the old man died. It was just punishment for his many sins!"

"She was such a stubborn old woman," Hyman recalls. "Dora and Esther went once with her to help her buy a hat. The salesgirl was frightened of this stout, glaring woman who looked exceedingly displeased with everything. The girl showed them one hat after another, each of which our mother would plunk down on her wiry, white, dishevelled hair, then look in the mirror and scowl. Dora and Esther tried to persuade her to buy this one, or that. They told her what looked becoming, what was stylish, and so on, trying to humour her into getting one. Finally she brushed them all aside and pointed to one that was tucked away in the far corner of the room. Without even trying it on, she insisted on buying it."[2]

Betty recalls that, until she died, Keine treated Irving like a little boy. "I remember her seizing his plate at the table, cutting up his food into little pieces and starting to spoon-feed him before he grabbed the plate back."[3]

"One summer, before my mother became really sick in 1957, I took her to Ste. Sophie," Layton recalls.[4] "I just wanted to give her a little holiday. We arrived at a hotel and checked in and she immediately sat down and began to wail and cry. She wanted to go back home. Right away. I can still picture us getting right back in the car and heading for Montreal. It soon got dark and she was terrified that I would have an accident on the narrow road. The headlights were stuck on high beam, so all the cars coming the other direction kept flashing their lights at me. She carried on and screamed at me, cursing and shouting in every language she knew all the way back to the city. 'I'll leave my money to Dora — or one of the others,' she'd threaten. She played us off against each other to the bitter end."

Her *Flamplatz*, meanwhile, was having trouble making up his mind about Betty and Aviva. On Christmas day 1957, he left Aviva in her basement apartment and returned to Betty and the children, a bunch of roses and a bottle of wine clutched in his fists, a gesture of apology and romantic hopes. "Bet and I, after many difficult and heartbreaking weeks, are back together again, the ghost of whatever misunderstandings were responsible for them at last laid away — I devoutly hope, forever," he had written to Desmond Pacey on 19 December 1957.[5] But a few weeks later, on New Year's Eve, he again had a foot in both camps: "I went to see my family, and then drove Betty to the Compton's where she had been invited for a New Year's Eve party. I left her at the door and returned to my semi-basement apartment for a quiet celebration with Aviva."[6] A week later he was trusting his fate to Aviva: "My little one, Aviva, and I very likely shall be spliced this summer. The separation [from Betty] will be legally effective sometime this month, since I'm not contesting Betty's right to the custody of the two children.... But Bet has a lovely, warm, human smile," he added wistfully.[7]

Layton would not ask Betty for a divorce, but he agreed to buy Aviva a wedding ring. On a lovely spring day in 1958, the date for the "wedding" was set. Leonard Cohen was to be the "best man" on this lark. He dressed up and so did Aviva, but Layton wore his usual crumpled, mismatched clothes.[8]

They went out for lunch together first. Everyone was in a good mood. They had some wine, joked and talked until the bill was paid. Then it was off to an exclusive little jewellery shop on Mountain Street, Montreal's boutique centre. Aviva headed straight for the ring section and, before long, was trying on gold bands, holding out her hand to see the light glint with promise, hopeful that this would make all the difference. She spoke to Irving, asking him which one he preferred. But he didn't answer; he didn't even hear.

Irving was busy at another display case, handling another piece of jewellery. It wasn't gold, but silver, and not even a ring, but a chunky bracelet. "I'll take it for my wife!" he exclaimed to the salesman. "Betty will really like this!" he went on, holding up the bracelet for Aviva to see.

It was Leonard who took the gold ring and jokingly slipped it on Aviva's finger. "She was feeling so bad," he recalls. "But Irving was so ambiguous. He's very gentle. He never meant to hurt anyone. He probably felt like living with both women. I think he could have handled them both, too. It was the *women* who demanded a resolution."[9]

"Though Irving told me not to," Aviva recalls, "I always called myself Mrs. Layton after that."[10]

The Sorcerer's Apprentice

"Lately I've begun to feel like the Sorcerer's Apprentice, as if someone had put a hex on me," Layton wrote to Pacey on 8 August 1958. As he contemplated his situation from the isolated comfort of Lac Provost Lodge where he was taking a short holiday with his two children, aged twelve and eight, he wasn't at all sure that he liked the tornado of events his passions had unleashed. Somehow it felt as if some blind fate was sporting with him. He tried to reckon things carefully: he had lost his wife; he had lost his best friend; and he had, briefly, lost his job at Herzliah. He enclosed three poems for Pacey. "For Mao Tse Tung: A Meditation on Flies and Kings" was "started by the article on Mao's poetry in the current number of Q[ueen's] Q[uarterly]." "A Bonnet for Bessie" was "definitely experimental." In the poem he literally invented his own language and supplied Pacey with a glossary[1] — "Faye" means used tea bag; "Joseph" means "a poet;" "Publer" means "a poet seeking publicity," and so on. "Love is an Irrefutable Fire" was a lyric that moved him deeply. Despite his pride in these poems, he claimed he was going to stop writing poetry. "I'm through with poetry! For a year or two anyway. Either that, or it'll be the loonie bin for me. Now that the 'Collected' is coming out in January, the demon inside me ought to be appeased, and be willing to lie quiescent for awhile."

Being close to his children, cooking and cleaning up for them and taking them swimming, boating and for long jaunts through the woods, Layton felt great tenderness and a sense of responsibility: "My two bairns are wonderful, and I blow up with fatherly pride every time I look at them. Max and Naomi both have their mother's good looks, but their temperament is mine. The chief reason I have resolved to abandon the writing of poetry, temporarily at least, is that I want to spend the next few years with them; I don't want them to be estranged from me. I want them to remember me as a father and not as someone who was too busy or too abstracted to notice them." Already Layton had ambitions for Max to become a writer, preferably a short-story writer or novelist. (Layton had seriously considered writing a novel more than once, and was planning to spend a year writing short stories.) For Naomi he had nothing specific in mind, though he thought her "gifted and temperamental."

Pacey, who had seven children, sensibly wrote back: "I simply can't believe that you are through with poetry — you're no more through with poetry than I am with fucking."[2]

The "collected" Layton referred to was *A Red Carpet for the Sun*.[3] The title was taken from the Mao Tse-Tung poem he sent Pacey. Layton had entertained three other titles, each of which highlighted his current state of mind: "Arrogant, The One-Armed Juggler," "Visions and Predicaments" and "The Theoretical Nipple." It was the first book he did not sponsor and distribute himself (though having acquired the habit, he would hawk it with the same vigour as the rest). Jack McClelland, coming into his own as the leading Canadian nationalist publisher, had finally noticed Layton and had proposed the book. It would include two hundred and ten poems, most of them "real" poems of the ironic complexity Layton could express so well, and only a few "verses" of the simple satiric attacks for which he was known. It was a book to be proud of. With its publication, in September, Layton attained full stature "officially" as a major Canadian poet.

Irving Layton had hit his stride, and that stride was formidable. Though he was short-legged physically, he took giant steps into the national literary arena, like a tall man on stilts, directly into the limelight. His energy seemed demonic.

In the fall of 1959, he was teaching two evenings a week at Sir George Williams (he taught a class on twentieth-century American and British poetry, and a seminar on Yeats); one evening a week at the Jewish People's Library (a class on English Romanticism); daily matriculation-level classes in history, composition and literature at Herzliah; and weekly sessions for three private students, each of whom was following a different curriculum in nineteenth- and twentieth-century prose. He also fitted in two evenings and Saturday-nightdinner visits to the children (after which he invariably made love to Betty — "the best love-making of our marriage,"[4] according to Betty), and a weekly visit to his mother, whom he now was supporting in the Old Peoples' Shelter and Home on Esplanade near Herzliah.

Visits to his failing mother were upsetting to Layton. "One feels so helpless," he wrote to Pacey. "[My mother] had grown very thin and as she lay on her bed, half-asleep, looking so pitiful, I stood in the doorway and sobbed like a child. It was my sobs that woke her and made her stir. She turned her head towards me and smilingly asked me why there were tears on my face. Then she made me sit on the bed near her and took my hand in her own and began to stroke it as if she were trying to comfort me. She knew it was I who needed comforting more than she."[5]

Somehow he found time for Aviva, for parties, for readings, for the occasional CBC appearance, for trips to Toronto where he now regularly was appearing on "Fighting Words" (a debate programme that offered the perfect outlet for the satirical diatribes he loved to indulge in), and for younger poets like Leonard Cohen, Henry Moscovitch, Eli Mandel and Al Purdy, who gave him their work to comment on or dropped in to drink and ruminate on literary matters. He also was writing letters, frequently long and argumentative ones, an average of three or four a week to Pacey alone, his main correspondent until 1975. And he was cultivating a new body for his new love by taking weight-lifting and calisthenics. Aviva had found a teaching job at Weston School for girls in Westmount, and began classes in the violin and ballet. "Now let's keep our fingers crossed for the Governor-General's Award for the *Improved Binoculars*," Pacey wrote in March

1957. But although Layton did win the Canada Foundation Award, worth four thousand dollars, the country's top poetry award went to *The Boatman* by Jay Macpherson, the "mythological" poet Layton disdainfully contrasted to himself.

But a groundswell was building on the poetry scene in Canada. Layton sensed it, and felt himself to be at the centre of it. Hugh Kenner had listed him in *Poetry, Chicago* (June 1958) as one of the poets doing the most exciting work in the 1950s. In late October 1957, Professor Malcolm Ross (who would become general editor of McClelland and Stewart's New Canadian Library series) had invited Layton to read his poems to the newly formed English Club at Queen's University. There Layton got his first taste of public acclaim. He was overwhelmed.

> The hall was jampacked, with many students standing through the hour-long reading, some sitting on the floor. All told I read about 21 poems, chiefly from the *Binox* [*The Improved Binoculars*], two or three from the *Pea-shooter*. The students' response — well, it was glory, glory all the way.... Unblushingly I confess this was a proud moment for me; for this was the acid test, and by all the rules of the game, I had passed it. In the evening about a dozen students with ambition to become poets crowded into Ross's rather small parlour: they read and I commented. They showed little talent, but much earnestness... They were charmingly naïve and innocent ...but poets are old, old bulls, full of malice and suspicion. Let them stay young and innocent; let them marry and breed.[6]

Layton's longing to become a public figure simultaneously — though briefly — took a quite different course. Already he was well-known as the most outrageous of Nathan Cohen's "Fighting Words" panelists. (The others included, for example, Morley Callaghan, Ted Allen, J.K. Galbraith, Charlotte Whitton and Kenneth Rexroth.) Soon Layton would be nicknamed "Mr. Fighting Words." But Aviva, who loved to sing and dance, had incited other ambitions in him. "Have written lyrics for songs that would be suitable hits if I could find anyone who's interested in doing a musical comedy," he wrote to Pacey on 12 November 1957, before Pacey knew anything about Aviva. "Do you know any such? My partner has a real genius for writing catchy tunes, the best since Victor Herbert." Layton and Aviva were written up in *Time* magazine in early July 1958. The article quoted Layton as saying he had "less and less time for serious verse" and was "ensnared" by the idea of writing a musical.[7] Layton quickly denied both quotations in letters and in a *Toronto Star* interview titled "Blue Suede Poetry," after Elvis Presley's hit.[8] In the accompanying photograph, Irving's plump face beamed self-satisfaction. Behind him, Aviva, in a girlish sailor dress, was perched on a desk, smiling enthusiastically. They were also on *Tabloid*, a television programme Layton had appeared on in 1957 to publicize *The Improved Binoculars*. But Layton's desire to be "a real gone lyricist" and "to set in motion...a revolution" by "getting thousands of people humming my words" to songs like "They Wanna Fix My Fixation" was never fulfilled. He settled for cutting an album with Folkways: he read some of his poems "for posterity."[9]

Layton had his second taste of glory riding on the coat-tails of Leonard Cohen, the younger *CIV/n* poet he thought had "the purest lyrical gift in the country." Jonathan Williams, Layton's young American publisher ("a tall, engaging man with a recognizable southern accent, and a taste for bourbon"), was spending a week in Montreal in March 1958. Layton arranged for a talk at the CBC and another at Sir George Williams University. One evening, they went out on the town: "we descended on Leonard Cohen's nest in Birdland, where he gives poetry readings to the accompaniment of a jazz orchestra. Daryl Hine was also present. It ended up with J.W., myself, and D.H. as well as *staple goods*, L. Cohen, all reading poetry. Since it was dark, it was not possible to see the expressions on the faces of the people who were there. A memorable night!"[10]

Even when it brought him trouble, Layton was unable to resist the hangers-on who wished to draw on his creative energy to fuel their own, or to bask in his rapidly accumulating glory. Ron Everson, a public-relations man with a Montreal firm who wished to become a poet, approached Layton for instruction. When Pacey berated Layton for getting involved with someone Layton thought was not very talented as a poet, and who was clearly a fairly well-to-do "philistine" of the sort Layton himself frequently attacked. Layton replied: "I should never have allowed the relation with Everson to go as far as it did. But damn it all, I like poetry and every poor devil who tries to write it is my brother. His stuff was no good, horrible, to begin with, but it improved with time and application."[11] Layton saw in every poetic ambition a reflection of his earlier self. Helping other poets re-enacted Layton's rise from nowhere to somewhere (no matter how low on the poetic scale), and provided him with a mirror in which to gaze at his own greatness.

Nor was Layton able to resist the still strong image he had of himself as a devoted father. On 22 April 1959 he wrote to Pacey:

> "[I went over to Côte] St. Luc...to try to persuade Betty to let me take an apartment on Westminster, not too far from my former home — so that I'd be able to see the children more often than I now can. She wouldn't hear of it however. While I put Sissyboo to bed with a story I created as I went along — something about a poor slum girl who fell in love with a pin that turned back into a prince whom she afterwards married, I gave the story a modern proletarian twist by having the prince renounce his former easy life and become a train engineer. Sissyboo is growing into a beautiful talented person with many taking airs. I'm vastly proud of her. Max turned thirteen on the 7th of this month. Had his father been an orthodox Jew, he should have had his bar mitzvah with all the traditional trimmings and fuss that go along with that event. Instead I bought him a guitar he very much wanted and now he's taking lessons in guitar and piano. He's a very promising boy with a wonderful flair for writing... I have great hopes for him. He's a handsome devil and not a streak of malice in him. After I had put Sissyboo to sleep I came downstairs and told Max stories about the prairie and Shelley."

Layton's third sampling of the heady brew of recognition on a grand scale came at the end of April with the announcement that he had been awarded a Canada Council senior fellowship (with Pacey's recommendation, among others) — funds for a year to write. He felt "euphoric." With visions in his head of "Childe Harold" making a pilgrimage around Europe, he set off for France and Italy without either of his women after classes were finished, ostensibly for a year of new experience and writing. He took up the role of expatriate poet with a vengeance, sitting in outdoor cafés and ostentatiously writing and revising poems in a book labelled "Journal."[12] He sent back a number of postcards and letters in which his "enthusiasm seemed boundless."[13] A card to Pacey reported that "The most beautiful women menstruate in Rome." Another to Jonathan Williams claimed, "Italian girls are going to be my favourite wet dream from now on. What figures on them, what faces! I feel twenty years younger."[14] But by mid-September he was back in Canada.

The main reason was Aviva. Although he had "married" her with the ring Leonard Cohen had bought that spring, and she was calling herself "Mrs. Layton" (not entirely to his liking), she had turned to John Mills after Layton left for Europe and was planning to move in with him.[15] "It was as if Irving somehow sensed this from all that distance," Aviva recalls. "I was all packed, ready to take a long trip across the United States with John, when a telegram from Irving arrived saying 'come and join me in Paris.' There was no money in the bank, and it cost four hundred dollars or so return to Europe, but I was determined to go to him. John was stunned, but I didn't care. I went to friends and borrowed the money that night. The next day I was in Paris. Irving met me at the end of the bus line (he would never have met me at the airport because it cost too much) and thrust the poem 'The Day Aviva Came to Paris' into my hand. It felt to me as if the poem had engendered the visit instead of the other way around."

THE DAY AVIVA CAME TO PARIS

The day you came naked to Paris
The tourists returned home without their guidebooks,
The hunger in their cameras finally appeased.

"Forever and forever, from this blazing hour
All Paris radiates from Aviva's nest of hair
— Delicate hatchery of profound delights —
From her ever-to-be-adored Arche de Triomphe!
All the languors of history
Take on meaning clear as a wineglass or the belch of an angel
Only if thought of as rushing
On the wings of a rhinoceros towards this absorbing event.
Voyeurs, voyez! The moisture of her delicate instep
Is a pool of love
Into which sheathed in candy paper
Anaesthetized politicians drop from the skies!"
(Word jugglery of course, my Sweet; but the French love it
— Mistake it in fact for poetry)
...
And when you were raised up
Into my hairy arms by the raving emotional crowds
Waving frenzied bottles of Beaujolais
And throwing the corks away ecstatically
(Not saving them!)
It was, my Love, my Darling,
As if someone had again ordered an advance
Upon the Bastille
Which we recalled joyously, face to face at last,
Had yielded after only a small token resistance.

Although Layton's poem was an exuberant tribute to Aviva (Al Purdy called it "a tour de force and a bloody masterpiece"),[16] travelling thrust the two lovers into unavoidable proximity. The differences between them became heightened, and it was not long before they both wanted to return to Montreal. In addition, Layton was worried about money. He was saving the fellowship that was supposed to sponsor his trip: "Sorry to be so crass," he wrote to Pacey, "but having to keep two households going has put a slight squint into my innocent blue eyes."[17] As his letters to Pacey reveal, financial anxieties were never far from his mind. On the sea voyage back, Aviva returned Layton's ring, but shortly afterwards they made it up again.

Another reason Layton could not comfortably travel for the year was Betty. Bill Goodwin recalls that Irving felt tremendous guilt about travelling on his first grant without sharing it with her; she had, after all, done several covers for his books, encouraged him as a poet for years and deserved to have a part in the spoils. "He told me that he really wanted to offer Betty the money to travel with him," Goodwin remarks. "The moral question weighed on him, not just at the time, but for years afterward. Though he seemed to be a philanderer, he had great, great conflicts. He hated himself for what he did."[18]

Layton's ascendance to the dizzying heights of the stage of public recognition helped to compensate for his personal troubles in 1959. In letter after letter to Pacey, he tried coming at things that bothered him from several different angles. He explained his "loss" of his wife at times as a case of physical or sexual or temperamental incompatibility. At other times, however, he launched into bewildering diatribes about D.H. Lawrence, Nietzsche and Yeats and their views of women. The diatribes irritated Pacey, a well-trained literary critic. As Layton expostulated about Lawrence's warnings to males against castration by females (an oblique "exploration" of his situation vis-a-vis Betty and Aviva), he sounded more Lawrencian than Lawrence. (On this subject, for Layton, Lawrence picked up where Shaw left off.) When Pacey recognized a blatantly Yeatsian image in "Because My Calling is Such," a poem Pacey thought one of Layton's worst and Layton thought one of his best, Layton quoted Yeats' words as if they were his own. In commenting on the poems he was sending Pacey, which he always linked directly to his own personal crisis, Layton obliquely expressed his bewilderment at the conflicting emotions he was experiencing. In all these ways, he used his "brother" Pacey ("we're as like as peas in a pod") as a sounding board against which he could bounce off the anger, anxiety and guilt that he otherwise would have to resolve. Although he seemed incapable of working out his own emotional priorities, waiting instead for "destiny," the Sorcerer, to inflict a fate upon him, Layton was aware that he was living more in a world of words than in life itself. Again with overtones of Lawrence, he wrote in June 1958: "Two things I must do: 1) Save enough money to buy myself a farm so that I can be truly independent and 2) Live more and write less." On another occasion he quoted Nietzsche: "Poets behave shamefully towards their experiences; they exploit them."[19]

The "loss" of his best friend, Louis Dudek, was apparently as painful as the "loss" of his wife, though since the two events were connected, his feelings about one tended to flow into his feelings about the other. In several heated letters, he drew Pacey into arguments about Dudek so he could give full vent to his bitter disappointment and pain. In 1957, Dudek had started up another little literary magazine, called *Delta*, in Montreal and had carefully excluded Layton on the grounds that his presence on the editorial board would preclude co-operative editing. This hurt Layton. But what really struck a nerve was a comment Dudek made in an article for *Culture*, which was published in the winter of 1958. Dudek had described Layton's poetry as "well-nigh demented verse." It was one thing, apparently, for Layton to accuse himself — as he often did — of madness. Madness was the enviable lunacy and genius of the poet. But for Dudek to make such a comment was an insult. Layton wheeled out the heavy artillery. First he wrote a personal and insulting essay about Dudek for the *Transparency*, a magazine published by Purdy and Milton Acorn. Then he wrote a childish parody of Dudek's imagist travel narrative, "En Mexico," called "Mexico as Seen by Looie the Lip."[20] Finally, in a chain reaction of explosions that might compare to nuclear fission, he fired off one blast about Dudek after another to Pacey, sometimes more than one a day, until his spleen was vented. "A fatal nervousness has begun [to] set in," he wrote in January 1959, "and the progress of this disease is as fascinating to observe as it was in the case of John Sutherland."[21]

"He [Dudek] and his wife are the Macbeth and Lady Macbeth of Canadian letters to me, the assassins of the creative spirit," he added in February. "For myself, I intend to keep after them until they both drop dead."[22] Dudek's off-and-on marriage, which recently had consolidated with the birth of a son, particularly offended Layton, probably because it highlighted by contrast his own marital break-up. "The big news is the birth of a son to Louis," he had written sarcastically in October 1958. "He's adored by every one as if he were the Messiah child himself... I'm waiting...before I visit him; let him have some strength in his infant composition before he see *this* harsh fact in the world he's let himself into... Louis got himself a house, bought furniture for it, hammered and sawed and painted, in general did all he could to smooth down the wisps of straw with his amatory breast."[23] In February, he wrote: "I talk to younger poets all the time, and I think I know better than you do what Louis' attitude can mean to them."[24] Later in February, as the storm began to abate, he wrote: "When I say that Louis' defection hurts me...it does not mean that I am *'personally'* hurt; it's the *poet* in me that's wounded."[25] Pacey remonstrated: "If you will be such a windmill, don't be surprised if your friends get caught in the turn of the blades sometimes."[26]

Pacey firmly suggested that Layton was being almost completely irrational. "I think your present fulminations against Louis are unworthy of you...you are exaggerating things grossly," he wrote. "Your Canada Foundation Award might just as readily be taken to imply that you are now safe and respectable and castrated."[27] Indeed, Pacey noted, as the American poet Creeley had, that in debate Layton did not play fair. At various times Pacey accused Layton of name-calling, thick-headedness, shifting the ground in the middle of a discussion and flaunting irrelevant knowledge. In March 1959, he wrote:

> Why do you feel it necessary to be so arrogant, so overbearing? I have to keep reminding myself that you have a tender, humble aspect of your personality to prevent myself from becoming disgusted with you... You seem determined to put me in the wrong, even if it involves deliberate distortion...[you try] not to further the argument, but to put me in the wrong by fair means or foul.... If Scott and Dudek are such minnows, how can you be sure that you're such a bloody big shark.[28]

Layton replied, "Why am I so hostile, even with you, who

mean me nothing but friendship and goodwill? Because I want you down in the abyss with me."²⁹

At the launching of *A Red Carpet for the Sun* on 24 September, Layton had his third intoxicating taste of glory. Jack McClelland was taking less than his usual publisher's margin to keep the price of the book down, and had spent more than usual on promotion. It was definitely a risk.³⁰ The launching party in Montreal was quite a change from Layton's last launching (for the second edition of *A Laughter in the Mind* at which Layton had supplied the sherry.)

> Last night — there was a cocktail party for RCFTS at the Windsor Hotel which Jack McClelland threw. I was quite a lion, having let my hair grow for the occasion since the middle of July. By now my head looks quite massive, almost Yeatsian, though with only streaks of poetic silver; however, I have an impressive lock of hair falling across my forehead which, if I weren't the moral man I am, would be good for a dozen swift & easy seductions. Anyway, the party was a great success. Bob Weaver and several others having come from Toronto with J. McC for it. From the hotel we went to McC's agent's house where the party flourished until 2 AM. Everyone in TV or Radio, in the Newspaper or Bookselling game was present when I made my great entry — and what an entry it was! I was flanked by Aviva on one side, and by Leonard Cohen on the other, and I needed both of these to run interference for me as the mob bore down. For the next hour I was busy autographing, grimacing, talking, having my hand pumped vigorously, and what not while everyone waited for me to do a Dylan Thomas act. I didn't even pretend to try! That's not called for in the contract, you know, though Jack was hovering around me flash bulbing all over the place. It was a great evening. Aviva overheard two booksellers disputing as to who had given the book the better window-display and who was selling the book faster. Sales seem very brisk, and several booksellers have assured Jack the book will sell out — all 5,000 of them. If they do, this will of course make history.

But that's enough happy hugging for one letter. In the midst of the celebration I was overheard to say, "all this is fine, but it has nothing to do with the poem I'm presently working on." So help me, I did say those words. And I also embarrassed a banker by flatly contradicting him when he said to me (with the best of intentions) that my "success" was like that of his own, or like that of anybody who strives hard, sacrifices, etc., etc. I told him I hadn't striven for success, that no poet really does, but only to write a good poem, and then another one, and so on. He searched for an answer to that at the bottom of his whisky glass, but not finding it there he finally gave up.[31]

Jack McClelland had been late to take notice of Layton, but was not slow in promoting what looked like a sure thing. He apologized to Layton for his "hucksterish" approach to his writers,[32] and held a second "launching" in Toronto soon after the Montreal party. "It's fun to be lionized," Layton reported to Pacey. "Everyone connected with radio, TV, and journalism was there: Ralph Allen, [Arnold] Edinborough, John Marshall of the Toronto *Telegram*. E.J. Pratt turned up also, and I was very touched by that since I had been told his health was poor and he never leaves the house. However, he seemed hearty enough and got in his usual quota of stag jokes. His greeting to me was: 'How are your gonads?' 'Fine,' I said, 'How are yours?' He's got the most unself-regarding look I've ever seen on a man's face."[33] From all over the country came letters of congratulation, including one from Lorne Pierce, who regretted that Ryerson Press had lost Layton just as he was entering his prime. "It must be a source of great satisfaction to you to know that already you have taken your place among the major voices of our time. The years will bring you sorrow and joy and many things to bless and hurt, but you will continue to transmute all of it into precious metal. Much of it will survive, a candle in the window against the dark night of the world, a bell ringing in the sanctuary that men may find their spiritual home."[34] Reviews of *A Red Carpet for the Sun* were mainly ecstatic.

The "lionization" of Irving confirmed the self-image his

mother had fostered of a Messiah destined to become great. With confidence born of public recognition, Layton began to draw together all the bits and pieces about poets and poetry he had read for decades and had mimicked with an almost perfect ear in his classes and elsewhere. He deemed himself not just one of a group of Montreal modernists, but a kind of oracle. When Pacey received from Layton a copy of *A Red Carpet for the Sun* in mid-July 1959, he wrote: "The poems are so uniformly excellent that no one can any longer have any doubts that you are the best Canadian poet ever, and my feeling is that there isn't a poet alive today with a more impressive output except Eliot and possibly Frost. In the Canadian race, there just isn't any competition — you win by a mile."[35] And shouldn't Pacey know? He had broken new ground in Canadian literary criticism with his *Ten Canadian Poets*; he was busy preparing his section of the *Literary History of Canada*; he was close to the literary scene through Fred Cogswell, editor of *Fiddlehead* magazine; and he had written and published some short stories and poems himself. Layton took seriously the praise of a man who was emerging as one of Canada's few literary critics. Furthermore, other critics — such as A.J.M. Smith, Milton Wilson at *Canadian Forum* and Northrop Frye — were, to some extent at least, saying many of the same things.

To Layton, all this meant that he was the last word on Canadian poetry, and on poetry and poets generally. He had certainly offered his opinions on the subject freely enough before his "lionization," but afterwards he did so without the least doubt that his statements, no matter where they were gleaned from and no matter how inconsistent, were indisputably true. When Pacey termed him a "romantic," Layton pompously replied, "If you want to write an essay on my work, first read Nietzsche, especially his 'Joyful Wisdom.' I *am* a romantic, but with a difference...with scars. I know all about nihilism, skepticism, disgust, of the dark side of the sky farthest from the shining, fructifying sun." He argued that, had he been a clerk instead of a poet, he would not have "lost" his wife and best friend,[36] since poets are "more susceptible to women." He saw himself as a poet-martyr ("every poet is the resurrected Christ")[37] creating "new life"

out of "the death of a part of [himself]. Monstrous paradox!..."
"I'll fight anyone who exalts reason above imagination and
intuition, anyone who refuses to see that the creative process
is supra-rational,"[38] he wrote to Pacey. In an image picked up
from Milton Wilson,[39] Layton saw Pacey as playing a doltish
Sancho Panza to his fervent Don Quixote (an interesting
turnabout of their physical complementarity). Layton seemed
to have forgotten his earlier descriptions of the poetic
process, which would be better summed up as "sub-rational"
than as "supra-rational." Being Jewish (though he had frequently bragged that he was not orthodox) seemed to
intensify the poetic process into something almost superhuman, certainly into something enviable. "Being a Jew," he
wrote to Pacey, "combines fanaticism and irony, passion and
doubt. Both are equally real. It is what gives [the Jew] his
dramatic flair."[40] "To be a poet," he was beginning to believe,
"is to see things with a terrible clarity [a comment reminiscent
of Yeats] where everybody else is blind or asleep."[41] He
returned to some of his earlier poems — "Karl Marx," for
example — and saw them as miraculously prophetic.[42] "Poets
live, professors speculate on life," he pronounced with a
Nietzschean ring. "Poets *must* be arrogant," he retorted to
Pacey, who had called him a stuffed shirt. "Like Blake, 'the
tigers of wrath are wiser than the horses of instruction.'"[43]
Layton's pronouncements on poets and poetry swelled and
puffed up like a stomach with wind. Poets, to Layton, must
be angry because he was: "I find my peace," he wrote in one
of the more convincing of his theories, "by pitting my whole
nature against something and the greater the tension, the
greater my self-knowledge."[44] If any one dictum came close
to the truth, it was an admission he made when humbled
once by Pacey: "Beneath my self-dramatization, abuse, and
sheer nonsense there's a good poet buried somewhere — one
growing stronger and wiser with the years' passing."[45] Or, as
he also put it, "Like Yeats, I played with masks. And yet —
have I really? We're all of us so many different people: it's
only the poet and the novelist who can give each one of them
a tongue and a separate identity. A total identity — maybe
only a stone ever achieves that."[46] Though it is tempting to
accept much of what Layton wrote that year in light of his

own qualifier — "Every great writer writes quantities of unedifying shit, embarrassing to his admirers"[47] — there was something that rang more true in his statement: "[Poetry] is the voice of the innocent child in each of us refusing to accommodate itself to the counsel of experience.... Poetry is the only realm where freedom is absolute."[48]

Though Layton claimed there was a note of "self-irony" in his descriptions of his roaring acclaim, and insisted that "all this hullabaloo is no compensation for the break-up of my marriage, and the loss all at the same time (and pretty much for the same reasons) of my best friend," he felt that "people and critics have finally begun to concur in my own opinion of my self — I mean of my poetry. The only thing that astonishes me is that they were so slow in getting there!... A poet has at last broken the sound barrier!... and turned the trick.... I'd like one day to win the Nobel Prize for literature. Why not? Say in ten or fifteen years... this is my latest and best dream."[49]

Layton's notions of poetry and poets, which floated around in his mind in varying and fluctuating degrees of vividness, found their most coherent and palatable expression in the foreword to *A Red Carpet for the Sun*, which he wrote in the calm, unhurried, affectionate atmosphere of Lac Provost Lodge in the summer of 1958. Northrop Frye called it his "first articulate statement in prose;"[50] but Robert Weaver turned it down as a CBC "Anthology" piece.[51] In contrast to some of his earlier prefaces, Layton's facts are correct (unlike McClelland and Stewart's jacket promotion blurb, which locates his birth in Bucharest and places him in the tradition of Dylan Thomas, whose poetry Layton disliked). Though a number of inconsistencies inevitably creep in, Layton wrote in lively, measured, expository prose his "Sermon on the Mount." He attacks philistinism in a way that echoes E.K. Brown's 1943 concerns with the anti-art bias of Canada's largely puritanical attitudes;[52] he cogently presents the case against aestheticism (its unearthliness); he attacks modern women (as "furies striving to castrate the male") in an early version of male response to feminism; he asserts the importance of remaining sensitive to the contemporary world, seeing the poet, much as Pound had, as "the antennae of the human race;" he quotes Byron and Nietzsche and Hebrew tradition without undue excess; above all, he combines these, gains a little perspective on his own views (as opposed to the many other views, which he knew so well), and conveys his ideas lucidly and without overbearing arrogance:

> I am not at ease in the world (what poet ever is?); but neither am I fully at ease in the world of the imagination. I require some third realm, as yet undiscovered, in which to live. My dis-ease has spurred me on to bridge the two with the stilts of poetry, or to create inside me an ironic balance of tensions... all poetry, in the final analysis, is about poetry itself; creating through its myriad forms a world in which the elements of reality are sundered; are, as it were, preserved for a time in suspension.... The poems in this collection are all leaves from the same tree. A certain man living between 1942 and 1958 wrote them. That man is now dead, and even if he could be resurrected wouldn't be able to write them in the way they were written. Nor would he want to. They belong to a period of my life that is now behind me: a period of testing, confusion, ecstasy. Now there is only the ecstasy of an angry middle-aged man growing into courage and truth... For me, a poet is one who explores new areas of sensibility. If he has the true vocation he will take risks.

Layton dedicated the book to his mother, Klara Lazarovitch, who had died in May 1959, four months before the book was published. She would have appreciated the fine puns in its title. *A Red Carpet for the Sun* not only suggested that her "son" was getting the royal treatment, it also carried reverberations of his politically revolutionary past ("a Red") and contained a word dear to her own heart, "carp." Layton's compression of many levels of personal significance into poetic phrases was characteristic of his work. He claimed that he owed this, among his many other gifts, to his mother. In a strong poem written too late to appear in the volume (in which her birthdate is given as 1870, not 1873 as in the dedication to *A Red Carpet for the Sun*) is Layton's tribute to the woman to whom he owed his "vigorous constitution" and whose "gift for cadenced vituperation" awakened what he modestly called "my impeccable ear for rhythm":

Keine Lazarovitch
1870–1959

When I saw my mother's head on the cold pillow,
Her white waterfalling hair in the cheeks' hollows,
I thought, quietly circling my grief, of how
She had loved God but cursed extravagantly
    His creatures.

For her final mouth was not water but a curse,
A small black hole, a black rent in the universe,
Which damned the green earth, stars and trees in its
    stillness
And the inescapable lousiness of growing old.

And I record she was comfortless, vituperative,
Ignorant, glad, and much else besides; I believe
She endlessly praised her black eyebrows, their thick
    weave,
Till plagiarizing Death leaned down and took them for
    his mold.

And spoiled a dignity I shall not again find,
And the fury of her stubborn limited mind;
Now none will shake her amber beads and call God
    blind,
Or wear them upon a breast so radiantly.

O fierce she was, mean and unaccommodating;
But I think now of the toss of her gold earrings,
Their proud carnal assertion, and her youngest sings
While all the rivers of her red veins move into the sea.[53]

The poem, which was first published in *Tamarack Review*, won the President's Medal for the best poem published in a magazine in 1960.

    When the Governor-General's Award for poetry published

in 1959 was announced in the spring of 1960, Layton's *A Red Carpet for the Sun* swept the stage, outdoing the other twenty-three books. And justifiably so. It was the single best collection of poetry to emerge from Canada to that point. "I'm particularly thrilled to see how your verse — the form of it I mean — has improved during the last two years," William Carlos Williams wrote, pleased that Layton had taken some of his advice to heart. "You have broken away from a too slavish adherence to the stanzaic form at the same time adhering to a miminal [sic] of regularity, not completely breaking down to a formlessness as has happened with some of our so called 'beatniks.'... With your constantly growing grasp of the art of poetry... you will be leading us all without delay... no one can succeed in stopping you... but yourself."[54] As Williams' remarks suggested, Layton had managed to forge a unique type of poetry. Because of his ability to maintain mutually inconsistent theories in suspension, he had been able to draw on the florid, formal British tradition and at the same time draw on the more colloquial, free-form American one. Each had tempered the other, and a poetry entirely representative of Canada's ambivalent position as an extension of Britain and a satellite of the United States had been born.

Not fully grasping his symbolic position, but simply unable to choose between apparently contradictory poetic theories, Layton greeted the news of his award with jubilation.

> I took Aviva and Max... with me to Ottawa for the presentation of the [$1000]... award [on 28 March 1960]. Max made a hit with everyone. Northrop Frye, Douglas Grant, Trueman, MacLennan, etc. were all there, and it was a fine party. The laurels were pinned to our distinguished brows while the TV cameras clicked, and the chefs prepared the tastiest shrimps and wines. The Vaniers [Georges and Pauline] are a nice old couple — it must be awful to lead their lives... I didn't get a chance to talk to Frye, though Aviva did.[55]

"He and Aviva were hilarious preparing to go to Ottawa," Marian Scott recalls. "They spent hours practicing curtsying and bowing and so forth."[56] Hugh MacLennan, who thought Layton "the best poet now producing steadily within the language,"[57] recalls that Vanier, then governor-general, had read neither his novel (*The Watch That Ends the Night* won the fiction award) nor Layton's poems. "Vanier and I were sitting on a sofa chatting, and he leaned over to me and, nodding towards Layton, said, 'You know, I can always tell an Irish face when I see one. I'm half-Irish myself.' To which I replied, 'Well, you know, sir, I always thought he was a Romanian Jew'."[58]

Though Layton had spoken, in his foreword, of putting his past life of "confusion" behind him, it had not been possible. Tensions were building with both Betty and Aviva. Just as he had been unable to choose between Faye and Betty, he found he could not select either Betty or Aviva. Though a crisis eventually was provoked by Layton, a decision finally was made by Betty. Custody of the children had been the real issue from the outset. Though Betty thought Layton did not give her enough money, she was never to change her contempt for the work-ethic, and he continued to contribute towards her support until she died in 1983. Money was not a serious issue, but the children were. Though he at first agreed that Betty should have custody, it had not taken him long to change his mind. First, he balked at the prospect of having them only a week each summer. Then, as the initial all-consuming excitement with Aviva calmed a little, he became more possessive of Max and Naomi.

With some of the money from his Canada Council fellowship, he bought Max the television he so much wanted to watch, something Betty never could have afforded. "I despised him for kow-towing to materialism like that — especially since he was the one who went around preaching against middle-class philistines all the time," Betty recalled. "He got the car from me by coming in one Sunday evening for dinner with us and 'borrowing' it to take the kids somewhere. When he came back, he said he'd lost the keys. I gave him my set to make another. I never saw the car again — not that it was anything much. He really went after those children — Max especially. He and Aviva would promise him trips to Australia, a chance to see kangeroos — that kind of thing. Worst of all was an evening when he came over near the end and asked me if I wanted him back. I fell for it, even though he'd been playing me and Aviva off against each other for over two years. Suddenly, he changed his mind, said he had to leave the house. I fell to my knees and grabbed hold of his legs, pleading with him not to go, to stay with us. He got free and left. Naomi, unfortunately, saw all this. Next he wanted to move into our neighbourhood with Aviva so that he could see the children anytime. Stephanie Dudek, who was a psychologist, advised me to take them as far away from Irving as possible, for their own sanity. For Max it was too late. Irving had bribed him with the TV and then with a new bike. But I did keep Naomi with me. I didn't even trust him to take her on an outing."[59]

"I haven't seen Naomi for nearly six months," Irving wrote to Pacey on 12 July 1960:

> and I've almost forgotten what she looks like. B's fears and anxieties have rubbed off on Sissyboo and now she says she won't see me; hangs up the receiver when she hears my voice. It's heartbreaking, but there it is. Bet's so fearful Sissyboo might also want to come and live with me, she's filled her mind with her own phobias. Otherwise, why should the child refuse to see me? I've shown her nothing but love and concern. She's never heard an unkind word from me, and I'm sure the one or two ugly episodes between Bet and me that she witnessed wouldn't matter all that much... it's the one thing I find it hard to forgive her for; it's the one thing that's really unforgivable.

That summer, Betty and Naomi left for San Francisco with Avi Boxer and his wife.

Max moved into the tiny basement bed-sitter on Ridgewood with his father and Aviva. "It was horrific," Aviva recalls. "Max thought that Irving would pay attention to him for the first time, that he would have his father to himself. But he mainly saw me, not Irving. Irving didn't want that domestic thing. He stayed away a lot. I was in my mid-twenties, and young for my age. I had no clue how to look after a thirteen-year-old. The only advice Irving gave me (which I took as gospel) was 'Never tell Maxie no — just suggest it. He doesn't like being told no.' Max seemed to be having an identity conflict: he called himself Sutherland for a while. The worst of it was that he was sexually attracted to me. He used to ask to put his head on my breast. I was attracted to him too. I wanted him to insist on physical closeness. I half thought I was making up for the loss of his mother. It was something I never discussed with Irving."[60]

Herzliah also forced Layton's hand. Trouble had been brewing since he had been fired briefly in May 1958, when he had led the teachers' federation in drafting a letter to the board of directors of the United Talmud Torahs about the use of the school telephone. Then parents who did not share his views of D.H. Lawrence, Nietzsche and other writers had begun complaining about the "corrupting" influence Layton's anti-Jewish ideas had on their children's minds.

> It's a parochial school, in theory very orthodox. And my Jewishness is neither parochial nor orthodox. As long as I was an obscure nobody, my views and opinions called for no investigation or surveillance. Now the question of my "influence" becomes rather important, especially to the rabbinical and conservative-minded...but...how slough off Canada's "most controversial poet" and some would say her best, without raising a hue and cry... So for the time being the axe hasn't fallen. But one day it will.[61]

That day came two years later. After 30 August 1960, he was informed, his contract would not be renewed. In response, Layton wrote the scathing "Jewish Cantata" and a searing poem to Benjamin Beutel, "pants manufacturer and Chairman of the United Talmud Torah School Board of Montreal," called "Mr. Beutel Lays a Cornerstone."

> Near forlorn beaches
> Turtles drop their eggs;
> So do ostriches
> And great blue herons
> With delicate legs.

> He so proudly furred
> On his large estate
> — No reptile or bird —
> Lays his cornerstones
> Stamped with name and date.

"No other word for him — obscene!" Layton wrote to Pacey. "As you see, I don't intend to let them forget."

The loss of his job at Herzliah brought Layton face-to-face with financial crisis. "It's a good thing I'm getting these calls [with offers of honoraria to give readings]," he wrote to Jonathan Williams, "for I'm without a job and am likely to stay so for many bleak years to come... I'm beginning to have nightmares in which the empty fridges look at me reproachfully, asking like childless, unfulfilled women to make them bulge."[62] To help out, Aviva returned to work as an x-ray technician at the Montreal General Hospital and Max got a job as a delivery boy for the corner grocery.

Later, Layton wrote another poem for Beutel, called "Beutel's Name Is Inscribed for Eternal Life."

> As the angry hawk flies towards the sun,
> Taking some small creature into the skies,
> So shall your fame be taloned fast to mine
> And like the clawed rodent rise as I rise.

Betty knew she would be safe from Irving in the United States. His reputation as a poet was beginning to spread there, but he was blocked from taking advantage of it because American Immigration still would not allow him to enter the country. Hugh Kenner, in California, had asked for permission to reprint the poems "Golfers" and "Cain" (which Milton Wilson thought his best poem to date) in his collection *The Art of Poetry: Best Articles and Poems of 1958*.[63] Someone from Detroit wanted to set up a reading tour of American colleges and universities "with Harvard and Princeton on the circuit"[64] for 1959, but, as Layton explained to Pacey, "My first hurdle is the U.S. Immigration that has me confused with Khruschev [sic] or Tim Buck despite everything I've said in letters, telegrams, and three separate hearings. I've now got a lawyer working on it, but he seems to be no more successful in shedding their delusions than I am. As a last desperate measure, I may see my MP and ask him to interest himself in this gross miscarriage of justice. I'm almost moved to send the Immigration officials a copy of 'The Ugly American' with my sincere un-compliments."[65]

Layton was restricted — physically at least — to Canada, and was probably impeded from what otherwise would have been some degree of acclaim in the United States. Nonetheless, he applied for and received a special "waiver" to give a poetry reading at the YM/YWHA in New York with Frank Scott and Leonard Cohen on 12 November 1959.[66] Finally, on 20 June 1960, he received word from the consulate-general of the United States in Montreal that the United States attorney-general had authorized his admission to the country.[67] Layton took advantage of the long-sought authorization to make a late-summer trip, in 1960, with Aviva and Max. He met William Carlos Williams (who made a pass at Aviva when Layton was out of the room)[68] and Walter Lowenfels. As if to thumb his nose at the authorities, he also met Ben Davies, then head of the Communist Party of the United States, and got into a terrible row with him.[69]

Layton continued to play a central role in Canada's cultural surge of the 1950s. His struggle to write "modern" poetry, to make the writing and reading of poetry a vital, necessary and important pursuit, to use his overlapping skills as teacher-satirist-poet both to revolutionize a staid and, to him, sterile society, and to demonstrate what a poet and poems ought to be like, was allegorical. Canadian society during the 1950s had become more self-critical, and the need for increased cultural activity on almost every level was being felt and enunciated. It was also beginning to be answered. The 1951 report of the Massey Royal Commission on National Development in the Arts, Letters, and Sciences (about which Layton had written a squib suggesting that money would be best spent on him)[70] had highlighted both the necessity of a strong national cultural environment and the danger to Canada of American mass media. Soon after the report was published — in 1953 — Stratford's tent was pitched and Glen Gould began to record his music; Malcolm Ross edited *Our*

Sense of Identity in 1954; photographer Roloff Beny snapped Canadian images and an Ottawa Syrian, Paul Anka ("the real gone lyricist" Layton had briefly wanted to be), had made the United States top-ten charts with his song "Diana" in 1957. CBC-television audiences cherished "our pet Juliette," "Front Page Challenge," with Pierre Berton and Gordon Sinclair, and "Hockey Night in Canada." "Painters 11," an informal association of artists including Jack Bush, Jock Macdonald, William Ronald and Harold Town, was turning the old Royal Canadian Academy of Arts upside-down. On the west coast, *Tish* (an anagram of "shit") and *Prism* — small literary magazines — had sprung up. The Canada Council (from which Layton had received his senior fellowship) slowly made its way into existence in 1957 as a direct result of the Massey report. By the end of the sixties, Jack McClelland had taken his father's company in hand and set out with a more flamboyant and nationalistic publishing policy than any Canada had seen.

The decade had been one of enormous cultural stress and change, an unprecedented blossoming into self-awareness. Layton had played a direct part in this larger sweep of cultural self-assurance, and his career could be seen as utterly representative of it. He emerged as a major, central and representative figure in Canada at the end of the fifties because he stood for the principle of change. He took on mythic proportions as everything the old, solid WASP Canadian society was not: dark, as if on the side of the devil himself; aggressive amongst peace-lovers; ethnic in a country that had once seen only a clean-cut homogenous image of itself; emotional where reason had dominated; imaginative amidst those who espoused the work-ethic; and volatile in a society that feared disorder. He had begun saving his letters, sorting them into brown envelopes, for a "literary historian."

"How did I know that the 1950s would be the most brilliant decade in Canadian poetry? Intuition," Layton bragged to Pacey on 7 February 1959. Layton was alive to the reverberations of his rapidly developing career. "The barriers are breaking down," he reported after a poetry reading he gave with Frank Scott, Michael Gnarowski and Al Purdy at the Art Gallery in Montreal in late March 1960.

It was an enormous success! You'll find it hard to believe, but 150 people were turned away. The place was packed and those who were unlucky enough not to find seats had to stand for more than two hours... Westmount Society (represented by Ogilvie's Flour Mills, the Baxters, etc.) rubbed shoulders that night with "proletarian soupspoons." It was altogether right that poetry should have been the means to dissolve the class differences and induce a kinder fellow-feeling. After all, in this strange world we're all fellow-travelling mortals.[71]

Though he took real pleasure in the rise of his younger poet-friends like Leonard Cohen (who in 1959 went to London on a Canada Council junior fellowship to write a novel) and Al Purdy, whom Layton thought was "beginning to hit his stride" ("He's got lots of talent; all that he's wanted is control and direction"),[72] he saw himself as dominating the literary scene in English Canada. An audience for poetry, quite a large and entranced one, had arisen. It seemed to him that he had created it.

It was not surprising that the American "beats" (beatnik poets) attracted Layton's attention. Their social criticism, revolutionary ideals and ethnic dress struck strong chords of identification. When he had read his poetry at Queen's University in 1957 and evoked such overwhelming response, he sensed that at last he had found "his" generation: "I felt I had something to say to them, that this was the generation for whom my poems had been written."[73] "Humanity has turned a sharp corner," he wrote to Pacey at the beginning of 1959,

> into a world where pity and sensitivity, or where ordinary decency, have no address. Where the viciously perverse has become the normal... We need another kind of writer, someone who'll touch the diseased heart of mankind, someone who will open our eyes to our bloodthirstiness... The "Beat" writers are saying it, but not very well or very successfully, and they'll end up by destroying themselves rather than the conditions that produced them.[74]

By the end of the year, he lay in hospital over Christmas "with a fistula on my bum." ("I'll be left with a permanent smile in that region.... Just think of it, no matter how sullenly I may frown...my smiling contradictory behind will be putting a good face on [things]."). From his bed he wrote to Pacey, "If the Beatniks have done nothing else, they've at least put the Squares on the defensive...a small revolution." By mid-March 1960, about the time of his ecstatic poetry reading in the Montreal Musée de Beaux Arts, he gave a lecture, called "The Political Significance of the Beatniks," to the McGill political-science faculty. The Beats were on the right track, he was convinced, but he would be able to convey what they had to say more effectively. He had sniffed out the perfect revolution for himself.

As Layton stood poised at the brink of what he would call, when speaking on a CBC "Anthology" show, "The Frightening Sixties," he felt more like the Sorcerer than an apprentice. Pacey warned him that the urge to plunge ahead was seductive but possibly catastrophic: "I do think...that you have a real dilemma before you: having made your name & face as a critic of bourgeois values, you are now enjoying being lionized by the proud possessors of those values. But the dilemma is to some degree a false one, because bourgeois society is to a large degree self-critical & will permit you to be a bit of a *wild* lion. You may survive intact, though I think you'll have to be doubly alert."[75]

The Day Aviva Came to Paris

When Layton set off for Europe on his Canada Council senior fellowship in the summer of 1959, it had seemed the culmination of longings that could be traced back to 1953, when he had envied Robert Creeley's Mallorca residence and had begun to try to figure out how he, too, could arrange some time abroad. Actually, his image of the poet freewheeling through sunny climes predated his recognition of Creeley's expatriate poetic stance. It originated in his readings about the lives of the romantic poets who had travelled in Europe and written profusely as they went.

From the outside, Irving Layton had begun his summer trip in fine style. Anyone spotting him in his crumpled clothes emerging from his cheap hotel on the Left Bank in Paris to spend the day at a sunny café table making entries in his journal, encouraging various women he met to sign their names or draw little pictures in it,[1] or writing and revising poems that he dated meticulously for posterity, would have concluded that *there* was a poet.

Though he had been lonely and had summoned Aviva in a way that might have seemed distinctly unadventurous and not quite in keeping with the great tradition of unhampered creativity he claimed to espouse, his mighty poem to her had compensated for this by presenting the two of them as larger-than-life lovers, for whom even the fabled city of Paris was too mundane a context. The poem was romantic, exuberant, a celebration of the great poet and his mistress.

Aviva's version of her arrival was quite different. At first Irving's enthusiasm proved contagious. When she entered the little Left Bank hotel, his poetic tribute clasped in her hand, and stood with him at the window looking out on teeming rue St. Germain, she was filled with excitement. The next day, Layton had promised her, they would go to the famous Shakespeare and Company Bookstore, where he had befriended the owner. Like writers everywhere, Layton and Aviva knew that the store had been a mecca for writers in Paris during the twenties and thirties, when it was run by Sylvia Beach, an American with a passion for the arts. Beach published James Joyce's work, which brought fame to her book-store, a little store-front shop tucked away on rue de l'Odéon in one of the oldest sections of Paris on the Left Bank. The store attracted all the major writers of the western world. T.S. Eliot, André Gide, Ernest Hemingway, Ezra Pound, Gertrude Stein, Paul Valéry, Samuel Beckett, Elizabeth Bishop, Leon Edel, Archibald MacLeish and Thornton Wilder had patronized Shakespeare and Company, wending their way past quaint courtyards and cafés to be welcomed for coffee and conversation.[2] It had been the obvious place for Morley Callaghan to begin looking for Hemingway when he arrived in Paris in 1929.[3] Though the store had long since changed owners, a visit there with Layton, who was rapidly becoming a major twentieth-century poet, promised the utmost in excitement to Aviva.

"I sensed something wasn't quite right when I met the owner," Aviva recalls. "He was an emaciated American who seemed to me to be on heroin or something. At least he was raving and screaming. He asked us to come in and have coffee and pointed to a ladder that led to a loft. So up the ladder we went.

"Irving's always had a nervous stomach. He really couldn't take Parisian food. He likes Jewish food — eggplant and soups, salamis and pickles. Anyway, that morning he needed a toilet. He couldn't control himself. There was simply no time to go looking for one. So he went out onto the roof to relieve himself and I closed the window. Almost at once, the corrugated tin roof gave way under him and he fell through the ceiling into the art gallery below where — I think — a *vernissage* or something was going on. There was utter chaos — everybody screaming and yelling. Irving was mostly concerned with doing up his pants. The owner of Shakespeare and Company was furious. He came storming up and insisted that we replace the roof. We had to go short on rations to pay for it. We wasted a whole day in Paris finding the right kind of roofing. We had to carry it across Paris to the bookstore because no taxi would take it.

"That man never forgave us. 'What an animal!' he kept saying. Over the years Irving and I have laughed and laughed about it.

"Things were better in Italy," Aviva continues. "At first we took the train to Milan. But once there, Irving insisted on staying in terrible places and eating the cheapest food. He was determined not to spend any more money than was absolutely necessary. We hitch-hiked to Venice and to Rome. I was wearing pedal-pushers and a quite bare halter top which was offensive to the Italians. Because my arms were bare, we were forbidden to enter the Vatican. Irving came up with a wonderful solution to this problem: he took a lot of those huge Italian lire notes and pined them to my halter top as sleeves."

But, though Aviva admired his unconventional ingenuity, Layton expressed attitudes that she found distinctly un-bohemian and downright offensive. As they hitch-hiked from place to place, entirely dependent on the goodwill of local people, she recalls his looking out at the Italians they passed and saying loudly, "I could buy and sell that bastard!"

By the end of the trip, the two had not agreed, in many particulars, on just how a bohemian trip in Europe ought to be conducted. On the boat back from Naples to Montreal they quarrelled dramatically and, it seemed, conclusively. "We were too much the same," Aviva speculates. "We ought to have separated after that trip, but neither one of us could bear to lose anything. We were both afraid that there might be a terrible vacuum."[4]

A Very Rich, Rich Year

In the late fifties Layton seemed to be caught up entirely in his role as a poet. His conversations and letters were preoccupied with high-minded, metaphysical speculations about art and society. In his poems, too, he continued to praise creativity and to attack ordinary men and women who lived life on a material level, thinking not of life's great philosophical questions, but of respectability and the practical exigencies of every-day life. He especially vaunted the unworldly attitude of poets who were disdainful of possessions when they answered their glorious "calling." "I'll fight anyone who exalts reason above imagination and intuition,"[1] he thundered characteristically.

His life-style in the late fifties would have impressed any observer as consistent with his beliefs. He had moved in with Aviva and shared her basement bedsitter on Ridgewood Avenue. There the two lovers lived in bohemian bliss. By day, Layton continued his part-time teaching at Herzliah and Sir George Williams University. But at night, seated at Aviva's kitchen table, he would drink endless cups of tea and look up out the window to the street, pencil poised, waiting for the Muse to strike. If she failed to do so he would disappear and walk up and down the streets of Montreal — over the mountain, perhaps, or back down towards the river to the tawdry area he cherished from his childhood. Aviva quickly learned the teaching trade with Layton, reading huge Russian novels and controversial modern fiction with the well-bred girls of Weston School who, at age seventeen or eighteen, were only six or seven years younger than she was. She encouraged them to challenge conventional attitudes and "old-fashioned" morality.[2]

The rumblings of Layton's imminent dismissal from Herzliah in 1958 had unsettled him. He was not financially secure. At the first opportunity that presented itself — the death of his mother and her final decision to leave her property to *Flamplatz*, the son who had nursed her through her asthma and visited her at the home regularly — he decided to hedge his bets behind the scene.

In the spring of 1959, Carl and Gertie Katz, a Jewish couple in their early thirties who ran an insurance brokerage and dabbled in real estate, placed an advertisement in the paper to sell a small property in the lower-class district of Pointe Saint Charles, Montreal. The place needed new plumbing. "I answered one phone call," Gertie recalls, "and heard a booming voice at the other end — a man who said that he'd like to go and see the property. He didn't sound at all like the other callers we had. I was curious and asked who he was. 'Irving Layton,' he replied. I'd heard about him already. His neice was a neighbour of ours, and she had told me of her uncle 'Mr. Fighting Words.' I had also read and admired some of his poems — especially 'Cat Dying in Autumn' — in a study group I belonged to as a young mother. I explained to him about the plumbing and advised him not to buy the property. He was non-plussed. He said he'd like to see it anyway. He explained he had inherited his mother's money, and it just happened to be the same amount we were asking for the Pointe Saint Charles property. I gave him the address, but tried to discourage him. In the end, he didn't go to see it. He phoned us back and asked to meet us to discuss real estate.[3]

"I invited him over. We all got along. He picked our brains (Carl accurately predicted inflation would increase and real estate would be the only way to secure capital) for about four hours. Before he left, he wrote us a cheque for the full amount of his mother's money and asked us to invest it for him. I was aghast! You never do that in real estate! Especially when you've been burned — as he had been. He'd already given a student some money to invest in some stock, and it went down and he lost his money. What he said to us was, 'You know your business: real estate. I know mine: people.' I thought to myself. 'Is this man a fool or is he right?' In fact, he was right to trust us.

"We refused to accept the money. Then he suggested a partnership. He explained that he was concerned about getting old and finding himself in the gutter, penniless. He felt very insecure. The result was that Carl formed a corporation of the three of us and made Irving the president. Oddly, he thought we did this to *shame* him in some way, but he didn't refuse either. At first he kept yelling at us, 'Why are you doing this to me?' I suppose because his poetry was *against* bourgeois materialists. He was like Duddy Dimwit. The dollar underneath the pillow made him uneasy, but he had no idea how to do something with it. On the practical level he knew nothing about managing a property, but he did the things we told him to do with alacrity and he was very happy in his bouncy way doing it. Each year we'd have a splurge using our joint account. We started with a small property owned jointly with Carl's brother-in-law. When he wanted out to invest in something else, we bought a larger property, and so on. Later, I'd say he gained a *little* skill in real estate. He had a degree in economics, so he thought he could forecast the economy. I don't think he ever knew very much about it. He came with us once to demolish a house and watch the rats run out."

In October 1960, Layton wrote to Pacey, "I have been endowed with a good share of my mother's realism and have saved my money and invested it wisely. I have no intention of being a 'starving genius' and getting my carcass thrown into a pauper's grave like Mozart."[4]

Layton's "dealings" in real estate struck the Katzes as amusing. Gertie recalls: "The funny part of it was that he used to go around bragging that he was a real dynamo in real estate. He'd repeat some of the things about inflation and real estate values that Carl and I told him and later we'd get it all back third-hand. Amazingly, it came back quite straight, absolutely recognizable as what we'd said.

"The summer after that, I had a hand at writing poetry. He'd meet me at Murray's on St. Catherine's. I'd read my poems and he'd tell me they were awful. Then my mother died and I wrote more seriously. That fall I met him for brunch and told him about my new poems. He looked as if to say, 'Oh! No!' but after I dropped him off at Somerled, he shrieked at me that I should join his poetry workshop at Sir George. I joined it a year later and asked him why he'd been so angry. Then he showed me how to divide it into lines and stanzas. He expected a lot of me. Reviewer Alan Pearson was in that class; so was someone writing for the *Star*; and my nephew Seymour Mayne — who later became a poet, professor of Canadian literature and a specialist on Layton — was auditing the class at about age fifteen or sixteen. Irving's an incredible teacher. In the fall of 1960 I had a poem accepted for *Canadian Forum* and another for *Fiddlehead*. I felt myself very fortunate that our paths crossed. It was a very rich, rich year."[5]

A Tall Man Executes a Jig

"The last word is always the poet's," Layton claimed in May 1961.[1] He did not mean what Shelley meant when he had declared that "Poets are the unacknowledged legislators of the world," though Layton echoed the idea. Layton meant something closer to "Poets are the *acknowledged* legislators of the world." Once he felt that the rest of the world concurred in his own view of himself as a genius, a poet above and beyond rational thought, though more than capable of that, too, he started to become the very myth he had created. "As I grow older," he commented after one of his many attempts to reflect upon himself, "I see people and events arranging themselves with a sort of pattern for me, with all things becoming larger than life. They take on the finality and inexhaustible suggestiveness of myth. A poet's life is a great symbol, or ought to be: a strike of jagged lightning illuminating the blackness briefly and fiercely."[2]

In 1960, Layton, Aviva and Max moved to a new, much bigger place. The third-floor flat at 5731 Somerled Avenue was a lovely old apartment with a wooden verandah where they could all sit out in fine weather and a fireplace in the main room where they could gather cosily in the winter. At last Max had his own room, and Irving had a proper study where he could keep his books attractively shelved and ready for reading. Aviva loved the place. "We had good times there. Harry Moscovitch was on the scene — most of Irving's friends were younger even than me. We saw Leonard [Cohen] a lot. We had the most fabulous evenings, talking and talking. Irving was writing a lot. To me it seemed like the first time we had a real place together, the first time there was recognition of our being 'married.'"[3]

In the early sixties, it seemed to Layton that the sky was his only limit. Desmond Pacey was writing successful short stories? Then Layton would resume his own efforts along those lines. With a canny sense that his early stories might go the rounds again, he began to revise and circulate them. Robert Weaver included his *Northern Review* story, "Vacation in La Voiselle," in his *Canadian Short Stories* in 1960 and took his 1944 *First Statement* story "A Game of Chess" for *Tamarack Review* in 1961. Pacey picked "A Plausible Story" from a 1954 *Origin* for his *A Book of Canadian Short Stories* in 1962. For all Layton's determination to write short stories, the impression he aimed for in *The Swinging Flesh* (which was half stories and half poems) that he was adding a new string to his bow, he had only one new story, "Osmeck." Although Bob Weaver bought another of Layton's short stories, "Dislocation" ("The World We Live In") for a thousand dollars in March 1960, Jack McClelland thought the story was "one of those bad ones that a writer must get out of his system now and then" and advised Layton to discard it. Leonard Cohen, after finishing a novel that M&S rejected as "too hot,"[4] had turned his hand to plays. Layton followed suit, and was soon collaborating with Cohen in his new apartment on plays they both thought would bring them fame and fortune:

> We've set ourselves a goal of six plays before we end our collaboration for this year (1961). That ought to take us up to May, after which he and I might fly over to Europe... If the CBC and some American stations take our plays (they had better!), we intend to make this a source of livelihood for both of us.[5]

The three plays Layton and Cohen completed ("Lights on the Black Water," "A Man Was Killed" and "Up With Nothing"

["Enough of Fallen Leaves"],[6] which they insisted on handing in person to Bob Weaver with a partial reading), made neither their fame nor their fortune. Weaver sent on the plays as possibilities for "Q for Quest," "Shoestring Theatre" and "Festival 61," but he was not sanguine. Of "Lights on the Black Water," he wrote bluntly:

> I doubt very much if this is a ninety minute play...it seems to me likely to be a rather thin hour. I suspect it is not for television or in fact for any kind of dramatic presentation. It is terribly wordy and if you will forgive my saying so ideology takes over to the point where the characters are destroyed. In spite of your description of the characters at the beginning of the play, they turn out really to be stereotypes of black or of white. Dear Irving, people just don't talk this way to one another even in the most ideological circumstances. I have never heard you talk to me in this way.[7]

About "Enough of Fallen Leaves" Weaver wrote, "neither the basic idea nor the structure of the play is strong enough to sustain interest through ninety minutes....[it] has all the earmarks of having been tossed off with energy and exuberance, but without the close attention to method...which always underlies good comedy construction."[8]

Reviving an older ambition, Layton announced from time to time that he was about to write a novel. Perhaps his most typical statement of his aims was made to Pacey: "I do want to live fully and exuberantly the next ten or twenty years, travel, fuck all the beautiful girls I can, drink the choicest wines and meet all the worthwhile, interesting people. I've changed my mind on a whole lot of things, except to keep changing them. When I'm sixty I'd like to sum it all up in the single poem that will live forever."[9]

It probably seemed to Layton that he could go almost anywhere and do almost anything. As the universities across Canada became more interested in Canadian culture and young people everywhere more interested in poetry, the Canada Council began to sponsor poetry readings. After 1960, it was not unusual for even small universities and colleges to have half a dozen poets read to them during the course of a year. Between the fall of 1960 and the end of 1962, Layton was invited to lecture or read at ten universities, and he had been offered teaching jobs at San Francisco, "Rutgers or some other such place," York University in Toronto and an unspecified university Frank Scott knew of that was looking for a "poet-at-large." Wherever he did read or lecture, bulging audiences were spell-bound. It was intoxicating.

Layton's excitement at this recognition took an increasingly sexual form. "Tomorrow I'm going up to Queen's... I hope [Malcom Ross] has invited a couple of seductive and seducible coeds, firm-breasted and golden-thighed [to his party],"[10] he confessed to Pacey in the fall of 1960. He began to see women from the point of view of a semi-Byronic notion of the poet; they were merely his due reward. "Daddio is getting around," he boasted to Pacey in "beat" slang.[11]

It seemed to Layton that he must be right on every issue. He took up the cause of John F. Kennedy immediately after his election, calling him "my boy" and praising him as a "tough" fighter. In fact, Layton seems to have viewed the president much as he viewed his fourteen-year-old son. Max, who had taken guitar lessons from Leonard Cohen and wanted to become a musician, was reading the books his father thought he must understand if he was to become the great Canadian novelist: Plato's *Apology*, the *Phaedo* and Arthur Koestler's *Darkness at Noon*. With a similarly paternal enthusiasm, Layton sent off Hadley Cantril's book *Soviet Leaders and Mastery Over Man* to President Kennedy in late February 1961 to help him "save the day for free human nature" during the Cuban-missile crisis. With the book, he sent a letter "advising him exactly how he should go about fighting Communist totalitarianism." He told Pacey, "it may be the most decisive letter in history.... I have an idea that he ought to make effective use of the many great writers in his country to do ideological battle with the Russians."[12] Layton also enclosed a copy of *A Red Carpet for the Sun* and a poem — titled "Why I Don't Make Love to the First Lady" — for Kennedy's wife, Jacqueline. He invited her to attend his reading of the poem at an American Arts Festival (which honoured Canada)[13] and compared her face to "the Rosa Mystica." "Maybe he'll invite me to spend a week-end at the White House!" Layton wrote Pacey.

> Of course I could have her!
>
> In a flash, with a snap of my fingers.
>
> An arrogant magician,
> I'd put words under her perfect feet
> and make her fly to me.
> She'd land in my arms
> reciting one of my poems.
> She'd remember nothing of the White House
> except what I told her.
> To draw from her one of her exultant smiles
> I'd persuade her my lips
> were official Washington.
>
> Pah, I'm a degenerate poet
> with a sense of honour!
>
> I shall not take her.
>
> Not while serene contractors
> build kindergartens
> for robots and goons,
> and skinny Caribs
> with beards sprouting from machine-guns
> clamour
> for blood, education, and cheaper roulette;
> or the Chinese have a leader
> who writes flawless verse.
>
> President Kennedy does not write verse.
>
> Not while Africa
> explodes in the corridors of the U.N.
>
> Lumumba, Kasavubu: a
> D'Oyly Carte of exotic names;

but the drums,
East & West,
thwack unearthly rhythms,
and the opera-loving Congolese
lie much too still
on their dead faces.

A President
must stay up night after night
deliberating such matters:

My lovely, unlucky Jacqueline!

Still, when a husband
is so harassed,
shall I add to his burdens
by running off with his attractive wife?

Not I, not Irving Layton.

I'll wait until
the international situation has cleared.
After that it's every poet for himself.

It didn't take A.J.M. Smith long to think up a little squib mocking Layton's poem. The squib appeared in the April issue of *Canadian Forum*. (Layton's poem had appeared in the previous issue.)

Come off it, cocky Layton, what has Jacky got
(Save a devoted husband) sweet Aviva's not?
But if you want variety to warm old bones,
Stick to the Commonwealth: try Mrs. Armstrong-Jones.[14]

Layton's diatribes against Castro were astonishing, for Castro was exactly the type of left-wing revolutionary Layton would have supported and, indeed, did support during the 1930s. What had happened to his left-wing sentiments? Was it possible that the student-agitator who had invited Norman Bethune to speak at Macdonald College was supporting

Kennedy's resistance to an anti-fascist Cuban revolution? "He never could have stomached Communism," Betty one speculated. "When it dawned on him what *his* life would be like in a place like Russia, he became fiercely anti-Communist. Why he wouldn't have been allowed to carry on the way he did — say the things he said in public — and he knew it. That's why he was so keen on 'democratic freedom.'"[15] It was true that Suzanne Rosenberg's detailed descriptions of Russia had shown Layton that it was no place for him. But, like so many people at the time, he also was entranced with the Kennedy charisma: JFK stood for youth, energy, power, freedom. Though Castro also had charisma, his views were too idealistic and anti-capitalist for the middle-aged Layton, who had property interests. He had struggled hard to make it, and he felt as if he had achieved power. He was no longer one of the ignorant lumpenproletariat, except when it served his purposes. He had triumphed over a WASP society, and he had much to teach them. Now was the time to go main-line, to enjoy the fruits of his labours, to be a legislator, acknowledged by the establishment.

Pacey — who like most intellectuals and artists at the time supported Castro — tried to argue with Layton, calling him a reactionary, an old conservative and a Fascist, and accusing him of confusing might with right. But Layton only sneered to "Pinky Pacey" that he was done with "socialist blabbermouths." When Pacey confronted him with some facts about the Cuban-missile crisis and suggested that Kennedy was promoting "American imperialism," Layton stuck to his guns. He was convinced that Kennedy would go down in history as one of the "great" presidents, just as he was convinced that he would go down in history as a "great" poet. Nothing could alter that view. But Layton had spent most of the fifties concerned with his success as a poet, and not with political issues; his letters of the early sixties sounded curiously out of date. He was using Cold War rhetoric for what rapidly was becoming a new political era of anti-American sentiment in the west. Was he really out of date? Was he pitting himself against majority views on principle? Or had he just become addicted to fighting?

Though Layton claimed that his poem for Jackie Kennedy

was really an oblique compliment to her husband, it revealed his conviction that the poet was sexually irresistible. Well, wasn't he? Didn't every woman swoon when a poem was composed for her? Wasn't Byron a rake? Wasn't every poet worth his salt a rake? After all, his "marriage" to Aviva really had not taken place. Whatever he did, he hardly could be called an adulterer. Anyway, Aviva understood about the creative spirit: she was starting to write herself — children's short stories and poems that were wonderful.[16] She wouldn't expect to tame his free, fierce nature. It wasn't long before Layton openly was advocating "free love." "I am in favor of sexual relationships outside marriage," he argued in a debate at Sir George Williams in November 1961 to "mostly male" applause. "Love must be free, unrestrained and spontaneous," though it "must not be confused with licentiousness and temporary amours." Layton said that marriage was the deathbed of love because it led to the decay of physical passion. He thought that a more liberal attitude towards extra-marital relationships could save many a marriage, a frustrated partner or a broken home. To liberate men and women from "the whore/madonna complex," people must "get rid of the subconscious feeling that there is something evil about sex."[17] At home, he sometimes liberated his two goldfish, Franny and Zooey, out of their confining bowl and put them in the bathtub. "Irving sits on the toilet-seat and watches them for hours and hours," Aviva wrote to Leonard Cohen. "He really is becoming curiouser and curiouser as a person you know!"[18]

At the end of 1962, Layton began to seek out sensational sex in the night-clubs of Montreal. One belly-dancer named "Fawzia" especially intrigued him. "She's about the best advertisement for the Swinging Flesh I've ever seen. I think I'll try to persuade Jack McClelland to hire her to go up and down the country, selling my book. All she'd have to do is paste a copy of the S.F. on her navel or between her ample breasts. Neon lights would flash on and off between her thighs, and then you'd see the sales mount and mount. And not only the sales."[19] In public, Layton was lauding D.H. Lawrence for his portrayal of "healthy and frank" sexuality between men and women,[20] forgetting for the moment that he previously had condemned Lawrence in private as "an inverted Puritan and a passive male."[21] Layton also enthusiastically espoused what later would be called "open marriage," apparently convinced that within a monogamous marriage sexual fulfillment was impossible. This was surprising, for his main correspondent, Desmond Pacey, frequently wrote to him about the warm intimacy of his marriage to his wife, Mary, who was a successful painter. Though Pacey was an earthy man who enjoyed the "bed-time stories" Aviva told him, sometimes in black bra and red panties, on his occasional visits with his wife to the Laytons, he was in love with his wife. "I'm kept pretty busy satisfying an amorous woman of my own these days," he wrote Irving in April 1962. "We've quite often been on a three a day schedule lately, and if you can beat that after twenty-three years of marriage, I'd like to see the evidence. We've never felt as amorous as we have the last few weeks — not even on our honeymoon. Mary's such a terrific bed-partner that I have nothing left for those other hypothetical lovely ladies... for the first time all the children are off to school — so each day after lunch we have what we periphrastically describe as a 'twenty-minute nap.'"[22] Layton wrote back in amazed admiration, as he had when he first learned of Pacey's prowess in 1956. ("My erotic superman, three times a day. Whew!... I can't manage that many in a week.... How was I to suspect that anyone from New Zealand was such a hot-blooded creature. Anyway, here's to you... may your prostate hold out!") Pacey's revelations did not prompt Layton to re-examine his own notions of sexuality. He preferred to listen to Pacey's frequent teasing remarks about his "aphrodisiacal kiss" and sexual prowess. He also did his best to get Pacey to write pornography and "break loose and screw all the lovelies who've read about your critical acumen and your cock."[23]

Layton's larger-than-life notions about himself acquired mythic proportions. He began to believe that his personal likes and dislikes were not simply relative matters, but absolute truths. It was not in keeping with his mythic persona to dislike women, since male poets were supposed to love women. But there were some types of men — again defined partly by the "myth" of the poet — whom he believed were absolutely without redeeming qualities. One "type" of man he could not stand was the successful businessman. Layton usually pictured him as married and Jewish. Such men reminded him of his "failure," by his family's criteria, to become respectable, wealthy and stable, his "failure" to become the kind of man he might have become had he stayed with Faye. When such men seemed content or when they held power over him (like Mr. Beutel, whom he held personally responsible for his firing from Herzliah), Layton lashed out with all the venom he could muster. But the "type" he loathed most, the men he attacked with a black and energetic spite, were quiet, reflective men. To him they seemed to have no guts, no life, no balls. Such men were usually poets with principles different from his own, or they were scholars. He accumulated a "tradition" of names, including poet John Sutherland, poet-professors Frank Scott, Louis Dudek and A.J.M. Smith, and professor Northrop Frye. Though each of these men was unique, Layton tended to subsume their identities into a simple cartoon of ineffectual dessication. He was particularly vicious about Northrop Frye, whose *Anatomy of Criticism* had revolutionized English literary criticism and whose prestige as the top literary critic in Canada had been established in the 1950s. When Frye, with poet-professors Roy Daniells and Alfred Bailey, judged Robert Finch's *Acis in Oxford* the best Canadian book of poems for 1961 and gave Finch his second Governor-General's Award instead of awarding it to Layton's friend Leonard Cohen for his first volume, *A Spice Box of Earth*, Layton's fury was intense.

> There isn't a single poem in the Finch book that won it. It's dull, academic stuff with not one alive line that can seriously be called poetry. *Exercises*, bloody, or rather, bloodless exercises. Nothing else. What an arsehole of a country this is, when this sort of crap can win prizes, but Leonard's genuine lyricism can't and doesn't. But why in the name of hell did Frye ask a pair of ailing sextagenarians to select the prize-winner? But wait a minute!

Isn't Frye well into the ailing sixties himself? Sextagenarians of the world, unite; you have nothing but your chilblains to lose.[24]

Daniells was fifty-nine, Bailey was fifty-six and Frye was forty-nine — exactly the same age as Layton.

Somewhere Layton seemed to have lost sight of the fact that Daniells had supported him in 1957 for his award of four thousand dollars from the Canada Foundation, and that Northrop Frye had declared *A Red Carpet for the Sun* "an important volume" and in 1961 called Layton "the best English-language poet in Canada."[25]

The intensity of Layton's hatred for the kind of men he frequently labelled "eunuchs," "castratos" and "corpses" was unleashed specifically as a result of an invitation, in April 1962, from Earle Birney to teach "creative writing" at the University of British Columbia. The salary would be about $25,000 a year, a startling improvement on the $1,800 Layton claimed to be earning at Sir George Williams. Birney explained that he was trying to make UBC the centre for creative writing in Canada. He also mentioned that he was inviting Layton's American poet-correspondent from the mid-fifties, Bob Creeley. At Birney's suggestion, Layton applied to the head of the English department, Roy Daniells. In a bizarre pageant of university politics,[26] which amounted to Daniells' fear of Layton's potentially disruptive presence in his department and Birney's power struggle with Daniells over how the department was to be shaped, Layton got caught in the cross-fire. Though Daniells sought letters of reference for Layton (one from Pacey), he and his staff decided that UBC could do without Canada's leading poet. Layton previously had resisted all attempts to draw him into academic positions. ("I don't wish to become a tamed university pet.... I want to grow wilder and fiercer with my flame controlled to the discipline of a blow-torch").[27] He had asked Pacey, "Can you imagine a Faulkner or a Hemingway in a university?"[28] (Pacey had replied that for several years Faulkner had been associated with the University of Mississippi.) But the lure of a lucrative creative-writing post near Creeley at a potential "centre" for writing drew Layton's hopeful interest. "I don't think the 'academic' surroundings are going to deaden or paralyze me; I'm too old for that, too set in my rebellious ways."[29]

When he was turned down, Layton was as furious as a thwarted two-year-old.

> I've always known there were brown-nosed shits in universities, but I never thought my toe would turn up so fine a specimen as this. Ugh! Now, more than ever, I am convinced that a writer has no business being found within five miles of a university.... Ha! If that's the sort of person Daniells is, I'd want to be as far away from him as possible: shits like that offend my nostrils... I shall never let myself be trapped — not by anything. If I ever weaken, I have only to think of Birney, Dudek, Smith, etc. No, thank you. No university is ever going to geld me, no Canada Council Fellowships, no titles and no honours.[30]

Apparently he did not consider Sir George Williams a university.

Layton's association of academic positions with a eunuch-like state; his fears of being "tamed" or "gelded" if he joined a university department; and his perception of his exact contemporary, Frye, as a "sextagenarian" were central to his view of life. Many of his friends disagreed with him. Pacey took him to task many times on the subject. Malcolm Ross, an English professor and the editor who chose several of Layton's poems for *Queen's Quarterly*, wrote, "I see no necessary *causus belli* between poet and professor. I see the need of an alliance, an uneasy alliance perhaps — but nonetheless an alliance... an 'entente cordiale'."[31] Milton Wilson, also an English professor and Layton's editor at *Canadian Forum*, said much the same thing: "About pernicious academia and poets. I think we might agree on individual cases, but not on the general principle... I don't see Mandel or Reaney as blinkered poets, and I'm not convinced that they would write better poems if they'd never seen the inside of a university."[32] Layton stubbornly held his ground. Was it the other side of his conviction of greatness, and especially of his exaggerated notion of his sexual power? Did the cliché of the sacrosanct "ivory tower" suggest to him a bedroom where a depressed, ineffectual man studied books, contemplated the ineffable mysteries of the universe and ignored him? Did contemplative scholars and metaphysical poets seem to him to have "defected" from real life at his expense? Did the insults he had heard flung daily at a fastidious man who lacked the energy to try to keep his family alive automatically fly forth from his own lips? Did rejection by universities mean exclusion from that room, from a man he wanted to love? Weren't scholarship and metaphysics and aesthetics the forerunners to terrifying paralysis and death? When his friend Pacey played father to Layton's childish outbursts, seeing through the bombastic tirade to the hurt little man inside, Layton responded with profound gratitude. "Thank you for your understanding letter. I felt a whole lot better after I had read it. It was kind and sensible and full of warm humanity."[33] For Birney's sake, Layton apologized to Daniells.

He also went to some lengths to explain himself to Pacey. "I must let you into a writing secret of mine. If anyone is going to keep writing in this country, he *must* pretend every bush is an ogre, *must* exaggerate, distort, and blow everything up.... I've no Napoleon III as Victor Hugo had. I must insert him in the first innocent mediocrity I meet...this country is so ordinary and commonplace — both in its virtues and vices.... In short, there's a method in my madness, and there always has been."[34]

Very few people saw this vulnerable side of Layton. His Messianic quest to become "a poet like Isaiah"[35] and to sustain his image as a genius consumed him and his public alike. Even though he often shifted around, he claimed that his remarks had been and were prophetic. He frequently reminded Pacey of "predictions" he had made that had come true, ignoring, with apparent ease, those that had not. He raved about books he had read as if everyone ought to know them: Pasternak's autobiography, *Safe Conduct*; Edmund Fuller's *Man in Modern Fiction*; G.S. Fraser's *Vision and Rhetoric*; Douglas Woolf's *The Hypocrite Days* and *Fade Out*; C. Wright Mills' *The Sociological Imagination*; and J.P. Donleavy's *The Ginger Man*. What seemed to appeal most to him in these books was the prose style. He used them as idea-banks and as fuel for his rhetoric.

Increasingly, he considered himself fellow to the "greats" of human history. When Pacey called his short stories "arch" and "stiff," Layton bragged, "they are the best thing since Joyce's *Dubliners* and they have much more to say."[36] He claimed that he was a modern Byron (ignoring or ignorant of the fact that Byron had savoured aspects of real life Layton certainly was not prepared to sample, such as drugs, homosexuality and sibling incest). He considered himself on a par with Shakespeare, Mailer, Catullus, Hemingway and Pasternak. "I've finally come up with the real meaning of *Hamlet*, the one Shakespeare himself had in mind when he wrote the play," Layton wrote to Pacey as he turned over ideas for his lecture ("Hamlet and the Beats") at St. Lawrence University in Canton, New York late in 1961. "Everybody from Coleridge on has missed the point. My theory also explains why they did. It's really fabulous, and I'm immensely excited by it."[37] He also became, in his own mind, the one true interpreter of modern European films, which had begun enjoying a vogue in North America. "I liked *La Dolce Vita* very much, and helped everyone around me to understand what it was all about."[38]

Such outrageous claims to omniscience and power invited retaliation, and it was not long before Layton suffered direct attacks. Poet Milton Acorn warned Layton that he intended to write a novel called *The Poets*: "He wanted my permission beforehand because he expects to say a whole lot of nasty things about me. I wrote back that I was extremely touched by such a display of 'fairness' and told him to go right ahead."[39] Layton was also criticised for his attack on the Romantic poets in a book called *Poems For 27 cents*, a collection of poems from his creative-writing workshop. In the preface Layton wrote:

> What has poetry got to do with the dead? And most people are dead. Dead, dead, dead. Poetry is the most subversive force in the world. It demands humanity from humans, here and now. Is there anything more revolutionary than that? It should surprise no one that thousands of mediocre, soul-less creatures in every State, especially in monolithic Russia and its satellites, are hired

to draw its teeth and claws. But the stuffed tiger is not poetry. Imagine what the real living tiger would do with the sterile culture of our own country, predominantly White, Protestant, and Anglo-Saxon. My eyes have seen the glory... Yeh, some glory![40]

In response, *Montreal Star* columnist Walter O'Hearne drew a cartoon of Layton, with his newly sprung little goatee,[41] kicking copies of Wordsworth and Keats around a study where a tiger stands grinning in the background. O'Hearne also wrote a parody of A.E. Housman's "To A Shropshire Lad" and called it "To A Slopshire Lad":

....Young men will always rise and yammer
And match the written word to tongue.
But — lad, excuse my modest stammer —
Lad, art thou really, truly young?

....Young men will always flaunt their
    banners,
Deride their elders, mock the past,
Ravage the salons with bad manners,
But, lad, their rage is quickly past.

Why, lad, when I was one-and-twenty,
(a way of saying twenty-one),
I had my say, and I said plenty,
And shocked the bourgeois, and had
    fun.

When young men gibe, I still endure them,
Remembering follies that were mine.
And try to answer, and just bore them.
(Laddie, aren't you forty-nine?)[42]

Layton fought back angrily and at once. In his reply to "O'Hernia," which appeared two days after the parody was printed, he concluded, "Reduced to its barest fundamentals what is, after all, the issue between us? Mr. O'Hearne is an undistinguished scribbler who cannot forgive mediocrity:

I am a genius who has written work that will survive with the best of Shakespeare, Wordsworth and Keats."[43] A comment from O'Hearne appeared at the bottom of Layton's letter: "Mr. Layton has confirmed every point I sought to make, plus a few I didn't dare to make."[44]

There is no doubt that several of the poems Layton wrote during the early 1960s were abominable. "Librarian at Asheville,"[45] for example, mimicked Creeley's and Olson's compact, slangy free verse. The poem described a librarian experiencing orgasm at the mere touch of first editions of her favourite writer's books, then performing fellatio on the speaker-poet, who is visiting the library. "The Fictive Eye,"[46] though technically more expert and rhythmic, is cloyingly self-adulatory. It pictures a "grave sage and hero" putting aside "Venus' hand" to "rise" and "go/to caress my exalted destiny." Such simple-minded, self-advertising poems underestimated the poetry-reading public, which was accustomed to Layton's skill at juggling complex emotional states and the images that expressed them. In several of his poems, he veered close to pornography: sexual description for sensation without much reference to art. But as Layton's role as spokesman for "free love" fell into place, it became a sound business proposition to market such material. Certainly, he would not hear criticism. He was a genius, and no one knew better than he did the subtleties of his craft. "I had a deal with Jack McClelland about censorship," Layton admits. "I didn't interfere with his business as a publisher and he didn't interfere with mine as a poet."[47] Characteristically, he sent off new poems to the prestige journals: *Canadian Forum*, *Tamarack Review* and *Queen's Quarterly*. Whatever was rejected there was sent to the minor journals, where editors were thrilled to have any original Layton poem. Why should he listen to Pacey, who thought the poem "The Gifts" was "slight," "Mysteries" was "sheer junk" and "There Were No Signs" was mediocre? As long as someone praised each poem, he chose to believe what the praiser said. He ignored this advice from Jack McClelland: "Your best poems — and they are fantastically good — are so much better than your worst poems that a lot of thought should be given to evolving a means of separating the two that will satisfy you."[48]

Yet beneath the showy, superficial poems there was evidence of true creativity. Layton sent the manuscript of short stories and poems, called *The Swinging Flesh*, to M&S at the end of November 1960; he had "that anti-climactic feeling, that drained, empty feeling — all fucked out!... I feel like giving myself a long, long rest.... What a stupid way of living, when there's so much to be looked at and enjoyed...[but] when a poem begins [to] take shape — that is ecstasy." Poems continued to take shape for Layton, often at the least convenient times. Sometimes inspiration struck when he was exhausted from marking exams: "God, when will I get off this treadmill? Miraculously, I've been overflowing with poems, some excellent ones too, but they're much too long to type."[49] On another occasion, he woke in the middle of the night filled with momentum:

> The ideas became power! O what a life! Here I am buried under hundreds of term papers and exams, and the muse pulls me out of bed at 4 AM to write a poem when I'm dog-tired and need the rest. Once a poem gets hold of me, it won't leave me alone... I no sooner sat down at the desk when a familiar drumming voice began to nag at me till I had to put aside what I was doing and take up the poem [I'd written] to eject [the] unsuitable word. I was at it for more than six hours! Precious time I needed for other things. But the poem was so tight rhythmically, and so organic by this time that the word simply had to be the right one. Finally, I found I had to switch a line in order to get the word in that would do. And almost immediately after, another line popped into my head, the beginning of a new poem, which also kept at me until I sat down and wrote it... The fact is, with the coming of warm weather (!) I've been writing like a frog, and I must have written about a dozen poems in less than three weeks.[50]

Layton felt the drumming "itch" to write poems more freely during the summer months: he had fewer teaching responsibilities, and responded physically to the contrast to winter provided by the summer climate.

It was in July 1961, while he was on holiday with Aviva in Berlin, New Hampshire (he had "postponed" a trip to Cuba because he feared it would be too hot) that he wrote one of his best poems, "A Tall Man Executes a Jig." Though he and Aviva had acquired sores and bruises ("stigmata") from riding horses without the proper gear, they were happily ensconced in a comfortable cottage beside a small lake. To Layton, the poem, dedicated to Malcolm Ross, stood out from his others:

> [it] has a music I've not achieved heretofore, plus some interesting ideas and imagery. I wasn't quite happy with Section III, so I'm enclosing what I think is an improved version. The image of the wheeling circle of sun and gnats meshing is both audacious and symbolically significant. In Section I, please change "mites" to "gnats" for I've since learned that that is what they are.[51]

"A Tall Man Executes a Jig" was Layton's most complex, sustained, craftsman-like poem to date. In the simple six-section narrative, which approximates Shakespearian blank verse, Layton depicted an ordinary man's insight into the beauty and terror of life through contemplation of the details of the natural countryside: a swarm of gnats, sunlight, a dying grass snake.

> III
> He stood up and felt himself enormous.
> Felt as might Donatello over stone,
> Or Plato, or as a man who has held
> A loved and lovely woman in his arms
> And feels his forehead touch the emptied sky
> Where all antinomies flood into light.
> Yet jig jig jig, the haloing black jots
> Meshed with the wheeling fire of the sun:
> Motion without meaning, disquietude

> Without sense or purpose, ephemerides
> That mottled the resting summer air till
> Gusts swept them from his sight like wisps of smoke.
> Yet they returned, bringing a bee who, seeing
> But a tall man, left him for a marigold.[52]

Through the poem, Layton conveyed his knowledge of life's complexities in unforced images and language so entrancing and melodious it effortlessly drew the reader into a place where fantasy and reality merged. For one of the poem's most vivid images, that of the "violated grass snake that lugged/Its intestine like a small red valise," Layton drew on recollections of the humiliated pedlar. The poem's title explored all the ambiguities of the word "execution." Something must suffer and be "executed" so a revelation can occur. To "execute" a poem, the poet must be destructive, even self-destructive. The "jig" is both an intentionally deceptive performance (as in "the jig is up") and a lively dance. To attain aesthetic beauty and stature, Layton's poem suggests, the poet must be an immoral hypocrite.

The poem was immediately recognized as Layton's best. Leonard Cohen wrote from Greece:

> *A Tall Man Executes a Jig* is a masterpiece! It's the poem you've always wanted to write and it includes everything you knew up to the day you wrote it. That kind of generosity has been missing from our verse since the metaphysicians. And your language makes everything being written around you fragmentary. Well, it's a masterpiece, that's simple to see, and there's no point even congratulating the author, regardless of the polishing, because poems like that are handed down.[53]

Al Purdy responded in a similar vein: "You have finally attained the upper echelons with this poem. People can understand it. The dirty old man has become the grand old man full of sound and fury."[54] "Smith was in town," Layton wrote to Pacey two months later:

> We had a lively get-together at Frank's home. I read

several of my new poems, and Art endeared himself to me for all time by sobbing openly when I read [them]. I've completed a revised version of "A Tall Man Executes a Jig"... I've added another stanza to [it], bringing the total to seven, and ninety-eight lines. I think its the best poem I've yet written, and had I done nothing else this summer but write that, I'd still feel it was a very good summer indeed.[55]

He told McClelland that it was "the most ambitious thing I've ever done, and the best single poem of mine to date."[56] Jay Macpherson, whose poetry and personality Layton had ridiculed and whose sensibility was entirely different from Layton's, greatly admired the poem:

Any poet who's ever read with Layton must hate him on one level — because Irving always sees to it that he reads last, uses very shameless means (I mean non-poetic means) to seduce his audience, and then reads & talks so long that in effect he's turned the whole occasion into his personal triumph — the rest of us supposed to be sharing the evening then get trampled in the stampede of most of the audience up to the front to make some connection with him — or so it used to be in the days when he & I & a few other people were in our prime. And anybody who's ever tried to get him to sign any sort of human-rights appeal knows what a conservative old slum landlord the beast is. But under all the rubbish there's that splendid poet — that's where the generosity & integrity went to: no nonsense for Irving about the poet's having to be also a good *man* — why should he, if his weaknesses feed his work? I wouldn't wish to see an exemplary husband-father-neighbour replace the author of "A Tall Man Executes a Jig".[57]

The poem first appeared in *Queen's Quarterly* in 1961; it was snapped up for the 1962 collection *Poet's Choice* (published in New York) and was reprinted in a large number of anthologies by different publishers, including Margaret Atwood's 1982 collection, *The New Oxford Book of Canadian Verse*.

Ironically, the very conditions that had brought him to the pinnacle of success were Layton's worst enemy. Times were changing quickly, and the age had thrown him into prominence as its representative because of his unpredictable changeability. The western world was taking part in a social revolution that raised questions of human values Layton had been pondering, though not resolving, for several years. A new generation was challenging the materialism of the "consumer society" and trying to recapture spiritual values that were rapidly eroding. Resentful at the hypocrisy of their parents, young people lashed out on several fronts: politically to the left, educationally for drastic reform, sexually against puritanical conventions. In an age made vulnerable by the rapid loss of religious faith, young people were beginning to drop out of the educational institutions an earlier age had revered, and were actively looking for "causes" to replace those institutions. Through eastern mysticism, popular music — both folk-song and rock — astrology, "flower power," communes, drug "trips," and in a host of other ways, they sought the ideals they felt certain their parents had lost. It was an era ripe for spell-binders, for gurus and guides who, through music or language, could seize leadership of a young population in search of perfect harmonies. Layton was a spell-binder by temperament, and his own concerns meshed sufficiently with those of an angry experimental generation to throw him into prominence as a spokesman. His down-to-earth attitude to all bodily functions seemed like the answer to puritanical fastidiousness. When D.H. Lawrence's *Lady Chatterley's Lover* was on trial in Montreal in 1960, Layton was ready, before his audiences, with quotations from Lawrence and with his affirmation-of-life-and-sex philosophy. Then he edited a collection of Canadian erotic poems. *Love Where the Nights are Long* (published in 1962) featured his introduction (excerpted by *Maclean's*), "What Canadians Don't know About Love." "Singlehandedly I'm going to change the image of my countrymen," he wrote to his publisher. "When I'm done with the book, no one in Canada will [think] of sleeping any more, only of sleeping around."[58] For years he had been criticizing the Canadian educational system. Now the majority of young people chimed in. The angry tone of so much of his poetry, particularly when directed against his favourite targets, the polite and the moneyed, struck a responsive chord among students who were fed up with an "irrelevant" system. The collection sold more than five thousand copies in three months.

The corresponding surge of Canadian nationalism that sky-rocketed in the sixties was also related to what Layton was saying. His criticisms of the Canadian people in poems like "From Colony to Nation"[59] or "Family Portrait" were embarrassingly accurate. Not surprisingly, it had taken the detachment of an eye from outside the mainstream WASP culture to see middle-class limitations. But even that mainstream culture was changing in ways that situated Layton nearer the centre of things. As he was sounding the note of a different voice, that voice from lower down on the social scale of which he had been so proud in the early days with Louis Dudek, a new generation was going "hippie," dressing with ethnic flamboyance in revolt against grey-flannel suits and turning to confrontational politics. While Layton was being lionized, a scholar called John Porter was investigating the real nature of Canadian society and finding it no longer a homogeneous WASP civilization, but a "vertical mosaic" of ethnic groups. Though Layton had taken his stances for personal reasons at a time when he seemed like an odd-ball outsider, and had accepted his fate in Canada only because he couldn't move to the United States or Europe when he wanted to, he found himself in the eye of the hurricane in the Canadian cultural scene of the early 1960s.

He had been right that Canadian poetry, like all art, needed a strong dose of realism and earthiness, even vulgarity, if it were to have vitality. But hadn't he simply been trying to justify his own existence? Hadn't his attacks on professors come from a deep-seated distaste for contemplative men, and from his unfortunate personal experiences? Yet, here again, Layton was partly right: he *had* been exploited. He still was being exploited. By 1962, he had been assigned to teach more courses at Sir George to compensate for his loss of the Herzliah job. He taught four courses (one of which had swelled from thirty-five to one hundred and seventy-five students) at eight dollars an hour — fifteen hundred dollars a year — when tenured professors were earning many times that amount. When Max returned from a visit to Betty (after Betty sent a collect telegram asking for a hundred dollars plus bus fare to Montreal to prolong Max's visit into October, which Layton paid), he announced that he wanted to move into a room downtown. Layton took on the financial responsibility for three households and added to his busy schedule regular morning classes at the Ross Tutorial School. Aviva had begun pressing for a baby; that would mean more expenses. His outrage at educational institutions was understandable. It was understandable, too, that students saw his anger as their anger.

Layton's power as a poet-maker was formidable and he wielded it recklessly and instinctively. In some cases, he was right. His assessment of Cohen's lyrical gifts was accurate, but his encouragement of young men like Henry Moscovitch (whose sensibility and poems could not have been less like Layton's) was based on hunches that were far from the mark. Though he played a crucial role in encouraging poets who were, by their own natures, likely to write in a similar vein, poets like Purdy and Acorn, he was blind to the merits of other sensibilities, like Reaney's and Macpherson's.

As 1962 drew to an end, Layton occupied an unenviable position in Canadian letters, though he was convinced that he was the "cynosure of every eye," in a word, "unstoppable." In 1960, the first academic thesis[60] on his poetry had been completed in Manitoba (an examination of "Layton's universal philosophy"), and Professor Wynne Francis at Sir George had completed her article "Montreal Poets of the Forties,"[61] "with a slight assist from me,"[62] Layton told Pacey. A.J.M. Smith, for one, regretted having his poems in Layton's erotic collection, *Love Where the Nights Are Long*. "That is a horrible book," Smith wrote to John Glassco, whose work also had been included. "Looking over it I'm ashamed for us both to be in it — most of the stuff is just plain crap."[63] As Layton waited with "pins and needles" for the eighty new poems in *Balls For A One-Armed Juggler* to appear in 1963, Pacey warned him in a friendly manner: "You can't have it both ways. You can't be the daimonic man attacking academicism and yet be yourself an academic... What you say about being too 'innocent' for academic life is in a sense quite true. And I believe that Jack McClelland is exploiting you for his own monetary gain. There *is* something vulgar and phoney about *Love Where the Nights Are Long* and its Harold Town illustrations and limited signed editions and its general aim of 'look how shocking I'm being!' I am genuinely afraid that you are becoming a victim of your own cult. It's easy to be a big frog in the little pool of Canadian narcissism — but you've got to go beyond that if you're going to win the Nobel Prize. Many of the poems in *Balls for a One-Armed Juggler* are not worthy of you."[64] The fact that *Balls* sold more than two thousand copies in a month and won the four-thousand-dollar Prix littérature de Québec struck Layton as proof that Pacey was wrong. "Imagine a lady from Westmount," he wrote gleefully to Earle Birney, "going into a bookstore and asking for Layton's *Balls*.... I frequently tickle myself with that idea."[65]

Mirror Reflections

"I can never over-estimate my debt to Murray's," Layton wrote in mid-December 1962. He was referring to a very ordinary little restaurant, one of a chain, that stood at the corner of St. Catherine and Guy streets in downtown Montreal, where he frequently shared the steamy, smoke-filled atmosphere with students eager to prolong their class discussion, or with his "coffee romances" that had openly begun to boil over. "In my 'office' at Murray's...there's never a week passes that I do not meet with young poets, frustrated wives, students, businessmen, etc. I have only to dip my spoon! There are hundreds of stories waiting to be written or melted down into a single poem or a single line.... The critics...will take [the preface to *Balls for a One-Armed Juggler*]...as some more attitudinizing on my part. I don't care. Nobody likes them except the public whose heartbeat I know because I've so often listened to it. My words echo people's own fears, ideals, and ambivalencies and they do this because nobody spends more time than I do learning of them."[1]

Layton saw himself as sort of proletarian Messiah whose individual efforts had the power to transform for the better the lives he touched. Young poets needed advice on what to write about and how to write and, more importantly, on how to live. Frustrated wives needed to discover what was wrong with their relationships, possibly to have a sample of what love could really be like with a truly free spirit, and to be encouraged to break free of life-denying, middle-class morality. Students needed to know that not all professors were dessicated, remote sticks with no more blood and guts in them than a scarecrow. They needed to see a professor who was a real human being, one with strong feelings, companionable concern and the right values in life. Businessmen needed a good dose of Layton's philosophy of life if they were to be saved from desperately narrow existences based on the respectable accumulation of wealth. They needed to know that life had loveliness: it cost nothing and it was free for the asking to those who revered the arts and gave creativity its due. Such encounters, as Layton admitted, had the added advantage of providing the insatiable poet with stories more bizarre and tortured than any he could have imagined. If he listened carefully, he'd have an endless supply of subject matter for his stories and poems.

Layton's influence on the lives into which he so eagerly "dipped his spoon" was almost always extreme. Those who did not like him or his philosophy of exuberant living hastily made themselves scarce. But those who were attracted to him were drawn to his relaxed sensuality like moths to an incandescent flame, never dreaming that anything but freedom, pleasure and success would result from their relationship with the "master poet." Layton never doubted for a moment that the opportunities he so generously provided could do anything but good. He did not see his revolutionary philosophy as a catalyst that might trigger unforeseen results.

In March, 1961, a freckle-faced twenty-three-year-old housewife in the tiny Ontario village of Angus sent a letter to Irving Layton. She had read about him in an article by June Callwood, "The Lusty Laureate from the Slums,"[2] published in the *Star Weekly Magazine*. The woman had been struck by Layton's slum background. It was one with which she could sympathize. She had dropped out of high school in nearby Barrie at age sixteen. Within seven years, she had five daughters. Her husband was an artist. He painted portraits and abstracts, which were sold in Eaton's. She was horribly miserable, but as a Catholic she could not hope for divorce. What should she do? Maybe Irving Layton would know. He seemed like someone who knew all about life, and how to solve problems.³

"At first he was really encouraging," Joyce Dawe recalls. "I felt he approved of everything, of all the mean, awful things about life that I kept writing him about. It was therapeutic. Eventually, after months of corresponding during which I couldn't make up my mind what I wanted to do, he wrote that he didn't know whether I'd make it in life or not. That did it. I left my husband and sneaked away to find Irving in Montreal.

"I talked and talked with him and Aviva. I used to meet them every week at the Murray's on Church Street opposite Eaton's. I told them all about my terribly puritanical upbringing. My mother, for example, had told me that the girls in the neighbouring town of Minnesing grew breasts because they were bad. When I began to develop breasts myself, I felt so guilty. Irving made up a poem about it. It went something like this:

> Her mother used to tell her
> only bad women
> had well-developed busts.
>
> When her young breasts
> began to grow
> she was certain Herr Satan
> had marked her for his own
> and would grab her from below.
>
> They grew & grew,
> and their very size
> has made Gretchen bold:
> one fine swing of them, she says,
> would knock the devil out cold.
>   ("Moral With a Story")⁴

"Irving and Aviva really supported me until I found a job in Montreal. Aviva gave me some of her clothes. I spent a lot of time crying because I was so afraid I would not get custody of the children. I knew the Catholic welfare people would consider that I had no right to them, since I had abandoned my husband. I did get them in the end. I saw a psychiatrist — Doctor Hesselstein — whom Irving claimed was the only good psychiatrist in Montreal. He advised me to get a divorce, which I did."

"Joycey-Oisey," as Irving and Aviva called her, gradually pulled her life together. In 1965, she got a job with the Toronto Symphony. By 1966, she was executive secretary for the Chicago Symphony. A year later, she was promoted to office manager. That was the year she met Jay Freedman, who took up the position of principal trombone with the orchestra. They married in 1972. Joyce gave up her job as assistant manager to run their fifteen-acre horse-farm. In 1974, a daughter consolidated their marriage.

In late March 1963, Layton received a letter at his Sir George Williams office from a forty-ish housewife.

> Dear Sir:
> Forgive a fan letter from a convert you made in London [Ontario] last week.
> The significance of the "planted name" is that I asked you to include my name in your autograph in the hope that you might recognize it in *Fiddlehead*.
> Please return the poem [enclosed was "Avant-Midi Avec un Faun"].
> Sincerely,
> Dorothy Rath[5]

Dorothy Rath had had a disruptive childhood. Her mother died when she was four, and she was sent to live with her mother's sister, a stern, loud woman who "scared her to death." "I was a short, fat girl who was very unhappy. Next, I was sent at age eleven to my father's sister who was gentler and quiet. My father came to see me then on Sundays. He was a romantic figure to me. I always wished I could go and live with him."[6]

In 1963, when Dorothy met Layton, who had come to

give a reading for the Poetry Writing Club she belonged to, he reminded her of her father. "I was fascinated by him," she recalls. "He looked to me like that movie star [Hungarian Laslo Benedek] that played in *Death of a Salesman*. I set off to find out everything I could about him. It was a hobby, kind of. At first I kept scrapbooks. Then I began collecting tapes, photos, articles, poems about Irving — anything at all that was connected to him. It was an obsession."

Layton encouraged her. He wrote regularly to her, analysing her poems, sending her clippings and information about himself, discussing his philosophy of life with her. At intermittent intervals, they met. She would visit Montreal and stop in; he would contact her when he was in Toronto or London. Their fifteen-year correspondence was published in 1980 by Layton's former Herzliah student, Howard Aster of Mosaic Press. The book's title, originally "Winterfire," was changed to *An Unlikely Affair*.[7]

"It's an authentic bit of Canadiana," Layton explained to a friend when the book appeared. "It also tells a fascinating, humourous and poignant story between a poet and a dowdy-appearing middle-aged woman who has [been] energized by poetry to reveal hitherto untapped resources of passion and imagination."[8]

Rath's obsession for information about Layton was almost incredible. Soon she was surrounded by heaps of clippings, photographs — some of herself and Layton, others she took of Layton — scrapbooks, video-tapes of television programmes he was on, tapes and, of course, his letters, which she cherished.

"I think my husband felt overshadowed at times," Rath remarks. "He didn't agree with Irving Layton's philosophy. Now that my infatuation for Irving is gone, I have a sense of loss, not that I don't like him as he is."

Henry Moscovitch had been a student of Layton's at Herzliah. He looked like a clone of Layton. "Irving influenced me a great deal," Moscovitch recalls.[9] "He encouraged me to write poetry, sent me to the second-hand book-stores and told me all about Marx and Nietzsche. He suggested that I study political science and philosophy just as he had at McGill. He was the one who helped me select the poems that appeared in my first collection when I was fourteen: *The Serpent Ink*. Betty designed the cover for it. He also encouraged me to publish my second book, *The Laughing Storm*, when I was nineteen."

In 1962, after an afternoon at Murray's spent drinking coffee and reading aloud to Moscovitch from J.P. Donleavy's scandalous novel, *The Ginger Man*, Irving felt pleased with his Pygmalion-like accomplishment. The Romanian Jew Moscovitch, in his opinion, was well on the way to becoming a distinguished man of letters. "Moscovitch is writing a longish essay," Layton wrote proudly to Pacey, "setting forth the 'poetics' of the *Cataract* school. He's going to take cracks at almost everybody and everything, and quite probably you'll be one of the few people he'll spare. He's won a Woodrow Wilson scholarship to Columbia, and will be going there this autumn...Lucky fellow. Not twenty-one, in good health, loved by a beautiful girl who adores him, author of two books of poems — what could be sweeter? The world's really his oyster."[10]

Layton had no idea that, beneath the surface, Moscovitch was a very troubled young man. Because he was flattered by Moscovitch's devotion to him, he did not see that Moscovitch had chosen him as a model because he was everything Moscovitch wasn't. Though he imitated his mentor's confident, virile panache, Moscovitch was experiencing a crisis in his career and struggling with serious sexual problems. The world was certainly not his oyster.

At the age of twenty-five, Henry Moscovitch had a nervous breakdown. One of his symptoms was impotence. "I had just broken up with a girl," he recalls. "I was uncertain about my career. My father wanted me to go into business. He did not want me to continue writing poetry. I was diagnosed as a schizophrenic. Later I was considered a manic-depressive. My mind wanders sometimes."

In 1979, Henry Moscovitch threw himself off one of the bridges that crosses Decarie Avenue, a busy Montreal freeway. Miraculously, he survived, but first to a life in the Douglas Hospital for mental patients and then to a half-way house in the west end of Montreal, where he shared a room with two other Douglas patients. He needed constant dosages of stabilizing drugs.

"I feel profoundly guilty about having encouraged Henry," Layton admits. "I was stunned when I found out he was so seriously troubled — especially when I learned that he was impotent. I thought he was fine, a good, outstanding poet. He's an albatross around my neck. It's painful for me to think about him."[11]

A Greek Tragedy

"He had walked in smelling so strongly of perfume I demanded an explanation," Aviva recalls.[1] "I was making dinner after finishing teaching. I couldn't believe it. That perfume was *visible!*"

"I bumped into a former student," he said. "She was so happy to see me she ran up and embraced me. I guess she was wearing some perfume. You really should meet her."

"That," says Aviva, "was the beginning of the nightmare."

Musia Schwartz, a blonde, Polish beauty with vivid features, intense dark eyes and a husky, Marlene Dietrich voice, had been a student of Layton's at the Jewish Library in 1948. At the evening class of English for new immigrants, she met another student, Leon. Two years later they married, then settled into the usual pattern of middle-class life: Leon was an energetic manufacturer of hats and Musia was a housewife with two children to raise. Layton had lost sight of them for almost a decade when Musia spotted him in the corridors of Sir George Williams, where she had begun taking night courses, and ran up to embrace him. She had become restless and frustrated at home, she explained.[2] It wasn't enough to be a housewife. Her enthusiasm and curiosity had no outlet. Leon understood. He was satisfied with things as they were, but she needed something more. A university education was sure to help.

Musia's life had been like a Greek tragedy before she arrived in Montreal. She had been only twelve when both her parents disappeared into a Nazi death-camp not long after her father had obtained for her a Christian birth certificate and German identification papers. She had worked as a maid or a baby-sitter in one Christian home after another, depending on her quick wits to avoid detection and to negotiate the sudden changes in immigration policy to which she was subject. In 1944, after the Polish uprising, she was among those who were evacuated to the countryside and forced to do manual labour. By chance, she ran into an aunt, who had her transferred to a displaced-persons camp in Germany. There Musia began to make the transition back to a normal life.

Clever as well as beautiful, Musia took private lessons to complete her matriculation in German. She was given special status to take language and literature in her mother tongue. In 1947 she matriculated, then spent one semester at Johann Wolfgang Goethe Universität in Frankfurt. Eventually, under the auspices of the Canadian Jewish Congress, she had the opportunity to emigrate to Canada. Knowing no English, and having heard only of Ottawa and Montreal in Canada, she found herself one of forty-eight passengers on a ship bound for Montreal in 1948.

Immediately after arriving, she was taken, with her group, to a reception centre on Jeanne Mance Street, where an "open evening" was being held. "It was like a cattle show," she recalls. "The place was full of sociologists, social workers and well-to-do Montrealers who had come there to choose us to do whatever jobs they needed help with. Because of the education I had acquired, I stood out like a shining star in that group. I had been a voracious reader and had spent most of my time, aside from the period of manual labour, in relatively civilized surroundings. Most of my peers were barely literate."[3]

Musia was quickly chosen by a rich family from Westmount who needed a maid. But she didn't last long. "I had been on my own since I was twelve," she explains. "I couldn't fit into that highly structured household." She entered business college, where she completed the year's course in six months.

Then she became an assistant book-keeper with Samuelson Limited, a men's clothing manufacturer, and signed up for Layton's evening classes in English.

"I was amazed, stunned and *intimidated*," she recalls of Irving's classes. "He had a very genuine interest in the students, an interest wed to compassion. I never spoke to him; he was always surrounded by many others. But his voice was enough to start you on fire. He would read us poems like Wordsworth's 'Daffodils.' His eyes would fill with tears. This was beautiful. He was never sarcastic, but remained patient and respectful. He would fish for stories. He was a good listener, a collector of stories."

In the fall of 1960 Musia, nearing thirty, registered in Layton's modern-poetry course. "His teaching had changed," Musia observed. "He was more expansive. His classes were pretty directed and structured compared to other teachers. He would never knock a poet. He brought out the strengths of each. He didn't mention his own poetry.

"We began meeting for conversations. We had marathon talks about literature, life, appearance and reality, personal problems, films, plays and poems. He and I were alike emotionally. We're both like happy puppies. We're big-hearted people whose feelings overflow like lava. I remember especially Irving coming round to discuss movies he'd seen. He'd come striding in rubbing his hands together and ask, 'What do you think about *Suddenly Last Summer* or *Cat on a Hot Tin Roof* or *The Night Porter?*' He liked the modern film method of free association. He'd sit down at my kitchen table, and I'd get him coffee and something to eat. He would try to construct the consciousness of the author, but it was really his own that he revealed. His relationship to me remained that of mentor to student, but I never felt eclipsed. If he disapproved of what I said, he was reduced to insults, but that never affected the core of our friendship. Sometimes we'd shout in duet, then later have a loving conversation. He also used to come to me after his frequent fights with Aviva."

"I was jealous," Aviva remembers. She confirms that Hella, "Our Lady of the Perpetual Perfume" in *Nobody's Daughter*, was partly based on Musia.[4] "I was always yelling at Irving. I refused to believe it, knowing it was true. There were double lies going on all the time. He kept coming home smelling of that perfume. It got worse and worse. I would cry. I spied on him. I'd lie there late at night knowing that his classes at Sir George had ended at nine-thirty or ten o'clock. I'd be rigid, my heart pounding. I'd get up at midnight and take sleeping pills. The stress was horrifying. Musia began to turn up everywhere — at parties Irving and I were invited to, at conferences and readings of his, at our apartment when I was out. They'd disappear from parties we were all at for four hours or so and then return."

"Aviva certainly did get hysterical," recalls Bill Goodwin, who was often on the scene. "When Irving was visiting Musia, she was convinced he was deserting and betraying her. 'Women are my workshop,' he used to tell me. Musia offered him relaxation. She was down-to-earth, talkative and admiring. He needed relief from Aviva. I think he also enjoyed creating a disturbance."[5]

"Aviva wanted to twine around me like an ivy and choke me," Layton recalls.[6] "Someone told her that they had seen me ringing Musia's doorbell. There was no liaison at that time. It was a 'coffee romance.' But Aviva wouldn't listen. The poem 'If I Lie Still' was written about my despairing mood at the time. We agreed — not for the first time — to separate. But we couldn't. Musia gave me what Aviva couldn't. She was older, closer to my own age. [In fact, Musia was only three years older than Aviva.] We have a similar background. I devoured her stories of Warsaw and ghetto life. She had had a terrible adolescence. I was fascinated. There was an instant bond of sympathy and affection — also physical desire. It was strange and sinister, but the more she told me about her other sexual experiences — even about another lover she took soon after she became involved with me — the more I desired her. Her husband was occupied with his business and she was lonely. We talked endlessly about Donne, Shakespeare, politics, everything. She introduced me to the great Russian and European writers like Kafka and Babel. I helped her with her MA thesis, 'The Holy Fool in the Novels of Nathaniel West.'" (Her Ph.D. in comparative literature, on Isaac Babel, was called

"Prophets for a Cold Age.") Layton tried to persuade Jack McClelland to publish her recollections in 1959.[7]

"She never looked to me as if her life was a Greek tragedy," Aviva remarks, certain that the incestuous relationship she had endured with her father as a child was as tragic as anything Musia had known. "She had money, cars, cleaning ladies. Irving and I had much less."[8]

A Question of Value

"What do you really value?" Pacey asked Layton in June 1963. "I see [from an article in the *Globe*]...that you are still emitting a stream of platitudes about poetry, professors & penises.... I still think you are playing a dangerous game: rhetoric is a habit that grows on one & is no substitute for, but rather an antidote against, real thought. Instead of allowing your tongue — or pen — to freewheel all the time, I'd like to see you really engage the fears of your mind some time.... I'd like to see you spell out just what you do believe... and not keep evading the crucial issues by taking pot-shots at straw-men of your own contriving."[1]

From the "grand height" of "Old Smoky Face," his rented villa in Lista del Correos, Spain, a sun-drenched Layton wrote back condescendingly.

> I look down at your poor frustrations and unease and offer you absolution from all sins present or to come — and they *will* come.... It's well-intentioned fellows like you and Frye who are a menace to the creative life in Canada. Please don't take offence: I know more about these matters than you do.... For me the poet is the complete man... It's because there's a great danger the spirit might be smothered by bald-headed fartless academics

that poets like myself...have spoken out as savagely as we have.... You will probably dismiss [this] with the word "rhetorical" and accuse me of "posturing" — two doombird shrieks you habitually give the barren, pathetic air when confronted by an experience you cannot comprehend.[2]

Layton had read Shakespearean and Greek tragedy, but somehow the concepts of *hubris* and *nemesis* had eluded him.

Half a year later, Pacey still was pressuring his friend "to discuss [the] basic problem of values by which men should and can live in the present world. Although you show your faith in the dionysian way, it seems to me that you are never very clear or very subtle in defining it or in recognizing its limitations... As Yeats said, 'In dreams begin responsibilities!'... For god's sake try to be clear and exact and relevant and [don't] subject me to a drench of cloudy misty rhetoric of your usual variety. I don't want to be faked as if I were a love-sick sophomore in one of your classes."[3]

Pacey's question was sincere, and it was timely. During the mid-sixties, Layton would have been forced to face the question of values if Pacey posed it or not. There simply wasn't enough time for him to develop fully in each of the many worlds he inhabited. He was unsure about his own priorities and preferred to rely on the mood of the moment for his sense of direction. Consequently, his aims were erratic, complicated and often conflicting. Should he write more poems or turn to short stories, a novel or an autobiography? Should he give up teaching to write or give up writing to teach and meet his increasing number of opportunities to read to, record for or lecture to the public? Should he concentrate on strengthening his marriage to Aviva or serve as mentor, guide and moral support for the large number of young poets, students and fans who approached him for help? Did he have an obligation to live up to his reputation as Canada's Dionysian lover-poet? Or did he have a greater obligation to the three households to which he was contributing? These questions became most acute in 1963 when Aviva, after two disappointing miscarriages, became pregnant with what they hoped was a girl. (They jokingly planned to call her "Fanny

Hill Layton.") Should he list "father" as top-most among the roles he illogically wished to play simultaneously?

He tested one hypothetical self after another on Pacey and others. Perhaps the most ludicrous was that of "scholar," a role he suddenly exhumed from his graduate-school days at McGill.

> I'm living up to my resolution made in July 1964 and broken in December 1964 not to write any poetry this summer. Instead, I've settled down to a fairly steady routine in which I spend several hours each day doing Maths, French and philosophy. All three subjects are coming along fine. I'm reading Maupassant in the original, as well as Verlaine and Musset. Maths I intend to make a lifetime study — *there's* thinking for you, *thought*.... In the fall I'll either get myself a tutor or register at the University.[4]

Layton's theories of the poet also had become more complicated and brought him face to face with a paradox he could not resolve. "It's hard to be a poet," he complained to Pacey,

> and harder, I suppose to be married to one. As you know, I've always maintained that a poet must take risks and be prepared to pay a price to see that his sensibility doesn't go stale in time. He must adventure into new and strange modes of feeling *or* become a tom cat spouting oratund [sic] pieties. Perhaps cats mixes up my metaphor badly. Let's say "eunuch" then. If and when I decide I'm no longer willing to pay the price, I shall stop writing poems and tell all my friends including yourself, never to mention poetry in my presence. Everything else but *intense* living and the writing that [it] makes possible I consider literary palaver, "culture". Don't misunderstand me here. In the classroom I can be as academic as the next fellow, but as someone who has lived, suffered, enjoyed, and written while "on the run" so to speak, I know the difference between the two activities; and if sometimes I bore or irritate you by insisting on that difference it's surely because better

than anyone else, in this country, anyhow, I've had the chance to apprehend that difference. Any poetry that's worth anything, that's going to mean anything to anybody and be remembered comes from an excited awareness of the beauty and terror of existence. I'm fifty-two now. Few poets have so consistently and unremittingly tried to become acquainted with those "terrible truths" as I have for the past quarter-of-a-century. You'd be close to the mark if you thought of me as a cold-blooded scientist who deliberately injects a malevolent virus into himself to study its effects. If that sounds too clinical, let me add that the experiment in "controlled irrationality" has yielded me experiences that no one could have predicted and insights and emotions I could have had in no other way. I was determined that middle-age was not going to douse my flame as it has so many of my contemporaries. Life is what I'm after. I have a never-to-be satisfied curiosity about one stretch of human emotions. For me that's the real stuff of poetry; everything else is commentary. I've little use for that monstrous hybrid "philosophical poetry" — if I want philosophy or religion I know where I can get it pure. From the philosophers and mystics. Narrative poetry in our day of TV and movies, is boring and archaic. Which leaves only the lyric — which is fine, since that's the authentic core of all true poetry. So to cut back to what I was saying before — no emotion, no poetry. So much of contemporary poetry strikes me as being devoid of feeling or a sterile harangue that wishes to cover up for the absence of personal experience.[5]

In the euphoria that accompanied the birth of Peter Herschel Layton on 24 July 1964, Layton felt confident that Aviva, who had published several children's stories, would make an excellent, "warm" mother. His priority, he said, was fatherhood:

> I look forward to a great deal of happiness with Aviva and my son. When I had my other children, Max and Naomi, I was lost to this world — five teaching jobs to hold down, private lessons, a sick mother, debts, and

turning out two volumes of poetry each year — to have much time or thought for them. I shall always regret this, yet looking back on that period I know for a certainty there was no other way of living possible for me at the time. Something drove me on, a feverish delirium, that gave me no rest. I marvel I'm still alive when I recall some of the mad things I got myself into — or that I'm not in a sanatorium or a looney-bin.

Well things are going to be different now. I intend to spend a lot of time with my family, and if I don't write another line of poetry for the next three or four years, it wouldn't bother me in the least.[6]

Layton was reminded of all his paternal responsibilities when Peter (who was soon renamed David) was born, for Max unexpectedly arrived from San Francisco that very day "looking great." Layton had been toying for some time with the possibility of "retiring." 'I want to be independent so that I need never be afraid of speaking my mind — and it's that I'm after, not great wealth, though I don't doubt that if I put my peculiar business talents [for real estate] into the making of money, I could end up this country's first millionaire poet."[7] He had considered permanently leaving Canada. He had even attempted (unsuccessfully) to buy the villa he and Aviva had stayed at in Spain. But his responsibilities to Betty, Max and Naomi preyed on him. These responsibilities arose from an odd combination of guilt and ambition. He was helping to pay off Betty's mortgage for her; he had sent her a hundred dollars to buy a car to drive to Montreal, and had loaned her their Somerled apartment for the summer of 1965, when he and Aviva were in Greece, so that she had somewhere to stay with the children. He promised Max a thousand dollars a year to spend in Greece to work on his novel, provided he liked the first draft. (Max did not show him sections of the novel, but friends of Layton's who had seen parts of it reported that Layton was a central character, a victim of women.) Layton also offered Naomi (who had taken up modern dance and classical guitar) money for a trip to Greece after she finished high school.

Though Betty later would complain that Layton was erratic

about sending money and that he was more generous to Max than to Naomi, his on-going sense of obligation to the three was never absent. His financial planning during the next two decades always figured varying amounts of money for each according to his or her needs as he perceived them. This made retirement impossible.

Financial matters were not really a serious problem. But his conflicts about fatherhood were. Aviva's long-sought-after pregnancy had not been halcyon. Disputes over Musia came to a crisis around the seventh month. Irving had taken a separate room at 6420 Somerled, very near Musia's home, to write undisturbed during Aviva's pregnancy. He often came home well-perfumed. Finally, "I telephoned her and really grovelled," Aviva recalls.[8] "I asked her to come over and talk about it. I was pregnant, lying on the sofa when she arrived. She was wearing a miniskirt up to her crotch over patterned stockings and a patent belt around her waist. She looked like someone going to a discotheque. I begged her to keep away from Irving until the baby was born. It was like a scene from a Bette Davis movie. She told me that Irving wouldn't leave her alone. 'He breaks down my door,' she said. She explained that Irving needed and wanted her."

"I wanted to have it out with Aviva," Musia recalls.[9] "I told her that Irving only loved her. He had no intention of eloping with me nor I with him. He was important to me as a teacher, a father-surrogate and a friend. I thought her worries were fantasies, chimeras. Aviva was too possessive."

Two days after David was born, Layton left with his nephew, Bill, for "a few weeks" to visit Betty and Naomi in San Francisco. How could this desertion, as Aviva thought of it, be reconciled with Layton's apparently genuine pledge to "spend a lot of time with the family"?

As Betty had observed, Irving was not good at birth times, despite the fact that he wanted children. Was there something about the whole idea of birth that disturbed him? He had referred, in his preface to *The Laughing Rooster,* written five months before David's birth, to a time without writing poems as "barrenness;" he described the state of readiness to write as "my head felt like a cloud pregnant with rain."[10] Later, he had referred to poetic inspiration in a letter as a "great impregnation."[11] Poems seemed to him like things inside him that were delivered into objective form when the time was ripe. Did a pregnant woman present a flesh-and-blood delivery of life that was more alive than his poems? Were women the very paradigms of creativity? Was this an experience from which he was forever excluded? One with which he could not compete?[12]

"Irving took more interest in his mistresses' children than he did in David," Aviva observed. "He'd send them flowers, go to their bar mitzvahs and so on. I often couldn't sleep with him. I had spent most of the pregnancy by myself. He slept in his study when he wanted. I was hurt when he went away after David was born. Before he went he'd look at me and David and ask, 'Do you like him?' 'Do you *love* him?' David got the short end of the stick. Irving didn't take much notice of him."

Shortly after Irving returned from San Francisco to begin a heavy teaching load (two new courses at the YMHA and a new grade-twelve class at Ross Tutorial School), Aviva took David and left for Australia to stay with her mother. "Going to Australia was leaving Irving," Aviva observed.[13] It felt permanent.

In the political sphere, Layton had conflicts to resolve, too. He had been angered by Pacey's charge, in his review of *Balls for a One-Armed Juggler*, that Layton had lost his Marxism. Layton claimed that he was as Marxist as ever. He had little hope of being believed, since he favoured American intervention in Vietnam. He thought the Americans should have begun getting tough with the Russians over Suez, and mentioned to Pacey his contempt for John Foster Dulles, who was too soft. He came close to asking himself whether his political views were really knee-jerk reactions against whatever was fashionable among intellectuals:

> Whenever F.R. Scott takes up a political position, all one has to do is to take up the contrary one and be proven right in the long run....Sterile intellectualism personified. That gray, rationalistic, goody-goodness that has undone the CCF and now the NDP. Not even a touch of

imagination... The man has a deep distrust of life, a distrust of its unpredictable upsurge. He's going around preaching fascism and blue ruin (the usual socialistic balderdash) and repeats or encourages the nonsense that his friend Blair Fraser is writing in *Maclean's*.[14]

In December 1963, Layton predicted that Richard Nixon would be the Republican candidate to run against Johnson in the 1964 election. *"And it wouldn't surprise me if Nixon were elected.* He's a complex, Dostoevskian character whom failure has taught a great deal about himself and the world. I think he'd surprise everyone by making an extraordinary president.... Nixon in some ways resembles Lincoln. Both are introverted, complex, shifty. Both knew poverty and humiliation. And both have guts. How's that for heresy?"[15] But on another tack altogether, he also was reflecting the new left-wing preoccupation with peace. "The great issue of our time is PEACE (with honour)."[16] Layton never had developed any true sense of political consciousness. He was anything he wanted to be, no matter what the contradictions.

Was he Marxist or right-wing? Did he believe in war or peace? Or were his political views taken up on the spur of the moment on account of their heresy? He seemed unable to think this through.

A situation he got into with Pacey about some poems seemed typical of his confusions in almost every one of his many worlds. Pacey had written in April 1964 to ask for "first call" on five poems, "At the Iglesia del Sacromonte," "Silly Rhymes for Aviva," "For My Green Old Age," "My Queen, My Quean" (a poem about Musia) and "Encounter."[17] Irving had sent him the poems for publication in the *Literary Review* Pacey was editing. Layton agreed Pacey could have first call. On 3 June, Pacey wrote to report that Fred Cogswell had told him that Layton had submitted "For My Green Old Age" to Cogswell, and that it was to be in the February issue of *Fiddlehead*. "Are the other four clear of entanglements?" Pacey asked. On 6 June, Layton assured him they were, said he had no recollection of sending Cogswell the poem and instructed Pacey to tell Cogswell that he would send a replacement poem if Cogswell would give the first poem to

Pacey. Cogswell reported that it was too late. On 4 December, Pacey wrote an irritated letter after seeing the four poems he believed "clear of entanglement" in Layton's latest collection, *The Laughing Rooster* (named, tentatively, "Poems in Bad Taste," then "A Wind Out of Hades"). Pacey demanded some new unpublished poems. Layton sent him "Beauty" and "Strange Turn."[18] Pacey wrote back to complain that they were not "you at your best." He thought "A Strange Turn" was "not sincere or logical." He rather liked "Beauty." He did not recognize that it was a poem from Layton's 1953 collection (now out of print), *Love the Conqueror Worm*. Was Layton deliberately dishonest with his closest friend? Or did his right hand not know what his left hand was doing? Was anything in his life clear of entanglements and confusion?

There is some indication that Layton knew that contradictions were overwhelming him. During the mid-sixties, he found himself in occasional depressions and "black moods," and expressed his "bafflement and terror" at life. There was something touching about the thought of him standing amid the vast collection of letters, manuscripts and papers he had collected together to sell for $3,600[19] to the University of Saskatchewan in 1965:

> When I finished putting things in order, tears stood in my eyes when I surveyed the mass of correspondence, etc on the large dining-table. They were tears of self-pity, elation, pride, and, yes, relief. If the evidence wasn't before my own eyes I'd never believe that anyone holding down five teaching jobs, looking after a sick mother and an ailing wife, and turning out two books annually could have done it. And done it single-handedly, without any secretaries, or anyone else to help him. I know I'm bragging, but let me go on, and consider the outburst as a sort of delayed nervous breakdown. Man, I must have been insane in those years. My correspondence alone, apart from letters to yourself, runs into the thousands. There's hardly a Canadian poet, young or old, that I haven't been writing to over the years. I have about 75 letters from Purdy alone, and from Souster and Dudek about one hundred apiece. I have an extended

correspondence with Robert Creeley, Cid Corman, Jonathan Williams, Earle Birney, Hugh Kenner, Milton Wilson, — putting these altogether, the Canadian poets and critics, and the American ones, I've corresponded with almost sixty persons. And this does not include miscellaneous correspondence, dealing with lecture tours, readings, advice to countless Canadians who have written to me for one reason or another, or the hundreds of letters relating to the publication of my books.... Relief, man, relief is what I feel. And gratitude that I've come through without my mental or physical health impaired. I know all this must sound like babbling to you, but when I think back over the past two decades, so full of tension and glory, the haste, the heat, the broken marriages, what astonishes me is the stubbornness and excellent health that saw me through it all. And now my intuition is to leave all that behind me. Let some one else take up the quarrel with the foe. And here, I can't help remarking somewhat wryly that no one appears too eager to do so — in fact, it would seem that I've been hacking away all alone for more than two decades, and not a single individual willing to risk either skin or reputation to draw the fire away from me for even a moment. Brave country mine, I applaud you![20]

Layton's recognition that he was having "a delayed nervous breakdown" and his relief that he was physically and mentally all right were not surprising, given what had happened to some of the people he knew. "I could have ended up [mad] like A.M. Klein," he later commented.[21] For several of his brothers and sisters, too, ill health and mental breakdown had been all too real. If his eldest brother, Avram, had been struck down merely for breaking an engagement, how had Layton, with his increasingly flamboyant sexual escapades, escaped punishment? When a little cheese-making had been enough to break his father's health, how had he, with his high-voltage existence, maintained his? Layton came very close, in that room of his, surrounded by the massive evidence of the delirium of his previous years, to learning from his experience. But he did not change. He would not or could not subjugate any one aspect of his life to any other, no matter how inconsistent or mad their co-existence might be. He clung to each of his many worlds as if his life depended on it.

Just as he stubbornly refused to establish rational priorities in his life, he had trouble doing so with his art. "At present I'm working on my *Collected Poems*, which will be published next autumn," he wrote to Pacey in the letter that announced David's birth. The volume, as he saw it, was to be a sum-up of his poetry, a milestone marked before he turned to prose. Pacey urged him, as Jack McClelland had, to "be really ruthless and excise all...trash."[22] But from the 425 poems that remained "after considerable pruning,"[23] Layton had great difficulty selecting. "I'm very pleased with the selection I made," he wrote to Pacey when the volume appeared in October 1965, "though it was not made without a good deal of heartburning. I almost drove myself mad, putting in and taking out poems, and even now I have one or two regrets for poems I kept out... Say: 'Afternoon of a Coupon Clipper' — why in the devil did I omit that one from the collection? Or the poignant 'Mother, This Is Spring.' Ah well, maybe two years from now McStew [Jack McClelland] will bring out another Collected, and this time I'll throw [in] the works."[24] Though he was at times clear-sighted and critical of his own work ("some poems...I've already extracted from...my nightmare...for *The Laughing Rooster*," he admitted to Pacey, "are hit-and-miss affairs, ejaculations rather than the omniscient, compassionate things I want them to be"[25]), he never declined to publish whenever and wherever he could. In his life he could not bear to cut off any side of his nature; in his poems, he was not prepared to sacrifice any expression of his multi-faceted life. Making the best of the situation, the advertising for Layton's next book, *Periods of the Moon* (a more "bitter" book), took this line: "He is often criticised for being too prolific, and for publishing everything that he writes, the bad along with the good. I see this not as pride but as a form of humility: Layton knows that he is not always at his best, but he is willing to let us see him in his off-moments as well as in his moments of magical success. More power to him: it enables us to see his development, to measure his best poems by his worst, and to savour the tiny pleasure that can be found even in his mistakes."[26]

Layton's insistence on preserving and indulging in all sides of nature and his inability to withhold publication of work he felt was inferior did seem like a fault to some and a virtue to others. To Pacey, who had continued to urge a sense of perspective on his friend by pressing him to examine his "values and make choices among his women, his publishers and his poems," it was a fault. "You should be red with shame, to prostitute your talent (*once* genuine, however limited) to such crass Madison Avenue capers," he reprimanded Layton when he heard that Layton had gone across Canada with Leonard Cohen, Earle Birney and Phyllis Gotlieb as a publicity stunt for Canadian poetry engineered by Jack McClelland and filmed by the National Film Board. "Can you imagine Donne or Yeats parading around with two other dancing bears to make a Roaming Holiday?"[27] To Leonard Cohen, who had just won the Prix littéraire de Québec for his novel *The Favorite Game*, and whose poetry collection *Flowers for Hitler* came out simultaneously with Layton's *The Laughing Rooster* and Birney's *November Walk Near False Creek Mouth*, it was a virtue. "Irving is a good custodian of his talent," Cohen says. "He hasn't let self-destruction get a foothold. He has an innocence, a purity, that is absolutely unsoiled. That innocence has allowed him to examine everything and to be affected by everything. It is the source of his health which is considerable. It is why he will never grow, his work or himself. His sense of the urgency of the poetic identity is unparalleled. He's lived it, examined it and knows how it can survive, if we want it to survive. He understands the role of the artist as a self-maintained identity whose very existence is in jeopardy. His poems come from many points of view, from many postures. Some are Sermons on the Mount (from a high place with a large vista); some are delivered upright; some are given lying down; others reclining on one elbow; some are prayers written while on his knees; others are glimpsed through a key-hole. But none of them are written from a crouch. He has danced through the whole world and embraced it with assertions, celebrations and judgements."[28]

Whether it was a rationalization of problems he was unable

to face and helpless or afraid to deal with, Layton refused to establish his values, as Pacey had urged him to do. He seemed genuinely to believe that he would lose more than he would gain. Even his bluffing, overly rhetorical arguments seemed to serve his purpose. "I cream off [from them] the requisite emotions I need for my poems," he acknowledged to Pacey, "which is a rather nasty thing I do with life in general."[29] (He attributed "Icarus" to Pacey's accusation that he was bluffing.) It was not just that he needed total immersion in life to feed his poetry; he needed even more the conflicts his erratic inconsistencies engendered if he was to maintain his "metaphysical sense of evil," what he called "the dark heart and centre" of his work. "The poet is not a gentleman," he explained to Pacey as he considered calling his next book of poems (eventually titled *The Laughing Rooster*) "Poems in Bad Taste." "His whole aim and purpose is to upset the canons of good taste. The older I grow the less patience I have with 'society,' which I'm coming to see more and more as a block of ice that must be melted by the poet's passion. Society is only a variant spelling of hypocrisy. It's forever at war with whatever is fresh, vital and creative.... The poet is alone with his experience: that's his *unique* glory and martyrdom. That's the live coal that everyone else waits for to cool down and become a clinker."[30] He seemed not to hear Jack McClelland's warning: "If the collection is something less than your best, I wonder if it's advisable [to publish it]. I'm not that convinced that the market here is good enough to absorb a book a year."[31]

Armchair Traveller

"I see Leonard Cohen almost every week; have wonderful talks with him," Layton wrote in April 1964.

For hours at a time, sometimes all night, the elegant, patrician Cohen and his "fellow-traveller," the bumptious, proletarian Layton, would engage in "talkathons" that attempted to fathom the mysteries of the universe. "We had a deep interest in each other's experience," Cohen observes. "We enjoyed the intoxication of friendship."[1] Subjects ranged from politics, to poetry (for a time they "took Wallace Stevens apart to find out what his poems meant") to movies, their families and, of course, their women. "Irving never took an avuncular or paternal position towards me," Cohen insists, trying to shake free of the common view that Layton was his mentor. It would be just as true to say that Cohen was Layton's mentor, for Layton quickly absorbed and sometimes mimicked the younger poet's sayings and life-style. "My stance when he got talking about movies," Cohen recalls, "was that he didn't understand. [Cohen had commented once to Layton that Layton "didn't need an original to construct an interpretation."[2]] He, of course, thought that I didn't understand. Irving's a great talker and a great listener, though he's more attached to his opinions than I am. Those were marvellous evenings."[3]

In one of their talks, Cohen persuaded Layton to try some LSD. Layton had dismissed drug trips. What was an LSD experience compared to what went on in his imagination all the time? These kids were nuts, he claimed. There really wasn't any chemical effect. By dropping acid, they merely gave themselves permission to hallucinate, let go of their every-day repressions for once.

"I had come back from Mexico with a vial of LSD," Cohen recalls. "Probably enough to disturb the social equilibrium of the entire city. I wasn't evangelical about drugs. I thought they were kind of dangerous. But I had told Irving about my experiences. Irving has a delicate stomach. He didn't drink much then. He couldn't smoke much either. He got a stomach-ache if he smoked too long.

"Aviva was out, I remember. We were sitting in Irving's book-lined study. I gave him a pin-head of powder. I didn't take any at the same time. He took it. When nothing happened right away he boomed out, 'You've been taken, Leonard. You've been taken by these gangsters in Chicago. I'd better take more.'

"I told him he'd better wait. But he dipped the pin in and took another quite substantial dose. We waited another half hour. Irving said, 'Not only have you been taken, but this stuff gives me a stomach-ache!'

"Then he said, 'Did you notice? The books are moving. Baudelaire has just moved out of the shelf and bowed to Victor Hugo. There's Shakespeare. Can you hear him? The carpet's moving. Did you see that?'

"He was in some kind of gathering of the greats, amidst the intercourse of mighty minds. Plato was there. Shakespeare was there. I guess it was the pedagogical habit. He kept explaining it all to me. I watched with admiration and delight. His mind was so pure. Filled with such light and understanding of himself and this world of spirits. His was a classical beatific vision.

"Then he looked at the square portrait of his mother on the wall. He said, 'The whole room is undulating like petals underwater in the wind. In the centre is my mother. Everything — the emanating rose petals — are coming from her.' It was a vision of innocence. He was alive in that pure infant vision."[4]

Où Sont Les Jeunes?

There was one thing Pacey and Layton agreed on, though they had reached an ethical impasse about values and their correspondence began to wane until it ended in 1975 with Pacey's death from cancer. They agreed that the younger poets in Canada didn't measure up. "The sad thing is that there doesn't seem to be a single good poet under thirty," Pacey had said in June 1964. "I should love to represent 'les jeunes' [in *The Literary Review*], but where are their poems? The stuff I got from Boxer, Coleman, Pearson, Davey, Bowering, etc. would make us [Canadians] look like laughingstocks abroad."[1] Layton wrote back:

> What you say about the young poets in Canada agrees with my own feeling about them. They seem a dispirited lot, with not very much to say. The Tishbites [poets in *Tish*, the west-coast magazine] have been ruined by an excessive interest in prosody and by the influence of [Charles] Olson, [Robert] Creeley, and [Denise] Levertov. However, had [Frank] Davey, [George] Bowering et al been true poets they would have assimilated the influence and eventually found their own voice-levels. But a poet *is* a teacher, and these have no doctrine in them. The desire to make fastidious bric-a-brac, all the coquettings with words and line-placements will not conceal the

empty heart. If a man urgently wishes to improve the lot of his fellow-man, the quality of their lives, he'll discover or invent the means for reaching them — always presupposing he has the necessary talent with words, without which, of course, his good intentions will count for nil.[2]

In "To a Generation of Poets," a pithy little verse he thought was "mordant and Swiftian," Layton recorded his opinion:

> I don't wish to make you more nervous
>   than you already are
> but truthfulness compels me to say
>   I find jars
>
> Of pickled foetuses
>   more interesting in every way
> than the self-lacerated hearts
>   you display in your verses.[3]

Modern poetry in Canada had moved into a new phase. Layton was no longer at its centre. Indeed, to many younger poets he was not a relevant figure. He had served his purpose, a crucial one in the development of modern poetry, but it was time to make way for the next generation. Layton was not prepared to budge. Al Purdy, he thought, lacked form. James Reaney, who had won Governor-General's Awards for *A Suit of Nettles* in 1958 and for *Twelve Letters to a Small Town* in 1962, was too "mythopoeic" and "aesthetic" for Layton's taste. He dismissed Reaney as one of the Toronto set — Northrop Frye, Robert Finch and Jay Macpherson — he despised so much. His inability to see merit in any of the younger poets except Leonard Cohen was exactly the kind of blindness that would have infuriated him beyond measure had it been directed at his own youthful poetic efforts.

A number of factors had resulted in a shift of focus in Canadian poetry, and contributed to the widespread feeling, expressed succinctly by Raymond Souster in his preface to *New Wave Canada: The Explosion In New Canadian Poetry* (1966), that "after one hundred years of our history," Canadian poetry was "at last vigorous and very sure of where it is going."[4]

The arduous struggle of the Montreal modernists, even their struggles with each other, had contributed greatly to the widening circles of poetic endeavour that were rippling across the country. By example, the poets of the forties had demonstrated that poetry was something Canadians could and should take seriously and that it was possible for committed poets to collect and publish Canadian poetry on a shoe-string budget without going through the "formal" channel of established magazine editors or publishers. By insisting that poetry express the voice of the ordinary man, the three "proletarian poets" of *Other Canadians* had succeeded in dragging poetry down from the ivory tower and out of the stuffy drawing-room into the market-place. In 1963, Jack McClelland rightly observed that "poems...sell in greater quantity than the average novel or work of non-fiction."[5]

Dudek asserted that "the most important single factor behind the rise and continued progress of Canadian poetry" was "the little magazine." To the *Canadian Forum* (established in 1920) and university magazines like *Queen's Quarterly* (established in 1893), neither of which were dedicated primarily to publishing poetry, had been added a number of literary magazines across the country. In 1967, Canada's centennial year, they numbered about eighty. The growth had been gradual at first: *Fiddlehead*, at the University of New Brunswick, in 1945; *Tamarack Review*, a Toronto literary journal conceived by Robert Weaver to replace John Sutherland's *Northern Review*, in 1956; and *Tish*, in Vancouver, in 1961, to mention but a cardinal few.[6] The poetry centre of Canada was no longer Montreal, though in the forties Montreal had been the crucible of the future. "In the last two years," Frank Davey wrote excitedly in 1962 in an article called "Anything But Reluctant: Canada's Little Magazines,"[7] "*Moment* (edited in Toronto by Al Purdy and Milton Acorn, then by Acorn and his wife, Gwen MacEwen), *Mountain* (put out by David McFadden in Hamilton), *Evidence* (edited by Alan Bevan in Toronto), *Cataract* (edited by Sydney Aster, a former Layton student, in Montreal), *Tish* and *Motion* (Vancouver's newsletters) have all appeared. In Vancouver alone, three new ones are projected." Davey criticised *Cataract*'s writer-editors for "spending more time thumbing their noses than...writing poetry." He disapproved of Irving Layton's "Open Letter to Louis Dudek" because it seemed merely a defense of "Layton's own waning reputation." He thought Layton's poem "To a Lily" (a satire, which Layton believed "pretty well drives a stave through [Smith's] entrails")[8] in the same issue of *Cataract* "defensive and high-schoolish."

It wasn't that Layton's submissions to the little magazines were falling off — both his productivity and the level of his verse remained much as they had been throughout the fifties. His remoteness from the centre of poetic activities was the result of his abandoning responsibility for fostering the little poetry magazines and, through them, experiencing a direct involvement with the growing corps of younger writers. He certainly had direct contact with large numbers of aspiring poets, but they were his students, his "coffee romances" and the fans who read his books or met him at readings and public lectures. He did not have access to the infrastructure of literary magazines he had once helped to launch. Unlike Dudek, who laboured at his own press, and sometimes at his own expense, to bring out the work of younger poets in *Delta*, and Souster, who continued his Contact Press, which undertook his fourth little magazine, *Combustion* (1957-1960), Layton laid himself open to the criticism that he hadn't directly worked at a magazine any longer than necessary to see his own poems published.

Just as he had unceremoniously dropped the American poets — Creeley, Olson and Corman — when they no longer served his purposes (after William Carlos Williams introduced Layton's *The Improved Binoculars* in 1956), he had removed himself from the editorial scene in the little magazines that were the life-blood of younger poets and the central network for the expression of new confidence and variety in Canada's poetic voice.

In 1952, when Layton wrote his preface for *Cerberus*, he had observed that "The Canadian poet...is an exile condemned to live in his own country. He has no public, commands no following, stirs up less interest than last year's licence plate."[9] But fifteen years later, a revolution had been effected. Though it was an exaggeration to claim, as Leonard Cohen did, that "Irving Layton converted a whole generation to poetry,"[10] he had made a strong impact. The initiation of the CBC in 1932 and the appearance of producers like Robert Weaver, who saw and acted on the potential entertainment value of Canadian poetry and Canadian culture generally; the founding of the Canada Council and the beginning of new awards and fellowships; the sudden accessibility of television in the mid-fifties and the possibilities for widespread media coverage; the popularity of poetry with the younger "beat" generation in the late fifties; the incursion of "poetic" lyrics through folk-songs into the broad popular music scene; and the successful proliferation of little poetry magazines across Canada all played key roles, too. Still, Layton had been a central figure. Dudek singled out William Carlos Williams's introduction to Layton's book as the point at which "a radical change" occurred, "the beginning of a new direction" in Canadian poetry.[11] Joan Finnegan pointed to the Canadian Conference of the Arts at Toronto's O'Keefe Centre (4 to 6 May 1961) as symbolic of Canada's entrance into "a golden age" of poetry. "Take away the socialites, hangers-on, 'culturettes' and merely curious," she wrote in the *Globe and Mail*, "and it might be safely claimed that the remaining crowd of earnest listeners was one of the largest live audiences ever faced by Canadian poets."[12] At the conference, which addressed visual, literary and dramatic arts and music in English and French Canada, poetry was read by Earle Birney, Leonard Cohen, Jay Macpherson and Layton in English and by Gilles Hénault in French. As Finnegan saw it, "Layton, as usual, stole the day. First he delivered a pithy off-the-cuff dissertation on the boring pomposity of the speakers who had opened the conference." [These included Claude Bissell, Northrop Frye and Jean-Charles Falardeau.] Then he read some of his most valid poems, such as 'The Bull Calf.' Finally, he delighted his audience with a new poem, '*Why I don't make love to the first Lady*,' a eulogy to Jacqueline Kennedy.... more and more Canadian poets are being listened to."[13] Layton's powerful stage presence, his debating skills, his long-haired "movie-star" appearance, his strong, resonant voice and his "feel" for his audience lent themselves to media coverage in a way no other poet could compete with. "Charisma" was a word unheard of at the time, but perhaps it was no coincidence that Pierre Elliott Trudeau, the man who would give the word a popular meaning for Canada in the late sixties, was coming into the national limelight. Both men had the kind of appeal that could sweep large audiences, and audiences were ready to be swept. Partly because of Irving Layton, poets and poetry in Canada became "news."

But a subtle shift had taken place since Layton's emergence at the top of Canada's poetic heap in the early sixties. Layton, like the "beats" in America and the "angry young men" in England, had "given vent to open rage and revolt" to shatter the "intense exclusivity" of the more aesthetic modern poets. But now that they had accomplished their aim, something else was called for.

Dudek speculated that Leonard Cohen would emerge as "the key figure" in the post-war generation of Canadian poets.[14] Layton had been a rebel with a cause, but Cohen, like the James Dean hero who seemed to speak for a younger group of affluent, disaffected idealists, was a rebel without one. He spoke on behalf of a group like himself. Innocent of the Depression and the Second World War, they suffered from a peculiar malaise, the result of leading pampered lives in a "consumer society" that, paradoxically, faced possible atomic annihilation. As this social shift took place, the tone of voice in poetry changed correspondingly. The bombastic rhetoric of Layton's satiric verses, the touching irony of his metaphysical speculations and the majestic inflections of his tragic relevations seemed too grand, too forced, too confident of right and wrong to express the more muted anxieties of the next generation. "Modernism" had been replaced by "post-modernism." Like Layton, against the wall of whose mind he had been bouncing his poems, his ideas and his feelings for several years, Cohen had the kind of personality the media could exploit. He was tall, dark and gently attractive. His stance and even his voice (which Purdy described as seductively "poppied") resembled those of American singer Bob Dylan. His love poems were modest, unassuming, delicate; they expressed the sexual longings of a generation that wasn't as sure as Layton's that it believed in love. By 1966, at age thirty-two, Cohen had published three excellent volumes of poetry and two best-selling novels, *The Favorite Game* and *Beautiful Losers*. His books were selling better than Layton's.

The shift from Layton to Cohen took place almost allegorically in the fall of 1964. *Red Carpet* had sold 7,500 copies. Jack McClelland sent the two writers, with Earle Birney and Phyllis Gotlieb, on the Ontario-Quebec university-campus tour that McClelland swore would "ultimately benefit the cause of poetry in this country."[15] *Time* magazine reported that the two poets read to "jammed audiences" everywhere they went. The report reveals much about the differences between their public images:

> The rumpled, twinkling Layton, whose showmanship mainly carried off the readings, was careful not to let down his image offstage. At Queen's, he gamely grinned at a rapt semicircle of coeds and announced: "If Dylan were here, he'd be pinching bottoms." With Layton's image puckishly in mind, the junior English instructors who threw the party invited not a single coed whose comeliness did not merit invitation. With Cohen gone home, and the chairman of the English department tolerantly thumbing a book of Byzantine mosaics across the room, Layton propped an elbow on an ornate rosewood chest, surveyed the surrounding cleavage, and talked earnestly about the pill, the morality of seduction, necrophilia. One delightful thing hung so raptly on Layton's every word that before leaving, he promised to write her a little poem. It would be called, he said, "Dylan Thomas and the Coed."
>
> At Western Ontario, Leonard Cohen, in a black leather jacket, Caesar haircut and expertly mismatched shirt and tie, looked around and asked: "Is this a church?" When an undergraduate demanded to know "What makes a poem?" Cohen replied: "God. It's the same kind of operation as the creation of the world." All of which worried the paternal Layton. "Leonard," he advised, "you don't eat enough, drink enough, smile enough."[16]

National Film Board producer Don Owen called Layton "romantic" and Cohen a "hipster." The documentary film he produced on the four poets somehow ended up as a film about Leonard Cohen, *Ladies and Gentlemen...Mr. Leonard Cohen*. The hipster had succeeded the romantic.

But though Cohen may be the central figure in the shift that took place towards the end of the sixties, he was by no means the only fine poet enjoying success in Canada.

Times were changing rapidly. In 1959, when Layton published *A Red Carpet for the Sun*, twenty-four books of poetry were published. In 1970 almost five times that number (120 by George Woodcock's count) appeared.[17] In the mid-sixties Michael Ondaatje, Alden Nowlan, John Newlove, John Robert Colombo, Milton Acorn, Al Purdy, Dennis Lee, Gwendolyn MacEwen, George Bowering, George Johnston, Victor Coleman, Lionel Kearns, James Reaney, bill bissett and George Jonas, and in French Canada Anne Hébert, St.-Denys-Garneau, Suzanne Paradis, Rina Lasnier and Jacques Godbout were well on their way to becoming established. And, in 1966, a new voice was heard that would soon take a central place in Canadian poetry. Margaret Atwood, a poet groomed by Jay Macpherson and Northrop Frye at the University of Toronto's Victoria College, won the Governor-General's Award for her first collection of poems, *The Circle Game*.

"Until I, fabulist, have spoken they do not know their significance": Layton in the mid-50s.
CREDIT: BRIAN MERRETT
DONATED BY AVIVA LAYTON

A gaggle of poets: from left to right Earle Birney, E.J. Pratt, Irving Layton and Leonard Cohen in Toronto in the late 50's.
CREDIT: BRIAN MERRETT
DONATED BY AVIVA LAYTON

"I am this misty slate and a lump of chalk": Layton before a class at Sir George Williams University, Montreal in the late 1950s.
CREDIT: BRIAN MERRETT
DONATED BY AVIVA LAYTON

Irving and his "little one," Aviva Cantor, camping in the Laurentians early in their relationship.
CREDIT: BRIAN MERRETT
DONATED BY AVIVA LAYTON

"But I am burning flesh and bone": a poet in his prime.
CREDIT: ALINE, MONTREAL

The opening of the Seven Steps Bookstore on 13 June 1960 in Montreal: left to right, Henry Moscovitch, Irving Layton, Robert Silverman (owner), Frank Scott and Louis Dudek.
CREDIT: BRIAN MERRETT
DONATED BY PUBLISHERS WEEKLY

Musia Schwartz on holiday in Mexico during the 1960s.
CREDIT: BRIAN MERRETT
DONATED BY AVIVA LAYTON

Max, Naomi and David in the late 60s.
DONATED BY AVIVA LAYTON

"The girl with the wide-apart eyes": Marion Wagshall on the Promenade des Anglais in Nice, France 1967.
CREDIT: BRIAN MERRETT
DONATED BY AVIVA LAYTON

Leonard Cohen and the friend he called the "incomparable master of inner languages" of the Greek island of Hydra in 1968.
CREDIT: BRIAN MERRETT
DONATED BY AVIVA LAYTON

Layton with Desmond Pacey, the man he thought of as a brother, and Pacey's wife, Mary, after a poetry reading in Fredericton in 1970.
CREDIT: JOE STONE, THE *FREDERICTON GLEANER*
DONATED BY MARY PACEY

"On the lam" with Aviva at Molibos, Greece in the early 70s.
DONATED BY AVIVA LAYTON

Irving Layton gets off the train at Milan, Italy where he was met by his translator Francesca Valente (on his left) and her students from the Liceo Scientifico in 1974.
DONATED BY IRVING LAYTON

Layton becomes an Officer of the Order of Canada, 20 October 1976, wearing two-tone red and blue shoes.
CREDIT: BRIAN MERRETT
DONATED BY AVIVA LAYTON

A "My Fair Lady" wedding: Harriet Bernstein and Irving Layton.
CREDIT: BRIAN WILLER, *MACLEAN'S*

"Squire Layton" working his garden at Niagara-on-the-Lake in 1978.
CREDIT: DAVID McILVRIDE, *ST. CATHERINES STANDARD*

"Your mother's smile was your benediction": the birth of Samantha Clara Layton, January 1981.
CREDIT: *GLOBE AND MAIL*

At home with words 1982.
CREDIT: REG INNELL, *TORONTO STAR*

"*If I had married her in the first place, I probably would never have written any poetry*": "*Anna-Panna*" *and her* "*Bad Biscuit Boy*" *in Oakville, 1983.*
CREDIT: NOEL TAYLOR, *OTTAWA CITIZEN*

Over-Exposed

As Canada's centennial year dawned, Layton's persistent worry was "over-exposure." He had explained the puzzling centrality of Leonard Cohen in the filmed tour of 1964 as the result of Layton's too-frequent appearances before the public. "I didn't need the extra publicity," he rationalized to Pacey, "since I'd already appeared this year at Carleton University [before one thousand students], and had two readings scheduled at Toronto. Moreover, I'd already appeared in London Ont.; and about one week before the tour commenced, at McGill University. I was definitely running the risk of over-exposure in Montreal, Ottawa, Toronto, and London, and was therefore, extremely reluctant to take part in the tour."[1] Layton didn't need the money, either. He told Pacey that McClelland had vaguely suggested he might pay each of the poets a hundred dollars. (In fact, McClelland had offered two hundred dollars.[2]) But Layton was usually paid between one and two hundred dollars for readings that were less time-consuming and stressful.

What looked to Layton like the mismanagement of his career was actually a shift in the development of Canadian poetry. Though he was much in demand still, he was losing ground to the next generation. People were now turning to Leonard Cohen and his guitar, or to Margaret Atwood and the stiletto precision of her feminism. Layton was no longer Canada's literary lion, though his doings and pronouncements would continue to occasion press coverage. Fashions were changing fast, and no amount of *chutzpah*, vituperation or exuberance could turn the clock back.

It is possible to see, with hindsight, that Layton sensed that he no longer could dominate and mesmerize the poetry scene in Canada. He thought of his best poems as "anthology pieces." Poems that were anthologized were usually rigorously selected in competition with other poets' works, and also from among a writer's other pieces. Judging from the number of his poems that were widely anthologized, the mid-sixties represented a falling-off in the desireability of his poems as anthology pieces. During the 1940s, five of his poems had found their way into two or more collections, and during the 1950s, an impressive twenty-five poems had been selected by a range of editors in Canada and elsewhere for inclusion in anthologies: eleven of them had appeared in more than five collections. But during the 1960s, the number of Layton poems selected for more than one or two collections had dropped to fifteen, and the majority of those had been written in the early part of the decade. By the 1970s, only two of his poems were chosen for a significant number of editions. In the 1980s, only one. The seven poems most widely anthologized suggested the same arc of influence: "The Cold Green Element" (1954), "The Bull Calf" (1955), "The Birth of Tragedy" (1956), "Berry Picking" (1958), "Song for Naomi" (1960), "Keine Lazarovitch" (1960) and "A Tall Man Executes a Jig" (1961).[3] The high point in his career had been the late 1950s. As he felt increasingly usurped by younger poets in a literary scene he was accustomed to controlling, his frustration built. "Your reading is so boring it's putting me to sleep," he had roared at a Margaret Atwood reading. "Women are only good for screwing, men are good for screwing plus!" he had added insultingly.[4] To a friend, he wrote that the monotony of Atwood's voice reminded him of "Piss on a platter."[5] His personality was ill-suited to assuming the role of senior statesman.

By 1965, Layton had frequently remarked that he ought to leave Canada. "I feel I need a long rest from controversies and arguments that I myself began," he wrote. "The last thing I want to see happen to me is to be taken captive by my own image. I want freedom and blessed independence — even from myself. Perhaps mostly from myself."[6]

"It is not what you call my amazing productivity I want to take a rest from," he wrote to Pacey,

> but from being a one-man poetry corporation. [It's] the correspondence, the handing out of advice, the sending of the books, the replying to enquiries, the readings, etc. etc. — all this I must leave behind now if I'm to do the big things I have it in me to do both in poetry and fiction. I shall need solitude, peace of mind. If I can find it here in Canada, I'll stay here — otherwise, I'll do a Leonard Cohen disappearing act. The main thing is to cut free to hide from the public view for a couple of years, wrap myself in a black shell of anonymity from which I can pounce on a startled world five or six years from now — put an end to, for me now, one more stultifying dialogue I've been pouring in for nearly two decades with my countrymen. I know what my further development needs and I intend to get it.[7]

One of the things he thought he needed for his "further development" was more sexual experience. In the fall of 1965, Aviva had returned with him to their Somerled apartment after a hysterical and strained summer reunion in Hydra Greece with Layton, Leonard Cohen and Cohen's Norwegian love, Marianne. Aviva took up her marriage and worked at Weston School part-time. But Musia still was very much on the scene, and Layton's frankly predatory attitude towards his students and "groupies" raged on unabated. Six months earlier, Pacey had raised a disturbing question concerning Layton's seductions. After accompanying Layton to a party at Sir George Williams, he wrote, "[I] was particularly delighted to be able to witness your amatory art in practice. You are a smooth seducer — the only pity was that the woman concerned seemed scarcely worthy of your talents. My standards are high, so high in fact that I've yet to see a woman other than my own wife that I'd want to bother seducing."[8]

Layton did not want to think about wives. His relationship with Aviva had deteriorated; they were living separate lives under the same roof. "I was dead to Irving sexually by then," Aviva comments.[9] "It was mainly because of Musia. Some people think that an 'open marriage' has no basic trust. In my opinion an 'open marriage' must be based on very intimate trust. Between Irving and me that basic trust was very shaky. On the one hand he didn't like to acknowledge me publicly. On the other hand he hated the idea that we weren't married. It got to the point where I dreaded supper. He'd come in and shout, 'Dinner! Aviva! Tea!' and so forth. But all I could think of was, Where has he been? Does he smell of that damned perfume again? I'd have to concentrate hard to think up topics we could talk about at dinner without getting into dangerous territory. Then there was his relationship with David. He had no sense of responsibility for him. David always came to me when he was hurt or when something was wrong. I couldn't have left him with Irving. He wouldn't have known how to look after him."

One of the things that Layton most wanted to escape from by the late sixties was the domestic scene on Somerled Avenue. Visits from the Paceys grew fewer and fewer, as did the letters between the two men, for Layton could not continue to confide completely in a man he knew was overexposed to the contradictions in his behaviour.

In January 1967, Layton confessed to Pacey that the past two years had been extremely hard on him. Pacey couldn't understand. On 24 April, after hearing that he had been awarded a Canada Council special arts award of seven thousand dollars plus travel expenses, Layton still was complaining of his "uncertain moods and feelings." Though he vowed he would remain a Canadian, he looked forward to living and writing in Asia. "I'm excited by the visions my poor head has had to harbour since I've heard the great news. Kashmir, India, Burma, Hong Kong, Singapore, Tokyo — and many, many other fabulous places the poets & novelists have inflamed my imagination with. Ah, to be 55, with money in my pockets, and dreams of geisha girls and houris in one's head."

Layton announced that he would go, via Lisbon and Spain,

to Bondel, about thirty miles east of Marseille, for four or five months. Then he would move eastward to Turkey, Israel and Kashmir. He planned to be out of Canada for about two years.[10]

What Layton did not tell Pacey, or Jack McClelland or anyone else, was that he planned to spend the next year travelling not with Aviva and their three-year old son, David, but with a young Montreal painter called Marion Wagshall.

Marion

Marion Wagshall had been born in Trinidad to Jewish parents who had fled Koningsberg, Germany in 1938. Her mother had seen Hitler in an open car and knew what was in store for Jews. Because of the "crystal-night raids" in their town, all the family's beautiful household goods had been destroyed. The year after emigrating to Trinidad, the Wagshalls had a son. Marion, their only other child, was born five years later. But family life for the Wagshalls was unsteady after Germany. The sudden trauma of falling from great wealth to lowly displaced-persons status in an alien climate and culture proved too difficult for the German couple. In 1947, when Marion was only four, they divorced. Marion came to Montreal with her mother and brother in 1953. She was ten.[1]

She first heard about Irving Layton when she was fourteen. A friend's brother had been at Herzliah and brought back reports of a teacher there who had written something called *The Long Pea-Shooter*. He was a really stimulating teacher, very excited about poetry, an excellent teacher for high school.

Eight years later, as Marion toyed with painting, trying to make up her mind about her own life, another friend began raving about Irving Layton, whose creative-writing course at

Sir George Williams she was taking. He was wonderful, she told Marion, a terrific teacher. Out of curiosity Marion went along to audit a class. "He was generous, a truly great teacher," she recalls. "He listened to the poems students had written and analysed them carefully and seriously." She began to attend his classes regularly.

By coincidence, Marion had begun dropping in to Layton's poetry classes the same year that she began to paint seriously. The comments on creative writing she heard in his sessions helped convince her that creativity in any form was a worthwhile endeavour. By the end of that year, at age twenty-one, she had her first show, at the Jason Teff Gallery. Her career as a painter was launched.

Like many students before her, Marion found Layton readily accessible. They began to meet for coffee at Murray's. There they would talk for hours: the fifty-three-year-old poet and teacher, grey-haired, authoritative and enthusiastic, and the twenty-two-year-old budding painter, diminutive, dark-haired and reticent. "Irving was very supportive to me at a time when I had many doubts about myself," Marion recalls. "He bought my paintings and drawings. He really thought they were good. He spoke about me to other people who also bought my work and encouraged me to keep at it. Because I do large figurative painting on themes from history, politics and the Bible, there are literary elements in my work. I was not working with pure aesthetics — especially then, when I started painting. He thought that my vision was significant, that my subject matter was very important. What he didn't understand was that paintings communicate in a different language than words. He tended to read literary things into them that I didn't think were there. So we would argue and discuss my work for hours. We explored all the concepts and ideas about art that were most significant to me at the time. I was trying to present my vision of reality in a literary context. I did drawings of Abraham and Isaac which were both personal and literary, for example. He had a great interest in the Bible, but he tended to see the literary and not the personal implications of my work. Mainly, we had a million things to talk about. We were two individuals with much in common."

With her blue eyes, stocky figure and strong profile, Marion looked like a tiny, voluptuous, female replica of the much older Layton. Within a year, they began a romantic fling. "We were strongly drawn to one another," comments Marion, who describes herself as "someone who attracts Casanova types." "He seemed to me like a secure parental authority. I saw him as all-powerful and strong. He made it clear that he was getting frustrated in his marriage to Aviva and his home life with David. He told me he wanted to leave, but that he would feel guilty if he did. He was always upset about his various commitments — not just to Aviva, but to Betty and her children and even to Musia. Now that I'm older, I see that he was someone who could not reconcile 'ideal' marriage with the day-to-day actuality."

Marion couldn't have suited him better. She spoke in an outright fashion about her hatred of homes and families. Domestic life, she thought, was boring and archaic. Conventional marriage inevitably provoked a complexity of emotions that were destructive: hostility and gratitude became relentlessly intertwined. By contrast, she lived by a code that was based on fun, humour, lust, perversion, love and — as a release for tension — violence.[2]

For Irving, Marion held out the possibility of a relationship with a deeply creative woman who appeared to be even more liberated than Aviva, with her philosophy of "open marriage," had been. He was swept away with someone new and exciting who promised never to tie him down, someone who believed that any bonds were destructive. "I think he wanted to return to the stage of life I was in. He wanted to be carefree, younger. It was convenient for him that I was younger," Marion observes. "I really had no expectations of him. I was in a daze generally. I was flying high on youth. Everything then was a wild experience for me. I was in a transitional state. I felt honoured that he paid so much attention to me."

When Layton secured his Canada Council award in 1967, he began to imagine how exciting a year abroad with Marion might be. Aviva, he often complained, was too garrulous. She was too involved with words. She had published her children's stories and now seemed determined to complete her graduate work on Patrick White for a critical book. Marion was more like Betty: talkative when you wanted her to be, but more predictably engaged in the silent, wordless world of painting. Marion had altogether a more serene temperament than Aviva.

In May 1967, Irving and Marion flew together to France. Contrary to the plan Irving had outlined to Pacey about going by himself to Bondel, he rented an apartment with Marion in Nice, on the second floor of an old building near the beach.

"That place was lovely," Marion recalls. "It had a little garden with a big palm tree which I used to sketch. Our life fell into a relaxed routine. Irving would get up early to catch what he called 'the champagne light' and go out for four hours or so. He would rent a *fauteuil* on the Promenade des Anglais, or go and lie on the beach. That's where he wrote the poem about a jaded cosmonaut eying the girls by the sea, 'For the Girl with Wide-Apart Eyes.'[3] While he was out, I would shop. I was into 'pleasing' him. I experimented with cooking for the first time. I found an ancient copy of *The Joy of Cooking* in an English bookstore and used to prepare incredible, enormous meals. I would cook things like pig's knuckles and sauerkraut — six-course meals — on hot, hot days. In the afternoons it was my turn to work. While Irving read or napped, I used to paint for hours every day. At night we'd go out and sit in cafés or look around Nice."

Defining the bohemian existence proved to be as thorny a problem with Marion as it had been with Betty and Aviva. Though Irving wanted his women to be casual and anything but middle-class, he disliked chaos at home. "In my living habits I was a real slob," Marion admits. "I never put my clothes away, for instance. But Irving's very neat. He used to yell at me: 'I'll put them all in a pile and burn them!' He's actually a very irritable person. It's hard to live with an independent artist like that. The only reason we didn't fight much about such things was that I did my best to be easy to get along with. I wanted him to like me."

By the end of the summer, the romance that was meant to last a year, perhaps longer, had crumbled. It was Irving who terminated the relationship. The very fact that he took such pains to conceal the situation from his friends suggests that he was treating the summer with Marion as a kind of "trial" or "experiment." "I've been in Nice for the last six weeks," he wrote to his friend Barry Callaghan, the journalist and writer, "and I haven't spoken to a single person, apart from tradesmen and my concierge. I sit on my ass all day long on the quay and write my poems under the wonderful Nicoise sun. I've had a marvellous burst of energy and inspiration since coming here and the poems are literally pouring out of me [in]...my self-imposed solitude."[4]

Layton felt guilty about Aviva and David, back in Montreal. Perhaps more importantly, he had been invited to take part in the World Poetry Conference at Expo. The opportunity to contact major poets from around the world and the chance to make a Canadian come-back with his new collection, *The Shattered Plinths* (a copy of which he sent off to President Lyndon Johnson), seemed too good to miss. Worried about leaving Marion alone, Irving arranged for Betty and Naomi, who were travelling in Europe that summer, too, to come and stay with her for a while. Nonetheless, when the two parted at the airport before Irving boarded his plane for Montreal, Marion burst into uncontrollable, embarrassing tears, certain that she would never see him again. The man she had planned to live and work with for a long time, perhaps forever, seemed like an impersonal tourist. Had she even known him?[5]

"We separated," recalls Layton, who in August appeared with Aviva at Expo as if nothing had happened, "because the disparity of age and psychology between us was too great. Here's the poem I wrote about our parting."[6]

END OF THE SUMMER

Already the sun burns less intensely;
its deepest passion is for other skies, other lands;
wedged between two clouds
it seems embarrassed by its sudden loss of power.
The foam now whitens my melancholy
and even the waves speak in a voice not heard before:
more tumultuous yet sadder
like people who shout at each other
at the end of a love affair.

It makes me think
of quiet Mediterranean cemeteries I've known
to see the sunlight limp across the beach
stuffing black leaves of shadow between the stones:
of old women with white skins
and fields of despoiled windflowers.
Where's its force, its fiery heat?
Is this the July monarch that reigned here? This slave
to a calendar, this enfeebled lecher
with not one good squint, one amorous gleam
left in its red eyes?
Slowly the sun mounts the stone steps of the Plage
and stares at my bronzed chest and arms
like a woman failing to recognize
her former lover.[7]

Sceneshifter

It was a cold January day in 1969. Irving and Aviva stood uncomfortably on the slushy sidewalk outside her uncle's apartment in Toronto and waited for a taxi. Eli Mandel, who began to teach at York University in 1967, had set up an interview for Layton with Jack Saywell, York's dean of arts. Perhaps they would offer him a job. Layton didn't want to be an English professor. Nor did he want to leave Montreal, especially for Toronto, a city he had long hated. But he had tried to parley his job at Sir George Williams into something more substantial and had failed to get anything more than his three-thousand-dollars-a-year position. He had tried McGill and the Université de Montréal, but they would give him only part-time work at two or three thousand dollars. "As we stood there freezing," Layton recalls, "I thought to myself, 'If a taxi doesn't come in ten minutes, I'll take it as an omen that I should not take a job here.'" A taxi arrived in exactly eight and a half minutes.[1]

York University was launched in response to the rapidly increasing demand for higher education that had characterized the decade. The institution set out to provide experimental and progressive programmes, emphasizing the humanities and social sciences. In its early years, the spirit had been one of buoyant optimism. It was a lively place, interested in up-to-date, even unorthodox instruction, and for this reason the university had approached Layton, first in 1962. The school's architecture resembled the huge stone brutalities of the fashionable southern California campuses. But unfortunately, the landscape in Downsview, flat, open, farm land north of Toronto, was anything but Californian. In summer it baked under an unrelenting sun, swathed in wisps of smog from nearby industrial areas. In winter, the north wind swept with such devastating force across the mammoth campus between the large boxey towers that eventually underground tunnels connecting the main buildings were constructed. York, wishing to benefit from the publicity Layton's presence would attract, offered him a tenured position as a full professor. He would teach the theory and practice of poetry and a seminar on creative writing for eighteen thousand dollars a year.[2] "It all looks like fun," he reported euphorically to Pacey, "and the increase in earnings will let me do more for Betty and Naomi in San Franscisco and Max, who has his own share of worries just now, in Montreal. Also for a couple of painters who suffer from the familiar affliction of talent without money."[3]

Layton's first Toronto reading seemed to him to augur well:

> about 35 girls from South Ontario listened to me reading the erotic poems of Ovid, Cohen, Layton, Cummings. At first their royal and loyal posteriors stiffened them against the raw emotions and the raw words. They were embarrassed because they didn't know how they were expected to behave. But after awhile they relaxed their guards and let their smiles and juices run naturally over their upper and lower parts. When at the end I said I'd better stop reading or they wouldn't be able to sleep at night, they all looked at one another with a knowing lasciviousness and broke into unrestrained laughter. In the meantime, of course, my hands had been stroking their hidden and delicious parts, squeezing them with an energy that only an imagination fired by erotic poetry and frustration can muster. If anyone spent a sleepless night I think it was I.[4]

To some observers, however, Layton was not affecting his audiences quite the way he imagined. His charisma was disintegrating:

> he has become a fixture, has practically joined the penates of Westmount and households across the land....in turtleneck and chained medal (the insignia of a later rebellion, now alas obsolete), jabs away with the familiar needle, looking around benignly for gasps and frissons — and receiving only the polite chuckles of unshockable students come to witness a venerable institution.[5]

Leaving Aviva and David in Montreal so that Aviva could complete her master's degree, on Australian novelist Patrick White, at the Université de Montréal, Layton took a small apartment on Keele Street near York and put in the rest of the 1969 winter term as writer-in-residence teaching appreciation of poetry and a writing workshop at the University of Guelph.[6] In the fall of 1969, he took up his new position at York, commuting from the new house he and Aviva had bought in Hampstead in Montreal.

Before the year was out, he was complaining vociferously to Pacey about his new environment. He produced a blistering poem, called "York University," comparing the university to Belsen.[7] "I stubbornly cling to the notion that the poet is a free man who functions best when he's able to cut his social obligations and commitments to a minimum. The strange device on his banner is not *power* but *love*. Respectability has never suited him. He makes a better figure as madman, heretic, clown, buffoon, or idol-smasher, and the university doesn't want such people — except, perhaps, as show-pieces!... Anyone who's really an artist — that is, a free soul — will escape institutionalization, and only those who aren't allow themselves to get tamed."[8] By the end of the year, Layton felt like the Sorcerer's Apprentice again. The job was taking over. "This isn't one job I've gotten myself into; it's a thousand. Or it's one whose many heads keep popping up and grinning fiendishly at me, like those of the fabled monster. Why didn't you tell me what a professor's life was really like?" he complained to the very man who, as he rose through the ranks to become president of the University of New Brunswick, had been describing the inner workings of a university to him for years.

> No, it's being poet-and-prof. that does it. That's harrying me prematurely into the land of gray haired dodderers anxiously scanning the horizons for friends or strangers bearing obligations and commitments on their honeyed palates. The black signs on my calendar would make you weep — they're the hieroglyphics of my self-betrayal.... Readings, readings, readings. And lectures, lectures, lectures. Promises to write prefaces, introductions, recommendations for grants, for scholarships, for acceptance into graduate schools. And MANUSCRIPTS! Everyone has been bitten by the mania for writing poetry. My desk has become the dumping ground for all the bad poetry in this country... how on earth can I stop the flood I seem to have started? Why don't the protesters and marchers call for a moratorium on poetry?
> For a start, why doesn't some benefactor of the human race shut down all the English departments and tell the profs & instructors to go off and fuck minnows — or something larger if they can manage it.[9]

It seems not to have occurred to Layton that he could say no.

When Layton received his first honourary degree, from Bishop's University in 1970, he took the opportunity to show the world he was no tamed puma. He took both Aviva and Musia to the proceedings. Though the ceremony took place on the same weekend on which Trudeau announced that he was invoking the War Measures Act, Layton's letters at the time suggest that his thoughts were mainly elsewhere. The political tensions that were rife that weekend — especially in the Eastern Townships of Quebec, where Bishop's was located — took second place to his personal triumph. "I had a difficult time," he confessed to Pacey, "keeping my face on an even keel between solemnity and amusement, especially when the Bishop of Quebec and the Bishop of Montreal were murmuring their congratulations and shaking my hand. Still, I guess history was made... Issie Lazarovitch, a Jew from the wrong side of the track receiving an Honorary Degree from the educational citadel of Quebec Waspdom! It's a remarkable event from whatever perspective you see it, mine or Bishop's. If I feel proud and gratified it's not only for myself, but for my country as well. O Canada...."[10] In his thank-you letter to poet Ralph Gustafson, with whom he had stayed in the Eastern Townships, Layton claimed that he had tried to write a poem expressing his gratitude, but that his Muse had "fled down the corridors of York."[11]

One of the things that most irritated Layton at York was the conversation of academics in the senior common room. "I was disappointed in my discussions with faculty," he recalls. "It made me see how rare fresh thinking really is." Layton meant that he found himself a majority of one on most subjects under discussion. His political views were usually the opposite of those of colleagues.

In the spring of 1966, he had created a stir in Canada, especially in the Jewish community, by reporting after a reading and a lecture tour in Germany that the world had nothing to fear any longer from the Germans and ought to forgive them for past events.

"A number of my own immediate family ended up as chimney smoke," Layton was quoted as saying. (All his immediate family — in the commonly understood use of the phrase — had emigrated safely from Romania.) He was attempting to identify himself closely with the Holocaust to do an abrupt about-face. "But it must be said that the first layer of ashes in the...crematoria was that of Germans — pacifists, liberals, socialists and Communists: they were the earliest victims of Hitlerism."[12] In an article in *Maclean's* he asked that people wipe the slate clean and not pursue the "new Germany" with complaints about the old.[13] This pro-German stance infuriated many readers, especially Jews; one of them, Peter Lust, noted in the *Canadian Jewish Chronicle* that Layton's views could not have been less timely, since the neo-Nazis of the NPD party in Germany made large gains in the election that followed Layton's return to Canada.[14]

Layton also upset and alienated the intellectuals around him by arguing that Trudeau had been right and "courageous" to invoke the War Measures Act in response to the FLQ terrorist activities that led to the "October Crisis" of 1970 in Quebec, an unpopular view that, for completely different reasons, was shared by Frank Scott. He also argued that the Americans were right to be backing the South Vietnamese against the Communist North. To take the opposite side in political matters seems to have provided an outlet necessary for his emotional stability. He publicly supported Trudeau's Quebec policy in the Toronto *Star* and the *Globe* and later bragged, "I've managed to rouse myself out of any depression that might try to assault me by firing off shots in all directions in defense of Trudeau and the War Measures Act, and I must say the tonic is having effect. There is nothing like a good fight to get the adrenalin working in the system."[15] There was much truth in Pacey's observation at the time that Layton was a "reactionary" who divided the world into great abstract entities: "the United States and Soviet Union, the good nations and the bad nations, the small states and the big states."[16] Such words made Layton, whose poem "Hymn to the Republic"[17] in Purdy's collection *The New Romans* was the only completely pro-American entry, bristle:

> For me the issue is *not* Vietnam, but the fate of Southeast Asia, and ultimately of the free world. I cannot, like yourself and others, close my eyes to the nature of communist tyranny... I can't pretend the Russians aren't probing for advantage and power in the Middle East and Latin America. Just as firmly as in the 30s when the danger to the human spirit took the form of National Socialism, so today I'll fight the mental fight against the present enemies of the open society. What free man doesn't rejoice that South Vietnam hasn't fallen into the hands of the N. Vietnamese communists, and that its recently held elections were meaningful, fair, and democratic? *You* would have given them over, all twenty or twenty-two million of them, to be trussed up by the communist thugs who rule in N. Vietnam — without a free press, a constitution, or the right to assembly. And *you* have the indecent gall to call me a *reactionary*![18]

Layton's views on Israel, which he had expressed in print

after visiting Israel for a few months in the winter of 1967–1968, after the Six Day's War, came closest of any to the views of his peers — but he was much more pro-Israel than they were. While most thought Israel ought to exist but remained sceptical of the country's reliance on American and Canadian financial support and feared the imperialistic tendencies that could result, Layton approved without qualifications Israel's aggressive attitude.

"My colleagues at York were so simple-minded and idealistic," he complained. "Unlike them, I'm very *experienced* in politics."[19] His colleagues, like Pacey, dismissed him as an old rectionary.

Though Layton complained about the burdens he had assumed as a professor and poet, and was disappointed with his colleagues as he had been in the WASPish environment of Macdonald College, he thought Toronto a good place for contacts with the CBC and other media. He also enjoyed teaching. "I like teaching," he wrote as his collection *Nail Polish*, which he predicted would win him the Nobel Prize,[20] went into final proofs.

> I enjoy meeting different people and getting into different situations. I've the certainty moreover of knowing that everything I do, everything that happens to me, will eventually flower into some lines that would otherwise never have gotten themselves written. I've tested myself too often and too variously not to have this certainty. I've an amazing ability to assimilate my experience, to reach out and ingest just about everything that surrounds me. I'm the sceneshifter of my own poems, arranging the episodes of my life to provide poems — vampires, every damned one of them — with the nourishment they need. There are times when I feel that my phsyical being is under the collective ownership of all the poems I've written or ever will write, or rather that I'm being manipulated by some creative hoola who pushes me into different lives or episodes so that I can co-operate with him in his need to expose himself. Luckily for both of us, I like his rage and range.[21]

Layton literally had become the "sceneshifter" of his poems.

After his plans to spend a year abroad with Marion Wagshall had disintegrated, he made other attempts, sometimes by himself, at other times with Aviva and David, to savour as many different environments and situations as he could. He met Betty and Naomi in India and went with them to Nepal in 1968. The same year, he met Aviva in Greece. In the summer of 1969, he went to Ireland and Portugal. He took Aviva to Molibos, in Greece, every summer from 1971 to 1974, and spent Christmas holidays in Zihuatanejo, Mexico. In the fall of 1973, Layton and Aviva — sponsored by a Canada Council grant of $7,980, travelled through Bangkok, Thailand and Indonesia on their way to Sydney, Australia, where Layton promoted his poetry. In 1974, he went to Italy to give readings and to celebrate the translation of some of his poems into Italian.

Layton had the money to travel and a no-holds-barred open marriage to Aviva; his long-held wish to escape from his duties to some remote sunny spot frequently came true. All he needed was time, the right climate and peace to live high and write some of the best work — poems, short stories, novels — the world would ever see. Or so he believed.

Layton enjoyed his travels, but they were not especially stimulating for his art. Although he kept journals, "not to be one of those portentous travel-diaries intended for publication," but rather "for storing ideas or impressions that could be used later in stories or poems,"[22] he did not write any stories. Nor was he able to sit still long enough to produce the novel he'd talked about for more than a decade. Travel provided the chance to "grab life with both fists instead of telling others how to do it,"[23] but somehow his trips were often disappointing. Despite his "open marriage," domestic life with Aviva, who had transferred to York in 1971 as a graduate student and then a teaching assistant, was profoundly unhappy. When she was with him in the house they bought at 122 St. Clements Avenue, they frequently fought. But when they were apart, he felt frightened and anxious.

Aviva thought Layton was impossible to travel with.[24] "Irving's a mad traveller," she recalled. "He really wanted to travel alone, so that he could do whatever he wanted, but then he'd get lonely and want me to join him. He solved this by leaving a few days or so before me so that he'd have freedom for a short while, knowing I'd be arriving soon. Once I was there, he'd just disappear for a few days at a time whenever he felt like it. His attitude to money was terrible. He's from that generation who came impoverished to Canada and went through the Depression, so he was always worried, always scrimping. We'd never have a real 'splurge' evening. We always stayed in the cheapest places. On the other hand, he could be extremely generous. He could give away a thousand dollars. I don't think it seemed like real money when it got past pennies. It was worst of all when we travelled with David. I remember once when he was seven or eight, and we were in India. Irving insisted that we must live with the natives. We stayed where the untouchables stayed. The shitholes were festering; there were no sheets on the mattresses. He'd buy food from the street stalls and try to force David to eat it. He thought David was spoiled because he didn't like Indian food. He was always trying to toughen him up. He'd wander through the most incredible filth and degradation whistling gaily. We'd get on a train and I'd be urging him to look at the scenery. He'd sit there writing and hand me a poem that had already captured the essence of the scene. He really makes up the world as he goes along. He creates his own countries, and no one can enter them with him. Of course I was immature then. I used to freak out every so often."

One time Aviva freaked out in Ireland, during a brief visit in the summer of 1969. Aviva's friend Nima Ash, who travelled with them, used one evening as the basis of a chapter for a draft of a novel.[25]

It had been one of those mediaeval-castle feasts, staged in Galway especially for tourists. When the actors learned that a great poet was among their guests, they took advantage of the situation to enhance the festivities. Nima's fictional version, beginning with a speech from the "King" of the evening, ran as follows:

> "Each year I light a candle to honour a poet from one of our kingdoms. Tonight I dedicate this candle to the renowned bard, famous throughout the land, Maxwell

Stevens, and ask him to rise." Everyone clapped. Maxwell rose slowly as though he had been rehearsed in advance. The king lit the tall thick candle and said, "I ask the honourable bard to bring you greetings from the far off kingdom from which he has come." Maxwell hesitated, but only for a fraction of a second, and then, as though his entire career as a poet had been a preparation for this moment, he spoke with a passionate eloquence. He outdid himself. He began somewhat formally by first extending thanks to the king, on behalf of the assembled poets, for the feast prepared in their honour, and then extending thanks for himself, for the esteem bestowed upon him, by singling him out for the dedication. Then, with the fluency of an orator, he launched into a moving address about poetry. He talked about the rich heritage of Irish poetry which gave birth to the poets gathered in the castle. He talked about the important position they occupied in the kingdoms as seers and healers. He quoted poem after poem, never hesitating for a single word. He talked about the poet, not only as seer and healer, but as prophet and warrior.

"The poet follows a prophetic path to lead his fellowmen toward light and awareness, to expose 'the dark subtleties that plague the human soul.' The poet is a fierce warrior doing battle with man's folly, a warrior like the brave warriors of Ulster and Connacht, who has the courage to use words as his shafts and javelins to wage war on hypocrasy [sic] and repression. The poet is a bard, who sings with fullness of feeling, a song so sweet it would fill any person hearing it with peace and music. I propose a toast to Irish poetry and to all the great Irish poets yet to come who will follow in the tradition of Prophet, Warrior and Bard." He ended with Yeats's epitaph.

> "Cast a cold eye
>   on life, on death
> Horseman pass by."

He received a standing ovation although it was assumed that he was part of the presentation....

During dinner Maxwell received a note inviting him and his friends to the cottage on the castle grounds where the cast lived. He answered with an expansive "yea" for all of us. It was one of those rare magical evenings. Maxwell, elated by the reception his spontaneous presentation had received, was at his charismatic best, dynamic, witty, full of a pungent wisdom. "Let's have a poem by the famous bard Maxwell Stevens," Cathleen, one of the players, declaimed. He knew many of his poems by heart and spoke them in his rich mellow voice, to the delight of the adoring cast. He had everyone sitting at his feet. Cathleen was especially encouraging, smiling up at him, singing Irish folk tunes, bringing him her favourite poems so she could hear him read them. She was a beautiful coleen with burning red-gold hair twisted round her head and fastened by a silver pin, and green-irised eyes with dark lashes casting shadows down her cheeks. She had a quick bright Irish wit, which sparked Maxwell to his philosophical scintillating best.

"Who do you write your poetry for Mr. Stevens?" she asked imitating a BBC interviewer. "For God," he answered, "but you, my dear, are very welcome to eavesdrop." All Maxwell needed was a responsive adoring woman to flourish, and he had five adoring women as well as two adoring men. He soared. It was his night and he filled it with magic. I felt grateful to be present. Aliza did not. She looked on from her seat in the corner of the room, refusing to participate, casting her own special brand of "cold eye." She pulled into herself, tightening like a bow, growing increasingly rigid as Maxwell grew expansive and embracing. From time to time she took a resentful sip of wine and once I saw her lips clench as though the wine had grown bitter in her mouth.

It began to grow very late. "Where are you stopping tonight?" Cathleen asked. "We didn't have time to arrange anything," Maxwell answered, "we thought we could get rooms in the hotel in town." "They're probably booked up with guests who come for the Castle Night." "We have a car, we'll find somewhere to stay," Aliza interrupted like a slap on the hand. Cathleen turned toward her and took her hand, ignoring the sting. "Why don't you all stay here, in the cottage." "That's a very generous offer," Maxwell said warmly. "I would rather not stay," Aliza said, casting her arrow. "You can remain, I'll get a room in town." Immediately the silence became so intense we could hear the arrow bite the air. Maxwell said nothing for a moment, recognizing the force of Aliza's attack, familiar with its devasteting [sic] potential. He tried only one perfunctory, "Come on maidel, let's at least stay the night, it's late, we'll leave tomorrow." "Don't maidel me. I'm going now."[26]

As this episode, which was based closely on the real events of the evening, suggests, Aviva easily felt insecure. "I was in a wonderful mood that night," Layton recalls. "I gave the best extemporaneous speech I've given in my whole life. I was truly inspired. Aviva was jealous of the actress who had performed so beautifully and who was excited by me and enamoured of me. But she misunderstood where I was at completely. I was not interested in making the girl. I was in a state of poetic exhilaration. Aviva was determined that we were not going to spend the night under the same roof as that lovely actress. She threw a wet blanket on the whole thing. Nima Ash really captured it in her fictional portrayal."[27]

In Australia in late February 1974, Irving and Aviva were invited to have dinner with Patrick White, about whom Aviva had written her master's thesis and had begun to prepare her doctorate. As Aviva recalled the evening in an article for *Weekend Magazine* (1976),[28] the conversation with White and his other guests — his companion Manoly Lascaris, his literary agent, a visiting Swedish writer and a woman journalist — was "wary and brittle."

To her dismay, White advised her not to continue her work on him, advice she took to heart when she returned to Toronto. Layton's first impressions of Australia had been extremely negative. To him it had not seemed like the feisty, bohemian environment Aviva had always been so nostalgic for, but a sort of bland, cultural backwater. He was not, she knew, likely to endear himself to Patrick White, whose complex fictional representations of Australian life had won him the Nobel Prize in literature the year before.

White's house was intimidating. Far from being the casual and squalid "digs" so often associated with artists, it was a warm, homey place exquisitely arranged with a multitude of paintings and art objects. Aviva knew that Irving's silence and uncharacteristically spartan appetite at dinner boded ill:

> Irving sat down with an after-dinner liqueur in what was obviously the host's favorite armchair and announced in a loud and deliberately jocular voice that he thought he would read them a superb poem — a masterpiece, in fact — which he had just tossed off that afternoon. This being barely acceptable behavior in most Canadian living rooms, I cannot stress enough how entirely outrageous it was in an Australian one. There was a short but palpable silence, then Patrick's elegant tones: "My dear fellow, whatever for?" Another silence followed, longer and more palpable, while Irving considered. His response, when it came, was even louder, more determinedly jocular: "Now that I come to think of it, I think I'll read two poems." Then Patrick in a voice even more refined and quiet than before: "You do that, dear chap, and I'll read my whole frigging novel." Another black hole of silence through which I saw my entire academic career drain away, while Irving's mouth compressed itself so much it all but disappeared: "That ought to be a fair exchange, Patrick, as two of my poems just about equal one of your novels."
>
> We all remained suspended in the ruins of the living room, sixty-two-year-old steely eye locked into sixty-two-year-old steely eye until, thank heaven, the witty, charming lady journalist threw a witty, charming remark into the hiatus.
>
> Somehow the threads of politesse were taken up once more, with only one more relatively minor relapse in which literature again reared its ugly head. This time it was whether Shakespeare had a moral sensibility or not. Patrick said he didn't. Irving raised his voice about two hundred million decibels and, in tones which would

have been considered infuriatingly patronizing in a junior kindergarten, chided, "Come, come, Patrick you know better than that." At this point Patrick, an asthmatic, started wheezing dangerously and we realized that our little evening was over.[29]

In 1974, Layton made his most successful trip abroad, to Italy. Amleto Lorenzini, who in 1971 had begun translating Layton's *Selected Poems* and an introduction by Northrop Frye into Italian for the prestigious Italian publisher Einaudi Torino, arranged the visit through Francesca Valente, junior vice-president of the Italo-Britannica Anglo-Italian Association. Layton was invited to be on hand for the launching of *Il Freddo Verde Elemento (The Cold Green Element)*, one book in a series that included Yeats, Eliot, Williams and Marlowe. Layton was the first of several Canadian cultural figures to visit Italy. After him came Leonard Cohen, Northrop Frye and Eli Mandel. Layton spoke to the British Council in Milan, the Anglo-American Association, the University of Venice, ca' Foscari and the embassy in Rome. In Milan there was what Valente called "an historic meeting" between Layton and Vittorio Sereni, a major Italian poet. For Francesca, there was a poem. It was "the usual thing," she remarks. "When he can't own a woman, he writes a poem about her imagining he does... He was wonderful with the high school boys and girls I brought to hear him. He was wonderful with everyone. He made a real hit in Italy. He seemed European, somehow."[30] For Layton, who was ambitious to launch himself on the world and who had already arranged for the translation of nine of his poems to appear in *Romania Literaria*[31] (he chose a Romanian journal on the basis that Romania was his birth-place), his Italian visit gave him a foothold on glory. "Excuse me," he wrote to McClelland from Greece when he first heard that Lorenzini wished to translate his poems, "but is that the Nobel prize I see gleaming before me? Anyhow, it's a step, a very necessary one, in that direction.... Lorenzini assures me that publication by Einaudi means an almost automatic translation into five or six other European tongues."[32]

Layton's life on the Greek island of Molibos, where he stayed for a few months for several summers, was probably most typical of his travels. He liked to imagine that the spirit of Sappho, who had lived on nearby Mitylene, was trying to get through to him.[33] "There's a tradition in Mithyma (Molibos)," he wrote to Barry Callaghan, "that the body of Orpheus floated down to the inlet at the foot of the hill where I'm situated. There's an old Genoese castle on the summit and from a distance it looks like the proud neck of a Renaissance lady and the town's habitations like a colorful pendant on her full, aristocratic bosom.... Everyone works mornings & afternoons, but we meet in the evening and then the drinking and talking are likely to go on till the last taverna has closed and the town is locked in silence and darkness."[34] But, although he rhapsodized romantically in his letters, he later recalled his time at Molibos as "bright, black days."[35] There he and Aviva had their worst quarrels, as if disappointed that a paradisal setting did not bring idyllic love. More often than not, Aviva spent her time talking animatedly with friends like Nima Ash at one end of the beach while Layton sat alone communing with his muse at the other. The result of one inspiration in 1968 concerned *Othello*. Hoping perhaps to outdo his earlier interpretation of *Hamlet*, Layton sent off a page and a half, which he claimed was "the final word on *Othello*" and that proved all other critics wrong. *Othello*, he theorized as if struck by divine revelation, was Shakespeare's version of the Crucifixion story.[36]

Andy Wainwright, a young poet whom Layton had encouraged, recalls spending a couple of summers in a house near the Laytons'. "He and Aviva were stormy in an exuberant fashion, but I thought it was just letting off steam — a sort of necessary dramatizing. The Greeks at the little taverna where we'd go to drink wine and talk had a name for him which meant 'the white-haired poet.' Irving refused to learn any Greek. He got away with things like that which other people couldn't do. He used to go swimming a lot. He did a funny stroke that we all called 'the dead man's breast stroke'; it looked weird, but he could do it for hours. After dinner, Aviva and my wife would go to the *agora* and he and I would sit in the courtyard and play chess. Though we were both poor players, he loved the strategy. He was an intensely competitive player. He'd try to get me drunk on brandy or blow cigar smoke in my face to confuse me so I'd lose."[37]

Such madcap adventures, such freedom, ought to have produced better poetry, Layton thought, than what he had written in the days when he was draining off his vital energies into multiple jobs. Certainly it gave him great satisfaction "to see others slaving away at jobs they abhor while I lie on my back enjoying the sunlight and the singing of birds,"[38] and in his free time he wrote prolifically. Between 1968, when he published *The Shattered Plinths*, and 1975, he published four collections of new poems: *The Whole Bloody Bird* (tentatively called "The Indelicate Touch") in 1969; *Nail Polish* in 1971; *Lovers and Lesser Men* in 1973 and *The Pole-Vaulter* in 1974.[39] But, with a very few exceptions, the poems in these collections did not measure up to the best of Layton's earlier works. He still was capable of subtle and powerful poems, like "Osip Mandelshtam" (about one of the Russian poets who vanished in Stalin's purges of intellectuals and Jews),[40] "Stella" (about an old Greek woman who set herself on fire)[41] and "Elephant" (a rollicking grotesquerie for and about Northrop Frye),[42] but the majority of his poems were slight, occasional pieces that came not from Layton's depths and multi-faceted complexities, but superficially and from only one of his sides, usually his raging, satiric side.

Judging by the poems, Layton's mood often was one of black cynicism. He was less concerned than he had been a decade before with beauty, either of experience or expression, and much more concerned with man's degradation and death. "Man suffers from an incurable disease: himself," he wrote in his collection of aphorisms.[43] Elsewhere he wrote:

> Man is absurd,
> not because he kills and couples,
> but because he feels obliged
> to invent reasons
> for doing so.[44]

"An idealist," Layton candidly stated, "is a cynic in the

making."[45] Certainly he had moved far from the idealism of his youth. "To a poet there are only two holes that matter," he sardonically wrote to Steven Osterlund, a young American expatriate who had looked him up at York and who showed real promise as a poet: "one of them is the grave and the other is a woman's cunt. The best way to keep from falling into the former is by exploring as many of the latter as you can."[46]

Layton seldom celebrated life as he had done earlier. At times, it seems he did not want to produce poems at all, but felt that he must. Most of what he wrote was forced, heavy-handed and graceless. "He must be the only man in North America who feels called upon to write about his dinner before he gets around to eating it," one reviewer jeered in 1973. "Perhaps Layton believes that diamonds look better in an environment of rhinestones."[47] Another reviewer commented:

> It's a little pathetic that the Establishment *has* come to him, and that the sixties *have* given us all such freedom of expression. Victory must taste bitter to him; now that everything he has to say can be said, and heard by everyone, what does he have to say that all the younger poets around him, like a chorus of frogs, aren't croaking out with less wisdom and wit but with the invincible vigour of youth?...In other words, Mr. Layton has had his day, and he knows it; the operative words in this volume are no longer only "lovely", "sun" and "castrato" but also "joyless", "grey" and "old."...Mr. Layton no longer writes as well as he did during the "high period" leading up to *A Red Carpet for the Sun*.[48]

Though a few reviewers remained enthusiastic, most had the same criticisms: superficiality, triteness and repetitious themes and images.

The poem "Economy, Please, Toronto"[49] suggested that Layton sometimes tired of his own escapades, felt uprooted and sad and longed to return, even to Toronto. Poems that depicted his real or imagined sexual adventures seemed not to express the joy of sex, but the sordidness of human nature. He often had commented that poems came to him when he least expected them, but as he travelled as a kind of poet-in-residence for the entire world, he felt obliged to produce a certain number of poems a year. In part, he was egged on by Jack McClelland who, during the early years, had turned Layton's unremitting demands for publication into a one-man side-show. McClelland not only brought out his new poems (with advances of a thousand dollars)[50] but also his *Selected Poems* (1969), his *Collected Poems* (1971), his articles, letters to editors and other prose (*Engagements*, 1972) and more selected poems in two volumes (*The Darkening Fire* and *The Unwavering Eye*, 1975).[51] McClelland and Layton were a disastrous combination. McClelland saw Layton as a money-making entertainer, boosted his already over-blown ego and then failed to insist on the discipline Layton needed. Layton responded almost naïvely to McClelland's charm and hucksterism without thinking of the consequences. (The poem he wrote for Jack McClelland — "Poetry as the Fine Art of Pugilism"[52] — dealt with boxing.) Though Pacey was joking with his friend and actually praised many of his poems, his reaction to Layton's title "Nail Polish" had more than a grain of truth in it: "your own verse is like nail polish — has a high gloss but no function, is used mainly by women and a few effeminate men, is translucent because it has no substance — has its only practical application on the thighs of ladies (where it stops runs in nylons!), and has a distinctly unpleasant smell which lingers in the nostrils for some hours."[53]

As the journal entries he published in *The Whole Bloody Bird* reveal, Layton despised or was intolerant of most of the new people and new situations he encountered: youthful hippies, young women, sophisticated American journalists, erudite Englishmen and local townspeople. He described Nepal, where he travelled with Betty and Naomi in the summer of 1968, as a place where "a congregation of beards, bards and bums have made their headquarters."[54] "All of these paradisal places attract the kind of persons you describe," he wrote in 1970 to Andy Wainwright.

> I've met them everywhere. Time-wasters; their own, and yours if you let them. Some of them are charming for a

short while; most of them bore the ass off me. The worst lot I encountered was in Kathmandu, perhaps because the hash was so inexpensive and plentiful.... In Kathmandu no one pretended any longer that he was a writer or a painter; in Ydra some of them still kept up the pretense.[55]

His rule of thumb seemed to be, "If they won't go to bed with me, admire my views or do something useful for me, they can all be damned." The self-loathing this attitude engendered spilled forth in some of the most offensive, un-musical poetry he had written. Though he had been wrongly accused, earlier in his career, of excessive use of four-letter words, his poems now were peppered with them in what looked like a desperate attempt to be interesting and "modern." As some reviewers noted, it was surprising that a publisher would accept most of the poems as art. Perhaps, if McClelland had refused to publish the poems that were mediocre or downright dreadful, Layton might have produced something more worthwhile. It was surprising, too, that McClelland agreed to publish Layton's journal entries instead of insisting that Layton turn them into stories. As travel writings, they were unexceptional; as short stories, they might have become literature.

But, as Layton realized, prose was not his medium: "It's not a good idea...to siphon off my impressions into prose for that leaves very little left over for poems.... Some poets there are who can switch from one form to the other, from poetry to prose, but I'm simply not one of them. Once the intensity has drained out of me, the pressure, the steam, I find I can't start again towards making a poem."[56] As McClelland had long realized, one good collection instead of four mediocre ones would have served both their purposes better. "What needs to be asked at this stage of Layton's career, with huge retrospective collections chugging off the press, is whether the first person is big enough,"[57] one reviewer commented. As another observed, "Layton needed not to flex his muscles, but to show his range."[58]

Layton's muse simply did not function as well in "paradisal places" as it did in the more austere Laurentian landscapes.

And, at times, Layton seemed to realize the importance of the Canadian landscape on his work. He objected strenuously, for example, when Northrop Frye theorized that an international style was developing in the arts partly because of the universalizing pressures of modern technology, commerce and science.

> Only an ideologue who is unresponsive to the concrete nature of poetry — its rhythm, immediacy, and life-rootedness — would or could make the kind of abstraction out of the process that Frye does.... poems are made from feelings, sensations and moods... If I look out of my window and see snow five months of the year, I'm obviously going to be a different sort of poet than if I were living near a Mexican swamp or a Nicoise beach. My eyes are going to see different things, and my mind is going to form different images. My internal chemistry is going to be different, changing not only the colour of my voice but the colour of my saying. And what about the rhythms of this being — they certainly were not the same for me in Tel Aviv and New Delhi or later when I moved on to Kathmandu, and they're different again now that I'm in Toronto.[59]

Layton hoped that the new rhythms he chose to encounter would stimulate different and better poetry. But he was, as he recognized, "a Canadian poet...someone who experiences so dramatically the winter and summer solstices."[60] Geography, landscape, climate and culture had played a subtle part in his poetry. His "life-rootedness" drew nourishment from the antimonies of the Montreal scene and from its ethnic mosaic. Travel disrupted this "life-rootedness." Like the climate and life-style and even the wastrels he complained of meeting there, many of Layton's poems from the Mediterranean and other warm climes were decadent.

Though Layton had been translated abroad, Jack McClelland, despite many efforts, never had been able to place his books with either a British or an American publisher. This situation thoroughly frustrated Layton, who had been angling for British and American publication since 1955. When Jonathan

Cape in England turned him down a decade later, he was furious. A Jonathan Cape editor had written to McClelland that although he was impressed with Layton's work, "there is a great danger that one finally becomes bored by his boastful exuberance, talented as he is."[61] Like a volcano, Layton erupted to McClelland: "So I'm to be put in a corner as a naughty bright boy whose boastful exuberance has disturbed Jonathan Cape. Well, well. I have been told that to be published nowadays in England one must be 'gay,' but never exuberant... Let the old country keep her dreary fairies."[62] Leonard Cohen came to Layton's rescue in 1971 by opening a publishing house — Spice Box Books Limited — in London for the sole purpose of publishing Layton there.[63] Years later, Layton was angry at cumulative rejections from the numerous American publishers he and McClelland had approached. Athaneum Publishers in New York, implying in their rejection note that Layton lacked scope as a poet, turned down *Balls for a One-Armed Juggler*.[64] Layton was furious at publishers south of the border: "Americans no longer know what a poem looks like and would be unable to distinguish it from an Idaho potato.... Not all Americans, but the overwhelming majority whose soft-boiled brains have led them from one disaster to another.... My poems are not for softheads and numbskulls. They never were. But in Canada, my long creative life enabled me to educate my compatriots to an understanding of what my poems and stories were all about."[65] Layton accounted for the lack of interest in his poetry in the United States as he accounted for English indifference: poetry was a dead art there.

> Where are the giants of yesteryear...? Poets like Jeffers, Frost, Robinson, Pound. Mailer fucked up his talent and Bellow suffers from hyperthyroidism. He's become unreadable. Ginzberg is writing oracular schlock. Also unreadable. I see he's getting some kind of an award and Mailer is going to be one of his pall-bearers. The difficulty of being a writer and maintaining one's artistic integrity in the essay is shown in the careers of both. Both of them crippled giants. Horrible grotesques, Anderson never could have imagined.[66]

Layton knew he was getting old and did not like it.

> I don't like it
> the way some people
> have been saying lately
> that I'm mellowing
>
> what they mean
> is that I'm yellowing
> that I'm becoming
> a washed-out Canadian
> like themselves
> with all the good rage
> rubbed out of me
> and no more lead in my pencil
>
> Or that they wished I was
>
> Only they're too polite to come right out
> and say so
>
> Up against the wall
> motherfuckers[67]

His picture on the cover of *Lovers and Lesser Men* showed an unshaven man with the beer-belly of a habitual pub-crawler, the striped cotton pants of the North American tourist and the crude large silver medallion and unkempt long hair of a hippie. Layton wished to convey the glamorous decadence of a drunk, the naïve wonderment of a tourist and the "groovy" exuberance of a hippie. But he drank little, detested tourists and hated hippies.

Layton sensed that he was moving out of the limelight, and the edge of viciousness in his poetry suggests that he badly wanted to be back in centre stage. But that was impossible. Interest had shifted to a new generation of poets, and had turned from poetry to fiction. Margaret Atwood and Leonard Cohen were fast becoming celebrities and joining the ranks of a new wave of Canadian fiction writers — Margaret Laurence, Marian Engel, Mordecai Richler, Brian Moore. At the time Layton was spending most of his free time outside Canada, the country experienced a burst of cultural nationalism in which he did not take part. Nor did he share the leftist idealism that characterized more than one age group during the late sixties and early seventies. Like a boxer who was still punching after his opponent has left the ring, he was directing his increasingly scatalogical diatribes against issues that no longer mattered. The puritanism he had attacked in the forties and fifties had virtually disappeared from the Canadian literary scene. Cohen's *Beautiful Losers* (1966) treated a wide variety of sexual acts explicitly and humorously; Jane Rule's *Desert of the Heart* (1964) dealt with a lesbian relationship; Scott Symons' *Place d'Armes* (1967) portrayed a homosexual relationship and related it to Canadian nationalism. As a reviewer of Layton's *The Whole Bloody Bird* noted, "After twenty-two [books] he has still not been able to find his wastebasket, but is seen pressing on regardless, an ageing iconoclast, running with hammer among already shattered busts of Mammon and peeing on the smokeless ruins."[68]

By insisting that all words in the English language should be available to the writer and by asserting, in his own lower-class voice, that there could be beauty, power and majesty in vulgarity, Layton had played a crucial role in transforming Canadian criteria. He did not seem to realize that the fight was won. Verses like his attack on the governor-general's committee (written the year Layton and several other poets gathered a thousand dollars and a medal for Milton Acorn, their choice for the award) were likely to strike readers as inartistic, repulsive, boring or ludicrous:

> One day you'll butter your bread with my excrement
> And pour libations to one another with my staling.
>
> Gentlemen, may you choke on both.[69]

Nowhere was Layton more out of touch with the times than in his attitude towards the growing feminist movement. He was proud to be considered the archetypal male-chauvinist pig. ("Skirts going up and pantyhose coming down — that's the only kind of dialectics I'm interested in nowadays," he wrote to Pacey after a fling in Montreal in 1972.)[70] Freedom, it seemed, was fine for men; not so for women. After a CBLT-TV "Life Style" programme with Kate Millett, he wrote to Pacey:

> My native chivalry with women stopped me from cracking her on the head, which is what she was really asking for. She's a militant ignoramus whose book *Sexual Politics*, I now suspect was ghost-written by somebody in the office of Doubleday's, if not in whole, certainly in large part. She's a menace, not to men, but to her own sex; and if women know what's good for them — and they always do — they'll shut her up as soon as possible. She's doing them and their cause a great deal of harm. Beside her, that other prick-envying communist, Betty Friedan, is an intellectual giant.[71]

Many of Layton's poems at this time reflect a profound dislike of women, even those he hotly pursued. "She says she loves you," went one of his aphorisms, "Let me translate for you. She says that while eating you, she will arrange the bones neatly on the plate."[72] In "Teufelsdröckh Concerning Women," he wrote:

> Women are stupid.
> They're cunning but they're stupid.
> Life with a capital L wants it that way.
> They're cunning with their clefts
> Where nothing can dislodge it
> Not even Phil 301 at Queen's or Varsity.
> Women will never give the world a Spinoza,
> A Wagner or a Marx;
> Some lab technicians and second-rate poets, yes,
> But never an Einstein or a Goethe.
> Vision is strictly a man's prerogative,
> So's creativity
> Except for a handful of female freaks
> With hair on their chins and enlarged glands.[73]

Such poems were not likely to speak to a generation that

turned to Margaret Atwood for consciousness-raising about sex roles. Nor would the poem appeal to Aviva, whose career as a writer was steadily developing.

The freedom and leisure Layton had sought for so long came too late and at the wrong time. He experienced a profound disillusionment with life, which he could not fully understand. How could it be that women are so rotten when they were supposed to be so desireable? Why did he feel so jealous of Aviva and she so jealous of him when they had agreed in principle that open marriage was the ultimate in civilized behaviour? Why weren't people shocked at his vituperations any more? Why were reviews of his books so hostile? In a world he himself had reduced to the primitive level of survival of the fittest, Layton suffered most of all a crushing disgust with himself. "Vampire" reflected his view that poems sucked out the poet's essence; it is a curiously archaic piece, which captured an inner void:

> I'm not a dirty old man, my love
> O I am not at all what men say I am;
> For I am not wild over breasts and thighs,
> Before the sweetest cleft my nerves are calm.
>
> Be warned, my love, be warned and do not stay;
> I'm a vampire who'll drain your youthful blood
> For poems to feed him immortality,
> Who'll give you horrid fangs and make you mad.
>
> Young girls are what melts the ice in my veins;
> Their sighs, loving glances are what I need.
> When they awake my wanton lust for truth
> Not rival Death himself can stay my greed.
>
> And you daisy loveliness is your doom;
> Run, my darling, run far away and hide
> For I'm cursed to turn beauty into truth
> And you, my sweet, into my spectral bride.
>
> Ah, no, do not run but if you love me
> End my accursed lineage and my lust;

If you would see them wither into dust,
Drive this stake through my heart and let me die.[74]

"Poets do well to die young," he wrote bitterly to Pacey on a postcard from Mexico, where he lay basking in the sun at Christmas in 1973. The poet he had in mind was Robert Frost, whose biography he was reading.[75]

Gypsy Jo

"Since 1970, Layton has been waging battle against the forces of Dullness from his headquarters in darkest Downsview," went a 1978 *Globe and Mail* article:

> He chooses people for his workshops by inspecting manuscripts submitted for his scrutiny; but he's the first to admit that he's a pushover for anyone determined to attend — like the attractive young woman who strode into the classroom one day while a session was in progress. "Don't you remember me?" she asked Layton when he expressed curiosity as to who she was. "We met on a street corner a few months ago."
>
> How is the York Poetry Workshop conducted? Well, for the first two or three months, the group examines masterpieces — poetry by Blake, Shakespeare, Dylan Thomas — with an eye to the technical devices of poetry: meter, sound, structure. Layton presents his ideas; the students, theirs. Both sides agree that sessions are never boring. (Can anything presided over by Layton be boring?) According to Fred Gaysek, a creative writing major, "His biggest purpose is to instill excitement and inspiration into students, and he literally starts ranting to do that."
>
> Once students have become attuned to what makes a

well-crafted poem, they're ready to discuss their own poetry, both in the workshop and in regular private meetings with Layton, where he will often spend an hour going through a poem line by line, even word by word. All in all, Layton argues, "It's a beautiful way to learn poetry."

This is not empty bombast. For some, Layton's workshop develops into an addiction. They return year after year to marvel at Layton's ability to bring excitement to the same poems. "He's a fantastic teacher," insists Judith Doyle, who has spent two years in the workshop. "Every class is a performance about everything that's on his mind. His particular bias is toward the well-crafted poem. He's heavily attracted by the impassioned voice. But the way that he discusses things in class can be impassioned and quite cold and intellectual at the same time — that's the particular quality of Irving's voice."

This balance between thought and feeling is what Layton hopes his students will achieve in their poetry, but he never promises miracles. Only God can make a poet, and despite Layton's reputation as a prophet howling in the wilderness, divinity has still eluded him. What he does guarantee is that by the end of a workshop, students will know what makes a poet and what makes a poem. Not that he complains if someone does go on to become a poet, especially a good poet.

It's unlikely that you can even carry on a ten-minute conversation with Layton without hearing the names of all his former students who are now publishing verse and editing poetry magazines. He keeps track of all of them. He writes their names on the blackboard so that others will recognize them.[1]

The main point about writing that Layton conveyed so incisively to his students was described by a journalist:

> Layton says he knows he can inflict mortal wounds on students who bring in poems, but he makes a point of being absolutely honest. Then he tells them what to do to improve: remove plain, ordinary words, avoid rhetoric

and cliches; watch out for relative pronouns and prepositions, which lead to prose rhythms; use action verbs, not copulatives; try for good, strong rhythm and fresh imagery.

"If they're serious about being poets they'll take what I have to tell them seriously," he says. "I had to learn all those things. I can save somebody five years."[2]

In the fall of 1974, Layton was a "pushover" for Harriet Bernstein. Harriet was beautiful. She was twenty-six. Her long, straight, russet hair framed a head so perfectly shaped it might have been formed by a sculptor. Her body was stocky, compact, suggestive of European peasantry. She was all ruffles, flowers and tawny autumn colours. When she arrived at his office in York for an interview for one of the ten places in his workshop, Layton intended to tell her that the poems she had submitted were not good enough and that he could not accept her. His eyes strayed to her full, slow-moving lips. He looked into her rich, melancholy eyes. "She told me that she was going into the hospital to have a hemmorhoid operation. I felt sorry for her. I told her she had been accepted."[3]

Harriet, whom Layton would soon nick-name "Gypsy Jo," was in revolt against her background of wealth and position. Her father was Jack Bernstein, the powerful vice-president of Famous Players Theatres. He decided what pictures Famous Players would offer, where they would be shown and for how long. Her mother was the soprano Mary Simmons, a woman who had aspired to the stage. Harriet and her brother were their only children. They were given all that money could buy: a home in Toronto's most expensive area, Forest Hill, education in the United States, the works.

In the late sixties, Harriet, who had been a pudgy, unprepossessing teenager, dropped out of sight of her Toronto friends. When she resurfaced a few years later, she was gorgeous. She no longer seemed miserable and self-effacing: she radiated charm and self-confidence. People who knew her thought she looked like a different person: happier, very bright and funny.[4] She took a job doing publicity for Paramount [Pictures] Canada. She married Stephen Shuster, the son of the well-known comedian Frank Shuster.

The marriage didn't work. After only two months, the young couple separated. In a bid to develop her talents, Harriet left her publicity job and enrolled at York University.

In an early poem to Harriet, called "For My Incomparable Gypsy," Layton claims he virtually announced to her that he was not "marital material" and that he intended to resist the impulse to give her a child:

> The beauty that nature would fill
> with pregnancies I'd keep sterile
> forever, to be gazed at, not touched:
> a poem, a canvas under glass.
> What has the fine curve of your chin
> the trim perfection of your thighs
> to do with ripening and decay?
> ...
> From here on it's all downhill,
> downhill all the way. Fine manners,
> love and poetry and what once
> went by the name of form or style
> — all have been rammed up a baboon's
> red asshole. Or Hitler's. The world grows
> each day safer for knaves and goons.
> So my incomparable gypsy
> I decline the invitation
> your amazing body sends me,
> though brain and instinct are programmed
> to infecundate all beauty.
> Go fuck and fill your womb with child,
> in these lines you'll never grow old
> but stay as fresh as the first kiss
> you pressed on my impatient lips.
> Marriages are for common clay;
> for you I wish eternal day
> not pukes and the rounded belly.
> Only in this embalming poem
> my unravished beauty be mine.[5]

As a result of Layton's instruction in the poetry workshop, Harriet began publishing her own poems. One that appeared in the *Canadian Review* in 1975 was called "Musical Interlude":

> It pains me deep when my lover's unable
> To lay the record on the turntable,
> His years are many, his sight grows dim
> But it's clear to see that I love him.
>
> And while his fingers grope for the hole
> Of the disc, to slip on the player's pole,
> How sweetly content I admit to be
> That he never has had the same problem with me.[6]

Though Layton was officially living with Aviva at 122 St. Clements Avenue, he took Harriet on a holiday to Greece in the summer of 1975. People who saw them together were struck by the extreme nature of their romantic infatuation. They were like story-book lovers: the white-haired legendary poet who, despite the fact that he had false teeth and a hearing aid, was full of vim and vigour, and his beautiful, adoring mistress, another poet in the making.

They arrived in Athens by sea on the *Adonis*. As if inspired by the ship's name, which alluded to the handsome Greek god who loved Aphrodite, Layton made love to his beautiful flower-child in the ship's washroom on the crossing from Brindisi, an episode that both Layton and Harriet recorded in ecstatic verse.[7] They settled in the Plaka, a small hotel in the slummy part of Athens right below the Acropolis, around the corner from the place where Byron had once sojourned. Once settled, Layton began the solitary morning rambles that had always been his custom. Up at dawn, he would leave Harriet sleeping and, like a curious young boy, walk out into the white light of Greece to see the early morning sights, watch the city come to life in its bustling markets and crowded maritime quay, hopeful that his muse would speak.

After one of these morning forays, he returned to find their room empty. Harriet had unaccountably left for Toronto, leaving only a short note of explanation. Perhaps Harriet had doubts about their relationship, or perhaps, as Layton later claimed, a minor illness she had come down with depressed her and she had decided she did not want to trouble her lover with taking care of her. Whatever the reason, without warning she was gone. Layton felt profoundly abandoned.[8]

Athens without Harriet lost its glamour for him. He fled impulsively to Barcelona to think things over. He sensed he must have been crazy to expect a girl like Harriet to stick with him. He wrote to Aviva. He'd been wrong. Could she come and meet him? Scott Symons had always said they could visit him in Essaouira, a small village in Morocco perched on the Atlantic Coast. How about there?

Symons had fled Canada with his handsome, under-age lover years before, after setting the establishment on its ear by writing *Place d'Armes* (1967), an award-winning novel about a man who defects from his conventional life in Toronto to find homosexual love and a mystic sense of his nationality in Montreal. He had settled down in an abandoned country auberge on the outskirts of Essaouira. Layton, recognizing a kindred spirit in Symons, had recommended him for arts awards, and their paths had crossed periodically.

"He and Aviva were coming from different directions, and planned to hook up here," Symons recalls.[9] "Irving arrived the night before he was expected and was terrified. He was very aware that he was a Jew in an Islamic country. He spent the night on the sofa of the hotel where I had booked a room for Aviva. She hadn't arrived. At six-thirty the next morning, he came by taxi to the auberge where I was living with my lover. He could hardly wade through the sand drifts. He just leaned against the tree a hundred yards from my place screaming and howling, 'Scott, Scott...' When I got up and went to the window, he looked like an abandoned mediaeval creature. He was totally terrified. He thought that Aviva was lost. Once she got there he calmed down.

"They took a room at the Hotel de Tourism overlooking the harbour and visited me every day at my auberge. We all spent a lot of time sitting at outdoor cafés. Irving immediately began looking for girls. He could never sit still. He'd keep getting up looking as if he was about to take off in the cockpit of a plane. He would pace up and down the big terrace that ran along the waterfront and declaim about life, or read the poems he'd written, for hours. But it was Aviva who had the real adventures. She found a lover who was a Moroccan prince who came in his chauffeur-driven sports Mercedes to pick her up. Irving was jealous that she was getting it all, but everything remained friendly between them."

By September, Irving and Aviva were back on St. Clement's Avenue in Toronto and Harriet, whose divorce from Shuster had just been finalized, was back at York University.

The Meshugas

"I'll be damned if I let you or anyone else rob me of my true glory... *not now, not ever,*" Layton had written to Pacey in 1970.[1] He cast about for something, anything, to stop the distressing erosion of his importance to Canadian literature. He had attempted to "widen his range" by concentrating more on political issues since he had gone to Europe with Marion Wagshall in the summer of 1967 and produced the bitter political poems and theories in *The Shattered Plinths*. He knew that his views on Vietnam would sell absolutely zilch. He certainly couldn't take part in the women's liberation movement, which seemed absurd and offensively strident. He wasn't interested in civil rights or ecology or drugs. What cause could he espouse to astonish his public and revivify his sagging reputation?

After returning from the west coast, where he had objected to the "huge impersonal halls" at Simon Fraser University, the University of British Columbia and the University of Victoria, which he thought made his poetry readings sound "phony and affected," he wrote to Pacey.

> Did I tell you what my latest *"mishuggash"*[2] (lunacy) is? It's to reclaim Jesus for the Jews. In Victoria I fired the opening shot when I announced this intention of mine

to a black-eyed dumb beauty who interviewed me for *The Victoria Times*. I don't think she understood a single word I said but there's just a possibility the lovely dumbell will quote me verbatim... If my views do get into the paper, they might make a lot of people mad, including my fellow Jews to whom Jesus is still a nasty word. But I've developed a strong feeling that something can be done about the prevailing smell of hypocrisy that surrounds the entire Christian-Jew problem. Gentiles have got to be brought to their senses, or rather they've got to be brought to openly admit that on the question of Jesus' sonship to God and his resurrection — for which Jews have been mercilessly persecuted for nearly 2000 years — they were WRONG and the Jews who stubbornly held to the view that Jesus was a mortal Jew no different from themselves were RIGHT.[3]

It was indeed a *meshugas* for Layton to tackle such questions. He had cleverly and stubbornly eluded his father's attempts to teach him the rudiments of his orthodox heritage. He knew almost no Hebrew. He had not had a bar mitzvah. He had disagreed violently with A.M. Klein's Zionism. He spent a good deal of time disclaiming his Jewishness and proclaiming himself an atheist. What Jewishness remained with him had been acquired from the familiar surroundings of his home, the Yiddish his mother spoke and the books by Jews he had read among so many others. He was certainly more Jewish than, say, F.R. Scott or Louis Dudek, but he also was much less Jewish than A.M. Klein or Seymour Mayne, the young student who had become a poet and professor. As for Christianity, Layton knew even less. Claiming Jesus for the Jews was primarily an attempt to disrupt Canadian complacency by using the horrors of Gulag and Auschwitz, the most sensational images he could find of human evil. Looked at in its worst light, his *meshugas* was based on the assumption that the Holocaust posed almost endless market possibilities.

As early as 1966, Layton had attempted to "acquire" what might be called the heritage of the holocaust. He also had begun to read more books about Jews and Judaism, as if to cull ammunition he might launch against an unsuspecting world. "Surely it's no accident," he challenged Pacey in 1974, "that the most prominent and most spirited dissenters in that accursed land [Russia] have been Jews: [Boris] Pasternak, Daniel, [Maxim] Litvinov, [Osip] Mandelshtam, [Joseph] Brodski, Ginzberg and the eminent physicist, [Andrei] Sakharov, to select names at random. On the contrary, the fact of their dissent and fierce opposition lies embedded in the logic of Jewish history itself."[4] Layton immersed himself in writings about Jews and identified himself with the right-wing opinions expressed in the Jewish current-events magazine *Commentary* (published in New York) as a sort of bolster for his ego. There had been many great Jews in history and culture. He was (sort of) a Jew. Therefore, he was a great historical and cultural figure.

Reviewers lashed out at the political naïveté of *The Pole-Vaulter*, which had appeared in 1975. "*The Pole-Vaulter* is prefaced by a political statement of such adolescent prejudice, smugness and sheer irrelevance that [Layton's] editor deserves to be shot for permitting its appearance," blasted the young poet Susan Musgrave. "Layton seems like the man in Priestly's novel who had 'over-drawn on his intellectual bank balance.'"[5] "If Irving Layton's *The Pole-Vauler* were a first book of poetry, it would not be worth a review. It's that embarrassing," declared another reviewer. "He seeks a revelation from history which is impossible — for he is at the same time using, exploiting, history as fine sentiment and self-justification. Whoever has read Nelly Sachs' *O the Chimneys* will find the suffering of Jews reduced to a non-event in *The Pole-Vaulter*. Without any first-hand idea of what the suffering was, Layton does not bother with historical understanding either."[6]

For My Brother Jesus (1976) and *The Covenant* (1977),[7] two books that, in some poems at least,[8] attempted to carry out Layton's aim to claim Jesus for the Jews, created an even greater furor. The furor, however, was not quite as Layton imagined it. It centred not on whether Jesus was a Jew or whether Christians should bear the burden of guilt for Auschwitz and Gulag, though Layton did receive many letters from readers on these questions; it centred on whether Layton was worth listening to at all. "What does *For My Brother Jesus* prove?" asked one reviewer. "Only that time's scythe cuts away more than beauty, and that this once-admired poet has fallen into the spleen of senescence."[9] "Where Layton should be powerful and subtle and original, he's bombastic and simple-minded and trite," wrote Robert Fulford. "[He] doesn't bother to reconcile...contradictions, and if pressed he would probably say that he's a poet, not a philosopher. Nevertheless, he approaches great philosophical and historic problems. He should do them justice or leave them alone. The 6 million don't need any more easy answers."[10] "The repatriation of Jesus, a noble enterprise, remains to be done," wrote Michael Hornyansky in "Letters in Canada, 1976." "It awaits a champion not wholly deficient in religion, and having some memory of what the Man said."[11]

Layton thought the response from the public far outweighed the opinions of the critics.

> "My Brother Jesus" has gotten me piles of letters from dear old maids, of both sexes, eager to save my soul, phone calls from every part of the country and even one from Dearborn, Mich, and invitations to relieve myself of my burdensome thoughts in Temples and Churches ...Next to sex, there's nothing like the divineness of Jeezus to make people take time off from watching the boob tube and write letters. I'm contemplating a sermon "Did Jesus The Man Fart?" I've learned that the destruction of six million Jews within living memory doesn't agitate people as much as the question of who crucified their Saviour two thousand years ago. Did I ever tell you people were loony?...G-r-r-r- there are a lot of crazy people out there.... Did I tell you...the title for my next book? *For My Brother Mohammed*. The one after that I'll call *For My Brother Buddha*.[12]

To Layton, it seemed only his due when he received a five-hundred-dollar award from the J.I. Segal Fund for Jewish Culture through the Jewish Public Library of Montreal. He won in the category "English Literature on a Jewish Theme."

About this time, Layton was asked to appear on Pierre

Berton's TV debate show to comment on the situation in Israel. He approached professor Harry Crowe at York University, who was editor of *Middle East Focus*, to be briefed before the programme. Professor Sally F. Zerker, Crowe's associate editor, did the briefing. "I didn't know how he had the nerve to go on television," she recalls. "He didn't know anything about the situation. It wasn't his area. He didn't understand the complexity and volatility of the situation, but he thought he could represent a point of view he felt strongly about. I watched the programme to see how he would do. I thought he would make an ass of himself and he did."[13]

Layton also appeared on Global Television's "The Great Debate" near the end of 1975, to discuss the topic "Zionism versus Racism" with Sami Hadawi. Layton's contribution was well below par. "Layton blew it," remarks Jewish scholar Elaine Kahn, the wife of a rabbi and the director of public relations for the Canadian Friends of the Hebrew University. "Whereas Hadawi was very well prepared with facts, Layton was purely emotional. He was just pontificating. I can't imagine why he ever agreed to go on the programme. He was just horrible."[14]

Joe Rosenblatt, a young Jewish poet in Victoria, British Columbia (whose *Top Soil* [1976] had won a Governor-General's Award), and a friend of Layton's, felt that Layton knew little about Judaism: "Layton's a fool, he's obviously a dummy; he's a bigot, he's an ignorant man in terms of what Judaism is all about: he's a stup, a super-stup; but he's also one of our best poets."[15]

Even Jack McClelland was beginning to give up on Layton. For years, McClelland had been trying to get Layton to see that he was publishing too much that was no good too often. Layton asked McClelland to look through the reviews of *For My Brother Jesus* with an eye to finding an American publisher. Layton said the reviews were mainly positive, but McClelland had to shake his head. "The idea had been that with an impressive press file that we might be able to interest an American publisher in this book. I don't think this file is going to impress an American publisher," he wrote in a memo.[16] In a later memo, he admitted, "There is really no solution to Layton. He is going to continue writing. We will just have to continue dealing with him. He says his [next] book may be ready for the fall of 1977...but hell we will do it in the spring of 1978. It should be no trick to convince him of that."[17]

The Covenant (Layton's proposed "awful" title was "Bravo Layton"), contrary to McClelland's plan, came out in 1977. Layton feebly announced that the book contained "several minor pieces" to "lighten the seriousness" of the volume. It drew more fire than his previous books. The poems were described as "some of Layton's worst moments ever,"[18] "deflated and unmusical"[19] and "works of inspired puerility."[20] One critic thought the rancour in them was "contrived."[21] In the most thoughtful review, Gary Geddes compared Layton's present work to what had gone before:

> [There is] distance here from the absolute rightness of lines in "Keine Lazarovitch," such as the "inescapable lousiness of growing old," where the community of sounds captures the ear and the word "inescapable," predictably hyperbolic in an elegy, is rendered acceptable by juxtaposing it with a completely unexpected colloquial word such as "lousiness".... There is perhaps, too much of the public debater in Layton and not enough of the private man who has composed some of the greatest poems in our language.... Too many poems...are formless; the ideas do not dance, but sit there uncomfortably waiting for the poet to turn off the rhetoric and turn on the imagination.[22]

Geddes said Layton candidly admitted to him at a conference: "Geddes, you and I would probably agree on my dozen or so best poems. These don't come unless you keep writing; and no one would ever get to read those dozen masterpieces, given the realities of Canadian publishing, unless you throw in the warm-up pieces too."[23] As a last-ditch measure, Layton turned the kind of criticisms he had been receiving into a poem. It was, one critic noted,[24] "the review we even sense he somehow longs for":

> In this book Layton has stripped away

all the trappings of restraint and decency
and has revealed himself to be
the uninhibited megalomaniac
we always suspected he was.
...this rowdy silly tortured tender
feisty outrageous posturing egotistical
and somewhat pathetic excuse for a poet.[25]

Compared to *A Red Carpet for the Sun*, which had sold five thousand copies in its first year in 1959, *The Covenant* only sold 1,841 copies. Layton's next five volumes — *The Tightrope Dancer* (1978), *Droppings From Heaven* (1979), *For My Neighbours in Hell* (1980), *Europe and other Bad News* (1981) and *The Gucci Bag* (1983)[26] — did nothing to revive his reputation. His stature as a major poet had been set and was now also witnessed by the steady output of various kinds of re-arrangements of his previous work: *Il Freddo Verde Elemento* (the Italian translation of *The Cold Green Element*), *Seventy-five Greek Poems 1951–1974* (some of which were written long before Layton went to Greece), *The Darkening Fire — Selected Poems 1945–1968* and *The Unwavering Eye — Selected Poems 1969–1975, The Uncollected Poems of Irving Layton 1936–59, The Poems of Irving Layton, Selected Poems* (1977), *The Selected Poems of Irving Layton* (1977), *Il Puma Ammansito* (a translation of *The Tamed Puma*) (1978), *There Were No Signs*, a portfolio with drawing by Aligi Sassu that sold for two thousand dollars a copy, *The Love Poems of Irving Layton* (1980), *Shadows on the Ground*, another portfolio, *A Wild Peculiar Joy — Selected Poems 1945–82, Poemas de Amor* (the Spanish translation of Layton's love poetry) and a *Spider Danced a Cosey Jig* (1984),[27] a selection of animal poems for children and adults.

Droppings From Heaven (the title referred to semen plonking onto the ground after coitus interruptus on a fire escape)[28] called forth the most scorching diatribes from the critics. Reviews were dotted with words like "overkill," "clichés," "lost authenticity," "pontificating nastiness" and "juvenile malice." "I want to go into the sunset with both pitchforks blazing," Layton had claimed in his preface. The remark uncomfortably recalled Stephen Leacock's description of a rider "going off in all directions at once." But even former admirer Al Purdy had had enough. In a 1979 review that infuriated Layton, Purdy wrote:

> Irving Layton was the Great Liberator for me and others in Montreal, at a time when literary panjandrums like A.J.M. Smith and V.B. Rhodenizer were setting old standards of classic dullness and verbal constipation in poetry. Layton attacked them with both invective and calumny; in his best poems he was magnificent. I personally owed him much.
>
> All of which is by way of prelude for saying *that* time is no more. Layton has been imitating himself for years, in a perfect parody of his own style, and has written nearly all of his poems before, some many times. Vigor and self-righteousness he still retains, and these may be admirable as a bulldozer destroying a slum...
>
> And there is such a joyful sound of jubilee in describing human cruelties and evil, a piling-on of adjectives and bone-crushing epithets, lambasting of the obvious — that I suspect Layton's motives. Surely this is over-kill. What human being, self-righteous or fallible, would not condemn the Holocaust, human cruelty and evil, Stalin, Hitler, Franco, etc.? I suspect he enjoys this over-kill lambasting far too much.[29]

For another reviewer, Layton had simply become absurd:

> IRVING LAYTON. DROPPINGS FROM HEAVEN.
> McCLELLAND AND STEWART, 1979.
>
> Here is *Droppings From Heaven*, another sublime canto of the Canadian Dante who, as always, with great humility denounces social injustice and makes us mediocre citizens realize what we missed by not having his lucidity....
>
> We can certainly say that the author of *Droppings From Heaven* chooses his quotations well. Is anyone able "to forget reality" better than Irving Layton? Has anyone ever written anything truer than "Narcissus," a poem composed "Under a false sky" in Palm Beach? And it is from Palm Beach, San Francisco, Molibos,

Banff, Inverness, Toronto, Montreal and St. Marguerite that Irving Layton fights for the world's oppressed.

Of all the superb poems in this collection "The Canadian Epic" is perhaps the most beautiful. Right from the start it presents the "underprivileged" poet crying for "justice":

> It's when I'm in a faraway land
> in Greece or Italy
> that I think of my country

Then Layton proceeds to compare, with great originality — as we all know that it has never been done before — his country to a woman:

> As a young woman with a headache,
> an ice-pack on her head
> and fluttering her hands over forests and streams

But the amazing freshness of the poem is felt when, again with immense originality, the poet castigates a profession in which he never believed or engaged:

> ...And I say your Bible-belters and yokels
> with an M.A. or Ph.D. in Literature
> Should be in a thriving zoo or circus

It is sad to see that academics lack so much tact and that they persist in studying and teaching Layton just to embarrass him with honours, royalties and fame — things that the humble poet really dislikes; for, as he points out in his introduction, Layton is only here to remind us of "Auschwitz or Goulag [sic]."[30]

"Layton fails to convince us of the truth or clarity of his vision," wrote a reviewer of *Europe and other Bad News*, "because he lacks the experience of Whitman, the wisdom of Freud, the intuition of Sartre, or the omniscience of God. Layton's old man is a rather doddering intellectual adventurer in a land he doesn't know, with a passport he has forged. He exhibits little of the objectivity or understanding that come with lifetime of experience.... He is a man grown old with bitterness, guilt and lack of forgiveness. His thinking is repetitive. His wise old man becomes a wise guy, senile with rage."³¹

Layton alienated Jack McClelland who, in the rash of Layton books published by companies other than his own, had begun to wonder whether he could still call himself Layton's publisher. Layton had always been difficult to handle. He had brought forward a series of manuscripts from his "protégés" that had had to be awkwardly rejected (Musia's memoirs, Seymour Mayne's collection of critical articles on Layton, a biography and a critical book on Layton by Wynne Francis, a Layton bibliography by librarian Joy Bennett and James Polson and a drawing of himself by Marion Wagshall). McClelland had not been able to trust Layton to play fair by the understood rules of publishing. In 1962, Layton had gone behind McClelland's back to edit *Poetry '64* for Ryerson Press. McClelland had been furious: "It ain't kosher. It's like Dylan Thomas writing for the *Reader's Digest*, only less respectable becaue it's at least commercial... I would prefer to have you arrested for relieving yourself at the corner of Peel and St. Catherine than being exposed as the editor of an anthology of new poetry published by the United Church Publishing House.... You don't need a publisher; you need a wetnurse."³² After this, McClelland thought of Layton as enormously insecure, betrayed by his voracious appetite for more publications, more money, wider audiences. Layton's fear about books going out of print — a kind of literary impotence — was intense. In 1970, McClelland again took him to task, this time for agreeing to take part in an Oxford University Press Collection called *Fifteen Canadian Poets*.³³ Then, in 1972, Layton had his lawyer hold McClelland to the contracts that pledged to keep six of his books in print "in perpetuum."³⁴ In 1975, Layton peddled a collection called *Seventy-Five Greek Poems*, which he had had published in Greece. But he was selling the book not only in Greece, as McClelland understood he would, but in Canada, where the book competed with the increasing numbers of Layton stock that lined the shelves of the M&S warehouse. McClelland was furious.[35] In 1980, when Layton brought out *For My Neighbours in Hell* and the Dorothy Rath correspondence, both with Mosaic Press in Oakville, things came to a head. McClelland had not even seen the manuscript of *For My Neighbours in Hell*. "Of course you're my publisher," Layton had ingenuously written in reply to Jack's angry letter. "Who else? But the two books I published with MOSAIC PRESS should have come as no surprise because I had mentioned both of them to you or Linda [McKnight]... Frankly, the reason I didn't offer you *For My Neighbours in Hell* is that I didn't think it was a book for M&S and I wanted to spare you the embarrassment of having to reject one of my books."[36] Layton had never been able to see McClelland's point of view: that in the early 1970s he had so many books in print and others coming out that he had begun to compete with himself. "As many great artists have had to realize before him," McClelland confided to one of his staff in 1975, "there is a limit to the absorptive qualities of the market... The market for individual volumes of poetry in Canada is not as good today as it was five years ago because of over-production. The market for Layton is softer than it was and will deteriorate rapidly if too much Layton is made available."[37] Though McClelland repeatedly explained the market situation to Layton, his explanation had an effect opposite to the one he desired. He hoped that Layton would see the virtue of self-restraint. But Layton, who had never been keen on virtues anyway, only became more anxious about his reputation. His insecurity actually increased his determination to publish more often and to puff up his image as much as he could. If this meant bullying McClelland to keep his growing number of books in print while he went elsewhere to swell the number of his poems and collections further, *tant pis*.

Judging from Layton's advice to poet Andy Wainwright, Layton knew better. "Hold off. Hold off," he wrote to Wainwright in 1971. "Don't be in a hurry to publish. Let the poems mellow like good wine in your skull. I'm a good one to talk, I know. But I think now if I had to [do] it over I'd space my books more broadly tho' I dunno the momentum was important and the eagerness to see the next book in print kept me writing furiously as if my next poem was going to be my last."[38] He proferred the same advice to poet Steven Osterlund, who had written a study of Layton called *Fumigator* and who kept up a spirited correspondence with "The Chief." "Always bear in mind," Layton wrote from Australia to Osterlund, who was also travelling abroad, "that it's fatal for a poet to cut his roots. Culturally, North America is where it's at."[39] Layton knew better, but he couldn't help himself.

Two Bar Mitzvahs

AN EVENING of dining and dancing to honour
Irving Layton on the occasion of his sixty-fifth birthday
(or his second bar-mitzvah).

7:30 PM, Saturday the nineteenth of March, 1977
at *Casa Loma*, 1 Austin Terrace, Toronto.

$20.00 per person
Make cheques payable to Sylvia Fraser,
382 Brunswick Avenue, Toronto M5R 2Y9
(416) 921-5068.[1]

The invitation featured a three-inch-by-three-inch photostat reproduction of Layton's leonine head looking out somewhat benignly from beneath a shaggy grey mane. This large logo embellished his personal stationery from then on.

Toronto's fairy-tale castle, Casa Loma, was perched Fantasia-like on a mid-Toronto hill. Its lights flickered over the dark city. A mish-mash of architectural styles, it was the overwrought folly of Sir Henry Pellatt, a financier in the early 1920s. Sir Henry had had vision, but no foresight. Within a few years of the building's completion, he was unable to run the multi-million dollar establishment he had built.

The party there, arranged by Jack McClelland, was kept a secret from Layton. "His son David said it wasn't difficult," reported *Quill & Quire*. "His father is usually in his third floor study writing poems and is pretty oblivious to household matters."[2] Even Aviva's unprecedented attention to ironing a crease in his trousers did not give the show away. Toronto lawyer Julian Porter got Layton there by telling him that they were going to a political dinner where Layton could straighten out Ontario treasurer Darcy McKeough on the problems of Quebec. Layton had replied, "Of course."[3]

Close to two hundred members of Canada's publishing and media communities were there. Telegrams arrived from Governor-General Jules Léger, Secretary of State John Roberts, Margaret Atwood and Ontario Premier William Davis. One from Trudeau reminded Layton of Shakespeare's adage: "Commit the oldest sins in the newest kind of ways." Rabbi Reuben Slonim gave a traditional Hebrew blessing for the meal. The highlight of the evening was a huge cake. Out of it suddenly burst blonde-bombshell novelist Sylvia Fraser in a backless red gown, clutching a bouquet of daffodils. "Roses are red, Daffodils are yellow, I'm your doxie tonight, What a lucky fellow!" she recited. Irving Layton was officially old.

"It was shortly after that birthday party at Casa Loma that I realized Irving and Harriet were deeply involved," Eli Mandel recalls. "I would see Harriet coming often to his office at York. There was an aura of perfume and a lot of smoke from Irving's cigars coming from that room. She'd show up in the morning, and I'd hear Irving offer her a drink of sweet, red Vermouth. Aviva would come down the hall. Her nostrils would flare and she'd turn and walk away. I remember Irving saying to me, 'When I was a young man and my mother was taken from me, God looked after me. First he gave me Betty, then he gave me Aviva, now he's given me Harriet.'"[4]

The summer after the Casa Loma party, David turned thirteen. For his bar mitzvah, Aviva planned a holiday abroad: London, Paris, Amsterdam, Rome, Israel and Greece. Irving had been awarded a Canada Council senior arts fellowship of seventeen thousand dollars for a year abroad. Aviva did not know she would celebrate David's bar mitzvah without Irving.

"Irving said that he wanted to go ahead of us," Aviva recalls.[5] "I begged him to wait until David's school was out so that the three of us could travel together. When he refused that, I wanted him to agree to a fixed date on which we would meet in Jerusalem. He didn't want to be bound by dates." Irving went ahead; Aviva waited until David could leave.

In London, where Aviva began the trip with David, she ran into Leon Whiteson, a script-writer she and Irving had met on Molibos several years before. The three had written a "musical tragedy" in 1974. "I became involved with Leon in London mainly because I was so furious with Irving for going ahead without us," Aviva explains. "I knew I couldn't count on him to be in Jerusalem when we got there either. Leon wanted to come with me to Molibos. I decided that if by some miracle Irving did turn up in Jerusalem, Leon would be a sort of 'counter-weight' for me. I didn't think I could stand to be let down by Irving again. It was more than that, too: I had fallen deeply in love with Leon. Of course Irving wasn't there. Later he accused *me* of being the one who got the signals crossed. I stopped writing to him then. He had no sense of responsibility. David was nothing more than a hiccup in our relationship. It was hell before he was born and hell afterwards."[6]

It was almost August by the time Aviva got to Molibos, where Irving had been building up his own reservoir of anxiety since early July. "I knew she had arrived," Layton recalls,[7] "but she didn't come directly to the house I had rented. I didn't realize that Leon was there with her and David until the next day, but that's where she was, making dinner for them. At four AM she came reeling in. She was stinking drunk. She had fallen into a puddle and could hardly get up. She reeked of alcohol. She did the same thing the following night. During the day, Aviva and Leon cavorted on the beach, showing anyone who might be interested that they were lovers. The next morning I sat her down and told her to go to this man with my blessings. I knew she must be horribly upset. She didn't usually drink. I asked to talk to

Leon. I told him to take her. They should have come to me at the start. There was no need to humiliate me in front of my friends and my son."

To Andy Wainwright, Layton wrote quite cheerfully:

> because Aviva fell in love with a Rhodesian novelist, this has been the most pleasant tension-free summer I've spent in the last two decades. I think she'll marry him but whether she does or does not, the split is real and final. Leon, that's the lucky man's name, has been here since Aviva arrived nearly one month ago — or was it only three weeks? I think you met him — *Leon Whiteson*.... It's a good match and I approve it wholeheartedly.... My union with Aviva was never a happy one, but I could never bring myself to end it. Now that she's crossed the Rubicon, I am ready to take on the world.[8]

Two months later he confessed, "the break-up of my marriage has shaken me more than I'd like to tell."[9]

"It was a real war," recalls Bill Goodwin, who was with Layton at the time. "Irving wouldn't let Leon into his house. He was in a very bad state. As soon as he realized that Aviva had really left him, he told me to get on the telephone and call Harriet in Toronto. He told me to say that he loved her, that he had sent her a gift and that he wanted to marry her. Just as Betty had made up his mind for him about Aviva, now Aviva made up his mind for him about Harriet."[10]

"Irving and Aviva's most desperate periods were in Greece," Leonard Cohen recalls. "They were both 'on the lam' somehow. I knew what bad shape things were in, but Irving never mentioned it. He never complained. He'd go whistling down the alleys as if nothing had happened."[11]

"'Night Music' was written that night she left me to stay with Leon," Layton recalls.[12]

In my eyes are uncontrollable tears
for the frustration and futility
in each man's lot, the inadequacies
and confusions which are the burden

and *leit-motif* of the whole symphony.
No man so deaf that he can't hear it.
For me, from this night on all's changed.
I have hatched an asp that delays its bite:
there remains only to be desperate and brave.

Molibos
July 28, 1977[13]

All That I Prize

The marriage of Harriet and Irving on 23 November 1978 was called the culmination of a "*My Fair Lady* fairy tale."[1] So similar were their physiques that they looked like two of those Russian wooden dolls that fit inside one another. Rabbi Harvey Joseph Fields officiated in his study at Holy Blossom Temple in Toronto. Zena Cherry, *Globe and Mail* social columnist, described the wedding reception and buffet on Forest Hill Road with all the panoply of a major media event. Names from Layton's past were casually interspersed with those of Toronto Jewish socialites. For public consumption, Betty was his first wife, and Aviva, whom he had never married, his second. Layton was described as "a lieutenant in the Second World War." Max, then manager of Jefferson Press, a subsidiary of M&S, was present. Naomi, who called herself Naomi Seabird, was not there; she was studying guitar in Spain. David Herschel Layton, the story went, "lives in England with his mother." Leon, who was in England with them, was not mentioned. Layton's forthcoming collection, *Love Poems*, was highlighted. McClelland and Stewart produced a limited edition of two hundred for a hundred dollars each and a special edition of fifty, with five original lithographs by Graham Coughtry, for a thousand dollars. All copies were said to be sold in advance. *Maclean's* later reported that Harriet's parents "weren't too thrilled about the age gap." Her father (ten years Layton's junior) "made it clear he never wanted to be called 'dad.'"[2]

Layton finally had negotiated a divorce from Betty so he could marry Harriet. The summer of 1978, he had gone to California to take Betty on a holiday to Inverness, where they spent a tranquil time together. His poem "Divorce,"[3] which resulted from this sojourn, pictures them as "two grey-haired children...exchanging news of friends and the universe," walking with arms around each other's waists through rain and mist. "What is it about divorce/brings an estranged couple closer?" Layton asked in his poem. Now that the guilt associated with Aviva had dissipated, Layton could be friends with Boschka.

Aviva was distressed, though because of her new stability with Leon, she managed to be forgiving. News of Irving's marriage hit her hard:

> The "gesture," the commitment, I'd waited nearly ¼ century for you to make, was given to someone else. That's not an accident, my love. How could it have been. Harriet has achieved — if that's the word — through pressure, emotional blackmail, etc. etc. what I've been waiting for during our whole life together. She's a clever lady. When she didn't have things entirely her way — when she felt uncomfortable about my presence, when the road was the slightest bit rocky, off she went to the well-padded comforts of her middle-class furs. Not a thought did she give for your comfort or state of mind. *When*, however, I was safely off the scene, *when* you'd made your traumatic move, *when* you'd found your luxury apartment, then in sailed Harriet the Lariat, insisted on the whole middle-class trip — & there you are. God, Irving, would she have lasted even one minute of our early years together? The painful Betty separation — the basement apartment, the lack of money, the stream of ladies, etc., etc.... Now it's easy fame & Palm Beach & Croydons & marriage & trips & no money problems & I'm sure, babies.... No, my love, I couldn't take your offers of "marriage" etc. last year. I'd begged

you to divorce Betty, but you'd refused. It was really insulting to me. Harriet demonstrated it was for *her* you divorced Betty — & boy did you jump to it. What I'd failed in 25 years to receive from you — even after the birth of my son — she pressured [for] — & got. Maybe it's because she really is a heavyweight — a thick weight of wanting and insisting. Maybe it's because you are really deeply in love with her. Which I know isn't true, Irving. Because you love me in the same way as I love you — it's what Leon calls "gut affinity."...Somehow news of your marriage to Bernstein (now Layton) really cut me deeply. I feel a very real sense of rejection. Irrational isn't it? And ironic. She gets so easily & so quickly from you what I needed and wanted so desperately from you. I've said it before, my love, and I say it again. *Had you married me or even promised to before summer, this would not have happened.* And you *know* it's not because I'm bourgeois etc. etc. I needed that sign. It would have relieved so many tensions & frustrations & murkiness that expressed themselves in such shameful forms. Never mind marriage — had you come with David and myself and travelled with us for his 13th birthday; had you followed through on what was essentially 10 days of attention and love to me, before you cut it short by taking off with Bill. I've lived through so many other women in your life — serious, long-standing, searing (for me) affairs. You've left me — I've always been there for you.... So that's why I can't see you this Xmas, Irv. Marriage — & then winging over here a couple of weeks later. It's not that easy my love. Instead, I'll send David to you.[4]

In 1979, Layton moved back to Montreal with Harriet, firing volleys in all directions about the repugnant materialism of Toronto and the desireability of Montreal, especially for poets. His teaching at York, which had been extended by special request for two years past normal retirement age, was over. In gratitude for his contribution to the institution, Layton had been honoured with a D.Litt. To show his thanks, Layton had read a scatalogical poem attacking York.

Layton and Harriet set up an apartment in Montreal. The apartment he chose was in the old Croydon Apartments, the building where he and Aviva had once had their "love nest." He called his move "returning to my roots." One of Layton's friends was Sandra Beaudouin, a psychologist. Bill Goodwin, who was once again on the scene, reported: "Irving found Sandra — who was a divorcee in her late thirties — really charming. Once Harriet moved in and met Sandy, she was distressed about his friendship with her. I recall hearing them fight once or twice about her."[5] Layton wrote a couple of erotic poems for Sandy that fall.[6] Mainly, though, he was glad to move Harriet to Montreal, because he thought that her parents, who lived in Toronto, exerted too much influence over her.[7]

Although Layton for years had frequently blasted Toronto, he now claimed that his stay there had been ideal. In a Toronto *Star* article that featured a photo of Layton on Toronto's Bay Street in front of the Toronto Stock Exchange, his grey hair wild and unruly, his arms spread wide in a gesture of all-embracing exuberance, his widening girth bulged through his shirt and a huge silver medallion (which, he was soon to claim, was awarded to him in a competition in Morocco for deflowering fifteen virgins in half an hour)[8] gleamed on his chest.[9] "Toronto made my career," he says. "In one week I get more support from radio, TV, newspapers than I did in a year in Montreal.... I would have stagnated in Montreal the last nine years. But here, with no deep distractions, I've been immensely creative." To Andy Wainwright, he wrote, "[I'm] 'retired' and doing more handsprings & cartwheels than ever before."[10]

By St. Valentine's Day 1979, when his *Love Poems* had been released (with press coverage picturing him with Harriet amid red hearts), Layton had finished teaching the fall term of the writing workshop at Concordia University (the amalgamation of Sir George Williams and Loyola College) for the second year and was taking it easy in Florida, at his in-laws' West Palm Beach condominium. He and Harriet were working on a screenplay called *Amber Savage* (never produced, though they approached Paramount Pictures), "a psychological study of a modern woman in a modern world."

An obviously infatuated Layton claimed, "My marriages get better and better."[11]

Harriet did not like Montreal. Friends who visited Layton recall her as a quiet young woman, overshadowed by her husband. Even to Layton, she seemed lonely and sad. In November 1979, they moved to Niagara-on-the-Lake, an elegant old Ontario town where Layton started two vegetable gardens and took advantage of the peace and quiet to work on short stories and his autobiography. He referred to himself as "Squire Layton" and pictured the town as a "microcosm of the peaceable kingdom."[12] "I made a trip to the bank every day," he remarked sardonically in the summer of 1979, "a habit I acquired when I lived in Toronto. Banks are modern man's religious institutions. Each one has its own theology, also known as its interest-rate structure, and you can check them out daily and transfer your money accordingly, achieving renewed spiritual fulfillment."[13] Layton's favourite haunt was the old Prince of Wales Hotel, where he would drink coffee with the groupies, students and friends who flocked to visit him. His telephone number was unlisted. He boasted that Harriet was his "protection, barrier...that all calls have to come through her, and everybody has to first get past Harriet to get to me."[14]

Layton's old friends were astounded at his sudden strange "defection" to a conventional life of bourgeois comforts. "It was startling," Bill Goodwin observes. "Acquisitive philistines had been anathema to him for years, but now he wanted all the things they represented. Why? When I asked him, he replied, 'I want a family.' To him the Bernsteins represented a family. He wanted to feel secure and accepted. He'd tried everything else; now he wanted to know what bourgeois existence meant. It was not so much the money, though he certainly enjoyed the cars, the West Palm Beach condominium, the luxurious life of the Bernsteins. It was more that with them he had a feeling of 'home.'"[15]

Dean Baker, a young poet and songwriter who met Layton in 1971 and had kept up a correspondence and friendship with him, recalls inviting Layton and Harriet back to his apartment in Guelph after Layton had given a reading at the university. Dean and Layton drank Beaujolais, Harriet drank Coke. "Irving seemed blind to Harriet," Baker recalls, "though she was nice enough to me — and I had an uneasy feeling about how she saw him & how they both actually related... Later I talked with him and Harriet — and she must have told me 4 or 5 times that 'Leonard's new album is dedicated to Irving, you know' — yes, and you're Great too, lady, I thought."[16]

As Aviva had predicted, Harriet soon became pregnant. Layton immediately wrote a poem, modestly called "The Annunciation," and claimed he was the first in world literature to write a poem for such an event.[17] Her pregnancy was a major media occasion. "I'm going to abstain from publication until 1982, to coincide with my seventieth birthday," Layton claimed. "My wife will be delivering a baby in January, as proof of my other kind of creativity. I fully expect her to present me with triplets."[18] On 10 January 1981, Samantha Clara Layton was born. Layton saluted her arrival with a poem.[19] But behind the romantic façade, he was finding that the more mundane realities of fatherhood were less palatable. "I'm learning to be a parent again," he wrote to Steve Osterlund a couple of months after Samantha's birth. "It ain't easy, there are so many important trifles I've forgotten or simply never learned. Just now, sleep's the huge problem since S. is being breast-fed and is gluttonous for the tit. She wakes us at least twice during the night, and after that sleep takes a long holiday."[20]

As he had when his three other children had been born, Layton soon made himself scarce. He went off to Italy for a reading tour of Rome, Venice and Pisa ("up the boot like Hannibal and down like Napoleon") less than three months after Samantha's birth. In Rome, he read before a distinguished audience that included Alberto Moravia (who invited him to dinner afterwards) and Giorgio Bassani, the author of "The Garden of the Finzi-Continis." "Everything seemed to be staged for the one purpose of proving...that I'm a Mediterranean Jew out of place in North America, engendering those grotesque twins, puritanism and pornography,"[21] Layton reported.

Alfredo Rizziardi, Layton's Italian translator and a professor at the University of Bologna, reports that on this visit — as on all his visits to Italy — Layton was an enormous success: "He lectures and reads to large audiences who shower on him manifestations of their sympathy and love. He captures everyone. He is a link between Canada and Italy: an ambassador at the highest level. Those Italians who are interested in poetry — especially the young students — are fed up with the nonsensical obscurity of much modern poetry. They see in Layton's work the flesh-and-blood qualities of the body with all its desires. They admire him because he has the courage to write such poetry."[22]

Wilfrid-Guy Licari, the Canadian ambassador to Rome, thought Layton was "extraordinary" when he met him on another of Layton's visits to Italy: "We were having dinner in Rome with a group of very sophisticated and cultured people. Layton was wearing a white, short-sleeved shirt open to the waist. He was very expansive, holding forth about life with the most astonishing theatricality. At one point he grabbed up a cutlet from his plate with his bare hands and took a bite out of it, as if to show by this gesture what he meant about seizing life greedily. He seemed to me like Tarzan plunked down in the middle of civilization for the first time. It was an incredible spectacle."[23]

Shortly after Layton came back from Italy, his marriage to Harriet was over. "Irving was at his worst in Niagara-on-the-Lake," his agent, Lucinda Vardey, recalls. "Aviva had called me to say she'd heard he looked bad. Would I go and see him. I found him in the Prince of Wales. I was taken aback. He'd lost weight. He looked dishevelled. He was despairing about the house. We went back to it. I looked around. Harriet had turned it into a doll's house. It had a big Canadian kitchen, a huge, book-lined study for Irving and a child's room with a cot and trolley. But Harriet was not there. Nor was the baby. Her lawyers had been making several tormenting calls to him. He tried to make some soup, but he spilled it and then cleaned it up. After lunch he pleaded with me to explain Harriet to him. It was pissing rain outside. He wanted to go and sit out in the garden. I persuaded him to stay in the kitchen. He read his new poems from *The Gucci Bag* to me in a despairing mood. It was the best poetry reading I ever heard. I praised some of the poems as the best, and told him which ones I didn't think were so good. 'Well, luv, you could be right,' he said, 'but they're going in anyway.' I left feeling very concerned about him. I thought he was having a nervous breakdown."[24]

"I was having a breakdown," Layton recalls. "It was the only time in my life I went to a psychiatrist: Dr. Ed Kingstone, head of psychiatry at the Sunnybrook Medical Centre in Toronto. I told him that I kept hearing voices saying 'Kill! Kill! Kill!' The psychiatrist told me I wasn't going to kill anyone. He told me to write down what I felt in letters and not send them."[25]

"I went to see Harriet and the baby next," Lucinda remembers. "She was concerned about Irving's role as a father. He didn't get up in the night to help with the baby. I told her that Irving's a poet, not a liberated man. He can't change. What came out of it was this: Irving had to decide between what he was creating in his words and what he was creating in the flesh. That was his trauma."

Karen Pietkiewicz, who was about forty, was from Sault Ste. Marie. She was a housewife and mother of three. She contacted Layton for help with her poetry shortly after seeing the *Maclean's* article about his marriage to Harriet. She recalls meeting him at the Prince of Wales Hotel in the early summer of 1980, at Layton's request. When he came storming through the door, his resemblance to her father was striking. "My father is dead. Meeting Layton was like seeing a ghost," she recalls.[26] "He treated the place like a European café, and began reading me his poems. He listened carefully to mine. He told me he liked my poems because, unlike most women writers, I was able to transcend myself. He was wearing that big medallion. I noticed that the head on it was broken off. He told me that his wife was pregnant. I wondered why a young girl would want a baby with this old man. There was something perverse about that. How could a child be raised by a father whose style would be cramped by a baby? Though he made comments about how I looked and what I was wearing, he didn't make a pass at me.

"We met at a series of restaurants after that. He was always on time. Once I called him long distance and I could hear the baby screaming. He wanted to get a book or something. 'Oh, damn,' he said. 'It's upstairs and I'm holding this baby and can't put her down. Harriet is downtown.' When Harriet answered the phone, she didn't give him my messages.

"The next thing I knew he and Harriet were splitting up. I met him to discuss my poems. His personality had completely changed. He was like a chameleon: first he was 'the poet' and read his own poems; then he was 'the teacher,' put on his half-glasses, declared I had 'abominable spelling' and gently corrected it; then he became 'friend' and said 'Let's go eat.' We talked about Harriet. He seemed to need my support. He needed to know that someone else thought that he and Harriet were all wrong. He was torn. He was saddened that this marriage wasn't going to go.

"At the end of September, he called me to ask if I wanted to go to the Amnesty International Conference (The Writer and Human Rights) in October. He invited me to stay with him in his apartment in Toronto. He was writer-in-residence at the University of Toronto that year. After I arrived, we were driving in his car when he suddenly said, 'You have beautiful eyes,' as if it was an afterthought, as if he'd noticed it for the first time. We went over to see Max. I was wearing a purple and white spotted dress. As we pulled up in front of Max's house he turned towards me and said, 'Have you got breasts?' and reached over to peek. 'You do have,' he went on — feel, feel, feel — 'very nice breasts too. Your dress doesn't show them enough. Women should dress to show their breasts. Men get so much pleasure from looking.' Then he ran into Max's for a minute. When he came back, he looked abashed.

"He pulled out into the traffic and mentioned feeling me up. I said, 'Go ahead, the poetry is all that matters.' He said, 'I was just checking to see if you had any Christian hang-ups.'

"'You liar,' I said jokingly. He was like all men: very human, enjoyable, disarming.

"'That's my girl,' he said. We both knew we were lying.

"All during the conference that afternoon I was wondering, Does he have two beds? One bed? A couch? A sleeping-bag? Would he be insulted if he knew what I was thinking?

"His apartment was not much bigger than a room. There

was no sofa, no carpet on the floor and one bed. Irving was going berscrk with happiness because he'd just heard that he had been nominated by some Italian poets for the Nobel Prize. The press were interviewing him that night. People were calling from all over to congratulate him. Max came over. Irving wanted to be alone with the interviewers, so he asked me if there was anything I could do downtown. I went out.

"That night we went to Convocation Hall. He was tired. Margaret Atwood read some poetry. He looked at her and said so loudly that sixteen people in each direction could hear him, 'Doesn't she look like a mouse? Her nose wiggles like a delicate little field mouse.' He was not listening to her poetry. He fell asleep and began to snore. But when Jacob Timerman came on, he was really impressed. He was instantly awake. He's like that with people. If he doesn't like them, he just turns them off.

"After that we went back to his apartment. I felt shy at dinner and nervous. On the way back he had talked about sleeping with him. 'At my age, you know, you have nothing to worry about.' I got the impression he was reassuring himself as much as me. After dinner he became jovial. I put on my nightgown. He blithely took off his clothes and flopped into bed. He told me that he'd been so depressed since Harriet left him that he couldn't touch another woman. But eventually he became so turned on that he wanted sex. I told him I couldn't. I might get pregnant. I thought he was going to leap on me. I was terrified. When he saw how frightened I was, he calmed down. He was phenomenal. He kept changing expressions as if he were different men. In the end, he was not mad, he was understanding and compassionate.

"In the morning, he leapt out of bed early and made us some breakfast of tea, toast and peanut butter. He was singing opera arias as he worked. I invited him to come and read at the Soo [Sault Ste. Marie]. He came up there for $500 and gave a reading at the library on 16 March. He was nervous meeting my husband.

"The next time I came to Toronto, we went to see *Mephisto* with Max and his wife. Even though Max and Stephanie were sitting right behind us, he reached over in an obvious way and started to play with my body. Actually he was intent on the movie, but it was second nature to him to do this too. He couldn't get my jeans undone and I said, 'Don't bother trying. I'm packed into them. You'll never get your hand in there.' It was as funny as hell. This time we weren't involved. Neither of us was really interested.

"I think Irving has a crumbling image of women. He requires encounters, meetings, adulation, calendars full of up-and-comings. It helps reinforce his image of himself. He's wanted stable relationships with women, but he's not really confident. He doesn't like getting involved, but once he does he feels he owes them something. His need for women is intense. He's maintaining a dream."

By the end of the year, Layton was appearing on television with decidedly anti-marriage views: "Couples marry in a state of intoxication...you wouldn't let a man drive a car while intoxicated...but you let the bloody fool get married. I think that's the basic mistake...in this whole arrangement."[27]

When the nomination (made by Alfredo Rizziardi at the suggestion of Canadian poet Greg Gatenby) for the Nobel Prize was announced, Layton arranged a ten-day tour of Korea under the auspices of the Korean Cultural Association at the suggestion of his friend Kim Yang-shik ("First Violet"), for whose poems he had written an introduction in 1975.[28] Shortly after his return, it was announced that Korea supported his nomination for the award. Layton pined for the Nobel Prize because it would vindicate the compromises he knew he had made to continue writing. Not long before he went to Italy and to Korea, he had been prompted to assess his life by re-reading Lawrance Thompson's biography of Robert Frost. He had not liked what he saw. He wrote to Steve Osterlund:

> Since I never particularly liked Frost as much as I did his poetry, I am somewhat horrified to see lots of resemblances between us, e.g. a certain pig-headedness in pursuing our goal. Some unkind critics would call it selfishness and egocentricity. But what a cunning conniver he

was, getting all sorts of people to puff his wares and dividing people into two strict groups: those who liked his stuff and those who didn't. He was also both envious and vindictive, simply hated to hear another poet praised. For all that, credit must be given him for fighting the good fight and lambasting the genteel academicism of his time as I have in my own time and place.[29]

The Nobel Prize promised Layton not only a cash award of approximately $180,000, but also a salve for his conscience. Winning the prize would announce to the world that he had "fought the good fight" and that whatever wake of griefs and grudges rippled out behind him had been a necessary means to a glorious end. In anticipation, especially since Korea was backing the nomination, Layton announced to a reporter (who understandably concluded, and reported, that Samantha was Layton's grandchild), "Without [immortality] my life will be incomplete."[30]

Layton greeted his nomination "with great joy and anxiety — joy because of what it means, anguish because I don't know if I'll win." The year between his nomination and the announcement of a winner was one of destructive agony for Layton. He campaigned to get as many people as possible to write supporting letters. Although the nomination was not in itself a distinction, since nominations could be made by anyone at any time, Layton billed himself at readings as "Nobel Prize Nominee." As he waited to hear whether he had attained immortality in one area of his life, he saw immortality in another slip through his grasp. Harriet, buttressed with legal advice, had no intention of returning to Layton. He became desperate to see Samantha. His visits to her at fixed times became the centre of a legal controversy. The only sure sign of immortality that year was one that didn't fully please him: the appearance of Aviva's first novel, *Nobody's Daughter*, in which she had drawn on the negative side of her life with Layton to invent the character Alex Jacobs, a Montreal Jewish poet of an intensely megalomaniac disposition.

"Layton, 70, is in a suing mood," ran the headline for an article in the *Montreal Gazette*[31] about the three legal cases

Layton had underway: one against a *Globe* book reviewer, William French, for half a million in damages for naming him as the protagonist for Aviva's book; one against Harriet for property settlement and fuller access to Samantha; and one against his own lawyer, Linda Dranoff, over a disputed $11,000 bill for legal services over the second case.

Layton was most distraught about not having more access to Samantha. He claimed in May that he had seen her only about a dozen times since he and Harriet had separated the previous June. "It wasn't until the end of the summer that one brief visit was allowed," he complained. "It was on the street corner at Forest Hill and Eglinton. The Bernsteins' maid wheeled Samantha there in a pram, and I spent 25 minutes with her. Not what you'd call a comfortable family visit."[32] Harriet insisted that a baby-sitter be present during Layton's visits. Sometimes Layton found no one home, or was told that his daughter had a cold. His frustration built to unbearable heights. Like a literary Rumpelstiltskin, he launched scathing attacks on Harriet and her family in letters and sent copies to newspapers, individuals in the academic world and libraries that held his papers. In poem after poem, he also denigrated them. Harriet, who had appeared in his earlier poems as such a tender beauty, was now transformed:

> Lord, must I be punished and was it a sin
> to have loved her fat ass and pendulous chin,
> her many folds and bulges and hanging tits
> that each time I saw them disordered my wits?
> The thick wrists and arms and legs elephantine
> that dazzled me more than any silver mine?
> Because I once loved her fat thighs and fat knees
> must I now sweat to pay my lawyer's fat fees?[33]

His project became a collection of poems, to be called *The Gucci Bag* (so named because the Bernsteins had given him one as a present). The bag seemed to symbolize the material affluence and bourgeois success he had always attacked, but had, during the time he was with Harriet, fully enjoyed. "For Gypsy Jo, A wonderful flower child I used to know," went the book's inscription. The Gucci bag was transformed, in his opening poem, into a magic charm to be nailed on the outside wall of his house "like a transylvanian bat / to dismay the vampires of possessiveness / and scare them away." In his preface, he was pre-occupied with Jack the Ripper, a symbol he chose for the times in which he was living. Certainly his thoughts and writings were violent. As he gradually realized that he could not see Samantha more frequently, he became even more frenzied. Harriet's exclusion of him slid easily into apparent confirmation of his long-held belief that the bourgeoisie were soulless.

Layton's dilemma gained wider coverage in the press. The Supreme Court ordered Layton to desist from public discussion of his separation.[34] "Some of the letters were extremely angry and abusive and others were sensitive and anguished," one judge reportedly said. "Anyone would see them as written by a very honest and bewildered man." But the poetry, in the judge's opinion, was primarily a ploy to try to "shame" his wife into giving him access to his fourteen-month-old daughter.[35] Layton, ostensibly to preserve freedom of speech, wrote an "open letter" to Trudeau, father to father,[36] and deliberately flouted the Ontario Supreme Court order by selling, for five dollars, documents called, "The Cost and Consequences of a two-year marriage to an enchanting Jewish American Princess." According to Layton, the break-up cost almost $75,000: a $33,000 cash payment, $28,000 in legal fees and $13,500 in maintenance payments. "To take liberties away from a writer — a poet — is an absolute blasphemy," Layton self-righteously announced to the press.

Layton testified that he wrote the poetry because he was "overcome with grief" at being denied freer access to his child. "As a poet," he pleaded, "I have reacted to the enormous stress of this situation by using my creative talents to write about my frustrations."[37] Justice John Osler found much of the material Layton had written "of an insulting nature, some of it scurrilous, and some of it 'highly abusive.'"[38] But the letters and poems did not fall within the Family Law Reform Act's section on spousal harassment. Harriet's application for an injunction against her husband was rejected. The judge suggested the time-worn remedy for unsolicited mail: "simply to drop the material in the wastebasket."[39] Layton was granted access two days a week, but had to pay baby-sitting costs while with Samantha. Harriet was to receive $750 a month support, plus $500 a month for her daughter. It was a hard financial blow. As of 1 March 1982, Layton owed McClelland and Stewart $5,831.78 in unearned advances and outstanding purchases.[40]

At the end of October 1982, a year in which he had given a record fifty-five readings and public lectures, the announcement came. Layton, now seventy, had not won the Nobel Prize. Nor had Margaret Laurence or Josef Škvorecký, the two Canadian writers who were nominated by Canada. The prize went to Columbian writer Gabriel Garcia Marquez.

Anna

They met after one of Irving's poetry readings at Dalhousie University in the spring of 1981. Her name was Annette Pottier. She was an Acadian with the sturdy, wholesome cheerfulness of his sisters in their youth, and the gentle, benevolent face of a Tintoretto Madonna. She was going to Athens, she explained. Would he write her a letter? She had begun writing poetry. Perhaps he could advise her.

Her letter to him reached his 1560 Bathurst Street apartment in Toronto at the end of September 1981. He wrote back the same day. "I must admit that I can't remember what your face looks like," he commented, after dispensing advice about how to behave like a poet in Greece. "Are you beautiful? Tall and blonde or short and dark? Snubnosed and freckled or classical Greek? What makes you think you are a poet, except your defiance of advice? After all, you weren't born circumcised as I was! What, if any, were the heavenly signs when you dropped out from between your mother's bleeding legs?"[1] He imagined her, he wrote, with trim feet and ankles, going up the steps to the American Express office in Constitution Square in Athens to mail him her letter.

Anna did not have trim ankles. She was short and dark and smiling. She was twenty-two. "I carried his letter all around Europe," she recalls,[2] "and I sent him my poems.

When I got back I phoned and invited him to come down to visit me. He refused, but asked me to come there. He said he would put me up at Niagara-on-the-Lake. When I met him, he told me what books to get. He mapped out my life for the next two years: what I should read, whom I should study. I got a part-time job in Toronto as a companion to an elderly woman. I wanted to spend most of my time reading interesting books and writing poetry and short stories."

By November 1982, Layton had sold the house at Niagara-on-the-Lake and moved to Oakville. He offered Anna the job of housekeeper.

"I'm a *chatelaine*," she announced, clearly pleased with the arrangement and also clearly head-over-heels in love with Layton. She loves Irving the way he has always wanted to be loved — with no strings attached. "He's free to come and go as he wishes," she says of the man she affectionately calls "Poops." "When he's good, I call him my good biscuit boy; when he's not, he's my bad biscuit boy. Usually he's a good biscuit boy."

Anna understands how other women might have become annoyed with Irving. "When he gets working on his poetry, he cuts off everything. A nuclear bomb could fall in the back yard and he wouldn't notice or care. He also asks constantly about what we're having for breakfast, lunch and dinner. 'Tea!' he shouts as soon as he comes in the door. 'Anna! Bagels! Where are they!' He's so impatient. It can be a bit irritating sometimes. Then there are all those people I call his 'parishioners.' The young poets, the former students and groupies. He phones them from time to time and meets with them. He knows they need him. They really blossom under his care. Take his latest 'coffee romance,' for instance. She's a woman he met after a poetry reading. She invited him to lunch in Hamilton. He came storming in afterwards and threw down his hat and complained about her aggression and vulgarity. She told him she was frustrated in her marriage. She stroked his knee under the table, kissed him and thrust her tongue into his mouth and proposed going to a hotel room."

Not all Layton's "parishioners" feel satisfied with what

he gives. After years of tantalizing promises of assistance with his poetry, Dean Baker finally turned on his mentor. "Machiavelli was a piker compared to Layton," he wrote in his journal in the fall of 1983.

> Maybe I should have accepted the fact a lot earlier... that this famous poet stays public even with intimate friends, his moments of authenticity numbered on the knuckles of one finger per friend...and so he has to have many appointments with former students, etc. because each one is a different sounding board for the poet (besides it's good publicity) — so, who gets to really know him? Nobody...not Aviva (unless it's knowledge like this she puzzles over) and not Harriet (what could she think/feel upon receiving his letter — that manipulation doesn't take genius, simply a talent for defrocking the other so the spotlight doesn't focus on him or his actions). All his promises to "really look at your poetry"..."to visit me"..."to get together for a long chat"...are so much dust, ashes and sand.... A great poetic institution...he's become his own enemy: I wonder if he'll prove great enough to "inform" on himself — and bring the person and the poet into a unity of thought & word & deed.[3]

Such dissatisfactions, Anna thinks, come to anyone who tries to own Layton.

Anna doesn't want to own her bad biscuit boy. "I give you all, would deny you nothing, not even my life were you to ask for it. And I pray that this expression, this confession of sentiment does not leave you feeling fettered or hobbled in any way," she wrote to him in May 1983 when he was abroad as a "cultural ambassador," giving readings in England, Scotland and Spain. She loves his energy, his care for her development as a writer, his appreciation of her many gifts. She would consider marriage only because she fears she would not receive fair treatment financially if he died. "There are just so many wives and children, I wouldn't stand a chance." Nor does she want children. "Looking after Irving satisfies all my maternal instincts," she remarks.[4]

In November 1983, Layton sold his house in Oakville and bought one at 6879 Monkland Avenue in the west end of Montreal, not far from the Somerled Avenue apartment he once shared with Aviva. Layton is idyllically happy with his "Anna-Panna": "If I had married Anna in the first place, I probably never would have written any poetry at all. I would have been too happy."[5] Once Layton discovered that Anna had been born on the same day his mother died, he began telling friends that their union was fated. "I believe my mother's soul has passed into Anna," he told Aviva.[6] To Dean Baker, he wrote:

> My domestic troubles are a thing of the past. I've wiped the floor with the "opposition" each time I went to court...and now have assured access to my daughter. That was what was worrying me all the time, but my tenacity finally triumphed. Moreover, my ex-wife has shaken all the money she was able to get from me, and there's nothing else in the kitty for her...my two main anxieties are laid to rest.[7]

"For some time I was debating with myself whether the choice should be Montreal or Toronto," he said in another letter to Baker, "since both cities have their attractions. But I think my old stamping ground has more to offer me in the way of friends and stimulations. And my 3 older sisters whose joints are getting chalkier with each day that passes [are there]. I've never been able to warm up to Toronto. Too sterile, too *Waspy*. Since I'm working on my memoirs it's the logical and best place to be."[8] More important than these "sentimental" ties, however, may have been the dent his legal costs put in his budget, a dent he hoped would be covered by the Nobel Prize money he did not win: "The big factor [in choosing Montreal]," he confessed to Baker, "is that I can find a place for about half of what it would cost in Toronto." As he negotiated for a permanent half-yearly lectureship at the University of Bologna in Italy, he rented out a room in his house to one of Anna's girl friends.

Reunions

It is 5 March 1983. At the Montreal home of Simon Dardick, Véhicule Press editor, and his wife, Nancy Marelli, the poets from the old *CIV/n* days gather for the launching of a reprint of their 1950s poetry journal. Among the forty-odd guests is sixty-five-year-old Louis Dudek, now grey and balding but agile and vigorous. He's just retired from McGill. Frank Scott, who is eighty-two and who has been ill and rarely goes out, appears at the door. Dudek takes his coat and the cameras flash. His hearing aid, Scott complains, is not working properly. "I call it my blockade," he quips.[1] More flash bulbs illuminate the room.

Layton arrives with Veneranda McGrath, a former student who is working on a book based on her master's thesis, "Love and Loathing: the Role of Women in Irving Layton's Poetry."[2] Layton hasn't seen Frank and Marian Scott for twenty, maybe thirty years. "Marian, you beautiful woman," he exclaims, throwing his arms around her. "How do you do it?" When Dudek is asked about his notorious falling-out with Layton, he replies, "We've put our old quarrels behind us. We met twice at poetry readings last week in Toronto."[3]

The party is a warm tribute, a reunion of many of the front-runners from *CIV/n*, a pot-pourri of sculptors like Buddy Rozynski and Mort Rosengarten, painters like Louise

Scott and journalists like Sheila Arnopoulos and Dominique Clift, the "Don Clift" contributor to *CIV/n*. More flashes record literary history.

The only tense moment occurs when Leo Kennedy thrusts his gnarled walking stick at Seymour Mayne and charges that Mayne had Kennedy booted out of the most recent edition of the *Oxford Book of Canadian Verse*. But the wine and cake restore order and a sense of comfortable perspective on an era long gone. Layton takes advantage of the journalists to pontificate as usual. "Poetry has abdicated," he declares. "Frankly it doesn't matter any more. Language is no longer central to communication. There hasn't been a truly important poetic statement since *The Waste Land* in 1922. It's film which now communicates vital realities. Filmmakers are the real modern poets."[4] Of course, Layton doesn't fully believe this, but it is his way of refusing to acknowledge the developments in poetry since his heyday. It sounds impressive and dazzles some.

"Look at him," says Veneranda McGrath, gesturing across the room towards Layton, who cannot hear her. She has arranged "a wild Laytonian night" to celebrate his seventy-first birthday. They will go to La Portugaise on the Main later. "He never changes. Can't decide between the ham sitting on his knee and the one on the table."[5]

And there in the press photograph, like a pictorial representation of the first "cell division" of Canada's vertical mosaic, are the three old war-horses: Polish Roman-Catholic Louis Dudek; English-Quebec Anglican Frank Scott; and Romanian Jew Irving Layton. These white-haired men, now well past their prime, had once thrust modern poetry into the forefront in Canada. The little magazines that spun out from presses bought and worked by these men had widened the audience for poetry in Canada. They had been among the vanguard that prepared the way for generations to come. It is, as the media report, a great night for Canadian poetry.

Layton's particular contribution to poetry has been something of a phenomenon. On the simplest level, Issie Lazarovitch from the Montreal slums had made it big. From the age of forty, he had been financially successful through teaching and poetry and in real estate. Like many Jewish immigrants to North America, he had made an important contribution to the arts and to culture. He is a major figure in Canada's Jewish literary establishment, an honour roll that includes A.M. Klein, Miriam Waddington, Adele Wiseman, Mordecai Richler and Leonard Cohen. He was awarded the country's top literary prize, the Governor-General's Award (in 1959); he received many of the country's other major awards and grants; he was made a Companion of the Order of Canada (in 1976); and he received three honourary degrees from the nation's universities. His poems have been translated and anthologized (he was, finally, published through Leonard Cohen by Charisma Books in England [1977] and by New Directions paperback in the United States [1977]), and he was nominated for the Nobel Prize.

Layton's poems are a truly remarkable achievement. Of the approximately one thousand poems he has published, roughly fifteen are world-class poems that could stand with the best modern poetry in English. Another thirty-five are extremely good. Such an assessment must vary with the critic, but the list of Layton's poems most often anthologized serves as a rough guide. All his best poems are relatively short. Layton was no epic poet; nor did he tackle long narratives or dramatic verse. His major poems can be recognized for striking combinations of styles and phraseology that normally would not be juxtaposed. It is as if he were able to infuse elegant, old-fashioned forms, like the lyric and Shakespearian blank verse, with the life-blood of peasant vitality and the colloquialism and sprung rhymes favoured by modern American and Canadian poets. Most of his best poems treat simple, personal situations — quite often family relationships — to draw close to the vulnerability of human life and its paradoxical tenacity. Humour, tenderness, sensuality, grief and ironic self-mockery characterize his strongly textured reflections on the poet and on creativity generally. Although he is noted for his use of four-letter words, such language appears in what he knew was his more superficial vein of satiric verse. In his best work, he does not employ coarse language. Layton has emerged as one of the great poets of the twentieth century, and certainly one of the very best in Canada.

"Nappy" or "Mr. Fighting Words" was a born scrapper. His lower-class Jewish background provided him with a vantage point from which he could clearly see the effete gentility and conservative repressions of Canadian society. Entering the Anglophone community from the Montreal slums, he challenged and commented on English Canada. In the face of puritanism, he championed rude earthiness; he baited elitism with revolutionary threats; he disarmed gentility with vulgarity; he countered materialism with idealism. In a culture that was conservative, rational and tight, he celebrated the life of the body, the emotions and the spirit. Though his views had little relevance for French Canada, he gloried in his role as the thorn in English Canada's side. His public life had strong sado-masochistic overtones: he was the man people loved to hate. Layton fought for and gained a necessary freedom in Canada's poetry; he smashed barriers of language, subject and style for all who would come after.

One early name he chose for himself, "Isadore Lazarre," suggested a poet in the grand romantic style. Layton responded first to the British romantics, models he never entirely abandoned. He liked to think of himself as the kind of poet who sang his brief song, then died young: an inspired Chatterton, perhaps, or a sensual Keats or an ethereal Shelley. Someone sensitive and tender, to whom the beauty of language was an exquisite pleasure. Wordsworth's theory that poetry was the product of emotion recollected in tranquillity stayed with Layton, for his particular gift was for the lyric, the same kind of poem, curiously enough, that dominated Romania, the country of his birth, though he never deliberately linked himself with that heritage. His attachment to the English tradition, despite the fact that he was assailing English values, reveals a paradoxical conservatism in his make-up.

As a teacher in the many institutions in which he faced thousands of immigrant and Canadian students, he conveyed the beauty and importance of this poetic tradition. Because he himself was neither effete nor genteel, he could impress upon his students the view that poetry was not a peripheral activity carried out by gentlemen at leisure in their drawing rooms, but a flesh-and-blood activity seminal to man's understanding of the larger world and himself. By most accounts, Layton was an extraordinary teacher whose students generally emerged loving poetry and frequently writing it. Though most of them, like most students of piano, would be mediocre artists at best, they gained sufficient insight into the craft to become, to some extent, cultured. By his ease in the classroom, Layton helped to widen the audience for poetry and the arts generally in Canada. Standing before his students, he must have seemed a symbol of hope for the arts in an overwhelmingly materialistic world.

Layton's political views, which often found their way into his classrooms, too, pose an enigma in his life. He came from a working-class home at a time when the Depression spawned endless talk of revolution, oppression and exploitation. Marxist rhetoric provided Layton with ammunition in his assault on Anglophone Canada. It was the language of politics that first drew him, language of a type with which he felt at home and that roused his instinct to fight and dominate. That rhetoric offered an appealing outlet for the electric friction between the poor Romanian Jewish immigrant and a conservative WASP society he did not like. Layton approached politics not rationally, like an intellectual, but instinctively, by grasping its broad contours, and imitatively, by parroting its spokesmen. It was inevitable that he would deal with politics both directly — in letters to the press, articles, journal entries and other theoretical statements — and indirectly, in his poetry. As in other areas of his life, he learned much through trial and error. When he explored the tensions in society through the use of political rhetoric, he was not very convincing. That was why the CCF mistrusted him, and why the graduate work he did in political science obtained barely passing grades. But when he explored these tensions in a poetic way, he succeeded in conveying the atmosphere of his time and place.

Layton has observed wryly that he chose the name "Layton" because it rhymes with "Satan." And he has indeed been the dark "Satanic" poet on the Canadian scene, in touch with the mysterious powers of destruction and recreation. Such powers were believed real by his superstitious Romanian family. But they also are held valid as descriptions of the creative process by theorists of poetry and psychology alike. Layton's sense that he was a kind of Sorcerer's Apprentice, at the beck and call of forces much greater than his own, pervades his reflections from a very early date. Ultimately, he remained perplexed about the good poems he wrote. Writing instinctively and on an emotional level, he actually felt as if he were the agent of mysterious, even sinister powers that threatened to overwhelm him. "When I create my poems a demon possesses me," he said at a conference for poets in 1963, "and I am not capable of thinking like a normal person until the poem is completed. I am possessed by the Great White Goddess or some Anima Mundi which tosses me aside. During the moment [of creation] I am a prophet, the Delphic oracle through whom He or She spoke."[6] Irving Layton is essentially a word-juggler of instinctive abilities, whose rational mind enters the scene only to revise. As his early nickname, *Flamplatz*, suggests, his ingenious creations have been like spontaneous combustion, exploding fire, illuminating, but often destructive. The collisions of modes found in his best poems — archaic and modern, colloquial and formal, vulgar and refined, tragic and comic, graceful and grotesque — reflect both the dramatic extremities of the Canadian climate and landscape and the uneasy medley of peoples in the society he knew.

Layton's physical presence, especially in an era that saw the beginnings of radio and television coverage of poets, has been a powerful factor in his career. His prodigious, almost electric energy, his coarse peasant features, his mane of black, then grey, then white hair, his attractive, resonant, booming voice, the intensity of a healthy male presence that conveys the intention of dominating physically, sexually or rhetorically — all add up to a charisma that continue to be unmistakeable even in his mid-seventies. To some, Layton's physical presence is noxious in the extreme. But to a wide variety of people from all classes, ages, races and religious backgrounds, he has seemed magnetic. Over men and women alike, he has cast his spell of words. His friendships have been numerous and intense, as his voluminous correspondences attest. These have ranged from the mutual admiration of professionals to the sycophantic adoration of "groupies." To most of them, Layton has demonstrated enduring loyalty. Quick to apologize for his periodic, outrageous fireworks of insults, he has frequently befriended his former enemies.

In family relationships, too, he has been loyal, and his loyalty includes financial gifts which, though erratic, have been generous. As a husband, he has been cheerful, tender and fun, though also devious, unreliable and erratic. Though he has lived with his women in a bohemian manner, going anywhere, putting up with anything, "whistling down the alleys," he has worked at his many, often simultaneous, teaching jobs as if he were the very incarnation of the Protestant work ethic, fitting in his poems around teaching schedules that included eighteen-hour days. As with many immigrants working their way up, financial success did not allay the fear of destitution that drove him to overwork and, at times, to over-write. As a lover, Layton was exciting, bold, all-consuming and tender, though here, too, he has been less than forthright and notably unpredictable. It is as a father that he has been most vulnerable. He often aroused a protective instinct in his women, and tended to fall apart at the very thought of being a parent. As his wives turned their thoughts inward during pregnancy and then doted on their offspring, he could not be supportive. He would become more devious and unreliable than ever, seeking attention for himself elsewhere. He proved himself the perpetual child.

It is 6 September 1983, in Toronto. Boschka, as Betty now calls herself, has driven a scarcely road-worthy wreck topped with a badly wrapped bunch of her paintings all the way from California. She is going to read some of her newly published poems at Harbourfront with her former husband.[7]

She walks up the steps with her son, Max, and his wife, Stephanie. Boschka looks like a benevolent, aging hippie, her twisted face framed with such a luxuriance of grey curls that she somehow resembles a child dressing up in her mother's over-size cast-offs. Proudly, like a ship in full sail, she walks into the room and casually clambers up on the stage.

Layton stands in the hall talking and gesturing to a couple of policemen. He looks agitated. He points this way and that, stabbing the air with his thick finger. His car has been stolen. He went back out to get something and the car was gone, he expostulates. There will be a delay while he gives the police the details.

Inside, in a room meant for two or three hundred people, the audience is not big, a hundred at the most. But there is Aviva sitting near the front. Leon is not with her. She goes up to the stage to tell Boschka something. Boschka nods and smiles her lop-sided smile. A few groupies are there. Loyal Dorothy Rath sits off by herself to one side, expectantly. Howard Aster, whose Mosaic Press has published Boschka's first book of poems, *A Prodigal Sun*,[8] is beaming in anticipation.

Layton returns and clambers up on the stage. As the two of them take turns reading their poems, their Montreal past is nostalgically recreated. But now Layton's charisma has faded. His exaggerated rhetoric and dramatic gestures do not draw his listeners into a rhapsodic trance. As Boschka reads in her quiet, understated way, there is the sense of a woman who has been silent too long, someone who has taken a lifetime to come to terms with bitterness.

The spirit of that reading is captured best by poems that were not read at Harbourfront, but that epitomize the tongue-in-cheek affection of the former couple's new friendship. Layton long ago wrote "What Ulysses Said to Circe on the Beach of Aeaea":

> You are beautiful
> As a remembered song from one's homeland,
>   Snake-eyed enchantress,
> And desirable beyond compare;
>   Not even Penelope
> In the first marriage blaze of passion
> Could heat the red juice in my veins
> As you do.
>   Yet even you, all-puissant goddess,

> And your bewitched minions
> Must scrape the oozy mud of the seafloor
>   For squids and periwinkles
> To nourish me thereon
> Should you want, O lovely and divine Circe,
>   Another erection.[9]

Boschka has recently written a sardonic reply, "What Circe Said to Ulysses":

> I don't want you to make love to me.
> My legs are like a wrinkled dead hog's butt —
> the light catching four long crinkled hairs.
> I want to exchange ideas
> the way we did in Inverness:
> even though we've grown miles apart
> still there must have been a basis for it,
> something that held our popeyes
> glued like squids' on each other.
>
> Come to think of it
> I'm glad you didn't ask me.
> I might have found myself
> on my back
> in the slime.[10]

Another of her recent poems, called "Brief to Irving" (about his 1981 volume, *Europe and Other Bad News*), sums things up:

> I open your latest book
> of eighty-two poems
> another blitzkrieg
> and see you're taking up the cudgels
> against another wife:
> I wonder how she's taking it?
> I see. She's leaking headaches
> trembling in corners
> already

> and she's only had two years of you.
> The reason, perhaps, appears on page 75
> you squirm over your neighbour's crotch....
>
> After twenty years I am still angry
> I will say it for us all
> Faye, Aviva, Harriet, myself:
> We're not, Irving, merely strumpets
> for your pleasure;
> we're almost numerous enough
> your wives
> to unionize, vote you out
> if you think that makes poetry
> you've got another wife coming....[11]

Irving, leaning back in his chair onstage, simply smiles into the lights.

Some members of the audience return to Max's apartment for a party. In the living room, Boschka receives congratulations. In another room, Aviva and Layton sit very close together, earnestly discussing something. She is stroking his knee, like someone offering comfort and intimacy at the same time. Anna is cheerfully helping Max and Stephanie with an abundant table of food and numerous bottles of wine.[12]

The party gets underway. A group in the living room arrange themselves casually beneath hanging plants, on cushions or on the floor, and begin to trade anecdotes about the most erotic fantasies and dreams they've had. The atmosphere is reminiscent of the 1960s. Layton appears from the other room, listens a moment, then disappears again.

After a while, someone looks up and asks, "Where is Irving?" No one seems to know.

Boschka calls to Stephanie in the kitchen. He's not there, it seems. Aviva looks up from an intense conversation with one of the guests and remarks that she hasn't seen him for some time. She walks briskly into the back room and looks out onto the porch. He's not there. Anna puts down the plate of cheese she is carrying and looks down the stairs into the lower hall. He's not there.

She discovers him in the bedroom. "Oh, look!" she says. Boschka and Aviva come to see. There, on Max's bed beside the guests' coats, Irving has fallen asleep with his knees drawn up to his chest.

"Ah," sighs Aviva. "Isn't he *sweet*?"

"Yeh, really sweet," says Boschka wryly, but not without affection.

Anna just beams down at her bad biscuit boy.

Endnotes

ABBREVIATIONS USED IN ENDNOTES

BOOKS

ANV	*Anvil — A Selection of Workshop Poems*	LWNL	*Love Where the Nights are Long — An Anthology of Canadian Love Poems*
BC	*The Bull Calf and Other Poems*		
BFOJ	*Balls for a One-Armed Juggler*	MK	*Music on a Kazoo*
BH	*The Black Huntsmen*	NIP	*Now is the Place*
BP$_1$	*The Blue Propeller* (first edition)	NP	*Nail Polish*
BP$_2$	*The Blue Propeller* (second edition)	PAN	*Pan-ic — A Selection of Contemporary Canadian Poems*
CERB	*Cerberus*		
CGE	*The Cold Green Element*	PIL	*The Poems of Irving Layton*
COV	*The Covenant*	PM	*Periods of the Moon*
CP	*Canadian Poems 1850–1952*	PV	*The Pole-vaulter*
CP$_{65}$	*Collected Poems* (1965)	RC	*A Red Carpet for the Sun*
CPIL	*The Collected Poems of Irving Layton*	SF	*The Swinging Flesh*
		SG	*Shadows on the Ground*
DF	*The Darkening Fire — Selected Poems 1945–1968*	SP	*The Shattered Plinths*
		SP$_{69}$	*Selected Poems* (1969)
DH	*Droppings From Heaven*	SPIL	*The Selected Poems of Irving Layton*
ENGAG	*Engagements — The Prose of Irving Layton*	ST	*Shark Tank — York Poetry Workshop Anthology*
EOBN	*Europe and Other Bad News*	TD	*The Tightrope Dancer*
FMBJ	*For My Brother Jesus*	TP	*The Tamed Puma*
FMNH	*For My Neighbours in Hell*	TS	*Taking Sides: The Collected Social and Political Writings*
GB	*The Gucci Bag*		
GP	*Seventy-five Greek Poems 1951–1974*	TWNS	*There Were No Signs*
		UE	*The Unwavering Eye — Selected Poems 1969–1975*
HN	*Here and Now*		
IB$_1$	*The Improved Binoculars* (first edition)	UPIL	*The Uncollected Poems of Irving Layton 1936–1959*
IB$_2$	*The Improved Binoculars* (second edition)	WBB	*The Whole Bloody Bird*
		WPJ	*A Wild Peculiar Joy — Selected Poems 1945–1982*
IL:PC	*Irving Layton: The Poet and his Critics*		
IMF	*In the Midst of My Fever*		
LCW	*Love the Conqueror Worm*		
LIM 58	*A Laughter in the Mind* (1958)		
LIM 59	*A Laughter in the Mind* (1959)		
LLM	*Lovers and Lesser Men*		
LP	*The Long Pea-Shooter*		
LPIL	*The Love Poems of Irving Layton*		
LR	*The Laughing Rooster*		

MANUSCRIPT LOCATIONS

CJC	Canadian Jewish Congress, National Archives
CU	Concordia University, Irving Layton Collection
JPL	Jewish Public Library
MU	McGill University Archives
PA	Public Archives of Canada
US	University of Saskatchewan Archives
UT	University of Toronto, Thomas Fisher Rare Book Library
UTEX	University of Texas, Humanities Research Center
UTS	University of Toronto, Thomas Fisher Rare Book Library, A.J.M. Smith Collection
YU	York University

Romania/4

1. Details of the Romanian landscape and life are taken from two collections edited by Henry Baerlein, *The Romanian Scene: Anthology on Romania and her People by Writers in English* (1945) and *Romanian Oasis: A Further Anthology on Romania and her People by Writers in English* (1948). Both were published in London by Frederick Muller Ltd. I am indebted to Arnold J. Toynbee's essay, "Description of Greater Romania" (*The Romanian Scene*, p. 144) for the image of Romania as a crescent moon.
2. James O. Noyes, "Customs and Beliefs," *Roumania: the Border Land of the Christian and the Turk* (New York: Rudd & Carleton, 1863), pp. 170–171.
3. Tereza Stratilesco, "The Funeral," *From Carpathian to Pindus* (London: Fisher, Unwin, 1906), pp. 291–292.
4. See Radu Florescu and Raymond T. McNally, *Dracula: A Biography of Vlad the Impaler 1431–1476* (New York: Hawthorn Books, 1973).
5. Noyes, p. 177.
6. Marcu Beza, "The Creation," *Paganism in Roumanian Folklore* (London: J.M. Dent & Sons, 1928), p. 125.
7. Romulus Vuia, "The Romanian Hobbyhorse, the Călusari," *The Romanian Scene*, pp. 197–199.
8. William J. Entwhistle, "The Ballads," *The Romanian Scene*, pp. 205–207.
9. Arnold Toynbee, "Spotlight on Rumania" (London, *The Listener*, 26 January, 1939), p. 220.
10. W. Beatty-Kingston, *A Wanderer's Notes: 1864–76, Romanian Oasis*, p. 108.
11. For more complete details of the situation of Jews in Romania during this period, see Carol Iancu, *Les Juifs en Roumanie 1866–1919: de l'Exclusion à l'Émancipation* (Aix-en-Provence: Éditions de l'Université de Provence, 1978).
12. Queen Marie [of Romania, King Carol's wife], "Carol I at Sinai," *The Romanian Scene*, p. 106.
13. Leonard A. Magnus, "Negotiations Between Austria and Romania Preceding the First World War," *Romanian Oasis*, p. 101.
14. W. Beatty-Kingston, *A Wanderer's Notes, The Romanian Scene*, p. 85.
15. Edmund Ollier, "After the Campaign," *The Romanian Scene*, p. 72.
16. See Carol Iancu, pp. 19–23.
17. Iancu, p. 23.
18. Iancu, p. 137.
19. Iancu, p. 28.
20. William Goodwin to E.C. (Elspeth Cameron), interview, 28 October 1983, Montreal; a confirmation that such were the clothes his mother and her family wore in Romania.
21. Iancu, p. 28.
22. Iancu, p. 137.
23. For details of the Congress of Berlin and its stipulations, see Iancu, pp. 153–180.
24. Iancu, pp. 24, 147. For detailed statistics of the occupations of Jews, Christians and "others" in Romania during the last decades of the nineteenth century, see also Verax, *La Roumanie et Les Juifs* (Bucarest: I.V. Socecu, 1903).
25. Iancu, p. 182.
26. Iancu, p. 26; "Les Juifs sont notre malheur!"
27. For these and other detailed population statistics, see Iancu, pp. 142–144.
28. Iancu, p. 26.
29. Harry Latch to E.C., interview, 9 July 1982, Petaluma, California.
30. Iancu, pp. 201–205, p. 186.
31. Gazella Goldberg to E.C., interview, 23 February, 1982, Montreal.
32. Details of the Lazarovitch family life in Romania come from Gazella Goldberg to E.C., interview, 23 February 1982, Montreal and Harry Latch to E.C., interview, 9 July 1982, Petaluma, California. "Cruminas" comes from the Yiddish "crum," meaning "crooked," and "nas" meaning "nose." "Megele" does not literally mean "as stupid as a donkey," which all the Lazarovitch family took it to mean. It is a diminutive form of the Yiddish word "mogn," meaning "digestive tract"; hence, "little digestive tract." By implication, this nickname suggests that there is nothing more to the child than his digestive system; that is, that he lacks brains and so on. (It does ulti-

mately mean "stupid.") "Shegetz" is a Yiddish term used in a pejorative sense for Christian boys. When applied, as here, to a Jewish boy, it means a person who is not attentive to scriptural studies or religious laws and is consequently an "imp" or "devil" who lacks moral character. "Guzlin," a Hebrew word, means literally "thief" or "bandit"; hence, "one who is dishonest and uses force to take what is not his."

33. For further details about the birth of Yiddish theatre, which took place during this period in Romania, see Iancu, p. 148.
34. Iancu, p. 148.
35. Marcu Beza, "English Influence on Romanian Literature," *Romanian Oasis*, pp. 118–119.
36. Beza, pp. 201–205.
37. Beza, pp. 192–196.
38. Beza, pp. 196–201.
39. Beza, pp. 189–192.
40. Gazella Goldberg to E.C., interview, 23 February 1982, Montreal.
41. Iancu, pp. 189–192.
42. Gazella Goldberg to E.C., interview, 23 July 1982, Montreal.
43. Christine A. Galitzi, "Romanian Immigrants in the United States," *A Study of Assimilation among the Romanians in the United States* (New York: Columbia University Press, 1929), p. 110.
44. Iancu, p. 264.
45. Iancu, p. 257; the song, in Romanian and French versions, is cited as originating in Piatra Neamt in 1900.
46. Figures taken from the entries under "Tirgul Neamt" and "Piatra Neamt" in *The Encyclopedia Judaica*.

Montreal/16

1. Gazella Goldberg to E.C., interview, 23 July 1982, Montreal. Dates of birth must remain approximate in a family that kept no records. Layton gives his date of birth variously as 5 March 1912, 9 March 1912 and 12 March 1912. In a note to Desmond Pacey, he said his mother told him only that he was born right after Passover.
2. Israel: the name of honour given to Jacob after his mysterious struggle with the angel ("Thou hast striven "sarita," from the Hebrew root "sarah"] with God [from the Hebrew "El"] and with men and hast prevailed"). Layton claimed his middle name was "Pinchas" to John Brebner (10 September 1975, property of John Brebner, Gagetown, New Brunswick). Since there is no evidence prior to 1975 that this was so, it is possible that Layton invented the name as the Hebrew equivalent of "Peter," the name he began using, as a first name and then as a middle name, when he enrolled at MacDonald College.

   Flamplatz: a nickname made up from the Yiddish *"flam,"* meaning "flame," and *"platz,"* meaning "blast" or "explosion."

   "Lazarovitch" means "the son of a beggar." Layton claims that the family's name was originally "Leizer,' but was changed some time ago in Romania.
3. Details regarding the nature of Montreal in 1913 are taken from: John Irwin Cooper, *Montreal: A Brief History* (Montreal: McGill-Queen's University Press, 1969), pp. 122–131; Leslie Roberts, *Montreal* (Toronto: Macmillan, 1969), pp. 304–316; Kathleen Jenkins, *Montreal* (New York: Doubleday, 1966), pp. 428–453; W.P. Percival, *The Lure of Montreal*, rev. ed. (Toronto: Ryerson Press, 1964), pp. 1–27; Leonard L. Knott, *Montreal: 1900–1930* (Toronto: Nelson, Foster and Scott, 1976); Luc d'Iberville-Moreau, *Lost Montreal* (Toronto: Oxford University Press, 1975); and Julius Chambers, *Montreal* (Montreal: International Press Syndicate, 1914).
4. Chambers, p. 55.
5. William Goodwin to E.C., interview, 33 February 1982, Montreal.
6. Judith Seidel, "The Development and Social Adjustment of the Jewish Community in Montreal," M.A. thesis (unpublished), McGill University, 1939, p. 110, pp. 143–145. *Landsleute* means "a fellow-countryman, one of those who emigrated from the same town or country in Europe."

7. Details of family history from Harry Latch to E.C., interview, 10 July 1983, Petaluma, California and I.L. to E.C., interview, 3 October 1983, Oakville, Ontario.
8. "Area of first settlement" is a term used by Judith Seidel to define the geographic location in Montreal where the first wave of Jewish immigrants settled.
9. Seidel, p. 51.
10. Seidel, pp. 7–11.
11. Arthur Ruppin, *The Jews in the Modern World* (London: Macmillan, 1934), p. 127.
12. Seidel, p. 18.
13. Seidel, p. 187–188.
14. Seidel, p. 143.
15. Christine A. Galitzi, "Romanian Immigrants in the United States," *A Study of Assimilation among the Romanians in the United States* (New York: Columbia University Press, 1929), p. 66.
16. Galitzi, pp. 62–66. Galitzi observes that the most "striking feature" of the distribution of Romanian immigrants in the United States is "their concentration in cities," a disruption of their traditionally rural lifestyle, which was "the direct outcome of circumstances."
17. Seidel, pp. 142–143.
18. William Goodwin to E.C., interview, 23 February 1982, Montreal.
19. Hyman Latch to E.C., interview, 6 July 1982, San Francisco.
20. Latch to E.C.
21. I.L. to E.C., interview, 3 October 1983, Oakville, Ontario.
22. Latch to E.C.
23. A.M. Klein, "The Seventh Scroll," *A.M. Klein, Short Stories*, ed. M.W. Steinberg (Toronto: University of Toronto Press, 1983), pp. 105–108.
24. I.L. to E.C., interviews, 6 and 13 January 1982, Toronto.
25. Latch to E.C.
26. Latch to E.C.
27. Family details derive from interviews with Gazella Goldberg, 23 February 1982, Montreal; Harry Latch, 9 July 1982, Petaluma, California; Dora Pleet, 12 March 1982, Montreal; Hyman Latch, 6 July 1982, San Francisco; I.L., 13 January 1982, Toronto and 3 October 1983, Oakville, Ontario.

Death/31

1. Based on reminiscences of I.L., 6 January 1982, Toronto; Dora Pleet, 12 March 1982, Montreal; and Gazella Goldberg, 23 February 1982, Montreal.
2. William Goodwin to E.C., interview, 23 February 1982, Montreal.
3. Saul Muhlstock to E.C., 3 September 1982; and interview, 1 September 1982, Montreal.
4. I.L. to E.C., interview, 20 January 1982, Toronto.
5. Hyman Latch to E.C., interview, 6 July 1982, San Francisco.
6. I.L. to E.C., interview, 13 January 1982, Toronto.
7. I.L. to E.C., interview, 3 October 1983, Oakville, Ontario.
8. Irma Zack (Miss Benjamin's daughter) to I.L., 11 April 1982.
9. I.L. has frequently referred to this in interviews and letters. See, for example, I.L. to Robert Creeley, 10 August 1953, Robert Creeley Papers, Washington University Libraries, St. Louis, Missouri.
10. I.L. to E.C., interview 3 October 1983, Oakville, Ontario.
11. Hyman Latch to E.C., interview, 6 July 1982, San Francisco.
12. I.L., "A Death in the Family," *Northern Review*, 1, No. 4 (1946), pp. 2–11; reprinted in *Engagements: The Prose of Irving Layton*, ed. Seymour Mayne (Toronto: McClelland and Stewart, 1972), pp. 311–319.
13. "*Strulick*," Keine's Yiddish endearment for her youngest son, literally means "little Israel"; "*srulickel*" means "darling little Israel." "*Maidele*" means "maiden" or "sweetheart." "*Mama bakele*," Layton's endearment for his mother, literally means "mummy with the soft cheeks."

Transitions/37

1. This date must remain approximate. The province of Quebec has no record of Moses Lazarovitch's death. Family

members have given various dates; some have given different dates during the same interview. For example, Layton said, "My father died in 1925 when I was nine" (to E.C., interview, 6 January 1982). Layton would have been twelve or thirteen — not nine — in 1925, since he was born in 1912. Under oath in Montreal before U.S. Immigration on 4 August 1953, Layton gave the date 1925 for his father's death. (Documents provided by the R.C.M.P., Ottawa.)
2. Hyman Latch's descriptive term for his mother.
3. Judith Seidel, "The Development and Social Adjustment of the Jewish Community in Montreal," M.A. thesis (unpublished), McGill University, 1939. Details for the street scenes that follow are taken from this thesis.
4. The Steinberg boys eventually founded a vast grocery empire that still thrives. See Peter Newman's portrait of them: "The Steinberg Brothers (1905–)," *Flame of Power* (Toronto: Longmans, Green & Co., 1959), pp. 171–182.
5. Seidel, p. 60.
6. I.L. to E.C., interview, 3 October 1983, Oakville, Ontario.
7. In all probability, I.L. was born with minor hypospadias, the most common birth defect of male or female genitals (one in every three hundred male births). This speculation is even more probable in a case like Layton's, where the mother is older than forty at the time of conception and birth; the older the woman, the higher the incidence of minor hypospadias. See R.B. Brown, *Clinical Urology Illustrated* (Lancashire: MTP Press, Ltd., 1982), pp. 20–21; and Meredith Campbell, *Urology*, Vol. 1 (Philadelphia: W.B. Saunders, 1954), pp. 421–422. When Layton's second wife, Betty Sutherland (called, by then, Boschka Layton), asked Layton's older brother Harry Latch whether Irving really was born circumcised, Latch replied indignantly, "Of course not!" (Betty Layton to E.C., interview, 8 July 1982, Guerneville, California).

Revenge/43

1. Alfred Lord Tennyson, "The 'Revenge': A Ballad of the Fleet," *Tennyson's Poetry*, ed. Robert W. Hill, Jr. (New York: W.W. Norton & Co., 1971), pp. 433–436.
2. Amos Saunders to E.C., interview, 22 February 1982, Montreal.
3. Saunders to E.C.
4. I.L. to E.C., interview, 2 April 1982, Toronto.
5. I.L. to E.C., interview, 13 January 1982, Toronto.
6. Handwritten sketch, dated "28th June 1927," was donated by Amos Saunders, who kept it for more than half a century because it always seemed to him an exceptionally accomplished piece of writing for a fifteen-year-old boy, especially one whose mother tongue was not English.

Suzanne/47

1. Details for Issie's imaginary departure are assembled from Layton's semi-autobiographical short stories, his personal recollections and those of his family about life at home.
2. Suzanne Rosenberg, "Memoirs" (unpublished), 1982, p. 67, pp. 71–72. The actual delivery of groceries by Issie to Suzanne occurred in the early spring, not the late winter, of Suzanne's tenth year.

Adrift/50

1. I.L. to E.C., interview, 13 January 1982, Toronto. In this interview, Layton recalled Hershorn's first name as "Zisa," but he gave the name "Kalman" under oath in Montreal at U.S. Immigration, 4 August 1953. (Documents provided by the R.C.M.P., Ottawa.)
2. William Goodwin to E.C., interview, 23 February 1982, Montreal.
3. I.L. to E.C., 31 July, 1984.
4. I.L. to E.C., interview, 13 January 1982, Toronto.
5. I.L., "Irving Layton Remembers Chopped Liver and Humble Pie," *Maclean's Magazine* (31 January 1959), p. 30.

6. This book is currently in the possession of William Goodwin.
7. I.L., "The Philistine," *Engagements: The Prose of Irving Layton*, ed. Seymour Mayne (Toronto: McClelland and Stewart, 1972), p. 252.
8. Hyman Latch to E.C., interview, 6 July 1982, San Francisco.
9. I.L. to E.C., interview, 20 January 1982, Toronto.
10. I.L., "The English Lesson," *Engagements*, p. 259.
11. I.L. to E.C., interview, 3 October 1983, Oakville, Ontario.
12. "The English Lesson," p. 259.
13. "The English Lesson," p. 260.

Revolution/57

1. Carol Iancu, *Les Juifs en Roumanie 1866–1919: De L'Exclusion a l'Émancipation* (Aix-en-Provence: Éditions de l'Université de Provence, 1978), p. 244.
2. Iancu, p. 245.
3. Iancu, p. 248.
4. See John Kolasky, *The Shattered Illusion: The History of Ukrainian Pro-Communist Organizations in Canada* (Toronto: Peter Martin Associates, 1979); Tim Buck, "The Founding of the Party of Communists," *Our Fight for Canada* (Toronto: Progress Books, 1959); and Ivan Avakumović, *The Communist Party in Canada: A History* (Toronto: McClelland and Stewart, 1975), p. 144.
5. Tim Buck, *Thirty Years 1922–1952: The Story of the Communist Movement in Canada* (Toronto: Progress Books, 1952), p. 38.
6. Buck, p. 51.
7. Buck, pp. 76–77. For an exposé of the monopolist elite in Canada, see the booklet by Francis William Park, *The Power and the Money* (Toronto: Progress Books, 1958).
8. I.L. to E.C., interview, 2 March 1982, Toronto.

The Politics of Love/60

1. Suzanne Rosenberg to E.C., interview, 30 January 1982, London, Ontario.

2. Suzanne Rosenberg, "Memoirs" (unpublished), 1982, p. 64.
3. Rosenberg, p. 64.
4. I.L. to E.C., interview, 20 January 1982, Toronto. Layton translates this Yiddish word as "soft and desirable, the flesh firm but not yielding — like a good pillow." "Zaftig" literally means "soft, in the sense of pinchable."
5. Rosenberg, p. 68.
6. Rosenberg, p. 72. Lazarovitch was a member of the Young People's Socialist League in 1929. (Documents provided by the R.C.M.P., Ottawa.)
7. I.L. to E.C., interview, 20 January 1982, Toronto.
8. Suzanne Rosenberg to E.C., interview, 2 April 1982, Toronto.
9. Rosenberg, p. 69.
10. Rosenberg, p. 75.
11. Rosenberg, p. 75.
12. Rosenberg, p. 77.
13. Rosenberg, p. 64.
14. Rosenberg, p. 82.
15. Anne Madras to E.C., interview, 2 April 1982, Toronto.
16. Suzanne Rosenberg to E.C., interview, 30 January 1982, London, Ontario.
17. Rosenberg to E.C.
18. Rosenberg to E.C.
19. Rosenberg to E.C.
20. Rosenberg, "Memoirs," p. 83.
21. Rosenberg, p. 80.
22. Rosenberg, p. 81.
23. Suzanne Rosenberg to E.C., interview, 30 January 1982, London, Ontario.
24. "Vigil," *The McGilliad* (April 1931), p. 108. Reprinted in the *McGill Daily* (26 January 1938); *First Statement*, I, No. 1 (1943); *CP, CPIL, LR* and *MS:CU*.
25. Rosenberg, "Memoirs," pp. 86–87.
26. Rosenberg, p. 88. Report on "I. Lazarre's" speech provided by the R.C.M.P., Ottawa.
27. Rosenberg, p. 89.
28. Rosenberg, p. 89.

Russia/67

1. See Suzanne Rosenberg's descriptions of Baron Byng High School, "Memoirs," pp. 77–80.

2. Layton claims today that the book he was reading was his favourite at that time, the encyclopaedic overview of human history by H.G. Wells, *The Outline of History* (London: Georges Newnes Ltd., 1920), parts 1–24.
3. I.L. to Richard G. Adams, interiew, cited in "Irving Layton: The Early Poetry, 1931–1945," Ph.D. thesis (unpublished), the University of New Brunswick, 1983, p. 31.
4. I.L. to E.C., interview, 20 January 1982, Toronto.
5. I.L. to E.C.
6. Suzanne Rosenberg to I.L., 1 June 1932, Irving Layton Collection, Concordia University Library, Montreal.
7. Extract of a report made on this thirty-five minute speech was provided by the R.C.M.P., Ottawa.
8. I.L. to E.C., interview, 6 January 1982, Toronto. Ghitta Caiserman-Roth (b. 1923) has won numerous awards and has exhibited in the United States, Europe and Canada. Her work, in the social-realist mode, is represented in the permanent collections of the National Gallery of Canada, the Montreal Museum of Fine Arts, the Vancouver Art Gallery and numerous other public and private collections.
9. Miriam Waddington to E.C., interview, 14 June 1983, Toronto.
10. Suzanne Rosenberg to I.L., 10 January 1934, Irving Layton Collection, Concordia University Library, Montreal.

Seeing Red/74

1. *Failt-ye Times*, 25 October 1935. "Failt-ye" means "welcome" in Gaelic.
2. *Failt-ye Times*, 6 December 1935.
3. *Failt-ye Times*, 31 January 1936.
4. John Ferguson Snell, *Macdonald College of McGill University: A History from 1904–1955* (Montreal: McGill University Press, 1963).
5. Snell, p. 206.
6. Snell, p. 203.
7. Snell, p. 212.
8. Snell, p. 210. The text of Dr. W.H. Brittain's address, "The First Fifty Years," Special Semi-Centenary Convocation, Macdonald College (4 June 1955).
9. I.L. gave the name as "Alec Alveiroff" to George Edelstein in an unpublished interview, 11 April 1962. See Edelstein, "Irving Layton: A Study of the Poet in Revolt," M.A. thesis (unpublished), Université de Montréal, 1962, p. 26. I.L. gave E.C. the name as it appears here in an interview, 6 January 1982, Toronto.
10. I.L. to E.C., letter from Montreal, 31 July 1984. A notice in the McGill University Calendar for 1933 indicates that "Quebec students from farming communities" were each entitled to a grant of nine dollars a month to study agriculture at Macdonald College (p. 492). How Lazarovitch, from Montreal, qualified for this grant remains a mystery.
11. I.L. to George Edelstein, interview, 11 April 1962, cited in Edelstein, pp. 27–28.
12. Name witheld to E.C., interview, 16 February 1984, Toronto
13. Name witheld to E.C.
14. Edelstein, p. 32.
15. Official transcript of record of Irving Peter Lazarovitch, Macdonald College, McGill University.
16. I.L. to E.C., 31 July 1984. Layton wrote, "'Pero' was a name I invented because I liked the sound."
17. I.L., President of Social Research Club, statement of aims as published in *The Macdonald College Annual*, 1934–1935.
18. Edelstein, p. 32.
19. *Failt-ye Times*, 18 December 1935.
20. I.L. did not recall using this pseudonym, but internal evidence suggests that this was his work. "Blissless Carmine" was a sarcastic allusion to poet "Bliss Carman" (a poet Lazarovitch thought was effete); as well, "Carmine" (carmen) means "red" and alludes to Communism (Lazarovitch's current political interest). If the poem was not written by Lazarovitch, it was probably written to mock him.

21. *Failt-ye Times*, 18 December 1935.
22. Edelstein, pp. 41–42.
23. *Failt-ye Times*, 31 January 1936 and 27 March, 1936.
24. I.L., "A Game of Chess," *First Statement*, 2, No. 7 (May 1944); reprinted in *Tamarack Review*, 18 (Winter 1961) and in *Engagements*, p. 225.
25. Bevan Monks to George Edelstein, cited in Edelstein, p. 30.
26. Official transcript of record of Irving Peter Lazarovitch, Macdonald College, McGill University.
27. Rochel Eisen (commonly known as "Eisenberg") to E.C., interview, 31 August 1982, Montreal.
28. I.L. to E.C., interview, 6 January 1982, Toronto; and Rochel Eisen to E.C., interview, 31 August 1982, Montreal.
29. W.J. Wright, registrar, Macdonald College, to Oscar Lazarovitch, 25 September 1936, Irving Layton Collection, Concordia University Library, Montreal.

Feeling Blue/87

1. I.L., "Vacation in La Voiselle," *Northern Review*, 1, No. 4 (1946), pp. 12–16; republished in *Canadian Short Stories*, ed. Robert Weaver (London: Oxford University Press, 1960), pp. 248–269; and in *Engagements*, p. 209. According to Layton, this story is based on his friendship with the Cusinières. (To E.C., 3 October 1983, Oakville, Ontario.) Layton wrote another story "The Parasite," based on his association with the family. In the original version of it, he used the name "Cusinier" [sic for the family of *maman*, Mimi and Calan [sic], *First Statement*, 1:14 (1943) pp. 3–9. In a revised version, "Unemployed," he changed the family name to "D'Alembert." *Engagements*, pp 302–310.
2. "Vacation in La Voiselle," p. 206.
3. Mimi Cusinière to I.L., undated [1936], Irving Layton Collection, Concordia University Library, Montreal.
4. As mentioned in a number of letters from the Cusinières to I.L., summer 1936, Irving Layton Collection, Concordia University Library, Montreal.
5. I.L., "The Philistine," *First Statement*, 2, No. 6 (April 1944), pp. 5–13; reprinted in *The Swinging Flesh* (Toronto: McClelland and Stewart, 1961) and in *Engagements*, pp. 247–256.
6. Mimi Cusinière to I.L., undated, Mardi [1936], Irving Layton Collection, Concordia University Library, Montreal.
7. "Vacation in La Voiselle," p. 210.
8. Mimi Cusinière to I.L., Mardi [1936], Irving Layton Collection, Concordia University Library, Montreal.
9. Calin Cusinière to I.L., September 1936; and Mouchkette Cusinière to I.L., Saterday [sic] [1936], Irving Layton Collection, Concordia University Library, Montreal.
10. Mimi Cusinière to I.L., 24 September [1936], Irving Layton Collection, Concordia University Library, Montreal.
11. Mimi Cusinière to I.L., undated [1936], Irving Layton Collection, Concordia University Library, Montreal.
12. Calin Cusinière to I.L., 24 September 1936, Irving Layton Collection, Concordia University Library, Montreal.
13. Mimi Cusinière to I.L., undated [1936], Irving Layton Collection, Concordia University Library, Montreal.
14. Mimi Cusinière to I.L., undated, Saterday [sic] [1936], and Calin Cusinière to I.L., September 1936, Irving Layton Collection, Concordia University Library, Montreal.
15. I.L. to E.C., interview, 3 October 1983, Oakville, Ontario.
16. "Vacation in La Voiselle," p. 207.
17. Mouchkette Cusinière to I.L., 1 October 1936, Irving Layton Collection, Concordia University Library, Montreal.
18. Mouchkette Cusinière to I.L.
19. Hyman Latch recalls that the Cusinières kept a list of bills for food and other expenses incurred by Layton and pursued him — unsuccessfully — to pay them for several years after he left.

(Hyman Latch to E.C., interview, 6 July, 1982, San Francisco.)

The Sultan of Sixth Avenue/*192*

1. This chapter is based on an interview with Hyman Latch, 6 July 1982, San Francisco.

The Farmer Thinks/*95*

1. Eugene Forsey to David Lewis, 2 September 1937, Public Archives of Canada, CCF Records, MG28, IV-I, vol. 94, Forsey file, Ottawa.
2. Eugene Forsey to E.C., 12 March 1984.
3. I.L. as cited by Richard G. Adams, Ph.D. thesis (unpublished), University of New Brunswick, 1983, p. 55.
4. As reported by Lucy L. Woodsworth to David Lewis, 25 November 1937, Public Archives of Canada, CCF Records, MG28, IV-I, vol. 107, J.S. Woodsworth file, 1937–1942, Ottawa.
5. David Lewis to Mrs. J.S. Woodsworth, 3 December 1937, Public Archives of Canada, CCF Records, MG28, IV-I, vol. 107, J.S. Woodsworth file, 1937–1942, Ottawa. According to his own sworn statement of 4 August 1953, Layton had spoken at a meeting of the Labor Progressive Party in Ontario Hall in 1937 or 1938, and he had subscribed to the *Canadian Tribune* for six months in 1939 or 1940. (Documents provided by the R.C.M.P., Ottawa.)
6. Eugene Forsey to David Lewis, 6 December 1937, Public Archives of Canada, MG28, IV-I, vol. 94, Forsey file, Ottawa.

Lynched/*101*

1. I.L. to E.C., interview, 29 January 1982, Toronto.
2. Hyman Latch to E.C., interview, 6 July 1982, San Francisco.
3. Mordecai Richler, *The Apprenticeship of Duddy Kravitz* (Penguin Edition, 1964), pp. 67–103.
4. I.L. to E.C., interview, 17 February 1982, Toronto.
5. Irving Layton Collection, Murray Memorial Library Archives, University of Saskatchewan, Saskatoon.
6. Hyman Latch to E.C., interview, 6 July 1982, San Francisco.
7. I.L. to George Edelstein, unpublished interview, 11 April 1982, cited in Edelstein, p. 51.
8. Edelstein, p. 54. "Medley For Our Times," *McGill Daily* (28 November 1938), p. 2. Reprinted in *UPIL*.
9. Official transcript of record of Irving Peter Lazarovitch, Macdonald College, McGill University.
10. I.L., "Machiavelli," dated 1938, unpublished Ms., 10 pp. Murray Memorial Library Archives, University of Saskatchewan, Saskatoon.

A Fuller Brush Man/*105*

1. Lattimer's letter, 16 December 1938, claimed Layton was "a first-class student" in economics, farm management and marketing, and praised him as "a forceful and competent speaker"; Brittain's letter, 3 May 1939, mentions his "absorbing interest in political and social problems" and describes him as "an accomplished public speaker" likely to be "a first class teacher" and "a very wide reader, very well informed in regard to literary, social, economic and political problems, particularly those of an international character." Both letters in the Irving Layton Collection, Concordia University, Montreal.
2. I.L. to H.M. Caiserman, 18 May 1939, Irving Layton Collection, Concordia University, Montreal.
3. H.I.S. Borgford to David Lewis, 27 November 1939, Public Archives of Canada, CCF Records, MG28, IV-I, vol. 27, Ottawa.
4. I.L. to Dean W.H. Brittain, 11 October 1939, as quoted by Edelstein, p. 55.
5. Samuel Margolian to E.C., interview, 24 August 1982, Toronto.
6. I.L. to E.C., 31 July 1984.

7. I.L. to Andy Wainwright, 30 August 1972, Irving Layton Collection, Concordia University, Montreal.
8. I.L. to E.C., interview, 17 February 1982, Toronto.
9. Hyman Latch to E.C., interview, 6 July 1982, San Francisco.
10. "English for Immigrants," *Northern Review*, I, No. 1 (December/January 1946), p. 22. Reprinted in *BH, CPIL* and *NIP*.

The Farmer Leaves A Wife/110

1. Rochel Eisen (Eisenberg) to E.C., interview, 31 August 1982, Montreal.
2. Rochel Eisen letters to I.L., 10 July to 27 August 1941, Irving Layton Collection, Concordia University Library, Montreal.
3. Rochel Eisen to I.L., 1 August 1941, Irving Layton Collection, Concordia University Library, Montreal.
4. Rochel Eisen to I.L., 14 July 1941, Irving Layton Collection, Concordia University Library, Montreal.
5. Rochel Eisen to I.L., 15 August 1941, Irving Layton Collection, Concordia University Library, Montreal.
6. Rochel Eisen to I.L., 6 August 1941, Irving Layton Collection, Concordia University Library, Montreal.
7. Rochel Eisen to I.L., 10 July 1941, Irving Layton Collection, Concordia University Library, Montreal.
8. I.L. to Rochel Eisen, as quoted by Eisen to I.L., 10 July 1941, Irving Layton Collection, Concordia University Library, Montreal.
9. Rochel Eisen to I.L., 22 August 1941, Irving Layton Collection, Concordia University Library, Montreal.
10. For information about Ravitch and samples of his writing, see *Canadian Jewish Anthology*, ed. Chaim Spilberg and Yaacov Zipper (Montreal: Canadian Jewish Congress, 1982), pp. 134–143. Layton claims that he was not influenced by Ravitch's work on Spinoza in writing his poem "Spinoza": "The title...just popped into my head. Why, I really don't know. It could be that I felt the pantheistic tenor of the poem called for it. Also...no name thrills me more when I hear it or see it." (To E.C., 25 October 1984.) Nonetheless, Ravitch was a serious scholar of Spinoza at the time.
11. Rochel Eisen to I.L., 6 August 1941, Irving Layton Collection, Concordia University Library, Montreal.
12. Rochel Eisen to I.L., 22 August 1941, Irving Layton Collection, Concordia University Library, Montreal.
13. Rochel Eisen to I.L., 9 August 1941, Irving Layton Collection, Concordia University Library, Montreal.

Many Worlds/114

1. Loaned by Rochel Eisen, Montreal.
2. Reprinted as "Harold Laski" in *Engagements: the Prose of Irving Layton*, ed. Seymour Mayne (Toronto: McClelland and Stewart, 1972), pp. 3–8.
3. "Harold Laski," p. 4.
4. *The Forge*, 18 December 1941, p. 46.
5. Faculty of Graduate Studies and Research records, McGill University, transcript #39433.
6. "Debacle," *Canadian Forum* (April 1941), p. 19. Reprinted in *UPIL*.
7. "Beneath the Bridge," *Saturday Night*, 57 (18 October 1941), p. 21. Reprinted in *LIM; UE; UPIL* and MS:CU.
8. "Providence," *Saturday Night*, 57 (1 November 1941), p. 21. Reprinted in *First Statement* (1943), *Voices* (1943), *CP65; CPIL; HN; LIM59; RC* and MS:MU.
9. For a scholarly treatment of these early poems, see Richard G. Adams, "Irving Layton: The Early Poetry, 1931–1945," Ph.D. thesis (unpublishd), McGill University, 1983. I am greatly indebted to this thesis for factual detail from this period.
10. "To R.E." ("To Rochel Eisen") *McGill Daily*, 27 February 1942. Reprinted in *UPIL* and MS:CU.

Icons/120

1. Louis Dudek to E.C., interview, 13 October 1983, Montreal.

2. Dudek to E.C. See also Dudek as quoted by Frank Davey, *Louis Dudek and Raymond Souster* (Vancouver: Douglas and McIntyre, 1980), p. 23.
3. *New Provinces*, ed. F.R. Scott and A.J.M. Smith (Toronto: Macmillan, 1936).
4. Originally two prefaces: Scott's, which appeared in the original 1936 edition, and Smith's (which was shelved because the publisher judged it too controversial), which was resurrected thirty-five years later in *Canadian Literature*, No. 24 (Spring 1965). Both are reprinted in *The Making of Modern Poetry in Canada*, ed. Louis Dudek and Michael Gnarowski (Toronto: Ryerson Press, 1967), pp. 38–41.
5. *The Making of Modern Poetry in Canada*, p. 41.
6. David Latham, "Leo Kennedy," *The Oxford Companion to Canadian Literature*, ed. William Toye (Toronto: Oxford University Press, 1983), p. 406.

Modernism/124

1. Louis Dudek and Michael Gnarowski, *The Making of Modern Poetry in Canada* (Toronto: Ryerson Press, 1967), p. 3.
2. In *Poetry: A Magazine of Verse* (Chicago), March 1913.
3. *The Making of Modern Poetry in Canada*, p. 4.
4. Bliss Carman, "Vestigia," *Canadian Anthology*, ed. Carl F. Klinck and Reginald E. Watters (Toronto: Gage, 1974), p. 118.
5. Archibald Lampman, "Reality," *Canadian Anthology*, p. 134.
6. Leon Edel, "The Young Warrior in the Twenties," *On F.R. Scott*, ed. Sandra Djwa and R. St. J. Macdonald (Kingston and Montreal: McGill-Queen's Press, 1983), p. 6. This excellent article gives many factual details as well as the atmosphere of McGill in the mid-twenties.
7. Edel, p. 12.
8. Edel, p. 7.
9. Edel, p. 14.
10. Leo Kennedy, "The Future of Canadian Literature," *The Canadian Mercury*; reprinted in *The Making of Modern Poetry in Canada*, pp. 34–37.
11. Leonard C. Marsh, *Canadians In and Out of Work — A Survey of Economic Classes and Their Relation to the Labour Market* (Toronto: Oxford University Press, 1940), pp. 346–349, 464–469.
12. Louis Dudek, *The Making Of Modern Poetry in Canada*, p. 45.

War/131

1. Statement of Service of Irving Peter Layton in the Canadian Armed Forces, Public Archives of Canada, Ottawa. Records issued 21 July 1983.
2. I.L., "A Game of Chess," *First Statement*, 2, No. 7 (May 1944), pp. 1–8; reprinted in *Tamarack Review*, 18 (Winter 1961), pp. 60–70 and in *Engagements*, pp. 222–232.
3. I.L. to E.C., interview, 3 October 1983, Oakville, Ontario.
4. Hyman Latch to E.C., interview, 6 July 1982, San Francisco.
5. I.L. to A.J.M. Smith, 2 January 1943, A.J.M. Smith Collection, Thomas Fisher Rare Book Library, University of Toronto, Toronto.
6. George Edelstein, "Irving Layton: A Study of the Poet in Revolt," M.A. thesis (unpublished), Université de Montréal, 1962. See Edelstein's personal reminiscences in his introduction, pp. 1–4.
7. Edelstein, pp. 1–4.
8. I.L. to E.C., interview, 3 February 1982, Toronto.

The Hat-Check Girl/136

1. I.L. to E.C., interview, 29 January 1982, Toronto.
2. Betty Layton to E.C., interview, 8 July 1982, Guerneville, California.
3. Margaret Day, Bruce Ruddick and Neufville Shaw were also involved in beginning the magazine. See "Four of the Former *Preview* Editors," transcript of a taped discussion (1965) with F.R. Scott, Bruce Ruddick, Neufville Shaw and Margaret Surrey, *Canadian Poetry*, No. 4 (Spring/Summer 1979), pp. 93–119.

P.K. Page joined the editorial board in April 1942, and A.M. Klein in March 1944.
4. John Sutherland, "Editorial," *First Statement*, 1, No. 1 (September 1942), p. 1.
5. I.L. compared Betty's appearance to both film stars (to E.C., interview, 29 January 1982, Toronto). Others who knew her at the time (Marian Scott, Frank Scott, Audrey Aikman) remarked only her resemblance to Ingrid Bergman.
6. Betty Layton to E.C., interview, 8 July 1982, Guerneville, California.
7. Betty Layton to E.C.
8. David O'Rourke, "John Sutherland," *The Oxford Companion to Canadian Literature*, ed. William Toye (Toronto: Oxford University Press, 1983), pp. 778–779.
9. Betty Layton to E.C., interview, 8 July 1982, Guerneville, California.

Here and Now/*139*

1. Betty Layton to E.C., interview, 8 July 1982, Guerneville, California.
2. "Drill Shed," *Poetry 63* (1944), p. 256. *BH*, *CP65*, *CPIL*, *HN*, *RC*, MS:MU.
3. Marian Scott to E.C., interview, 2 September 1982, Montreal.
4. Betty Layton to E.C., interview, 8 July 1982, Guerneville, California.
5. Eugene Forsey to E.C., 12 March 1984.
6. I.L. to E.C., interview, 3 February 1982, Toronto.
7. Betty Layton to E.C., interview, 8 July 1982, Guerneville, California.
8. "Vigil" had appeared in *The McGilliad*, 2, No. 5 (April 1931), p. 108, and in *The McGill Daily* (26 January 1938); "A Jewish Rabbi" ("My Father") had appeared in *The McGill Daily* (8 November 1938); "Providence" had appeared in *Saturday Night* (1 November 1941) and in *Voices*, 113 (1943); and "Petawawa" ("Training Camp") had appeared in *Direction*, 3 (1943) and in *Canadian Forum* (January 1944). For a full account of Layton's poems in *First Statement*, see Richard G. Adams, "The Early Poems of Irving Layton," Ph.D. thesis (unpublished), University of New Brunswick, 1983. "Vigil" reprinted in *CP65*; *CPIL*; *LR* and MS:CU. "A Jewish Rabbi" ("My Father") reprinted in *HN* and MS:MU. "Providence" reprinted in *CP 65*; *CPIL*; *HN*; *LIM 59*; *RC* and MS:MU. "Petawawa" ("Training Camp") reprinted in *Other Canadians* (Montreal: First Statement Press, 1947); *BH*; *HN* and MS:MU.
9. The poem had been published in *Canadian Forum* in July 1942. "Restaurant De Luxe" reprinted in *HN*, *UPIL* and MS:MU.
10. *First Statement*, 1, No. 14 (undated) [1943], pp. 3–9.
11. *First Statement*, 1, No. 16 (2 April 1943), pp. 6–7.
12. Patrick Waddington, *First Statement*, 1, No. 16 (2 April 1943), pp. 6–7.
13. Betty Layton to E.C., 8 July 1982, Guerneville, California.
14. As described on the fly-leaf of *Here and Now* (1945).
15. Betty Layton to E.C., 8 July 1982, Guerneville, California.
16. Louis Dudek to E.C., interview, 13 October 1983, Montreal.
17. I.L., *Here and Now*, Writer's Series Chapbook 1, ed. John Sutherland (Montreal: First Statement Press, 1945).
18. "Mortuary," *Canadian Forum* (February 1943), p. 33. Reprinted in *CP65*; *CPIL*; *DF*; *HN*; *RC*; *SP69* and MS:MU.
19. "Mother, This is Spring," *Here and Now*.
20. "Spinoza," *Canadian Forum* (July 1944), p. 90. Reprinted in *HN* and MS:MU.
21. "Waterfront," *Canadian Forum* (February 1945), p. 258. Reprinted in *HN* and MS:MU.
22. "Epitaph For a Wit" ("For a Wit"), *McGill Daily* (27 February 1942) and *Canadian Forum* (May 1942), p. 55. Reprinted in *BH*; *CP65*; *CPIL*; *HN*; *RC* and MS:CU.
23. "The Modern Poet," *First Statement*, 1, No. 16 (2 April 1943), p. 4. Reprinted in *HN* and *NIP*.
24. "De Bullion Street," *First Statement*, 2, No. 5 (March 1944), p. 3. Reprinted in *Other Canadians* (Montreal: First Statement Press, 1947); *BH*; *CP65*; *CPIL*; *DF*; *HN*; *IB1*; *IB2*; *RC*; *SP69*; *TWNS* and MS:CU.

25. *Unit of Five*, ed. Ronald Hambledon (Toronto: Ryerson Press, 1944).
26. Margaret Avison, *Canadian Forum* (May 1945), pp. 47–48.
27. I.L., *Canadian Forum* (June 1945), pp. 64–65. "The Swimmer," *First Statement*, 2, No. 10 (December–January 1944–1945), p. 8. Anthologized widely and reprinted in *BH*; *CP*; *CP 65*; *CPIL*; *DF*; *IB 1*; *IB 2*; *HN*; *NIP*; *PIL*; *RC*; *SP 69*; *SPIL*; *WPJ* and MS:CU. "Newsboy," *Direction*, 2 (1943), p. 9. Anthologized widely and reprinted in *BH*; *CP 65*; *CPIL*; *DF*; *IB 1*; *IB 2*; *NIP*; *RC* and MS:CU. "Proof Reader," *Canadian Forum* (March 1945), p. 286. Reprinted in *BH*; *CPIL*; *DF*; *HN*; *NIP* and *SP 65*.
28. Margaret Avison, *Canadian Forum* (June 1945), p. 65.
29. F.W. Dupee, *The Nation* (1 September 1945), p. 208.
30. D.A.M., *Canadian Author and Bookman*, 21, No. 4 (December 1945), p. 40.
31. Alfred C. Ames, *Poetry: A Magazine of Verses*, 67, No. 5 (February 1946), pp. 282–284.
32. E.K. Brown, *University of Toronto Quarterly*, 15, No. 3 (April 1946), pp. 274–275.

Yes, Sir!/*154*

1. I.L., "A Plausible Story," *Engagements: The Prose of Irving Layton*, ed. Seymour Mayne (Toronto: McClelland and Stewart, 1972), p. 245.
2. As described by Alvin Neiss to E.C., interview, 11 January 1984, Montreal.
3. Professor Ruth Wisse to E.C., interview, 11 October 1983, Montreal.
4. Judith Seidel, "The Development and Social Adjustment of the Jewish Community in Montreal," M.A. thesis (unpublished), McGill University, 1939, pp. 26–29.
5. Faculty of Graduate Studies and Research records, McGill University, transcript #39433, entries dated 1945–1950.
6. McGill transcript.
7. An edited version of the thesis appears in *Taking Sides*, pp. 19–40.
8. *Taking Sides*, pp. 21–22.
9. Under oath before U.S. Immigration officials at Montreal, 4 August 1953, Layton stated that he had belonged to the Labor Progressive Party for one week in 1946 after attending only one meeting, which took place at Baron Byng High School. There, he signed an application for membership and "very likely" paid his dues. "Within a week my eyes were opened to the anti-democratic, anti-Canadian position of the Communist Party. I saw that the Communist Party was nothing but a tool for the extension of the Soviet Union — that it did not have the interests of the Canadian people at heart but was interested in teaching people like myself how to engage in spying or sabotage activities that might help the Soviet Union." (Documents provided by the R.C.M.P., Ottawa, Ontario.) A letter in File: A 7 991 801 from the Assistant Commissioner, Examinations, of the United States Immigration and Naturalization Service of the United States Department of Justice re: Irving Peter Layton, 10 June 1960, states that Layton had "membership for one week during 1946 in the Labor Progressive (Communist) Party" and that "Layton has testified that since his withdrawal from the Labor Progressive Party in 1946, he has had no affiliations with the Communist party." Betty Layton remembers that I.L. belonged to the party "for one weekend, and then destroyed his card" (to E.C., interview, 8 July 1982). I.L. maintains, "I was never a card-carrying member of either the Communist Party or the Socialist Party" (to E.C., 31 July 1984).
10. Patrick Anderson, "Montreal Journal" (unpublished), 3 (Winter/Spring 1945), Public Archives of Canada, Ottawa.
11. Stanley Ryerson to E.C., September 1982, Montreal.
12. Eugene Forsey to E.C., 12 March 1984.
13. Prof. Ethel Roskies to E.C., interview, 13 October 1983, Montreal.
14. Roskies to E.C.
15. Alvin Neiss to E.C., interview, 11 January 1984, Montreal.

16. First published in *Origin*, first series, 14 (1954), pp. 91–104. Reprinted in *A Book of Canadian Short Stories*, ed. Desmond Pacey (Toronto: Ryerson Press, 1962), pp. 144–159; *The Eye of the Beholder*, ed. Bruce Vance (Toronto: Thomas Nelson, 1970), pp. 116–127; *Engagements*, pp. 233–246 and *The Swinging Flesh*, pp. 32–46.
17. I.L. to E.C., interview, 3 October 1983, Oakville, Ontario.
18. "A Plausible Story," *Engagements*, p. 233.
19. Inscribed copy owned by Ethel Roskies, whose first husband, she claims, blamed Layton for giving her the principles of intellectual freedom, which caused conflicts and eventually ended their marriage. (Ethel Roskies to E.C., interview, 13 October 1983).
20. 24 June 1955. Copy owned by I.L.
21. 24 June 1955.
22. 24 June 1955.
23. 24 June 1955.
24. 19 June 1952. Copy owned by I.L.
25. 19 June 1952.

Bohemia/*166*

1. Betty Layton to E.C., interview, 8 July 1982, Guerneville, California.
2. Audrey Aikman to E.C., interview, 12 October 1983, Montreal.
3. Betty Layton to E.C., interview, 8 July 1982, Guerneville, California.
4. I.L. to E.C., interview, 17 February 1982, Toronto.
5. Betty Layton to E.C., interview, 8 July 1982, Guerneville, California.
6. Betty Layton to E.C.
7. Gwethalyn Graham, *Earth and High Heaven* (London: Jonathan Cape, 1944).
8. Audrey Aikman to E.C., interview, 12 October 1983, Montreal.
9. Louis Dudek to E.C., interview, 13 October 1983, Montreal.
10. Louise Scott to E.C., interview, 11 October 1983, Montreal.
11. Betty Layton to E.C., interview, 8 July 1982, Guerneville, California.
12. Audrey Aikman to E.C., interview, 12 October 1983, Montreal.
13. Betty Layton to E.C., interview, 8 July 1982, Guerneville, California.
14. Audrey Aikman to E.C., interview, 12 October 1983, Montreal.

The "Proleterian Poets"/*171*

1. Finch would later publish *The Sixth Sense: Individualism in French Poetry 1686–1760* (1966) and an anthology, *French Individualist Poetry* (1971).
2. Robert Finch, "Train Window," *The Book of Canadian Poetry*, ed. A.J.M. Smith (Toronto: W.J. Gage and Co. Ltd., 1943), p. 364.
3. John Sutherland, "Review of *Poems* by Robert Finch (Toronto: Oxford, 1946)," *Northern Review*, I, No. 6 (August–September 1947).
4. John Sutherland, letter to the Editors, *Preview* magazine, 27 March [1945], Public Archives of Canada, MG30D211, Vol. 26, Poetry 1945–1946 file, Ottawa.
5. Editors of *Northern Review*, "Notices of Resignation," *Northern Review*, II, No. 1 (October–November 1947).
6. See Louis Dudek and Michael Gnarowski, eds., *The Making of Modern Poetry in Canada*, p. 84.
7. Smith, "Introduction," *The Book of Canadian Poetry*, p. 29.
8. Northrop Frye, *Canadian Forum* (December 1943).
9. Louis Dudek, "Academic Literature," *First Statement*, 2, No. 8 (August 1944).
10. *Canadian Anthology*, ed. Carl F. Klink and Reginald E. Watters (Toronto: Gage Educational Publishing, 1974).
11. John Sutherland, "Introduction," *Other Canadians* (Montreal: First Statement Press, 1974). Reprinted in *The Making of Modern Poetry in Canada*, pp. 47–61.
12. Louis Dudek, "The New Poetry: A Manifesto," *The Making of Modern Poetry in Canada*, p. 45.
13. "Words Without Music," *Here and Now*.
14. I.L., "Foreword," *Now is the Place: Stories and Poems by Irving Layton* (Montreal: First Statement Press, 1948).

15. "To the Lawyer Handling My Divorce Case" ("The Existentialist"), *Now Is the Place*. Reprinted in *BH*; *CPIL* and the *Toronto Sun* (11 February 1975).
16. "The Eagle" ("Lenin"), *Northern Review*, 1, No. 6 (August–September 1947), p. 15. Reprinted in *BH* and *NIP*.
17. "Karl Marx," *Northern Review*, 1, No. 6 (August–September 1947), p. 14. Reprinted in *CP 65*; *CPIL*; *DF*; *NIP* and *SP 69*.
18. "A Poor Poet is Grateful For a Sudden Thaw" ("Sudden Thaw"), *Northern Review*, 1, No. 5 (February–March 1947), p. 25. Reprinted in *BH*, *CPIL* and *NIP*.
19. Robert Weaver, "Focus on '48," CKEY radio (18 July 1948).
20. Robert Weaver to I.L. [undated], attached to typescript of his radio review, 18 July 1948.
21. John Sutheland, *Northern Review*, 2, No. 2 (July/August 1948), pp. 34–35.
22. "Jewish Main Street," "De Bullion Street," "Excursion to Ottawa" and "Stolen Watch."

Poet by Default/*187*

1. Faculty of Graduate Studies and Research records, McGill University, transcript #39433.
2. "School Teacher in Late November" and "A Plausible Story," for example.
3. Betty Layton to E.C., interview, 8 July 1982, Guerneville, California.
4. I.L. to Frank Scott, Public Archives of Canada, F.R. Scott papers, MG30D211, Vol. 24, Ottawa.
5. F.R. Scott to I.L., Irving Layton Collection, Concordia University, Montreal.
6. I.L. to Robert Creeley, 17 April 1953, Robert Creeley Papers, Washington University Libraries, St. Louis, Missouri.
7. I.L. to E.C., interview, 13 January 1982, Toronto.
8. Betty Layton to E.C., interview, 10 July 1982, Guerneville, California.
9. "Church Parade," *Canadian Forum* (August 1943), p. 115. Reprinted in *BH*; *HN*; *NIP* and MS:MU.
10. "Stolen Watch" ("Young Thief"), *Canadian Forum* (April 1945), p. 24. Reprinted in *Other Canadians*; *BH*; *CP 65*; *CPIL*; *HN* and *NIP*.
11. "The Modern Poet," *First Statement*, 1, No. 16 (2 April 1943), p. 4. Reprinted in *HN* and *NIP*.
12. "Gents' Furnishings," *First Statement*, 2, No. 3 (October 1943), pp. 16–17. Reprinted in *BH*; *CPIL*; *HN*; *NIP* and MS:CU.
13. I.L., "Preface," *The Laughing Rooster* (Toronto: McClelland and Stewart, 1964), pp. 19–20. I.L. describes the events leading up to the writing of this poem. See also a similar, but inferior, later poem, "Thoughts in the Water," *Origin*, first series, 18 (Winter–Spring 1956), p. 85. Reprinted in *BC*, *CP 65*, *CPIL*, *IB 1*, *IB 2*, *RC* and MS:CU. See also the excellent later poem "The Cold Green Element," *Origin*, first series, 14 (1954), pp. 68–69. Anthologized widely and reprinted in *CGE*, *CP 65*, *CPIL*, *DF*, *IB 1*, *IB 2*, *PIL*, *RC*, *SP 69*, *SPIL*, *WPJ* and MS:CU, US.
14. Anne Marriott, *Canadian Forum* (February 1952), p. 262.
15. Northrop Frye, "Letters in Canada: 1951," *The University of Toronto Quarterly*, 21, No. 3 (April 1952), p. 255.
16. I.L. to Earle Birney, 22 July 1951, Earle Birney Papers, Thomas Fisher Rare Book Library, University of Toronto, Toronto.
17. Earle Birney to I.L., 2 August 1951, Earle Birney Papers, Thomas Fisher Rare Book Library, University of Toronto, Toronto.
18. "Auspex" ("Haruspex"), *Commentary*, 12, No. 1 (July 1952), p. 75. Reprinted in *BH*; *CP 65*; *CPIL*; *IB 1*; *IB 2*; *RC* and MS:CU.
19. "Mrs. Fornheim, Refugee," *The Black Huntsmen*. Reprinted in *CP 65*; *CPIL*; *DF*; *IB 1*; *RC*; *SP 69* and MS:CU.
20. "Mont Rolland," *Contact*, 1, No. 1 (January 1952), p. 8. Reprinted in *BH*, *CP*; *CP 65*; *CPIL*; *DF*; *IB 1*; *IB 2*; *RC*; *SP 69*; *WPJ* and MS:CU.

21. "The World's A Tavern," *The Black Huntsmen.*
22. "The Poet and the Statue," *The Black Huntsmen.* Reprinted in *CPIL.*
23. "Elan," *The Black Huntsmen.* Reprinted in *CP 65* and *CPIL.*
24. "Gothic Landscape," *Commentary,* 10, No. 1 (July 1950), p. 41. Reprinted in *BH; CP 65; CPIL; DF; RC* and *SP 69.*
25. I.L. to Earle Birney, 8 August 1951, Earle Birney Papers, Thomas Fisher Rare Book Library, University of Toronto, Toronto.

Target Practice/*196*

1. Raymond Souster, "Some Afterthoughts on *Contact* Magazine," in *Contact 1952 – 54: Notes on the History and Background of the Periodical and an Index,* ed. Michael Gnarowski (Montreal: Delta Canada, 1966), p. 1. For details surrounding Souster and Dudek between 1951 and 1953, see Frank Davey, *Louis Dudek and Raymond Souster* (Vancouver: Douglas and McIntyre, 1980).
2. Louis Dudek to E.C., interview, 13 October 1983, Montreal.
3. Louis Dudek to E.C.
4. Davey, pp. 12–15.
5. Davey, p. 13.
6. Davey, p. 15.
7. I.L., *Cerberus* (Toronto: Contact Press, 1952), p. 45.
8. "Good-Bye Bahai," *Cerberus.* Reprinted in *CP 65; CPIL* and *RC.*
9. "Little David," *Cerberus.*
10. "The Excessively Quiet Groves," *Cerberus.*
11. "News of the Phoenix," *Cerberus.*
12. "Poetess," *Cerberus.*
13. "Letter To Raymond Souster," *Cerberus.*
14. "Lines on the Massey Commission," *Cerberus.*
15. As quoted by Norman Levine, "The Modern Canadian Author," *Ottawa Citizen* (11 August 1953).
16. Vernal House, "Avant-Garde Poets," *Globe and Mail* (9 August 1952).
17. Raymond Souster to I.L., 30 December 1952. Irving Layton Collection, Concordia University Library, Montreal.
18. James Reaney, *Canadian Forum* (December 1952), p. 213.
19. B.K. Sandwell, "Poets Now Suffer in Groups," *Saturday Night,* 27 (September 1952), p. 7.
20. Northrop Frye, "Letters in Canada: 1952," *University of Toronto Quarterly,* 22 No. 3 (April, 1953), pp. 279–280.
21. Office of the Secretary to the Governor General to I.L., 3 June 1957, Irving Layton Collection, Concordia University Library, Montreal.
22. Raymond Souster to I.L., 24 November 1952, Irving Layton Collection, Concordia University Library, Montreal.
23. Louis Dudek to E.C., interview, 13 October 1983, Montreal.

Vexed Questions/*204*

1. I.L. to Robert Creeley, [January] 1953, Robert Creeley Papers, Washington University Libraries, St. Louis, Missouri.
2. A full description of the genesis, contents and significance of *CIV/n,* as well as Michael Gnarowski's index to the contents of its seven issues, can be found in *CIV/n: A Literary Magazine of the 50s,* ed. Aileen Collins (Montreal: Véhicule Press, 1983).
3. I.L. to Robert Creeley, 25 August 1953, Robert Creeley Papers, Washington University Libraries, St. Louis, Missouri.
4. Ken Norris, "The Significance of *Contact* and *CIV/n,*" *CIV/n: A Literary Magazine of the '50s,* pp. 253–266.
5. Betty Layton to E.C., interview, 8 July 1982, Guerneville, California.
6. I.L. to Cid Corman, 18 July 1953, Cid Corman Papers, Humanities Research Center, the University of Texas, Austin.
7. Cid Corman to I.L., 25 June 1953, Irving Layton Collection, Concordia University Library, Montreal.
8. Audrey Aikman to E.C., interview, 12 October 1983, Montreal.
9. I.L. to Cid Corman, 4 September 1953, Cid Corman Papers, Humanities Research Center, the University of Texas, Austin.

10. Raymond Souster to I.L., 25 January 1953, Irving Layton Collection, Concordia University Library, Montreal. "Ah Rats!!! (A Political Extravaganza of the 30s)," *McGill Daily* (5 October 1938). Reprinted in *UPIL* and *LCW*.
11. I.L. to Cid Corman, 1 January 1954, Cid Corman Papers, Humanities Research Center, the University of Texas, Austin.
12. "Vexata Quaestio," *Artisan*, 6 (Autumn 1954), pp. 2–3. Reprinted in *CP*; *CP 65*; *CPIL*; *DF*; *IB 1*; *IB 2*; *LCW*; *RC*; *SP 69*; *WPJ* and MS:CU.
13. Robert Creeley to I.L., 17 February and April 1953, Irving Layton Collection, Concordia University Library, Montreal.
14. Robert Creeley, "For W.C.W.," *CIV/n*, No. 4 (October 1953). I.L. to Robert Creeley, 25 August 1953, Robert Creeley Papers, Washington University Libraries, St. Louis, Missouri.
15. Charles Olson, "These Days," *Contact*, II, No. 1 (November–January 1952–1953), p. 6.
16. Robert Creeley to I.L., 26 April 1953, Irving Layton Collection, Concordia University Library, Montreal.
17. I.L. to Robert Creeley, 1 January 1953, Robert Creeley Papers, Washington University Libraries, St. Louis, Missouri.
18. I.L. to Robert Creeley, 17 April 1953, Robert Creeley Papers, Washington University Libraries, St. Louis, Missouri.
19. Robert Creeley to I.L., 26 April 1953, Irving Layton Collection, Concordia University Library, Montreal.
20. I.L. to Robert Creeley, 26 May 1953, Robert Creeley Papers, Washington University Libraries, St. Louis, Missouri.
21. I.L. to Cid Corman, 12 August 1953, Cid Corman Papers, Humanities Research Center, the University of Texas, Austin.
22. I.L. to Robert Creeley, [early October] 1954, Robert Creeley Papers, Washington University Libraries, St. Louis, Missouri.
23. I.L. to Cid Corman, 16 August 1954, Cid Corman Papers, Humanities Research Center, the University of Texas, Austin. "O.B.E." ("Imperial"), *Origin*, first series, 14 (1954), p. 84. Reprinted in *CP 65*; *CPIL*, *LPS* and *RC*. "Sensibility," *The Long Pea-Shooter*. Reprinted in *CPIL*.
24. Charles Olson, "Projective Verse," *Human Universe and Other Essays*, ed. Donald Allan (New York: Grove Press, 1967).
25. I.L. to Ann Creeley, [13 June] 1953, Robert Creeley Papers, Washington University Libraries, St. Louis, Missouri.
26. I.L. to Robert Creeley, 8 July 1953, Robert Creeley Papers, Washington University Libraries, St. Louis, Missouri.
27. Robert Creeley to I.L., 11 July 1953, Irving Layton Collection, Concordia University Library, Montreal.
28. I.L. to Robert Creeley, 22 July 1953, Robert Creeley Papers, Washington University Libraries, St. Louis, Missouri.
29. Robert Creeley to Charles Olson, 31 July 1953, Charles Olson Papers, Special Collections Department, University of Connecticut Library, Storrs, Connecticut.
30. Charles Olson, "The Crisis of the Third Foot" (unpublished) [1954], 2 pp., Charles Olson Papers, Special Collections Department, University of Connecticut Library, Storrs, Connecticut. See also Charles Olson to Robert Creeley, 30 September 1954, Robert Creeley Papers, Washington University Libraries, St. Louis, Missouri.
31. Olson, "Crisis."
32. I.L. to Robert Creeley, 5 December 1953, Robert Creeley Papers, Washington University Libraries, St. Louis, Missouri.
33. I.L. to Cid Corman, 20 December 1953, Cid Corman Papers, Humanities Research Center, the University of Texas, Austin. *Trio* would be published early in 1954.
34. Robert Creeley to I.L., 11 July 1953, Robert Creeley Papers, Washington

University Libraries, St. Louis, Missouri.
35. Robert Creeley to I.L., 23 December 1953, Robert Creeley Papers, Washington University Libraries, St. Louis, Missouri.
36. Robert Creeley to Charles Olson, 20 September 1953, Charles Olson Papers, Special Collections Department, University of Connecticut Library, Storrs, Connecticut. For further information about Black Mountain College (1933–1956), see especially Martin Duberman's *Black Mountain: An Exploration in Community* (New York: E.P. Dutton & Co. Inc., 1972), and also Fielding Dawson, *The Black Mountain Book* (New York: Croton Press, Ltd., 1970).
37. I.L. to Robert Creeley, 9 October 1953, Robert Creeley Papers, Washington University Libraries, St. Louis, Missouri.
38. I.L. to Robert Creeley, 24 August 1954 and 27 September 1954, Robert Creeley Papers, Washington University Libraries, St. Louis, Missouri.
39. I.L. to Cid Corman, 25 August 1953, Cid Corman Papers, Humanities Research Center, the University of Texas, Austin.
40. I.L. to Cid Corman, 8 May 1954, Cid Corman Papers, Humanities Research Center, the University of Texas, Austin.
41. I.L. to Cid Corman.
42. Raymond Souster to I.L., 15 March 1953, Irving Layton Papers, Concordia University Library, Montreal. Fraser Sutherland recalls John Glassco recounting how Layton's children sold their father's books at parties (to E.C., 3 August 1983).
43. Layton recorded three poems — "Maxie," "Snowfall at Lake Achigan" and one other in late November 1954 (I.L. to Robert Creeley, 8 May 1954).
44. I.L. to Robert Creeley, 17 October 1954, Robert Creeley Papers, Washington University Libraries, St. Louis, Missouri.
45. I.L. to Cid Corman, 9 November 1953, Cid Corman Papers, Humanities Research Center, the University of Texas, Austin.
46. I.L. to Cid Corman, 22 November 1953, Cid Corman Papers, Humanities Research Center, the University of Texas, Austin.
47. Cid Corman to F.R. Scott, 22 September 1953, Irving Layton Collection, Concordia University Library, Montreal.
48. I.L. to Robert Creeley, 30 December 1954, Robert Creeley Papers, Washington University Libraries, St. Louis, Missouri.
49. The poems that actually appeared in the 1957 edition of Smith's *The Book of Canadian Poetry* were: "The Fertile Muck," "Newsboy," "In the Midst of My Fever," "Poem," "Metzinger: Girl With a Bird," "Rain at La Minerve" and "The Birth of Tragedy."

Superman/224

1. I.L. to Robert Creeley, 16 June 1953, Robert Creeley Papers, Washington University Libraries, St. Louis, Missouri.
2. Louise Scott to E.C., interview, 11 October 1983, Montreal.
3. Miriam Waddington to E.C., interview, 14 June 1983, Toronto.
4. Betty Layton to E.C., interview, 8 July 1982, Guerneville, California.
5. Betty Layton to E.C. "When It Came to Santayana's Turn," *Origin*, first series, 14 (1954), p. 81. Reprinted in *CGE*; *CP65*; *CPIL*; *DF*; *IB1*; *IB2*; *RC* and MS:CU, US.
6. Marian Scott to E.C., interview, 2 September 1982, Montreal. "Eros Where the Rents Aren't High," *The Long Pea-Shooter*. Reprinted in *CP65*.
7. Betty Layton to E.C., interview, 8 July 1982, Guerneville, California.
8. I.L. to Cid Corman, 22 November 1953, Cid Corman Papers, Humanities Research Center, the University of Texas, Austin.
9. Louise Scott to E.C., interview, 11 October 1953, Montreal.
10. I.L. to Robert Creeley, 1 October 1953, Robert Creeley Papers, Washington

University Libraries, St. Louis, Missouri.
11. Betty Layton to E.C., interview, 8 July 1982, Guerneville, California.
12. I.L. to Cid Corman, 18 July 1953, Cid Corman Papers, Humanities Research Center, the University of Texas, Austin.
13. Betty Layton to E.C., interview, 8 July 1982, Guerneville, California.
14. Betty Layton to E.C.
15. I.L. to Robert Creeley, 17 April 1953, Robert Creeley Papers, Washington University Libraries, St. Louis, Missouri. "In the Midst of My Fever," *CIV/n*, No. 3 (July/August 1953), pp. 9–10 and *Artisan*, 6 (Autumn 1954), pp. 1–2. Anthologized widely and reprinted in *CP 65*; *CPIL*; *DF*; *IB 1*; *IB 2*; *IMF*; *PIL*; *RC*; *SP 69*; *SPIL*; *WPJ* and MS:CU, US.
16. Nathan Cohen to Louis Dudek, 3 January 1957, CBC Archives, Toronto.
17. "The Ambassador: A Political Farce" (unpublished), undated [ca. 1953], MS. in Irving Layton Collection, Concordia University Library, Montreal.
18. "The Old and Quiet Ones" (unpublished), undated [ca. 1953], MS. in Irving Layton Collection, Concordia University Library, Montreal. Notes for this play in Layton's handwriting, in University of Saskatchewan Archives, Saskatoon.
19. Nathan Cohen turned both these plays down.
20. I.L. to Robert Creeley, 10 August 1953, Robert Creeley Papers, Washington University Libraries, St. Louis, Missouri. "Bacchanal," *Origin*, first series, 12 (1954), pp. 200–201. Anthologized and reprinted in *CP 65*; *CPIL*; *IB 1*; *IB 2*; *IMF*; *RC* and MS:CU, US. "Portrait of Aileen," *Contact*, 9 (January–April 1954), p. 20. Reprinted in *CP 65*; *CPIL*; *DF*; *IB 1*; *IB 2*; *IMF*; *RC* and MS:CU, US.
21. I.L. to Robert Creeley, 5 June 1954, Robert Creeley Papers, Washington University Libraries, St. Louis, Missouri.
22. I.L. to Robert Creeley, 17 January 1953, Robert Creeley Papers, Washington University Libraries, St. Louis, Missouri; and I.L. to E.C., interview, 3 October 1983, Oakville, Ontario. The story was first published by Cid Corman in *Origin*, first series, 17 (Fall/Winter 1955–1956), pp. 25–40. Reprinted in *Engagements*, pp. 269–284; *SF* and MS:US.
23. I.L. to Robert Creeley, 16 August 1954, Robert Creeley Papers, Washington University Libraries, St. Louis, Missouri. Layton wrote to John Brebner: "The unpleasant JB in Mrs. Polinov was intended as a malicious caricature of myself. When I wrote the story I was teaching at the JPL and the model for Mrs. P. was one of my students. Alas, she died about ten yrs. ago. Cancer." (24 September 1974, property of John Brebner, Gagetown, New Brunswick.)
24. I.L. to E.C., interview, 29 September 1982, Oakville, Ontario. "Mildred," *In the Midst of My Fever*. Reprinted in *CP 65*; *CPIL*; *IB 1*; *IB 2*; *RC* and MS:CU, US. "For Priscilla," *In the Midst of My Fever*. Reprinted in *CP 65*; *CPIL*; *IB 2*; *LPIL*; *RC* and MS:US.
25. I.L., *The Long Pea-Shooter* (Montreal: Laocoon Press, 1954).
26. I.L., *The Blue Propeller* (Toronto: Contact Press, 1955). Also, a second edition with nine additional poems (Toronto: Contact Press, 1955).
27. "On First Looking Into Stalin's Coffin," *Music On a Kazoo*. Reprinted in *CP 65*; *CPIL*; *DF*; *RC* and *SP 69*.
28. "May Day Orators," *The Blue Propeller*. Reprinted in *BP 2*; *CP 65*; *CPIL* and *RC*.
29. "My Favourite Colour's Green," *The Blue Propeller*. Reprinted in *BP 2*; *IB 2* and *UPIL*.
30. "Prologue to the Long Pea-Shooter," *CIV/n*, No. 6 (September 1954), pp. 19–23. Reprinted in *CP 65*; *CPIL*; *DF*; *LPS* and *SP 69*.
31. "Address to the Undernourished," *The Long Pea-Shooter*. Reprinted in *UPIL*.
32. "No Moby Dick," *The Long Pea-Shooter*. Reprinted in *UPIL*.
33. See also "Latria" and "The Longest Journey," a poem about marriage.

34. "Look, the Lambs Are All Around Us!" *The Long Pea-Shooter*. Anthologized widely and reprinted in *CP65*; *CPIL*; *DF*; *IB2*; *LPIL*; *RC*; *SP69* and *WPJ*.
35. "How Poems Get Written," *Queen's University Journal*, n.d., p. 2. Anthologized widely and reprinted in *CP65*; *CPIL*; *LPS* and *RC*.
36. "Love's Diffidence," *Fiddlehead*, No. 26 (November 1955), pp. 10–11. Reprinted in *BP1*; *BP2*; *CP65*; *CPIL*; *DF*; *IB1*; *IB2*; *LPIL*; *RC* and MS:CU.
37. "Maxie," *McGill News*, 39, No. 3 (Summer 1958), p. 29. Reprinted in *CP65*; *CPIL*; *DF*; *IB1*; *IB2*; *IMF*; *RC*; *SP69*; *WPJ* and MS:CU, US.
38. "For An Older Poet in Despair With the Times," *The Long Pea-Shooter*. Reprinted in *WPJ*.
39. "Now That I'm Older," *The Long Pea-Shooter*. Reprinted in *CP65*; *CPIL*; *DF*; *IB2*; *RC* and *WPJ*.
40. "Against This Death," *In the Midst of My Fever*. Reprinted in *CP65*; *CPIL*; *DF*; *RC*; *WPJ* and MS:US.
41. I.L. to Robert Creeley, 9 November 1954, Robert Creeley Papers, Washington University Libraries, St. Louis, Missouri.
42. "Impotence," *Origin*, first series, 14 (1954), p. 83. Reprinted in *LPS* and *UPIL*.
43. "Mr. Ther-Apis," *CIV/n*, No. 4 (October 1953), p. 5. Reprinted in *CP65*; *CPIL*; *IMF*; *RC* and MS:US.
44. "Composition in Late Spring," *Contact*, 8 (September–December 1953), p. 20; and *Artisan*, 6 (Autumn 1954), pp. 4–5. Anthologized widely and reprinted in *BH*; *CP65*; *CPIL*; *DF*; *IB2*; *SP69*; *WPJ* and MS:CU, US.
45. "What Ulysses Said to Circe on the Beach of Aeaea," *The Long Pea-Shooter*. Reprinted in *CP65*; *CPIL*; *GP*; *IB2* and *RC*.
46. "The Greeks Had a Word For It," *The Blue Propeller*. Reprinted in *BP2*, *CP65* and *CPIL*.
47. "Marius," *The Long Pea-Shooter*. Reprinted in *CP65* and *CPIL*. "Marie," *The Long Pea-Shooter*. Reprinted in *CP65*; *CPIL*; *IB2* and *RC*.
48. "Misunderstanding," *The Long Pea-Shooter*. Anthologized widely and reprinted in *CP65*, *CPIL*, *DF*, *LPIL*, *PIL*, *RC*, *SP69*, *SPIL*, *WPJ* and MS:CU.
49. "Enigma," *Black Mountain Review*, 6 (Spring 1956), p. 32. Reprinted in *BP2*; *LIM59*; *MK* and *UPIL*.
50. "Lines on Myself," *The Long Pea-Shooter*. Reprinted in *CPIL*; and MS:CU.
51. "Human Being," *The Blue Propeller*. Reprinted in *BP2*; *CP65* and *CPIL*.
52. "Portrait of Aileen."
53. "The Ants," *Contact*, 9 (1954), p. 21. Reprinted in *CP65*; *CPIL*; *DF*; *IB1*; *IB2*; *IMF*; *RC* and MS:CU.
54. "Author, With a Pipe in His Mouth," *The Long Pea-Shooter*. Reprinted in *UPIL*.
55. "Metzinger: Girl With a Bird," *Origin*, first series, 12 (1954), pp. 202–203. Reprinted in *CPIL*; *DF*; *IB1*; *IB2*; *IMF*; *RC*; *SP69* and MS:US.
56. I.L. to Robert Creeley, undated [July 1954], Robert Creeley Papers, Washington University Libraries, St. Louis, Missouri.
57. Betty Layton to E.C., interview, 8 July 1982, Guerneville, California.
58. "The Birth of Tragedy," *Encounter* (December 1956), p. 38. Anthologized widely and reprinted in *CP65*; *CPIL*; *DF*; *IB1*; *IB2*; *IMF*; *PIL*; *RC*; *SPIL*;

An Attractive Bulldozer/239

1. I.L. to Robert Creeley, 20 March 1955, Robert Creeley Papers, Washington University Libraries, St. Louis, Missouri.
2. I.L. to Desmond Pacey, [late October] 1955, Desmond Pacey Papers, property of Mary Pacey, Fredericton, New Brunswick.
3. I.L. to Robert Creeley, 9 January 1955, Robert Creeley Papers, Washington University Libraries, St. Louis, Missouri.
4. I.L. to Robert Creeley. "Canadian Skiers," *Fiddlehead*, No. 26 (November 1955), p..10–11. Reprinted in *BP1*; *BP2*; *CP65*; *CPIL*; *RC* and MS:CU, UTEX.
5. Cid Corman to I.L., 4 August 1955, Irving Layton Collection, Concordia University Library, Montreal.
6. I.L. to Robert Creeley, 19 March 1955, Robert Creeley Papers, Washington University Libraries, St. Louis, Missouri.
7. Raymond Souster to I.L., 4 July 1954,

Irving Layton Collection, Concordia University Library, Montreal.
8. Cid Corman to I.L., 8 February 1954, Irving Layton Collection, Concordia University Library, Montreal.
9. I.L. to Robert Creeley, 19 March 1955, Robert Creeley Papers, Washington University Libraries, St. Louis, Missouri.
10. Layton uses "fuckers" once; the rest are scatalogical words: "shit," "ass," "asshole," "fart," "crap," "turd," "piss" and so on.
11. William Carlos Williams to I.L., 14 January 1955, Irving Layton Collection, Concordia University Library, Montreal.
12. Hugh Kenner to I.L., 23 September 1955, Irving Layton Collection, Concordia University Library, Montreal.
13. Northrop Frye, "Letters in Canada: 1954," *University of Toronto Quarterly*, reprinted in *The Bush Garden: Essays on The Canadian Imagination* (Toronto: Anansi, 1971), pp. 40–42.
14. Desmond Pacey to I.L., 13 February 1955, Irving Layton Collection, Concordia University Library, Montreal.
15. Steve Cumas to E.C., interview, 30 August 1982, Montreal.
16. George Johnston to I.L., 13 October 1955, Irving Layton Collection, Concordia University Library, Montreal.
17. Milton Wilson, "Turning New Leaves," *Canadian Forum* (October 1955), pp. 162–164.
18. Al Purdy, "Memoirs" (unpublished), Queen's University Archives, pp. 1–11, Kingston.
19. Lorne Pierce to I.L., 15 December 1956, Irving Layton Collection, Concordia University Library, Montreal.
20. Lorne Pierce to I.L., 10 January 1957, Irving Layton Collection, Concordia University Library, Montreal.
21. I.L. to Lorne Pierce, undated note [late December 1956], Irving Layton Collection, Concordia University Library, Montreal.
22. Lotta Dempsey, "Poet Attacks Publisher's Attitude," *Globe and Mail* (14 January 1957). Layton was quoted as saying, "I have no desire to shock or say something nasty scrawled on an outhouse." He claimed that his poetry "aims to chasten morals through the imagination." Gerald Yur'echek, "Frustrated Canadian Poet Victim of 'Philistines,'" Toronto *Telegram* (26 January 1957) and I.L., "A Poet Explains," Toronto *Telegram* (2 February 1957). In this letter, Layton wrote: "my quarrel is not with the publisher [Dr. Lorne Pierce of Ryerson Press], but with a puritanical mores that makes it possible to confound pharisaism with religion."
23. I.L. to Desmond Pacey, 24 April 1956, Desmond Pacey Papers, property of Mary Pacey, Fredericton, New Brunswick.
24. I.L. to Jonathan Williams, 31 December 1955, Poetry/Rare Books Collection, University Libraries, State University of New York, Buffalo.
25. I.L. to Jonathan Williams, undated [December 1956], Poetry/Rare Books Collection, University Libraries, State University of New York, Buffalo.

Dear Desmond/250

1. This letter is printed in its entirety. Desmond Pacey Papers, property of Mary Pacey, Fredericton, New Brunswick.
2. Pacey had observed (24 June 1955) that "Frye praises your *In the Midst of My Fever* to the skies."
3. In his review, Frye had remarked that "most of the world of *The Long Pea-Shooter* is a depressingly unreal world." "Letters in Canada: 1954," *University of Toronto Quarterly*. Reprinted in Frye, *The Bush Garden* (Toronto: Anansi, 1971), pp. 40–41.
4. Layton was omitted from the original 1943 edition and from the revised 1948 edition, but would be included in the revised 1957 edition of A.J.M. Smith's *The Book of Canadian Poetry*.
5. Ralph Gustafson, ed., *The Penguin Book of Canadian Verse* (Harmondsworth, Middlesex: Penguin Books Ltd., 1958).
6. Earle Birney, ed., *Twentieth Century Canadian Poetry, An Anthology* (Toronto: Ryerson Press, 1953).
7. Carl F. Klinck and R.E. Watters, eds., *Canadian Anthology* (Toronto: W.J. Gage, 1955).

8. A written version of Smith's assessment appeared in A.J.M. Smith, "The Recent Poetry of Irving Layton — A Major Voice," *Queen's Quarterly*, 62, No. 4 (Winter 1955–1956), pp. 587–591. Reprinted as "A Salute to Layton — In Praise of his Earliest Masterpieces," *On Poetry and Poets* (Toronto: McClelland and Stewart, 1977), pp. 70–71.
9. George Woodcock, "The New Books — Recent Canadian Poetry," *Queen's Quarterly*, 62, No. 1 (Spring 1955), pp. 111–115.
10. "Cemetery in August," *Love the Conqueror Worm*. Reprinted in *CP 65*; *CPIL*; *DF*; *IB 1*; *IB 2*; *RC*; *SP 69* and MS:CU. "Lacquered Westmount Doll" ("Westmount Doll"), *Black Mountain Review*, 1, No. 1 (Spring 1954), p. 19. Reprinted in *CP 65*; *CPIL*; *IB 1*; *IB 2*; *IMF*; *RC* and MS:CU, US, UTEX.
11. "A Plausible Story" eventually was anthologized: once in Pacey's collection *A Book of Canadian Short Stories* (1962) and also in Bruce Vance's *The Eye of the Beholder* (1970). "Mrs. Polinov" has not been anthologized to date. Of the other three stories Layton mentions here, only "Vacation in La Voiselle" was anthologized, in Robert Weaver's *Canadian Short Stories* (1960).
12. *The Blasted Pine: An Anthology of Canadian Satire*, ed. F.R. Scott and A.J.M. Smith (Toronto: Macmillan, 1957).
13. Pacey had published two books of poems for children, *The Cow With the Musical Moo* (1952) and *Hippity Hobo and the Bee* (1952), and had asked Layton to assist in finding bookstores that would take copies to sell.

At Odds/256

1. I.L. to Robert Creeley, 28 March 1955, Robert Creeley Papers, Washington University Libraries, St. Louis, Missouri.
2. Fred Cogswell to E.C., interview, 8 October 1982, Fredericton, New Brunswick.
3. I.L. to Desmond Pacey, 22 August 1955, Desmond Pacey Papers, property of Mary Pacey, Fredericton, New Brunswick.
4. "Letter From A Straw Man," *Black Mountain Review*, 6 (Spring 1956), pp. 110–111. Reprinted in *BC*; *CP 65*; *CPIL*; *IB 1*; *IB 2*; *LPIL*; *RC*; *SP 69* and MS:CU.

Anti-Romantic/259

1. Aviva Layton to E.C., interview, 20 October 1982, Toronto.
2. Aviva Layton, *Nobody's Daughter* (Toronto: McClelland and Stewart, 1982).
3. "The Newer Critics," *Music on a Kazoo* (Toronto: Contact Press, 1956), p. 15. Reprinted in *UPIL* and MS:CU.
4. "If You Can't Scream," *Delta*, 1 (October 1957), p. 11. Reprinted in *CP 65*; *CPIL*; *LIM 58*; *LIM 59* and *RC*.
5. "Anti-Romantic," *Combustion*, 1 (1957), p. 8. Reprinted in *CP 65*; *CPIL*; *IB 2*; *LIM 59* and *RC*.
6. Fred Cogswell to E.C., interview, 8 October 1982, Fredericton, New Brunswick.
7. *Nobody's Daughter*, p. 124.
8. Louise Scott to E.C., interview, 11 October 1983, Montreal, and Betty Layton to E.C., 8 and 10 July, Guerneville, California. The disease, still not completely understood, is thought to be caused by a virus and exaggerated by stress. Its technical name is "sub-acute bacterial endocarditis."
9. I.L. to E.C., interview, 2 March 1982, Toronto.
10. Aviva Layton to E.C., interview, 20 October 1982, Toronto. "Esthetique," *Music on a Kazoo*. Reprinted in *CP 65*, *CPIL* and *RC*.
11. Aviva Layton to E.C.
12. I.L. to Jonathan Williams, 27 February 1957 and 30 December 1957, Poetry/Rare Books Collection, University Libraries, State University of New York, Buffalo. In a letter 26 January 1957, I.L. asked Creeley to write on his behalf to say that his appearance in the U.S. would be "beneficial." Creeley replied 11 February 1957 to say that he had done so.
13. Aviva Layton to E.C., interview, 20 October 1982, Toronto.
14. John Mills, "The Road Runner: A Rigmarole," *Evidence* (1968), p. 20.
15. I.L. to Desmond Pacey, 28 February 1958, Desmond Pacey Papers, property

of Mary Pacey, Fredericton, New Brunswick. "A Roman Jew to Ovid" ("An Errant Husband"), *A Laughter in the Mind* (Toronto: McClelland and Stewart, 1958). Reprinted in *CP65*; *CPIL*; *LIM58*; *LIM59* and *RC*. "Individualist," *Tamarack Review*, 9 (Autumn 1958), p. 24. Reprinted in *CP65*; *CPIL*; *LIM58*; *LIM59* and *RC*. "Whatever Else Poetry is Freedom," *Canadian Forum* (February 1958), p. 252. Anthologized widely and reprinted in *CP65*; *CPIL*; *DF*; *LIM58*; *LIM59*; *PIL*; *RC*; *SP69*; *SPIL*; *WPJ* and MS:CU. "On Seeing the Statuettes of Ezekiel and Jeremiah in the Church of Notre Dame" ("On Seeing the Statues of Ezekiel and Jeremiah in the Church of Notre Dame, Montreal"), *Origin*, first series, 17 (Fall/Winter 1955–1956), p. 22. Anthologized widely and reprinted in *BC*; *CP65*; *CPIL*; *DF*; *IB1*; *IB2*; *PIL*; *RC*; *SP69*; *SPIL*; *WPJ* and MS:CU.

16. All poems under discussion here are from Layton's three 1956 volumes: *The Improved Binoculars*, *Music on a Kazoo* and *The Bull Calf and Other Poems*. In a letter to A.J.M. Smith, 16 March 1956, I.L. described his intentions in *The Bull Calf* as follows: "As no other book of mine, it's organized around a central theme symbolized by the execution of the bull calf. I've put 'Sacrament By the Water' as the last poem, because that's the movement of the book, though the movement, as you'll notice, is a dialectical one. History, what man makes of himself ('Boys Bathing' and 'One View of Dead Fish') and Sex, not religion, not mysticism, are the answer. Though the thing is never that simple: Vide 'A Dark Nest' sandwiched between 'Earth Goddess' and 'Sacrament By the Water.' I've arranged the poems to make this movement by antimonies, modifications or contrarities apparent. In one sense 'The Bull Calf' is a single poem for several voices." Trent University Archives, A.J.M. Smith Papers, 78–007/4 (5), Peterborough, Ontario.

17. "The Longest Journey," *In the Midst of My Fever*. Reprinted in *CP65*; *CPIL*; *IB1*; *IB2*; *RC* and MS:CU, US, UTEX.

18. "Poem," ("I Would For Your Sake Be Gentle"), *Direction*, 3 (1943), p. 5

19. "Song for Naomi," *The Bull Calf*. Anthologized widely and reprinted in *CP65*; *CPIL*; *DF*; *IB1*; *IB2*; *PIL*; *SP69*; *SPIL*; *WPJ* and MS:CU, US. "Berry-Picking," *Tamarack Review*, 9 (Autumn 1958), p. 25. Anthologized widely and reprinted in *CP65*; *CPIL*; *DF*; *LIM58*; *LIM59*; *LPIL*; *PIL*; *RC*; *SP69*; *SPIL* and *WPJ*.

20. "Autumn Lines For My Son," *A Laughter in the Mind*. Reprinted in *CP65*; *CPIL*; *LIM59* and *RC*.

21. I.L. to A.J.M. Smith, 2 May 1955, A.J.M. Smith Papers, Thomas Fisher Rare Books Library, University of Toronto, Toronto.

22. "Odysseus in Limbo" ("The World's Tavern"), *Contact*, 1, No. 1 (January 1952), p. 6. Reprinted in *BH*; *CP65*; *CPIL*; *DF*; *GP*; *IB1*; *IB2*; *LCW*; *RC*; *SP69* and MS:CU. "Nausicaa," *The Improved Binoculars*. Reprinted in *CP65*; *CPIL*; *DF*; *GP*; *IB1*; *IB2*; *LPIL*; *RC*; *SP69*; *WPJ* and MS:CU. "Lesbia," *Fiddlehead*, No. 29 (August 1956), pp. 2–3. Reprinted in *BC*; *CP65*; *CPIL*; *IB1*; *IB2*; *RC* and MS:CU.

23. "Earth Goddess," *The Bull Calf*. Reprinted in *CP65*; *CPIL*; *IB1*; *IB2* and *RC*.

24. "By Ecstasies Perplexed," *The Improved Binoculars*. Reprinted in *CP65*; *CPIL*; *DF*; *IB1*; *IB2*; *LPIL*; *MK*; *RC*; *SP69* and MS:CU.

25. Al Purdy to I.L., undated, Irving Layton Collection, Concordia University Library, Montreal.

26. "How Domestic Happiness is Achieved" ("Marital Bliss Explained"), *A Laughter in the Mind*. Reprinted in *CP65*; *CPIL* and *RC*. "From a Lawnchair," *Music on a Kazoo*. Reprinted in *UPIL*.

27. "The Bull Calf," *Origin*, first series, 17 (Fall–Winter 1955–1956), pp. 23–24. Anthologized widely and reprinted in *BC*; *CP65*; *CPIL*; *DF*; *IB1*; *IB2*; *RC*; *SP69*; *WPJ* and MS:CU.

28. "Cain," *Queen's Quarterly*, 65, No. 2 (Summer 1958), pp. 294–295. Anthol-

ogized widely and reprinted in *CP 65*; *CPIL*; *DF*; *LIM 58*; *LIM 59*; *PIL*; *RC*; *SP 69*; *SPIL*; *WPJ* and MS:CU. In a letter to A.J.M. Smith, 29 October 1957, I.L. "explained" his poem "Cain" as follows: "of the two ["Berry Picking" and "Cain"] "Cain" is the more powerful and vastly more original. You're disturbed by the 'wanton cruelty' and the absence of compassion when the whole bitter point of the poem is that man is either damned or self-deluding — or both. Cain is mankind. In Genesis not once does God address any words to Abel; only to Cain. It is not the victim, but the victim's slayer who has this concern and compassion. For man is an animal who must kill in order to survive, yet suffers on occasion the most exquisite agonies of conscience. Therein lies the source of his self-disgust, his 'madness': his dilemma is insoluble and eternal." Thomas Fisher Rare Book Library and Archives, A.J.M. Smith Papers, University of Toronto.
29. "Firecrackers," *The Bull Calf*. Reprinted in *CPIL*.
30. "Fiat Lux," *The Bull Calf*. Reprinted in *CP 65*; *CPIL*; *RC* and MS:US.
31. Ernest Jones, *The Life and Work of Sigmund Freud*, 3 vols. (New York: Basic Books, 1953–1957). "The Love Dream of W.P. Turner" ("Love Dream of W.P. Turner! English Poet"), *A Laughter in the Mind*. Reprinted in *LIM 59* and *UPIL*.
32. "Rose Lemay," *The Bull Calf*. Reprinted in *CP 65*; *CPIL*; *IB 1*; *IB 2* and *RC*.
33. William Carlos Williams to I.L., 19 and 21 March 1956, Irving Layton Collection, Concordia University Library, Montreal.
34. William Carlos Williams, "A Note on Layton," *The Improved Binoculars*, 2 pp.

Portrait of the Artist/272

1. Louis Dudek to E.C., interview, 13 October 1983, Montreal.
2. Louis Dudek to E.C.

Backflips/274

1. I.L. to E.C., interview, 2 March 1982, Toronto.
2. Hyman Latch to E.C., interview, 6 July 1982, San Francisco.
3. Betty Layton to E.C., interview, 8 July 1982, Guerneville, California.
4. I.L. to E.C., interview, 2 March 1982, Toronto.
5. I.L. to Desmond Pacey, 1 January 1958, Desmond Pacey Papers, property of Mary Pacey, Fredericton, New Brunswick.
6. I.L. to Desmond Pacey, 7 January 1958, Desmond Pacey Papers, property of Mary Pacey, Fredericton, New Brunswick.
7. I.L. to Desmond Pacey.
8. The details for this episode are taken from Leonard Cohen to E.C., interview, 16 May 1983, Toronto; and from Aviva's fictional presentation based on the event in *Nobody's Daughter*, pp. 134–136.
9. Leonard Cohen to E.C., interview, 16 May 1983, Toronto.
10. Aviva Layton to E.C., interview, 24 November 1982, Toronto.

The Sorcerer's Apprentice/278

1. Layton included this glossary in *The Whole Bloody Bird* (Toronto: McClelland and Stewart, 1969), p. 45. "For Mao Tse Tung: A Meditation on Flies and Kings," *Canadian Forum* (November 1958), p. 179. Reprinted in *CP 65*; *CPIL*; *DF*; *LIM 59*; *PIL*; *RC*; *SP 69*; *SPIL*; *WPJ* and MS:CU. "A Bonnet For Bessie," *A Laughter in the Mind*. Reprinted in *RC*. "Love is an Irrefutable Fire," *Canadian Forum* (November 1958), p. 178. Reprinted in *CP 65*; *CPIL*; *LIM 59*; *RC* and MS:CU.
2. Desmond Pacey to I.L., 8 September 1958, Irving Layton Collection, Concordia University Library, Montreal.
3. I.L., *A Red Carpet for the Sun* (Highlands, North Carolina: Jonathan Williams and Toronto: McClelland and Stewart, 1959).
4. Betty Layton to E.C., interview, 10 July 1982, Guerneville, California.
5. I.L. to Desmond Pacey, 24 May 1963, Desmond Pacey Papers, property of Mary Pacey, Fredericton, New Brunswick.
6. I.L. to Desmond Pacey, 2 November 1957, Desmond Pacey Papers, property of Mary Pacey, Fredericton, New Brunswick.

7. "Far Out," *Time* (7 July 1958), p. 9.
8. I.L. to Desmond Pacey, 18 July 1958, Desmond Pacey Papers, property of Mary Pacey, Fredericton, New Brunswick, and *Toronto Star* (23 July 1958).
9. "Six Montreal Poets — 1957," Folkways LP. Layton read "The Birth of Tragedy," "The Fertile Muck," "Maxie," "The Bull Calf," "The Cold Green Element," and "The Improved Binoculars." The other poets on the LP are A.J.M. Smith, Leonard Cohen, Louis Dudek, F.R. Scott and A.M. Klein.
10. I.L. to Desmond Pacey, 23 March 1958, Desmond Pacey Papers, property of Mary Pacey, Fredericton, New Brunswick.
11. I.L. to Desmond Pacey, 7 January 1958, Desmond Pacey Papers, property of Mary Pacey, Fredericton, New Brunswick. A lengthy and troubled correspondence between Layton and Everson can be found in the Irving Layton Collection, Concordia University Library, Montreal. Ronald G. Everson has published several volumes of poetry since 1957 to date.
12. This "Journal," which contains several handwritten drafts, with revisions, of the poem "The Day Aviva Came to Paris," is located in the University of Saskatchewan Archives, Saskatoon. Arithmetical calculations in the journal in Layton's handwriting suggest that he was able to live on less than forty dollars a week.
13. I.L. to Desmond Pacey, 1 June 1957, Desmond Pacey Papers, property of Mary Pacey, Fredericton, New Brunswick.
14. I.L. to Desmond Pacey, 14 September 1959, Desmond Pacey Papers, property of Mary Pacey, Fredericton, New Brunswick. I.L. to Jonathan Williams, August 1959, Poetry/Rare Books Collection, State University of New York, Buffalo.
15. Aviva Layton to E.C., interview, 24 November 1982, Toronto.
16. Al Purdy to I.L., undated [1959], Al Purdy Papers, Queen's University Archives, Kingston, Ontario. "The Day Aviva Came to Paris," *Canadian Forum* (February 1960), pp. 256–257 and *Galley Sail Review* (Winter 1959–1960), pp. 35–37. Anthologized widely and reprinted in *CP 65*, *CPIL*; *DF*; *LPIL*; *LWNL*; *SF*; *SP 69*; *WPJ* and MS:CU, US.
17. I.L. to Desmond Pacey, 25 November 1958, Desmond Pacey Papers, property of Mary Pacey, Fredericton, New Brunswick.
18. William Goodwin to E.C., interview, 30 August 1982, Montreal.
19. I.L. to Desmond Pacey, 1 June 1958 and 22 February 1959, Desmond Pacey Papers, property of Mary Pacey, Fredericton, New Brunswick. "Because My Calling Is Such," *Queen's Quarterly*, 66, No. 1 (Spring 1959), p. 26; and *Canadian Jewish Congress Bulletin* (1959). Reprinted in *CP 65*; *CPIL*; *DF*; *LPIL*; *SF* and *SP 69*.
20. "Mexico As Seen By Looie the Lip" ("Mexico As Seen By the Reverent Dudek"), *Moment*, 1 (1960), p. 8. Reprinted in *BFOJ*; *CP 65*; *CPIL* and *LR*.
21. I.L. to Desmond Pacey, 25 January 1959, Desmond Pacey Papers, property of Mary Pacey, Fredericton, New Brunswick.
22. I.L. to Desmond Pacey, 1 February 1959, Desmond Pacey Papers, property of Mary Pacey, Fredericton, New Brunswick.
23. I.L. to Desmond Pacey, 18 October 1958, Desmond Pacey Papers, property of Mary Pacey, Fredericton, New Brunswick.
24. I.L. to Desmond Pacey, 3 February 1959, Desmond Pacey Papers, property of Mary Pacey, Fredericton, New Brunswick.
25. I.L. to Desmond Pacey, 16 February 1959, Desmond Pacey Papers, property of Mary Pacey, Fredericton, New Brunswick.
26. Desmond Pacey to I.L., 15 January 1959, Irving Layton Collection, Concordia University Library, Montreal.
27. Desmond Pacey to I.L., 4 February 1959, Irving Layton Collection, Concordia University Library, Montreal.
28. Desmond Pacey to I.L., 24 March 1959, Irving Layton Collection, Concordia University Library, Montreal.
29. I.L. to Desmond Pacey, 30 March 1959,

488 Irving Layton: A Portrait

Desmond Pacey Papers, property of Mary Pacey, Fredericton, New Brunswick.
30. Jack McClelland to I.L., 13 February 1963, McClelland and Stewart Papers, McMaster University Library, Hamilton, Ontario.
31. I.L. to Desmond Pacey, 25 September 1959, Desmond Pacey Papers, property of Mary Pacey, Fredericton, New Brunswick.
32. Jack McClelland to I.L., 17 August 1959, McClelland and Stewart Papers, McMaster University Library, Hamilton, Ontario.
33. I.L. to Desmond Pacey, 8 October 1959, Desmond Pacey Papers, property of Mary Pacey, Fredericton, New Brunswick.
34. Lorne Pierce to I.L., 11 December 1959, Irving Layton Collection, Concordia University Library, Montreal.
35. Desmond Pacey to I.L., 13 July 1959, Irving Layton Collection, Concordia University Library, Montreal.
36. I.L. to Desmond Pacey, 1 February 1959, Desmond Pacey Papers, property of Mary Pacey, Fredericton, New Brunswick.
37. I.L. to Desmond Pacey, 12 March 1959, Desmond Pacey Papers, property of Mary Pacey, Fredericton, New Brunswick.
38. I.L. to Desmond Pacey, 1 February 1959, Desmond Pacey Papers, property of Mary Pacey, Fredericton, New Brunswick.
39. Milton Wilson to I.L., 29 January 1959, Irving Layton Collection, Concordia University Library, Montreal. Wilson had observed that Layton reviewing Pacey's *The Picnic* in *Fiddlehead* struck him "like Don Quixote reviewing Sancho Panza."
40. I.L. to Desmond Pacey, 18 February 1959, Desmond Pacey Papers, property of Mary Pacey, Fredericton, New Brunswick.
41. I.L. to Desmond Pacey, 8 February 1959, Desmond Pacey Papers, property of Mary Pacey, Fredericton, New Brunswick.
42. I.L. to Desmond Pacey, 16 February 1959, Desmond Pacey Papers, property of Mary Pacey, Fredericton, New Brunswick.
43. I.L. to Desmond Pacey, 29 March 1959, Desmond Pacey Papers, property of Mary Pacey, Fredericton, New Brunswick.
44. I.L. to Desmond Pacey, 18 February 1959, Desmond Pacey Papers, property of Mary Pacey, Fredericton, New Brunswick.
45. I.L. to Desmond Pacey, 30 March 1959, Desmond Pacey Papers, property of Mary Pacey, Fredericton, New Brunswick.
46. I.L. to Desmond Pacey, 8 October 1959, Desmond Pacey Papers, property of Mary Pacey, Fredericton, New Brunswick.
47. I.L. to Desmond Pacey, 21 March 1959, Desmond Pacey Papers, property of Mary Pacey, Fredericton, New Brunswick.
48. I.L. to Desmond Pacey, 26 March 1959, Desmond Pacey Papers, property of Mary Pacey, Fredericton, New Brunswick.
49. I.L. to Desmond Pacey, 24 October 1959, Desmond Pacey Papers, property of Mary Pacey, Fredericton, New Brunswick.
50. Northrop Frye, "Letters in Canada: 1959," *University of Toronto Quarterly*, 29, No. 4 (July 1960), p. 447. I.L., "Foreword," *A Red Carpet for the Sun* (Toronto: McClelland and Stewart, 1959), 4 pp.
51. Robert Weaver to I.L., 19 February 1959, Irving Layton Collection, Concordia University Library, Montreal.
52. E.K. Brown, *On Canadian Poetry* (Toronto: Ryerson Press, 1943).
53. "Keine Lazarovitch 1870–1959," *Tamarack Review*, 15 (Spring 1960), p. 22. Anthologized widely and reprinted in *CP65*; *CPIL*; *DF*; *PIL*; *SF*; *SP69*; *SPIL*; *WPJ* and MS:CU.
54. William Carlos Williams to I.L., 19 February 1960, Irving Layton Collection, Concordia University Library, Montreal.
55. I.L. to Desmond Pacey, 5 April 1960, Desmond Pacey Papers, property of Mary Pacey, Fredericton, New Brunswick.
56. Marian Scott to E.C., interview, 2 September 1982, Montreal.
57. Hugh MacLennan to I.L., 18 March 1960, Irving Layton Collection, Concordia University Library, Montreal.
58. Hugh Maclennan to E.C., interview, 10

February 1982, Montreal.
59. Betty Layton to E.C., interview, 8 July 1982, Guerneville, California.
60. Aviva Layton to E.C., interview, 24 November 1982, Toronto.
61. I.L. to Desmond Pacey, 1 June 1958, Desmond Pacey Papers, property of Mary Pacey, Fredericton, New Brunswick. A copy of Layton's letter of appeal to Joseph S. Caplan, Honorary Secretary of the United Talmud Torahs of Montreal, 30 April 1960, is in the Irving Layton Collection, Concordia University Library, Montreal. In this letter, Layton casts himself as one of "the scholarly poor" engaged in the on-going struggle within the Jewish community against "the unlettered rich." He calls Mr. Beutel "autocratic and bullying" and accuses him of heading a "camarilla" (Layton here probably meant a "camorra"—a secret society resembling the nineteenth-century Neapolitan one that specialized in blackmail and robbery). Layton compares himself to Socrates, whose trial tested the moral fibre of the community at large. He justifies his own participation in the Teacher's Federation which, for the first time, brought the board before a court of arbitration to negotiate new contracts for the teachers, as helping give the teachers "a modicum of independence and self-respect."
62. I.L. to Jonathan Williams, 13 July and 24 November 1960, Poetry/Rare Books Collection, University Libraries, State University of New York, Buffalo. "Mr. Beutel Lays a Cornerstone," *Moment*, 3 (1960), p. 9; and *Canadian Forum* (September 1960), p. 137. Reprinted in *CP65*; *CPIL* and *SF*. "Beutel's Name is Inscribed For Eternal Life," *Canadian Forum* (September 1960), p. 137. Reprinted in *CP65*, *CPIL* and *SF*.
63. *The Art of Poetry*, ed. Hugh Kenner (New York: Holt Rinehart and Winston, 1960), pp. 26–28. "Golfers," *Origin*, first series, 14 (1954), p. 76. Anthologized widely and reprinted in *BP1*; *BP2*; *CP65*; *CPIL*; *DF*; *IB1*; *IB2*; *PIL*; *RC*; *SPIL*; *WPJ* and MS:CU.
64. I.L. to Desmond Pacey, 25 November 1958, Desmond Pacey Papers, property of Mary Pacey, Fredericton, New Brunswick.
65. I.L. to Desmond Pacey, 22 February 1959, Desmond Pacey Papers, property of Mary Pacey, Fredericton, New Brunswick. Layton refers here to the novel *The Ugly American* by William J. Lederer.
66. William J. King, District Director, Immigration and Naturalization Service, United States Courthouse, Buffalo, New York, 5 November 1959, granted "alien" Irving Peter Layton (or Issie Lazarovitch) admission to the United States for "a period of four days." Records of the United States Department of Justice, Washington, D.C., File: A7 991 801. The poetry reading was broadcast on CBC "Anthology" 5 March 1960.
67. William Kane, Consul of the United States of America, to I.L., 20 June 1960, Irving Layton Collection, Concordia University Library, Montreal.
68. Aviva Layton to E.C., interview, 24 November 1982, Toronto.
69. I.L. to Desmond Pacey, 5 September 1960, Desmond Pacey Papers, property of Mary Pacey, Fredericton, New Brunswick.
70. "Lines on the Massey Commission," *Cerberus*, p. 57:
> Do you want culture?
> I'll tell you what to do:
> Subsidize a talented
> Italian or Jew —
> A neurotic Roumanian
> Would also do!
71. I.L. to Desmond Pacey, 5 April 1960, Desmond Pacey Papers, property of Mary Pacey, Fredericton, New Brunswick.
72. I.L. to Desmond Pacey, 15 February 1960, Desmond Pacey Papers, property of Mary Pacey, Fredericton, New Brunswick.
73. I.L. to Desmond Pacey, 2 November 1957, Desmond Pacey Papers, property of Mary Pacey, Fredericton, New Brunswick.

74. I.L. to Desmond Pacey, 18 February 1959, Desmond Pacey Papers, property of Mary Pacey, Fredericton, New Brunswick.
75. Desmond Pacey to I.L., 3 November 1959, Irving Layton Collection, Concordia University Library, Montreal.

The Day Aviva Came to Paris/305

1. See I.L., "Journal" (unpublished), University of Saskatchewan Archives, Saskatoon. There is, for example, a sketch of Irving with the handwritten title "Mister Okei" on one of the pages.
2. See Noel Riley Fitch, *Sylvia Beach and the Lost Generation: A History of Literary Paris in the Twenties and Thirties* (New York: W.W. Norton, 1983).
3. Morley Callaghan, *That Summer in Paris* (Toronto, Macmillan, 1963), pp. 89–91.
4. Aviva Layton to E.C., interview, 24 November 1982, Toronto.

A Very Rich, Rich Year/308

1. I.L. to Desmond Pacey, 6 February 1959, Desmond Pacey Papers, property of Mary Pacey, Fredericton, New Brunswick.
2. Aviva Layton to E.C., interview, 24 November 1982, Toronto.
3. Gertrude Katz to E.C., interview, 12 October 1983, Montreal. "Cat Dying in Autumn," *Yes*, 2, No. 1 (1957), p. 11. Reprinted in *CP65*; *CPIL*; *DF*; *LIM58*; *LIM59*; *RC*; *SP69*; *WPJ* and MS:CU.
4. I.L. to Desmond Pacey, 17 October 1960, Desmond Pacey Papers, property of Mary Pacey, Fredericton, New Brunswick.
5. Gertrude Katz to E.C., interview, 12 October 1983, Montreal.

A Tall Man Executes a Jig/312

1. I.L. to Desmond Pacey, 17 May 1961, Desmond Pacey Papers, property of Mary Pacey, Fredericton, New Brunswick.
2. I.L. to Desmond Pacey, 2 December 1961, Desmond Pacey Papers, property of Mary Pacey, Fredericton, New Brunswick.
3. Aviva Layton to E.C., interview, 30 December 1982, Toronto. Max Layton wrote a short story partly based on this period of his life: "My Yarmulka," *Antigonish Review*, No. 53 (Spring 1983), pp. 57–66.
4. "Dislocation" was broadcast under the title "The World We Live In," 24 August 1960 on CBC's "Wednesday Night" series. Jack McClelland to I.L., 27 April 1960, McClelland and Stewart Papers, McMaster University Library, Hamilton, Ontario. I.L. to Desmond Pacey, 28 December 1960, Desmond Pacey Papers, property of Mary Pacey, Fredericton, New Brunswick.
5. I.L. to Desmond Pacey, 28 December 1960, Desmond Pacey Papers, property of Mary Pacey, Fredericton, New Brunswick.
6. "Enough of Fallen Leaves" (unpublished), 30 January 1961, MS., Irving Layton Collection, Concordia University Library, Montreal, was later titled "Up With Nothing," March 1961. "Lights on the Black Water" (unpublished) [ca. 1961], MS., Irving Layton Collection, Concordia University Library, Montreal. "A Man Was Killed," MS. Irving Layton Collection, Concordia University Library, Montreal, also published in *Canadian Theatre Review*, No. 14 (Spring 1977), pp. 56–58. This play was performed by a high school in Montreal in 1983.
7. Robert Weaver to I.L., 18 January 1961, Irving Layton Collection, Concordia University Library, Montreal.
8. Doris Gauntlett and Doris Mosdell, editors, Special Programs TV, CBC, to I.L., 2 May 1961, Irving Layton Collection, Concordia University Library, Montreal.
9. I.L. to Desmond Pacey, 19 May 1962, Desmond Pacey Papers, property of Mary Pacey, Fredericton, New Brunswick.
10. I.L. to Desmond Pacey, 17 October 1960, Desmond Pacey Papers, prop-

erty of Mary Pacey. Fredericton, New Brunswick.
11. I.L. to Desmond Pacey, 31 December 1961, Desmond Pacey Papers, property of Mary Pacey, Fredericton, New Brunswick.
12. I.L. to Desmond Pacey, 27 February 1961, Desmond Pacey Papers, property of Mary Pacey, Fredericton, New Brunswick.
13. I.L. to Jacqueline Kennedy, 19 April 1961, Irving Layton Papers, Concordia University Library, Montreal. "Why I Don't Make Love to the First Lady," *Canadian Forum* (March 1961), p. 267. Reprinted in *CP 65*; *CPIL*; *SF* and *SP 69*.
14. A.J.M. Smith, "To Irving Layton (On his Passion for the First Lady)," *Canadian Forum* (April 1961), p. 4. Reprinted in *The Blasted Pine*, ed. F.R. Scott and A.J.M. Smith (Toronto: Macmillan, 1967).
15. Betty Layton to E.C., interview, 8 July 1982, Guerneville, California.
16. Aviva's children's stories would eventually include *The Singing Stones* (New York: Abelard-Schuman, 1963), later published as *The Magic Stones* (Toronto: McClelland and Stewart, 1977); *How the Kookaburra Got His Laugh* (Toronto: McClelland and Stewart, 1975); and *The Squeakers* (Oakville: Mosaic Press, 1980). In addition to *Nobody's Daughter* (1982), Aviva assisted writing *Lotfi Mansouri: An Operatic Life* (Toronto: Mosaic Press/Stoddart Publishing, 1982).
17. "Layton, McCullogh Differ As to Cost of Love," *Sir George Williams University Georgian* (28 November 1961).
18. Aviva Layton to Leonard Cohen, undated [ca. 1961 or 1962], Thomas Fisher Archives, University of Toronto Library, Toronto.
19. I.L. to Desmond Pacey, 2 December 1961, Desmond Pacey Papers, property of Mary Pacey, Fredericton, New Brunswick.
20. Jerry M. Cohen and Moses Znaimer, "Irving Layton," *The Hillellight* (20 November 1959).
21. I.L. to Desmond Pacey, 9 November 1954, Desmond Pacey Papers, property of Mary Pacey, Fredericton, New Brunswick.
22. Desmond Pacey to I.L., 16 April 1962, Irving Layton Collection, Concordia University Library, Montreal.
23. I.L. to Desmond Pacey, 7 May 1956 and 12 April 1962, Desmond Pacey Papers, property of Mary Pacey, Fredericton, New Brunswick.
24. I.L. to Desmond Pacey.
25. Northrop Frye to a meeting of the Canadian Association of University Teachers, as reported in the *Montreal Star* by Morris Fish (13 June 1961), p. 12.
26. See Birney's letter to I.L., 27 August 1962; and I.L. to Desmond Pacey, 28 April and 11 June 1962. An extensive correspondence, including Birney's resignation over the matter, can be found in the Thomas Fisher Rare Book Library, University of Toronto.
27. I.L. to Desmond Pacey, 17 October 1960, Desmond Pacey Papers, property of Mary Pacey, Fredericton, New Brunswick.
28. I.L. to Desmond Pacey, 30 November 1960, Desmond Pacey Papers, property of Mary Pacey, Fredericton, New Brunswick.
29. I.L. to Desmond Pacey, 19 May 1962, Desmond Pacey Papers, property of Mary Pacey, Fredericton, New Brunswick. In fact, though Faulkner had gone to the University of Mississippi for part of a year, he had not been associated with the academic side of the University, as Pacey apparently thought. He had been the university postmaster from 1921 to 1924 and supervisor of the university power plant in 1930, jobs that supported him while he wrote.
30. I.L. to Desmond Pacey, 11 June 1962, Desmond Pacey Papers, property of Mary Pacey, Fredericton, New Brunswick.
31. Malcolm Ross to I.L., 8 December 1961, Irving Layton Collection, Concordia University Library, Montreal.

32. Milton Wilson to I.L., 20 June 1960, Irving Layton Collection, Concordia University Library, Montreal.
33. I.L. to Desmond Pacey, 1 July 1962, Desmond Pacey Papers, property of Mary Pacey, Fredericton, New Brunswick.
34. I.L. to Desmond Pacey, 8 July 1962, Desmond Pacey Papers, property of Mary Pacey, Fredericton, New Brunswick.
35. *The Montrealer* (August 1950), p. 8.
36. I.L. to Desmond Pacey, 13 May 1961, Desmond Pacey Papers, property of Mary Pacey, Fredericton, New Brunswick. The lecture, which took place 18 March 1962 at the Steinman Festival of the Arts, St. Lawrence University, Canton, New York, is reprinted as "Prince Hamlet and the Beatniks" in *Taking Sides*, pp. 50–62.
37. I.L. to Desmond Pacey, 28 December 1961, Desmond Pacey Papers, property of Mary Pacey, Fredericton, New Brunswick.
38. I.L. to Desmond Pacey, 8 November 1962, Desmond Pacey Papers, property of Mary Pacey, Fredericton, New Brunswick.
39. I.L. to Desmond Pacey, 19 May 1962, Desmond Pacey Papers, property of Mary Pacey, Fredericton, New Brunswick. Milton Acorn's letter to Pacey, 15 May 1962, asked permission to use Layton's real name in the novel (see Irving Layton Collection, Concordia University Library, Montreal). The novel was never published.
40. *Poems for 27 cents*, ed. I.L. (Montreal: Authors, 1961).
41. Photos of Layton with moustache and goatee appear in *Balls for a One-Armed Juggler* (1963).
42. Walter O'Hearne, the *Montreal Star* (21 October 1961), reprinted in *Engagements: The Prose of Irving Layton*, ed. Seymour Mayne (Toronto: McClelland and Stewart, 1972), pp. 168–169.
43. "Letter," the *Montreal Star* (23 October 1961). Reprinted in *Engagements*, pp. 168–169.
44. Alan Pearson, "Lost in the Feud: Is It Worth 27 Cents?" *Canada Month* (December 1961), pp. 39–40.
45. "Librarian at Asheville," *The Swinging Flesh*. Reprinted in *CPIL*.
46. "The Fictive Eye," *The Swinging Flesh*. Reprinted in *CP 65* and *CPIL*.
47. I.L. to E.C., interview, 29 September 1982, Oakville, Ontario.
48. Jack McClelland to I.L., 19 May 1961, McClelland and Stewart Papers, McMaster University Library, Hamilton, Ontario. "Gifts," *Balls For a One-Armed Juggler*. Reprinted in *CPIL* and MS:CU. "Mysteries," (unpublished). "There Were No Signs," *Canadian Forum* (October 1961), p. 158; and *Amythyst*, 2, No. 4 (Summer 1963), p. 14. Anthologized widely and reprinted in *BFOJ*; *CP 65*; *CPIL*; *DF*; *SP 69*; *TWNS*; *WPJ* and MS:CU.
49. I.L. to Desmond Pacey, 3 February 1962, Desmond Pacey Papers, property of Mary Pacey, Fredericton, New Brunswick.
50. I.L. to Desmond Pacey, 28 April 1962, Desmond Pacey Papers, property of Mary Pacey, Fredericton, New Brunswick.
51. I.L. to Desmond Pacey, 21 July 1961, Desmond Pacey Papers, property of Mary Pacey, Fredericton, New Brunswick.
52. "A Tall Man Executes a Jig," *Queen's Quarterly*, 86, No. 3 (Autumn 1961), pp. 456–458. Anthologized widely and reprinted in *BFOJ*; *CP 65*; *CPIL*; *DF*; *PIL*; *SP 69*; *SPIL*; *WPJ* and MS:CU.
53. Leonard Cohen to I.L., 8 December 1961, Irving Layton Collection, Concordia University Library, Montreal.
54. Al Purdy to I.L., undated [1961], Al Purdy Papers, Queen's University Archives, Kingston, Ontario.
55. I.L. to Desmond Pacey, 8 September 1961. See also I.L. to Desmond Pacey, 17 September 1962, Desmond Pacey Papers, property of Mary Pacey, Fredericton, New Brunswick.
56. I.L. to Jack McClelland, 10 September 1961, McClelland and Stewart Papers, McMaster University Library, Hamilton, Ontario.

57. Jay Macpherson to E.C., 1 February 1983.
58. I.L. to Jack McClelland, 20 March 1962 and 6 February 1962, McClelland and Stewart Papers, McMaster University Library, Hamilton, Ontario.
59. This satirical poem was titled after Arthur M. Lower's book of Canadian history, which had appeared in 1946.
60. Patricia Porth, "The Poetry of Irving Layton" M.A. thesis (unpublished), University of Manitoba, 1960.
61. Wynne Francis, *Canadian Literature*, No. 14 (Autumn 1962), pp. 21-34.
62. I.L. to Desmond Pacey, 12 October 1962, Desmond Pacey Papers, property of Mary Pacey, Fredericton, New Brunswick.
63. A.J.M. Smith to John Glassco, 5 December 1963, Public Archives of Canada, MG 30, D 163, vol. 14, Ottawa.
64. Desmond Pacey to I.L., 25 June 1962, 19 January and 27 March 1963, Desmond Pacey Papers, property of Mary Pacey, Fredericton, New Brunswick.
65. I.L. to Earle Birney, 28 September 1962, Earle Birney Papers, University of Toronto Archives, Toronto.

Mirror Reflections/336

1. I.L. to Desmond Pacey, 16 December 1962, Desmond Pacey Papers, property of Mary Pacey, Fredericton, New Brunswick.
2. June Callwood, "The Lusty Laureate from the Slums," *Star Weekly Magazine* (6 February 1960), pp. 10-12, p. 21.
3. Joyce Dawe Freedman to E.C., interview, 25 September 1983, Toronto.
4. "Moral With a Story," *Tamarack Review*, 25 (Autumn 1962), p. 86. Reprinted in *BFOJ*; *CP 65*; *CPIL* and MS:CU.
5. *An Unlikely Affair: The Irving Layton - Dorothy Rath Correspondence*, introd. Adrienne Clarkson (Oakville: Mosaic Press, 1980), p. 3.
6. Dorothy Rath to E.C., interview, 10 July 1983, Toronto.

7. *An Unlikely Affair: The Irving Layton - Dorothy Rath Correspondence*.
8. I.L. to Andy Wainwright, 24 October 1977, Irving Layton Collection, Concordia University Library, Montreal.
9. Henry Moscovitch to E.C., interview, 10 January 1984, Montreal. Max Layton wrote a short story partly based on this situation: "The Myth of Joel Ickerman," *Descant*, No. 77, (Summer 1982), pp. 82-102.
10. I.L. to Desmond Pacey, 19 May 1962, Desmond Pacey Papers, property of Mary Pacey, Fredericton, New Brunswick.
11. I.L. to E.C., interview, 3 October 1983, Oakville, Ontario.

A Greek Tragedy/343

1. Aviva Layton to E.C., interview, 24 November 1982, Toronto.
2. Musia Schwartz to E.C., interview, 22 February 1982, Montreal.
3. Musia Schwartz to E.C.
4. Aviva Layton to E.C., interview, 24 November 1982, Toronto.
5. William Goodwin to E.C., interview, 30 August 1982, Montreal.
6. I.L. to E.C., interview, 17 February 1982, Toronto.
7. Jack McClelland to I.L., 28 September 1959, McClelland and Stewart Papers, McMaster University Library, Hamilton, Ontario.
8. Aviva Layton to E.C., interview, 30 December 1982, Toronto.

A Question of Value/348

1. Desmond Pacey to I.L., 19 June 1963, Irving Layton Collection, Concordia University Library, Montreal.
2. I.L. to Desmond Pacey, 19 July 1963, Desmond Pacey Papers, property of Mary Pacey, Fredericton, New Brunswick.
3. Desmond Pacey to I.L., 6 January 1964, Irving Layton Collection, Concordia University Library, Montreal.

4. I.L. to Desmond Pacey, 15 July 1964, Desmond Pacey Papers, property of Mary Pacey, Fredericton, New Brunswick.
5. I.L. to Desmond Pacey, 13 April 1964, Desmond Pacey Papers, property of Mary Pacey, Fredericton, New Brunswick.
6. I.L. to Desmond Pacey, 27 July 1964, Desmond Pacey Papers, property of Mary Pacey, Fredericton, New Brunswick.
7. I.L. to Desmond Pacey, 1 March 1964, Desmond Pacey Papers, property of Mary Pacey, Fredericton, New Brunswick.
8. Aviva Layton to E.C., interview, 30 December 1982, Toronto.
9. Musia Schwartz to E.C., interview, 22 February 1982, Montreal.
10. Preface, *The Laughing Rooster* (Toronto: McClelland and Stewart, 1964), p. 22.
11. *The Laughing Rooster*, p. 21.
12. I.L. to Desmond Pacey, 26 December 1968, Desmond Pacey Papers, property of Mary Pacey, Fredericton, New Brunswick.
13. Aviva Layton to E.C., interview, 30 December 1982, Toronto.
14. I.L. to Desmond Pacey, 6 June 1964, Desmond Pacey Papers, property of Mary Pacey, Fredericton, New Brunswick. Blair Fraser, for example, had written articles in *Maclean's* criticising Canada's expensive defense policy (25 January 1964), supporting old-age pensions (22 February 1964) and favouring greater restrictions on centralized powers in the Pearson government (4 April 1964).
15. I.L. to Desmond Pacey, October 1963, Desmond Pacey Papers, property of Mary Pacey, Fredericton, New Brunswick.
16. I.L. to Desmond Pacey, 7 October 1963, Desmond Pacey Papers, property of Mary Pacey, Fredericton, New Brunswick.
17. "At the Iglesia de Sacromonte," *Prism International*, 4, No. 1 (Summer 1964), p. 32. Reprinted in *CP65*; *CPIL*; *DF*; *LR*; *SP69* and MS:CU. "Silly Rhymes for Aviva," *The Long Pea-Shooter*. Reprinted in *CP65*, and *CPIL*. "For My Green Old Age," *Fiddlehead*, No. 60 (Spring 1964), p. 20. Reprinted in *CP65*; *CPIL*; *LPIL* and MS:CU. "My Queen, My Quean," *The Laughing Rooster*. Reprinted in *CP65*; *CPIL*; *LPIL* and MS:CU. "Encounter," *The Laughing Rooster*. Reprinted in *CP65*; *CPIL* and MS:CU.
18. "Beauty," *Love the Conqueror Worm*. Reprinted in *CP65*; *CPIL*; *RC* and *Literary Review*, 8, No. 4 (Summer 1965). "A Strange Turn," *Literary Review*, 8, No. 4 (Summer 1965), p. 547. Reprinted in *CP65*; *CPIL*; *DF*; *LPIL* and *WPJ*.
19. I.L. to Earle Birney, 17 June 1963, Earle Birney Papers, Thomas Fisher Rare Book Library, University of Toronto, Toronto.
20. I.L. to Desmond Pacey, 6 January 1965, Desmond Pacey Papers, property of Mary Pacey, Fredericton, New Brunswick.
21. I.L. to E.C., interview, 17 February 1982, Toronto, Ontario.
22. Desmond Pacey to I.L., 12 March 1963, Irving Layton Collection, Concordia University Library, Montreal.
23. I.L. to Desmond Pacey, 27 July 1964, Desmond Pacey Papers, property of Mary Pacey, Fredericton, New Brunswick.
24. I.L. to Desmond Pacey, 15 October 1965, Desmond Pacey Papers, property of Mary Pacey, Fredericton, New Brunswick.
25. I.L. to Desmond Pacey, 1 March 1964, Desmond Pacey Papers, property of Mary Pacey, Fredericton, New Brunswick.
26. Half-page advertisement in the *Fiddlehead*, for 1967, copy in Desmond Pacey Papers, property of Mary Pacey, Fredericton, New Brunswick. "Afternoon of a Coupon Clipper," *Now Is the Place*. Reprinted in *BH* and *CPIL*.
27. Desmond Pacey to I.L., 25 November 1964, Irving Layton Collection, Concordia University Library, Montreal.
28. Leonard Cohen to E.C., interview, 16 May 1983, Toronto.

Endnotes 495

29. I.L. to Desmond Pacey, 9 August 1963, Desmond Pacey Papers, property of Mary Pacey, Fredericton, New Brunswick. "Icarus" (unpublished).
30. I.L. to Desmond Pacey, 7 October 1963, Desmond Pacey Papers, property of Mary Pacey, Fredericton, New Brunswick.
31. Jack McClelland to I.L., 16 April 1963, McClelland and Stewart Papers, McMaster University Library, Hamilton, Ontario.

Armchair Traveller/361

1. Leonard Cohen to E.C., interview, 16 May 1983, Toronto.
2. Leonard Cohen to I.L., 12 September 1961, Irving Layton Collection, Concordia University Library, Montreal.
3. Leonard Cohen to E.C., interview, 16 May 1983, Toronto.
4. Leonard Cohen to E.C.

Où Sont Les Jeunes?/363

1. Desmond Pacey to I.L., 3 June 1964, Irving Layton Collection, Concordia University Library, Montreal.
2. I.L. to Desmond Pacey, 6 June 1964, Desmond Pacey Papers, property of Mary Pacey, Fredericton, New Brunswick.
3. "To a Generation of Poets," *The Shattered Plinths* (Toronto: McClelland and Stewart, 1968), p. 67. Reprinted in MS:CU. "On Rereading the Beats," *Outsider*, 1, No. 3 (September 1963), pp. 42–43. Reprinted in *BFOJ* and *CPIL*.
4. Raymond Souster, ed., "Preface," *New Wave Canada* (Toronto: Contact Press, 1966). Reprinted in *The Making of Modern Poetry in Canada*, pp. 300–301.
5. Jack McClelland to I.L., 13 February 1963, McClelland and Stewart Papers, McMaster University Library, Hamilton, Ontario.
6. For a full treatment of the growth of little magazines in Canada, see *The Making of Modern Poetry in Canada*. See also Wynne Francis, "The Little Magazines: A Mysterious Phenomenon," *Montreal Star* (11 June 1966), p. 4.
7. *Canadian Literature*, No. 13 (Summer 1962), pp. 39–44. This growth continued after 1967 as well. According to Wynne Francis, there were sixty little magazines devoted to verse between 1968 and 1973. (See George Woodcock, "Place, Past and Poetry: Notes on Contemporary Canadian Poets" (unpublished), *Queen's Quarterly* Archives, Kingston, Ontario.)
8. I.L. to Jonathan Williams, [July] 1961, Poetry/Rare Books Collection, University Libraries, State University of New York, Buffalo. "To a Lily," *Cataract*, 1, No. 2 (Winter 1962), p. 22. Reprinted in *BFOJ* and MS:CU.
9. *Cerberus*, p. 45.
10. Leonard Cohen to E.C., interview 16 May 1983, Toronto.
11. Louis Dudek, "The Role of Little Magazines in Canada," *The Making of Modern Poetry in Canada*, p. 205.
12. Joan Finnegan, "Canadian Poetry Finds its Voice in a Golden Age," *Globe and Mail* (20 January 1962). Reprinted in *The Making of Modern Poetry in Canada*, pp. 235–240.
13. *The Making of Modern Poetry*, p. 235.
14. Louis Dudek, "Poetry Finds a Public," *The Making of Modern Poetry in Canada*, p. 232.
15. Jack McClelland to I.L., 9 December 1964, McClelland and Stewart Papers, McMaster University Library, Hamilton, Ontario.
16. *Time* (6 November 1964), p. 16 and *Montreal Star* (31 October 1964), p. 4.
17. George Woodcock, "Place, Past and Poetry: Notes on Contemporary Canadian Poets" (unpublished), p. 3. *Queen's Quarterly* Archives, Kingston, Ontario.

Over-Exposed/371

1. I.L. to Desmond Pacey, 9 December 1964, Desmond Pacey Papers, property of Mary Pacey, Fredericton, New Brunswick.
2. Jack McClelland to I.L., 20 October 1964, McClelland and Stewart Papers, McMaster University Library, Hamilton, Ontario.

3. Those of Layton's poems reprinted in two or more anthologies are listed below, by date. Among these, the poems that were anthologized five or more times are asterisked. The seven most anthologized poems are asterisked twice.

1940s: My Love, A Miracle/
A Spider Danced a Cosy Jig (1942)
Newsboy (1943)
Jewish Main Street (1944)
The Swimmer (1944–1945).
Excursion/Excursion to Ottawa/
Weekend Special/Words Without Music (1944–1945)

1950s: The Black Huntsmen (1952)
To the Girls of My Graduating Class/To the Girls of My Graduation Class (1952–1953)
*Composition in Late Spring (1953)
In the Midst of My Fever (1953)
**The Cold Green Element (1954)
First Snow: Lake Achigan (1954)
*Golfers (1954)
Look, the Lambs Are All Around Us! (1954)
Misunderstanding (1954)
Vexata Quaestio (1954)
**The Bull Calf (1955)
*On Seeing the Statuettes of Ezekiel and Jeremiah in the Church of Notre Dame/On Seeing the Statues of Ezekiel and Jeremiah in the Church of Notre Dame, Montreal (1955)
**The Birth of Tragedy (1956)
*From Colony to Nation (1956)
Family Portrait(1956)
*The Fertile Muck (1956)
Red Chokecherries (1956)
Sacrament by the Water (1956)
Cat Dying in Autumn (1957)
Against This Death (1958)
**Berry Picking (1958)
*Cain (1958)
Cote des Neiges Cemetery (1958)
*Whatever Else, Poetry is Freedom (1958)
The Day Aviva Came to Paris (1959)

1960s: *The Improved Binoculars (1960)
**Keine Lazarovitch (1960)
Piazza San Marco (1960)
**Song for Naomi (1960)
**A Tall Man Executes a Jig (1961)
*There Were No Signs (1961)
On My Way to School (1962)
Butterfly on Rock (1962)
The Well-Wrought Urn (1962)
Anglo-Canadian (1963)
El Gusano (1964)
For Musia's Grandchildren (1966)
How Poems Get Written (1967)
Marché Municipale (1967)
Osip Mandelshtam (1969)

1970s: The Haunting (1970)
If Whales Could Think on Certain Happy Days (1974)

1980s: The Search (1981)

4. Margaret Atwood, as quoted by Roy MacGregor, "Mother Oracle," *Canadian Magazine* (September 1976), p. 15.
5. I.L. to John Brebner, 23 July 1979, property of John Brebner, Gagetown, New Brunswick.
6. I.L. to Desmond Pacey, 6 January 1965, Desmond Pacey Papers, property of Mary Pacey, Fredericton, New Brunswick.
7. I.L. to Desmond Pacey, 14 January and 21 March 1965, Desmond Pacey Papers, property of Mary Pacey, Fredericton, New Brunswick.
8. Desmond Pacey to I.L., 8 March 1965, Irving Layton Collection, Concordia University Library, Montreal.
9. Aviva Layton to E.C., interview, 30 December 1982, Toronto.
10. I.L. to Desmond Pacey, 24 April 1967, Desmond Pacey Papers, property of Mary Pacey, Fredericton, New Brunswick.

Marion/376

1. Marion Wagshall to E.C., 16 February 1983, Montreal. Wagshall later became an art teacher at Sir George Williams University and the Saidye Bronfman Centre.

2. Marion Wagshall to I.L., undated [1967 or 1968], Irving Layton Collection, Concordia University Library, Montreal. In this letter Marion outlines her "code."
3. "For the Girl With Wide-Apart Eyes," *The Shattered Plinths*. Reprinted in *CPIL*; *DF*; *LPIL* and MS:CU.
4. I.L. to Barry Callaghan, 2 July 1967, property of Barry Callaghan, Toronto.
5. Marion Wagshall to I.L., undated [September 1967], Irving Layton Collection, Concordia University Library, Montreal. Wagshall apologized to I.L. for weeping at the airport and explained that suddenly he had looked like "a handsome rich tourist that really had never known me at all and I was imagining the whole thing."
6. I.L. to E.C., interview, 17 February 1982, Toronto, Ontario.
7. "End of the Summer," *Quarry*, 17, No. 1 (Fall 1967), p. 33. Reprinted in *CPIL* and *SP*.

Sceneshifter/*382*

1. I.L. to E.C., interview, 10 February 1982, Toronto.
2. Professor Michael Collie, Chairman of English, to I.L., 23 January 1969, Irving Layton Papers, Concordia University Library, Montreal.
3. I.L. to Desmond Pacey, 23 January 1969, Desmond Pacey Papers, property of Mary Pacey, Fredericton, New Brunswick. No doubt Layton had Marion Wagshall — with whom he was still closely in touch — in mind, among others.
4. I.L. to Desmond Pacey.
5. Michael Hornyansky, "Letters in Canada: 1971, Poetry," *University of Toronto Quarterly*, 41, No. 4 (Summer 1972), pp. 330-331.
6. The poem "Guelph Suite" depicts younger girls as more stand-offish toward a poet.
7. "York University," *Saturday Night* (December 1972), p. 10. Reprinted in *LIM* and MS:UT.
8. I.L. to Desmond Pacey, 17 March 1970, Desmond Pacey Papers, property of Mary Pacey, Fredericton, New Brunswick.
9. I.L. to Desmond Pacey, 15 June 1970, Desmond Pacey Papers, property of Mary Pacey, Fredericton, New Brunswick.
10. I.L. to Desmond Pacey, 23 October 1970, Desmond Pacey Papers, property of Mary Pacey, Fredericton, New Brunswick.
11. I.L. to Ralph Gustafson, 26 October 1970, Irving Layton Collection, Concordia University Library, Montreal.
12. I.L. as quoted in "Poet Irving Layton on German Tour," *Montreal Star* (10 May 1966), p. 8.
13. I.L., "Two Views of Germany," *Maclean's* (19 November 1966), pp. 18-21, 26, 28, 30-31.
14. Peter Lust, "Not Hatred, Mr. Layton — Common Sense," *The Canadian Jewish Chronicle Review* (11 November 1966), p. 4. See also, "Visitor to Germany Thoroughly Convinced Nation's Abhorrence of Hitlerism Sincere," *Montreal Star*, 19 May 1966. Reprinted in *TS*. (See letter by Peter Lust, *Montreal Star*, 25 May 1966); "Mr. Layton Defends his Insights Into Germany's Mind Against Criticism," *Montreal Star*, 21 June 1966. Reprinted in *TS*. (See Heinz Brodersen, F. Kenrick, G.A. Parr, "Readers, Two to One, Find Layton Reaction to Challenge of his Opinion Offensive" [*Montreal Star*, 23 June 1966]; and Peter Lust, "Fear of New Nazi Bid for Power in W. Germany Said Solidly Based on Fact" [27 June 1966]); "Situation in Germany Today Unlike That Leading to Fall of Weimar Republic," *Montreal Star* (28 November 1966), p. 5. Reprinted in *TS*. (See responses by Irving Borwick, Anne Hope and A.C. Thorn, *Montreal Star*, 1 December 1966; and Peter Lust, "Layton Claim to Full Understanding of German Political Scene Challenged" [3 December 1966, p. 6].) "Germany's New Chancellor Exhibiting Sincere Desire to Reassure Doubters," *Montreal Star*, 16 December 1966, p. 5. Reprinted in *TS*. "CBC Back Down 'Act of Poltroonery'," *Montreal Star*, 29 January 1967, p. 8. Reprinted in *TS*. (See replies by Susan Handman, "Neo-Nazi 'Fact'

Defies Dismissal," *Montreal Star*, 23 January 1967; Aviva Layton, 24 January 1967; Oscar P. Singer, 25 January 1967; and Peter Lust, *Canadian Jewish Chronicle Review*, 27 January 1967); "Another Danger Fills Mr. Layton's Mind to Exclusion of Proclaimed Nazi Rebirth," *Montreal Star*, 31 January 1967, p. 6. Reprinted in *TS*. (See responses by Aviva Layton, *Montreal Star*, 31 January 1967, p. 6; K. Wiseman, 1 February 1967; and Phyllis Mass, 6 February 1967); "Open Forum — Layton on Lust," *Canadian Jewish Chronicle Review*, 10 February 1967; "The Time for Illusions is Over, the Confrontation is Here," *Montreal Star*, 17 June 1967, p. 8. Reprinted in *TS*. (See Freda Bain, "Mr. Layton's Views Inspire Wonder," *Montreal Star*, 21 June 1967; and letter by A.C. Thorn, 22 June 1967); "Der Mensch ist ein Krankes Tier;" "Irving Layton: Mut ist das Wort — Stets," *Montreal Zeitung*, 9 November 1967, p. 9. (See Adolph Schmidt, "Irving Layton — Kurze Betrachtung Uber Einen Kanadischen Dichter," *Montreal Zeitung*, 9 November 1967, p. 9.)

15. I.L. to Desmond Pacey, 20 October 1970, Desmond Pacey Papers, property of Mary Pacey, Fredericton, New Brunswick.
16. Desmond Pacey to I.L., 28 June 1970, Irving Layton Collection, Concordia University, Montreal.
17. "Hymn to the Republic," *The New Romans*, ed. Al Purdy (Edmonton: Hurtig Publishers, 1968), pp. 62–64.
18. I.L. to Desmond Pacey, 5 July 1970, Desmond Pacey Papers, property of Mary Pacey, Fredericton, New Brunswick.
19. I.L. to E.C., interview, 10 February 1982, Toronto.
20. I.L. to Steven Osterlund (later known as DaGama), 5 February 1971, property of Steven Osterlund DaGama, Akron, Ohio.
21. I.L. to Desmond Pacey, 21 November 1970, Desmond Pacey Papers, property of Mary Pacey, Fredericton, New Brunswick.
22. I.L., "Foreword," *The Whole Bloody Bird* (Toronto: McClelland and Stewart, 1969), p. 9.
23. I.L. to Jack McClelland, 29 April 1964, McClelland and Stewart Papers, McMaster University Library, Hamilton, Ontario.
24. Aviva Layton to E.C., interview, 30 December 1982, Toronto.
25. Nima Ash to E.C., 5 April 1985.
26. The novel, titled *Light and Dark in Morocco*, was never published, but sections of it have appeared as short stories in *Men Only*.
27. I.L. to E.C., by telephone, 16 April 1985, Montreal.
28. Aviva Layton, "Steely Eye vs. Steely Eye," *Weekend Magazine* (8 May 1976), p. 17.
29. "Steely Eye," pp. 16–18.
30. Francesca Valente to E.C., interview, 28 September 1983, Toronto.
31. These were: "After Theoginis," "Everywhere, the Stink," "Love's Diffidence," Piazza San Marco," "Redemption," "T.S. Eliot," "Therapy," "There were No Signs" and "The Well-Wrought Urn." All were translated by Ion Caraion for the 23 April 1970 issue.
32. I.L. to Jack McClelland, 17 July 1971, McClelland and Stewart Papers, McMaster University Library, Hamilton, Ontario.
33. I.L. to Barry Callaghan, 18 August 1968, property of Barry Callaghan, Toronto.
34. I.L. to Barry Callaghan.
35. I.L. to E.C., interview, 17 February 1982, Toronto.
36. I.L. to Barry Callaghan, September 1968. Reprinted in *The Whole Bloody Bird*, pp. 67–69.
37. Andy Wainwright to E.C., interview, 22 February 1982, Toronto.
38. "Foreword," *The Whole Bloody Bird* (Toronto: McClelland Stewart, 1969), p. 9.
39. *Nail Polish* (Toronto: McClelland and Stewart, 1971); *Lovers and Lesser Men* (Toronto: McClelland and Stewart, 1973); *The Pole-vaulter* (Toronto: McClelland and Stewart, 1974).
40. "Osip Mandelshtam (1891–1940)," *Canadian Jewish News* (12 December 1969), p. 4. Reprinted in *Tamarack Review*, 54

(1970); *New American and Canadian Poetry* (1971), ed. John Gill; *Canadian Poetry: the Modern Era* (1977), ed. John Newlove; *CPIL*; *NP*; *PIL*; *UE*; *SPIL* and *WPJ*.
41. "Stella," *Queens' Quarterly*, 79, No. 4 (Winter 1972), pp. 503-504. Reprinted in *Selections from Major Canadian Writers* (1972), ed. Desmond Pacey; *GP*; *LIM*; *UE*; *WPJ* and MS:UT.
42. "Elephant," *Canadian Forum* (September 1968), p. 135. Reprinted in *How Do I Love Thee?* (1970), ed. John Robert Colombo; *CPIL*; *UE*; *WBB* and MS:CU.
43. "aphs," *WBB*, p. 83.
44. "aphs," p. 77.
45. "aphs," p. 87.
46. I.L. to Steven Osterlund (DaGama), 26 November 1970, property of Steven Osterlund DaGama, Akron, Ohio.
47. Perry Nodelman, "Review of Lovers and Lesser Men," *Winnipeg Free Press* (24 March 1973).
48. Edward Lacey, *Northern Journey*, No. 4 (1973), pp. 82, 83, 87.
49. "Economy, Please, Toronto," *Lovers and Lesser Men*, p. 74. MS:UT.
50. Layton's Contracts with McClelland and Stewart, Irving Layton Collection, Concordia University Library, Montreal; and McClelland and Stewart Papers, McMaster University Library, Hamilton, Ontario.
51. *Selected Poems* (Toronto: McClelland and Stewart, 1971); *Engagements: The Prose of Irving Layton*, ed. Seymour Mayne (Toronto: McClelland and Stewart, 1972); *The Darkening Fire: Selected Poems 1945 to 1968* (Toronto: McClelland and Stewart, 1975) and *The Unwavering Eye: Selected Poems 1969 to 1975* (Toronto: McClelland and Stewart, 1975).
52. "Poetry As the Fine Art of Pugilism," *Lovers and Lesser Men*, pp. 69-71. Reprinted in MS:UT.
53. Desmond Pacey to I.L., 29 November 1970, Irving Layton Collection, Concordia University Library, Montreal.
54. I.L. to Barry Callaghan, 12 April 1968, property of Barry Callaghan, Toronto.
55. I.L. to Andy Wainwright, 29 November 1970, Irving Layton Collection, Concordia University Library, Montreal.
56. I.L. to Barry Callaghan, 2 July 1967, property of Barry Callaghan, Toronto.
57. Michael Hornyansky, "Letters in Canada: 1971, Poetry" *University of Toronto Quarterly*, 41, No. 4 (Summer 1972), pp. 330-331.
58. Clare McCulloch, *Alive*, 28 (11 May 1973), pp. 46-47.
59. I.L. to Desmond Pacey, 15 January 1970, Desmond Pacey Papers, property of Mary Pacey, Fredericton, New Brunswick.
60. Desmond Pacey to I.L., 29 November 1970, Irving Layton Papers, Concordia University Library, Montreal.
61. Tom Maschler, Board of Directors, Jonathan Cape Ltd. to I.L., 14 January 1965, Irving Layton Papers, Concordia University Library, Montreal.
62. I.L. to Jack McClelland, 20 June 1965 and 22 December 1968, McClelland and Stewart Papers, McMaster University Library, Hamilton, Ontario.
63. See Leonard Cohen's correspondence on "Spice Box Books, Ltd." letterhead with Jack McClelland of McClelland and Stewart. This venture was superceded by an arrangement Cohen made with Charisma books to print from the M&S plates of *Selected Poems* (see Martin J. Machat to Jack McClelland, 5 November 1972, McClelland and Stewart Papers, McMaster University Library, Hamilton, Ontario). The book, edited by Wynne Francis, was published in England in 1977.
64. Athaneum Press to Jack McClelland, 7 February 1963, McClelland and Stewart Papers, McMaster University Library, Hamilton, Ontario. Robert Creeley speculated that when Layton "dropped" his American poet friends like Creeley and Olson in the late fifties, he cut his connection with the American poetry scene. Had he maintained these contacts, he might have developed an American market for his work. (Robert Creeley to E.C., taped interview, 7 August 1983, Buffalo, New York.)
65. I.L. to Jack McClelland, 4 August 1980, McClelland and Stewart Papers, Toronto, Ontario.

66. I.L. to Steven Osterlund (DaGama), 24 February 1979, property of Steven Osterlund DaGama, Akron, Ohio.
67. "I Don't Like It," *Lovers and Lesser Men*, p. 76. Reprinted in MS:UT.
68. Graham Dowden, *Quarry*, 20, No. 1 (Winter 1971), pp. 45–48.
69. "To the Gov-Gen's Poetry Awards Committee For 1971–1972," *Lovers and Lesser Men*, p. 84. MS:UT.
70. I.L. to Desmond Pacey, 24 May 1972, property of Mary Pacey, Fredericton, New Brunswick.
71. I.L. to Desmond Pacey, 23 October 1970, Desmond Pacey Papers, property of Mary Pacey, Fredericton, New Brunswick. This programme, with Helen Hutchison as moderator, was broadcast at 2:30 PM, 2 December 1970.
72. "aphs," *The Whole Bloody Bird*, p. 73.
73. "Teufelsdröckh Concerning Women," *Lovers and Lesser Men*, p. 85. MS:UT.
74. "The Vampire," *Poetry Readings by Irving Layton, 10 November 1972* (Toronto: Temple Sinai Congregation, 1972), p. 4. Reprinted in *LIM* and MS:UT.
75. I.L. to Desmond Pacey, 24 November 1973, Desmond Pacey Papers, property of Mary Pacey, Fredericton, New Brunswick. The biography was *Robert Frost* by Lawrance Roger Thompson, 3 vols. (New York: Holt, Rinehart & Winston, 1966–1976).

Gypsy Jo/408

1. Adele Freedman, *Globe and Mail* (18 March 1978), p. 41.
2. Judith Knelman, *University of Toronto Bulletin* (19 October 1981), p. 9.
3. I.L. to E.C., interview, 20 January 1982, Toronto.
4. Martin Knelman to E.C., telephone interview, February 1985, Toronto.
5. "For My Incomparable Gypsy" ("For The Incomparable Gypsy"), *Tamarack Review*, 68 (Spring 1976), pp. 40–41. Reprinted in *FMBJ*, *LPIL* and MS:CU.
6. "Musical Interlude," *The Canadian Review*, vol. 2, No. 4 (1975), p. 45.
7. I.L., "Adonis," *For My Brother Jesus*, p. 67; and Harriet Bernstein, "And For Making Love in the Washroom of the Adonis" (unpublished), MS. property of I.L., Montreal.
8. I.L. to E.C., telephone interview, 16 April 1985, Montreal.
9. Scott Symons to E.C., interview, 4 May 1983, Toronto.

The Meshugas/415

1. I.L. to Desmond Pacey, 1 April 1970, Desmond Pacey Papers, property of Mary Pacey, Fredericton, New Brunswick.
2. The phonetic spelling of this Yiddish word is *"meshugas."* "Meshugas" means "craze"; there is another word for "lunacy."
3. I.L. to Desmond Pacey, 4 October 1974, Desmond Pacey Papers, property of Mary Pacey, Fredericton, New Brunswick.
4. I.L. to Desmond Pacey, 9 January 1974, Desmond Pacey Papers, property of Mary Pacey, Fredericton, New Brunswick.
5. Susan Musgrave, *Open Letter*, series 3, No. 2 (Fall 1975), p. 102.
6. Leslie Mundwiler, *Canadian Dimension*, 10, No. 7 (March 1975), p. 102.
7. *For My Brother Jesus* (Toronto: McClelland and Stewart, 1976); and *The Covenant* (Toronto: McClelland and Stewart, 1977).
8. Only a quarter of the poems in *For My Brother Jesus* and a third of the poems in *The Covenant* actually deal with religion.
9. Patrick O'Flaherty, *Canadian Forum* (October 1976), p. 30.
10. Robert Fulford, *Toronto Star* (20 March 1976).
11. Michael Hornyansky, "Letters in Canada; 1976," *University of Toronto Quarterly* 46, No. 4 (Summer 1977), p. 368.
12. I.L. to Steven Osterlund (DaGama), 22 April 1976, property of Steven Osterlund DaGama, Akron, Ohio.
13. Professor Sally Zerker to E.C., interview, 28 November 1984, Toronto.
14. Elaine Kahn to Ruth Panofsky, 3 November 1982, Toronto.
15. "An Interview with Joe Rosenblatt" by Marianne Stenbaek-Lafon and Ken Norris, *CV II*, vol. 4, No. 1 (Winter 1979), pp. 32–37.
16. Jack McClelland to Anna Porter, 4 May

1976, McClelland and Stewart Papers, McMaster University Library, Hamilton, Ontario.
17. Jack McClelland to Anna Porter, 24 August 1976, McClelland and Stewart Papers, McMaster University Library, Hamilton, Ontario.
18. Brian Bartlett," Layton Slips Even Further," *Montreal Gazette* (21 January 1978), p. 39.
19. Russell Brown, "Layton's Quarrel," *Canadian Literature*, No. 80 (Spring 1979), pp. 90-92.
20. J.W. Charles, *Canadian Book Review Annual — 1977*, eds. Dean Tudor and Linda Biesenthal (Toronto: Peter Martin Associates, 1978), p. 172.
21. Robert Lecker, *Fiddlehead*, No. 117 (Spring 1978), p. 122.
22. Gary Geddes, "Our Most Erotic Puritan," *Books in Canada*, 6, No. 10 (December 1977), pp. 12-13.
23. Geddes, pp. 12-13.
24. Russell Brown, pp. 90-92.
25. "Review of 'Bravo, Layton'," *The Covenant*, p. 108.
26. *The Tightrope Dancer* (Toronto: McClelland and Stewart, 1978); *Droppings from Heaven* (Toronto: McClelland and Stewart, 1979); *For My Neighbours in Hell* (Toronto: McClelland and Stewart, 1980); *Europe and Other Bad News* (Toronto: McClelland and Stewart, 1981); *The Gucci Bag* (Toronto: McClelland and Stewart, 1983).
27. *Il Freddo Verde Elemento*, introd. Northrop Frye, trans. Amleto Lorenzini (Turin, Italy: Giulio Einaudi, 1974). Introduction reprinted in IL:PC; *Seventy-five Greek Poems 1951-1974* (Athens, Greece: Hermias Publications, 1974); *The Darkening Fire — Selected Poems 1945-1968* (Toronto: McClelland and Stewart Limited, 1975); *The Unwavering Eye — Selected Poems 1969-1975* (Toronto: McClelland and Stewart Limited, 1975); *The Uncollected Poems of Irving Layton 1936-1959*, ed. and afterword by W. David John, preface by Seymour Mayne (Oakville: Mosaic Press, 1976); *The Poems of Irving Layton*, ed. and introd. Eli Mandel (Toronto: McClelland and Stewart Limited, 1977); *Selected Poems*, ed. and preface Wynne Francis (London, England: Charisma, 1977); *The Selected Poems of Irving Layton*, introd. Hugh Kenner (New York: New Directions, 1977); *Il Puma Ammansito*, with Carlo Mattioli, trans. Francesca Valente (Milan, Italy: Edizioni Trentadue, 1978); *There Were No Signs* (Portfolio) with Aligi Sassu (Toronto: Madison Gallery, 1979); *The Love Poems Of Irving Layton* (Toronto: McClelland and Stewart Limited, 1980); *Shadows on the Ground* (Portfolio) (Oakville: Mosaic Press, 1982); *A Wild Peculiar Joy — Selected Poems 1945-1982* (Toronto: McClelland and Stewart Limited, 1982); *Poemas de Amor*, trans. Salustiano Maso (Madrid, Spain: Ediciones Hiperion, S.L., 1983); *A Spider Danced a Cosy Jig and Other Animal Poems*, ed. Elspeth Cameron (Toronto: Stoddart Publishing Co. Limited, 1984).
28. As described in the poem "Droppings From Heaven," *DH*, p. 26. Confirmed as a real incident by I.L. to E.C., 21 February 1985.
29. Al Purdy, "Layton and Lee: A Bulldozer vs. A Subtle Quester," *Toronto Star* (27 October 1979), p. F7.
30. Alexandre L. Amprimoz, *Quarry*, 29, No. 2 (Spring 1980), pp. 77-78.
31. Tecca Crosby, "Old Enough to Know Better," *Books in Canada* (May 1981), pp. 33-34.
32. Jack McClelland to I.L., 19 July 1962, Irving Layton Collection, Concordia University Library, Montreal.
33. *Fifteen Canadian Poets*, ed. Gary Geddes (Toronto: Oxford University Press, 1970).
34. The letter, from Hugh S.D. Paisley of Smiley, Allingham and Brown, Toronto to Don [sic] McClelland, 17 August 1972, said Layton's contracts with McClelland and Stewart specified that *Love Where the Nights Are Long, Selected Poems, The Collected Poems of Irving Layton, Engagements, The Whole Bloody Bird* and *A Red Carpet for the Sun* were to be kept in print "in perpetuum." McClelland and Stewart Papers, McMaster University Library, Hamilton, Ontario.
35. Jack McClelland to I.L., 11 February

1975, Irving Layton Collection, Concordia University Library, Montreal.
36. I.L. to Jack McClelland, 4 August 1980, McClelland and Stewart Papers, McMaster University Library, Hamilton, Ontario.
37. Jack McClelland to Anna Porter, 14 August 1975, McClelland and Stewart Papers, McMaster University Library, Montreal.
38. I.L. to Andy Wainwright, 8 January 1971, Irving Layton Collection, Concordia University Library, Montreal.
39. I.L. to Steven Osterlund (DaGama), 8 February 1974, property of Steven Osterlund DaGama, Akron, Ohio. *Fumigator: An Outsider's View of Irving Layton* (Ohio: Rumple Studios, 1975).

Two Bar Mitzvahs/427

1. Invitation Card, McClelland and Stewart Papers, McMaster University Library, Hamilton, Ontario.
2. Beverley Slopen, "Layton at 65," *Quill and Quire* (1 May 1977), p. 30.
3. Slopen, p. 30.
4. Eli Mandel to E.C., interview, 16 May 1983, Toronto.
5. Aviva Layton to E.C., interview, 30 December 1982, Toronto.
6. Aviva Layton to E.C.
7. I.L. to E.C., interview, 17 February 1982, Toronto.
8. I.L. to Andy Wainwright, 12 August 1977, Irving Layton Collection, Concordia University Library, Montreal.
9. I.L. to Andy Wainwright, 29 October 1977, Irving Layton Collection, Concordia University Library, Montreal.
10. William Goodwin to E.C., interview, 30 August 1982, Montreal.
11. Leonard Cohen to E.C., interview, 16 May 1983, Toronto.
12. I.L. to E.C., interview, 17 February 1982, Toronto.
13. "Night Music," *TD, TP, WPJ* and *ASDCJ*.

All That I Prize/432

1. Zena Cherry, "Poet Layton Marries Movie Publicist," *Globe and Mail* (24 November 1978).
2. Barbara Matthews, "People," *Maclean's* (6 July 1981), p. 27.
3. "Divorce," *Droppings From Heaven* (1979), p. 42. See also Boschka Layton, "Soft Death," *The Prodigal Son* (Oakville: Mosaic Press, 1982), p. 8.
4. Aviva Layton to I.L., undated [ca. Nov. 1978], Irving Layton Collection, Concordia University Library, Montreal.
5. William Goodwin to E.C., interview, 30 August 1982, Montreal.
6. "For Sandra" and "The Chastening Years," *Droppings From Heaven*, pp. 93-94.
7. I.L. to E.C., interview, 10 February 1982, Toronto.
8. As reported by Caterina Ricciardi, *Litterature d'America*, No. 7, Anna II (1981), p. 1.
9. Olivia Ward, *Toronto Star*, (21 July 1978), p. D5.
10. I.L. to Andy Wainwright, 19 December 1979, Irving Layton Collection, Concordia University Library, Montreal.
11. I.L. as quoted by Bill Brownstein, *Montreal Gazette* (14 February 1979), p. 33.
12. I.L. to Andy Wainwright, 20 July 1980, Irving Layton Collection, Concordia University Library, Montreal.
13. "A Day in the Life of Irving Layton," *Weekend Magazine* (25 August 1979), p. 7.
14. Dean Baker, "A Fool's Long Journey" (unpublished diary), January 1981.
15. William Goodwin to E.C., interview, 30 August 1982, Montreal.
16. Dean Baker, "A Fool's Long Journey" (unpublished diary), 6 November and December 1979. Baker claimed that Cohen had dedicated one of his record albums "For Irving Layton, incomparable master of inner languages. God bless him."
17. I.L. to John Brebner, 4 June 1980, property of John Brebner, Gagetown, New Brunswick.
18. Marsha Boulton, ed., "People," *Maclean's* (14 July 1980), p. 39.
19. "Samantha Clara Layton," *Canadian Literature*, No. 90 (Autumn 1981), p. 5. Reprinted in *GB, SG* and *WPJ*.
20. I.L. to Steven Osterlund (DaGama), 2 March 1981, property of Steven

Osterlund DaGama, Akron, Ohio.
21. I.L. to Steven Osterlund (DaGama), 23 April 1981, property of Steven Osterlund DaGama, Akron, Ohio.
22. Alfredo Rizziardi to E.C., interview, 30 March 1985, Selva di Fasano, Italy.
23. Wilfrid-Guy Licari to E.C., interview, 28 March 1985, Selva di Fasano, Italy.
24. Lucinda Vardey to E.C., interview, 22 September 1983, Toronto.
25. I.L. to E.C., interview, 28 September 1982, Oakville, Ontario.
26. Karen Pietkowitz to E.C., interview, 3 October 1982, Toronto.
27. *Man Alive*, CBMT-6 (Sunday, 29 November 1981), Toronto.
28. I.L. to Kim Yang-Shik, 10 August 1974, Irving Layton Collection, Concordia University Library, Montreal. See I.L. "Introduction," *Beyond Time and Space* by Kim Yang-Shik (Seoul: Modern Poetry Press, 1975).
29. I.L. to Steven Osterlund (DaGama), 2 March 1981, property of Steven Osterlund DaGama, Akron, Ohio. The biography is Lawrance Roger Thompson's *Robert Frost*, 3 vols. (New York: Holt, Rinehart & Winston, 1966-1976).
30. I.L. as quoted in the *Montreal Gazette* (13 October 1981).
31. *Montreal Gazette* (27 March 1982), p. E6.
32. I.L. as quoted by Olivia Ward, *Toronto Star* (2 May 1982), p. C-1.
33. "24," *The Gucci Bag* (Oakville: Mosaic Press, 1983), p. 24.
34. Supreme Court Justice George Walsh advised Layton to "stop divulging his legal wrangles to the media" (as reported by Kathy English, *Toronto Star* [27 September 1982], p. 21).
35. Justice John Osler, as quoted by Kirk Makin, *Globe and Mail* (11 May 1982), p. 8.
36. I.L., "An Open Letter to the Prime Minister of Canada [P.E. Trudeau]," undated [1983], Irving Layton Collection, Concordia University Library, Montreal. After describing himself as "a loving and caring father," Layton wrote: "Since you also have had to make a choice between vocations, I now appeal to you for any advice you can spare for someone who has learned there is only one law for the rich and the poor but only the rich can afford it.... What I want to know is this: am I living in the Soviet Union where a writer can be gagged on one pretext or another or am I living in a free democratic state with enforceable rights to protect the individual against self-righteous bullies robed in ermine?"
37. Report by Farrell Cook, *Toronto Star*, 11 May, 1982, p. A8.
38. As reported by Kirk Makin, p. 8.
39. Kirk Makin. p. 8.
40. "$1,500 for *New Selected Poems 1982*; $456.21 for *Droppings from Heaven*; $197.14 for *Love Poems*; $1,790.11 for *Europe and Other Bad News*; $1,500.00 for *Poems of Irving Layton*; $20.57 for *The Tightrope Dancer* and $367.75 for outstanding purchases," 1 March 1982, McClelland and Stewart Papers, McMaster University Library, Hamilton, Ontario.

Anna/447

1. I.L. to Annette Pottier, 29 September 1981, property of Annette Pottier, Montreal.
2. Anna Pottier to E.C., interview, 29 September and 11 November 1982, Oakville, Ontario.
3. Dean Baker, "A Fool's Long Journey" (unpublished diary), Fall, 1983.
4. Anna Pottier to E.C., interview, 29 September and 11 November 1982, Oakville, Ontario.
5. I.L. as quoted by Noel Taylor, *Ottawa Citizen* (5 November 1983), pp. 33, 42.
6. Aviva Layton to E.C., interview, 9 May 1985, Toronto.
7. I.L. to Dean Baker, 21 January 1983, property of Dean Baker, Toronto. In a letter to Harriet, 27 January 1983, I.L. stated: "In a few months from now, I shall be taking [Samantha] to my house for weekends. After that the law permits me to have her for several weeks at a time." A year and a half later, he wrote

to Harriet: "Settled in Montreal, I have neither the desire nor the means to fulfill the role of part-time father. I have resigned myself to the thought that I shall never again see my daughter in this life....But...let me have a picture of [her] every year or so and some news of her progress." (18 August 1984, Irving Layton Collection, Concordia University Library, Montreal.)
8. I.L. to Dean Baker, 13 November and 15 September 1983, property of Dean Baker, Toronto.

Reunions/451

1. Details for this event, taken from Doris Giller, the *Montreal Gazette* (12 March 1983), p. I-1 and Marianne Ackerman, *Globe and Mail* (8 March 1983), p. 12. F.R. Scott died 30 January 1985.
2. Veneranda McGrath, "Love and Loathing: The Role of Woman in Irving Layton's Vision," M.A. thesis (unpublished), Concordia University, 1980. McGrath is planning to publish her thesis (to E.C., interview, 17 February 1982, Montreal).
3. Giller, p. I-1.
4. I.L. as quoted by Ackerman, p. 12.
5. Veneranda McGrath, as quoted by Ackerman, p. 12.
6. I.L. in an opening address to the Foster Poetry Conference, 1963, as reported by Doug Jones to John Glassco, 25 December 1963, M.G. 30, 163, vol. 1, Glassco file, Public Archives of Canada, Ottawa. I.L.'s talk and Jones's commentary are reprinted in *English Poetry in Quebec*, ed. John Glassco (Montreal: McGill University Press, 1965). Boschka Layton died 13 February 1984.
7. E.C. was present on this occasion.
8. "What Ulysses Said to Circe on the Beach of Aeaea," *Erotic Poetry*, ed. William Cole (New York: Random House, 1963), pp. 349–350. Reprinted in *CP 65*, *CPIL*, *GP*, *IB 2*, *LPS* and *RC*.
9. "What Circe Said to Ulysses," unpublished poem, lent to E.C. by Boschka Layton.
10. "Brief to Irving," unpublished poem, lent to E.C. by Boschka Layton. The poems Boschka actually read at Harbourfront were: "Soft Death," "Finishing My Tea in the Sun," "Do the Trees Know It's Election Year?" "Where Is Sylvia?" "Pound," "Afternoon in the Sun," "Pin-prick," "What's For Dinner?" and "Women As Women Have a Problem." All but the last poem, which is unpublished, appear in *The Prodigal Sun* (Oakville: Mosaic Press, 1982).
11. E.C. was present on this occasion.

Bibliography

I. MANUSCRIPT AND PRIMARY MATERIAL COLLECTIONS CONTAINING MATERIAL BY AND/OR ABOUT LAYTON

Archives of Ontario, Toronto
Canadian Jewish Congress, National Archives, Montreal
Concordia University, Irving Layton Collection, Montreal
Jewish Public Library, Montreal
McGill University Archives, Montreal
McMaster University Library, Hamilton
Public Archives of Canada, Ottawa
Queen's University Archives, Kingston
Simon Fraser University, Special Collections, Burnaby
University of Calgary, Special Collections, Calgary
University of Connecticut Archives, Storrs, Connecticut
University of New Brunswick Archives and Special Collections, Fredericton
University of Saskatchewan Archives, Saskatoon
University of Texas, Humanities Research Center, Austin, Texas
University of Toronto, Thomas Fisher Rare Book Library, Toronto
Washington University, Special Collections, St. Louis, Missouri
York University Archives, Toronto

II. BOOKS BY LAYTON

Here and Now. Montreal: First Statement Press, 1945.
Now is the Place. Montreal: First Statement Press, 1948.
The Black Huntsmen. Montreal: Author, 1951.
Cerberus. With Louis Dudek and Raymond Souster. Toronto: Contact Press, 1952.
Love the Conqueror Worm. Toronto: Contact Press, 1953.
In the Midst of My Fever. Palma de Mallorca, Spain: Divers Press, 1954.
The Long Pea-Shooter. Montreal: Laocoon Press, 1954.
The Blue Propeller. Toronto: Contact Press, 1955.
The Blue Propeller. Another edition, with nine additional poems. Toronto: Contact Press, 1955. (A copy is housed at MU, Special Collections.)
The Cold Green Element. Toronto: Contact Press, 1955.
The Bull Calf and Other Poems. Toronto: Contact Press, 1956.
The Improved Binoculars. Introduction by William Carlos Williams. Highlands, North Carolina: Jonathan Williams, 1956. (Introduction reprinted in IL:PC.)
The Improved Binoculars. Second edition, with thirty additional poems. Highlands, North Carolina: Jonathan Williams, 1956.
Music on a Kazoo. Toronto: Contact Press, 1956.
A Laughter in the Mind. Highlands, North Carolina: Jonathan Williams, 1958.
A Laughter in the Mind. Second edition, with twenty additional poems. Montreal: Editions D'Orphée, 1959.

A Red Carpet for the Sun. Highlands, North Carolina: Jonathan Williams, 1959.
A Red Carpet for the Sun. Toronto: McClelland and Stewart Limited, 1959.
The Swinging Flesh. Toronto: McClelland and Stewart Limited, 1961.
A Hasty Selection From Irving Layton's Sixteen Volumes of Poetry. Canton, New York, 1962. (Photocopy) (The original is housed at Brown University Library, Providence, Rhode Island.)
Balls for a One-Armed Juggler. Toronto: McClelland and Stewart Limited, 1963.
The Laughing Rooster. Toronto: McClelland and Stewart Limited, 1964.
Collected Poems. Toronto: McClelland and Stewart Limited, 1965.
Periods of the Moon. Toronto: McClelland and Stewart Limited, 1967.
The Shattered Plinths. Toronto: McClelland and Stewart Limited, 1968.
Selected Poems. Edited with a preface by Wynne Francis. Toronto: McClelland and Stewart Limited, 1969.
The Whole Bloody Bird. Toronto: McClelland and Stewart Limited, 1969.
The Collected Poems of Irving Layton. Toronto: McClelland and Stewart Limited, 1971.
Nail Polish. Toronto: McClelland and Stewart Limited, 1971.
Engagements — The Prose of Irving Layton. Edited by Seymour Mayne. Toronto: McClelland and Stewart Limited, 1972.
Lovers and Lesser Men. Toronto: McClelland and Stewart Limited, 1973.
Il Freddo Verde Elemento. Introduction by Northrop Frye, translated by Amleto Lorenzini. Turin, Italy: Giulio Einaudi, 1974. (Introduction reprinted in IL:PC.)
Lovers and Lesser Men. Second printing. Toronto: McClelland and Stewart Limited, 1974.
The Pole-vaulter. Toronto: McClelland and Stewart Limited, 1974.
Seventy-five Greek Poems 1951–1974. Athens, Greece: Hermia Publications, 1974.
The Darkening Fire — Selected Poems 1945–1968. Toronto: McClelland and Stewart Limited, 1975.
The Unwavering Eye — Selected Poems 1969–1975. Toronto: McClelland and Stewart Limited, 1975.
For My Brother Jesus. Toronto: McClelland and Stewart Limited, 1976.
The Uncollected Poems of Irving Layton 1936–1959. Edited with an afterword by W. David John, preface by Seymour Mayne. Oakville: Mosaic Press, 1976.
The Covenant. Toronto: McClelland and Stewart Limited, 1977.
The Poems of Irving Layton. Edited with an introduction by Eli Mandel. Toronto: McClelland and Stewart Limited, 1977.
Selected Poems. Edited with a preface by Wynne Francis. London, England: Charisma, 1977.
The Selected Poems of Irving Layton. Introduction by Hugh Kenner. New York, New York: New Directions, 1977.
Il Puma Ammansito. With Carlo Mattioli, translated by Francesca Valente. Milan, Italy: Edizioni Trentadue, 1978.
Irving Layton: The Poet and his Critics. Edited with an introduction by Seymour Mayne. Toronto: McGraw-Hill Ryerson Limited, 1978.
Taking Sides: The Collected Social and Political Writings. Edited with an introduction by Howard Aster. Oakville: Mosaic Press, 1978.
The Tightrope Dancer. Toronto: McClelland and Stewart Limited, 1978.
Droppings From Heaven. Toronto: McClelland and Stewart Limited, 1979.
The Tamed Puma. Toronto: Virgo Press, 1979.
There Were No Signs. With Aligi Sassu. Toronto: Madison Gallery, 1979. (Portfolio.)
An Unlikely Affair: The Irving Layton — Dorothy Rath Correspondence. Introduction by Adrienne Clarkson. Oakville: Mosaic Press, 1980.
For My Neighbours in Hell. Oakville: Mosaic Press, 1980.

The Love Poems of Irving Layton. Toronto: McClelland and Stewart Limited, 1980.
Europe and Other Bad News. Toronto: McClelland and Stewart Limited, 1981.
Shadows on the Ground. Oakville: Mosaic Press, 1982. (Portfolio.)
A Wild Peculiar Joy — Selected Poems 1945–1982. Toronto: McClelland and Stewart Limited, 1982.
The Gucci Bag. Oakville: Mosaic Press, 1983.
Poemas de Amor. Translated by Salustiano Maso. Madrid, Spain: Ediciones Hiperion, 1983.
A Spider Danced a Cosy Jig. Edited by Elspeth Cameron. Toronto: Stoddart Publishing Co. Limited, 1984.
Waiting for the Messiah: Reflections on My Early Days. Toronto: McClelland and Stewart Limited, 1985.

Index

Achtman, Helen 230
Acorn, Milton ("The Poets") 287, 325, 334, 365, 370, 404
Aikman (Sutherland), Audrey 166-167, 169-170, 174
Alexandra Street School 32, 41, 127
Allen, Ralph 290
Allen, Stan 95, 106-107
Allen, Ted 281
Alvarine (Alveiroff), Alex 77
Amber Savage (with Harriet Layton) 435
Amnesty International Conference 440
Anderson, Patrick ("Montreal Journal," *A Tent in April*) 136, 156-157, 172-173, 178, 186, 205-206, 251, 254
Anka, Paul ("Diana") 302
Apollinaire, Guillaume 199
Arnold, Matthew ("Culture and Anarchy") 211
Arnopoulos, Sheila 452
Ash, Nima 390-393, 396
Aster, Howard 340, 458
Aster, Sydney 365
Atlantic Monthly 224
Atwood, Margaret (*The Circle Game*) 331, 370-372, 403, 406, 428, 441
Auden, W.H. 121, 148, 180, 209
Auschwitz 347, 416-417, 423
Australia 354, 389, 393, 425
Avison, Margaret 151-152, 198
Babel, Isaac 346-347
Bailey, A.G. 198, 321-322
Baker, Dean ("A Fool's Long Journey") 436-437, 448, 450
Balls for a One-Armed Juggler 334-335, 336, 354, 401
Baron Byng High School 42, 43-46, 53, 57, 59, 61-63, 67, 77-78
Bassani, Giorgio (*The Garden of the Finzi-Continis*) 437
Baudelaire, Charles 362
Beach, Sylvia 306
Beaudouin, Sandra 435
Bellow, Saul 402
Benedek, Laslo 340

Benjamin, Miss 34
Bennett, Joy 424
Beny, Roloff 302
Bernstein, Jack 410, 433, 436
Berton, Pierre 302, 418-419
Bethune, Norman 317
Beutel, Benjamin 299-300, 321
Bevan, Alan 365
Birney, Earle (*November Walk Near False Creek Mouth*) 173, 193-195, 198, 201, 222, 243, 251, 253, 322-324, 335, 357, 359, 367, 369
Bishop's University 385
Bissell, Claude 367
bissett, bill 370
Blackburn, Paul 242
The Black Huntsmen 191-195, 204, 206, 253, 255
Black Mountain College 199, 219, 246
Black Mountain Review 219, 251
Blake, William 125, 148, 229, 243, 292, 408
The Blasted Pine: An Anthology of Canadian Satire (ed. F.R. Scott and A.J.M. Smith) 244, 255
The Blue Propeller 230, 246, 268
The Book of Canadian Poetry (ed. A.J.M. Smith) 175-177, 186, 243, 251
A Book of Canadian Short Stories (ed. Desmond Pacey) 313
Booth, Louella 242
Borgford, H.I.S. (Ingi) 106
Bowering, George 363, 370
Boxer, Avi 205, 298, 363
Brewster, Elizabeth 252
Brittain, Miller 137
Brittain, W.H. 77, 82, 105, 107
Bronk, William 242
Browder, Earl (*The Democratic Front for Jobs, Security, Democracy and Peace*) 93, 102
Brown, E.K. ("On Candian Poetry") 152, 293
Brunt, H.D. 97
Buck, Tim (*Steps to Power*) 66, 82, 160, 300
Bukharin, Nickolai (*ABC of Communism*) 62
The Bull Calf and Other Poems 246-247
Bush, Jack 302

Bryon, Lord George Gordon 148, 284, 294, 315, 319, 325, 412
Caiserman, H.M. 105-106
Caiserman, Nina 71, 89, 105
Caiserman, Ghitta 71
Call, Frank Oliver *(Acanthus and Wild Grape)* 124-125
Callaghan, Barry 380, 396
Callaghan, Morley 281, 306
Callwood, June ("The Lusty Laureate From the Slums") 337
Camp Petawawa 133, 136, 139, 142
Campbell, Roy 152, 205
Canada Council 284, 297, 302-303, 305, 314, 323, 367, 374, 378, 428-429
Canada Foundation Award 281, 288, 322
Canadian Author and Bookman (Canadian Bookman) 124-125, 152
Canadian Authors' Association (CAA) 124, 129
Canadian Broadcasting Corporation (CBC) 221, 244, 249, 252-253, 280, 282, 293, 302, 304, 313-314, 367, 388
Canadian Conference of the Arts (1961) 367
Canadian Communist Party 58, 82, 107-108
Canadian Forum 118, 125, 151, 176, 182, 193, 253, 291, 311, 317, 323, 327, 365
Canadian Jewish Chronicle 386
Canadian Jewish Congress 106-107, 344
Canadian Labour Defense League 70
Canadian Mercury 129
Canadian Poems: 1850–1952 202, 242-243
Canadian Poetry Magazine 193
The Canadian Review 411
Canadian Short Stories (ed. Robert Weaver) 313
Cantril, Hadley *(Soviet Leaders and Mastery Over Man)* 315
Cape, Jonathan 401-402
Carleton University 371
Carman, Bliss ("Vestigia") 83, 121, 125-126
Castro, Fidel 317-318
Cataract 341, 365-366
Cat on a Hot Tin Roof 345
Catullus, Gaius Valerius 325
Cerberus 199-202, 207, 214, 218, 366
Chatterton, Thomas 454
Cherry, Zena 432
CIV/n 204-206, 215, 218, 272, 282, 451-452
Clift, Dominique ("Don Clift") 452
Cogswell, Fred 249, 259, 261, 291, 355-356
Cohen, Benjamin 27, 41, 51-52
Cohen, Leonard *(The Favorite Game, Flowers for Hitler, A Spice Box of Earth)* 205, 276-277, 280, 282, 284, 289, 301, 303, 313, 315, 319, 321, 330, 334, 359, 361-362, 364, 366-371, 373, 383, 395, 402-404, 430, 437, 453
Cohen, Nathan 228, 281
The Cold Green Element 240, 246, 421
Cole, Desmond 222
Coleman, Victor 363, 370
Coleridge, Samuel Taylor ("Christabel") 273, 325
Collected Poems (1965) 358
Collected Poems (1971) 399
Collins, Aileen 204, 228, 268
Colombo, John Robert 370
Combustion 366
Commentary 251, 417
Compton, Neil 241, 276
Concordia University (Sir George Williams University and Loyola College) 435
Contact 198-200
Contemporary Verse 182
Co-operative Commonwealth Federation (CCF) 95-96, 99-100, 105-107, 158, 354, 455
Corman, Cid 196-197, 199, 204-208, 214-215, 217, 221-222, 226, 241-243, 246, 273, 357, 366
Coughtree, Graham 432
The Covenant ("Bravo, Layton") 417, 420-421
Crawley, Alan 198
Creeley, Robert ("For W.C.W.") 196, 199, 204-205, 207-212, 214-219, 222-224, 226-228, 230, 234, 236, 240-243, 246, 256, 264, 266, 272, 288, 305, 322, 327, 357, 363, 366
Crowe, Harry 419
The Croydon Apartments (Montreal) 263, 433, 435
Culture 287
Cumas, Steve 245
cummings, e.e. 80, 180, 383
Currie, Bob 272-273
Cusinière, Calin 87-91
Cusinière, Mme. (Mouchkette) 87-91
Cusinière, Mimi 87-91
DaGama, Steven Osterlund *(Fumigator)* 398, 425, 437, 442
Dalhousie University 107
Daniells, Roy 185, 198, 321-324
Dardick, Simon 451
The Darkening Fire 399, 421
Davey, Frank 198-199, 363, 365

Davies, Ben 301
Davis, William 428
Death of a Salesman 340
de la Roche, Mazo 239
DeLeon, Daniel 94
Delta 287, 366
Donleavy, J.P. *(The Ginger Man)* 324, 341
Donne, John 148, 346, 359
Don Quixote 146, 288, 292
Dostoevsky, Fyodor 355
Dracula 5
Dranoff, Linda 444
Droppings From Heaven 421-422
Dudek, Louis (*Litererature and the Press*, "En Mexico," "An Air by Sammartini") 120-123, 137, 139, 143, 147, 150, 162, 171-173, 175, 177, 180, 186, 196-200, 202-205, 207, 218, 222-223, 225, 228, 242, 251, 254, 259, 261, 272-273, 287-288, 293, 321, 323, 333, 356, 365-368, 416, 451-452
Dudek, Stephanie 298
Dulles, John Foster 354
Dupee, F.W. 152, 250
Dylan, Bob 368
Edel, Leon 128, 306
Edelstein, George 133-134
Edinborough, Arnold 290
Eigner, Larry 242
Eisen (Eisenberg), Rochel 85-86, 110-115, 117, 119
Eliot, T.S. ("The Hollow Men," *The Love Song of J. Alfred Prufrock, The Waste Land*) 123, 124, 148-149, 176, 179, 209, 233, 243, 270, 291, 306, 395, 452
Engagements 399
Engel, Marian 404
Europe and Other Bad News 421, 423, 459
Everson, Ronald 282-283
Evidence 365
Failt-Ye Times 74, 80-85, 87, 97
Falardeau, Jean-Charles 367
Faulkner, William 322
Fawzia 319
Fearing, Kenneth 180
Fiddlehead 249, 259, 261, 291, 311, 339, 355, 365
Fields, Harvey Joseph 432
Fifteen Canadian Poets (ed. Gary Geddes) 424
"Fighting Words" (CBC) 280-281, 309
Files, Harold 130
Finch, Robert *(Poems, Acis in Oxford)* 121, 123, 171-176, 187, 198, 321, 364

Finnegan, Joan 367
Firestone, Marjorie 71
First Statement 136, 141, 143, 145-149, 158, 166, 173-175, 177, 206, 313
Fletcher's Field 18, 154, 274
The Forge 114-119, 155
For My Brother Jesus 417, 419
For My Neighbours in Hell 421, 425
Forsey, Eugene 95, 96, 99-100, 103, 129, 142
France 375, 379-381, 401, 428
Francis, Wynne ("Montreal Poets of the Forties") 334, 424
Fraser, Blair 355
Fraser, G.S. *(Vision and Rhetoric)* 324
Fraser, Sylvia 427-428
Frazer, Sir James 123
Il Freddo Verde Elemento (The Cold Green Element) 395, 421
Freedman (Dawe), Joyce 337-339
Friedan, Betty 405
French, William 444
Freud, Sigmund 179, 248, 270, 423
Frisch, Anthony 252
Frost, Robert 80, 291, 402, 407, 442-443
Frye, Northrop *(Anatomy of Criticism)* 129, 177, 201-202, 243-244, 249-250, 252-255, 291, 293, 296, 321-322, 348, 364, 367, 370, 395, 397, 401
Fulford, Robert 418
Fuller, Edward *(Man in Modern Fiction)* 324
Galbraith, John Kenneth 281
Gatenby, Greg 442
Gearing, Orlando 206
Geddes, Gary 420
Germany 98, 386
Gibbon, J.M. 124
Ginzberg, Alan 402
Glassco, John (Buffy) 334
Globe and Mail 201, 248, 348, 367, 387, 408, 432, 443
Gnarowski, Michael 302
Godbout, Jacques 370
Goldberg, Strul 27, 32, 41, 42, 51, 53, 94, 150
Goldberg (Goodwin), Vehlvel or William (Bill) 54, 59, 80, 110, 170, 226, 286, 346, 353, 430, 434-436
Goldfaden, Avram 12
Gotlieb, Phyllis 359, 369
Gould, Glenn 301
Gouzenko, Igor 156
Governor-General's Awards 168, 171-173, 175, 244, 280-281, 295, 321, 364, 370,

404, 419, 453
Graham, Gwethalyn *(Earth and High Heaven)* 168
Grant, Douglas 296
Greece 352, 389, 395-397, 412-413, 421-424, 428-431, 447
The Gucci Bag 421, 438-439, 444
Gulag 416-417, 423
Gustafson, Ralph 174, 198, 251, 386
Hadawi, Sami 419
Hambleton, Ronald 150, 178
Hamlet 12, 325, 396
Harvey, John Paul 237
Hébert, Anne 370
Hellman, Robert 242
Hemingway, Ernest 306, 322, 325
Hénault, Giles 367
Henty, G.A. 34
Here and Now 147-153, 182, 185, 250
Hershorn, Kalman (Zisa) 50, 65, 169
Herzliah Junior High School 154, 161-166, 188-191, 245, 264, 274, 278, 280, 299-300, 308-309, 321, 333, 340, 376
Hine, Daryl 282
Hitler, Adolf 105, 135, 143, 376, 386, 422
Homer *(The Iliad, The Odyssey)* 257
Hooten, Harry 259, 261
Horn's Cafeteria 61-64, 79, 88, 104
Hornyansky, Michael 418
Housman, A.E. ("To a Shropshire Lad") 326
Hugo, Victor 362
The Improved Binoculars ("Tibby" or "Binox") 246-249, 268, 270-271, 280-282, 366
In the Midst of My Fever 218, 240, 242-245, 250
India 374, 389, 401
Ireland 389-393
Isaiah 181, 324
Israel 240, 375, 387-388, 428-429
Italy 98, 240, 284, 307, 389, 395, 423, 428, 437-438, 442, 450
James, Cyril 249
Jeffers, Robinson 402
Jesus 5, 8, 27, 181, 247, 291, 396, 415-419
Jewish Colonisation Association 14
Jewish People's Library (Jewish Public Library) 70, 85, 108, 110-111, 117, 155, 161, 166, 188, 190-191, 221, 280, 343, 418
J.I. Segal Fund for Jewish Culture 418
Johnson, President Lyndon B. 355, 380
Johnston, George ("The Gentle Poet") 245, 370
Jonas, George 370

Jones, Douglas 205, 222, 236
Jones, Ernest *(The Life and Work of Sigmund Freud)* 270
Joyce, James *(The Dubliners)* 128, 242-243, 306, 325
Kafka, Franz 346
Kahn, Elaine 419
Katz, Carl 309-310
Katz, Gertie 309-311
Kearns, Lionel 370
Keats, John 54, 125, 148, 326-327, 454
Keewaydin Poetry Festival 236-237, 268
Kennedy, Jacqueline 315-319, 367
Kennedy, John F. 315-319
Kennedy, Leo 121, 123, 129, 452
Kenner, Hugh 243, 281, 300, 357
Kenyon Review 224
Kingstone, Ed 439
Klein, A.M. ("The Seventh Scroll") 23-25, 65, 68, 78, 98, 121, 123, 144, 148, 168, 174, 198, 206, 230, 245, 255, 357, 416, 453
Klinck, Carl 251
Knister, Raymond 125
Koestler, Arthur 157, 315
Korea 442-443
Krushchev 300
Labor Progressive Party (LPP) 58, 156-158, 160
La Dolce Vita (Frederico Fellini) 325
Lampman, Archibald ("Reality") 126
Laski, Harold 93, 114-117, 151, 155-160, 187, 189-190
Lasnier, Rina 370
Latham, Allan 129
Lattimer, J.E. 105
A Laughter in the Mind 289
The Laughing Rooster ("Poems in Bad Taste," "The Indelicate Touch") 211, 353-354, 356, 358-360
Laurence, Margaret 404, 446
Lawrence, D.H. *(Lady Chatterley's Lover)* 231, 233, 242, 286-287, 299, 319-320, 332
Lawrence, Frieda 256
Layton (Cantor), Aviva *(Nobody's Daughter,* "Steely Eye to Steely Eye") 259-269, 273, 276-277, 280-282, 284-286, 289, 296-301, 305-309, 312-313, 317, 319-320, 329, 338-339, 343, 345-347, 349, 351-355, 373-375, 378-380, 382, 384-385, 389-390, 393-396, 399, 406, 412-414, 428-430, 432-435, 437, 443-444, 450, 458, 460-461
Layton, David (Peter) Herschel 351-354,

374-375, 378, 380, 384, 389-390, 428-429, 432, 434
Layton (Sutherland), Elizabeth (Betty/Boschka) (*A Prodigal Sun*, "Brief to Irving," "What Circe Said to Ulysses") 136-147, 156, 166-170, 187, 189-191, 205-206, 211, 220, 224-227, 229, 231, 234, 236-237, 240-241, 245, 255-257, 260, 262-263, 266-269, 271, 273, 275, 276-277, 279-280, 283, 286, 293, 297-298, 300, 334, 341, 352-353, 379-380, 383, 389, 399, 428, 430, 432-434, 457-461
Layton (Lynch), Faye 89, 101-111, 121, 138, 141-143, 147, 167-168, 170, 297, 321
Layton (Bernstein), Harriet (Gypsy Jo) ("Musical Interlude") 410-414, 428, 430, 432-441, 444-446
Layton, Maxwell Rubin 169-170, 189, 220, 225, 232-233, 255-257, 269, 278-279, 283, 296-298, 300-301, 312, 315, 334, 351-353, 383, 432, 440-442, 457, 460-461
Layton (Seabird), Naomi (Sissyboo) Parker 189, 211, 255-257, 263, 278-279, 283, 297-298, 351-353, 380, 383, 389, 432
Layton, Samantha Clara 437-439, 443-446
Layton, Stephanie 441-442, 457, 460
Lazarovitch, Abraham (Avram) 11-14, 18, 20, 31-32, 36-37, 58, 102, 357
Lazarovitch, Dora 1, 3, 11, 27, 31, 42, 47, 53, 55, 94, 275-276
Lazarovitch, Esther 2, 11, 27, 51, 53, 55, 101, 275
Lazarovitch, Gazella (Gertie) 2, 10-14, 16, 18, 20, 27, 32, 36, 51-55, 78, 94
Lazarovitch (Latch), Harry 1, 3, 11, 13, 28, 35, 106, 249
Lazarovitch (Latch), Hyman 2-3, 11, 22, 26-27, 29, 33, 92-94, 101, 103, 106, 109, 131, 133, 249
Lazarovitch, Klara or Clara (Keine) 1-2, 10-13, 19, 21-22, 26, 29, 31, 35-42, 47-48, 50-55, 73, 84-86, 88, 102, 116-117, 143, 151, 159, 169-170, 181, 195, 213-214, 225, 228, 274-276, 294-295, 372
Lazarovitch (Latch), Larry (Oscar) 1-3, 11, 28-29, 35, 75, 86, 93, 106, 110, 220
Lazarovitch (Leizer), Moses (Moishe) 2-3, 7, 9-13, 18-28, 34-40, 50, 57, 116-117, 159, 357
Leacock, Stephen 421
Lederer, Williams (*The Ugly American*) 301
Lee, Dennis 370
Léger, Jules 428

Lenin, Vladimir I. 63, 68, 69, 89, 156, 176
Leonard, Benny 75
Le Pan, Douglas (*The Colour As Naked*) 251, 254
Levertov, Denise 199, 363
Levine, Norman 233, 240, 245
Lewis, David 62, 68, 73, 78, 81, 99, 106, 230
Licari, Wilfrid-Guy 438
Literary History of Canada (ed. Carl F. Klinck) 291
The Literary Review 355
Livesay, Dorothy 125, 173, 198
The Long Pea-Shooter 214, 222-223, 230, 240-241, 243-245, 250, 252, 254-255, 281, 376
Lorenzini, Amletto 395
Love Poems of Irving Layton 421, 432, 435
Love the Conqueror Worm 207-209, 221, 252-253, 356
Love Where the Nights are Long (ed. Irving Layton) 332, 334-335
Lovers and Lesser Men 397, 403
Lowenfels, Walter 301
Lust, Peter 386
Macbeth 287
Macdonald College 74-88, 95-105, 107, 142, 151, 220, 317, 388
Macdonald, Jock 302
MacEwen, Gwendolyn 365, 370
Machiavelli 104, 449
MacLean's 52, 332, 355, 386, 432, 439
MacLennan, Hugh (*The Watch That Ends the Night*) 198, 296-297
MacNeice, Louis 222
Macpherson, Jay (*The Boatman*) 270, 281, 331, 334, 364, 367, 370
Madras, Anne 63, 73
Mailer, Norman 325, 402
Mandel, Eli 205, 218, 222, 249, 280, 323, 382, 395, 428
Mandelshtam, Osip 417
Manolescu 12
Margolian, Samuel 107
Marlowe, Christopher 395
Marquez, Gabriel Garcia 446
Marriott, Anne 173, 193, 198, 253
Marsh, Leonard C. (*Canadians In and Out of Work*) 96, 130
Marshall, John 290
Marx, Karl 57, 68, 83, 89, 93-94, 96, 103, 115, 142, 148, 155-156, 158-160, 176, 179, 185-186, 197, 207, 245, 340, 354, 455

Mason, Mason Jordan 242
Massey *Report* 201, 301-302
Massey Royal Commission on National Development in the Arts, Letters, and Sciences 201, 301
Massey, Vincent 249
Mayne, Seymour 311, 415, 424, 452
McClelland and Stewart 199, 244, 248, 281, 293, 313, 328, 422, 425, 432, 446
McClelland, Jack 202, 248, 279, 289-291, 302, 313, 319, 327, 331-332, 335, 347, 358-360, 365, 369, 371, 375, 395, 399-402, 419-420, 424-425, 428
McFadden, David 365
McGill Daily 97-104, 127-128, 143, 150, 207
McGill Fortnightly Review 128-129
McGilliad 65
McGill University 17, 77, 82, 96-104, 114-120, 127-130, 134, 136, 138, 155, 158, 160-161, 163, 176, 181, 187-190, 197-198, 205, 221, 242, 249, 256, 304, 340, 350, 371, 382, 451-452
McGrath, Veneranda 451-452
McKeough, Darcy 428
McKnight, Linda 425
Mephisto 440
Messiah 3, 16, 42, 44, 59, 288, 291, 324, 336
Metcalfe, Paul 264
Mexico 389, 401, 407
Middle East Focus 419
Millett, Kate *(Sexual Politics)* 405
Miller, Henry 242
Mills, C. Wright *(The Sociological Imagination)* 324
Mills, John 264-266, 284
Milton, John 84
Moment 365
Monks, Bevan 85
Montreal Gazette 90, 443
Montreal Star 326
Moore, Brian 404
Moore, Marianne 180
Moravia, Alberto 437
Morocco 413-414, 435
Mosaic Press 340, 425, 458
Moscovitch, Henry *(The Serpent Ink, The Laughing Storm)* 245, 280, 313, 334, 340-342
Motion 365
Mountain 365
Muhlstock, Saul 32
Murray's 311, 336-338, 341, 377
Musgrave, Susan 417

Music on a Kazoo ("the bloody i") 246
Musset, Alfred 350
Nail Polish 388, 397, 399
The Nation 45, 54, 152, 250, 254
National Film Board (NFB) 359, 369-370
Neiss, Alvin 162
New Democratic Party (NDP) 354
New Directions Annual 251
New Mexico Quarterly 224
The New Oxford Book of Canadian Verse (ed. Margaret Atwood) 331, 452
New Provinces 121-122, 124, 139, 171, 175
New Republic 45, 54, 81, 256
The New Romans (ed. Al Purdy) 387
New Wave Canada: The Explosion in New Canadian Poetry (ed. Raymond Souster) 364
Newlove, John 370
Niagara-on-the-Lake, Canada 436, 448
Nietzsche, Frederich *(The Joyful Wisdom)* 159, 229, 231, 237, 245, 260-261, 286-287, 291-292, 294, 299, 340
The Night Porter 345
Nixon, Richard 355
Nobel Prize for literature 293, 335, 388, 394-395, 441-443, 446, 450
Nobody's Daughter 260-262, 345, 347, 443
Norris, Ken 205
Northern Review 174, 181-184, 198, 205, 313, 365
Now is the Place 181, 183-189, 192
Nowlan, Alden 370
October Crisis 1970 387
O'Hearne, Walter ("To A Slopshire Lad") 326
Olson, Charles ("Projective Verse," "These Days") 196, 199-200, 205, 207-208, 210, 214-217, 219, 241, 244, 264, 272, 327, 363, 366
Ondaatje, Michael 370
Order of Canada 453
Origin 196-197, 199, 204, 207, 251, 253, 313
Osler, John 445-446
Othello 396
Other Canadians 175, 177, 186, 189, 202, 207, 365
Ovid 383
Owen, Don (NFB) 369
Pacey, Desmond *(Ten Canadian Poets)* 222, 240, 244, 248-255, 278-280, 282-283, 285-294, 296, 298-304, 310, 313, 315, 318, 320, 322-325, 334-335, 341, 348-350, 355-356, 358-360, 371, 373-375, 379, 383, 385, 387-388, 405, 407, 415, 417

Pacey, Mary 320
Page, P.K. *(The Metal and the Flower)* 150, 172-174, 178, 186, 198, 206, 244, 254
Paradis, Suzanne 370
Partisan Review 197
Pasternak, Boris *(Safe Conduct)* 324-325, 417
Pearson, Alan 311, 363
Periods of the Moon 358
Philosophy 256
Pierce, Lorne 247-248, 290
Pietkiewicz, Karen 439-442
Plato *(Phaedo, Laws, The Republic, The Statesman, Apology)* 54, 221, 315, 329, 362
Plays by Layton: "The Ambassador" (with Louis Dudek) 228; "Lights on the Black Water" (with Leonard Cohen) 313-314; "A Man Was Killed" (with Leonard Cohen) 313-314; "The Old and Quiet Ones" (with Louis Dudek) 228; "Up With Nothing" ("Enough of Fallen Leaves") (with Leonard Cohen) 313-314
Poemas de Amor (Love Poems) 421
Poems For 27 cents 325
Poems of Irving Layton 421
Poetry by Layton: "Address to the Undernourished" 231; "Afternoon of a Coupon Clipper" 253, 358; "Against This Death" 233; "Ah Rats!!! (A Political Extravaganza of the 30's)" 207; "And Sendeth Milk" 84; "The Annunciation" 437; "Anti-Romantic" 261; "The Ants" 236; "aphs" 397-398, 405; "At the Iglesia de Sacromonte" 355; "Auspex" 195, 253; "Author, with a Pipe in His Mouth" 236; "Autumn Lines for My Son" 267; "Bacchanal" 228, 234; "Beauty" 356; "Because My Calling Is Such" 286; "Beneath the Bridge" 118; "Berry Picking" 267, 372; "Beutel's Name is Inscribed for Eternal Life" 300; "Birds at Daybreak" 223; "The Birth of Tragedy" 237-238, 372; "A Bonnet for Bessie" 278; "The Bull Calf" 269, 367, 372; "Butchevo, the Critic" 193; "By Ecstasies Perplexed" 268-269; "Cain" 269, 300; "The Canadian Epic" 423; "Canadian Skiers" 241; "Cat Dying in Autumn" 309; "Cemetery in August" 252; "Church Parade" 191; "The Cold Green Element" 223, 372; "Composition in Late Spring" 234; "Day" 144; "The Day Aviva Came to Paris" 284-285; "Death of Moishe Lazarovitch" 252; "Debacle" 118, 140; "De Bullion Street" 149, 152, 180, 191-192, 195, 247-248, 251, 255; "Divorce" 433; "Drill Shed" 139-141, 148, 195, 251, 253; "The Eagle" 182; "Earth Goddess" ("Elegy for Marilyn Monroe") 268; "Economy, Please, Toronto" 398; "Elan" 195; "Elephant" 397; "Encounter" 355; "End of the Summer" 380-381; "English for Immigrants" 109; "Enigma" 234-235, 268; "Epitaph for a Wit" 148; "The Epitaph for an Ugly Servitor" 223; "Eros Where the Rents Aren't High" 225; "Esthetique" 263; "The Excessively Quiet Groves" 201; "Family Portrait" 333; "Fiat Lux" 270; "The Fictive Eye" 327; "Firecrackers" 269; "For an Older Poet in Despair with the Times" 233; "For Francesca" 395; "For Louise, Age 17" 223; "For Mao Tse-Tung: A Meditation on Flies and Kings" 278-279; "For My Green Old Age" 355; "For My Incomparable Gypsy" ("For the Incomparable Gypsy") 411; "For Priscilla" 229-230; "For the Girl with Wide-Apart Eyes" 379; "From a Lawnchair" 269; "From Colony to Nation" 244, 333; "Gents Furnishings" 192; "The Gifts" 327; "Golfers" 300; "Good-Bye Bahai" 200-201; "Gothic Landscape" 195-251; "The Greeks Had a Word for It" 234; "How Domestic Happiness Is Achieved" 269; "How Poems Get Written" 231; "Human Being" 236; "Hymn to the Republic" 387; "Icarus" 360; "I Don't Like It" 403; "If You Can't Scream" 261; "Impotence" 233; 'Individualist" 266; "In the Midst of My Fever" 227; "Jewish Cantata" 299; "Jewish Main Street" 251; "A Jewish Rabbi" ("My Father") 150; "Karl Marx" 182, 292; "Keewaydin Poetry Festival" 223; "Keine Lazarovitch 1870-1959" 295, 372; "Lesbia" 268; "Letter from a Straw Man" 257, 268; "Letter to Raymond Souster" 201; "Librarian at Asheville" 327; "Lines on Myself" 235; "Lines on the Massey Commission" 201, 301; "Little David" 201; "The Longest Journey" 266-267; "Look, the Lambs Are All Around Us!" 231; "The Love Dream of W.P. Turner" 270; "Love Is an

Index 515

Irrefutable Fire" 278; "Love's Diffidence" 232; "Marie" 234, 255; "Marius" 234; "Maxie" 232; "May Day Orators" 230; "Medley for Our Times" 97, 103; "Metzinger: Girl with a Bird" 236, 266; "Mexico As Seen by Looie the Lip" ("Mexico As Seen by the Reverent Dudek") 287; "Mildred" 230; "Misunderstanding" 234; "The Modern Poet" 148, 191; "Mont Rolland" 195, 251, 253; "Moral with a Story" 338; "Mortuary" 148; "The Mosquito" 269; "Mother, This Is Spring" 148, 151, 358; "Mr. Beutel Lays a Cornerstone" 299-300; "Mr. Ther-Apis" 234; "Mrs. Fornheim, Refugee" 195, 251, 253; "My Favourite Colour's Green" 230; "My Queen, My Quean" 355; "Mysteries" 327; "Narcissus" 422; "Nausicäa" 268; "The Newer Critics" 260; "Newsboy" 152, 180, 191-192, 251; "News of the Phoenix" 201; "Night Music" 430-431; "No Moby Dick" 231; "Now That I'm Older" 232; "O.B.E." ("Imperial") 214; "Obstacle Course" 144; "Odysseus in Limbo" 268; "On First Looking into Stalin's Coffin" 230; "On Seeing the Statuettes of Ezekiel and Jeremiah in the Church of Notre Dame" ("On Seeing the Statues of Ezekiel and Jeremiah in the Church of Notre Dame, Montreal") 266; "Osip Mandelshtam" 397; "Poem" ("I Would for Your Sake Be Gentle") 267; "The Poet and the Statue" 195, 251; "Poetess" 201; "The Poetic Process" 223, 247-248; "Poetry As the Fine Art of Pugilism" 399; "A Poor Poet Is Grateful for a Sudden Thaw" 182; "Portrait of a Pseudo-Socialist" 97; "Portrait of Aileen" 228, 236; "Prologue to the Long Pea-Shooter" 230; "Proof Reader" 152, 192, 251; "Providence" 118, 144; "Restaurant de Luxe" 143-144; "Review of 'Bravo, Layton'" 420-421; "A Roman Jew to Ovid" ("An Errant Husband") 266; "Rose Lemay" 270; "Samantha Clara Layton" 437; "Say It Again, Brother" 144; "Sensibility" 214; "Silly Rhymes for Aviva" 355; "Song for Naomi" 267, 372; "Spinoza" 148; "Stella" 397; "Stolen Watch" 191-192; "A Strange Turn" 356; "The Swimmer" 152, 191-192, 195, 201, 251, 253; "A Tall Man Executes a Jig" 329-331, 372; "Teufelsdröckh Concerning Women" 405-406; "Thaumaturge" 97; "There Were No Signs" 327; "To a Generation of Poets" 364; "To the Gov-Gen's Poetry Awards Committee for 1971-1972" 404; "To the Lawyer Handling My Divorce Case" ("Existentialist") 182, 191; "To a Lily" 366; "To R.E." ("To Rochel Eisen") 119; "To a Very Old Lady" ("To a Very Old Woman") 202, 251; "T.S. Eliot" 233; "24" (*The Gucci Bag*) 444; "Vampire" 406-407; "Vexata Quaestio" 208-212, 214, 227, 242; "The Vigil" 65, 144; "Waterfront" 148; "Week-end Journey" 251; "Westmount Doll" ("Lacquered Westmount Doll") 233, 252; "Whatever Else Poetry Is Freedom" 266; "What Ulysses Said to Circe on the Beach of Aeaea" 234, 458-459; "When It Came to Santayana's Turn" 225; "Why I Don't Make Love to the First Lady" 315-316, 367; "Words Without Music" 180; "The World's a Tavern" 195; "York University" 384

Poetry: A Magazine of Verse (Chicago) (*Poetry Chicago*) 281
Poetry '64 424
Poet's Choice 331
The Pole-vaulter 397, 417
Polson, James 424
Pope, Alexander 84, 148, 184
Porter, John (*The Vertical Mosaic*) 333
Porter, Julian 428
Pottier, Anna 447-450, 460-461
Pound, Ezra 121, 124, 139, 176, 197-198, 204-207, 222-223, 239, 252, 293, 306, 402
Pratt, E.J. (*The Titanic, The Witches' Brew, Brébeuf and his Brethren*) 121-123, 126-127, 171, 186-187, 290
President's Medal 295
Presley, Elvis 239, 282
Preview 136, 158, 173-175, 205
The Prince of Wales Hotel 436, 438-439
Prism 302
Prix littéraire de Québec 335-359
Prose by Layton: "The Cost and Consequences of a Two-Year Marriage to an Enchanting Jewish American Princess" 445; "Culture and Capitalism" 98; "The

Frightening Sixties" (CBC radio talk) 304; "Hamlet and the Beats" 325; "Machiavelli" 103-104; "My Most Memorable Meal" 52; "The Political Significance of the Beatniks" 304; "What Canadians Don't Know About Love" 332

Proust, Marcel (*Remembrance of Things Past*) 134

Il Puma Ammansito [*The Tamed Puma*] 421

Purdy, Al 245-246, 269, 280, 285, 287, 302-303, 330, 334, 356, 364-365, 368, 370, 422

Queen's Quarterly 247, 252, 278, 303, 313, 323, 327, 365

Queen's University 137, 249, 281, 331, 369

Quill & Quire 428

Rath, Dorothy (*An Unlikely Affair*, "Winterfire") (with Irving Layton) 339-340, 458

Ravitch, Melech 112-113

Reaney, James (*A Suit of Nettles, Twelve Letters From a Small Town*) 198, 201, 243, 251, 323, 334, 364, 370

A Red Carpet for the Sun ("Arrogant, the One-Armed Juggler," "Visions and Predicaments" "The Theoretical Nipple") 278-279, 289-294, 296, 315, 322, 369-370, 398, 421

Rexroth, Kenneth 281

Rhodenizer, Vernon Blair 422

Richler, Mordecai (*The Apprenticeship of Duddy Kravitz*) 102, 404, 453

Rizziardi, Alfredo 437-438, 442

Robarts, John 428

Robinson, E.A. 402

Romania 2-15, 19-22, 26-28, 31, 57, 74, 78, 160, 176, 341, 386, 395, 454-456

Romania Literaria 395

Ronald, William 302

Rosenberg, Suzanne ("Memoirs") 47-49, 60-73, 318

Rosenblatt, Joe (*Top Soil*) 419

Rosengarten, Mort 451

Roskies (Goldstein), Ethel 161-164

Roskolenko, Harry 185

Ross, Malcolm 249, 281, 301, 315, 323, 329

Ross Tutorial School 334, 354

Ross, W.W.E. 125, 195

Royal Society of Canada 241-242

Rozynski, Buddy 204, 226-227, 451

Rule, Jane (*Desert of the Heart*) 404

Ryerson, Stanley 82, 157-158, 160

Ryerson Press 173, 199, 247-248, 290, 424

St.-Denys-Garneau 370

St. Laurent, Louis 249

Sandburg, Carl 124, 144, 180

Sandwell, B.K. 202

Sappho 396

Sartre, Jean-Paul 423

Sassu, Aligi 421

Saturday Night 118, 125

Saunders, Amos (Sandy) 43-46, 54, 56, 115, 260

Saywell, Dean John (Jack) 382

Schwartz, Louis 129

Schwartz, Musia 343-347, 353, 373-374, 378, 385, 424

Scott, Frank R. 121-123, 127-130, 136, 141, 158-160, 171, 173-176, 186-190, 197-198, 205-206, 222, 225, 237, 243, 251, 254-255, 259, 288, 301-302, 315, 321, 330, 354, 387, 416, 451-452

Scott, Louise 168, 224, 226, 260, 451-452

Scott, Marian 141-142, 225, 296, 451

Seidel, Judith 20, 21

Selected Poems (1969) 395, 399

Selected Poems (1977) 421

The Selected Poems of Irving Layton (1977) 421

Sereni, Vittorio 395

Seventy-five Greek Poems 1951-1974 421, 424

Shadows on the Ground 421

Shakespeare and Company Bookstore 306-307

Shakespeare, William 64, 84, 98, 148, 190, 202, 325, 327, 329, 346, 349, 362, 394, 396, 408, 428, 453

Shapiro, Karl 180

The Shattered Plinths 380, 397, 415

Shaw, George Bernard ("The Apple Cart" *The Intelligent Woman's Guide to Socialism and Capitalism*) 63-64, 141, 148, 164, 190, 252, 286

Shaw, Neufville 174, 198

Shelley, Percy Bysshe 98, 125, 148, 163, 283, 312, 454

Short stories by Layton: "A Death in the Family" 35, 36, 253; "Dislocation" ("The World We Live In") 313; "The English Lesson" 55; "A Game of Chess" 85, 131-133, 253, 313; "Osmeck" 313; "The Parasite" ("Unemployed") 145-146; "The Philistine" 54, 88; "A Plausible Story"

Index 517

163-164, 253, 313; "Mrs. Polinov" 230, 253; "Silhouette of a Man" 101; "Vacation in La Voiselle" 90-91, 253, 313
Shuster, Stephen 410, 414
Simon Fraser University 415
Sinclair, Gordon 302
Sir George Williams University (Concordia University) 190, 241, 243, 280, 282, 308, 311, 319, 322-323, 333, 339, 343, 346, 373, 377, 382, 435
Škvorecký, Josef 446
Slonim, Reuben 428
Smith, A.J.M. (ed. *The Book of Canadian Poetry*) 121-123, 127-129, 133, 171, 173-179 186-187, 201-202, 223, 243, 251-255, 268, 291, 317, 321, 323, 330-331, 334, 366, 422
Smith, Kay 143-144, 198
Socialist Labour Party 93
Souster, Raymond 150, 172, 175, 180, 198-202, 204-205, 207, 215, 244, 246, 254, 356, 364, 366
Spain 348, 352, 374, 413, 449
Spender, Stephen 121, 209
A Spider Danced a Cosy Jig 421
Stalin, Josef 69, 157, 397, 422
Star Weekly Magazine 337
Stein, Gertrude 128, 306
Steinberg family 39
Stevens, Wallace 199, 361
Stringer, Arthur 124
Suddenly Last Summer 345
Sutherland, Donald 137
Sutherland, Frederick (Fred) 137, 143, 168, 170
Sutherland, John 130, 136-138, 141, 143-144, 146-147, 150-151, 166, 168-169, 172-175, 177-181, 184-189, 191, 194, 198, 200-201, 205-207, 213, 233, 254, 287, 321, 365
Swift, Jonathan 202, 364
The Swinging Flesh 313, 319, 328
Symons, Scott (*Place d'Armes*) 404, 413-414
Tamarack Review 295, 313, 327, 365
The Tamed Puma 421
Tennyson, Alfred Lord ("The Revenge") 43-44, 243
There Were No Signs 421
Thomas, Dylan 180, 205, 239, 293, 369, 408, 424
Thompson, Lawrance R. (*Robert Frost*) 442
The Tightrope Dancer 421

Time 369
Timerman, Jacob 440
Times Literary Supplement 239
Tirgul Neamt 2, 4-7, 9-15, 18-19, 57, 104
Tish 302, 363
Torino, Einaudi 395
Toronto Star 282, 387, 435
Toronto *Telegram* 248, 290
Town, Harold 302, 335
Transparency 287
Trio 218
Trilling, Lionel 197
Trotsky, Leon (*The History of the Russian Revolution*) 69, 95, 99, 100, 136, 157
Trudeau, Pierre Elliot 368, 385-387, 428, 445
Tuck, Raphael 158-159
Turnbull, Gael 205, 218, 240, 247
The Uncollected Poems of Irving Layton 1936-59 (ed. Seymour Mayne) 421
Unit of Five (ed. Ronald Hambleton) 150
Université de Montréal 382, 384
University of British Columbia 322, 415
University of Guelph 384, 436
University of New Brunswick 240, 365, 385
University of Saskatchewan 356
University of Toronto 172, 177, 370, 440
University of Toronto Quarterly 152
University of Victoria 415
An Unlikely Affair 340
The Unwavering Eye 399, 421
Valente, Francesca 395
Vanier, Governor-General Georges 296-297
Vardey, Lucinda 438-439
Véhicule Press 451
Verlaine, Paul 350
Voice 251
Waddington, Miriam 71, 145-146, 198, 200-201, 224-225, 251, 453
Waddington, Patrick 145-147
Wagshall, Marion 375-381, 389, 415, 424
Wainwright, Andy 396-397, 399-400, 425, 430, 435
War Measures Act 385, 387
Weaver, Robert 183-185, 221, 249, 289, 293, 313-314, 367
Webb, Phyllis ("Elegy on the Death of Dylan Thomas") 198, 205, 218
Weekend Magazine 393
Wells, H.G. (*The Outline of History*) 64
White, Patrick 378, 384, 393-395
White, Thomas 242

Whiteson, Leon 429-430, 432-434, 458
Whitman, Walt (*Song Of Myself*) 80, 148, 193, 200, 423
Whitton, Charlotte 281
The Whole Bloody Bird 397, 399, 404
A Wild Peculiar Joy: Selected Poems 1945-82 421
Wilde, Oscar 63
Wilkinson, Anne 198
Williams, Jonathan 246-249, 264, 282, 284, 300, 357
Williams, William Carlos 196, 209, 216, 243, 247, 252, 270-272, 296, 301, 366-367, 395
Wilson, Edmund (*Axel's Castle*) 128
Wilson, Milton 245, 291-292, 300, 323, 357
Window 199
Wiseman, Adele 453
Woolfe, Douglas (*The Hypocrite Days, Fade Out*) 324
Woodcock, George 252, 370
Woodsworth, J.S. 70, 99
Woodsworth, Lucy 99
Wordsworth, William ("Intimations on Immortality") 125, 185, 193, 326-327, 345, 454
World Poetry Conference at Expo (1967) 380
Wreford, James 150, 178, 198
Yale Review 256
Yang-Shik, Kim ("First Violet") (*Beyond Time and Space*) 442
Yeats, William Butler 176, 201, 243, 280, 286, 289, 292, 349, 359, 391, 395
York University 315, 382-384, 386, 388-389, 408-411, 414, 419, 434
Young Communist League (YCL) 61-63, 71, 99, 107
Young Men's Hebrew Association (YMHA) 354
Young People's Labour League 65
Young People's Socialist League (YPSL, Yipsel) 62, 73, 95, 99, 129
Zerker, Sally F. 419